WHAT'S THAT SOUND?

Third Edition

AN INTRODUCTION TO ROCK AND ITS HISTORY

John Covach

UNIVERSITY OF ROCHESTER
AND THE EASTMAN SCHOOL OF MUSIC

Andrew Flory

CARLETON COLLEGE

W. W. NORTON AND COMPANY
NEW YORK • LONDON

W. W. Norton & Company has been independent since its founding in 1923, when William Warder Norton and Mary D. Herter Norton first published lectures delivered at the People's Institute, the adult education division of New York City's Cooper Union. The firm soon expanded its program beyond the Institute, publishing books by celebrated academics from America and abroad. By midcentury, the two major pillars of Norton's publishing program—trade books and college texts—were firmly established. In the 1950s, the Norton family transferred control of the company to its employees, and today—with a staff of four hundred and a comparable number of trade, college, and professional titles published each year—W. W. Norton & Company stands as the largest and oldest publishing house owned wholly by its employees.

Third Edition

Editor and Electronic Media Editor: Steve Hoge
Assistant Editor: Ariella Foss
Associate Editor: Justin Hoffman
Editorial Assistant and Electronic Media Editorial Assistant: Nicole Sawa
Project Editor: Rachel Mayer
Manuscript Editor: Lory Frenkel
Marketing Manager: Nicole Albas
Senior Production Manager: Ben Reynolds
Design Director: Rubina Yeh
Designer: Marc Cohen
Photo Editors: Stephanie Romeo and Peter Lesser
Permissions Manager: Megan Jackson
Composition and Layout: Carole Desnoes
Manufacturing: Courier—Kendallville, IN

Library of Congress Cataloging-in-Publication Data

Flory, Andrew.
    What's that sound? : an introduction to rock and its history / Andrew Flory, John Covach. — 3rd ed.
        p. cm.
    Includes index.
    ISBN 978-0-393-91204-3 (pbk.)
    1. Rock music—History and criticism.   I. Covach, John Rudolph.   II. Title.
    ML3534.C7 2012
    781.6609—dc23

                                                                            2011047224

W. W. Norton & Company, Inc., 500 Fifth Avenue, New York, NY 10110
wwnorton.com
W. W. Norton & Company, Ltd., Castle House, 75/76 Wells Street, London WIT 3QT

5 6 7 8 9 0

ABOUT THE AUTHORS

John Covach (Chair and Professor of Music, University of Rochester and Professor of Theory, Eastman School of Music) received his Bachelor of Music (1983), Master of Music (1985), and Ph.D. (1990) in music theory from the University of Michigan. He was also a Fulbright student in Vienna, Austria in 1987–1988. The recipient of several teaching awards and citations, Professor Covach teaches theory and analysis as well as courses in popular music. Since 1993, he has taught large-lecture courses on rock at University of North Texas; University of North Carolina, Chapel Hill; and University of Rochester and has lectured across North America and Europe. He is coeditor of *Understanding Rock* (Oxford 1997), *American Rock and the Classical Music Tradition* (Harwood 2000), and *Institutions, Traditions, and American Popular Music* (Harwood 2000). His extensive writing on twentieth-century music, popular music, and the philosophy of music have appeared in numerous books and journals. Professor Covach also maintains an active career as a performing and recording musician.

Andrew Flory (Assistant Professor of Music, Carleton College) received his bachelor of music from the City College of New York (1998), and Master of Music and Ph.D. from the University of North Carolina at Chapel Hill (2003, 2006). Professor Flory teaches courses in American music, focusing on rock, rhythm and blues, and jazz. Since 2004, he has taught courses on the history of rock to intimate groups, in the large-lecture format, as continuing education, and in the distance-learning environment at the University of North Carolina, Shenandoah University, and Carleton College. He has lectured internationally and written extensively about American rhythm and blues, and is an expert on the music of Motown. Working directly with Universal Records, Professor Flory has served as consultant for several recent Motown reissues. His book, *I Hear a Symphony: Listening to the Music of Motown*, is forthcoming from The University of Michigan Press.

Contents

The 1950s   74

CHAPTER 2

The Birth and First Flourishing of Rock and Roll   78

CHAPTER 3

The Demise of Rock and the Promise of Soul   112

The 1990s 488

CHAPTER 13

Widening Gaps 492

The 2000s: The New Millennium 538

CHAPTER 14

A Very Different Industry: The First Decade of a New Millennium   542

LISTENING GUIDES

WHAT'S NEW IN THE THIRD EDITION?

The structure and many features of the Third Edition will be familiar to users of the Second Edition. Yet, we have made some revisions and additions to the content in order to expand coverage of areas that seemed to require it, and to react to major changes in the music industry during the last decade.

Drawing on the tremendous reception of the "Backstage Pass" sections written by outside authors, we have commissioned a new essay on music and technology from Mark Katz, whose work in this area is well known among scholars of popular music. Additionally, new Listening Guides have been added for ten songs, including: the Chords, "Sh-Boom"; the Animals, "House of the Rising Sun"; the Rolling Stones, "(I Can't Get No) Satisfaction"; the Replacements, "Color Me Impressed"; R.E.M., "The One I Love"; Neutral Milk Hotel, "In the Aeroplane over the Sea"; Nickelback, "Photograph"; Carrie Underwood, "Before He Cheats"; OutKast, "Hey Ya"; and Wilco, "Ashes of American Flags." To support students' efforts to consolidate information from the Listening Guides we have also created summarizing Sound Check reference boxes at the end of each chapter. These boxes include pertinent factual information in a side-by-side format for each Listening Guide song in a given chapter.

Realizing the importance of rock's visual elements and the many instructors that have successfully integrated video into their teaching, we have also added a feature to this edition called Viewing Rock. Focusing on several of the most important genres of rock television and film, these eight boxes provide basic analysis with supporting screen shots of a made-for-television variety special (Martha and the Vandellas, "Nowhere to Run"), a popular variety program (Elvis on the *Ed Sullivan Show*), a rock film from the mid-1960s (The Beatles in *A Hard Day's Night*), a dance-oriented program from the 1960s (Temptations, "My Girl"), a live performance film (Jimi Hendrix at Woodstock), and music videos from the 1980s (Michael Jackson, "Thriller"), 1990s (Weezer, "Buddy Holly") and 2000s (OutKast, "Hey Ya").

The majority of the content and framework of the Third Edition is the same as the Second Edition with some notable exceptions. In order to facilitate basic skills in approaching rock as music at the beginning of a course, the three Interlude sections featured throughout the Second Edition—which covered song form, instrumentation, and studio techniques—have been folded into a larger section entitled "What to Listen for in Rock." Additionally, these three topics have been augmented with a short pedagogical discussion of "viewing rock," which supports the Viewing Rock boxes discussed above. Readers will also note an effort to reorganize Chapter 1, integrating the three "streams" of mainstream, country, and rhythm and blues.

This Third Edition also adds coverage to several of the later chapters, forming a larger theme that considers independent rock after the punk movement. Chapter 10 has a revised discussion of the emergence of punk in the United States and the UK; a section on American post-punk and hardcore has been added to Chapter 11; several sections were added in Chapter 12 to form a discussion of college rock and the emergence of the American indie scene; and a significant section on American indie rock was added to Chapter 13. While it was difficult to single out a loosely related family of underground movements as worthy of treatment in this manner, these

Preface

additions come after discussions with many instructors who found this lacking from the book. Moreover, an enhanced element focusing on independent music allows for richer discussions about the ever-present dynamic in rock between independent and mainstream concerns.

It has been a decade since John first began work on this text and the music industry has changed greatly during this time. A final structural goal of this edition was to refocus the discussion of the 1990s in Chapter 13 and create a new Chapter 14 that provides commentary on music and issues pertinent to the 2000s. Readers will note a slight change of rhetorical delivery in the new Chapter 14, which discusses music in a less comprehensive way, focusing instead on larger issues that help to summarize themes in the book while referring to recent historical trends most relevant to the history of rock.

Finally, a new four-color design greatly enhances this Third Edition in several ways. In addition to a more pleasing layout and typeface, adding color throughout the book allows for a wider array of photography and art related to rock, much of which uses color in significant ways. Similarly, we have made great effort to use color as a visual aid in the set of redesigned Listening Guides, which many instructors feel are a central feature of the text.

Ancillaries and Emedia

A talented team of Norton specialists and college instructors has created a new set of ancillaries and emedia to support teaching in the college environment. This Third Edition features a new StudySpace website (wwnorton.com/studyspace) with resources for students, including diagnostic quizzes, study outlines, and playlists that feature artist biographies and include links to music purchase downloads and embedded video from authorized channels.

Also available on StudySpace are interactive Listening Guides (iLGs). Easy to operate and designed for lecture presentation and individual study, this software synchronizes rock audio and author commentary. In order to function properly, the software requires that you have a recording of the work downloaded from the StudySpace links, or an MP3 of the same recording from your personal collection.

The Third Edition offers a test bank for instructors, which includes a variety of multiple-choice, short-answer, and matching questions, as well as several essay prompts per chapter. The test bank is available in a customizable ExamView format on CD-ROM and for download from Norton's Instructor's Resource site. Also available is the *What's That Sound?* Instructor's Resource Disc, which provides PowerPoint lecture outlines and a comprehensive set of art from the textbook. Additionally, Norton has integrated the test bank, practice quizzes, chapter outlines, and StudySpace content into a course pack available for your course management system. These resources are free to adopters.

Acknowledgments

Like most textbooks, the one you are about to read developed over the course of many years—in this case, over twenty years of teaching university-level courses in rock music. As a consequence of this prolonged period of gestation, we owe debts of gratitude to many more people than we can list here. Our apologies in advance to those we may have overlooked.

The genesis of the book occurred during John's time at the University of North Texas College of Music, where Thomas Sovik and David Joyner gave him the chance to teach courses in the history of rock music. At the University of North Carolina at Chapel Hill, John Nádas, James Haar, Jon Finson, and Mark Evan Bonds were especially supportive in helping John to establish a series of rock-music courses there. At the University of Rochester, John is most grateful for the continued support of Tom Leblanc (now at the University of Miami), Peter Lennie, Joanna Olmsted, Jamal Rossi, and Doug Lowry. These colleagues have supported his research and teaching in more ways than he can list here. Andy is especially grateful to current and former colleagues at Shenandoah University and Carleton College. At Shenandoah, Tracy Fitzsimmons, Bryon Grigsby, Michael Stepniak, Keith Salley, Adam Olson, and Golder O'Neil were especially helpful in establishing and inspiring courses in rock music, and at Carleton, Justin London, Ron Rodman, Melinda Russell, Hector Valdivia, Alex Freeman, Nikki Melville, Larry Archbold, and Lawrence Burnett have provided administrative support and personal encouragement.

We owe a significant debt to the thousands of students who have taken our courses over the years. Much of what is contained in this book was tried out on them first, and we have benefited immensely from their feedback. Over the years, many of John's students helped to educate him on a number of the finer points of rock history. This special group of students includes Mark Spicer, David Carson Berry, Tim Hughes, John Brackett, Paul Harris, Marc Medwin, Akitsugu Kawamoto, Sarah Nicholson, Jason Titus, Anna Stephan-Robinson, Martha Bausch, Christina Brandt, Jonathan Hiam, Joel Mauger, Joe Gennaro, Richard Rischar, Trevor deClercq, Crystal Asmussen, David Leblanc, and Christopher Gupta. Several incredibly knowledgeable students provided Andy with administrative assistance during in his early time working on this book, including Robbie Taylor, Alan Weiderman, Billy Barry, Miles Campbell, and Jen Winshop.

Many friends and colleagues have also given us wise, helpful, and encouraging advice and support, including Kim Kowalke, Walter Everett, Albin Zak, James Grier, Jocelyn Neal, Mark Butler, Betsy Marvin, Tim Riley, Carl Woideck, Dan Harrison, Lori Burns, Rob Wegman, John Buzby, Paul Cole, Chris Chamis, Stefan Zajic, John Howland, Phil Ford, Travis Stimeling, Annie Randall, Mark Clague, and Bob Fink.

Thanks are also due to the instructors who reviewed and commented on parts of various editions of the book: John Brackett, Theo Cateforis, Diane Cardarelli, John M. Crabtree, Marcus Dickman, Jr., Jeff Donovick, David Englert, Roberta Freund-Schwartz, Jennifer Gunderman, Mark Katz, Laura Lohman, Bente Hansen, Heather Miller, Richard Mook, Michael A. Morrison, David M. Moskowitz, Joseph Poshek, Gary Pritchard, Jr., Karl Raudsepp, Jerry Skelley, Richard Sorrell, Patrick Warfield, Arthur White, and Amy S. Wooley.

We would like to thank Gary Giddins, Albin Zak, John Jackson, Tim Riley, Ben Fong-Torres, Guthrie Ramsey, Graeme Boone, Susan Fast, Robert Bowman, Mark Spicer, Jeff Chang, Norma Coates, and Mark Katz for contributing their scholarship to the "Backstage Pass" sections. Thanks also to the authors of the emedia and ancillary materials which support this book: Laura Lohman for the StudySpace outlines and quizzes, Roberta Freund-Schwartz for the StudySpace Playlists, John

Husser for the interactive Listening Guide development, and Gary Pritchard for the test bank.

The excellent staff at Norton also deserve a big thanks, including Michael Ochs and Suzanne LaPlante, who convinced John to write the first edition of this book; Roby Harrington and Maribeth Payne, who offered wisdom and guidance along the way; Peter Lesser, who edited the first two editions of the book and served as photo consultant for this edition; project editor Rachel Mayer; production manager Ben Reynolds; photo editor Stephanie Romeo; and editorial assistants Ariella Foss and Nicole Sawa. Thanks also to Lory Frenkel, who copyedited the Third Edition. For his wisdom and one-liners, Steve Hoge deserves huge thanks for his work as the main editor of both media and text for this Third Edition.

Most of all, we would like to thank our families, Julie, Jonathan, and Ricky Covach, who suffered John's many obsessed moments over the years with grace and loving support, and Kate, Charlotte, Ben, and Alexander Flory, whose love and patience made the Third Edition possible.

John Covach
Rochester, New York

Andrew Flory
Northfield, Minnesota

September 2011

WHAT'S THAT SOUND?

Third Edition

AN INTRODUCTION TO ROCK AND ITS HISTORY

STUDYING ROCK

Rock music was born out of controversy, and its rebellious image has always appealed to fans. In the mid-1950s, many adults accustomed to the fatherly crooning of Bing Crosby and the suave, swinging delivery of Frank Sinatra were shocked by Elvis Presley's emphatic **blues**-influenced singing and suggestive dance moves. Teenagers, of course, loved him. Similarly, the Beatles' moptop haircuts upset a lot of parents in the mid-1960s, while setting a fashion trend among youngsters. Rock continued to push the envelope in later years: artists such as Jim Morrison, Alice Cooper, and David Bowie challenged cultural values in the late '60s and early '70s, while Madonna and Prince did the same in the 1980s. Issues such as payola and obscene lyrics have even been the focus of federal government hearings. While only a small portion of rock has been the source of controversy or cultural struggle, nonconformity and misbehavior are central to the rock movement.

Considering rock's frequent (and sometimes militant) opposition to the status quo, some people are surprised to learn that colleges and universities across the country have been offering courses in rock for many years. As music historians look back on the last century, it is obvious that popular music has played an enormous role in the recent development of the Western musical tradition, and rock music has been dominant among popular styles. Even music historians whose work focuses on other genres and decades must take into account the many and often far-flung effects rock has had on the world of music in general.

Despite the acknowledged importance of rock music, determining exactly what "rock" means is not easy. Some scholars use the term "rock and roll" to describe the first wave of rock from 1954 to 1959 (covered in Chapter 2). Other scholars describe music after 1964 as "rock." Using these two distinct terms preserves what many scholars and fans see as an important difference. This book will employ the term "rock" in a broad sense, however, using the term to designate popular music that is produced specifically for a youth audience. But even this more encompassing usage is still problematic and includes seeming contradictions. Is rock defined by race, or musical style, or specific musical elements, such as instrumentation or lyrical content? Can 1960s soul be considered rock? How about folk or rap? Is all pop also rock, and is all rock also pop? Moreover, how do we think about rock music after its musicians and audience have grown up? Few will argue that artists such as Elvis Presley, the

Recorded in 1951 by Jackie Brenston and His Delta Cats, "Rocket '88'" is considered by many to be the first rock and roll record. Though it was first released as a 78-rpm single, this is a photograph of a 1955 pressing—one of only a handful of "Rocket '88'" 45s still in existence.

Beatles, the Rolling Stones, Jimi Hendrix, Led Zeppelin, the Police, and U2 were central to the rock movement. But artists like the Supremes, Madonna, and the Kingston Trio are harder to categorize.

This book will not completely resolve these kinds of questions. Rather, it will tell a history of popular music that focuses on rock but includes many other styles. The chapters that follow consider rock in an inclusive manner, discussing artists as diverse as the Andrews Sisters, Bessie Smith, Bill Haley and the Comets, the Supremes, Santana, Parliament Funkadelic, Metallica, and Britney Spears. The main purpose of the book is to organize this repertoire—an enormous body of music that covers over fifty years of popular-music history—to make it easier to understand and appreciate. Today there is more popular music available to listeners than at any other time in the history of recorded music. The rock era included a vast amount of music, more than can be covered in a typical university course, which only scrapes the surface of rock music. In the chapters that follow, we will organize the music into styles and eras to make the rock repertoire easier to understand and appreciate, and to provide broad stylistic and historical perspectives.

ELEMENTS TO CONSIDER

Rock History in the Media. Studying rock is not new, and most fans will have had some exposure to background information on artists and their music. For those who have not studied rock as an academic subject, this historical information will probably have come from general interest publications, radio, television, or the Internet. Magazines such as *Rolling Stone* and *Mojo* provide readers with useful information about rock musicians, their music, and aspects of the entertainment industry. Books targeted at the general reader—often written by journalists and music critics—are plentiful and varied. Cable networks such as VH-1 and MTV regularly offer profiles of artists and styles, frequently taking larger historical patterns into account. The development of the classic-rock radio format in the early 1990s also encouraged a growing sense of rock's history, along with the time-tested oldies format that has existed for decades. All these sources of information about the history of rock can be useful, and many have been employed in the writing of this textbook—a list of some of the best general sources follows this Introduction, and references to more focused material are provided at the end of each chapter. Be aware, however, that a scholarly approach to rock will differ significantly from general interest books or media accounts. In many cases, information found in the popular media is designed primarily for entertainment rather than educational or research purposes. Some of this information may be accurate, well researched, and balanced, but some of it is also skewed, gossipy, and unreliable. Remember that magazines and broadcast stations generate revenue through the sale of advertising; the worst thing that can happen in such businesses is for people to put the magazine down, change the radio station, or turn off the TV. It is in the best interests of media outlets to deliver what they believe people want most, which can lead to a focus on the more sensational and titillating aspects of biography, rather than serious consideration of musicians and their music.

This textbook will attempt to provide a balanced and fair account of the history

Rock is difficult to define. Almost any listener would agree that "rock" includes Jimi Hendrix (top left). But what about Taylor Swift (bottom left) or the Supremes (bottom right)?

of rock music. Many more artists and groups will enter the story than may typically appear in general interest accounts. Some artists or groups were more important in their day than they have been since. Other artists have become more popular over time. There will be no attempts to convince you to like a style of music, to elevate one style over another, or to dismiss or otherwise discredit any artist or group. The following chapters will provide reliable information, historical context, and informed debate. Hopefully, this book will elicit informed discussion of contested issues in rock, such as the relevance of popularity to historical importance, the role of gender and masculinity in rock's history, and the responsibility of music executives to share profits with musicians.

I Know What I Like: The Fan Mentality. Many fans of rock are passionate about the music they like. But what does it mean to be a fan? Fans of rock music listen frequently to the music of a particular artist, group, or style and gather interesting facts about both the artists and the music. As fans, there is absolutely nothing wrong with ignoring artists, groups, or styles that do not interest us. This is perfectly natural. But as students of rock music, we cannot simply ignore music we do not like. We must strive to be balanced as we study rock's history and development, which often forces us to consider carefully music we probably wouldn't choose to listen to otherwise. If you were studying American history, it wouldn't be acceptable to study only those presidents who shared your political persuasion. An objective history of the last few decades would consider John F. Kennedy *and* Richard M. Nixon, Ronald Reagan *and* Jimmy Carter, and Bill Clinton *and* George W. Bush. When it comes to studying music, you don't have to suspend your sense of judgment, but you do have to work to keep the fan mentality at bay.

The Ups and Downs of Chart Positions. This book will make frequent reference to chart positions. Almost everyone is familiar with charts that rank hit songs and albums by popularity for a given week, and the best-known American charts appear in *Billboard* magazine. Charts help us draw general conclusions about the popularity of a song or album at the time it was released. It can also be useful to compare how certain songs did on pop charts with the way they fared on rhythm and blues or country charts, or even on the British charts. More importantly for this book is that charts can help us avoid the fan mentality—in a sense, they keep us honest. Among scholars, charts are viewed with understandable suspicion because little is known about how they have been put together in the past, making them susceptible to manipulation. Clearly, charts are not precision instruments for measuring a song or album's success or popularity, and they do not accurately reflect the popularity or influence of some songs or albums. A record can chart well and have little influence, or chart moderately well (or even poorly) and have a lot of influence. But in a broad sense, charts are still the best instruments we have available to judge listeners' changing tastes, even if chart measurements are flawed. Ideally, we would have access to comprehensive radio playlists of various eras, or the actual number of records sold of any song or album. However, playlist data is not plentiful and record companies often manipulate sales numbers (a frequent complaint of artists and bands since the beginning of recording). The Record Industry Association of America (RIAA) does award gold records for sales of 500,000 units and platinum records for sales of one million units, which can be helpful in measuring the success of an album or single. The RIAA website (www.riaa.com) allows you to look up any hit record and track its award history. The popular Google Books search engine also provides access to an extensive collection of *Billboard* magazines, allowing us to consider aspects of advertising and industry news at a particular date.

The Four Themes. The following chapters each take a three- to ten-year period of rock's history and organize the music along stylistic lines. Some chapters cover the same years from different angles. For example, the mid-1960s are covered in three chapters: Chapter 4, which is devoted to the British invasion; Chapter 5, which discusses the American response to it; and Chapter 6, which focuses on black pop. Each chapter also raises a set of interpretive issues that provide insight into scholarly and critical debates about the music and its historical circumstances or aesthetic impact and value. In the discussion of psychedelia in Chapter 7, for instance, the differences between mainstream popular culture of the mid-1960s and the hippie subcultures in both London and San Francisco are highlighted; the questions that arise in this discussion are representative of the issues that can surface whenever strong subcultures overlap. While interpretive angles change from chapter to chapter, four important themes are pursued throughout the book: social, political, and cultural issues; issues of race, class, and gender; the development of the music business; and the development of technology.

Each of these themes play an important role in the development of rock music as a musical style and a force in popular culture. The music business has changed dramatically since the early 1950s, as the rock element of the business has grown from small independent upstarts to some of the most successful and dominant corporations of the modern age. In the realm of technology, the rise of radio in the 1920s and the emergence of television after World War II are central factors in rock's explosion into mainstream American culture in the mid-1950s. Just as important is the development of cable television that facilitated the introduction of MTV in the early 1980s. Issues of race, class, and gender are also essential to understanding the origins of rock, the constant challenge of stereotypes in this music, and the ever present struggle for authenticity in a form that blends down-home vernacular sensibilities with public adoration and extreme wealth. As the chapters unfold, you will be urged to examine how these themes fit into the story of rock's development. No style of music exists in a vacuum, and consideration of these broader perspectives will help us identify and appreciate the forces that have shaped the repertoire, and the ways it has been interpreted, both by scholars in academia and by writers in the popular media.

Tracking the Popularity Arc. As we study rock's history and progress from the 1950s through the 1990s and beyond, you may notice a pattern of styles and their popularity. In many cases, a specific style will appear within a relatively restricted geographic region and remain unknown to most fans of popular music. For instance, few rock fans were aware of the punk scene in New York during the mid-1970s, and bands such as Television, the Ramones, and Blondie played to small, local audiences. The American punk style, which would morph into new wave by the end of the decade, developed within this small subculture before breaking into the national spotlight in 1978. By the early 1980s, some artists formerly associated with punk embraced styles and commercial strategies of the rock mainstream, while the more die-hard, aggressive groups retreated back into the punk underground. The rise of punk from a small, regional underground scene to mainstream pop culture, and its subsequent retreat, follows a pattern that we might think of as a "popularity arc." Over and over, the stories of specific styles in rock music follow this template. Typically, histories of rock music account for the time each style spends in the pop limelight—the peak of the popularity arc—creating a chronology without examining a style's pre-mainstream roots or existence after the commercial boom years. In a sense, it is difficult to avoid such a historical account, and similar problems arise in histories of other musical styles (such as jazz and classical music). To keep the popularity arc in mind for any given style, ask yourself the following questions: How did this style arise? When did it peak in popularity? Does it still exist in a sub-

culture somewhere? How are elements of this style incorporated into current mainstream pop?

This book will give you the information you need to answer the first two questions. But you will probably need to do your own research to answer the last two. You may be surprised to discover how many older rock styles are still thriving, often long after they have fallen out of the mainstream spotlight.

WHAT TO LISTEN FOR IN ROCK

Throughout the book, Listening Guides will direct your attention to individual songs that illustrate specific musical features of the styles discussed. While the circumstances surrounding a style, band, or song may be interesting, the way the music sounds is the element that attracts most listeners. The analysis of rock music can require a high level of specific music-analytical training. Books, articles, and doctoral dissertations in the past several decades demonstrate the many dimensions of rock's musical structure. The Listening Guides in this book will help you identify the structural features of rock music, with a focus on musical form. In the broadest sense, musical form refers to the structure and organization of different sections in a song or piece. Rock generally uses a limited number of common formal types; once you are familiar with these types, you will notice that most songs fit relatively neatly into one form or another (with certain exceptions). Understanding formal structure will help you hear new things in the music itself and perceive similarities between musical styles that may otherwise seem very different. The basic formal types are introduced below, along with short explanations of rhythm, instrumentation, and recording techniques. Instrumentation, or the types of instruments used in a given recording, can drastically change the way a song sounds and allow for variation within a performance. A familiarity with basic techniques used to record rock music will also help us understand some of the important differences between studio recordings, which form the bulk of the repertoire discussed in this book, and live rock performances. In addition to the sounds of rock, we will also consider the sights of rock with a special introduction to viewing rock in its multiple contexts.

"Rocket '88'." Before delving into greater detail, it may be helpful to look closely at some of these features in a brief analysis of a classic track: Jackie Brenston and His Delta Cats' 1951 single, "Rocket '88'." Recorded in Memphis and produced by Sam Phillips (Elvis Presley's first producer), "Rocket '88'" is considered by many to be the first rock and roll song. While it is legally credited to Brenston, he may have written only the lyrics and lifted the music from an earlier song called "Cadillac Boogie" (such "borrowings" are relatively common in early rock and roll). To show how the song is laid out, the book provides a **formal diagram** that breaks it into sections and lists them according to music timings. These timings simply give you an idea of where in the song a specific section begins and ends. Each section is also marked by a snippet of lyrics or some other description to help you locate it. The formal diagram for "Rocket '88'" is in the Listening Guide below. "Rocket '88'" is in what we call **simple verse form**. It repeats a single section of music eight times and, as you will see in the diagram, each section is labeled either **"Verse"** or **"Instrumental Verse."** The only exception is verse 2, which slightly alters the structure found in all the other sections. Simple verse form is common in rock music and we will see many instances of it in the chapters that follow.

In the first section, labeled "Instrumental Verse" in the diagram, note that the description "12 mm." is given. This indicates that the section is twelve **measures** in length ("mm." is commonly used to abbreviate measures in musical writing). You have probably heard musicians begin a song by counting out "one, two, three, four!" Musicians commonly count the **beats** in music in groups of four (though groups of two or three beats can also be found). This simply means that you count "one, two, three, four" and continue counting "one, two three, four" again rather than "five, six, seven, eight." Each group of four beats is called a "measure" or **bar** of music—these terms are synonymous and used interchangeably. Note that each verse and instrumental verse (except one) in "Rocket '88'" is twelve measures (bars) in length. You might count it like this:

mm.:	1	2	3	4	5	6	7	8	9	10	11	12
beats:	1234	1234	1234	1234	1234	1234	1234	1234	1234	1234	1234	1234

Verse 2 is the exception and is only eight measures in length; it seems to break off early compared to the twelve-measure pattern shown above. This is likely a mistake, because you can hear the musicians scrambling a bit to come back together as a band. Verse 2 can be counted like this:

mm.:	1	2	3	4	5	6	7	8	9??
beats:	1234	1234	1234	1234	1234	1234	1234	1234	???

Despite the irregularity of verse 2, if you count the measures and watch the music timings, you should be able to follow the diagram as the song plays. If you are having trouble keeping up, try pausing the music at the section boundaries given by the timings; this may help you hear the sections more clearly. When you have followed the form with the diagram, see if you can do so without the diagram. Once you begin hearing form in music, you may find that it can be difficult *not* to hear it!

In addition to form and rhythm in this song, it is also useful to listen for the instrumentation. This particular track uses drums, electric guitar, acoustic piano, two saxophones, and lead vocals. Try to listen to the song all the way through following only one of these instruments; don't let your attention be drawn away by what's happening in another part. Then, play the song again and see if you can follow a different instrument all the way through. Typically, our attention darts from part to part in a song, usually when something new comes in to grab our interest.

While listening to "Rocket '88'," for instance, we may focus on the piano in the first instrumental verse, the vocals in verse 1, the saxes in the next section, and so on. You may be surprised at the difficulty of focusing on one part as you listen, but if you can train yourself to do this, you will hear things in the music that you've never noticed before.

TYPICAL FORMAL TYPES IN AMERICAN POPULAR MUSIC

The analysis of musical form is a study of the way sections are structured in a piece of music, and the way these sections combine to produce larger structures. Most musical styles work within the constraints of a small number of formal types, so formal analysis of a single work usually consists of noting its similarities to and dif-

---

Listening Guide

Get Music Ⓢ wwnorton.com/studyspace

Jackie Brenston and His Delta Cats, "Rocket '88'" Chess 1458

Words and music by Jackie Brenston, produced by Sam Phillips. "Rocket '88'" hit #1 on the *Billboard* "Best Selling Retail Rhythm and Blues" and "Most Played Juke Box Rhythm and Blues" charts in 1951.

FORM: Simple verse.

TIME SIGNATURE: 4/4.

INSTRUMENTATION: Piano, drums, saxophones, solo vocals, distorted electric guitar playing a repeated boogie-woogie pattern.

Timings	Section	Description
0:00–0:19	Instrumental Verse	12 mm., piano featured.
0:19–0:38	Verse 1	12 mm., "You women have heard of jalopies . . ."
0:38–0:57	Instrumental Verse	12 mm., saxophones featured.
0:57–1:10	Verse 2 (partial)	8 mm., "V-8 motor . . .", breaks off early.
1:10–1:28	Instrumental Verse	12 mm., sax solo.
1:28–1:47	Instrumental Verse	12 mm., sax solo continues.
1:47–2:05	Instrumental Verse	12 mm., sax solo continues.
2:05–2:23	Verse 3	12 mm., "Step in my rocket . . ."
2:23–2:46	Instrumental Verse	12 mm., sax and guitar featured.

A Note on Rhythm and Meter

Generally, **rhythm** refers to the ways musical sounds are organized in time and **beat** refers to a regular rhythmic pulse. Most of the music in this book will employ four-beat measures. Measures may also contain two or three beats, and these are counted "one two, one two" and "one two three, one two three" respectively. It is even possible for a measure to contain five, six, seven, or more beats per measure. These ways of organizing rhythm and beats in music are called **meter**. A fuller consideration of a song's meter takes into account not only how many beats are in each measure, but also how each beat may be subdivided. A single beat can be divided into either two or three equal parts; in the first case you would evenly count, "one & two & three & four &," and in the second, "one & uh, two & uh, three & uh, four & uh." When each beat is evenly divided into two parts, we call this **simple**, and when each beat is divided evenly into three parts, we call this **compound**. Meters are grouped by combining the number of beats per measure with the way each beat is divided, as shown in the following chart:

	Simple (2 parts)	Compound (3 parts)
Duple (2 parts)	duple simple (2/4)	duple compound (6/8)
Triple (3 beats)	triple simple (3/4)	triple compound (9/8)
Quadruple (4 beats)	quadruple simple (4/4)	quadruple compound (12/8)

When the meter employs two beats per measure, and each beat is evenly divided into two parts, we classify the meter as "duple simple," and this can be seen in the chart. Notice that a time signature is given in parentheses next to each **meter classification**. In each case, the time signature given represents the most common one used to indicate this meter classification in written music. You may have noticed that sheet music almost always has a time signature provided at the beginning of the song or piece; this indicates what the meter classification of the rhythm will be in the song. Meter plays a crucial role in establishing the rhythmic "feel" of a song, though it is not the only element that influences this. In this book, most songs will be in quadruple time, with both simple and compound divisions in play. "Rocket '88'," for instance, is in quadruple compound time, which many musicians simply think of as a **"shuffle"** in four (4/4).

ferences from some formal design common to the style. Formal types and musical styles are often linked to one another. For our purposes, it will be useful to look at some common formal types that occur in rock music.

The 12-Bar Blues and the Doo-Wop Progression. Perhaps the best place to begin the study of form in rock is with the **12-bar blues**. This is a common structural pattern found in rhythm and blues, rock and roll, and many styles of jazz. A 12-bar blues is a structural pattern that consists of twelve groups of four-beat measures. The twelve-measure structure of the 12-bar blues is distinctive because of the way its measures fall into three groups of four. These groups can be seen in the measure length, phrasing, lyrics, and chord structure. Once this twelve-measure pattern is in place, an entire song will often repeat the structure several times, with new lyrics and instrumental solos added to make these repetitions fresh. The first four measures, which are called a **phrase**, often feature a lyric that is repeated in the subsequent four measures. The words of the final four measures often complete the thought begun in the repeated initial phrase. Think of this pattern as "question—question—answer" (although the lyrics don't literally have to ask a question). The first line in each verse is repeated in the second phrase, with the third phrase completing the thought with a new line.

Listen again to "Rocket '88'" and you will find that it uses a 12-bar blues structure. After you have listened to the song two or three times, you should begin to hear the 12-bar blues structure clearly. Notice that eight of the nine phrases in the song are twelve measures long—the only exception is the fourth phrase, which does not complete the structure (the Listening Guide notes that this phrase "breaks off early"). The entire 12-bar blues structure appears in the **introduction**, for example, and begins a second time with the vocals. Phrase one begins with the lyrics, "heard of jalopies"; phrase two, "yes, it's great"; and the third phrase, "ride in style." You will notice that, although "Rocket '88'" is constructed using the 12-bar blues, its lyrics do not follow the question/question/answer pattern. For an example of a 12-bar blues that uses this lyrical structure, see Big Joe Turner's "Shake, Rattle, and Roll," which appears in Chapter 1. Other examples of 12-bar blues in the book are Howlin' Wolf's "Evil Is Goin' On" (Chapter 1), Chuck Berry's "Johnny B. Goode" (Chapter 2), and Little Richard's "Tutti Frutti" (Chapter 2).

The chart below illustrates some of the structural properties of 12-bar blues. Notice that **Roman numerals** occur under each measure number. This shows the **chords** that are typically played in those measures. Chords are combinations of notes played together—think of somebody strumming chords on a guitar or banging them out on the piano. Chords in any **key** can be organized by the **scale** for that key, and the Roman numerals show which note of the scale the chord is based on. If we are in C, for instance, the scale goes C – D – E – F – G – A – B – C. The I chord is a C chord, the IV is an F chord, and the V is a G chord, since the notes C, F, and G are the first, fourth, and fifth notes of the scale. Why would musicians bother with arcane Roman numerals when they could just write C, F, and G? The reason is more pragmatic than you might think: this pattern can occur in twelve distinct keys, and the specific labels C, F, and G cover only one of these, while the Roman numerals generalize across all twelve. If a musician knows the Roman numerals, she can play the pattern in any key as easily as in C.

bars	1	2	3	4	5	6	7	8	9	10	11	12
chords	I	(IV)	I	I	IV	IV	I	I	V	(IV)	I	(V)
	1st phrase (question)				2nd phrase (question)				3rd phrase (answer)			

Another musical structure that appears in a lot of rock music is the **doo-wop progression**. Though it can occur in many styles of pop, this chord progression is most often associated with the doo-wop of the 1950s. Moreover, like the 12-bar blues, the doo-wop progression can form the underlying structure for many of the forms that we discuss below. Using our Roman numerals, we can characterize the doo-wop progression as a series of four chords: I – vi – IV – V. In the key of C, this progression would go C – A minor – F – G. This familiar chord progression can be heard in 1950s tracks such as the Five Satins' "In the Still of the Night" and the Del Vikings' "Come Go with Me." The chart below illustrates the doo-wop progression as it appears in the first vocal phrase of the Chords' "Sh-Boom" (labeled "verse 1" in the Listening Guide). Note that there is a chord on every beat, forming a harmonic pattern (or "progression") that repeats through the entire song except for the short section labeled **"bridge."** Like the 12-bar blues, it is not difficult to hear the repeating doo-wop progression that forms the basis for the song's musical content.

bars	1	2	3	4
chords	I	vi	IV	V

Life could be a **dream**… if I could **take** you up in paradise…

Simple Verse Form. Repetitive structures like the 12-bar blues and the doo-wop progression often combine to form larger structural patterns. As these patterns repeat, we may think of them differently depending on what aspects are repeated. A

Listening Guide

Get Music Ⓢ **wwnorton.com/studyspace**

The Chords, "Sh-Boom" Cat 104

Words and music by Jimmy Keyes, Carl Feaster, Claude Feaster, Floyd "Buddy" McRae, and Ricky Edwards. Reached #5 on the *Billboard* rhythm and blues "Most Played in Juke Boxes" chart in 1954. (This recording dropped quickly off of the charts after a cover version was released by the Crew Cuts.)

FORM: Simple verse with several **interludes** and a bridge.

TIME SIGNATURE: 4/4.

INSTRUMENTATION: Electric guitar, bass, piano, drums, saxophone, solo vocals, and lead vocals.

0:00–0:06	**Prelude**, 2 mm.	"Life could be a dream . . ."
0:06–0:22	**Verse 1**, 4 mm.	"Life could be a dream . . ."; solo vocal with background harmonies.
0:22–0:29	**Interlude (partial)**, 2 mm.	Nonsense syllables; "De dong e ding dong . . ."
0:29–0:43	**Verse 2**, 4 mm.	"Life could be a dream"; beginning of verse punctuated by vocal harmony.
0:43–0:57	**Bridge**, 4 mm.	"Every time I look at you . . ."; performed by bass vocalist.
0:57–1:11	**Verse 3**, 4 mm.	"Life could be a dream"; performed as harmony throughout (note the high range of the tenor vocalist).
1:11–1:25	**Interlude (full)**, 4 mm.	Nonsense syllables followed by entrance of saxophone.
1:25–1:39	**Instrumental verse**, 4 mm.	Saxophone solo.
1:39–1:53	**Instrumental verse**, 4 mm.	Saxophone solo.
1:53–2:07	**Verse 4**, 4 mm.	Repeat of verse 3.
2:07–2:23	**Interlude**, 4 mm.	Repeat of full interlude.

verse is defined as a section with repeating music and nonrepeating lyrics. A form that employs only verses is called a **simple verse form**. Look back at the Listening Guide for "Rocket '88'" and you will see that it is in simple verse form. Elvis Presley's 1956 recording of "Heartbreak Hotel" provides another clear example of simple verse form: each 8-bar verse is based on the same chord progression, which is actually an abbreviated version of the 12-bar blues (though it is not a 12-bar blues). As you listen to "Heartbreak Hotel," notice how the song consists of repetitions of the same music with different words for each verse (and one instrumental verse).

AABA Form. The song form most associated with mainstream pop before the birth of rock and roll is **AABA form**. This is one of the most common formal patterns in Tin Pan Alley songs and usually occurs in a 32-bar scheme that combines four 8-bar phrases. We use the designation AABA to show that the first two 8-bar phrases are very similar, the third 8-bar phrase is contrasting, and the last 8-bar phrase is similar to the first two.

A	A	B	A
8 mm.	8 mm.	8 mm.	8 mm.

Among the songs in later Listening Guides that employ the standard 32-bar AABA form are "Over the Rainbow," "I'm Sittin' on Top of the World," "Hey Good Lookin'," and "Blueberry Hill." As it turns out, most AABA songs would be

Listening Guide   Get Music ⓢ wwnorton.com/studyspace

Elvis Presley, "Heartbreak Hotel" RCA 47-6420

Words and music by Mae Boren, Tommy Durden, and Elvis Presley, produced by Steve Sholes. Reached #1 on the *Billboard* "Top 100" chart, #1 on all three *Billboard* country and western charts (sales, jukebox, and radio), and #3 on the *Billboard* rhythm and blues "Most Played in Juke Boxes" chart in 1956.

FORM: Simple verse.

TIME SIGNATURE: 12/8 (shuffle in four).

INSTRUMENTATION: Electric guitar, piano, acoustic bass, drums, and lead vocals.

0:00–0:22	**Verse 1**, 8 mm.	"Well, since my baby left me . . ."
0:22–0:42	**Verse 2**, 8 mm.	"Oh, though it's always crowded . . ."
0:42–1:01	**Verse 3**, 8 mm.	"Now, the bellhop's tears . . ."
1:01–1:22	**Verse 4**, 8 mm.	"Well, if your baby leaves you . . ."
1:21–1:42	**Instrumental Verse**, 8 mm.	Guitar solo for first 4 mm., then piano solo.
1:42–2:05	**Verse 5**, 8 mm.	"Oh, though it's always crowded . . ."

too short if the song did not repeat some or all of the 32-bar pattern. (In "I'm Sittin' on Top of the World" and "Hey Good Lookin'," the entire AABA form returns, but in "Over the Rainbow" and "Blueberry Hill," only part of the AABA structure is repeated.) When the entire AABA form is repeated, it is a **full reprise**, and when only part of the AABA form returns, a **partial reprise**. While the 32-bar AABA is common, this form can also be modified to include sections that exceed eight measures. Jerry Lee Lewis's recording of "Great Balls of Fire" provides a good example of this from the rock and roll repertoire. The A sections are 8 measures long, but each presentation of the bridge uses twelve measures of music. This extended bridge structure produces a complete AABA pattern of thirty-six measures, not the usual thirty-two. Note that "Great Balls of Fire" employs a full reprise of this 36-bar pattern to form the second half of the song.

Simple Verse-Chorus. A **chorus** is a section that repeats the same music and lyrics intact in each presentation. (Remember that verses use the same music with different words.) When a single musical pattern is used as the basis for both verses and choruses in a song, the resulting form is called **simple verse-chorus**. Note that the melody portion of a song may change from verse to chorus, while the chords underneath stay the same. Hence, the biggest difference between a simple verse and a simple verse-chorus is the presence of a repeating set of lyrics to form a chorus section. Consider "Can the Circle Be Unbroken" as recorded by the Carter Family. The verses and choruses in this song are built on the same 16-bar progression. While the verse and chorus may seem different on the first listen, repeated listenings reveal that the verse and chorus use the same melody and chord progression, with only slight changes made between sections. Listen to this track and see if you can hear the similarity.

In order to count the measures in "Can the Circle Be Unbroken," you will need to keep two things in mind. First, rather than the four-beats-per-measure rhythmic pattern we encountered in the 12-bar blues, this song uses a two-beats-per-measure pattern. You thus need to count "one-two, one-two," and so on. A second aspect of this song involves irregular counting of measures. When you try to count measures during the verses of this song, the twelfth bar contains only one beat, while in the choruses the fourth and twelfth measures contain only one beat. Musicians often refer to this as "dropping a beat," meaning that in each instance the second beat is dropped. The only instance of this 16-bar pattern not to drop these beats is the first instrumental verse on the guitar. In this verse the group "corrects" the dropped beats from the sung verses and choruses by playing sixteen full measures of two beats.

Contrasting Verse-Chorus. Unlike a simple verse-chorus, in which the verse and chorus sections share the same musical material, when the verses and choruses of a song employ different music, we call this **contrasting verse-chorus**. Forms like contrasting verse-chorus may also include a bridge, or a section that provides a contrasting, nonrepeated section of music and lyrics and returns to a verse or chorus. A rock and roll example of contrasting verse-chorus with a bridge is Buddy Holly's "That'll Be the Day." As you listen to this track, note the differences between the 8-bar verse and chorus sections, in addition to the instrumental bridge formed out of a 12-bar blues pattern.

The diagram on p. 18 summarizes the four common formal types found in rock

Listening Guide

Get Music ⑤ wwnorton.com/studyspace

Jerry Lee Lewis, "Great Balls of Fire" Sun 281

Words and music by Otis Blackwell and Jack Hammer, produced by Sam Phillips. Reached #2 on the *Billboard* "Top 100" chart, #1 on the country and western "Best Sellers in Stores" chart, and #3 on both the "R&B Best Sellers in Stores" and "Most Played R&B by Jockeys" charts in 1958.

FORM: AABA, with full reprise.

TIME SIGNATURE: 4/4.

INSTRUMENTATION: Piano, drums, acoustic bass, and lead vocals.

0:00–0:13	**A-Verse**, 8 mm.	Vocals delivered in stop time, "You shake my nerves . . ."
0:13–0:25	**A-Verse**, 8 mm.	Full band in, "I laughed at love . . ."
0:25–0:43	**B-Bridge**, 12 mm.	"Kiss me baby . . ."
0:43–0:55	**A-Verse**, 8 mm.	"I chew my nails down . . ."
0:55–1:06	**A-Instrumental Verse**, 8 mm.	Raucous piano solo.
1:06–1:18	**A-Instrumental Verse**, 8 mm.	
1:18–1:37	**B-Bridge**, 12 mm.	"Kiss me baby . . ."
1:37–1:49	**A-Verse**, 8 mm.	"I chew my nails . . ."

music. While we will encounter more complicated formal designs later in the book, these four will apply to a large majority of the songs we study. Listening for form in rock music helps us gain a deeper understanding of how music is structured. It provides fans and students of this music with a glimpse of how musicians, songwriters, producers, and arrangers organize these songs. In many ways, understanding form helps us hear the larger patterns in the music and gives us a sense of the "bigger picture."

WHO'S PLAYING WHAT: INSTRUMENTATION IN ROCK

Beat It: Drums and Percussion. The musical instruments used in rock music, and especially the ways these instruments are combined, are central to the myriad musical styles discussed in this book. While most rock fans can tell the difference between an electric guitar and a keyboard, or a drum set and a saxophone, far fewer listeners understand exactly how these instruments typically work together in songs. Instruments in rock frequently have specific roles within the music. The task of the **rhythm section** is to establish a solid foundation for singers, instrumental soloists, and other members of the group that focus on melody. At the heart of the rhythm section is the drummer, whose role is to establish not only the tempo and meter, but also the "feel" of each song. Most rock drummers employ a set consisting of a snare drum (which sits on a stand between the drummer's legs), a bass drum (played by the right foot), and a high-hat (two cymbals that can be clamped together using

Listening Guide   Get Music ⓢ wwnorton.com/studyspace

The Carter Family, "Can the Circle Be Unbroken" Columbia 37669

Words and music by A. P. Carter, recorded in 1935. Released before the era of country charts in the United States. (There were no *Billboard* country charts until 1944.)

FORM: Simple verse-chorus.

TIME SIGNATURE: 2/4, with dropped beats.

INSTRUMENTATION: Acoustic guitar, two female and one male voice, with one female voice taking the lead during verses and choruses sung in three-part harmony.

0:00–0:06	**Introduction**, 3 mm.	Guitar accompaniment.
0:06–0:26	**Verse 1**, 16 mm. (only one beat in m. 12)	Solo vocal, "I was standin' . . ."
0:26–0:44	**Chorus**, 16 mm. (only one beat in mm. 4 and 12)	Choral vocal, "Can the circle . . ."
0:44–1:04	**Instrumental Verse**, 16 mm. (no dropped beats)	Guitar solo.
1:04–1:23	**Verse 2**, 16 mm.	As before, "I told the undertaker . . ."
1:23–1:41	**Chorus**, 16 mm.	As before, "Can the circle . . ."
1:41–2:00	**Verse 3**, 16 mm.	As before, "I followed close behind her . . ."
2:00–2:18	**Chorus**, 16 mm.	As before, "Can the circle . . ."
2:18–2:28	**Instrumental Verse** (partial), 8 mm.	Guitar solo.
2:28–2:47	**Verse 4**, 16 mm.	"Went back home, Lord . . ."
2:47–3:04	**Chorus**, 16 mm.	"Can the circle . . ."

Listening Guide

Get Music Ⓢ **wwnorton.com/studyspace**

The Crickets, "That'll Be the Day" Brunswick 55009

Words and music by Buddy Holly, Jerry Allison, and Norman Petty, produced by Norman Petty. Reached #1 on the *Billboard* pop "Best Sellers in Stores" chart, and #2 on the *Billboard* "R&B Best Sellers in Stores" chart in 1957.

FORM: Contrasting verse-chorus with instrumental bridge.

TIME SIGNATURE: 12/8 (shuffle in 4).

INSTRUMENTATION: Electric guitar, acoustic bass, drums, lead and backup vocals.

0:00–0:04	**Introduction**, 2 mm.	Solo guitar featured.
0:04–0:19	**Chorus**, 8 mm.	"Well, that'll be the day . . ."
0:19–0:34	**Verse**, 8 mm.	"Well, you give me . . ."
0:34–0:49	**Chorus**, 8 mm.	"Well, that'll be the day . . ."
0:49–1:12	**Instrumental Bridge**, 12 mm.	Guitar solo over 12–bar blues.
1:12–1:27	**Chorus**, 8 mm.	"Well, that'll be the day . . ."
1:27–1:42	**Verse,** 8 mm.	"Well, when Cupid shot . . ."
1:42–1:58	**Chorus**, 8 mm.	"Well, that'll be the day . . ."
1:58–2:14	**Ending**, 8 mm.	Based closely on chorus, "That'll be the day . . ."

Four Common Formal Types

Simple verse	All verses based on same music, no chorus.
Simple verse-chorus	Verses and choruses based on same music.
Contrasting verse-chorus	Verses and choruses based on different music.
AABA	Verses and bridge based on different music; can employ full or partial reprise.

12-bar blues or the doo-wop progression may occur as the basis for any of the sections in these forms.

Simple verse, simple verse-chorus, and contrasting verse-chorus forms may also employ a bridge.

a stand controlled by a foot pedal). Most drummers also use medium-sized drums called tom-toms. Tom-toms that are mounted on the bass drum are called ride toms; those that stand on the floor are called floor toms. A drummer may also use several cymbals, most often a larger ride cymbal and a smaller crash cymbal. The rhythmic patterns drummers play work something like the gears of a clock, with some gears moving quickly and others moving more slowly. The high-hat or ride cymbal is often used for the fastest notes, played in a regular stream. The bass and snare drums are generally played at slower intervals, and often seem to be in dialogue with one another. A typical drumbeat is shown below; the numbers across the top show how the rhythm would be counted, while the x's show which drums (or high-hat) are used on which beats:

Count:	1	&	2	&	3	&	4	&			1	&	2	&	3	&	4	&		
High-hat	X	X	X	X	X	X	X	X		X	X	X	X	X	X	X	X	
Snare			X				X					X				X		
Bass	X			X	X					X			X	X				

The drum set can be enhanced by the addition of other percussion instruments, such as tambourine, cowbell, conga drums, or even hand claps. Most drummers will use one pattern for verses and another for bridges or choruses, and also break the pattern to play "drum fills" that help lead the music from section to section.

The Low Down: Electric Bass. The bass player's job is to "lock in" with the drummer rhythmically, and to provide the important bass notes to the chord progressions played by the guitar and/or keyboards. Within the rhythm section, the bassist is a kind of bridge between the rhythmic and harmonic (or chord-based) dimensions of the music. Often the bass player will create their part around the rhythmic pattern played on the bass drum, stressing those notes rhythmically while filling in other notes to provide an interesting bass line. Much early rock music used the acoustic upright bass, which could be amplified; but by the early 1960s, the more easily amplified electric bass guitar was the preferred instrument for most popular music except jazz and country. The bass (both acoustic and electric) usually has four strings that match the bottom four strings of the guitar. The distance between the tuning of guitar and bass strings is what musicians call an **octave**, a lower or higher version of the same note. If you sing the pattern Do-Re-Mi-Fa-Sol-La-Ti-Do, the two "Do" notes are an octave apart, and represent the distance between the typical tuning of strings on a bass and a guitar.

Harmony in Motion: Rhythm Guitar and Keyboards. While the bass usually provides the foundation for a song's harmony within the rhythm section, the rhythm guitar fleshes out the harmonic dimension by playing full chords. Rhythm guitar can be played on either acoustic or electric guitar. The electric guitar produces little sound on its own, but can reach high volume levels when connected to an amplifier. In 1950s rockabilly, the acoustic rhythm guitar often replaces the drum set and provides the rhythmic propulsion that drives the song forward. More often, though, the rhythm guitar part complements the bass and drum parts, and these three instruments work together to establish the harmonic and rhythmic basis

Adolfo "Fito" de la Parra, drummer for Canned Heat, performing at the Woodstock Music and Art Fair (see Chapter 7). Here, de la Parra performs on a standard rock drum set: bass drum (bottom right), snare drum (center), two mounted toms (attached to a second bass drum), a floor tom (left), a ride and crash cymbal (left) and a high-hat (right).

for the song. The rhythm guitarist also has to be careful to fit his part in with the bass and drums. Sometimes if the bass locks in with the bass drum, the rhythm guitar will lock in with the snare, emphasizing the snare part while filling in the remaining space between beats. Sometimes the piano, organ, or synthesizer is used along with, or even in place of, the rhythm guitar. If keyboards or organs are used with rhythm guitar, they may play the same rhythmic figure as the guitar or simply sustain chords while the guitar plays its more rhythmic part. However the parts are organized, rhythm guitar and keyboard players have to be careful not to conflict musically.

In the Spotlight: Lead Singers and Backup Vocals. With the rhythmic and harmonic dimensions of the piece firmly secured by the rhythm section, the singer focuses on the melodic dimension of the music. Singers are sometimes very free with the rhythmic placement of their melody notes, which translates into a lively dialectical tension with the tightly structured grid of the rhythm section. The singer's job is to create melodic interest and deliver the lyrics in a convincing manner—one that does not seem contrived or unnatural in comparison with normal speech. Many listeners attend as closely to the lyrics as to the melody that projects them, so a vocal performer has to be sure that the words come across effectively. Many solo vocalists are also accompanied by background vocals. A singer may have no backup vocals (Elvis Presley's "That's All Right (Mama)"), or the singer's melody will be accompanied by harmony vocals that follow the melody (The Beach Boys' "Surfer Girl") or support and echo some part of it (The Beatles' "Twist and Shout"). Like the rhythm section parts described above, the vocals are usually coordinated (with one another and with the rhythm section) to avoid conflict between parts.

Steppin' Up: Instrumental Solos. In order to create contrast in arrangements, an instrumental solo is often introduced somewhere past the midpoint in a song. This might be a saxophone solo (the Coasters' "Yakety Yak"), a guitar solo (Jimi

Hendrix's "Purple Haze"), or a piano solo (Jerry Lee Lewis's "Great Balls of Fire"). Sometimes an arrangement can feature several solos, as in Yes's "Roundabout." In all of these cases, the instrumental soloist is the central focus of the music for the duration of the solo, taking the place usually reserved for the singer. The job of the rhythm section remains the same as it was during the other sections of the song: to support the soloist. The instrumental solo often makes the return of the vocals sound fresh, since there is usually no singing during the solo. In this regard the solo is itself subordinate to the sung sections of the track (although with some bands—like Santana—this relationship can be reversed).

Horns and Strings: Sweetening the Sound. Some arrangements use horns or strings to add the finishing touches to a track. Horn sections often consist of a combination of trumpets, trombones, and saxophones used to give a tune a little more "punch." This approach is evident in much of the soul music recorded in Memphis and Muscle Shoals (Chapter 6). Strings can make an arrangement sound bigger and more elegant. Strings are often saved until late in the arrangement and are employed to give the end of the track a convincing lift. An arranger has to be careful that the horns or strings added to sweeten a track stay out of the way of the rhythm section and singers, creating a backdrop that enhances the song without drawing too much attention to itself.

How It All Fits Together: "Smoke on the Water." Now that we have discussed the instruments used in rock music and outlined their respective roles, we will explore an example to observe how instrumentation works. Deep Purple's "Smoke on the Water" is a prime example of how rock music from the mid-1960s (and beyond) is organized in terms of instrumentation. The track follows the **contrasting verse-chorus** formal pattern: after a lengthy introduction there are four verse-chorus pairs (the third of which is instrumental), with a **coda** rounding the tune off. It is easy to hear each instrument during the introduction, since the band brings them in almost one at a time. The song begins with the electric guitar alone, playing a four-measure blues-inflected **riff** that is then repeated. Notice the guitar's distorted tone, which is a result of overdriving the amplifier; this tone is used extensively in rock. The third time through the guitar riff, the drums enter (0:17); first the high-hat alone, and on the fourth time through, the snare drum as well. Notice that the guitar is also doubled by the organ here, although the effect is subtle because the organ is also distorted and sounds like a second guitar. With the fifth occurrence of the guitar riff (0:34), the bass guitar is added, and the sixth time through (0:43), the bass is doubled by the bass drum. As the vocals enter for the first verse (0:51), notice that the drummer is primarily playing the high-hat, bass drum, and snare, using crashes on the cymbal and bass drum to mark the beginning and end of vocal phrases. The guitar and bass are playing almost the same part, while the organ takes the "rhythm guitar" role, playing the chords off the drums

Parliament Funkadelic's Bootsy Collins playing the electric bass in concert. The electric bass plays a prominent part in rock and is central to funk music.

Keyboard instruments most common in rock music are piano, organ, synthesizer, and digital piano. Keyboardist Rick Wakeman from the progressive rock group Yes, who uses both synthesizers and electric piano in this photo, was known for his large battery of instruments.

and bass. As the chorus begins (1:25), note that the organ becomes more sustained, as do the guitar and bass, while more crashes and drum fills and a second vocal harmony are added. The verses and choruses that follow are mostly the same as the first pair, although the verse and chorus during the guitar solo are different (2:58). The bass moves in faster notes during the solo, while the drum part emphasizes the snare on the faster notes rather than the high-hat. The arrival of the chorus during the solo is particularly dynamic (3:30), as is the return to the guitar riff in the passage before the beginning of the last verse (3:40).

Listening to this example analytically helps us focus our attention on the separate elements that make up "Smoke on the Water." Most listeners never really attend to the ways the musical parts in a track work together; they may only notice individual parts when one stands out in some way, and then only for a moment. As we continue our study of rock music, try to listen more carefully to each song's instrumentation to hear how the musicians are working together to make the music sound the way it does. As mentioned above, it sometimes helps to follow a single part all the way through a tune, for example listening to the bass only, then playing the song again and focusing only on the drums. While rock music sometimes gives the impression of musical simplicity, there are often layers of complexity waiting to be discovered. The tapestry of musical texture often does not draw attention to itself; a good rhythm section helps the listener's focus on the vocals or solos, making the background instrumentation relatively transparent.

IN THE STUDIO: THE ROLE OF RECORDING TECHNIQUES IN ROCK MUSIC

Because of the importance of recordings to the history of rock music, some scholars argue that the rock repertoire is not simply a collection of songs, but a collection of *specific recordings* of songs. There is, for instance, only one recording of *Sgt. Pepper's Lonely Hearts Club Band* that we value: the one made by the Beatles in 1967. Many recordings have what might be thought of as "sonic signatures"—features that distinguish them in terms of where and when they were recorded, as well as by whom. Elvis's early recordings with Sam Phillips at Sun Records have a distinctive sound that is, in a sense, separable from the songs themselves or the actual performances of them. For scholars with this view, rock is largely a recorded art, and when we talk about rock songs, we are almost always talking about rock *records*, even if we don't realize it.

Is It Live or Is It Memorex? There are two principal approaches to thinking about what a recording represents. The first is to think of the recording as an "audio snapshot." In this case, the recording is meant to reproduce a live performance as faithfully as possible and the listener should be unaware that a recording process is involved. On these types of recordings, the sounds should seem natural and indiscernible from an actual performance. This approach to recording is frequently used in classical, jazz, and folk music. The second approach to recording is to exploit the possibilities offered by the studio. This often produces sounds that would be impossible to re-create in a live setting. The records of Les Paul and Mary Ford (see Chapter 1) are early examples of this second approach. By progressively building up tracks of his guitar and Ford's voice, Paul was able to create a recorded sound that was very much a consequence of the recording technology that produced it. The recording studio also allows instruments to be combined in ways that would not easily work in a natural acoustic setting. Since the early 1970s live performance technology has made it increasingly possible to combine acoustic instruments with louder electric ones, which is largely a result of sounds that first occurred in the studio. Since the days of Elvis Presley's Sun recordings in the 1950s, rock music has been more dependent on exploiting the possibilities of the studio than creating audio snapshots.

Reverb and Echo. Whether we are aware of it or not, every space we enter has specific acoustic properties. Whenever a sound is made, it is the result of a series of vibrations moving through the air. Some of these vibrations reach our ears directly from the source while others bounce around the room and reflect back to us. Hard surfaces reflect sound; more porous ones (like carpeting, curtains, or furniture) absorb sound. Architects who design concert halls are keenly aware of this, and they devote considerable energy to determining the balance of harder and softer surfaces in a hall and how these surfaces will be angled. The idea, of course, is to create a space that makes the performances in the hall sound as acoustically rich as possible. If there's too much reflection, the sound can be too bright or boomy; if there's not enough, the music can sound dry and lifeless. When taking the audio snapshot approach, it is crucial to find a space with "good acoustics"—that is, with the right kind of reflected sound for the ensemble or soloist involved. Major record companies have in the past maintained their own studios that have been acoustically engineered for the best natural sound. For them, the task is not only to capture the way the musicians sound but also to commit to tape how those musicians sound in that specific room. Stories abound of vocals that were recorded in bathrooms, or guitar parts that were recorded in hallways or stairwells in order to take advantage of the natural acoustics of those spaces.

It is also possible to artificially create a room sound—often referred to as **ambience**—via electronic means, and this effect is called **reverb**. Most commercially available electronic reverb units (or digital plug-ins) offer settings that reproduce the sound of small rooms, medium-size rooms, large rooms, auditoriums of various sizes, churches, and a number of "unnatural" spaces. When an engineer knows that she will use reverb, she may record the original sounds with as little natural ambience as possible, often called a "dry" recording. This dry sound is then fed through the reverb device to produce the desired sound. Reverb is used on almost all rock recordings, meaning that the "spaces" captured on tape are often not real spaces at all. Different kinds of reverb can also be used on different instruments or voices, producing sounds that are the result of multiple "spaces," none of which could naturally coexist in a world with only three dimensions.

Reverb is different from **echo**. In the natural world, an echo occurs when sound bounces back to our ears to create two sonic images of the same event—we hear the original and then its reflection. This sound can be produced electronically as well, though some recording studios have built their own trademark "echo chambers" (the chamber at Gold Star Studios in Los Angeles—now destroyed—has a mythical standing within the recording world). Echo tends not to be of much concern to those who employ the audio snapshot approach; mostly they try to avoid it. In rock, echo is used extensively and often on voices. Together with reverb, echo can make the singing voice sound much richer and even mask certain imperfections in tone or intonation. The beginning of the Supremes' "Where Did Our Love Go?" offers an example of studio reverb. The clapping (actually two-by-fours being slapped together) is drenched in a rich reverb that creates the sound of a large gymnasium or some other big, reflective space. The most famous echo can be found on Elvis Presley's Sun recordings. For many years after Elvis's success, studio engineers around the world tried to reproduce the distinctive echo found on songs such as "That's All Right (Mama)," in which the quick echo (often called "slap-back echo") gives Presley's voice a quality that he could never have produced live. Reverb and echo provide what might be thought of as the ambient dimension of the music, and these effects can make instruments sound closer to or farther from the listener, depending on how much reverb or echo is employed—the more reverb or echo, the farther away the sound seems to be.

River Deep, Mountain High: Equalization (EQ).

Frequency also plays a major role in recording techniques, as **equalizers** are used to affect the quality of most sounds. Each note played by an instrument is called its "fundamental," but along with this note, every instrument also subtly produces other, higher notes that help to form the tone, or **timbre** (pronounced to rhyme with "amber") of the instrument. You may have noticed that if you adjust the treble and bass settings on your stereo you can greatly affect the sound—more treble and the sound is brighter, less treble and it sounds muffled. These tone settings adjust the volume of the frequencies in the sounds you hear and affect not only the fundamentals but also the higher notes that are generated in each case (called "upper partials" or "harmonics"). In the process of recording instruments, an engineer has a significant amount of control over the timbre of each recorded sound; for each microphone in use there may be multiple controls that work like the treble and bass on your stereo. Adjusting frequencies of sounds is often called "EQ," which is short for equalization. A good recording is "EQ-ed" to produce a balanced distribution of frequencies. EQ can also help to highlight certain instruments, and keep instruments in a similar range from covering each other up, resulting in a crisper, clearer, more defined sound.

Every Breadth You Take: Stereo Placement. For its first decade or so, most rock music was recorded and released in monophonic sound, **mono**, meaning that there was assumed to be only one speaker for playback and no possibility of stereo imaging. Almost all of the Beatles' records, for instance, were originally released in mono, with later **stereo** versions being prepared mostly (and sometimes hastily) for hi-fi enthusiasts, often without the band participating in the stereo mixes. Among the most successful producers to work in mono was Phil Spector. By the late 1960s, however, stereo was the preferred format for albums and FM radio, and by the mid-1970s complex stereo mixes had become the norm. The development of more and more tracks, greater use of the stereo field, and increasingly ambitious musical projects progressed in tandem throughout the late '60s and '70s, as listeners purchased more sophisticated stereo equipment to get the full effect of the music.

When we hear sounds in the natural world, we can locate the position of a sound source because the sound enters each of our ears in a different way. Our mind calculates where a sound is coming from on the basis of the "stereo" effect. In music that is recorded in stereo, the engineer can control whether a sound comes out of the right or left speaker, or some combination of the two. In order to hear this clearly, use headphones to listen to a stereo recording and close your eyes: you will notice that there is a kind of "sonic landscape" in the space between the two headphones. Some sounds seem to come from the center, while others seem to come from the right or left, or mid-right or mid-left. It is, of course, impossible for the sounds that seem to be coming from the center to really be coming from there; after all, you are sitting between the headphone speakers and there is no center speaker physically present. Stereo sound is thus an aural illusion that we construct as a result of how we hear. Engineers use this phenomenon to separate sounds so we can hear more detail in the recording. For instance, if a rhythm guitar and organ are playing almost the same thing in the same frequency range, the listener may not be able to distinguish them from one another—one will cover up or "mask" the other. If you adjust one to sound like it is coming from the right and the other from the left, each will be much more distinct. So, in a stereo recording, the instruments and voices are arranged across the stereo field and the result is that the recording sounds clearer and more sonically complex.

Mixing. These dimensions of recorded sound—ambience, EQ, stereo placement, and overall volume—are controlled from a mixing board. A mixing board is used in two ways: first, to record the sound to tape (or more recently to a digital recorder) and second, to play the recording back. In classical music, the engineer's job is to capture the sound in the natural ambient space as faithfully as possible; a playback should not color the sound (though it may, and sometimes adjustments are made at this second stage). In rock, sounds are often recorded dry (except when special room effects are desired) and stored for playback. Until the 1960s, most popular music was recorded using a single performance. The use of tape after World War II allowed engineers to begin experimenting with multi-track tape, creating recordings from multiple performances. Early recording tape could store three **tracks** of music (meaning that three performances could be played back simultaneously), but as the '60s and '70s progressed, tapes could contain eight, sixteen, twenty-four, forty-eight, or even more tracks. As computer hardware and software have become less expensive, in the last decade more musicians have turned to **digital audio workstations** (or DAWs) to record music, shedding the need for large, expensive recording studios. Although now encased in computer software, modern recording programs such as GarageBand and Pro-Tools still incorporate the same principles as older mixing boards. However, with the advance of digital technology in recent years, the number of tracks available is so large that track space is no longer a technical limitation. Regardless of the process used to capture the sounds (analog or digital), once all the tracks are recorded, the engineer is ready to **mix down**, meaning that she will adjust the ambience, EQ, stereo placement, and relative volume of the tracks to produce the final version of the song. (Notice that the word "track" is used in recording to designate a recorded part, but it is also used more generally among fans and writers to mean "song.") Mixing is a complicated and creative process undertaken by highly skilled professionals who are often known for their distinctive "sound." Since the mid-1960s, bands have often spent more time mixing an album than recording the individual tracks.

Putting It All Together: "Josie." Some of the most sophisticated recorded sounds in rock were created by Steely Dan. Taking a closer look at Steely Dan's "Josie" will allow us to observe many of the techniques explained in this "What to Listen For in Rock" section at work in a single recording. "Josie" is structured according to the **compound AABA form**, meaning that each section of the AABA form is made up of smaller verse and chorus sections. After an angular introduction featuring the electric guitar, there are several measures of vamp before the first verse begins. Two verse-chorus pairs make up the large-scale A sections, followed by an instrumental bridge making up the B section. The return to the verse-chorus pair in this case features a guitar solo over the verse material, with the vocals returning for the chorus. A return to the introduction and vamp close the song as it fades out. In terms of the instrumentation, the track uses a fairly standard rhythm section of rhythm guitars, electric piano, bass, and drums. The vocals are mostly solo, with some backing vocals added during both the verse and chorus sections. Horns, percussion, and synthesizer strings are also added to "sweeten" the mix. The stereo aspect of the record can be heard most readily in the drums: note that the snare and bass drums are in the center, the high-hat is panned right, and tom-toms and cymbals are panned both right and left. As is usual for rock, the lead vocals and bass are in the center. Three electric guitars are involved in the rhythm section: two of these are panned right and left and play a part almost identical to the piano, which is panned center. The third guitar, which plays a funky single-note part, is panned right. When the synthesizer

(1) Phil Spector in the producer's role at the famous Gold Star studios in California. This 12-input mixing board shows the limited resources of producers and engineers in the recording studio during the early 1960s.

(2) The sheer size of the sound board in this 1979 photo of producer and engineer Alan Parsons shows the development of recording technology during the 1970s.

(3) Modern digital audio workstations such as GarageBand and Pro-Tools are commonly used to perform the functions of a mixing board and tape machine. This screen shot of a Pro-Tools session shows how digital recording software often directly emulates physical sound recording equipment.

strings enter in the second chorus, they are panned left. Note that the horns and backup vocals are both panned mid-right and mid-left to keep them distinct in the mix. Listen for the reverb and echo that have been added to the lead vocals and the heavy reverb on the synthesizer strings and solo guitar; by contrast, the bass, bass drum, and high-hat are very dry. Thus, in addition to the separation that occurs through stereo placement, ambience is also used to help keep the parts distinct. The distribution of instruments and equalization across the full frequency range makes the recording sound full, with plenty of low end balanced by bright highs.

VIEWING ROCK

Formal structure, instrumentation, and studio techniques are among the most important aspects of recorded sound. Yet, rock music became popular in an age after the Second World War, when images of musicians were often inextricable from sound. Various forms of video-based media—including television, films, and music videos—have enabled rock musicians to reach audiences visually as well as aurally. Thus, images of rock have been vital to the formation of cultural tastes for dance, fashion, and behavior that would not have been possible without the combination of rock music with the moving image.

Although the average listener often has experience with the visual aspects of rock, when studying rock in an academic setting it is informative to consider the relationship between music and images. For one, when viewing a musical performance on video it is important to observe whether the musicians perform live or lip-synch to a prerecorded audio track. Similarly, knowledge of the original context can change how we might view a video performance. Among television broadcasts, for example, there are noteworthy differences between late-night talk show appearances, prime-time variety shows, and daytime talk shows. Moreover, dramatic feature films starring rock musicians and performances have been popular for decades, and serve a different function than documentaries that compile footage from live performances.

Rock Television. Prior to their demise in the 1980s, variety shows presented compelling rock performances on network television. They featured comedy, skits,

Listening Guide

Steely Dan, "Josie"

Words and music by Walter Becker and Donald Fagen, produced by Gary Katz. Reached #26 on the *Billboard* "Hot 100" chart in 1978. Contained on the album *Aja*, which reached #3 in the United States and #5 in the UK in late 1977.

FORM: Compound AABA form, with A sections employing a verse-chorus pair.

TIME SIGNATURE: 4/4.

	0:00–0:32	**Introduction**, 16 mm.	8 mm. guitar figure then 8 mm. vamp.
A	0:32–1:03	**Verse 1**, 16 mm.	"We're gonna break out . . ."
	1:03–1:28	**Chorus**, 12 mm.	8 mm. chorus then 4 mm. link to verse 2.
A	1:28–1:59	**Verse 2**, 16 mm.	As before, "Jo would you love . . ."
	1:59–2:15	**Chorus**, 8 mm.	No link this time, "When Josie . . ."
B	2:15–2:31	**Bridge**, 8 mm.	Instrumental.
A	2:31–3:03	**Instr. verse**, 16 mm.	Guitar solo.

dancing, and musical performances, among many other odd acts. Important variety shows in the history of rock included the Ed Sullivan Show (officially called *Toast of the Town*) on CBS and *The Hollywood Palace* on ABC. While many readers can easily conjure iconic images of the Beatles appearing on Ed Sullivan's variety hour, many have not considered these performances in the context of the variety show, in which the band performed alongside ventriloquists, acrobats, and magicians that rounded out Sullivan's nightly lineup. Other variety shows in the 1960s, such as *Hullaballoo, Shindig!, and Shivaree,* were more youth oriented, featuring Technicolor sets and go-go dancers. Although rock purists might find it odd to celebrate variety show appearances, the shows are often historically valuable because they included real-time (not lip-synched) musical performances.

While variety shows were often marketed to adults in prime-time slots, teen-oriented dance programs also became extremely popular during the 1950s. These programs were often locally produced, and broadcast in late-afternoon time slots to reach kids at home after school. Early dance shows popular during the 1950s included *American Bandstand* and *The Arthur Murray Party*, both of which became nationally syndicated. Dance-oriented television shows usually featured a room full of young dancers, both professional and amateur, who demonstrated new

Get Music ⓢ **wwnorton.com/studyspace**

3:03–3:19	**Chorus**, 8 mm.	As second chorus, "When Josie . . ."
3:19–4:24	**Coda**, 32 mm.	8 mm. as intro, then 24 mm. vamp and fade.

INSTRUMENTATION

Rhythm section	*Singing*	*Solos*	*Sweetening*
Electric piano	Solo w/ some backing	Electric guitar	Horns
2 rhythm guitars	vocals on verse and		Synth strings
"Funky" guitar	chorus		Percussion
Drum set			
Bass			

MIX

Left		*Center*		*Right*
Cymbal	Solo guitar	Lead vocal	Backup vocals	High-hat
Rhythm guitar	Backup vocals	Electric piano	Horns	Cymbal
Tom-tom	Horns	Percussion		"Funky" guitar
Synth strings		Snare drum		Rhythm guitar
		Bass		Tom-tom
		Bass drum		

moves and fashion trends to a soundtrack of popular recordings. In many cases, these shows featured a special guest performance, but most artists did not perform their music live in this context, lip-synching instead. The dance show format maintained popularity well past the 1960s, with *American Bandstand* running until the late 1980s. During the 1970s, disco-oriented shows such as *Soul Train* and *Dance Fever* continued this tradition, while 1980s audiences enjoyed programs like *Solid Gold* and *Dance Party USA*. MTV also played an important role in producing dance-oriented television shows, with *Club MTV* in the 1980s and later with *TRL* (or *Total Request Live*) in the 1990s and 2000s. *TRL* was certainly created out of the same mold as *American Bandstand*: it aired in an after-school time slot, centered on a live studio audience, and featured live performances by the most popular teen-oriented groups of the time.

Television has also been an important forum for artists starring in musical sitcoms. Beginning with *The Monkees* in the mid-1960s, there have been numerous script-based comedies that featured rock musicians or musical performances. The Partridge Family was a fictional musical group, popularized during the 1970s, in a self-named television series starring teen heartthrob David Cassidy and his real-life step-mother, Shirley Jones. A decade later, the series *Fame* (based on a feature film of the same name) offered a similar musical-dramatic construct that included notable elements of theater and dance. Although no real-life rock stars were featured in this series, much of the music became quite popular, especially in the UK. A modern brand of this same musical sitcom can also be found in *Glee*, which has struck a chord with television audiences while racking up dozens of hit singles and millions of worldwide album sales.

Rock Film. From the beginning of the rock movement, many rock music performances were featured in motion pictures. While early depictions of rock music in films like *Rock Around the Clock* and *Blackboard Jungle* characterized rock musicians and fans as "hoodlums," rock performances were increasingly common in major motion pictures only a few years later. After signing to RCA in the mid-1950s, Elvis Presley made dozens of films, most of which featured musical performances. Some of Presley's most iconic video performances came from his work in films, including the famous "Jailhouse Rock" sequence from 1957. Presley's move into motion pictures helped to usher rock and roll into Hollywood, and during the early 1960s it became common for low-budget teen-oriented films to feature musicians and rock performances. The most popular of these were the "beach party films" produced between 1963 and 1967, many of which starred Annette Funicello and Frankie Avalon. In addition to music performed by the stars, many of these films included a house band (often Dick Dale and the Del-Tones), and various pop and R&B stars of the time.

Throughout the 1970s and 1980s rock musicians continued to star in films. Some of these might be considered serious works, while others simply served as popularity vehicles. KISS famously starred in the cult-classic *KISS Meets the Phantom of the Park* in 1978, a made-for-television film that is best known for its embarrassing and campy acting. The Ramones were central to the plot of the 1979 film *Rock and Roll High School*. Many conceptual rock albums of the 1970s also translated easily into dramatic film, producing rock-oriented movies such as *Tommy* (1975) and *Pink Floyd The Wall* (1982). Prince also starred in a series of films during the 1980s, including *Purple Rain* (1984), *Under the Cherry Moon* (1986), and *Graffiti Bridge* (1990). These are only a few of the many films after the 1960s to blur the line between music video and Hollywood feature, exposing the visual aspects of rock music to a wider audience.

Concert films have also been important to the history of rock music. The first notable film in this genre was *T.A.M.I. Show*, a 1964 feature film shot at the Santa Monica Civic Auditorium that included performances by many of the most popular rock stars of the time, ranging from British invasion groups to James Brown. The tradition of concert films has produced many of the most notable visual images in the history of rock, which include Otis Redding coaxing a newfound audience in *Monterey Pop* (1968), Jimi Hendrix playing "The Star-Spangled Banner" in *Woodstock* (1970), and the Rolling Stones' catastrophic performance at Altamont in *Gimme Shelter* (1970). As rock became more prominent, attracting the attention of Hollywood and the financial clout to secure important directors, the artistic quality of the concert film continued to improve. These include Martin Scorcese's depiction of the 1976 Thanksgiving farewell concert by the Band at San Francisco's Winterland Ballroom portrayed in *The Last Waltz* (1978) and Jonathan Demme's documentary of the Talking Heads' 1983 three-night stand in a Hollywood theater released as *Stop Making Sense* (1984). While films such as these were notable in their time, documentary films and high-quality concert footage are now released frequently, providing fans with ongoing opportunities to experience the visual element of rock without actually attending live performances.

Music Videos. Since the advent of rock, artists have also used films as a vehicle for advancing their careers and increasing their popularity. Short films made to promote singles date back at least to the 1960s, although these were more a part of the European market than the American one. The Beatles created some of the earliest promotional videos, intended to promote their music after they stopped performing live. In 1966, the band made videos for "Rain" and "Paperback Writer." Judged by later standards, these seem unimaginative and bland: the band lip-synchs performances in various scenes shot in the same outdoor garden setting. But because the Beatles were weary of touring, these and later videos—most especially those for "Penny Lane" and "Strawberry Fields Forever"—became important tools in promoting new Beatles releases. The promotional video, which later became called the music video, has an extraordinary history that eventually made a massive impact on the entire popular music industry. The emergence of 1980s music videos and the rise of MTV will be covered in depth later in the text.

Visual and Contextual Aspects of "Nowhere to Run." For the purposes of this introduction to the video elements of rock, a useful example is a famous performance by Martha and the Vandellas for their hit single "Nowhere to Run." This well-known video footage was filmed for a summer 1965 television special hosted by disc jockey Murray the K and sponsored by the national Office of Economic Opportunity. The lip-synched video features Martha and the Vandellas in a car factory in Detroit, riding down the assembly line in a Ford Mustang as it is being

assembled (see image 1 on this page). Images taken from this footage have often been associated with Motown, the Vandellas' record company. As the most important record company to emerge from Detroit, historians often associate Motown's creative process with an assembly line, akin to the city's many car factories (2). This footage might seem like an effort on the part of Motown to create this association, but the video actually comes from a larger television special called *It's What's Happening, Baby*, not created by Motown, that featured many of the most popular acts of the period, including Ray Charles, the Righteous Brothers, Johnny Rivers, and the Ronnettes. The purpose of the special was to get young viewers to mail employment concerns to a government-sponsored organization called New Chance. Moreover, at the end of the Vandellas clip, Murray the K drives the Mustang created during the performance to a beach-oriented setting, segueing into a video featuring Jan and Dean (3). From this clip we learn several things about the connection between video and musical performances during the early rock era. First, we see how the government was attuned to the power of musical performances to inspire youth to action. We also see how specific settings can enhance regional and cultural stereotypes of musical sounds. Finally, we witness how the larger context of a video performance can be lost over time, and how reconnecting these settings is valuable to the study of rock music and its history.

Throughout the remainder of the book, many notable performances in films, on television, and in music videos are discussed in special Viewing Rock boxes. Additionally, many of the Backstage Pass sections provide commentary on historically significant performances that are available on commercial video, including DVD and Internet media services like Netflix, Amazon, and iTunes. Further study of these performances can be a rewarding experience that enhances the aural consideration of rock recordings.

Now that we have discussed the organization of the book, listened carefully to some music, and considered some visual aspects of rock, it is time to dive in and explore rock music's history and repertoire. Before we consider the emergence of rock and roll, however, we will need to get a clear picture of how the music business was configured in the first half of the twentieth century. Chapter 1 will help us understand what the popular music world was like before the advent of rock and roll.

FURTHER READING

Mark Cunningham, *Good Vibrations: A History of Record Production* (Sanctuary, 1996).

Simon Frith, *Sound Effects: Youth, Leisure, and the Politics of Rock 'n' Roll* (Constable, 1985).

Theodore Gracyk, *Rhythm and Noise: An Aesthetics of Rock* (Duke University Press, 1996).

Greil Marcus, *Mystery Train: Images of America in Rock 'n' Roll Music*, 5th rev. ed. (Plume, 2008).

Howard Massey, *Behind the Glass: Top Record Producers Tell How They Craft the Hits* (Backbeat Books, 2000).

James Miller, *Flowers in the Dustbin: The Rise of Rock and Roll, 1947–1977* (Fireside, 1999).

Robert Palmer, *Rock & Roll: An Unruly History* (Harmony Books, 1995).

Dafydd Rees and Luke Crampton, *Rock Stars Encyclopedia*, new rev. ed. (Dorling Kindersley, 1999).

The Rolling Stone Encyclopedia of Rock & Roll, 3rd ed., eds. Holly George-Warren and Patricia Romanowski (Fireside, 2001).

The Rolling Stone Illustrated History of Rock Music, eds. Anthony DeCurtis and James Henke (Random House, 1992).

Martin C. Strong, *The Great Rock Discography* (Canongate, 2000).

Ed Ward, Geoffrey Stokes, and Ken Tucker, *Rock of Ages: The Rolling Stone History of Rock & Roll* (Simon & Schuster, 1986).

Albin Zak III, *The Poetics of Rock: Cutting Tracks, Making Records* (University of California Press, 2001).

VISIT STUDYSPACE AT WWNORTON.COM/STUDYSPACE

Access free review material such as:

- music links
- performer info
- practice quizzes
- outlines
- interactive listening guide software

1920s-'40s

The decades of the 1920s, '30s, and '40s in America were to a great extent shaped by three crucial events: the end of World War I ("The Great War"), the stock market crash of 1929, and World War II. Before and after these crushing events, Americans conquered flight, fought for the right to vote, battled for and against prohibition, danced new dances, and made new music.

When World War I ended, 10 million soldiers were dead. Although American casualties accounted for only 1 percent of the total, the Great War had taken a costly toll on American culture. The war was bloody, fought with gas as well as bullets and with old-world strategies that could not accommodate modern weaponry. The modern world was torn apart and people everywhere were horrified.

With the war finally over, Americans felt simultaneous relief and fear, and the result was a sense of desperate recklessness. Upheaval in world politics was reflected in the arts, with the emergence of riotous new forms of literature, dance, and music. Songs remained the dominant form of popular music in the 1920s, but the radical sounds of Louis Armstrong, Duke Ellington, and others helped define the decade musically. F. Scott Fitzgerald (author of *The Great Gatsby*) dubbed the 1920s "the

jazz age," and jazz's strong rhythms, jagged melodies, and big sound made people get up and dance, with young, single, female "flappers" dancing (and smoking and drinking) right alongside their male counterparts.

But the excitement and freedom of the "roaring" twenties were quickly snuffed out in one day, with the stock market crash of October 29, 1929, forever known as "Black Tuesday." The crash sent the American economy into turmoil: 26,000 businesses failed in 1930. By 1932, 11 million Americans—25 percent of the labor force—were out of work. People were forced to move from their homes into shantytowns and many stood in line for bread every day.

In 1932, with the nation out of work and looking to its government for help, Franklin Delano Roosevelt was elected president. Roosevelt promised Americans a "New Deal" and used the power of the federal government to get people back to work, creating government-paid jobs to improve the nation's roads, bridges, tunnels, and forests and national parks. Roosevelt also established the Works Progress Administration (WPA), which contributed significantly to the arts. With the creation of federal agencies like the WPA, along with the establishment of the Social Security

At
early 25
American
out of
ndreds of
nemployed
ne seeking
York in

system, Roosevelt defined a new role for the federal government that some argue broke the United States out of its psychological, if not its economic, depression.

No sooner had Americans started to leave the Great Depression behind than a new enemy emerged: Adolf Hitler. Like Roosevelt, Hitler was dealing with a severe economic crisis in his nation. Hitler, however, began to solve Germany's economic problems in a different way. He chose expansion, eventually leading his military forces into Austria, Czechoslovakia, and Poland and pitting the German "master race" against "undesirables," most notably Jews—6 million of whom were killed in Nazi death camps by 1945. Joining forces with Italy and Japan, Germany led the Axis powers in what soon became World War II. At first the United States did not join in the fighting, but when Japan attacked Pearl Harbor on December 7, 1941, the country entered the fray in the Pacific, and after Germany declared war on the United States, in Europe as well. The war on the European front ended with Germany's surrender in May 1945. The Japanese fought until September when they surrendered after the United States dropped atomic bombs on Hiroshima and Nagasaki. The war was over but the world had entered the atomic age.

While war had ravaged Europe and rocked the world, American soldiers returned home as conquering heroes. Optimism reigned at home, signaled by the G.I. Bill, which allowed more Americans to attend college than ever before, and by a dramatically increased birth rate—a "baby boom" that would have long-range consequences for American culture, especially for popular music and its audience. Being such a large (and prosperous) generation had its benefits. There were lots of baby boomers and soon they would have their own money to spend. Many would spend it on music, a music that was also all their own: rock and roll.

CHAPTER 1

THE WORLD BEFORE ROCK AND ROLL

I n 1956 a young, handsome Elvis Presley appeared on *Toast of the Town*, a weekly television variety program hosted by Ed Sullivan that aired Sunday evenings on CBS. Presley's appearance on the show was the source of considerable controversy. In an earlier performance of "Hound Dog" on *The Milton Berle Show*, Elvis had launched into an improvised ending to the tune, grinding his hips suggestively as he sang. Such on-stage antics caused a public uproar and earned the singer the nickname "Elvis the Pelvis." In spite of heated protests from parents, Elvis became the central figure in a new kind of popular music intended especially for teenagers: rock and roll.

Elvis and his music will be discussed in further detail in the next chapter. For now, recognizing the importance of Elvis's early television performances can help us understand important aspects of the development of rock and roll in the mid-1950s. Consider, for instance, that Presley appeared before a national audience, eliciting simultaneous reaction from the entire country. As rock and roll erupted in 1955 and 1956, a unique feature of its success was that it didn't spread gradually from town to town and region to region, but broke onto the national cultural scene relatively suddenly. How was it possible for this first wave of rock and roll to saturate American culture so quickly and thoroughly? What cultural conditions and commercial means of production and distribution were necessary for a new musical style to "catch fire" as rock and roll did? And what were the sources of this new style?

This chapter will examine these issues and outline the world of popular music in the United States before rock and roll made its rowdy entrance onto the national scene. Few musical styles emerge fully formed in isolation from other styles of their time, and rock and roll is no exception. Rock and roll developed out of three principal sources that preceded it: mainstream popular music, rhythm and blues, and country and western. This chapter will examine how these styles developed in the 1930s, '40s, and early '50s, providing a historical backdrop and musical and stylistic context that will help us

Irving Berlin's "White Christmas" is one of the most successful songs in the history of popular music. Originally featured in the 1942 movie *Holiday Inn* starring Bing Crosby and Fred Astaire, the song has been recorded by a wide range of performers, including Crosby, Frank Sinatra, Perry Como, Clyde McPhatter and the Drifters, Elvis Presley, and Al Green. Crosby's version is reported to be the biggest selling record in history, and it returned to the upper regions of the pop charts during the Christmas season almost every year until 1962, hitting number one in 1942, 1945, and 1946. While the song has come to conjure up nostalgic and warm images of snowy winter nights in front of a crackling fire, the original opening (shown on the previous page) has the singer stuck in sunny southern California during the Christmas season, lamenting the balmy climate.

understand how and why rock and roll emerged as it did and when it did. It will also explore how the development of new technologies like radio and television played a crucial role in the critical shift in the pop-music landscape brought by rock and roll.

BUILDING A NATIONAL AUDIENCE FOR MUSIC AND ENTERTAINMENT

Sheet Music Publishers and Professional Songwriters. The mainstream popular-music business was shaped by a number of factors in the decades before rock and roll. Newly developed radio and television technologies made a huge impact on distributing performances, while the business of music publishing determined how songs were sold. In the first half of the twentieth century, sheet music was the principal method of selling music. The sheet music business was concentrated in an informal district of New York City often referred to as Tin Pan Alley, where songwriters and producers clustered to form the geographic heart of the industry. The area got its name from the high concentration of songwriters plunking out their ideas on rows of pianos, which sounded to the locals like a bunch of people banging on tin pans. The term "Tin Pan Alley" has become shorthand not only for the body of music produced at that time, but also for a way of doing business and a style of American popular music. The body of music consists of the thousands of songs written and made popular, mostly in the first half of the twentieth century, by professional songwriters such as Irving Berlin, Cole Porter, George and Ira Gershwin, and Jerome Kern.

Musically speaking, Tin Pan Alley songs follow a standard, though very flexible, formal pattern. Many of these songs make use of a **sectional verse-chorus** format, in which the chorus is the part of the song listeners are likely to recognize, while the verse is an introduction that sets the scene for the song. Most listeners, for instance, know only the chorus of the perennial favorite "White Christmas." Far fewer listeners will know the song's verse, which explains how Christmas doesn't seem the same in California with all the bright sunshine. Tin Pan Alley choruses are often cast in a 32-measure AABA form. "Over the Rainbow"—a song featured in the classic 1939 film *The Wizard of Oz*—provides a representative example of this form in a Tin Pan Alley context. While there are some standard variations on this common structural pattern in the Tin Pan Alley repertoire, the basic 32-bar chorus appears in many songs. Thus, what holds these songs together musically is a fairly uniform approach to musical form, practiced by a majority of the professional songwriters of Tin Pan Alley, along with a consistent approach to the many other musical elements that are used to help delineate the form. While the sectional verse-chorus form is rare in rock and roll, the AABA form common to so many Tin Pan Alley choruses plays a central role in rock.

This repertoire was also unified by the way it was marketed. In rock music, the basic unit of trade would become a specific recorded performance, available in formats ranging from records and tapes to MP3 files. But in the Tin Pan Alley era, the basic unit of trade was the song itself, not a specific recording of the song. A successful song was recorded by a series of artists, each trying to tailor the tune to his or her personal style. More recorded versions of a song allowed the songwriter

and publisher to earn more money. Professional songwriters composed songs, and publishers worked to get each tune heard by the public. The songwriters themselves were rarely performers, so publishers had to "pitch" songs to artists who might consider performing them. Songs were pitched in all kinds of ways—some more ethical than others. The usual path to popularizing a song was convincing a professional to perform the tune as part of a show.

With the rise of musical theater in the 1930s, Broadway musicals became a prime vehicle for bringing songs to the public's attention. Many early Broadway shows had very skimpy plots, which were created merely to tie the show's songs together (later musicals were far more integrated). The first movies had no sound, although music was often furnished by local musicians—sometimes even an orchestra—and sheet music was occasionally provided by the film studio. When sound films became popular in the 1930s, musicals were often released in film versions, and new musicals were composed expressly for the movies. Records also helped to promote songs, although in the prerock era the central element in a record was still not a particular performance. By far the best way to promote a song during the 1930s and '40s was to get it on the radio, which was dominated by big bands from 1935–45 and by star singers from 1945–55. If a song was performed on national radio, a publisher could expect the best chance of success. In some instances, sales of a recorded version of a song might outsell the sheet music, but sheet music sales were the key to success in the Tin Pan Alley business model.

National versus Regional. In today's world, where satellite TV and the Internet provide convenient and instant access to remote parts of the globe, it is difficult to imagine an America in which culture was largely regional. But at the end of the nineteenth century, the majority of Americans lived in a world very much conditioned by their local and regional surroundings. People did not travel as much as we do now, and in many parts of the country there was limited access to national and world news. This meant that musical styles could often be identified with par-

Listening Guide

Judy Garland with Victor Young and His Orchestra, "Over the Rainbow" Decca 2672

Words by E. Y. Harbaugh, music by Harold Arlen. Reached #5 on the *Billboard* pop chart in fall 1939.

FORM: This example uses AABA form which is closely associated with Tin Pan Alley songwriting and is one of the most common of the mainstream pop formal designs used during the 1900–1950 period. Typically an AABA form presents two verses, followed by a contrasting bridge, and a return to the verse. To fill out a particular performance arrangement of an AABA song, verses and the bridge may be repeated. Here two verses are repeated, as well as part of the bridge, after the complete AABA structure has been presented. Note that the verses within the AABA form are not the same as the verse employed in the sectional verse-chorus form.

TIME SIGNATURE: 4/4. Note the frequent speeding up and slowing down of the tempo. These tempo variations help shape the vocal phrases and make them more expressive. Such changes of tempo are not common in dance music or any style that uses a drummer. In this case, a conductor directs the changes of tempo and dynamics.

INSTRUMENTATION: Vocalist with orchestra.

ticular regions of the country. Mail-order catalogs from Sears, Roebuck and Co. and Montgomery Ward made recorded performances available via gramophone cylinders and 78-rpm discs, but the music that people knew best were pieces that they could either play or hear performed in person, perhaps at a vaudeville show. Many Americans read music and played the piano, and could purchase the sheet music to a favorite song at the local Woolworth's five-and-dime store, which had pianists on hand to play songs for customers trying to decide among competing titles. A wealth of music was also available through the oral tradition, and one could learn to play tunes by ear, without having to read music. During the first few decades of the new century, however, technological and marketing developments in radio and motion pictures made the same kinds of popular entertainment available throughout the country, in many ways breaking down regional differences. The 1930s and '40s are often thought of as a golden age in the history of motion pictures, as Hollywood churned out a wide variety of films that proved popular across America. Later, we will consider the role films played in the music business during those years.

While films were undeniably influential, the most important technological innovation for the music business was radio. Radio technology was developed at the end of the nineteenth century and used initially for military purposes and communication with ships at sea. Radio was first used to broadcast commercial music in 1920, when KDKA in Pittsburgh and WWJ in Detroit went on the air with a blend of news, local

Get Music ⓢ **wwnorton.com/studyspace**

0:00–0:11	**Introduction**, 4 mm.	String melody with pulsating winds accompaniment sets the dreamy mood for the song.
0:11–0:34	**A-Verse**, 8 mm.	Vocal enters, "Somewhere . . . way up high . . ." Listen for the large leap in the melody, which then works its way back to Earth, paralleling the words.
0:34–0:55	**A-Verse**, 8 mm.	As before, "Somewhere . . . skies are blue . . ."
0:55–1:18	**B-Bridge**, 8 mm.	"Some day I'll wish . . ." Notice how the first half of each vocal phrase seems to rush forward, then slow down toward the end.
1:18–1:40	**A-Verse**, 8 mm.	As before, "Somewhere . . . bluebirds fly . . ." Note the melodic support in the orchestra.
1:40–2:01	**A-Verse**, 8 mm.	Vocal gets a rest and the melody is played by clarinet and answered by orchestra.
2:01–2:25	**A-Verse**, 8 mm.	Vocal returns with variations that make the melody seem fresh, "Somewhere . . . bluebirds fly"
2:25–2:46	**B-Partial Bridge**, 4 mm.	Beginning of bridge serves as the basis for the ending, "If happy . . ."

information, and live music. It is hard to exaggerate the marked effect radio had on American culture, especially the history of popular music. Large groups of listeners within range of a regional radio station enjoyed music that might otherwise have been unavailable. Listeners in rural areas could hear live performances from far-off big-city nightclubs. NBC went coast-to-coast with its national radio network in 1928, which was an important step in blurring the regional boundaries of popular culture. The same news, music, drama, and comedy became simultaneously available to significant portions of the country. Network radio audiences were now national audiences.

Some pop styles became national, while others kept their regional identities. This can be attributed to network programming: the mainstream pop of Bing Crosby, the Andrews Sisters,

Many of the first radio stations developed from modest beginnings. This photo shows the original facilities used to broadcast the results of the 1920 presidential election. This small set-up, originally housed in a garage, would soon become Pittsburgh's KDKA.

the big bands, and later Frank Sinatra was heard frequently on network radio, while country and western and rhythm and blues were not. Mainstream pop was similar in most markets, and was targeted to a white, middle-class listening audience. Music marketed to low-income listeners (rural or urban) was mostly excluded, or given a marginal role in network radio programming. Since country and western and rhythm and blues were considered music for low-income listeners, these styles were often not played on network radio; as a consequence, they retained their regional distinctions.

The Rise of the Radio Networks in the 1920s. The early years of radio were an exciting time. As broadcasters worked to get radio into every home in America, they discovered two reliable ways to reach larger audiences. First, they broadcast radio signals via high-power transmitter. Under the most favorable atmospheric conditions, such "superstations" could reach listeners within a radius of several hundred miles. The federal government also licensed a few stations for exclusive use of a particular frequency. Without local stations to mask the signal, these "clear channel" stations could regularly reach entire multistate regions. Other enterprising broadcasters placed their transmitters in Mexico, just south of the border where the U.S. government had no licensing authority. These "border radio" stations could sometimes be picked up as far north as Chicago.

A second, more effective way to reach a large audience was linking a number of local and regional stations together to form a network. NBC used telephone lines to link sixty-nine stations across the country for its first coast-to-coast broadcast in 1928. Soon NBC was running two networks and other companies followed suit. The network system had a number of distinct advantages: programming could be run from a central location (most often a studio in New York), and it was possible to run live broadcasts from member stations (called "affiliates"). This gave the networks a tremendous range of programming from which to choose. When networks could get one of the clear-channel stations on board, this offered the best of both worlds. Today, the network system still exists in the television industry, where most prime-time programming originates from studios in Los Angeles or New York, while other shows and newscasts originate locally. Talk radio also employs this model, with shows originating from many parts of the country and playing to a national audience.

Live radio was also an important vehicle for music publishers, who had to convince bandleaders and singers not only to perform a song, but also that using the song in their live shows would serve their career interests. For most musicians during the 1930s and '40s (much as today), "career interests" meant future bookings for more money. Publishers bargained with bandleaders, singers, and radio producers to get their songs into live radio broadcasts that the bands and singers were using to generate future bookings. The radio networks, performers, and song publishers relied on one another to succeed, and much of the music business during those years focused on pairing artists with songs and appropriate radio shows.

Today, *Amos 'n' Andy* is considered politically incorrect, but in the heyday of radio, the show was enormously popular nationwide. Amos (Freeman Gosden) and Andy (Charles Corrrell) are shown here broadcasting their show in 1935.

Network radio programming offered listeners a wide range of entertainment: soap operas, adventure shows, and comedies were all popular, as were variety shows and live music. *The Guiding Light* appeared in 1937, while shows like *The Lone Ranger* and *Superman* entertained listeners throughout most of the 1930s and '40s. One of the greatest successes of the era was the comedy *Amos 'n' Andy*, which premiered in 1929. Its use of racial stereotypes, drawn from the minstrel tradition, would be unacceptable today, but the adventures and mishaps of Amos and Andy held the attention of the entire United States (not unlike the success later enjoyed by television shows such as *All in the Family, Cheers,* and *Seinfeld*). Network radio created an audience that stretched from coast to coast, and in so doing, it created a national popular culture in which music played a central role. Through the medium of radio a song could become popular almost overnight, eliminating the need for word of mouth to spread gradually from town to town and region to region. With radio, a song could be heard far and wide in a single performance.

Radio in the 1930s and '40s was unlike modern radio because most of the music was performed live. While modern radio listeners expect that the music they hear is recorded, early radio listeners assumed that what they heard over the airwaves was live. Before 1945, it was considered unethical to play records on the air. Consensus dictated that by playing a record you were trying to fool people into believing a performance was live when it was not. This was a benefit to live musicians, who eagerly took advantage of the work opportunities afforded by radio. Even though affiliates were fed network programming for large segments of the broadcast schedule, most larger stations employed a studio band for local programming. In addition, stations had to fill the gaps between network programs, which created plenty of opportunities for entrepreneurial local bandleaders. In this context, it is not surprising that the musician's union (American Federation of Musicians) took strong political steps in the 1940s to keep records ("canned music") off the airwaves—keeping music live meant keeping musicians (and union members) working.

REGIONAL STYLES OF COUNTRY AND WESTERN MUSIC

"Country" Music in the Southeast in the 1930s. Country and western music remained mostly regional until after 1945. Unlike the mainstream pop heard on radio networks, several musical styles that would come together under the umbrella of "country and western" after World War II kept distinctive regional accents until the late 1940s, when Nashville became a hub for this type of music. For our purposes, these regional styles can be divided into "country" music from the southeast and Appalachia, and "western" music from the West and southwest. Country music can be traced to the folk traditions of the region, largely derived from the folk music of the British Isles. Some of the first recordings later associated with the American country music industry were made by Ralph Peer, a producer who roamed the South in search of what record companies called "hillbilly music." Peer recorded many of the earliest country performers, including "Fiddlin'" John Carson and Gid Tanner and His Skillet Lickers. Peer traveled from one small town to another, setting up his gear as he went, and local musicians lined up to record on his equipment. Among the acts "discovered" by Peer was the Carter Family, who became seminal figures in the history of country music. Accompanied by an acoustic guitar and an autoharp (played by Maybelle and Sara Carter, respectively), the voices of Maybelle, Sara, and A. P. Carter sing together in a style very much influenced by white gospel music. "Can the Circle Be Unbroken" (1935) captures both the musical style and confessional spirit of this music, as does "Great Speckled Bird" (1936) performed by Roy Acuff and His Crazy Tennesseans. The Acuff group added the slide guitar to the mix, which was associated with both country and blues music. A more developed version of the slide guitar, the pedal steel guitar, would come to play a central role in later country and western instrumentation.

"Western" Music in the Southwest and California in the 1930s. If country music was most often associated with the Appalachian Mountains, western music reflected the wide open prairie of the cowboys—or at least Hollywood's portrayal of it. Gene Autry was the first singing cowboy to appear in a long line of Wild West films. His "Back in the Saddle Again," complete with cattle call "whoopie ti yi yo," is representative of the songs that he and Roy Rogers sang throughout their careers in recordings and on the silver screen. Patsy Montana made her mark as the singing cowgirl with "I Want to Be a Cowboy's Sweetheart" (1935) and featured a yodeling style influenced by Jimmie Rodgers (discussed below). Historians may dispute how authentically western some of this music was, but for the national movie-going public, these artists defined "cowboy music."

Popularized by Bob Wills and His Texas Playboys and Milton Brown and His Musical Brownies, western swing also helped to define western music as a style that put a cowboy twist on the big band idea. In addition to a rhythm section and horns, as one might expect of a radio dance band, western swing featured fiddles, a steel guitar, and occasionally, mariachi-style trumpet parts imported from Mexico. Wills's "New San Antonio Rose" (1940) is an example of this eclectic blend of urbane dance band and rough-and-tumble western hoedown. Wills's band greatly benefited from Bing Crosby's 1941 remake of the song, which became a national hit and brought western swing far more attention than it might have received otherwise. By the 1940s Wills and the Playboys were appearing in Hollywood films and expanding Americans' sense of western music beyond cowboy songs.

Jimmie Rodgers: The First Star of Country Music. The historical and cultural contexts in which country and western music reached a mainstream pop audience are essential elements to understanding the overall development of these styles. Western music's biggest stars were Gene Autry and Roy Rogers, but the

Often considered the first star of country music, Jimmie Rodgers appears here in his "Singing Brakeman" attire. Although Rodgers's career was short, his musical influence was felt for decades.

most important figure in the early history of country music was Jimmie Rodgers. Rodgers's music and performances made him a national star, although his career was cut short when he died from tuberculosis in 1933 at the age of thirty-six. He was primarily a solo performer, who sang and played the acoustic guitar. Rodgers's "Blue Yodel" (1927)—often called "T for Texas"—is representative of his style, including his trademark yodel. Rodgers's singing style was much imitated by later country and western singers, including Gene Autry, Ernest Tubb, and Eddy Arnold.

During his brief career, Rodgers was known as both "The Blue Yodeler" and "The Singing Brakeman." The Blue Yodeler image cast Rodgers as a kind of rustic back porch guitar picker and singer, while his Singing Brakeman persona was a roving hobo, wandering the country in the back of a freight car, only stopping long enough to sing a song about his lonely, nomadic existence. Neither was an accurate portrait of Rodgers, who, according to many reports, frequently performed in stylish clothes. These rustic images played on stereotypes of the time, and show an early awareness of the importance of marketing. Constructing homespun images would become the specialty of the country barn-dance radio shows, the most successful of which was the *Grand Ole Opry*. Rodgers's legacy to country includes not only his music, but the way he, and those around him, crafted its reception.

RURAL AND URBAN BLUES

Migration Patterns from the Rural South to the Urban North. After World War I, popular music played by black musicians and intended for black listening audiences was called "race" music. It was not until the late 1940s that a journalist at *Billboard* magazine named Jerry Wexler (who would later play a major creative role at Atlantic Records) coined the term "rhythm and blues." During the first half of the twentieth century black popular music developed almost completely outside the infrastructure created for mainstream pop. While country and western had at least a marginal presence in mainstream American pop, middle-class white listeners were largely unfamiliar with rhythm and blues before rock and roll. This was a reflection of racial segregation in American culture; most white, middle-class Americans were simply unaware of most aspects of black culture. Yet a great migration of African Americans from the South to northern industrial centers helped to integrate regional African-American popular styles into the American cultural mainstream. Many black Americans left the South in hopes of finding better work in the North, and when they arrived in St. Louis, Chicago, and Detroit, they brought their music

Pictured in the center of this advertisement for "race" records, Bessie Smith was one of the most famous blues singers of the 1920s. Her 1923 recording of Alberta Hunter's "Down Hearted Blues" sold over a million copies. Her style influenced many singers, including Billie Holiday and Janis Joplin.

Legend has it that Robert Johnson (left) made a deal with the devil to acquire his forceful skill as a blues guitarist. Johnson's 1930s recordings were embraced by the 1960s British blues revival, making him a guitar hero decades after his death.

with them. Before rock and roll, rhythm and blues was not a single musical style. Rather, it was a collection of popular-music styles tied together by its audience and its specific musical characteristics. Within the music business, if a record was expected to have a black listening audience, it was classified as race or rhythm and blues, and which led to a number of distinctive black pop styles being grouped together under one label.

After World War I, blues enjoyed several years of popularity with mainstream white pop listeners, partly through the sheet music of W. C. Handy, whose "Memphis Blues" and "St. Louis Blues" sold well nationally. Composers like Handy also became popular through recordings of their material featuring female black singers. The history of selling blues records can be traced to the 1923 million-selling song "Down Hearted Blues," sung by Bessie Smith. Originally from Tennessee, Smith enjoyed enormous success for years after this popular recording. As a child, Smith toured the South performing in tent and minstrel shows where she was undoubtedly exposed to early blues music. In spite of her Southern blues style, Smith's recordings were made in New York, where she was able to use the best jazz musicians of the day, including Louis Armstrong. By the end of the decade, however, Smith's career began to fade as blues fell off the commercial radar.

Many of the blues recordings of the 1920s and '30s exist because record companies scoured the South in an attempt to find new rural blues artists who might repeat Bessie Smith's success. One example is Robert Johnson, whose 1936–37 recordings became enormously influential on rock guitarists in the 1960s, largely based on Eric Clapton's enthusiastic endorsement (discussed in Chapter 5). Like many rural blues singers, Johnson was a solo performer who sang to the accompaniment of his own acoustic guitar playing. The rural blues style allowed for tremendous flexibility, and artists could easily add extra beats or measures as the spirit moved them. This can be heard clearly in Johnson's "Cross Roads Blues" (1936), as he alters the regular blues structural patterns to suit his sense of musical expression. As African Americans migrated to urban areas, blues musicians moved into city bars and clubs, often forming combos using electric guitars, bass, piano, drums, and harmonica (in addition to microphones to amplify the singer's voice). This arrangement forced them to stick more closely to a prearranged structure.

While much of the development of rhythm and blues during the 1940s remained regional and outside the pop mainstream, the jump blues of Louis Jordan and His Tympany Five became popular with main-stream listeners through a series of hit singles, including "G.I. Jive" (1944), "Caldonia Boogie" (1945), and "Choo Choo Ch'boogie" (1946). Jordan adopted the fast tempos of swing dance music but pared down the instrumentation to only a rhythm section and saxophone, a move that worked both musically and financially, considering the expenses of traveling with a larger band. Jordan's vocal delivery was upbeat and often comical, although his humorous lyrics often touched on pressing social issues such as racism and poverty. In "Saturday Night Fish Fry" (1949), for example, Jordan describes a typical weekend evening party scene in the New Orleans African-American community, which ends when the police take everyone to jail and book them on "suspicion."

Regional Radio and the Black Experience in 1950s America.
In the 1950s, a new approach to radio disseminated rhythm and blues outside of regional black communities. To understand how radio changed after the introduction of television it is important to know what makes a radio station work financially. Commercial radio makes its profits by selling advertising time; to reach a particular kind of listener, radio stations program music they hope will attract a specific group. These stations offer that audience to sponsors, who have an interest in targeting groups that might be interested in their products. By the early 1950s, the national audience for popular music had largely shifted from radio to television. This meant that radio needed to adapt considerably to survive, and many stations opted for a local or regional approach. As black populations began to grow in urban areas, it soon became clear that they constituted a distinctive community with needs for particular goods and services. In 1948, WDIA in Memphis began programming and advertising especially to the local black population, playing rhythm and blues records supported by a roster of sponsors who welcomed a black clientele. Soon black stations—or programs directed to a black audience on otherwise white stations—began to pop up around the country. These programs and stations provided African-American listeners with music they could enjoy and informed them of which advertisers would welcome their business. In the days of racial segregation, this was useful information.

Independent Labels Target Regional Audiences.
As radio stations devoted to rhythm and blues arose across the country, so did record labels specializing in black popular music. Sun Records in Memphis, Chess Records in Chicago, King Records in Cincinnati, and Atlantic Records in New York were just a few of the more successful new rhythm and blues labels after World War II. Most of the new record companies were independents—that is, they were not part of a larger corporate conglomerate like the major labels that dominated the music industry at the time, including Decca, Mercury, RCA-Victor, Columbia, Capitol, and MGM. Major labels had enormous financial resources, manufacturing plants, and sophisticated distribution networks that allowed them to get their newest records out quickly to most areas of the country. At their smallest, independent labels were staffed by only a few people, perhaps the owner and a secretary, which required driving from store to store and distributing records out of the trunk of a car. This meant that smaller independents had to focus on local or regional markets. Independent labels prospered precisely because the major labels were so big; and since the rhythm and

blues market was not nearly as profitable as mainstream pop, the majors tended to devote their resources to pop, leaving room for the independents to survive—and in many cases, to thrive. In both radio and records, then, rhythm and blues in the period between 1945 and 1955 was popular music intended specifically for black urban listeners. Nobody expected that white listeners would hear this music. White teenagers could pick up black stations on their radios just as well as anybody, however, and when they developed a taste for rhythm and blues, the stage was set for rock and roll to emerge.

THE SINGER STEPS FORWARD

The Singers and the Big Bands. As country and western and rhythm and blues were beginning to infiltrate wider markets during the 1930s and '40s, large-scale changes were also occurring in mainstream pop, especially after the end of World War II. During the period from about 1935 to 1945, often considered the big band era, much of the most popular music was created by dance bands that employed a rhythm section of bass, drums, piano, and guitar combined with a horn section of trumpets, trombones, and saxophones. These groups created arrangements of Tin Pan Alley songs designed to provide music appropriate for dancing, while also featuring the instrumental prowess of the musicians and the virtuosity of the arranger. Big bands were led by instrumentalists such as Tommy Dorsey, Jimmy Dorsey, Benny Goodman, Duke Ellington, and Glenn Miller, and singers were used sparingly as featured soloists. Thus, the celebrity in the band was its leader, as the musicians and singers often changed frequently. Arrangements during the big band era emphasized the band, often allotting only one time through the chorus of a song for the singer. Sections of the band, and perhaps instrumental soloists, were also featured both before and after the singer. Many swing arrangements, such as the Glenn Miller Band's 1942 number-one hit "A String of Pearls" employed no vocals at all. Such emphasis on the band may seem strange to rock listeners. In much rock music the vocalist is the focus of the song, while an instrumental solo takes a verse of the song to provide variety. In big band music, however, the vocalist provides the variety. Because of the emphasis on instrumental playing in the big bands, there was a close relationship between big band music and jazz, which developed both within and alongside big band music. In fact, many important jazz musicians played in big bands, and several bands figure heavily in most accounts of jazz history.

Despite the general focus on bands during the big band era, a number of performing artists developed careers independent from any particular band. The most important pop singer in the 1930s and 1940s was Bing Crosby, whose relaxed, easygoing crooning made him a favorite in both the United States and abroad. Crosby enjoyed a long string of hit recordings, including "I've Got a Pocketful of Dreams" (1938), "Only Forever" (1940), "Swinging on a Star" (1944), and "White Christmas." In addition to being perhaps the most successful solo performer of his era, Crosby acted in films (often with comedian Bob Hope) and hosted his own radio variety show (sponsored by Kraft Foods). In contrast to some of the pop singers who would come to fame after World War II, Crosby projected a wholesome, friendly, and paternal image; in many ways, he was America's dad (or favorite uncle).

Duke Ellington (at the piano) was an important band leader in the swing music scene during the 1930s and '40s. Shown here in a poster for the 1943 movie *Reveille with Beverly*, Duke's band was joined by Frank Sinatra, the Mills Brothers, and the Count Basie Orchestra in a film that gave radio listeners across the country a chance to see and hear performances of these popular artists in the years before the rise of television.

Many vocal groups also became popular during the swing era. The Andrews Sisters and the Mills Brothers were important figures during the 1935–45 period, each ringing up a long series of hit records. Both groups made extensive use of dense vocal harmony, relating closely to big band horn arrangements. The Andrews Sisters enjoyed their greatest commercial success with "Bei Mir bist du Schoen" (1938), " Shoo-Shoo Baby" (1943), and "Rum and Coca Cola" (1945), while the Mills Brothers scored with "Tiger Rag" (1931), "Paper Doll" (1943), and "You Always Hurt the One You Love" (1944). The groups' approach to harmony singing served as one precursor to the doo-wop and girl groups that played an important role in rock and roll during the 1950s and 1960s. Moreover, the Mills Brothers and the Ink Spots, along with solo vocalist Ella Fitzgerald and vocalist and pianist Nat "King" Cole, were among the first African-American artists to enjoy mainstream success in the record industry.

Frank Sinatra. Before 1942, entertainment insiders would have thought it crazy to even consider that a big band singer could strike out on his own and have a viable career. Bing Crosby had enjoyed considerable success as a solo act, but he was viewed as the exception to the rule. Frank Sinatra, however, established a new model for the pop-music singer; building in part on Crosby's accomplishments, Sinatra made the singer the star of the show, paving the way for later rock and roll singers like Elvis Presley and Pat Boone. For three years Sinatra was a singer with the Harry James and Tommy Dorsey bands, singing the occasional solo but mostly sitting on the sidelines. He went solo in late 1942, changing the emphasis of the music to the vocalist. Perhaps owing to his good looks and slightly rebellious sensuality, Sinatra became a teen idol almost immediately. In a preview of the rock and roll hysteria to come a decade later, teenage girls mobbed Sinatra performances, and exhibited audience behaviors that would later become commonplace in rock, such as fainting and grabbing at the artist. Although Sinatra enjoyed the fanatical attention and advantages of a successful solo singing career, he was extremely dedi-

THE INVENTION OF BING CROSBY

by Gary Giddins

Bing Crosby accumulated more unbroken statistics than any other figure in pop music history. Unrivaled in the sheer number of his studio recordings, his discography included 368 charted singles under his own name and 28 more as a sideman. He scored more number-one hits (38) than any other twentieth-century performer, among them the best-selling record of all time, "White Christmas." As a movie star, he ranked as a top box office attraction for 20 years, five times in the number one slot. He was nominated for an Oscar three times (he won for *Going My Way*) and introduced

more Oscar-nominated songs than anyone else.

Crosby was also a major radio star for three decades, practically inventing the modern talk-music-comedy variety hour with the *Kraft Music Hall*, which he began hosting in 1936. At the peak of the show's success, 50 million listeners tuned in every week to hear him. During World War II, he raised an unparalleled $14,500,000 in war bonds. As an innovator of musical technology, he was the first to use the microphone as a musical instrument (leading one critic to observe, "he sang to you, not at you"); the first to prerecord on radio; and the first to record on tape—an invention he helped finance. Even his leisure pursuits made history: he created the first celebrity pro-am golf championship and was the central figure in the development of the Del Mar racetrack in Southern California.

All of which directly underscores the irony inherent in one of his least known yet most prescient achievements. Crosby was the first American singer to actively invent a persona—a part real and part fabricated character, polished with the detail worthy of a novelist. Comedians like Jack Benny or Laurel and Hardy had previously invented

personae using their own names, and nightclub singers created personalities suitable to their performances. But Crosby prefigured the postures and attitudes of rock by presenting the illusion of a figure no different in song than in life.

It wasn't just Crosby's baritone voice, phrasing, range, and articulation of lyrics that sold his songs, but also his personality. Before Frank Sinatra recreated himself as a 1950s jet-set swinger or Elvis Presley perfected his pompadour and sneer or the Beatles settled on cheery irreverence and jackets without lapels, Crosby incarnated a unique temperament in American song—the everyman performer, the modern minstrel, friend to all.

The beloved Bing of the Depression and war years was a far cry from the young jazz crooner of Prohibition, who indulged his share of stimulants, both illegal (alcohol) and legal (marijuana), and women (mostly legal). In many respects, an unknowable and private man, Crosby had a live-and-let-live attitude that put him ahead of the curve when it came to racial and gender politics. But he was hardly a portrait of personal reliability or professional affability.

The Crosby persona was

reshaped with the aid of two close advisers—his wife, Dixie Lee, who threatened to end their marriage if he didn't stop drinking and take his career more seriously; and his record producer, the legendary Jack Kapp, who founded Decca records and convinced Crosby that he should not limit himself to the "hip" audience of jazz fans and Broadway habitués. With Kapp's prodding, Crosby's repertoire grew to encompass more musical styles than any singer had ever attempted, all handled with unpretentious authenticity that won him fans in each field: jazz, mainstream pop, Irish and Hawaiian songs, country and western, operetta, French and Spanish songs (he was fluent in both languages), waltzes, Christmas carols, even rhythm and blues—he recorded duets with Louis Jordan.

Yet his persona was that of an incorrigibly lazy man: self-sufficient, unperturbed, shrewd, cool—a grown-up Tom Sawyer, complete with a pipe, battered hat, mismatched clothes, and jive lingo. Crosby invented a character so resonant that even those who knew and worked with him had a hard time separating it from the real Bing, though in reality he was the least lazy man in town. Despite being a ubiquitous presence in American culture, turning out three films a year (a full-time career by itself), a weekly radio show and frequent recording sessions, he was known as a guy who didn't like to work, preferring to laze around, play golf, and hang out at the track.

Crosby routinely spoke of how idle and lacking in ambition he was, and media stories played it up. Feeding into the fiction were his easy charm and off-handed way of speaking, careless way of dressing,

and cool independence, which came off as admirably aloof and paradoxically warm. He didn't seem to give a damn about Hollywood propriety. For example, Crosby lost his hair as a young man and wore toupees in movies. Yet he was the only star of his era who didn't wear one at private parties or when entertaining the troops during World War II. He demanded the maximum number of exterior scenes in his films so that he could wear a hat instead of the hated "scalp doily." Even his vocal style offered the illusion of effortlessness. It was often said that every man singing in the shower thought he sounded like Crosby.

The success of the Crosby persona may be measured by its incalculable popularity throughout

society: young and old, men and women, black and white, urban and rural, above and below the Mason-Dixon line. But it also contributed to the ebbing of his success in the rock era, when the casual, unperturbed attitude that proved so engaging during the Depression and war suddenly seemed remote, grandfatherly, safe, and irrelevant. In the 1950s, rock and roll changed the nation's tempo and temperature, but it never changed Bing Crosby. He had grown older while the country grew younger.

Gary Giddins is the author of Bing Crosby: A Pocketful of Dreams, Visions of Jazz, *and the textbook* Jazz *(with Scott DeVeaux).*

Despite being a tireless worker and performer, Bing Crosby represented himself as a carefree "everyman." Crosby cultivated this image, often wearing mismatched clothes, a battered hat, and sporting a pipe. He was someone you could relate to, someone you wanted to be around and (because of his immense popularity) often were—whether at the movies, on the radio, or in the concert hall.

Starting out as a featured singer with the Harry James and Tommy Dorsey bands, Frank Sinatra struck out on a solo career in 1942. Sinatra was especially popular with young women, who often swooned when the slim, handsome singer crooned.

cated to his craft and frequently acknowledged that much of his vocal phrasing and technique was based on his study of the musicians he worked with during the big band era. Among Sinatra's many important records from the late 1940s, his rendition of "I've Got a Crush on You" (1948), with a text that reinforces his teen idol image, illustrates his distinctive singing style. Sinatra went on to become one of the most successful singers of the post–World War II era, selling millions of records and playing to packed houses well into the 1980s. In the wake of his first success, Sinatra drew many imitators, as singers replaced the big bands as the focus of the music business and many former big band vocalists took center stage. At the same time, financial pressures forced many of the big bands to break up. After 1945 it simply became too expensive to employ so many musicians, and smaller combos became a more cost-effective way to make a living playing dancehall gigs.

The Sound of Pop in the Early 1950s. Pop music in the first half of the 1950s is sometimes dismissed as being hopelessly corny and stiff, especially in comparison to the rhythm and blues of the same era. Patti Page's "The Doggie in the Window" (1953) might be thought of as representative of the generally wholesome and inoffensive approach found in much early to mid-1950s pop, but there was more to pop than hopelessly happy tunes with canine obbligato. Singers such as Eddie Fisher and Tony Bennett scored hit records in the new, youth-oriented mold cast by Sinatra; Fisher's sentimental "Oh! My Pa-Pa" (1953) and Bennett's swinging "Rags to Riches" (1953) each placed the musical focus squarely on the singer with the orchestra in a supporting role. Johnnie Ray took the male vocalist role from suave and controlled to overtly emotional and romantically melodramatic with his ballad, "Cry," creating an international hit in 1951. In addition to the success enjoyed by Page—whose "The Tennessee Waltz" topped the charts for thirteen weeks in 1950—female vocalists were well represented in the pre–rock and roll hit parade. Jo Stafford's "You Belong to Me" (1952) and Kay Starr's "Wheel of Fortune" (1952) both follow the emerging practice of featuring the singer and relegating the band to an accompanimental role.

Before rock and roll, mainstream pop music was produced for a family audience and teenagers were expected to enjoy the same music as their parents and grandparents. As family entertainment, pop music mostly avoided topics that might be considered unsuitable for general audiences. "I'm Sittin' on Top of the World," a hit in 1953 for guitarist Les Paul and vocalist Mary Ford, is just one example of the happy, wholesome sound of early 1950s mainstream pop and a showcase of the duo's trademark layering of guitars and vocals.

As discussed in the next chapter, early rock and roll was directed primarily at young people, serving as a marker of generational difference. In the first half of the 1950s, however, mainstream pop was designed to appeal to a broad, mostly white middle-class audience. Aspects of this music that might seem corny and naïve in retrospect resulted from trying to produce music that would be acceptable to a wide range of listeners. Even within this relatively constrained context, however, it is possible to detect elements of the rowdier, youth-oriented rock and roll that would emerge mid-decade: a focus on the singer, the sensual appeal of Sinatra and the emotional directness of Johnnie Ray, the acceptance of select African-American musicians into the mainstream, and the popularity of jump blues and boogie woogie.

As some aspects of popular music were preparing the way for rock and roll, Tin Pan Alley was caught entirely off guard by the new style. Part of this was to do with the rise of rhythm and blues and country and western, which the big music publishing houses had previously ignored. Big publishers and major record companies like Columbia, Decca, and RCA-Victor, did not invest themselves in the rhythm and blues and country and western markets because they considered their profitability to be limited in these areas, and major labels had a tradition of poor sales outside of mainstream pop. Before the rise of rock, rhythm and blues and country and western were largely separate from mainstream pop, with few artists achieving popularity in more than one of these markets.

Les Paul and Mary Ford were among the most popular acts during the first half of the 1950s. The couple is shown here recording at home, using a roomful of Paul's custom modified equipment.

Listening Guide

Les Paul and Mary Ford, "I'm Sittin' on Top of the World"
Capital F2400

Words and music by Sam Lewis, Joe Young, and Ray Henderson, produced by Les Paul. The song reached #10 on the *Billboard* "Most Played in Jukeboxes" chart in 1953 and had been featured in the 1946 film *The Jolson Story*.

FORM: AABA, with three presentations of the complete verse-verse-bridge-verse structure. The first and third presentations are sung, while the second one features a guitar solo. The verses in the second presentation are adapted from the sung verses and do not match these earlier and later verses exactly. During the first two verses in the third presentation, the time signature changes from 2/4 time to 4/4 time, and while the tempo does not change, this creates the impression that the music slows down. The 2/4 time signature returns at the bridge and continues to the end. The change of key that occurs in the last verse helps drive the music toward a big ending.

TIME SIGNATURE: 2/4, with verse in 4/4 as indicated.

INSTRUMENTATION: Layered electric guitars and lead vocals. The highest and fastest guitar lines were recorded at half speed, creating a "chipmunk" sound.

0:00–0:09	**Introduction**, 8 mm.	Layered guitar melody; note the echo effect on the guitar—this is the trademark Les Paul sound.
0:09–0:17	**A-Verse**, 8 mm.	Multitrack harmony vocals, all recorded by Mary Ford, with "chipmunk" guitar lines filling in the gaps, "I'm sittin' . . ."
0:17–0:25	**A-Verse**, 8 mm.	As before, "I'm quittin' . . ."

RECORDINGS AND RADIO FURTHER A NATIONAL SOUND FOR COUNTRY AND WESTERN MUSIC

Superstation Radio Broadcasts in Prime Time. As far back as the 1930s, mainstream pop played to a national audience, while country and western was mostly limited to regional radio exposure. In 1922, Atlanta's WSB went on the air featuring local country music (like "Fiddlin'" John Carson and Gid Tanner), while WBAP in Fort Worth began a barn-dance program, featuring hoedown fiddle music. Within a few years, local and regional radio stations across the nation were programming country music, especially WSM in Nashville and WLS in Chicago. WSM broadcast the popular country-oriented program the *Grand Ole Opry*, while

0:25–0:34	**B-Bridge**, 8 mm.	Harmony vocals continue, layered guitars create a nice descending cascade effect, "Hallelujah . . ."
0:34–0:43	**A-Verse**, 8 mm.	As before, "I'm sittin' . . ."
0:43–0:51	**A-Instrumental Verse**, 8 mm.	Guitar solo, music adapted from earlier verses. Les Paul's skill as a jazz soloist comes to the fore throughout this sectional verse.
0:51–0:59	**A-Instrumental Verse**, 8 mm.	Guitar solo continues.
0:59–1:08	**B-Instrumental Bridge**, 8 mm.	Guitar solo continues, high and fast "chipmunk" guitar lines created as described above.
1:08–1:16	**A-Instrumental Verse**, 8 mm.	Guitar solo continues.
1:16–1:33	**A-Verse**, 8 mm.	As before but now in 4/4 time, creating a sense that the music slows down. Note the addition of new backing vocals, "I'm sitting . . ."
1:33–1:50	**A-Verse**, 8 mm.	Continues in 4/4, "I'm quitting . . ."
1:50–1:58	**B-Bridge**, 8 mm.	Music goes back to 2/4, creating a sense that the music is speeding up, "Hallelujah . . ."
1:58–2:06	**A-Verse**, 8 mm.	This last verse changes key and this helps drive the song effectively to its ending, "I'm sittin' . . ."
2:06–2:15	**Coda**, 8 mm.	A showy ending adapted from last verse, "I'm sittin' . . ."

WLS produced the *National Barndance*. Initially broadcasting to the middle Tennessee region, in 1932 WSM became a clear-channel station whose signal reached most of the southeast and could even be picked up in Texas. This made *Opry* broadcasts available to a significant portion of the country, and when NBC picked up a half-hour version of the show in 1939, the *Opry* could be heard coast-to-coast. As the listening audience for the show increased, so did the clamor from musicians to appear on these broadcasts. In 1943, the *Grand Ole Opry* became a live broadcast of a stage show from the Ryman Auditorium in Nashville. Performers were happy to make the trip to Nashville to sing and play on the show, since the large radio audience and presence on the city's most important stage could provide enormous exposure.

While the *Grand Ole Opry* blanketed southern evenings with country music, the *National Barndance* did the same for the Midwest. Although the *Opry* eventually became more prominent and influential, the *Barndance* reached a national audience much sooner when a one-hour segment of it ran on the NBC network in 1933.

Les Paul, Electric Guitars, and Multitrack Recording

A new role for the electric guitar in pop was pioneered by guitarist and inventor Les Paul, whose innovations in electronics and recording during the 1950s had a lasting impact on popular music. Paul's innovations manifested themselves stylistically and technologically. Some of the most important examples are below.

As Guitarist and Arranger for Les Paul and Mary Ford Les Paul was one of the country's leading guitarists during the big band era. While his own musical preference was for up-tempo jazz, he was a master of many styles. In fact, early in his career he posed as the country singer Rhubarb Red, singing traditional "hillbilly" music on a local radio show in his home state of Wisconsin. Paul met country singer Mary Ford in 1945, and in 1949 they married and formed a musical duo that featured spirited husband-and-wife banter and gags on stage. Paul arranged all of the duo's music, playing guitar and employing his latest electronic inventions to create a distinctive pop style that made Les Paul and Mary Ford records unmistakable and enormously successful.

As Inventor of the Solid-body Electric Guitar Les Paul was one of the first to experiment with this type of instrument. Before Paul's experiments, electric guitars were traditional hollow-body jazz guitars with an electric pickup attached. Paul was convinced that to produce the purest electric sound the pickup must to be free from vibrations caused by the guitar body on which it was mounted. In 1941 this led Paul to design a guitar with a solid body that would vibrate less. By mounting a pickup on this guitar—which he constructed out of a railroad tie and called "the log"—Paul invented one of the first solid-body electric guitars. He later negotiated with the Gibson Guitar Company in 1951 to produce the Gibson Les Paul guitar, which has become one of the most frequently used models in the history of rock music. Leo Fender was experimenting with the same idea in southern California in the late 1940s, resulting in his Broadcaster and Telecaster guitars. Fender's later Stratocaster design rivals that of the Les Paul in popularity among rock guitarists.

As Inventor of Sound-on-Sound Recording ("Overdubbing") Les Paul was one of the first musicians to experiment with sound-on-sound recording—the process by which a musician records one instrumental part and then another part so that the two parts sound together when played back. By extending this process, one musician can record several parts to an arrangement that would take many musicians to play in real time. Using discs in his first recordings, Paul figured out how to lay one take over the previous one, painstakingly building up the parts according to a method that allowed for no error—a mistake could only be corrected by starting the process all over again. In the early 1950s, Paul developed the first multitrack tape machine by synchronizing several tape machines to produce a more flexible method of **"overdubbing."** On his hit records with Mary Ford, such as "How High the Moon" (1951) and "I'm Sittin' on Top of the World" (1953), Paul overdubs choruses of guitars and vocals to create complex arrangements that reveal his big band roots. Paul also developed a technique of recording guitar parts at half speed so that when the machine ran at full speed the parts were not only higher, but much faster (the same technique was originally used to record the voices of the cartoon Chipmunks).

The electric guitar is central to rock music, and two models have achieved particularly iconic status. The Les Paul guitar (left) was developed by Paul in collaboration with the Kalamazoo-based Gibson company, while the Fender Stratocaster (right) was developed in Southern California by Leo Fender.

With her trademark "Howdy!" Minnie Pearl (left) would launch into one of her stand-up comedy routines on the *Grand Ole Opry*. Like many *Opry* regulars, Pearl played up the idea that country folk are simple and honest, but somewhat backward and naïve.

Combined with numerous other barn-dance shows that emanated from local and regional stations across the United States, at least some country and western music was readily available to radio listeners, even if the style remained something of a novelty on network radio, receiving far less exposure than mainstream pop of the day. Moreover, country music radio shows proliferated during the 1940s, with shows like *Big D Jamboree* (Dallas), *Hayloft Hoedown* (Philadelphia), *Hometown Jamboree* (Los Angeles), *Louisiana Hayride* (Shreveport), *Midwestern Hayride* (Cincinnati), and *Wheeling Jamboree* (Wheeling).

Country Music during World War II. Other important factors that led to the dissemination of country music among northerners (and those outside the South generally) developed as a result of World War II. Military personnel hailing from all regions of the country lived together overseas during the war, and as people got to know one another they naturally shared their favorite music. Many listeners got their first sustained exposure to country and western music from their fellow soldiers. During the war, country singers became so popular among the U.S. Armed Forces that Roy Acuff was voted best singer by the troops in Munich (over Frank Sinatra); and hoping to insult American soldiers, Japanese attackers on Okinawa raised the battle cry, "To hell with Roosevelt! To hell with Babe Ruth! To hell with Roy Acuff!" When the troops returned home, many retained their newfound affection for country and western music and sought it out in their hometowns. On the home front, white workers migrated north to fill factory jobs created by the war effort. Country music fans moved to many of the same industrial centers as black workers migrating from the South, and during the early 1940s a number of cities—including Baltimore, Washington, D.C., Cincinnati, Chicago, and Los Angeles—became home to southerners from the surrounding regions as they followed wartime production jobs. These relocated country and western fans brought their music with them, and jukebox records in these cities show that in some places country and western music was the most popular style in local bars and clubs.

Nashville Becomes Country and Western Headquarters. After the war, Nashville became the center of most of the professional activity in country and western music. Nashville had been home to the *Grand Ole Opry* since 1925, and by the late 1940s the *Opry* had become the most highly regarded radio show in country music. Nashville also became the center of country music recording and publishing. To meet the demand created by the nation's new interest in this music, the business of country and western became more sophisticated. Musicians increasingly made their way to Nashville to record (especially in the studios of Castle Recording Company). Promoters, booking agents, and record company representatives also moved their offices there. A major factor in music industry growth in Nashville was the success of the publishing firm Acuff-Rose, which was established in 1942 by singer Roy Acuff and songwriter Fred Rose. Unlike typical Tin Pan Alley publishers, Acuff-Rose did not rely on sheet music sales. Instead, they worked to have the firm's songs recorded and performed by country artists. When Patti Page's version of "The Tennessee Waltz"—an Acuff-Rose song—became a hit pop record in 1950, the resultant financial success allowed the company to expand its operation and extend its influence. Even though country and western publishers focused on recordings during the post-war years, they still employed songwriters using the Tin Pan Alley model. Many later country greats started out as songwriters. For example, in 1946 Fred Rose signed the then-unknown Hank Williams to Acuff-Rose—not as a singer, but as a songwriter.

THE BROAD RANGE OF RHYTHM AND BLUES

The Influence of Gospel Music (Rural Southern Church Traditions). Like country and western music, African-American pop styles, which were known generally as rhythm and blues after 1949, were wide ranging. One trait shared by most rhythm and blues styles during this era was a debt to gospel music. Much like the southern white musicians who performed country music, many African Americans who would go on to sing in secular pop styles learned to sing in church. While the sophisticated harmony singing that characterized doo-wop certainly had roots in the vocal arrangements of the Mills Brothers, the Ink Spots, and the Andrews Sisters, it also was clearly influenced by gospel singing. The vocal emphases and embellishments that rhythm and blues singers frequently employed, as well as the **call and response** between the soloist and the chorus, were drawn from typical gospel practices. Sometimes—as in the case of Ray Charles's "I Got a Woman" (1954)—religious lyrics to gospel songs were changed to make them pop songs. (Charles changed the lyrics of the Southern Tones's "It Must Be Jesus," which was popular in mid-1954.) Borrowing from religious music to create secular hits was a source of controversy within the black community, as some considered it sacrilege. Ambivalence toward using gospel elements in popular music would continue to confront both white and black singers after the emergence of rock and roll.

Chess Records and Chicago Electric Blues. As a talent scout for Sam Phillips's Sun Records in Memphis, Ike Turner has claimed that he typically searched two types of places for new performers: churches and bars. While gospel was clearly grounded in the sacred, blues was strongly secular. After decades of African-

American migration, by the early 1950s Chicago had become the most important scene for electric blues in the United States, in part due the success of an independent company called Chess, founded in 1947 by two white fans of black music, Phil and Leonard Chess. Chess amassed an impressive roster of blues artists, including Howlin' Wolf, Muddy Waters, John Lee Hooker, Little Walter, and Bo Diddley. The Chess style emphasized a sometimes rough-edged emotional directness, with vocals that were more expressive than beautiful or technically accomplished, and instrumental playing that blended technical prowess with raunchy bravura. Early Chess recordings were made with simple equipment, producing a raw, technically unsophisticated sound, in marked contrast to the polished records released by major

Leonard Chess (left) is shown here in the Chess recording studio with three of the most influential artists in electric blues: (from left) Muddy Waters, Little Walter, and Bo Diddley. Chess blues recordings defined the sound of Chicago electric blues. Their style was often rough-edged and direct, with expressive vocals. Early Chess recordings used simple equipment, which produced a raw, unsophisticated sound—contrasting with records released by major labels.

Listening Guide   Get Music ⓢ wwnorton.com/studyspace

Howlin' Wolf, "Evil Is Goin' On" Chess 1575

Words and music by Willie Dixon, produced by Leonard and Phil Chess and Willie Dixon. Released as a single in July 1954. Did not chart.

FORM: Simple Verse. Note that while the lyrics for each verse begin differently, they always close with the same lyrics. Returning lyrics that occur within a verse as they do here are called a **refrain**.

TIME SIGNATURE: 12/8 (shuffle in 4).

INSTRUMENTATION: Piano, guitars, bass, drums, harmonica, and lead vocals. Howlin' Wolf provides both lead vocals and harmonica. The song's composer and coproducer, Willie Dixon, plays bass, as legendary Chess musicians Hubert Sumlin and Otis Spann contribute on guitar and piano, respectively.

0:00–0:32	**Verse 1**, 13 mm.	After a 1-measure introduction, the vocal enters with a 12-bar verse that includes a refrain in the second half. "If you're a long way from home . . ."
0:32–1:00	**Verse 2**, 12 mm.	Begins as before but introduces a change in the first half of the lyrics, "A long way from home . . ."
1:00–1:28	**Instrumental Verse**, 12 mm.	High-register piano and harmonica share a solo, as Howlin' Wolf adds vocal interjections related to the story unfolding in the lyrics between harmonica bursts.
1:28–1:55	**Verse 3**, 12 mm.	Vocal returns as lyrics pick up the story, "If you call on the telephone . . ."
1:55–2:22	**Instrumental Verse**, 12 mm.	Harmonica and piano share a solo again, with Howlin' Wolf focusing more on his harmonica playing this time.
2:22–2:52	**Verse 4**, 12 mm.	Vocal returns and story in the lyrics reaches its conclusion. The final measures are adjusted slightly to create an ending for the song. "If you make it to your house . . ."

labels. This lack of studio refinement, combined with a direct performance style, gave Chess records an aura of honesty for many later white rock and rollers. Howlin' Wolf's "Evil Is Goin' On" (1954), Muddy Waters's "I Just Wanna Make Love to You" (1954), and Bo Diddley's "I'm a Man" (1955) are representative examples of Chicago electric blues, with adult-oriented lyrics delivered with more gusto than polish accompanied by accomplished instrumental playing. Although best known for blues, Chess also recorded artists like the Moonglows, who released crooning, doo-wop-oriented singles such as "Sincerely" (1955), which had the potential to appeal to a white audience. Yet, the company's electric blues records, which made few concessions to white, middle-class sensibilities, had the most impact on rock and roll.

Atlantic and Black Pop. Atlantic Records in New York was an independent company that reached a broad audience with recordings made by African-American performers in the 1950s. Founded in 1948 by Ahmet Ertegun and Herb Abramson, Atlantic's recordings often featured a polished pop sound influenced by the production practices of the mainstream and showcasing singers such as Ruth Brown, Big Joe Turner, Clyde McPhatter, and Ray Charles. While Atlantic also recorded blues records, its best-known releases focused on the singer and the song rather than instrumental playing, with backup arrangements that were structured and controlled and rare solos. In this way, a typical Atlantic single, such as Ruth Brown's "Mama, He Treats Your Daughter Mean" (1952), has clear ties not only to blues and gospel, but also to big band pop. Taken together, the music of Chess and Atlantic exhibits the wide stylistic range of 1950s rhythm and blues. Although these were among the most prominent independent companies of the period, there were many other regional labels that produced R&B records during this era.

Doo-Wop. Immediately following World War II, doo-wop groups began to emerge from urban neighborhoods. The singers in these groups often could not afford instruments, so their vocal arrangements were completely self-contained and did not require accompaniment (the musical term for these all-vocal arrangements is "a cappella"). A common practice was for groups from one neighborhood block to challenge groups from nearby blocks, leading to group-singing contests in the street. As independent labels sought out local talent to record, many invited these groups into the recording studio. Professional studio musicians learned the group's arrangements in order to accompany them. These recordings formed a body of music called "doo-wop," after the nonsense syllables singers used in their arrangements. Doo-wop groups typically featured a solo singer against the vocal accompaniment of the other singers, with one section of the song, usually toward the end, reserved for a sophisticated harmony-vocal rendition of one of the verses. The songs were sometimes in the AABA form derived from Tin Pan Alley and cast in a rolling, compound rhythm pounded out as chords on the piano (imagine this as one-and-uh, two-and-uh, three-and-uh, four-and-uh). The Chords' "Sh'Boom" (1954) is a representative example of doo-wop, with the syllables "sh'boom" used in the vocal accompaniment as a solo singer delivers the initial verses (see the Introduction for a Listening Guide of this song). A contrasting section highlights different singers from the group, and the last verse features the entire group singing together in harmony. "Sh'Boom" is a bouncy up-tempo number, but doo-wop songs were frequently ballads appropriate for slow dancing. The Five Satins' "In the Still of the Night" (1956) is a good example of this kind of song. Doo-wop is easily distinguished stylistically from Chicago blues and Atlantic pop (although Chicago blues labels and Atlantic also recorded doo-wop groups), but in the eyes (and ears) of the market, it was all rhythm and blues.

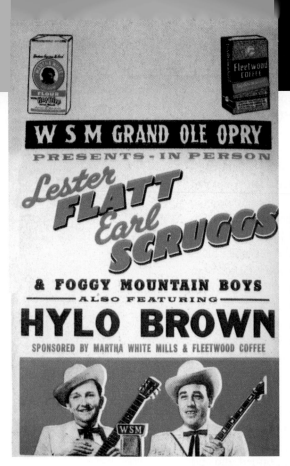

W S M GRAND OLE OPRY

PRESENTS - IN PERSON

Lester FLATT *Earl* SCRUGGS

& FOGGY MOUNTAIN BOYS

ALSO FEATURING

HYLO BROWN

SPONSORED BY MARTHA WHITE MILLS & FLEETWOOD COFFEE

THE BIG BUSINESS OF COUNTRY AND WESTERN

Bill Monroe and His Blue Grass Boys. During the 1940s, as country music began to thrive and Nashville became the hub of the country industry, new styles emerged. The most prominent of these was bluegrass. To most ears, this music sounds old-fashioned, but bluegrass actually developed during the late 1930s as a form of commercial music. The origin of the style can be traced to Bill Monroe and His Blue Grass Boys, who first performed on *Grand Ole Opry* in 1939 but gained far greater popularity in the late 1940s. The group's lineup after 1945 featured Monroe playing mandolin and singing high harmony, Robert "Chubby" Wise on fiddle, Lester Flatt on guitar and lead vocals, and Earl Scruggs on banjo. This version of the Blue Grass Boys cast a musical mold that later bluegrass groups would imitate and develop further.

Bluegrass bands typically play upbeat, dance music that features instrumental soloing, "high and lonesome" solo vocals, and close vocal harmonies. The bluegrass repertoire is often based on older songs, drawing from white gospel, Tin Pan Alley, and western swing. Monroe's late-1940s band had three dynamic and technically accomplished soloists—Wise, Scruggs, and Monroe himself—and the solos were more the focus of the group's music than the singing. Banjoist Earl Scruggs's playing is especially noteworthy in this context: Scruggs developed a technique called the "three-finger roll," which allowed him to play passages of greater complexity than previous banjo players. Along with developing other technical innovations, Scruggs raised the level of banjo playing to new heights. In 1948, Flatt and Scruggs left the Blue Grass Boys to form their own group. Inspired by the playing of Monroe's classic lineup, artists such as the Stanley Brothers, Jimmy Martin, and Mac Wiseman were attracted to bluegrass in subsequent years.

Hank Williams: A Short Career that Cast a Long Shadow. During the early 1950s, Hank Williams became an iconic figure in country and western music. Jimmie Rodgers, Gene Autry, and Roy Acuff had enjoyed considerable commercial success before this time, but none matched the popular appeal of this singer-songwriter from rural Alabama. Williams performed regionally for much of the 1940s, appearing as a regular on the *Louisiana Hayride* radio show on KWKH in Shreveport (a young Elvis Presley would get his start on the same show only a few years later). Williams's first important hit was not one of his own songs, but a Tin Pan Alley number entitled "Lovesick Blues" (1949). On the strength of its popularity, Williams became a regular on the *Grand Ole Opry* in the summer of 1949 and enjoyed tremendous success until his death on New Year's Day, 1953, at age thirty-three. While Williams himself enjoyed fewer than five years of national success, his music was recorded by later generations of country singers. The story of the hard-living singer-songwriter who died too young became a romantic image for future rock singers as well.

Williams's singing style shows the influence of both Roy Acuff and Ernest Tubb, and his many vocal inflections create an impression of sincere emotional expression. He pours out his personal romantic anguish in "Your Cheatin' Heart" (1953), "Cold, Cold Heart" (1951), and "I'm So Lonesome I Could Cry" (1949); he radiates confident excitement in "Hey, Good Lookin'" (1951); and offers prayerful testimony in "I Saw the Light" (1948). Williams's lyrics are direct and simple, and his performances seem to come straight from the heart. Whether his songs really are autobiographical (some are) is less important than the fact that most people understood them to be so. To listeners in the early 1950s, Hank Williams was "pure country"—a country boy right down to the bone. His music and performance style became an important influence on subsequent country performers and writers.

By the early 1950s, country and western music had grown from a mostly regional musical style to a national phenomenon. Building on a growing audience for cowboy and western swing music in the movies, the success of barn-dance shows that played on network radio stations, and the appeal of stars such as Gene Autry, Jimmie Rodgers, Roy Acuff, and Hank Williams, country and western began to make its mark as a national style just as rock and roll was poised to explode. Despite its growth throughout the 1930s, '40s, and '50s, however, country and western music remained separate from mainstream pop, which still had a national market share that dwarfed country and western in terms of sales and profitability. Early rock and roll would challenge the lines that separated pop and country and western, but for the time being that boundary was clear and secure.

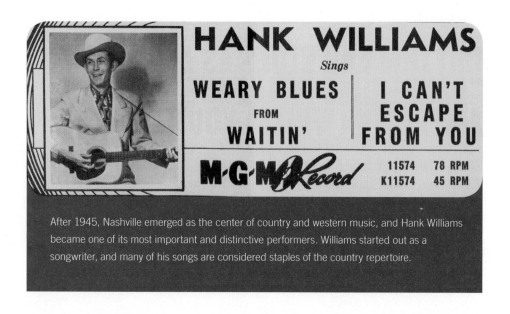

After 1945, Nashville emerged as the center of country and western music, and Hank Williams became one of its most important and distinctive performers. Williams started out as a songwriter, and many of his songs are considered staples of the country repertoire.

Listening Guide

Hank Williams, "Hey Good Lookin'" MGM-K11000

Words and music by Hank Williams, produced by Fred Rose. Hit #1 on the *Billboard* "Records Most Played by Folk Disc Jockeys" chart in 1951.

FORM: AABA, with three presentations of the complete verse-verse-bridge-verse structure. The arrangement of the song is similar to "I'm Sittin' on Top of the World." But where the Les Paul and Mary Ford track devotes the middle presentation of the AABA to a guitar solo, Williams's track splits the solo between the steel guitar and fiddle, with the steel taking the verses and the fiddle taking the bridge. Note also that Williams composes two sets of lyrics for the AABA structure, turning what was a formal chorus with unchanging lyrics in typical Tin Pan Alley music to a type of verse, with different lyrics for every presentation of the form.

TIME SIGNATURE: 4/4.

INSTRUMENTATION: Acoustic guitars, bass, steel guitar, fiddle, and lead vocal. Note that there are no drums, which were forbidden in the early years of the *Grand Ole Opry*. The piano and steel guitar take turns playing fills behind the vocals, seeming to comment on each vocal line, often echoing some part of it at the ends of phrases.

0:00–0:07	**Introduction**, 4 mm.	The steel guitar is featured, its notes sliding gracefully into one another.
0:07–0:21	**A-Verse**, 8 mm.	Vocal enters, "Hey good lookin' . . ." Note how the rhythm of the accompaniment is driven by the acoustic guitars and piano. The piano echoes the vocal at the ends of phrases.

RHYTHM AND BLUES AS A "DANGEROUS INFLUENCE" ON AMERICAN (WHITE) YOUTH

Stagger Lee and the Black Male Swagger. In many ways, the growth of rhythm and blues parallels the rise of country and western, but perceptions of racial difference influenced the way in which mainstream America received rhythm and blues. As white teenagers were increasingly drawn to rhythm and blues in the early 1950s, their parents worried about the effects this music might have on their children. Much of this concern—which at times ran to fear—resulted from racial stereotypes circulating within the white community. Of these, the image that seemed the most threatening is what scholars call the

		Get Music ⓢ wwnorton.com/studyspace
0:21–0:34	**A-Verse**, 8 mm.	As before, "Hey sweet baby . . ."
0:34–0:47	**B-Bridge**, 8 mm.	"I got a hot-rod Ford . . ." The chords now change more quickly beneath the melody, creating a sense of excitement and anticipation. The steel guitar steps forward.
0:47–1:01	**A-Verse**, 8 mm.	As before, "Hey good lookin' . . ." Piano commentary returns.
1:01–1:15	**A-Verse**, 8 mm.	Steel guitar solo, plays an arrangement of vocal melody.
1:15–1:28	**A-Verse**, 8 mm.	Steel guitar solo continues. This simple solo is considered a classic by fans of the steel guitar.
1:28–1:41	**B-Bridge**, 8 mm.	Fiddle picks up the melody to provide contrast.
1:41–1:55	**A-Verse**, 8 mm.	Steel guitar returns to round off this AABA presentation.
1:55–2:08	**A-Verse**, 8 mm.	Vocal returns, "I'm free and ready . . ." Now steel echoes vocal, instead of piano.
2:08–2:22	**A-Verse**, 8 mm.	Note that the story develops this last time through the AABA form, "No more lookin' . . ."
2:22–2:35	**B-Bridge**, 8 mm.	"I'm gonna throw my datebook . . ." Piano adds new part in its high register.
2:35–2:51	**A-Verse**, 8 mm.	As before, "Hey good lookin' . . ." Steel "commentary" returns as song drives to ending.

Stagger Lee myth: the idea that some black men are especially defiant, and often driven sexually. This type of swaggering black man was frightening to law enforcement due to his lack of compassion, and was thought to be constantly on the lookout for virginal white women. This is not the place to explore the origins of such ugly stereotypes; it is enough to realize that when many white listeners heard Muddy Waters singing "I Just Wanna Make Love to You," it aligned with a certain social myth. From a musical standpoint, we can see that these ideas were often based on fundamental sociocultural misunderstanding. A song that was understood one way within the black community was often interpreted in an entirely different way by white listeners unfamiliar with African-American literary forms and humor. This had the unfortunate consequence of convincing many white parents that rhythm and blues was a dangerous influence on their teenagers, and many worked to have this music, and the rock and roll that later developed out of it, abolished.

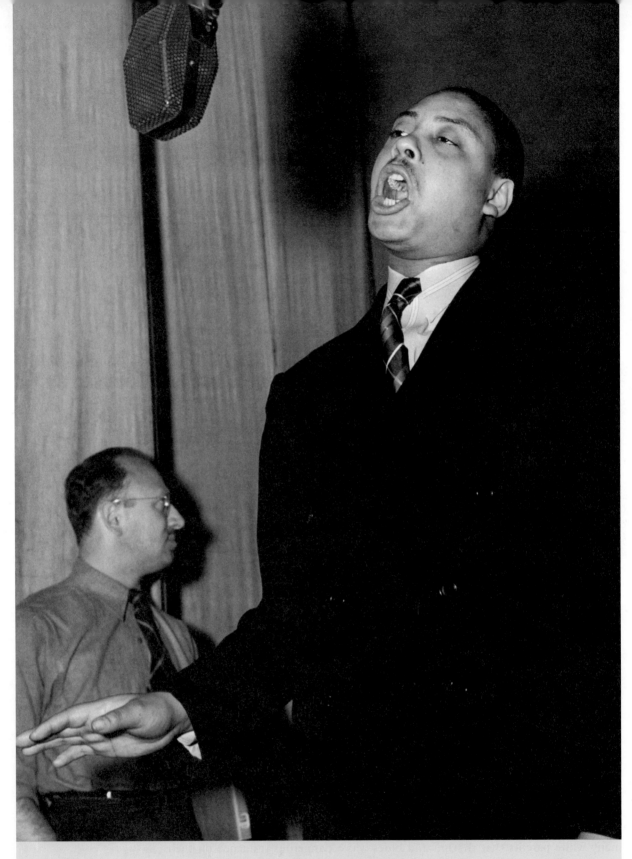

Although rock fans know his 1950s recordings for Atlantic Records, Joe Turner's success in rhythm and blues music dates back to the late 1930s. Turner is often considered the premiere blues shouter of the postwar years, possessing a voice that could rock a club even without the benefit of a microphone.

Listening Guide   Get Music ⑤ wwnorton.com/studyspace

Big Joe Turner, "Shake, Rattle, and Roll" Atlantic 1026

Words and music by Jesse Stone (Charles Calhoun), produced by Ahmet Ertegun and Jerry Wexler. Reached #1 on the *Billboard* rhythm and blues "Most Played in Jukeboxes" chart in late 1954.

FORM: Simple verse-chorus. This song is based on 12-bar blues, which appears in both the verse and chorus sections.

TIME SIGNATURE: 12/8 (shuffle in 4).

INSTRUMENTATION: Piano, saxes, guitar, bass, drums, and lead vocals.

0:00–0:07	**Introduction**, 4 mm.	Piano featured. Note the easy, rolling rhythmic feel.
0:07–0:25	**Verse 1**, 12 mm.	Vocal enters and musical focus remains almost entirely on the singing, with the saxes answering the ends of vocal lines "Get out of that bed . . ."
0:25–0:43	**Verse 2**, 12 mm.	The story begins to unfold, "You're wearin' those dresses . . ."
0:44–1:02	**Verse 3**, 12 mm.	"I believe to my soul . . ." New horn lines added.
1:02–1:21	**Chorus**, 12 mm.	This sing-along type chorus uses the same background music as the verses; at this point, it still is not clear how these lyrics relate to the verses, "Shake, rattle, and roll . . ."
1:21–1:40	**Instrumental Verse**, 12 mm.	Sax solo.
1:40–1:58	**Verse 4**, 12 mm.	Sexual innuendos increase, "I'm like a one-eyed cat . . ." Simpler sax commentary returns.
1:58–2:17	**Chorus**, 12 mm.	The connection is getting clearer, "Shake, rattle, and roll . . ."
2:17–2:36	**Verse 5**, 12 mm.	This verse almost stops having a double meaning, horn parts from earlier return, "I said, over the hill . . ."
2:36–3:00	**Chorus** with ending, 12 mm.	Now the connection is clear, "Shake, rattle, and roll . . ."

Hokum Blues and Fun with Double Meanings. Within black culture at mid-century, there was a well-established musical tradition of songs called "hokum blues" that poked fun at various aspects of adult relationships, mostly centered on sexual relations and the many situations that can arise in this context. Hokum stemmed from the minstrelsy tradition, which centered on stereotypes of African Americans using song, dance, and comedic dialogue. Although rhythm and blues of the 1950s was far removed from this original hokum context, the prevalence of sexual innuendo through double entendre carried into these later forms of black pop. Recordings of hokum blues numbers like "Papa" Charlie Jackson's "You Put It In, I'll Take It Out" (1934) and Tampa Red's "Let Me Play with Your Poodle" (1942) took this kind of fun as far as possible while maintaining a double meaning. Later elements of hokum in rhythm and blues were far gentler in their references. For example, "Hound Dog," recorded by blues singer Big Mama Thornton and written by white songwriters Jerry Leiber and Mike Stoller, features the lines: "You ain't nothin' but a hound dog, snoopin' 'round my door. You can wag your tail, but I ain't gonna feed you no more." In the context of such a tradition, the words "snoopin' 'round my door," "wag your tail," and "feed you" might be heard through the filter of double entendre.

Big Joe Turner's "Shake, Rattle, and Roll," released on Atlantic Records in 1954, provides a representative example of the hokum blues tradition as it appeared in rhythm and blues of the 1950s (the lyrics are provided on p. 72). In the text of Turner's recording the "one-eyed cat" is a metaphor for something more anatomical, as is the "seafood store." When Turner gets to gritting his teeth during the last

Sound Check

Artist	Judy Garland	Les Paul and Mary Ford	Howlin' Wolf	
Title	Over the Rainbow	I'm Sittin' on Top of the World	Evil Is Goin' On	
Chart peak	p5 1939	p10 1953	1954	
Form	AABA	AABA	Simple verse	
Rhythm	4/4	2/4 4/4	12/8	
Instrumentation	Orchestra	Electric guitars Lead vocal	Electric guitar Bass Drums Lead vocals Piano Harmonica	
Comments	Tempo variations Repetition of two verses and part of the bridge Conversation between voice and orchestra	Echo effect on guitar Multitracked guitars and vocals Jazz influence	12-bar blues Harmonica and piano solos Gritty vocal performance	

verse of the song, there is no doubt that the phrase "Shake, Rattle, and Roll" is a veiled reference to sexual activity. As innocuous as this song may be by today's standards, it was considered obscene in white middle-class culture in the mid-1950s. Interestingly, Bill Haley and His Comets (a band made up entirely of white musicians) also recorded "Shake, Rattle, and Roll" during the same period, adapting the song to make the lyrics acceptable to white audiences. Haley changed the words just enough to make the song seem harmless: the references to bed and sensuality were replaced with more wholesome images. Note that while Haley retained the line about the one-eyed cat, it no longer seems sexual in this new context. Another aspect of the song that changed in Haley's version is the rhythmic feel. While Turner's version projects a laid-back metric feel, Haley's version is somewhat frantic by contrast, pushing the beat as if the musicians can't wait to get to the next measure. This makes Haley's version seem peppier and happier, and helps in creating the impression that the song is really only about good, clean fun. In many ways, Haley's recording of "Shake, Rattle, and Roll" is a prototype of the pop adaptation of rhythm and blues that came to define rock and roll in its early years.

	Hank Williams	Big Joe Turner
	Hey Good Lookin'	Shake, Rattle, and Roll
	c1 1951	r1 1954
	AABA	Simple verse-chorus
	4/4	12/8
	Steel guitar Acoustic guitar Bass Lead Vocal Fiddle	Electric guitar Bass Drums Lead vocal Piano
	Piano and lead guitar alternate fills Instrumental solos through an entire AABA cycle No drums	Piano featured in introduction 12-bar blues Double entendre in lyrics

Two versions of "Shake, Rattle, and Roll"

TURNER'S VERSION (Atlantic 1026):	HALEY'S VERSION (Decca 29204):
Get out of that bed, wash your face and hands (well you) get in that kitchen, make some noise with the pots and pans	Get out in that kitchen and rattle those pots and pans (well) Roll my breakfast 'cause I'm a hungry man
(well) You're wearin' those dresses, the sun comes shinin' through I can't believe my eyes, all of this belongs to you	(I said) Shake, Rattle, and Roll (well) You'll never do nothin' to save your doggone soul
I believe to my soul you're the devil in nylon hose (well) the harder I work, the faster my money goes	Wearin' those dresses, your hair done up so nice You look so warm but your heart is cold as ice
(I said) Shake, Rattle, and Roll (well) you won't do right to save your doggone soul	(I said) Shake, Rattle, and Roll (well) You'll never do nothin' to save your doggone soul
I'm like a one-eyed cat, peepin' in a seafood store (well) I could look at you till you ain't no child no more	I'm like a one-eyed cat, peepin' in a seafood store I can look at you till you don't love me no more
(ah) Shake, Rattle, and Roll (well) you won't do right to save your doggone soul	I believe you're doin' me wrong and now I know The more I work, the faster my money goes
(I said) Over the hill and way down underneath you make me roll my eyes, baby make me grit my teeth	(I said) Shake, Rattle, and Roll (well) You'll never do nothin' to save your doggone soul
(I said) Shake, Rattle, and Roll (well) you won't do nothing to save your doggone soul	

The ways white musicians adapted rhythm and blues for the pop market are discussed in more detail in the next chapter. For now, remember that in the first half of the 1950s rhythm and blues, like country and western, was in many ways very different from mainstream pop. Until 1955, the music business remained highly segregated into pop, rhythm and blues, and country and western markets, with most of the media exposure and industry dollars devoted to pop. Pop was deeply invested in Tin Pan Alley music publishing and focused on the song. Although the market for rhythm and blues was assumed to be distinct, as industry insiders believed that nobody but black listeners would buy this music, white middle-class teenagers became quite interested in both rhythm and blues and country and western by the middle of the decade. Because these styles were available over the radio, white teens could hear this music, which often emanated from neighborhoods and communities their parents would prefer they avoided. When rock and roll broke out in 1955, it not only challenged the boundaries of style but threatened the way the popular music business was run—as well as some white Americans' sense of moral decency. Elvis the Pelvis seemed to assault middle-class sensibilities and Tin Pan Alley appeared to be under siege by styles and practices that originated in the other, smaller areas of the music business. The next chapter focuses on the first tumultuous years of this musical and cultural onslaught: rock and roll.

FURTHER READING

Glenn C. Altschuler, *All Shook Up: How Rock 'n' Roll Changed America* (Oxford University Press, 2003).

Philip K. Eberly, *Music in the Air: America's Changing Tastes in Popular Music, 1920–1980* (Hastings House, 1982).

Phillip H. Ennis, *The Seventh Stream: The Emergence of Rocknroll in American Popular Culture* (Wesleyan University Press, 1992).

Gary Giddings, *Bing Crosby, a Pocketful of Dreams: The Early Years, 1903–1940* (Little, Brown, 2001).

Charlie Gillett, *The Sound of the City: The Rise of Rock and Roll*, rev. and expanded ed. (Da Capo, 1996).

Charles Hamm, *Yesterdays: Popular Song in America* (Norton, 1983).

Tom Lewis, *Empire of the Air: The Men Who Made Radio* (Perennial, 1993).

Bill C. Malone, *Country Music U.S.A.* (University of Texas Press, 2002).

Russell Sanjak, updated by David Sanjek, *Pennies from Heaven: The American Popular Music Business in the Twentieth Century* (Da Capo, 1996).

Mary Alice Shaughnessy, *Les Paul: An American Original* (William Morrow, 1993).

Nick Tosches, *Unsung Heroes of Rock 'n' Roll: The Birth of Rock in the Wild Years before Elvis* (Da Capo, 1999).

Jerry Wexler and David Ritz, *Rhythm and the Blues: A Life in American Music* (St. Martin's, 1994).

After the roaring 1920s, the depressed '30s, and the war-ravaged '40s, the 1950s seemed to some a kinder, simpler, and more innocent decade. Many of the 1950s' conservative (and, some would say, puritanical) values were reflected in popular TV shows like *Father Knows Best* and *Leave It to Beaver*, and grandfatherly President Dwight Eisenhower. But the decade also saw the birth of the modern civil rights movement, *Playboy* magazine, and rock and roll.

While visible wars erupted in Korea and began to boil in Vietnam, Americans were much more aware of an ideological battle being fought: the Cold War. During World War II, the Americans and Soviets had been allies in the struggle against the Axis powers. But this partnership arose almost entirely out of necessity, and both parties remained acutely suspicious of one another. Many Americans were convinced that communists were trying to infiltrate their culture and overthrow the U.S. government. In 1948 former State Department official Alger Hiss was indicted for smuggling secrets to the Soviets (he was convicted in 1950), and Julius and Ethel Rosenberg were tried and convicted on espionage charges in 1951 (they were executed in 1953). Riding what many viewed

as a wave of communist paranoia (often called the "Red Scare"), Senator Joseph McCarthy, chairman of the Committee on Government Operations of the Senate, used his position to lead an anti-communism campaign (some would call it a witch hunt) during the early 1950s. McCarthy's subcommittee undertook a series of well-publicized hearings and private investigations dedicated to exposing communists thought to be lurking among U.S. citizens in politics, film, and labor unions.

The Soviets did have secrets: while the United States had stunned the world with the development and use of the atomic bomb in 1945, the Soviets launched the first satellite into space in 1957. Called *Sputnik*, this satellite reinforced American fears of Soviet ambitions and fueled an intense race for technological superiority between the two countries, which was won when America landed the first men on the moon in 1969.

Out of this strange brew of technology, spaceflight, and communist paranoia came a distinctly American passion for science-fiction stories and movies. Evil aliens seemed to drop out of the skies every night, and films such as *Invasion of the Body Snatchers* (1956) captured the sense that these intruders might well be lurking among us, waiting for the right moment to execute their nefarious plan for world domination.

Along with communist paranoia, economic prosperity increased after World War II. The American economy boomed, spurred by strong demand for new houses and consumer goods like televisions, home appliances, and cars. Most new homes were constructed in the suburbs, and new highways and automobiles made commuting to and from these towns easy.

With the rise of the suburbs, many Americans became reliant on the automobile for transportation during the 1950s. This 1958 photo of a Utah drive-in movie theater during a showing of *The Ten Commandments* depicts the decade's "car culture."

Racial segregation was one of the most controversial issues of the 1950s. This picture's original caption says it best: "9/4/1957—Little Rock, AR: Arkansas National Guardsmen turn away Elizabeth Eckford, a Negro Girl, as she attempts to enter Central High School here, Sept. 4th. The troops stopped eight Negro students from entering the school. The soldiers, called out to prevent the desegregation of the school because it might set off rioting between Negroes and whites, stopped the students in defiance of a federal judge's order that the school was to be integrated." President Eisenhower eventually sent troops in to enforce the judge's order and integrate the school.

Americans spent more time in cars than ever before, and many automobiles were equipped with AM radios. Car radios would play a signifi-cant role in the development of rock and roll, allowing teenagers to listen to rock and roll and rhythm and blues well out of earshot of their parents.

By contrast, traditional middle-American values were strongly reinforced on 1950s television (evi-denced by the popularity of *Leave It to Beaver*). Sexuality was almost totally absent from the small screen. In fact, most married couples on TV slept in twin beds, and if a couple

CHAPTER 2

JOHNNY B. GOODE
(C. Berry)

CHESS

Arc Music
BMI 8633
2:30

CHUCK BERRY
1691

MANUFACTURED BY CHESS PRODUCING CORP. CHICAGO ILLINOIS U.S.A.

THE BIRTH AND FIRST FLOURISHING OF ROCK AND ROLL

Historians love to define historical periods with specific beginning and end dates. In American history, for instance, we think of 1776 as the year when the United States broke with England to become a country in its own right. Of course, more careful study reveals that many events before and after 1776 influenced how the United States came to be organized as a sovereign nation. Important years and specific dates allow historians to organize the past, but they must be understood as representative markers in the flow of a broad range of historical events. Music historians also use important dates to account for the development of musical styles. While many scholars distinguish 1955 as the first year of rock and roll, there is not a clean dividing line between rock and roll, rhythm and blues, and even some country music until a few years later. However, 1955 is a useful marker and will help us draw a line between the world before rock and roll and everything that follows.

In the last chapter we saw that country and western and rhythm and blues were clearly established styles by the early 1950s and how regional radio made this music available to middle-class white youth. This audience was essential to the emergence of rock into the popular-music mainstream. Before 1955, rhythm and blues and country and western were still mostly outside the mainstream of American popular music, which was dominated by the major record labels and the Tin Pan Alley publishers. But as a youth culture developed in America after World War II, rhythm and blues became the music of choice for young people. When rhythm and blues broke into the mainstream in 1955, rock and roll was born.

Many elements came together to create this eruption of rock and roll in the later 1950s, primarily the rise of a youth culture and the emergence of independent radio and record labels. Rock and roll played a crucial role in challenging Tin Pan Alley's dominance of the music business and removing the divisions between

A fan of both country and western music and rhythm and blues, Chuck Berry came to Chicago to record with Chess Records on the advice of Muddy Waters. One of the first African-American rock artists to achieve success on the pop charts, Berry incorporated into his music tales of cars and school that easily applied to most American teenagers. Beginning with one of Berry's trademark guitar riffs, "Johnny B. Goode" tells the story of a young country boy who is destined to be a big star, because he can "play the guitar like ringing a bell." Notably, the song steers clear of any suggestive language, eliminating an obstacle that kept many rhythm and blues hits off mainstream pop radio until white artists rerecorded them in cover versions more appropriate for teenage ears. Berry was happy to write about typical topics of teenage life (school, dancing, parents), although he is perhaps most admired for the clever wordplay found in many of his lyrics.

the three industry markets: mainstream pop, country and western, and rhythm and blues. In 1955 and the years that followed, songs and records moved freely among these three markets and astounded the major labels. Since these markets had been divided along racial and socioeconomic lines, the integration of musical styles was bound to have reverberations throughout American culture. But none of this could have happened without the middle-class teenage audience, which created a lucrative market for record companies, radio stations, and others involved in the pop-music business.

This chapter will consider the "first wave" of rock and roll, loosely encompassing the period between 1955 and 1960. During this time, artists such as Fats Domino, Little Richard, Chuck Berry, Bill Haley, Elvis Presley, Jerry Lee Lewis, and Buddy Holly established rock and roll as a distinct style. As mentioned earlier, white teenagers thought of rock and roll as their music—something distinct from the culture of their parents and grandparents. White adult culture mostly viewed rock and roll as a dangerous influence, leading to juvenile delinquency or adoption of unacceptable attitudes and cultural practices. In many cases, adult opinions of rock were either tacitly or explicitly based on its association with black culture.

Due to a variety of factors, most of rock's originators and many of the independent labels they worked for were out of the music business by 1960. But these early years were crucial in establishing rock as a musical style and a central element of youth culture. Later musicians would frequently look back on these years as the Golden Age of rock and roll. Popular music had crossed a line, and in many fundamental ways, the music business would never be the same again.

THE RISE OF YOUTH CULTURE IN THE 1950S

The First Wave of War Babies Reach Adolescence (This Is Not Your Father's Pop Music). The end of World War II saw the rise of a new and significant phenomenon in American society: a pop culture devoted exclusively to teenagers. While earlier generations had been expected to assimilate into adult culture as soon as they left high school, in the 1950s white, middle-class teens were allowed to avoid adult responsibility longer than any group in history. They had fashion, music, dancing, movies, magazines, and a bevy of slang terms that belonged exclusively to them. In part, this phenomenon arose from the country's relative political stability and affluence in the post–World War II years: teens had money to spend on leisure activities and luxury items. There was also an attempt within the middle class to return to "normalcy" following the war. Parents, in many cases recovering from the domestic disruption of the war, now focused increasingly on family life, devoting considerable attention and resources to the health, education, and overall happiness of their children. Children born just before the American involvement in the war (December 1941) were the first beneficiaries of this new attention. By 1955 many of them were in high school. In a pattern that has since become familiar, these adolescents wanted music that did not sound like that of their parents or their

In the mid-1950s, several films helped establish the image of restless and rebellious youth that soon would become associated with rock and roll. Directed by László Benedek, *The Wild One* (1953, top) starred Marlon Brando as the charismatic and troubled leader of a motorcycle gang. James Dean also played a troubled youngster in *Rebel Without a Cause* (1955, middle), becoming a legend after his untimely death in an automobile accident. Also in 1955, *Blackboard Jungle* (bottom, starring, from left, Vic Morrow, Sidney Poitier, and Glenn Ford) gave rise to adult concerns when teenage viewers got rowdy as the song "Rock Around the Clock" was played in the film.

older siblings. To these kids, rhythm and blues—available via local black radio—seemed exotic, dangerous, and sexual in ways that excited them.

Listening to rhythm and blues was not simply a forbidden pleasure to white teens. It was also an act of social rebellion—a way to resist assimilation into the adult world of responsibilities and commitments. Conversely, juvenile delinquency was a major concern for adults during the 1950s. Several contemporary films reflect this societal confict. In *The Wild One* (1953), Marlon Brando plays the rebellious young leader of a motorcycle gang. When asked at one point what he's against, he replies simply, "Whaddya got?" *Rebel Without a Cause* (1955) features James Dean in a classic portrayal of a tragically misunderstood teenager. Before the film was released, Dean was killed in a car crash and his untimely death at the age of twenty-four made him an icon for misunderstood youth and teenage tragedy. While both of these films directly addressed teen angst and rebellion, neither reflected this musically, relying on traditional orchestrated film soundtracks. By contrast, *Blackboard Jungle* (1955)—a film about the perils of juvenile delinquency in an urban high school setting—featured Bill Haley's "(We're Gonna) Rock Around the Clock" over the opening credits. The success of the movie, which actually led to youth riots in some theaters in both the United States and the United Kingdom, catapulted the Haley song to the top of the pop charts. This marked an important moment in the emergence of rock and roll. Not only was "Rock Around the Clock" one of the top pop records of 1955, but its inclusion in a film dealing with juvenile delinquency cemented the association of rock music with teenage rebellion and rowdiness. Haley was among a growing number of artists to score pop hits with rhythm and blues records. Once it became clear that such records would sell, the market was flooded with them.

RADIO AND RECORDS

The Rise of the Disc Jockey. Many white teenagers were first exposed to rhythm and blues by hearing it on the radio. During the early 1950s, small and inexpensive tube-driven tabletop radios were common among the white middle class, and the majority of black urban households had at least one radio. By mid-decade, the development of the transistor had made small portable radios affordable to almost everyone.

As radios became more available to teenagers, disc jockeys (DJs) emerged as the most important tastemakers of early rock and roll. In 1951, Alan Freed was an announcer at a radio station in Cleveland, hosting an evening classical-music show sponsored by one of the city's largest record stores—the Record Rendezvous, owned by Leo Mintz. Mintz noticed that teenagers were buying significant numbers of rhythm and blues records, and he offered to sponsor a late-night radio show devoted to this music, with Freed as the host. Freed was reluctant at first, but on July 11, 1951, *The Moondog Show* premiered on WJW, a clear-channel station with a signal that reached far beyond the Ohio state line. Radio programming that had been targeted at a black audience was now being enjoyed by white teens. Freed was among the first of a new wave of disc jockeys to develop rhythm and blues program-

ming, and he is often cited as the most influential DJ in rock and roll's breakthrough to the popular music mainstream.

As it turns out, Freed was not the first disc jockey to play rhythm and blues on the radio. In 1949, Dewey Phillips began his *Red, Hot, and Blue* show on WHBQ in Memphis, while Gene Nobles, John R. Richbourg, and Hoss Allen were playing rhythm and blues at WLAC in Nashville, as were Zenas "Daddy" Sears in Atlanta (WGST), and Hunter Hancock in Los Angeles (KFVD). Freed was reportedly a WLAC listener and modeled his early shows on those from Nashville, even calling occasionally to find out what records were hot there. All of these early DJs were white, though most listeners assumed they were black on the basis of their on-air voices. According to one survey, of the three thousand or so disc jockeys on the air in the United States in 1947, only sixteen were black. However, during the late 1940s and throughout the '50s black DJs made their mark on radio throughout the country, including Vernon Winslow ("Doctor Daddy-O") in New Orleans, Lavada Durst ("Doctor Hepcat") in Austin, William Perryman ("Piano Red" and "Doctor Feelgood") in Atlanta, Al Benson in Chicago, Jocko Henderson in Philadelphia, and Tommy Smalls ("Jive") in New York. WDIA in Memphis featured an all-black on-air staff, including Rufus Thomas, B.B. King, and Martha Jean ("The Queen") Steinberg. When he debuted his rhythm and blues show in Cleveland in 1951, Freed was simply emulating something that was already going on in other parts of the country.

Freed was enormously successful in Cleveland, and reports of his popularity there drew the attention of WINS in New York. In September 1954 he debuted in the Big Apple, where he repeated his midwestern success on a much larger media stage. Freed renamed his show *The Rock and Roll Party* (after a dispute over the Moondog moniker) and was soon syndicated nationally and eventually in Europe. Thus, in the waning months of 1954 and into 1955, Freed created a considerable buzz over rhythm and blues among white teenagers in one of the country's major markets. He extended his involvement in bringing rock and roll to the masses by promoting concerts, producing films, and eventually working in television, capitalizing on the tremendous success of his radio show. He took his 1958 concert show, *The Big Beat* (which included Jerry Lee Lewis and Buddy Holly), on the road across the United

States. Freed starred in hastily produced films like *Rock Around the Clock* (1956) and *Don't Knock the Rock* (1957), which had flimsy plots and featured appearances by early rhythm and blues and rock and roll acts, including Bill Haley, Chuck Berry, Frankie Lymon, and the Moonglows. He also hosted a TV dance show from 1958 to 1960. To many teenagers, Alan Freed was the father of rock and roll, so it came as no surprise when the almost continual backlashes against the music were directed at him, and especially his concert shows, which the press often portrayed as teen riots. As Freed enjoyed celebrity on the national level, his popularity was paralleled in every major city by local DJs who were stars in their own communities. These DJs also aggressively promoted the new youth music—now widely known as rock and roll thanks to Freed's influence.

Aggressive Marketing by Independent Labels. Most of the rhythm and blues that teens heard on the radio during the 1950s was recorded by and released on independent labels. In the previous chapter, we noted that these labels were much smaller operations than the major labels, and while the majors were national, the indies were mostly regional. The majors—Decca, Mercury, RCA-Victor, Columbia, Capitol, and MGM—had their own manufacturing plants and national distribution networks; most indies had to farm out manufacturing and improvise distribution systems, at first cooperating with indie labels in other parts of the country to establish reciprocal arrangements ("You distribute my records, I'll distribute yours") until independent distributors were established. This competitive disadvantage was significant and meant that a successful indie label had to be aggressive about marketing. For independent labels success was dependent on gaining radio play for their records and getting them into stores and jukeboxes. To get a record played, it was necessary to develop relationships with DJs, who could be influenced by gifts ranging from cash and merchandise to nights on the town and even vacations. Stores might receive extra copies of records to sell at full profit in order to push a particular record. Jukeboxes were a fixture in many bars and restaurants; if a label could get a regional distributor to pick up a record for use in jukeboxes, this constituted significant sales and stimulated jukebox listeners to buy even more records. In this context, the practice of paying disc jockeys to play music on the radio was later called "payola."

Both independent and major labels used payola, but it was most beneficial to the independent labels, who used this practice more readily in order to compete with the greater resources shared by major labels. Employees at a major label were often working with the company's money, but the owner of an indie label often had his own money on the line with a record. In the early 1950s, the conventional wisdom held that an indie could not beat a major label in the pop market, so rhythm and blues and country and western were markets in which independents could make money. In many ways, the emergence of rock and roll in the 1950s can be attributed to the entrepreneurship of both indie labels and DJs, each working on the outskirts of their respective business worlds: indie labels were fighting for a place on the margins of the recording industry, while independent radio stations were battling in regional markets with the local affiliates of the national networks. Rhythm and blues had been largely ignored by the major corporate powers, mostly because these companies found that the profit generated by such music did not justify the effort to develop, record, and market it. All of this occurred, for the most part, outside the powerful corporations and institutions that had shaped popular music in the United States for decades. When rhythm and blues records started showing up on the pop charts in the early 1950s, however, the industry was headed for a significant shake-up.

CROSSOVERS AND COVERS

Hit Records and the Charts. In order to be successful, people who sell music for a living ultimately have to view it as a business. It is great if a record company executive, radio station manager, record store owner, or jukebox distributor likes some of the music they sell, but this is by no means a necessity. Businesspeople need to think in terms of markets, product, distribution, and promotion—especially given the fickle character of many listeners when it comes to popular music—and it is tremendously beneficial to be able to identify trends. If you can spot a trend, your chances are greatly increased for having the right amount of product where it needs to be, timed precisely to meet the peak consumer demand. If your timing is right, your profits soar; if you time it wrong, they plummet. Such "inside" information is usually not very interesting to most listeners, who just want to hear the music, so magazines devoted to the more dollars-and-cents aspect of the business have developed for industry professionals. The most important of these in the history of rock and roll in the United States were *Cashbox* and *Billboard*. Both of which contained sales charts that attempted to predict trends in record and jukebox sales. Based on the most recent issue of *Billboard*, a store owner might have decided to order additional copies of a record that was climbing the charts, while making sure to get rid of extra copies of a record that was falling. Likewise, jukebox owners wanted the most popular songs in their machines; the more jukeboxes were played, the more they paid. Jukebox distributors would use the most recent *Cashbox* charts to decide which records to add and remove on their regular visits to service their regional clients.

The charts in these industry periodicals were divided according to the professionals' assessment of how consumers could most effectively be separated, so they were driven by purchasing patterns. Thus, pop charts listed records that would likely be marketed to white, middle-class listeners. Rhythm and blues (originally called "race" and then "sepia") charts followed music that was directed to black urban audiences, and country and western (originally called "hillbilly" and then "folk") charts kept track of music directed at low-income whites. This system of parallel charts was based on assumptions about markets and audience tastes, not musical style. The arrangement suggests that rhythm and blues listeners would not enjoy country and western or pop, but all it really tries to predict is who is most likely to buy records or play them on the jukebox. According to this system, if you owned a record store on Main Street that had few black customers and almost none from the country, you would not pay much attention to the rhythm and blues and country and western charts, since most of your customers would have been interested in pop records. Contrary to beliefs about such segregated listening, anecdotal evidence suggests that many black listeners enjoyed pop and country and western, and that many country and western listeners enjoyed pop and rhythm and blues. Young, middle-

Reading the Chart Numbers

Throughout this book, *Billboard* chart positions will be noted and often these numbers will be cited in an abbreviated form. Rhythm and blues positions will be abbreviated with an "r": "r1, 1955" indicates a record that hit the number one slot on the R&B charts in 1955. Pop records will be abbreviated with a "p," and country positions will use the letter "c." Later in the book, British chart positions will be abbreviated with the letters "uk" (these numbers come from *Record Retailer*). Using these abbreviations, a record's chart success might be cited as "r1 p3, 1956," meaning it rose as high as number one on the R&B charts and number three on the pop charts in 1956. Bear in mind that chart numbers are not precision instruments and are subject to manipulation in some cases; they provide only a general indication of a record's success. We are using them here mostly for comparison purposes and to keep the "fan mentality" in check, as discussed in the Introduction.

class white listeners already knew some country and western from network broadcasts, although most white adults were apparently not interested in rhythm and blues. One of the most significant changes to these business practices that occured during the early 1950s was when middle-class white teens discovered rhythm and blues, which led to the softening of the boundaries between chart classifications.

When a record or song holds a prominent position on more than one of the three types of charts, this is called "crossover." Crossover can occur in many ways. The record itself or the song, recorded by a different artist, may cross over. A new version of a song is called a "cover," and the original recording or a cover version might cross over. Until 1955, chart boundaries were relatively reliable; for the most part, records and songs popular on one chart stayed on that chart and crossovers were more the exception than the rule. From 1950–53, for instance, about 10 percent of the hits appearing on the rhythm and blues charts crossed over. Beginning in 1954, however, a clear trend can be seen, as rhythm and blues records began to cross over onto the other charts; 25 percent of the rhythm and blues hits crossed over that year, and by 1958 the figure increased to 94 percent. Sometimes two versions of the same song would appear on the pop charts—the original rhythm and blues performance, most often performed by a black artist, and a cover version, usually performed by a white artist. With only a few notable exceptions, the versions by white artists performed better on the pop charts than the rhythm and blues originals. When the original version appeared on a small independent label, a larger independent label (or a major label) could record a cover and distribute its records faster and more widely; to some extent, this explains the greater success of these versions and why we call them "covers." Race played a significant role in pop listeners' tastes, which was the source of much resentment among the black artists whose records were copied.

THE FIRST ROCK AND ROLLERS CROSS OVER

Fats Domino. Among the first of the early rockers to enjoy consistent crossover success was Antoine "Fats" Domino. Based in New Orleans and recording on the West Coast independent label Imperial, Domino scored a series of rhythm and blues hits in the early 1950s, including "The Fat Man" (r6, 1950), "Goin' Home" (r1, 1952), and "Something's Wrong" (r6, 1953). "Ain't It a Shame" was a number one hit on the rhythm and blues charts in 1955 and crossed over to the pop charts, rising as high as number ten that summer. Between 1955 and 1963, Domino released thirty-seven Top 40 singles, the most successful of which were "I'm in Love Again" (r1 p3, 1956), "Blueberry Hill" (r1 p2, 1956), and "I'm Walkin'" (r1 p4, 1957).

Listening Guide Get Music Ⓢ wwnorton.com/studyspace

Fats Domino, "Blueberry Hill" Imperial 5407

Words and music by Al Lewis, Larry Stock, and Vincent Rose, produced by Dave Bartholomew. Reached #1 on all three *Billboard* rhythm and blues charts (best sellers, jukeboxes, and radio) and #2 on the "Most Played in Jukeboxes," pop chart in 1956.

FORM: AABA form, with only the bridge and last verse repeated (BA).

TIME SIGNATURE: 12/8, with a characteristic easy, loping New Orleans feel. Each measure contains four beats, with each beat divided into three parts (compound). Note how the piano chords play these three parts of each beat, creating a rolling 1 & uh, 2 & uh, 3 & uh, 4 & uh rhythmic undercurrent.

INSTRUMENTATION: Piano, electric guitar, acoustic bass, drums, horns, and lead vocal.

0:00–0:12	**Introduction**, 4 mm.	Piano featured as the New Orleans feel locks in.
0:12–0:33	**A-Verse**, 8 mm.	Vocal enters. Note the repeated chords high on the piano, and the rolling line in the bass and guitar below. Sustained horns support the vocal, "I found my thrill . . ."
0:33–0:53	**A-Verse**, 8 mm.	As before, "The moon stood still . . ."
0:53–1:14	**B-Bridge**, 8 mm.	New horn line enters to emphasize contrast, "The wind in the willow . . ."
1:14–1:35	**A-Verse**, 8 mm.	As before, "Though we're apart . . ."
1:35–1:56	**B-Bridge**, 8 mm.	Supporting horn line returns, "The wind in the willow . . ."
1:56–2:18	**A-Verse**, 8 mm.	As before, "Though we're apart . . ."

Domino delivered his songs from the piano, gently tapping out repeated triplet chords and singing his often lyrical melodies in a relaxed manner. He projected a warm, friendly image that was unlikely to trigger the kind of racial anxiety in white listeners that Big Joe Turner might. According to Domino's producer, Dave Bartholomew, close musical associates thought of Domino as a country and western singer. His biggest pop song, "Blueberry Hill," had been a hit for Glenn Miller in 1940, and provides a representative example of Domino's easygoing crossover style.

Chuck Berry. Charles Edward Anderson (Chuck) Berry grew up in St. Louis and was introduced to Leonard Chess of Chess Records by blues great Muddy Waters. Berry's first hit for Chess was "Maybellene," his version of a traditional country fiddle tune called "Ida Red," which had been recorded by both Roy Acuff and Bob Wills. There are several stories about how the lyrics and title of the song changed—

Based in New Orleans, Fats Domino had a series of rhythm and blues hits before crossing over onto the pop charts. His easygoing style is characterized by rolling triplets on the piano and a smooth vocal delivery.

Chess reported that he got the idea from a makeup case and Berry claimed it was the name of a cow in a book he read as a child. Either way, "Maybellene" became a number one hit on the rhythm and blues charts and crossed over to reach number five on the pop charts in the fall of 1955. Berry followed with several more hit singles, including "School Day" (r1 p3, 1957), "Rock and Roll Music" (r6 p8,

Doo-wop and Crossover

Doo-wop music played an important role in rhythm and blues before 1955. Doo-wop originated with the vocal quartets of urban areas. The vocal quartet had been a long-standing tradition among African-American men that could be traced back decades, and groups like the Mills Brothers and the Ink Spots had brought vocal-group music to the top of the pop charts during the 1940s. One of the first doo-wop records to cross directly over to the pop charts was "Cryin' in the Chapel" by the Baltimore-based Orioles (on the Jubilee independent label). The Chords' "Sh'boom" was also a crossover hit on Atlantic in 1954, though it was quickly covered for the white market by the Crew Cuts. The success of these records led independent labels to search the streets for vocal groups. In such cases, the label brought a group into the studio, added a rhythm section—often consisting of drums, bass, piano, and guitar—and recorded the tunes the group had worked up, releasing the best of them. Some groups used their own arrangements, giving many classic doo-wop recordings an amateurish quality that fans of the style find especially endearing. Consequently, most doo-wop groups had only one or two hits; follow-up hits were difficult because the first hit was often the best arrangement a group had, and it had developed over months of rehearsing. In some cases a label would work with a group to help them develop material and arrangements, as Atlantic did with Clyde McPhatter and the Drifters, who had a series of rhythm and blues hits, including "Money Honey" (r1, 1953) and "Whatcha Gonna Do?" (r2, 1955). Recording for Mercury, the Platters were among the most successful of the 1950s vocal groups, charting eighteen pop Top 40 hits during the 1955–60 period, including "Only You (and You Alone)" (r1 p5, 1955), "The Great Pretender" (r1 p1, 1955), "My Prayer" (r1 p1, 1956), "Twilight Time" (r1 p1, 1958), and "Smoke Gets in Your Eyes" (r3 p1, 1958).

1957), "Sweet Little Sixteen" (r1 p2, 1958), and "Johnny B. Goode" (r2 p8, 1958). His vocal delivery in these early rock hits is heavily influenced by his love of country music. In fact, reports from early personal appearances chronicle a sense of surprise among many audience members who had assumed from his records that Berry was white. Berry had a more showy performance style than Fats Domino, and the iconic "duck walk" he performed during his guitar solos became a Berry trademark. Like Domino, however, there was little about Berry's music or performances that struck white audiences as threatening or menacing.

Unlike the many cover versions that toned down adult-oriented songs, Berry has stated that his intention was not to reach adult black listeners but to write songs specifically geared toward the average teenager. "Roll Over Beethoven" gently celebrates the idea that the practice of teens listening to rhythm and blues music—which is playfully cast as a contagious virus—would probably make Beethoven turn over in his grave. Of course, the real target here is not classical music, but what classical music stands for—conservative and serious adult culture. Early in his professional career Berry developed an affection for what he called "story songs," and "School Day" (originally titled "A Teenager's Day") is one such song, chronicling the daily life of the average teen—off to school in the morning, classes, lunch, and the final bell, after which everyone goes down to the local meeting place to play rock and roll on the jukebox. In this case, the conservative and oppressive institution is not the stuffy world of classical music and culture, but school life, and rhythm and blues (here referred to as "rock and roll") is the music of resistance. The ending chorus of the tune, "Hail, hail, rock and roll," has been an anthem for rock fans ever since.

Such lyrics might have been delivered with an earnestness that could prove tedious or directly rebellious. But Berry's clever allusions and good humor make his songs more of a friendly ribbing of adult culture than a full frontal assault advocating or affecting social change. Later rock musicians such as John Lennon and Bob Dylan, among many others, admired Berry's lyrics and imitated his careful and creative wordplay. Berry's songs do not all deal with teen life, and some can be interpreted on many levels. "Memphis, Tennessee" (1963) is perhaps the best example of a more adult story song that expertly plays on the expectations of the listener. Throughout the song the listener believes that Berry is trying to reach his estranged wife by telephone, revealing details of his personal life to the operator; in the last line we find out that this is not the case. (Listen to the song to hear its conclusion.) Even "Maybellene," which alternates between seemingly unrelated stories of the singer racing Maybellene's Cadillac in his Ford and a chorus complaining of Maybellene's unfaithfulness, can be read at a second level. The problem with Maybellene is that she is a "fast woman," represented in this case by a fast car (the Cadillac). Trying to keep up with her is like a race, as the allusions follow one after another. The singer begins by "motorvatin' over the hill" but soon they are "bumper to bumper, rolling side to side"; later Berry describes "rainwater flowin'

A consummate showman, Chuck Berry decided early on that he would write and perform songs that didn't need to be changed for white radio. Berry's attention to lyrics provided a model for many songwriters who followed, as did his bursts of lead guitar.

Listening Guide   Get Music ⓢ wwnorton.com/studyspace

Chuck Berry, "Johnny B. Goode" Chess 1691

Words and music by Chuck Berry, produced by Leonard and Phil Chess. Reached #8 on the *Billboard* "Top 100" chart and #5 on both rhythm and blues charts (jukeboxes and best-sellers) in 1958.

FORM: Simple verse-chorus.

TIME SIGNATURE: 4/4, with a tendency to blend in a shuffle.

INSTRUMENTATION: Electric guitars, piano, acoustic bass, drums, and lead vocal. Note how the drums tend to shuffle, while the guitar stays stubbornly in simple time.

0:00–0:17	**Introduction**, 12 mm.	Famous guitar intro using double stops, with stop time in first 4 mm. and band entering in m. 5.
0:17–0:34	**Verse 1**, 12 mm.	Vocal enters; note the constantly changing piano fills in the background throughout the song, "Deep down in Louisi-ana . . ."
0:34–0:51	**Chorus**, 12 mm.	Vocal punctuated by characteristic Chuck Berry guitar bursts, "Go, Go Johnny . . ."
0:51–1:08	**Verse 2**, 12 mm.	As before, note Berry's vocal sound—does it sound country-influenced? "He used to carry . . ."
1:08–1:26	**Chorus**, 12 mm.	As before.
1:26–1:43	**Instrumental Verse**, 12 mm.	(Like Intro), guitar solo, more double stops, full of rhythmic drive but technically simple.
1:43–2:00	**Instrumental Verse**, 12 mm.	(Like Intro), guitar solo continues.
2:00–2:18	**Verse 3**, 12 mm.	As before, "His mother told him . . ."
2:18–2:38	**Chorus**, 12 mm.	As before, driving to ending.

all under my hood, knew that was doin' my motor good," and at the end of the song the Ford catches the Cadillac "at the top of the hill." It is not difficult to interpret this as a thickly veiled song about sexuality, ultimately not much different from "Sixty Minute Man" or "Shake, Rattle, and Roll."

Most of Berry's songs are in simple verse or simple verse-chorus form, often employing a chord structure influenced by the 12-bar blues. His songs are relatively easy to learn, and with their catchy lyrics, they have been favorites with rock bands since the late 1950s. Most of the musicians who created the rock music of the '60s and '70s could have played half a dozen Berry tunes without even thinking about it, and many often did so in live shows. Berry's guitar style became one of the most imitated in rock. His chordal accompaniments often featured a characteristic two-string boogie-woogie pattern on the low strings, and his solos used frequent double stops (playing two notes at the same time) on adjacent high strings. These can be heard clearly on a number of songs, but "Johnny B. Goode" is perhaps the best example.

Little Richard. The most flamboyant performer in the early years of rock and roll was probably Little Richard, born Richard Wayne Penniman. Recording on the Hollywood-based Specialty independent label, Richard's high-energy "Tutti Frutti" climbed the rhythm and blues charts in late 1955, hitting number two and crossing over to the pop charts where it peaked at number seventeen. In subsequent years, Richard placed nine hits on the pop Top 40, including "Long Tall Sally" (r1 p6, 1956), "Keep a Knockin'" (r2 p8, 1957), and "Good Golly, Miss Molly" (r4 p10, 1958). With his sometimes-maniacal singing and screaming, aggressive piano pounding (he frequently played with one leg propped up over the piano), and strong driving beat in the rhythm section, Richard provided a remarkable contrast to the gentler Fats Domino. Little Richard was the first rock and roll artist to cultivate the "wild man" persona. While this made him attractive to white teens, it also made it more difficult for him to advance his career in the mainstream pop market. A clear country and western influence may have made it easier for white audiences to accept Fats Domino and Chuck Berry, but there was little of that influence evident in Little Richard. Lyrics such as "Good golly, Miss Molly, you sure like to ball" and "I got a girl named Sue, she knows just what to do" were not appropriate for pop audiences. Richard was a prime target for cover versions; if a white artist covered a song and took much of the sexual innuendo out of the lyrics, his record could often outperform Richard's on the charts and in sales, even if it was far less vital and exciting than the original.

Richard Penniman (Little Richard) was the most flamboyant figure in rock's first years. He often stood while playing the piano, which allowed him more flexibility to move during performances. Little Richard had a string of crossover hits before quitting rock music to enter the ministry.

Listening Guide

Get Music Ⓢ wwnorton.com/studyspace

Little Richard, "Tutti Frutti" Specialty 561

Words and music by Richard Penniman, Robert "Bumps" Blackwell, and Dorothy LaBostrie, produced by Bumps Blackwell. Reached #1 on the *Billboard* "Most Played in Jukeboxes" pop chart and #2 on both rhythm and blues charts (jukeboxes and best-sellers).

FORM: Simple verse-chorus, beginning with chorus.

TIME SIGNATURE: 4/4.

INSTRUMENTATION: Piano, acoustic bass, drums, saxophones, and lead vocal.

0:00–0:18	**Chorus**, 12 mm. + 2 mm.	Vocal intro, "Wop bop . . ."
0:18–0:34	**Verse 1**, 12 mm. (with slight change from chorus)	"I got a girl . . . Sue . . ."
0:34–0:49	**Chorus**, 12 mm.	"Tutti frutti . . ."
0:49–1:04	**Verse 2**, 12 mm.	"I got a girl . . . Daisy . . ."
1:04–1:20	**Chorus**, 12 mm.	"Tutti frutti . . ."
1:20–1:35	**Instrumental Verse**, 12 mm.	Sax solo.
1:35–1:50	**Chorus**, 12 mm.	"Tutti frutti . . ."
1:50–2:06	**Verse 3**, 12 mm.	Same lyrics as Verse 2.
2:06–2:22	**Chorus**, 12 mm.	"Tutti frutti . . ." ends on vocal intro "Wop bop . . ."

The "Whitening" of Rhythm and Blues. As we saw in the previous chapter, Bill Haley's version of "Shake, Rattle, and Roll" removes much of the sexual playfulness from Big Joe Turner's original song. These changes were clearly made so the song would be more appealing to white listeners. Indeed, the resulting record, like much of Haley's music that followed it, exudes a kind of innocent excitement by replacing references to sexuality with references to dancing. Many listeners would not think of it this way now, but when viewed in context, "(We're Gonna) Rock Around the Clock" might sound like a song that deals with sexual stamina. Prompted by the success of the Dominoes' "Sixty Minute Man"—a number one rhythm and blues hit in 1951 that briefly crossed over to the pop charts—a series of songs followed that dealt with this same topic, including Ruth Brown's "5–10–15 Hours" (r1, 1952), the Ravens' "Rock Me All Night Long" (r4, 1952), "Work with Me, Annie" (r1, 1954) and "Annie Had a Baby" (r1, 1954) both by the Midnighters with Hank Ballard. (In early 1955 Georgia Gibbs had a number two pop hit with "Dance with Me Henry," a reworked version of "Work with Me, Annie" that also substitutes dance for sex.) Adjustments to both the lyrics and the music of rhythm and blues began to establish a model for rock and roll in the early years, and Haley was an important figure in what might be called the "whitening" of rhythm and blues.

In the early 1950s William John Clinton Haley Jr. was a disc jockey who also played in a Philadelphia-area country swing band, Bill Haley and His Saddlemen. In 1954 Bill Haley and His Comets signed with the major label Decca and released "Shake, Rattle, and Roll" and "(We're Gonna) Rock Around the Clock." "Shake, Rattle, and Roll" was the most popular of Haley's early singles, rising to the top 10 of the *Billboard* pop "Best Sellers" chart. In late 1954, Haley released "Dim, Dim the Lights," which crossed over to the rhythm and blues charts. With the release of *Blackboard Jungle*, "(We're Gonna) Rock Around the Clock" enjoyed a new-found popularity, topping the pop charts for eight weeks in mid-1955 and rising to the upper reaches of the rhythm and blues charts. Even though Haley represented a whitened version of rhythm and blues, he still found popularity in black markets. Haley and the group placed nine more hits in the pop Top 40, including "Burn That Candle" (r9 p9, 1955) and "See You Later, Alligator" (r7 p6, 1956).

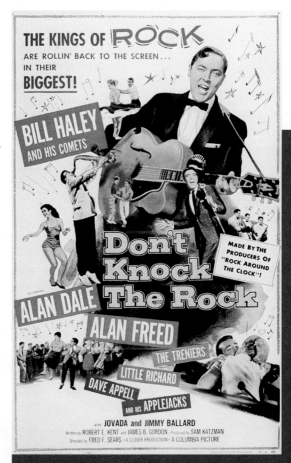

Many listeners who associate rock and roll with the raucousness of Chuck Berry and Little Richard might be surprised to learn that Charles Eugene "Pat" Boone (a direct descendant of Daniel Boone) was one of the most successful artists in the early years of rock and roll. Recording for the independent, Nashville-based Dot Records, Boone scored thirty-two Top 40 hits—sixteen of these in the Top 10—between 1954 and 1959. Boone's cover of Fats Domino's "Ain't It a Shame"—renamed "Ain't That a Shame"—outperformed the original on the pop charts, hitting number one for two weeks in the fall of 1955 (r13), and his covers of Little Richard's "Tutti Frutti" (p12, 1956) and "Long Tall Sally" (p8, 1956) equaled or surpassed the originals in the pop market. Rock historians and critics often consider Boone's contribution to rock and roll only in terms of these cover versions, but he had many other hit records during this period that were not derived from rhythm and blues material, including "Don't Forbid Me" (p1 r10, 1956), "Love Letters in the Sand" (p1 r12, 1957), and "April Love" (p1, 1957). Boone cultivated a polite, clean-cut personal image. His musical approach in many ways continued in the mainstream pop style of Frank Sinatra, but extended it to include the country and western, rhythm and blues, and gospel repertoire. If Little Richard presented a musical and personal image that many white parents found threatening, Boone's music and manner were much more readily assimilated into middle-class white culture. Most important for the history of early rock music, Boone's popularity was both dependent on and fueled by the rise of rock and roll. More than just a singer

Fueled by the success of "Rock Around the Clock," Bill Haley and His Comets became one of the first successful white acts in rock and roll. In addition to recording many popular hits in the early years of rock, the group also appeared in several rock-oriented films.

who covered rhythm and blues records for a white audience, Boone played a crucial role in establishing rock and roll within mainstream pop music.

The Controversy over Cover Versions.

With the success of Bill Haley, Fats Domino, Little Richard, Pat Boone, and Chuck Berry, it became common practice in the record business to watch the rhythm and blues charts for hits and then cover these songs for the pop market. This practice significantly reduced the crossover potential for both the original records and the original artists, who were almost always black. In many people's view, black artists were "ripped off." Rhythm and blues artists were often paid a flat fee for recording a number and frequently signed away any rights to future royalties they might be entitled to as songwriters. For musicians in the habit of going from town to town and gig to gig, it was far more prudent to be paid up front than to sign an agreement for future royalties with a small, financially fragile record company. Thus, the only beneficiaries of cover versions were record company people—who were almost always white—and white performers. Early rock and roll cover versions remain a controversial and hotly debated topic among scholars and critics of rock music. It is easy to see how many black rhythm and blues artists could resent white cover versions. In some cases, song arrangements were copied in great detail, the only substantial differences being that the new record was on a different label and the artist was white. Record companies seemed intent on having white cover versions replace the original versions on the charts, in jukeboxes, on the radio, and in stores.

If Elvis Presley seemed dangerous to middle-class parents, Pat Boone was the alternative. Boone's cover versions of songs by Fats Domino and Little Richard outperformed the originals on the pop charts, and together with his other hit records made him one of the top-grossing pop artists of the late 1950s.

However, the situation was not so clear-cut. The unit of trade within American popular music since the late nineteenth century had been the song, not a particular recording of it. This was still true in 1955, when the top thirty records featured three different performances of the same song, "The Ballad of Davy Crockett." It was a well-established practice among record companies to release a version of the latest popular song on their label to capitalize on its success. In fact, our current understanding of the term "cover version," in the strictest sense, is based on the idea that a particular recording is the primary source of reference. This understanding of the cover version did not develop until the 1960s, as rock musicians and producers explored the possibilities of the recording studio. It seems silly, for instance, to imagine a band covering *Sgt. Pepper's Lonely Hearts Club Band* in the same style as the Beatles only weeks after its release in June 1967. But in 1955, copying someone else's record was the norm, and the practice went back decades. There is an important difference with the early white covers of rhythm and blues hits, however. Record labels in the prerock music business invested in particular singers whose distinctive approach, it was hoped, set them apart and fostered "brand loyalty." If you liked a song, you might especially want to hear the Frank Sinatra or Tony Bennett version. The formula was largely a matter of matching songs with "song stylists." None of these stylists would dream of closely copying another version of a song, since that would diminish his or her own mark of musical distinction. The white rhythm and blues covers of the 1950s, however, are not distinctive versions but almost note-for-note replications of the originals.

If this seems to further complicate the issue, also consider that most of the Pat Boone and Bill Haley records were distinct versions that would not be confused with the originals. In fact, the extent to which Haley and Boone's covers can be distinguished from their rhythm and blues models illustrates the important features that will ultimately distinguish rock and roll from rhythm and blues. Pat Boone has remarked that the records he covered would never have been played on white radio anyway; to Boone, the changes were necessary to bring this music to a white pop audience. Haley might have said the same thing. Little Richard would strongly disagree. As we might expect, both Boone and Haley were most popular on the pop charts; however, both artists also placed their songs prominently on the rhythm and blues charts. Our discussion here does not settle the issue, but using the context established by this discussion, consider the issue for yourself: Were black artists ripped off, or were these cover versions understandable within the context of music-business practices of the day?

THE RISE OF ELVIS PRESLEY: IN STEPS CORPORATE AMERICA

Elvis at Sun. If the music of early rock musicians such as Haley, Domino, Boone, Berry, and Little Richard began breaking down the boundaries between pop, country and western, and rhythm and blues, then Elvis Presley would complete the job. He was the first rock and roller to draw intense interest from the major labels and have hits on all three charts simultaneously. When Elvis moved from Sun Records to RCA in November 1955, RCA mobilized its vast resources to support the rising star, which would not only lead to Elvis's success, but firmly establish rock and roll in the pop mainstream.

Born in Tupelo, Mississippi, Elvis and his parents moved to Memphis when he was only thirteen. Raised in a city with a rich and thriving black music scene, Elvis became well versed in both the country music of the South and the rhythm and blues of the black community. As a teenager he performed around the neighborhood and at school, gaining a reputation as a flashy dresser who seemed to buy much of his wardrobe at Memphis's leading clothing store for blacks, Lansky Brothers. In 1950, radio announcer and technician Sam Phillips opened his Memphis Recording Service, specializing in recording black blues singers (including Joe Hill Louis, B. B. King, Howlin' Wolf, and Roscoe Gordon) and taking whatever other recording jobs might come his way. Phillips initially licensed his recordings to other labels such as the Los Angeles–based Modern and Chicago-based Chess. Among these recordings was Jackie Brenston's 1951 rhythm and blues hit, "Rocket '88'," which he licensed to Chess. In 1952 Phillips decided to start his own label, Sun Records. He focused his efforts on black blues, releasing records by Rufus Thomas,

Listening Guide

Get Music ⓢ wwnorton.com/studyspace

Elvis Presley, "That's All Right (Mama)" Sun 209

Words and music by Arthur Crudup, produced by Sam Phillips. Recorded and released on Sun Records in July 1954. Did not chart.

FORM: Simple verse, with measures added and subtracted throughout.

TIME SIGNATURE: 2/4, employing a country two-step feel with alternating bass notes.

INSTRUMENTATION: Electric guitar, acoustic guitar, acoustic bass, and lead vocals. Note that what sounds like a snare drum is actually Bill Black slapping on his bass.

0:00–0:06	**Introduction**, 5 mm.	Note strummed guitar and country feel, and entrance of the slap bass after the guitar begins alone.
0:06–0:26	**Verse 1**, 18 mm.	Vocal enters, note electric guitar fills, "That's all right, Mama . . ."
0:26–0:47	**Verse 2**, 18 mm.	Listen to how Presley swoops and shades the vocal line, sometimes moving from a low chest voice to a higher and thinner head voice. "Mama, she done told me . . ."
0:47–1:10	**Instrumental Verse**, 20 mm.	Chet Atkins–influenced guitar solo, 18 mm. verse extended by 2 mm.
1:10–1:30	**Verse 3**, 18 mm.	As before, "I'm leavin' town . . ."
1:30–1:53	**Verse 4**, 20 mm.	Presley improvises using "di" during the first part of the vocal; the previous 18 mm. verse is shortened to 16 mm. then extended by 4 mm. to create the ending.

Little Junior Parker, Little Milton, and the Prisonaires, a group of singing inmates from the Tennessee State Penitentiary. In 1953, a teenage Elvis Presley showed up at Phillips's studio to make a private demo. Phillips decided to try using Elvis as a vocalist on two songs in 1954—"It Wouldn't Be the Same Without You" and "I'll Never Stand in Your Way." While Presley didn't ultimately seem right for these songs, Phillips asked guitarist Scotty Moore and bassist Bill Black to work up some other tunes with Elvis to see what he might be able to do.

Phillips had a flair for spotting talent. As a producer, he also had the patience to let performers loosen up and explore in the recording studio. Part of his routine was to roll tape and let the musicians keep working until they hit on something interesting. That was what happened in July 1954 when, after trying several numbers and perhaps feeling a bit tired and slap-happy, Elvis grabbed his guitar and started playing an Arthur "Big Boy" Crudup song called "That's All Right (Mama)." Bassist Black joined right in and Moore began fiddling with a guitar part. Phillips, who was busy doing something else in the studio at the time, asked the group to start again as he hit the record button. Before long they had recorded the single that would launch Presley's career and establish Sun Records as an independent label of national stature. The band recorded a rocked-up version of Bill Monroe's classic bluegrass number "Blue Moon of Kentucky" as the B-side. Phillips rushed a copy of the recording to DJ Dewey Phillips, who played it on his popular *Red, Hot, and Blue* radio show, making Elvis a local celebrity. Elvis and the group began touring, performing on the *Grand Ole Opry* (which did not go well) and landing a regular spot on the *Louisiana Hayride* out of Shreveport. Despite the strong rhythm and blues influence on his music, Elvis was marketed as a country and western artist, using the moniker "The Hillbilly Cat."

The Big RCA Deal. As Elvis's success increased and word spread about his dynamic performances, he drew the attention of professionals within the music business. Among these was Colonel Tom Parker, who had managed Hank Snow (one of the most popular country singers of the early 1950s). Parker began working with Elvis as a promoter and later became his personal manager. In the meantime, Sam Phillips received at least two serious offers to buy out the young singer's contract. Phillips turned these down, but as 1955 wore on he found himself in need of funds to keep Sun afloat. Parker believed that Elvis could never achieve national success with Sun; he felt Phillips did not have the necessary capital to promote Presley. Parker brokered a deal with the country division of RCA records that paid Phillips the unheard-of sum of $35,000 for Presley's contract, while Elvis received an additional $5,000. Phillips had asked RCA for an amount that he thought they would never be willing to pay; to his surprise, they took his offer. Phillips invested the money in Sun and a radio station he had purchased. He went on to produce artists such as Carl Perkins, Johnny Cash, Jerry Lee Lewis, and Roy Orbison.

Presley's first single for RCA was "Heartbreak Hotel," which hit number one on both the pop and country and western charts in early 1956 and rose as high as number five on the rhythm and blues chart. Television appearances followed in 1956, including the famous performance on Ed Sullivan's *Toast of the Town* variety show discussed in Chapter 1. Parker also began to work on movie deals for his young star. By the beginning of 1957, Presley had begun to ring up sales and chart numbers that would establish him as one of the most successful entertainers of all time. Tom Parker and RCA had elevated Presley from a regional sensation to an international star.

The importance of Presley's deal with RCA is hard to exaggerate. Before he moved to RCA, most major labels were not interested in rock and roll, considering it a fad. Columbia Records' Mitch Miller even saw his label's lack of involvement in rock and roll as a point of personal pride. But when industry leader RCA paid an enormous sum for a rock and roll singer, it was clear that the game was changing. The other major labels soon began to add rock and roll artists to their rosters, which pushed rock and roll even closer to the center of the pop mainstream. Compared with its place at the very margins of the business just a few years earlier, things had changed considerably.

Why Would Sam Phillips Sell Elvis's Contract?

Sam Phillips benefited from selling Elvis Presley's contract to RCA because of the way independent labels were forced to operate in the mid-1950s. When an independent put out a record, the owner had to pay up front for all manufacturing costs—the businesses making the labels, sleeves, and records were paid before any income from the record was realized. Independent distributors, however, paid for the records that were shipped to them *after* these records were sold. This meant that there was a lag of weeks or months between when labels paid for printing costs, and when they received money from distributors. Once records were being released on a regular schedule, profits and expenses could begin to balance out after the initial expenses were absorbed. Ironically, a hit record could throw everything into disarray. Due to the high upfront cost of manufacturing large numbers of records to meet demand, a label could face great financial jeopardy until the profits were realized. Elvis's fame was increasing around the time his contract was due to expire. Phillips judged that the smart thing to do was to sell Elvis's contract while it was still worth something and use the money to put his label in a better financial position.

Covers in Elvis's Early Career. Elvis Presley was not a songwriter. He is best thought of as a master song-stylist who had an exceptional ability to choose songs and discover engaging ways to interpret them. From the beginning of his recording career, Presley had almost total control over this aspect of his music. If there was a song or version of a song he didn't like, neither Sun nor RCA would release it (since his death in 1977 many of these recordings have been issued). Presley's recording sessions were often a series of experiments with a wide variety of songs. Some songs Presley learned from commercial recordings, while others were supplied on acetates (inexpensive demonstration records not designed for commercial release) by professional songwriters. Among the songs offered to him was "Don't Forbid Me," but Pat Boone recorded it first and had a number one hit. With his focus on style, Presley joined Boone as a singer in the pop tradition of Bing Crosby, Frank Sinatra, and Tony Bennett. Presley extended this tradition by drawing broadly from folk, country and western, rhythm and blues, and gospel sources for his tunes. His first sessions for Sun featured not only Crudup's "That's All Right (Mama)" and Monroe's "Blue Moon of Kentucky," but also "I Love You Because," which had been made famous by traditional vocalist Eddie Fisher, and "I Don't Care If the Sun Don't Shine," which had been recorded by Patti Page.

The Sun recordings are often viewed as some of Elvis's best, and they helped to establish a style that came to be called "rockabilly." These songs were mostly recorded without drums, featuring Presley singing to the accompaniment of his acoustic guitar, Black's acoustic bass, and Moore's Chet Atkins–influenced electric guitar. Warm reverberation and "slapback echo" are sonic features that Sam Phillips pioneered, and this general ambience has been imitated by rockabilly artists since Elvis's first release. Although these recordings often featured light percussion, the absence of drums is a clear marker of their country and western roots: drums were important to pop dance music and rhythm and blues generally, but country musicians tended not to use them. The *Grand Ole Opry* even had a long-standing policy against using a drum set in performances. Even in his

Viewing Rock

TELEVISION IN THE 1950S: ELVIS ON ED SULLIVAN

Elvis Presley's first appearance on Ed Sullivan's *Toast of the Town* in September 1956 was a historic moment in television, offering an example of the role of rock performance on a prime-time television variety show during the mid-1950s. A conflict between the "old guard" of prerock entertainment and the youthful exuberance behind Presley's popularity is evident in the program. Because Sullivan had recently been in a serious car accident, the program was hosted by stage actor Charles Laughton, whose proper British mannerisms con-

trasted sharply with the down-home ways of Presley (1).

Despite an evident cultural gap, Presley's first Sullivan appearance was hardly shocking and controversial. The singer was filmed from Hollywood, where he was working on his first film, *Love Me Tender* (2).

Laughton referred respectfully to Presley's remarkable record sales, and displayed four recent gold records. In response, Presley commented that his appearance was "probably the greatest honor that I've ever had in my life." Presley performed in two segments.

The first was remarkably tame. Flanked by the Jordanaires vocal group, Presley performed the mid-tempo "Don't Be Cruel" and the ballad "Love Me Tender" (3).

The second segment included the upbeat "Ready Teddy" and a single chorus of "Hound Dog," which ventured into the dance-oriented rock of the Sun years. These offered only glimpses of the physical movements that we closely associate with Presley's television appearances. Upon returning to host Laughton, he remarked in clear mockery to the laughter of the mostly adult audience in New York, "Music hath charms to soothe the savage breast"(4).

very first recordings, Elvis's distinctive vocal style is as much a stylistic hybrid as his repertoire. Much of the swooping in his voice can be traced to early '50s pop singers like Dean Martin, while other vocal mannerisms derived from rhythm and blues.

Presley's Move to RCA for Broader Appeal. While Presley's move to RCA signaled the greater involvement of the major labels in rock and roll, the plan almost from the beginning of his tenure with RCA was to broaden his appeal beyond a teenage audience. The movies he made were part of that strategy, but the mainstreaming process can be seen most clearly after 1960. Presley's career was interrupted by a stint in the U.S. Army from 1958 to 1960. While much happened in

ELVIS PRESLEY'S VISUAL APPEAL

by Albin Zak

From the very beginning, rock and roll has been defined by both its sound and its look. Between 1955 and 1957, rock erupted on the world stage with widespread radio exposure, mass distribution of records and images seen by millions on television and in films. On its initial release in 1954, Bill Haley's "(We're Gonna) Rock Around the Clock" barely made the *Billboard* charts, fading after a single week. But the following year, when it was used as part of the soundtrack to *Blackboard Jungle*, it became one of the best-selling singles of all time. The film gave visual form to the record's sonic barrage, and young audiences responded as if to a call. Now the record's disembodied sounds were linked to specific images confirming and heightening rock and roll's association with youthful rebellion. And although the song played only over the opening credits, the film's images somehow mingled in the public consciousness with the sound of rock and roll.

Teenagers' favorite DJ, Alan Freed, also brought rock and roll into film, capitalizing on his celebrity by starring in such films as *Rock Around the Clock* (1956), *Rock, Rock, Rock* (1956), *Don't Knock the Rock* (1956), and *Mr. Rock and Roll* (1957). These films had little in the way of plot or characters, but in presenting performances by stars of the day—including Haley, Fats Domino, Little Richard, Chuck Berry, and Frankie Lymon and the Teenagers—they provided mass exposure to the sounds and images of the new pop idols. To the consternation of many critics, those pictures included an unprecedented concentration of black faces.

Elvis Presley was especially suited to the visual medium. With good looks, sex appeal, and an electrifying performance style, his television appearances thrust him onto the national stage, linking his musical energy to a visual spectacle. He set off a firestorm of both adulation and scorn, depending largely on the age of the viewer. When audiences saw his hip gyrations, leg shakes, and lip curls—his seemingly reckless physical abandon—the responses were almost immediate. No mainstream pop singers made these moves, which many critics considered aggressive and even dangerous in their overt sexuality. Once again, the music was associated with specific images that became identifying markers. Presley's style invoked familiar rock and roll themes—the rebellious outsider persona typified by his favorite actor, James Dean; a repertoire and performance style drawing heavily on the music of black performers; and a powerful sexual presence. This explosive package was apparent to those who had seen him perform live, but television would bring it to a huge nationwide audience.

Following the release of his first Sun recording on July 19, 1954, Presley was known primarily in the South, where he played dozens of one-nighters in venues from Florida to Texas. His biggest media stage was provided by radio, when he performed on the *Louisiana Hayride* or the *Grand Ole Opry*. In 1955 his three hit records showed up only on the country charts. But in January 1956, after leaving Sun and signing with RCA and Parker, Presley appeared on television in a series of four weekly performances on *Stage Show*, a variety show hosted by Tommy and Jimmy Dorsey. His first appearance was on January 28, the day after RCA released "Heartbreak Hotel."

Stage Show had poor ratings and at first relatively few people saw his performances. At his first show, the theater audience was sparse; the promoter recalled being "unable even to give away" the dozens of leftover tickets. Publicity mentioning a "special guest" on the show referred not to Presley but to the famous DJ Bill Randle, who was brought in to introduce the young singer. But unlike any of Presley's previous shows, this one reached a nationwide audience. If it was small by television standards, it was still the largest stage he had yet played. Most importantly, it linked the musical and visual sides of the Presley persona. In the following weeks, Presley's fame increased with astonishing speed. "Heartbreak Hotel" began to sell more than any of his previous records; it not only put him on the pop chart, but rose all the way to number one. In turn, he was signed for two further Dorsey shows. Following his six appearances on *Stage Show* in the space of two months, he appeared twice on *The Milton Berle Show*, twice on *The Steve Allen Show*, and signed a three-show deal for Ed Sullivan's *Toast of the Town*.

Presley's appearances on television attracted widespread criticism in the press, most of it aimed at his look and style. One commentator summed up the general unease: "Where do you go from Elvis Presley, short of obscenity—which is against the law?" But the criticism only sharpened the generational divide, and his popularity with young people meant Presley's rise was unstoppable. Seven months before his first Sullivan performance on September 9, he had earned $1,250 for his *Stage Show* appearance. For the three Sullivan shows, he was paid $50,000. By January 1957, Presley was the biggest singing star in America and *Love Me Tender*, his first film, was playing nationwide. In less than a year of mass media exposure he went from regional hillbilly star to worldwide rock and roll icon.

Albin J. Zak III (SUNY Albany College of Arts and Sciences) is the author of The Velvet Underground Companion *(Schirmer Books),* The Poetics of Rock: Cutting Tracks, Making Records *(University of California Press) and* I Don't Sound Like Nobody: Remaking Music in 1950s America *(University of Michigan Press). He is also a songwriter and record producer.*

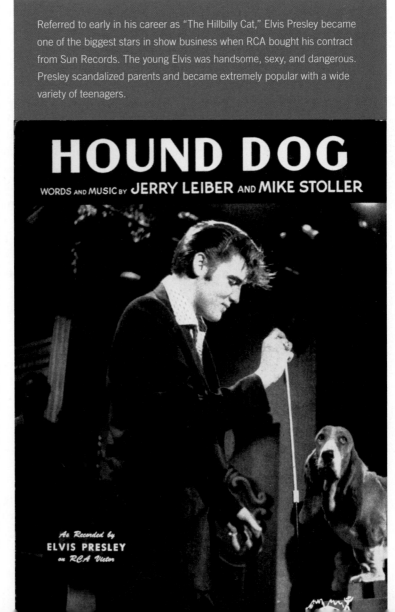

Referred to early in his career as "The Hillbilly Cat," Elvis Presley became one of the biggest stars in show business when RCA bought his contract from Sun Records. The young Elvis was handsome, sexy, and dangerous. Presley scandalized parents and became extremely popular with a wide variety of teenagers.

HOUND DOG

WORDS AND MUSIC BY JERRY LEIBER AND MIKE STOLLER

As Recorded by
ELVIS PRESLEY
on RCA Victor

When Elvis (center in background, choosing his uniform from clothing bins) was drafted into the U.S. Army, many predicted his career would be over. However Elvis's manager, Tom Parker (second from right, talking to two RCA executives), calculated that military service would show that Presley was a good, upstanding American boy. This image would position the singer closer to the center of the entertainment business mainstream. Presley recorded several records before he shipped out to boot camp, and these singles were released while he was away, keeping his career alive until his return.

popular music while he was stationed in Germany, his return to civilian life was celebrated by a television performance hosted by Frank Sinatra and featuring some of Sinatra's Rat Pack buddies, including Sammy Davis Jr. The plan was to turn necessity into a virtue, and Presley was transformed from the hip-swiveling menace to society into a patriotic G.I., doing his part to protect the American way of life. Musically, his three number one hits from 1960 show this transition. "Stuck on You" (p1 r6 c27, 1960) is a clear continuation of Presley's earlier RCA hits such as "Hound Dog" (p1 r6 c10, 1956), "Too Much" (p1 r3 c3, 1957), and "Teddy Bear" (p1 r1 c1, 1957). But "It's Now or Never" (p1 r7, 1960) is reminiscent of Italian crooner Mario Lanza, while "Are You Lonesome Tonight" (p1 r3 c22, 1960) features a narration in the middle that contrasted sharply with Elvis's bad boy image. Separating Presley from his close association with rock and roll was a prudent business move at the time. Rock and roll had been viewed by many in the music business as a fad that would pass with time. By the late 1950s (as we'll see below), the first wave of rock and roll was about to enter a new era. Since so much had been invested in Presley, it was important that his popularity was sustained even as the public grew tired of rock and roll. By mid-1960, Presley was a pop song-stylist who had established himself in rock and roll but had moved on. Despite an excellent 1968 television special intended to reestablish his rock roots, the music he made before 1960 became the most important to his legacy as a pivotal figure in rock and roll.

ROCKABILLY IN THE WAKE OF PRESLEY

Carl Perkins, Johnny Cash, and Jerry Lee Lewis at Sun. After Presley left Sun, Sam Phillips focused on other artists who would help develop rockabilly. Only weeks after signing over Elvis's contract, Phillips recorded Tennessee guitarist-vocalist Carl Perkins. In one December session in 1955, Perkins laid down four songs, including "Honey, Don't" and his biggest hit, "Blue Suede Shoes." In the first half of 1956, "Blue Suede Shoes" rose to number two on the pop charts; more importantly, the record was a hit on all three charts (r2 c1). While some popular records crossed over from the rhythm and blues charts and others from the country and western charts, it was rare for the same record to climb all three. Beginning with "Heartbreak Hotel," which raced up all three charts neck-and-neck with Perkins's "Blue Suede Shoes," Presley's records did this routinely. "Blue Suede Shoes" was the first million-selling single for Sun and likely served to reassure Phillips that he had acted wisely in selling Presley's contract to RCA. Perkins's career was dealt a severe blow when he and his band were involved in a serious auto accident. Despite the fact that he was unable to capitalize on the success of "Blue Suede Shoes" through live performances, several of his songs were later covered by the Beatles. (George Harrison admired Perkins so much that at one point before the Beatles became famous he adopted the stage name Carl Harrison!)

In 1956, Johnny Cash was another of Sam Phillips's young hopefuls at Sun. Early that year he had become a regular on the *Louisiana Hayride* broadcasts out of Shreveport, barely overlapping with Presley, who was moving into the mainstream market with RCA. Cash's "Folsom Prison Blues" (c4, 1956) was on the country and western charts at the same time as "Heartbreak Hotel" and "Blue Suede Shoes," but it did not cross over. By late 1956, however, "I Walk the Line" did make the leap, reaching number seventeen on the pop charts and becoming the first of four Top 40 pop singles Cash would release on Sun. By the end of 1957, Cash and Perkins had followed Elvis's lead and signed new contracts with the same major label, Columbia.

In July 1957—about a year after Elvis's first provocative national television appearances—viewers of *The Steve Allen Show* tuned in for new Sun artist Jerry Lee Lewis's energetic performance of "Whole Lotta Shakin' Goin' On." Lewis pounded the piano as he belted out the lyrics, at one point tossing the piano bench across the stage only to have Allen toss it back. This performance fueled the record's ascent on all three charts. Lewis's manic style was nothing new—Little Richard had beat him to that punch by two years. Nevertheless, in the following twelve months Lewis would have three additional hits on all three charts: "Great Balls of Fire" (p2 r1 c1, 1957), "Breathless" (p7 r3 c4, 1958), and "High School Confidential" (p21 r5 c9, 1958). Lewis might have turned out more hit records for Sun had he not been involved in a scandal: On a concert tour of Britain, Lewis let it slip that his new bride, Myra Gale Brown, was fourteen years old (she was actually thirteen and also his cousin). The British press picked up on this, also revealing that Lewis had already been married twice before. These stories played into the negative stereo-

After Elvis left RCA, Sam Phillips invested in a number of other artists, including the blonde-haired, piano-banging Jerry Lee Lewis. Lewis enjoyed a string of hits but was chased briefly from the business when reporters learned that his wife was only thirteen.

types of American southerners and rock and roll musicians. Because of public back-lash, Lewis was not active in the entertainment business for several years afterward.

Gene Vincent and Eddie Cochran.

Gene Vincent and Eddie Cochran. While Sam Phillips continued to develop new talent at Sun, new rockabilly artists also emerged on other labels. Bearing a striking stylistic resemblance to Elvis Presley, Virginian Gene Vincent scored three Top 40 hits for Capitol, the most noteworthy of which was his "Be Bop a Lula," which rose to number seven in 1956 (r8 p5). Guitarist-vocalist Eddie Cochran hailed from Oklahoma City and recorded three Top 40 hits for Liberty, including "Summertime Blues," which hit number eight in 1958 (r11). Both artists appeared in the 1956 film *The Girl Can't Help It*, and Cochran's performance of "Twenty Flight Rock" in that movie made an impression on the teenage Paul McCartney. Both rockabilly stars were very popular in England, and they were involved in an auto accident during a UK tour in 1960; Cochran was killed and Vincent was seri-ously injured.

Rockabilly Ladies. Several female performers also made an impact on the rocka-billy movement of the late 1950s. Although she is more often remembered for her hit singles from the early 1960s, such as "I'm Sorry" (p1 r4, 1960), Brenda Lee started her career singing rockabilly. Her 1956 single, "Bigelow 6-200," is credited to Little Brenda Lee. Lee was only twelve when the song was recorded in Nashville with experienced session musicians backing her up. Janis Martin was known as "the female Elvis" and enjoyed moderate success in 1956 with her self-penned debut single, "Drugstore Rock 'n' Roll" and "My Boy Elvis." Martin was signed to RCA just weeks after Elvis and used some of the same musicians, though the two met only briefly. Wanda Jackson did know Presley well, however, and credits him with convincing her to sing rockabilly. Jackson released a series of singles in the second half of the 1950s, enjoying her greatest rockabilly success with "Let's Have a Party," which hit the Top 40 in 1960. The rest of Jackson's career was spent in country music, and she was active on the country charts for the remainder of the 1960s.

Buddy Holly. As rockabilly moved into the pop mainstream, new artists emerged who put greater stylistic stress on pop at the expense of the country and western and rhythm and blues influences. Among these were the Everly Brothers and Ricky Nelson, who will be discussed in Chapter 3 since both acts continued to have hits after 1960. Another important figure, Buddy Holly, was killed in a tragic plane crash in early 1959, so his contributions to the history of rock music were complete by the beginning of the new decade.

Charles Hardin (Buddy) Holly was one of the first major figures in rock music who was significantly influenced by the rock and rollers who emerged in 1955 and 1956. Growing up in Lubbock, Texas, Holly was first exposed to the music of Elvis Presley, Little Richard, and Chuck Berry by listening to the radio. Like many teenagers, Holly was glued to the screen when Elvis appeared on *Toast of the Town*. Holly had seen Presley perform in Lubbock in January 1955, and he spent time with both Presley and Little Richard when they passed through Lubbock on tour.

In early 1956 the Columbia and Decca offices in Nashville were searching for young rockabilly artists to compete with Presley on RCA, so Decca signed Holly. The recording sessions did not go well, and when the records from them were not successful, he was dropped by the label. Buddy Holly and his band, the Crickets, began recording for Norman Petty in his independent studio in Clovis, New Mexico. When some of these recordings were shopped around to labels, Coral, ironically a Decca subsidiary, was interested. It was decided that another subsidiary, Brunswick, was a better home for the Crickets. Later, Decca shifted again and released Buddy Holly records on Coral. This explains why some Holly hits are credited to him while others are credited to the Crickets, despite the fact that there is little difference in personnel on the actual recordings.

The Crickets' first hit, "That'll Be the Day," was released on Brunswick and reached number one on the pop charts in the second half of 1957 (r2). Between his emergence onto the national scene in August of 1957 and his death in early February of 1959, Holly had seven Top 40 hits, including "Peggy Sue" (p3 r2, 1957), "Oh, Boy!" (p10 r13, 1957), and "Maybe Baby" (p17 r4, 1958). Despite being a clean cut, white performer who wrote his own material, Holly's biggest hits were also very popular in the rhythm and blues market. He also recorded a number of other tracks that have since become classics covered by later groups, such as "Not Fade Away" (the Rolling Stones), "It's So Easy" (Linda Ronstadt), and "Words of Love" (the Beatles). Holly's early death has prompted much speculation about what his music would have sounded like had he lived longer. One indication is provided by two of his last recordings, "It Doesn't Matter Anymore" (p13, 1959) and "True Love Ways." Both employ orchestral accompaniment and suggest that Holly might have joined Presley in moving to a more mainstream pop style.

In many ways, Buddy Holly and Chuck Berry offer an interesting comparison: both were guitarists who wrote most of their own songs and performed them in a distinctive manner. They also wrote music intended for a pop audience that was strongly influenced by country and western and rhythm and blues. The country elements of Berry's music can be heard in his vocals, his penchant for telling stories with his lyrics, and occasional upbeat tempos (as heard in "Maybellene," for instance). However Berry's guitar playing is derived strongly from the electric blues tradition, often relying on muted, low-register chords for rhythm playing and distorted string bends and double stops for leads. Holly, by contrast, tends to strum full chords energetically with an open, clean tone on his electric guitar, much the way traditional country guitarists do on an acoustic guitar. Combined with a clear country twang in his voice and the vocal hiccups that came to be his trademark, Holly's west-Texas musical roots are perhaps the most obvious feature of his style. But Holly was also fascinated by Elvis's assimilation of rhythm and blues singing, and with the records of Clyde McPhatter and others who influenced Elvis. The development of Holly's distinctive sound, using the same styles that had influenced so many other early rockers, offers a fascinating musical case study.

Much of the distinctiveness of Holly's stylistic approach can be heard in his recording of "Oh, Boy!" (one of the few Holly hits not from his own pen). A very open, country-style guitar accompanies Holly's eager and excited delivery of the lyrics. A closer listen reveals that the song is in AABA form with verses based on a 12-bar blues structure, showing the influence of both country and western and rhythm and blues. "Peggy Sue" is perhaps the best example of Holly's vocal technique. Holly never delivers any of the verses in exactly the same way. To vary them, he not only changes the notes and rhythms, but the timbre of his voice, producing the sound either back in his throat and chest or very forward and through his nose.

Hailing from Lubbock, Texas, Buddy Holly blended country twang with R&B rhythm to become an important songwriter and performer during rock's first wave. Shown here with the Crickets, Holly died in a plane crash in February 1959—an event singer-songwriter Don McLean would later describe as "the day the music died."

This manipulation of timbre is an extension of Presley's approach. (Holly's direct tribute to Elvis can be heard on his "Rock Around with Ollie Vee.") The drums on "Peggy Sue" are also noteworthy: Crickets drummer Jerry Allison employs only tom-toms in the drum set—no cymbals or snare drum are heard.

As engaging as his recorded performances may be, Buddy Holly was most influential among later rockers as a songwriter. While his lyrics are not exceptional in the way that Chuck Berry's are, the fact that Holly wrote his own songs served as a model for many rock musicians in the 1960s and '70s. If Berry's songs were more lyrically accomplished, Holly's were much more adventurous in terms of formal design. Holly employed 12-bar blues, AABA, simple verse-chorus, and contrasting verse-chorus forms in his songwriting, thereby avoiding the impression that a song was simply poured into a preexisting mold. In addition, his stylistic range was broader than most rock and roll songwriters of the time. Comparing the excitement of "That'll Be the Day" or "Maybe Baby" with the gentle pop lyricism of "Words of Love" or "True Love Ways" clearly illustrates his range. Buddy Holly and Chuck Berry were definitive examples of the successful songwriter-performer—a model that would come to define much rock music after the Beatles used it to shake up the music industry in early 1964.

THE DAY THE MUSIC DIED

The Misfortunes of Many in Rock and Roll's First Wave. The 1950s ended with rock and roll suffering a series of setbacks that removed some of its principal figures from the music business. At the height of his success in 1957, Little Richard believed he received a calling to go into the ministry. He promptly quit music and began a course of study that led to his ordination as a minister in the Seventh Day Adventist Church. Elvis received his draft notice in December 1957, and after a deferment and boot camp at Fort Hood, he was on his way to Germany by late September 1958. In May 1958, the British press broke the story of Jerry Lee Lewis's marriage to his thirteen-year-old cousin—a scandal that sent his career on a steep decline. Buddy Holly's plane went down on February 3, 1959, a date singer-song-writer Don McLean dubbed "the day the music died." Fellow rock and roll singers Ritchie Valens and the Big Bopper were also killed in the crash. Also in 1959 Chuck Berry was charged with violating the Mann Act (transporting a minor across state lines for immoral purposes). He was convicted but the verdict was overturned on appeal. He was tried again and convicted in February 1961, receiving a three-year sentence (of which he served less than two years). By the end of 1959, many of rock and roll's most important figures were out of the pop-music picture, and rock and roll seemed to be a played-out fad, fading away just as many of its biggest critics had predicted it would.

The Payola Investigations. A series of legal and political proceedings fed a nationwide scandal over payola in the record business beginning in late 1959. As mentioned above, record labels and distributors often paid disc jockeys to play records on the radio—sometimes the payment was cash; other times it was in goods or services. This practice of paying to get your song heard goes back to the nine-teenth century in the American popular music business. In the early twentieth century, singers received payola to include particular songs in their acts; during the big band era, bandleaders received payment to play and record certain numbers; and during the 1950s, disc jockeys were paid to play records on the radio. In each era, certain professionals were "gatekeepers"—they had the power to expose a song to a broad audience and hopefully increase record or sheet music sales by doing so. In the first half of the century, there were periodic squabbles over this, either because the publishers resented having to pay the fees or because they paid the fees and did not get the song played as much as they wanted. So from inside the music business, there was nothing new about payola.

By the end of the 1950s, however, a major shake-up had occurred in the music business. Early in the decade, most hit pop records were recorded and released by major labels. By 1958, because of rock and roll's breakthrough to the pop main-stream, a significant portion of the hit pop records were on independent labels. From the perspective of major-label executives, these new indies presented a sub-stantial competitive threat that had to be eliminated. In addition to the record company money at stake in this shake-up, there was also a struggle between the two organizations that collected public performance royalties for songwriters. ASCAP (the American Society of Composers, Artists, and Performers) represented the tradi-tional pop song composers. They were very selective about who could be a member, and composers of rhythm and blues or country and western songs were not welcome to join their ranks. BMI (Broadcast Music Incorporated) was a newer organization that embraced the kinds of songwriters ASCAP was proud to reject. The majors and ASCAP therefore represented music's powerful and well-entrenched old guard (Tin Pan Alley and Hollywood songwriters, mainstream pop performers and their record companies), while the indies and BMI represented rock and roll. Clearly the musical establishment had much to gain by attacking both the indie labels and the songwrit-ers who provided their material. The payola scandal was the means by which the old guard attempted to win back its market share.

It is important to understand just how little respect rock and roll had in the minds of many seasoned musical professionals in the late 1950s. Most music executives had come up in the business during the 1930s and '40s, achieving their greatest success promoting the music of big bands and song-stylists. They considered rock and roll—and the rhythm and blues and country and western from which it developed—to be crude and unrefined. Of course, most listeners over the age of thirty felt the same way, and many people had a tough time understanding how rock and roll could have become so popular so fast. Many adult listeners questioned this new music's quality given its ubiquity on the radio. One explanation made particular sense to opponents of rock and roll: these ragamuffin indie labels were buying their time on the air—paying the disc jockeys to play that primitive musical garbage—and *that's* why people were buying it. The argument was presented in just such terms to the listening public as the industry began creating controversy over payola. As it happened, a congressional committee was just winding up its investigation into television quiz shows (some of which were rigged, they discovered) and now decided to turn its attention to payola in the music business. In November 1959 the House Special Subcommittee on Legislative Oversight, chaired by Oren Harris (an Arkansas Democrat), began taking testimony.

Sound Check

Artist	Fats Domino	Chuck Berry	Elvis Presley
Title	Blueberry Hill	Johnny B. Goode	That's All Right (Mama)
Chart peak	p2, r1 1956	p8, r5 1958	1954
Form	AABA	Simple verse-chorus	Simple verse
Rhythm	12/8	4/4	2/4
Instrumentation	Electric guitar Acoustic bass Drums Lead vocal Horns	Electric guitar Acoustic bass Drums Lead vocal Piano	Electric guitar Acoustic guitar Acoustic bass Lead vocal
Comments	Loping New Orleans feel Repeated high chords and rolling low line in piano Horn lines support vocal melody	Famous double-stop guitar introduction Drums use a shuffle rhythm and guitar does not Constantly changing piano fills	Drum sound created by slapping bass Swopping vocal line Vocal improvisation in final verse

From the start, the committee's investigation focused on radio stations that played rock and roll. The testimony offered no significant acknowledgment that payola had existed in the music business for decades and that both majors and indies, marketing rock and roll as well as other styles, were involved. The committee manipulated deeply ingrained stereotypes that people involved in rhythm and blues were likely to be dishonest, bringing the cultural struggle over the segregation of black and white cultures to a new field of conflict. The Federal Trade Commission (FTC) and Federal Communications Commission (FCC) eventually got involved, causing most stations to take action, if only for show: disc jockeys were fired and formats were changed. Strangely enough, there was nothing illegal about taking money or gifts in exchange for playing a record on the radio. There were two catches, however: by FCC rules the gift had to be acknowledged on the air, and any money received had to be claimed on the recipient's income tax form. The problem for many of the disc jockeys under scrutiny was not that they took gifts, but that they never declared them. For most of the radio stations involved in the investigation, it was a matter of public perception and trying to guard against losing their broadcast license with the FCC.

The two highest profile subjects in the payola investigations were Alan Freed and

Elvis Presley	Little Richard
Heartbreak Hotel	Tutti Frutti
p1, r5, c1 1956	p21, r2 1956
Simple verse	Simple verse-chorus
12/8	4/4
Electric guitar Acoustic bass Drums Lead vocal Piano	Acoustic bass Drums Lead vocal Piano Horns
Heavy vocal reverb Refrain, "been so lonely, baby" Guitar and piano solo	Form begins with chorus Double entendre in lyrics Verse and chorus are slightly different in form, but still considered Simple verse-chorus

Dick Clark. Clark was extremely cooperative and emerged from the proceedings with his reputation intact, even being praised as a hard-working young business-man. However he was forced to divest himself of a number of financial holdings that might have created a conflict of interest with his broadcast activities. Freed, on the other hand, resisted the idea that there was anything wrong with his activities. He argued that he would never take money to play a record he didn't like, but if he'd played a record and a company wanted to show its appreciation, he was happy to accept the gift. Such honest but rebellious declarations made him a liability to his broadcast employers, and he lost both his radio job at WABC and his television show on WNEW-TV. There is little doubt that Freed took a wide variety of payments; he was even credited as one of three writers of Chuck Berry's "Maybellene," even though he had no role in its composition. (The practice of sharing publishing rights was common within the business; Norman Petty's name, for instance, appears on a number of songs that Buddy Holly composed alone.) But as a "gatekeeper," Freed was in the position to promote songs in which he had a financial interest, and the investigating committee considered this a questionable practice. In December 1962 Freed pleaded guilty to a charge of taking bribes. While he received only a six-month suspended sentence and a $300 fine, the damage had been done. The payola scandal had driven Alan Freed out of the music business. With the severe shake-up in both the personnel and the business of rock and roll, by 1960 it seemed to many that the Golden Age of rock and roll was over.

Rock and roll emerged in 1955 following a series of significant events: "Rock Around the Clock" became a pop hit associated with juvenile delinquency; Alan Freed's radio show rose to prominence in New York; and Fats Domino, Chuck Berry, and Little Richard enjoyed their first crossover hits, all on independent labels. By the end of the year, Elvis Presley was signed to RCA and on his way to becoming the most commercially successful entertainer in rock and roll. His popularity launched a major-label search for rock and roll singers that led to recording deals for figures such as Gene Vincent and Buddy Holly. As exciting as rock and roll was, it also represented a serious threat to established music-business interests, which pulled political strings to shut down the upstarts, and by 1960 the first wave of rock and roll was all but over.

The big record companies and music publishers were not about to let this new market in youth music fade away, however, because it was now a lucrative aspect of the business. In the years that followed, big companies took control of American popular music, primarily producing music for middle-class teens that would not offend their parents. In the next chapter we will explore how popular music returned to its Tin Pan Alley ways, with a wide variety of artists hoping to duplicate the success of Elvis Presley and other rock and roll artists.

FURTHER READING

Chuck Berry, *The Autobiography* (Faber & Faber, 2001).

Howard A. DeWitt, *Chuck Berry: Rock 'n' Roll Music* (Pierian Press, 1985).

Ahmet Ertegun, *What'd I Say: The Atlantic Records Story* (Welcome Rain, 2001).

Colin Escott with Martin Hawkins, *Good Rockin' Tonight: Sun Records and the Birth of Rock 'n' Roll* (St. Martin's Press, 1991).

Mark Fisher, *Something in the Air: Radio, Rock, and the Revolution that Shaped a Generation* (Random House, 2007).

Ben Fong-Torres, *The Hits Just Keep On Coming: The History of Top 40 Radio* (Backbeat, 2001).

Charlie Gillett, *Making Tracks: Atlantic Records and the Growth of a Multi-Billion-Dollar Industry* (E. P. Dutton, 1974).

John A. Jackson, *Big Beat Heat: Alan Freed and the Early Years of Rock & Roll* (Schirmer, 1995).

Ernst Jorgensen, *Elvis Presley: A Life in Music* (St. Martin's, 2000).

Myra Lewis with Murray Silver, *Great Balls of Fire: The Uncensored Story of Jerry Lee Lewis* (St. Martin's Press, 1982).

Craig Morrison, *Go Cat Go! Rockabilly Music and Its Makers* (University of Illinois Press, 1998).

Philip Norman, *Rave On: The Biography of Buddy Holly* (Simon & Schuster, 1996).

Kerry Segrave, *Payola in the Music Industry: A History, 1880–1991* (McFarland, 1994).

Wes Smith, *The Pied Pipers of Rock 'n' Roll: Radio Deejays of the 50s and 60s* (Longstreet, 1989).

Ⓢ VISIT STUDYSPACE AT WWNORTON.COM/STUDYSPACE

Access free review material such as:

- music links
- performer info
- practice quizzes
- outlines
- interactive listening guide software

CHAPTER 3

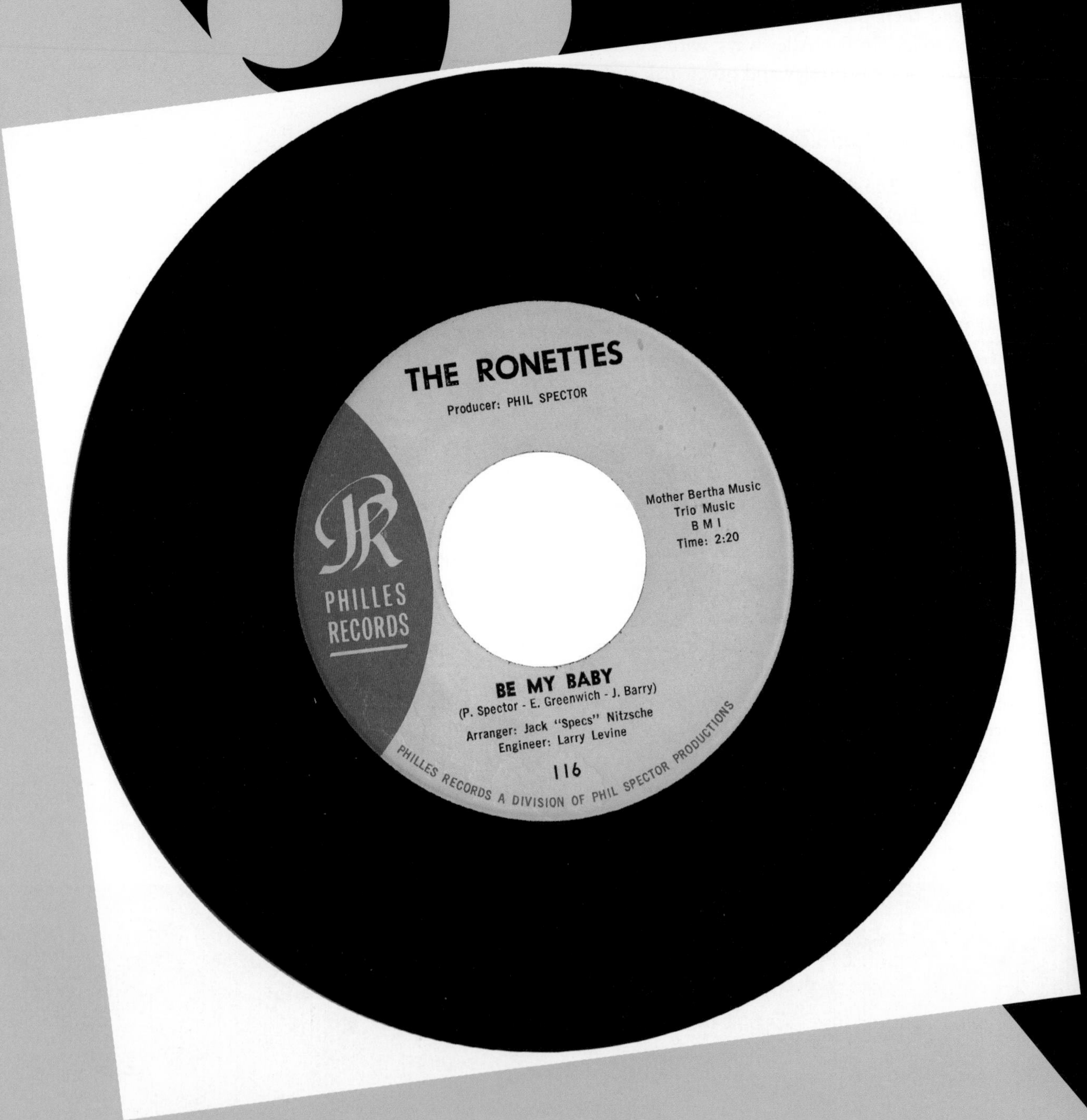
THE RONETTES
Producer: PHIL SPECTOR
PHILLES RECORDS
Mother Bertha Music
Trio Music
B M I
Time: 2:20
BE MY BABY
(P. Spector - E. Greenwich - J. Barry)
Arranger: Jack "Specs" Nitzsche
Engineer: Larry Levine
116
PHILLES RECORDS A DIVISION OF PHIL SPECTOR PRODUCTIONS

THE DEMISE OF ROCK AND THE PROMISE OF SOUL

B y the end of the 1950s, many important figures in rock and roll's first wave were out of the music business and radio stations and independent labels that supplied rock records had been shaken by the payola scandal. Rock and roll not only posed a cultural challenge to the values of many Americans, it also threatened the old guard music business. The basic problem, as some older hands saw it, was that the wrong people controlled rock and roll: musicians, disc jockeys, and independent label owners. According to the old pros, all this hustling led to a market for youth music that was destined to run into trouble because these small-time operators could not be depended on to act responsibly. Too much free choice resulted in too many unpredictable variables, and the entire enterprise fell apart. Despite these seeming failures, rock and roll *had* accomplished something important: it demonstrated convincingly that youth culture provided a significant and profitable market. Now seasoned professionals were needed to pick up the pieces and bring some order to the chaos. A lot of money could be made if the processes of creating and selling music to a youth market were more tightly organized and controlled. As we saw in the last chapter, however, rock and roll did not collapse entirely on its own; the music-business establishment played a significant role in hastening the demise of the first wave.

The period after the first wave and before the arrival of the Beatles is a source of controversy among rock historians. For some, the perspective outlined above explains why rock music was so mediocre during these years: corporate types tried to domesticate rock, turning it into a slick, cynically produced commercial product that was a shadow of its former self. Teen idols, girl groups, and songs composed and produced by professionals—exemplified by New York's Brill Building—are often seen to represent the severe decline of rock that was reversed only with the "British invasion" in 1964. However, some writers and historians take a more positive view of this period, arguing that it was filled with important music and musical accom-

An original pressing of the Ronettes' "Be My Baby," produced by Phil Spector in 1963. Although early 1960s rock and roll is seen by some as a mere pause between Elvis and the Beatles, others cite the period's many musical innovations. Spector was one of the most important producers of this era—drawing influence from Leiber and Stoller before him and influencing the Beatles and Brian Wilson after. Spector demanded total control over the music and was famous for his "Wall of Sound," which was created through a combination of his arrangements, the small size of the spaces in which he recorded, and a large group of (sometimes exotic) instruments. This complex, richly textured sound was often complemented by strong vocals from female singers like Darlene Love and Veronica Bennett (Ronnie Spector). "Be My Baby," featuring Ronnie Spector, is representative of Phil Spector's Wall of Sound.

plishments. They cite the music of Leiber and Stoller, Phil Spector, and the rise of sweet soul as marking an important maturation in rock and roll that was cut short by the British invasion.

This chapter surveys the variety of pop styles that comprised the youth market in the early 1960s. As we will see, the period between 1959 and 1963 was indeed filled with a wide variety of music. Rock and roll had brought an audience (and a market) together, but many considered it a fad that now seemed to be over. Nearly everyone in the music business was on the lookout for the "next big thing" that would seize the attention of youth culture the way Elvis and the early rock and rollers had done. As it turned out, the next big thing was the Beatles, but the Fab Four did not become popular in the United States until early 1964. In the interim, a number of styles vied for center stage—a spot that none would ultimately win.

SPLITTING UP THE MARKET: TEENYBOPPERS AND THEIR OLDER SIBLINGS

The period from 1959 to 1963 was a time of transition in the history of rock. Music executives took advantage of the opportunities provided by the youth market, noticing that by 1960 it was no longer a single entity. Many of the kids who had been excited by Little Richard, Chuck Berry, and Elvis in the mid-1950s had graduated from high school by the end of the decade and were now eager—in time-honored fashion—to be treated as adults. This meant that there were at least two distinct markets: one focused on the new generation of teenagers (the younger siblings of first-wave rock and roll fans) and another directed at former rock and rollers. Teen idols and dance music, concerned with nonsexual romance and dancing, were directed at the younger set. Folk, a style that grappled with social, cultural, political, and economic issues, had the greatest appeal for older fans.

The Adults in the Room: Brill Building and Aldon Publishing. The return of pre–rock and roll practices in teen pop music can be seen clearly in the Brill Building music of the early 1960s. The Brill Building is an actual place, but "Brill Building" is also a stylistic label and refers to a set of business practices (much like "Tin Pan Alley"). Located in midtown Manhattan, the building housed many of the most important music publishers. The business practices of Aldon Music, run by Al Nevins and Don Kirschner, provide an example of how Brill Building pop worked. The Aldon offices contained a number of small rooms equipped with pianos, where songwriters or songwriting teams would work all day writing new pop songs. Carole King and Gerry Goffin, Cynthia Weil and Barry Mann, and Neil Sedaka and Howard Greenfield were some of the best-known professional songwriters at Aldon, turning out a new song every day or so and competing to have their song recorded next. (Jeff Barry and Ellie Greenwich worked in a similar manner for Trio Music, while Doc Pomus and Mort Shuman wrote for Hill and Range Songs.) Once a song was selected by Aldon, it was then matched to the appropriate performing group, who were almost never the songwriters themselves. A professional producer organized the session and professional studio musicians would record the tune, which might be released on any of a number of record labels. This was a very methodical way of producing pop music, with duties assigned to specialists and songs cranked out with machine-like efficiency and precision. In such a situation, the actual recording artist was not at the center of the process. The Brill Building approach—which extended to many other publishers—was one way that professionals in the music business established more control after rock and roll's first wave. In the Brill Building practice, there were no unpredictable or rebellious singers, and none of the songs had lyrics that might offend middle-class sensibilities. Brill Building songs were written to order by professionals who could customize music and lyrics for the targeted teen audience. In many ways, the Brill Building approach was a return to typical business practices before rock and roll: it returned power to the publishers and made the performing artists more peripheral to the music's production. The public, however, focused on these performers, with teen idols and girl groups (discussed later) becoming the principal means of delivering Brill Building tunes to the pop audience.

Teen Idols for Idle Teens. The rise of Pat Boone and Elvis during the first wave established two distinct types of teen idol: the "good boy"—a clean-cut and respectable young man middle-class parents would allow their daughters to date, and the "bad boy"—a tough, sex-obsessed hoodlum whom parents tried hard to keep their girls away from. (These good and bad boy roles would be reworked in the 1960s, with the Rolling Stones cast as troublemakers and the Beatles as the charming, good boys.) During his stint in the army, Elvis's image was carefully reformed, suggesting that the strict discipline of army life had made a respectable man out of him. By 1957 it was clear that preteen and younger teenage girls were very eager to buy—or have their parents buy—records by young, handsome men singing songs about love. These "good boy" teen idols were cast as ideal boyfriends: well groomed and attractive, sensitive, and absolutely not interested in anything more than holding hands and an occasional kiss. It was another indication of how poorly regarded rock and roll was within the music business that record companies figured anybody could be a rock singer; if the songs were written by pros and the backing music was played by experienced studio musicians, all that was needed was somebody who could carry a tune, or be coached to do so. The crucial thing was that these teen idols look and act the part effectively.

Teen idols recorded for both independent and major labels with almost equal success between 1957 and 1963 (although the indies involved were usually not those that had previously released rock and roll). Philadelphia produced an especially high number of teen idol hits in this period, including Frankie Avalon's "Dede Dinah" (p7 r8, 1958) and "Venus" (p1 r10, 1959), Bobby Rydell's "Wild One" (p2 r10 1960), and Freddy Cannon's "Palisades Park" (p3 r15, 1962). Other teen idols with hits included Bobby Vee ("Take Good Care of My Baby"; p1, 1961), Bobby Vinton ("Roses Are Red"; p1 r5, 1962), and three singers who wrote many of their own songs: Paul Anka ("Diana"; p1 r1 1957), Bobby Darin ("Dream Lover"; p2 r4 1959), and Neil Sedaka ("Breaking Up Is Hard to Do"; p1 r12, 1962). Although teen idols were usually white (many were from Italian descent), they often found popularity among black audiences, with Bobby Rydell, Freddy Cannon, and Neil Sedaka all scoring Top 20 R&B hits during this period. Fabian Forte's "Turn Me

Loose" (p9, 1959), a product of Bob Marcucci's Philadelphia-based Chancellor label, is a good example of the musical problems that the teen-idol adaptation of rock and roll could produce for first-wave rock fans. The song was written by Brill Building songwriters Doc Pomus and Mort Shuman and the backup playing is proficient but nondescript—another day at the office for these musicians. Fabian's vocals are tenuous, creating the impression that he can just barely sing the tune. For many listeners who had experienced the excitement of the first recordings of Elvis and Little Richard, this was discouragingly tame stuff. Like many teen idols, Fabian's appearances on television and in films allowed him to appeal visually to audiences and were central to his success as a recording artist.

The emergence of the teen idols in the late 1950s inaugurated a segment of the market that has since been termed "bubblegum music." Despite the cynical system in which this strategically accommodating music was produced, there were some genuine highlights. Paul Anka, Neil Sedaka, and Bobby Darin all got their starts as teen idols, and each later translated that success into a career in songwriting and performing for a broader audience. Though their packaging would transform to follow changing fashions, ideal boyfriends would continue to be marketed to young girls for decades afterward. In the early 1960s, teen idols were marketed on the radio and special television shows devoted to teen pop, the most important of which was *American Bandstand*.

The Dance Craze, *American Bandstand*, and "The Twist." By the early 1960s many American teenagers were in the habit of heading straight home from school to watch a new television show developed especially for them. The idea of *American Bandstand* was simple: get a bunch of teenagers together in the studio, play current hit records as they dance, and have a few musical guests "performing" their most recent hits. *Bandstand* was another instance of the migration of entertainment from radio to TV. The show was essentially a rock and roll radio program adapted for television. Although he made it famous, Dick Clark was not the first host of the program. Bob Horn was the host when the show debuted on Philadelphia's WFIL in 1952, but was fired in 1956 after a series of personal problems. *Bandstand* was not the only television rock and roll show, but it was the one that survived and succeeded. Debuting nationally on the ABC network in 1957, the show was broadcast every weekday afternoon and on Saturday nights. In his first years of network broadcast, Dick Clark had almost every important rock and roll performer on his show. Unlike Jerry Lee Lewis on *The Steve Allen Show* or Elvis on *Toast of the Town*, *Bandstand* appearances were almost always lip-synched—another symptom of the industry's perceived need to control the music. There was no throwing of piano benches or provocative hip swiveling—just good clean fun and dancing. Of course, the lip-synching practice worked out well for the teen idols who were often featured performers on Clark's show, many of whom looked the part and could dance, but had less public performance experience than many of the first-wave performers.

Most of the focus of *American Bandstand* was not on these controlled "performances," however; it was on dancing. Dancing had never been absent from rock and roll, especially since dancing was the crucial substitute for references to sex in the original rhythm and blues that so much rock and roll appropriated. But during the first wave, dancing was often secondary, as the performance itself was the focus of the experience. The high profile of Clark's show created heightened interest in

dancing to pop music. For example, in 1960 Clark introduced a cover version of Hank Ballard's "The Twist" by a young singer named Ernest Evans, who went by the stage name Chubby Checker. The record quickly rose to number one on the pop charts (r2) and initiated a craze for named dances: the fly, the fish, and the mashed potato were among those that would be demonstrated by the teens on Clark's show. The popularity of the twist reached far beyond youth culture, as even affluent Manhattan socialites began frequenting the Peppermint Lounge in New York City to do the twist—prompting a hit spin-off song, Joey Dee's "Peppermint Twist" (p1 r8, 1962). Hoping to re-create the previous year's success, Checker released "Let's Twist Again" in 1961, which rose as high as number eight. "The Twist" then returned to the number one slot for a second time in 1962 (r4), a feat that had been accomplished only by Bing Crosby's "White Christmas."

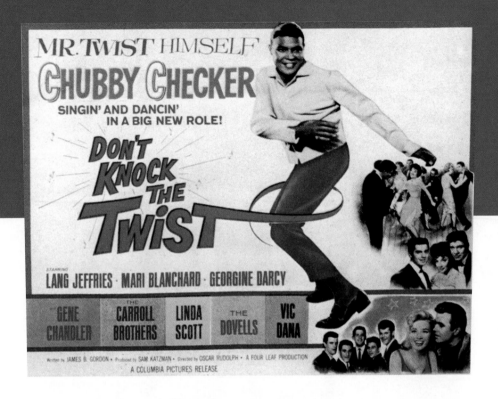

Chubby Checker is shown here dancing the twist on a 1962 film poster. Dick Clark, host of *American Bandstand*, said that "The Twist" was one of rock and roll's most important songs: it swept the nation (and reached into Europe), and everyone, young, old, black, and white, could all do the dance with ease.

While *American Bandstand* was responsible for igniting the early 1960s dance craze, its greater importance is the role it came to play in representing America's youth. Having a network television show dedicated to young people reinforced the idea that there was a national youth culture, and while there might be regional differences in the way people spoke and acted, when it came to music most teens were united by a common bond. Movies featuring well-known musicians also played a role in building this sense of community and shared concern. Elvis—at this point as much a teen idol as anything else—was making family-oriented films, and Frankie Avalon (among many other teen idols) made the jump to movies, appearing in a series of music- and dance-filled, teen-targeted beach movies with Annette Funicello (who had been a Mouseketeer on the original *Mickey Mouse Club* television show). As commercially successful as movie and television exposure was for pop music in the early 1960s, it also prepared the way for the Beatles—a group as charming as they were musically talented, who would become the darlings of television and movie audiences. *American Bandstand* also helped to make rock and roll more acceptable to adults. Although the show had been designed to appeal to teens, Clark soon discovered that adults were tuning in too. He has remarked that he considers "The Twist" to be one of the most important songs in the history of rock and roll because its reception constituted the first time that most adults could freely admit that they liked rock and roll. Hardliners might reply that this is precisely the problem: rock and roll should be about resistance to adult culture, not assimilation into it. But like "(We're Gonna) Rock Around the Clock" appearing in *Blackboard Jungle* and Elvis achieving mainstream success, the popularity of "The Twist," *American Bandstand*, and teen movies clearly indicated that rock and roll was becoming firmly established within American culture.

Folk Music and the Putting Away of Childish Things. While teens and their parents were enjoying *American Bandstand*, many college-age listeners were looking for music more consistent with their new standing as adults. They may have consigned rock and roll to their high school past, but many were not quite ready to enter the cultural world of their parents. Some remained devoted to first-wave rock, others assimilated into adult culture, but many—college students especially—began to enjoy music that seemed more "real" than the mainstream commercial music. As different as it sounded, folk music shared with early rock an "alternative" mindset that preferred music *not* embraced by the mainstream. Some older listeners were attracted to jazz, blues, or classical music, but folk became the most popular style of alternative music among these former rock and rollers.

Folk had enjoyed a certain amount of popular appeal throughout the 1940s, with traditional performers such as Pete Seeger and Woody Guthrie reaching larger audiences, both as soloists and then together in the Almanac Singers. During the first half of the 1950s, the Weavers (with Pete Seeger) had a series of pop hits, including "Good Night Irene" (p1, 1950), "So Long (It's Been Good to Know Ya)" (p4, 1951), and "On Top of Old Smoky" (p2 c8, 1951). Folk had a long history of addressing the problems faced by the less fortunate in American society, and folk singers often advocated social change from a markedly left-wing political position. As a consequence, many folk artists ran into problems during the Red Scare of the early 1950s, as the U.S. government vigorously attempted to identify communists within its borders. The Weavers' career, for instance, was cut short when they were blacklisted for reportedly being in sympathy with the Communist Party. By the mid-1950s, politically engaged folk music was forced out of mainstream pop. Only a few years later, however, fueled largely by its appeal to college audiences and downplaying any overt political connections, folk music experienced a revival that pushed it back into the pop mainstream. By the early 1960s, some folk artists were once again openly political, as many aligned themselves with the civil rights movement and, later, the opposition to the Vietnam War.

One of the key components of folk that attracted many listeners was its marked populist character. Folk seemed to be devoted to a greater sense of community than commercial pop: to its adherents, it was music for regular people, performed by regular people. Folk performers were not perceived to be above their audience; they were thought to be in some sense representative of it. Virtuosic or theatrical performance practices were rejected in favor of unpretentious and direct musical expression. Folk lyrics frequently told stories that illustrated various kinds of societal problems, and the meaning of the lyrics was much more important to folk listeners than the musical prowess of the folk singer, or his or her good looks. No matter how accurate such a description of folk-music culture during the original folk song movement (1935–48) might be, much of the untutored quality of folk singers and their audiences in the later folk revival period

One of the most important groups in American folk was the Weavers: (from left) Ronnie Gilbert, Pete Seeger, Lee Hayes, and Fred Hellerman. Characterized by its focus on social issues and musical and instrumental simplicity, folk appealed to a college (and decidedly nonteen) audience. After many hits, the Weavers' career was cut short when they were blacklisted for reportedly being sympathetic to the Communist Party.

THE RISE AND FALL OF AMERICAN BANDSTAND

by John Jackson

In 1960 America was thinking young. As the country sent John F. Kennedy to the White House, the nationally televised teenage dance show *American Bandstand*—taped in Philadelphia and seen in 135 cities coast-to-coast—was unchallenged as a shaper of pop culture. The show's youthful-looking emcee Dick Clark was the most powerful voice in American popular music. Although Clark could not create a hit record simply by playing it on his show, the publicity a song received from exposure on *American Bandstand* went a long way toward determining its success.

During the first three years *American Bandstand* was on the air, Clark stealthily cobbled together a pop music dynasty of his own. By 1959 he owned scores of music-related companies, including record labels and music publishing firms.

As Clark offered up a seemingly endless parade of white "teen-idol" singers—many of them home-grown products from Philly—who lip-synched their latest recordings to a rapt sea of adolescents, *American Bandstand* continued to introduce the latest hit records, spark the latest teen fashion fads, and inspire new dance crazes. Indeed, the show was instrumental in turning America into the land of a thousand dances. During the summer of 1960, Chubby Checker's recording of "The Twist" introduced the nation to solo, or open dancing, in which partners never touched. Because of "The Twist," *American Bandstand*'s exalted status as the premier purveyor of teen-oriented dance music reached its apex. Dance fads arrived and departed more rapidly than ever as teenagers and young housewives no longer had to leave the friendly confines of their homes to learn the latest steps.

American Bandstand's amplified status was a stark contrast to the show's modest beginnings. A local version known simply as *Bandstand* originated in Philadelphia in 1952. Hosted by disc jockey Bob Horn, *Bandstand* quickly became the most popular local television program in the City of Brotherly Love. But in 1956 Horn was cited for drunken driving and Clark replaced him as the *Bandstand* emcee. In 1957 Clark made a pitch to the ABC television network to broadcast *Bandstand* nationally. ABC, then a distant third behind NBC and CBS in the network ratings and desperate for any kind of cost-efficient daytime programming, agreed to broadcast Clark's show. Now called *American Bandstand*, the show could be seen for ninety minutes each weekday afternoon. It soon became the wellspring of American popular culture.

But *American Bandstand* eventually became a victim of its own success. As the popularity of Clark's show increased, so did ABC's stature. By 1961 the network was able to command larger commercial fees for new shows than it received from *American Bandstand*. To create space for these new shows, ABC began reducing *Bandstand*'s daily airtime, first to sixty minutes, then to thirty minutes. Distressed with

Bandstand's repeated reduction in airtime, Clark brashly predicted that, if handled properly, the show could run for thirty years. (It lasted for thirty-two!)

Early in 1963 *American Bandstand* lost much of its consequential spontaneity when, due to growing outside commitments, Clark abandoned the show's live format and began taping a week's worth of programs in one day. To exacerbate matters, *Bandstand* was stripped of much of its power to expose potential hit songs when later that year ABC ended the show's daily status and began showing it only on Saturday mornings.

In February 1964, less than three months after America was shaken to its core by the assassination of President Kennedy, two events portending *American Bandstand*'s future occurred. By then Clark had forsaken Philadelphia's blue-collar grit for California's glitz and permanently relocated his show to Los Angeles. The move went virtually unnoticed, a sure sign that America's youth had begun to look elsewhere for the latest trends in music and fashion. The West Coast debut of *Bandstand* occurred on Saturday, February 8. The following Sunday, as 70 million households tuned in to CBS-TV's *Toast of the Town*, the Beatles were introduced to America, touching off the "British invasion" of American pop. These two incidents marked the beginning of a steady diminution of *American Bandstand*. Save for its longevity, Dick Clark's fabled music and dance program was on its way to becoming just another television show.

John Jackson is the author of American Bandstand: Dick Clark and the Making of a Rock 'n' Roll Empire, *which received the Ralph J. Gleason Music Book Award and the ARSC Award for excellence in research.*

Dick Clark, host of *American Bandstand*, 1959. Unlike Elvis's performance on Ed Sullivan's show or Jerry Lee Lewis's performance on Steve Allen's, *Bandstand* was just good, clean fun: lip-synched performances by current pop stars with teenagers dancing. Clark's show featured both black and white artists and was seen as a force for racial integration.

The Kingston Trio—(from left) Bob Shane, Nick Reynolds, and Dave Guard—at a recording session. The group was the most popular of the "folk revival" of the late '50s and early '60s. Their first album, *The Kingston Trio* (1958), stayed on the pop album charts for 195 weeks.

(1958–65) was studied and self-conscious. To college-age people who were drawn to it, a big part of folk culture's appeal was its break with the norms of middle-class life. The music itself was in many cases not new to these young people; they had been humming and strumming folk tunes on camping trips and in school music classes almost all their lives. Its democratic ethos, combined with a seriousness of

Listening Guide

The Kingston Trio, "Tom Dooley" Capital 45-CL 14951

Words and music by Frank Warner, John Lomax, and Alan Lomax, produced by Voile Gillmore. Released in 1958 as a single and on the album *The Kingston Trio*. Reached #1 on the *Billboard* "Hot 100" chart and #9 on the "Hot R&B Sides" chart in 1959.

FORM: Simple verse-chorus, beginning with the chorus. The entire song repeats the same 8-bar music for verses and choruses. The verses are presented the same way each time, with the lead vocal supported by two-part backups. The chorus is presented first in unison (all three voices sing the same notes), then in three-part harmony, and then in a more complicated arrangement for three voices that introduces a new melody over the chorus melody. The last 2 bars of the chorus are repeated three times, a technique often used to close out a tune and called a **"tag."**

TIME SIGNATURE: 12/8, a gently rolling four-beat feel.

INSTRUMENTATION: Acoustic guitar, banjo, acoustic bass, lead vocal, and two backup vocals.

0:00–0:28	**Introduction**, 16 mm.	Spoken introduction, banjo plays melody.

purpose and cultural distinctions from adult culture, made folk music very popular on college campuses by the turn of the decade. One index of the popularity of folk is the steep increase in the number of acoustic guitars that were sold in the United States as collegiate folkniks were popping up throughout the country. Equipped with a passable singing voice and the ability to strum a few easy guitar chords, almost anyone could play it, which reinforced the idea that folk was "for the people and by the people."

The rise of folk was preceded by a brief fascination with calypso music. Harry Belafonte's "Jamaica Farewell" (p14, 1957) and "Banana Boat (Day-O)" (p5 r7, 1957) are the best examples of this easygoing, soft pop style featuring Caribbean folk inflections that seemed exotic at the time. Inspired by a Pete Seeger performance they heard while auditioning in a San Francisco club, Dave Guard, Bob Shane, and Nick Reynolds began performing folk to collegiate audiences and adopted a name inspired by Belafonte's Jamaican-drenched hits. The Kingston Trio's version of the traditional "Tom Dula"—which they called "Tom Dooley"—began to climb the pop charts in late 1958, hitting number one in early 1959 (r9) and initiating the folk revival in the mainstream pop market. This recording serves as a representative example of the group's easygoing and polished approach, with a carefully scripted verbal introduction to the tune, followed by an elegant arrangement. The Kingston Trio's pop-sensitive approach to folk proved to be a winner; the group placed ten singles in the pop Top 40 between 1958 and 1965, all of which were recorded for Los Angeles–based Capitol, including "Where Have All the Flowers Gone" (p21, 1962) and "Reverend Mr. Black" (p8 r15, 1963).

Get Music ⓢ **wwnorton.com/studyspace**

0:28–0:46	**Chorus**, 8 mm.	Choral unison vocal, strummed rhythm kicks in, "Hang down your head . . ."
0:46–1:01	**Verse 1**, 8 mm.	Solo vocal w/ backup vocals, "I met her on the mountain . . ."
1:01–1:16	**Chorus**, 8 mm.	Three-part harmony vocal introduced, "Hang down your head . . ."
1:16–1:32	**Verse 2**, 8 mm.	Solo vocal w/ backups as before, "This time tomorrow . . . Tennessee."
1:32–1:47	**Chorus**, 8 mm.	Energetic new solo melody against two-part harmony, music gets much louder, "Hang down your head . . ."
1:47–2:02	**Chorus**, 8 mm.	New texture continues, "Hang down your head . . ."
2:02–2:17	**Verse 3**, 8 mm.	Music gets quiet again, solo vocal w/ backups as before, "This time tomorrow . . . tree."
2:17–2:32	**Chorus**, 8 mm.	Three-part harmony vocal as in first chorus presentation, "Hang down your head . . ."
2:32–3:00	**Chorus**, 14 mm.	Music gets louder, energetic 8-bar chorus is extended by tag.

While pop singles give us some picture of an artists' success in the youth market, a better measure of pop success for folk artists among other listeners is album sales. Long-playing 33-rpm records were only a secondary concern for teen-oriented pop acts, but they were the primary format for two other "serious" styles of music at the time: jazz and classical. It suited the cultural aspirations of folk listeners to be part of the more sophisticated, album-buying—as opposed to singles-buying—public. Accordingly, the Kingston Trio had a series of nineteen Top 40 albums through 1964, thirteen of these reached the Top 10, including five number one albums. The group's first album, *The Kingston Trio* (1958), stayed on the pop album charts for 195 weeks. In the early 1960s, the Kingston Trio was among the most consistently successful acts in popular music and in many ways defined folk music for most general listeners.

In the years that followed the first hit records of the Kingston Trio, two sides of the folk revival developed. Listeners interested in folk's roots and tradition began exploring the rich literature of folk that had already begun to be documented by musicologists and folklorists such as Charles Seeger and Alan Lomax in the preceding decades. Singers such as Joan Baez and Bob Dylan emerged from this side of the folk revival, gaining popularity and respect among the folkniks; neither produced a hit single during this period, but both had Top 40 albums. To the discriminating fan, singers like Baez and Dylan were the real thing. The Kingston Trio, and other groups that followed in their wake such as the Highwaymen ("Michael Row the Boat Ashore"; p1, 1961), the Rooftop Singers ("Walk Right In"; p1 r3 c23, 1963), and the New Christy Minstrels ("Green Green"; p14, 1963), were oriented much more toward the pop market. Other pop-oriented groups that had successful albums but no hit singles were the Chad Mitchell Trio and the Limelighters. But however much uncompromising folk fans disparaged the Kingston Trio and other commercially successful folk groups, by music-business standards these acts were enormously successful and many within the business sought to stoke the fire that was now burning under folk music.

Formed in New York's Greenwich Village in 1961, the group known as Peter, Paul, and Mary eventually eclipsed the Kingston Trio as the most successful folk-pop group of the 1960s. After the success of "Lemon Tree" (p35, 1962), they followed up with "If I Had a Hammer" (p10, 1962), "Puff the Magic Dragon" (p2 r10, 1962), and a cover of Bob Dylan's "Blowin' in the Wind" (p2, 1963). The group released ten Top 40 albums during the decade: two hit number one, and their first album, *Peter, Paul, and Mary* (1962), stayed on the album charts for 185 weeks. The members of the group all had different musical backgrounds: Peter Yarrow had been a solo folk artist, Paul Stookey had played in a rock and roll band, and Mary Travers had sung in the chorus of an unsuccessful Broadway musical. While he was a full-fledged folkie, Yarrow was working as a stand-up comic when the group formed, and Travers was just getting back into singing. Manager Albert Grossman was responsible for bringing the group together, and the idea from the start was to capitalize on the folk revival ignited by the Kingston Trio. Peter, Paul, and Mary were assembled much the way other pop acts were put together. One might suspect that an act born of such music-business calculating would be rejected by the folk community, which often made a show of denouncing commercialism. But even though part of their fame rested on slick, pop-flavored cover versions of Bob Dylan originals, Peter, Paul, and Mary were mostly well received by die-

Peter, Paul, and Mary—(from left) Paul Stookey, Mary Travers, and Peter Yarrow—was a group constructed not for the small coffeehouses that had been the traditional home of folk, but for larger concert halls. Even though their music was decidedly more polished than that of many folk artists, die-hard folkniks embraced the group—mostly because of their passionate involvement in the civil rights movement.

hard folkniks, perhaps owing to their strong commitment to the civil rights protest movement. Their lasting popularity was a result of the group's ability to represent both strains of the folk revival, maintaining a believable sense of authenticity and an approachable performance style.

A comparison of Peter, Paul, and Mary's version of "Blowin' in the Wind" with Dylan's illustrates important differences between the folk music of this period. While Dylan makes no concessions to pop sensibilities, the Peter, Paul, and Mary version is professionally sung, played, and arranged (by Milton Okun)—increasing its likelihood of appealing to a pop audience. At the time, Dylan's performance would have seemed too rough and amateurish for pop radio. Of course, such perceptions of Dylan's marketability would change dramatically later in the decade when American folk rock emerged as a response to the music of the Beatles and other British bands (see Chapter 5). For now, it is enough to point out that folk's image of sincerity and authenticity—as it was perceived by pop audiences in the early 1960s—was largely constructed by the music industry. Like the old adage—"sincerity: if you can fake that you've got it made"—folk performers worked carefully to project a homespun image. (This parallels the "construction of authenticity" discussed in Chapter 1 regarding the development of the *Grand Ole Opry* and the country music business.) Such constructions of authenticity bear out the notion that no matter what sort of image a performer projects, he or she is still part of the entertainment business. Even if a performer actually is sincere and homespun in his or her everyday personal manner, it will never be enough simply to show up and be oneself; these qualities must be projected from the stage, and most performers must learn how to do this. The issue of authenticity will return in later chapters, since later rock musicians (the singer-songwriters especially) used the perceived authenticity of the folk revival as a model of artistic integrity.

The similarities between folk music and Brill Building pop are striking; these styles were indeed two faces of the same music business in the early 1960s. Each was carefully crafted to appeal to a distinct age group within the youth culture. The images of the two styles contrasted strongly—pop was superficial and cute, folk was serious-minded and intellectually engaging—but the business mechanisms that marketed the music were often the same. Both folk and Brill Building pop were strikingly polite in comparison to the first wave of rock and roll, and much of this family orientation can be attributed to the control being exercised within the music business during this period.

AMBITIOUS POP: THE RISE OF THE PRODUCER

Some of the most enduring pop songs of this period were created by well-known producers such as Leiber and Stoller and Phil Spector. To understand this aspect of early 1960s music, we must understand just what a "producer" is. During the early years of rock and roll, many performers brought their own fully worked-up arrangements of songs from the country and western and rhythm and blues repertoires into the recording studio. Less often, as with Chuck Berry and Buddy Holly, the songs were written by the artists. But regardless of who wrote the songs, many early rock and roll artists had a strong voice in the recording process, deciding what would be recorded and how the song would be arranged. In mainstream pop, by contrast, artists used songs written and arranged by professionals. Most record companies employed A&R (artists and repertoire) men whose job was to organize and coordinate the various professionals involved in making the record, including hiring the musicians who played on the tracks. This was an early version of the record producer. The mainstream pop approach put more of the crucial decision-making authority in the hands of the A&R man, leaving the artists relatively powerless. For example, Buddy Holly's unsuccessful sessions for Decca were the result of an A&R man who had no feel for Holly's strengths and weaknesses. As the business took greater control of rock and roll, the mainstream pop model became the norm for making rock and roll records. But as this aspect of the business was changing, the role of the A&R man/producer also shifted, and the role of the record producer began to develop. Replacing the mostly organizational role of the label's A&R man, the producer became a specialist in charge of shaping the sound of a record, from the details of arranging to fine points in the recording process, such as microphone placement or equalization. In some cases, the record became the result of the producer's vision rather than that of the artist or songwriter. In most cases, the producer, not the performing artists, was responsible to the record company for how a record turned out.

The first important production team was Jerry Leiber and Mike Stoller. Their success with a variety of artists was imitated by others such as Carole King and Gerry Goffin, Shadow Morton, and, perhaps most important, Phil Spector. As the role of the producer in pop developed, there was parallel growth in the ambition with which song ideas were executed. Producers increasingly experimented with ways to make their records more musically sophisticated, some establishing a trademark "sound" that distinguished their records. Drawing from classical music and musical theater, as well as sounds available only in the recording studio, early 1960s teen pop records initiated an important shift away from the idea that a record should represent a recorded version of a live performance (as it had been until then) to the concept of a record as a kind of performance in its own right. This increased focus on the recording studio and the sounds it could produce would resonate in almost all rock music that followed.

Leiber and Stoller with the Coasters.

During the early 1950s Jerry Leiber and Mike Stoller were the most important songwriting team in rock and roll. They had roots in the West Coast rhythm and blues scene and enjoyed hits on the R&B charts such as Charles Brown's "Hard Times" (r7, 1952), Big Mama Thornton's original version of "Hound Dog" (r1, 1953), and the Robins' "Smokey Joe's Cafe" (r10, 1955). In 1956, Elvis Presley's version of "Hound Dog" went to number one on the pop charts (r1 c1), prompting the team to write more songs for Presley, including "Jailhouse Rock" (p1 r1 c1, 1957) and "Don't" (p1 r4 c2, 1958). Almost from the beginning, Leiber and Stoller wanted more control over the recording process than songwriters were typically allowed. In 1953, they formed their own label in Los Angeles, Spark Records, and began "producing" their songs in what would soon become the standard sense of the term. The pair has often said, "We don't write songs, we write records." In many ways, Leiber and Stoller already had a clear idea of how a record should sound before the performers entered the studio, and the artists' task became more a matter of realizing Leiber and Stoller's concept for the song than finding their own interpretation of the tune.

Leiber and Stoller had already produced three rhythm and blues hits with the Robins on Spark when they got an offer to produce records for Atlantic. The duo had found the business end of running an independent label to be unrewarding, so they welcomed the chance to move to a bigger label and leave the bookkeeping chores behind. The arrangement they made with Atlantic was exceptional for its time: rather than become A&R men working exclusively for the label, as was the

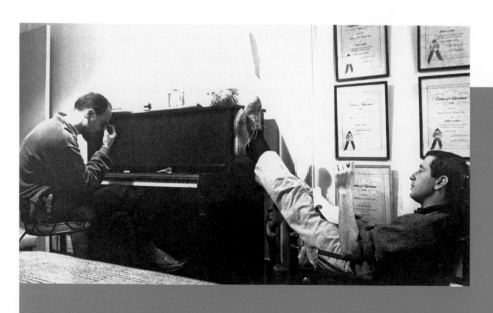

Mike Stoller (left) and Jerry Leiber (right) helped to define the important role producers would play in the music of the early 1960s. Their songs were characterized by strong rhythm and blues influences and complex arrangements, often recounting mini-dramas (called "playlets"), as in "Smokey Joe's Cafe" and "Down in Mexico."

industry norm, Leiber and Stoller retained the right to work with other artists and labels, making them among the first independent producers in pop music. They had had great success working with the Robins and wanted to take the group with them to Atlantic, but disagreement over the move meant only two members went with Leiber and Stoller. Two new members were added and the new group was called the Coasters; this group became the focus of Leiber and Stoller's most creative work over the next several years.

The Coasters recorded "playlets": short songs that often told a humorous story. In writing for the Coasters, Leiber and Stoller were inspired by Broadway and radio play traditions. As Jerry Leiber has remarked, the very first song they wrote for the Robins, "Riot in Cell Block #9," was inspired by a radio show called *Gangbusters*. The Coasters would frequently act the lyrics out in performance, sometimes using costumes, emphasizing the similarity to the Broadway stage. There were clear connections to older forms of vaudeville and minstrelsy in these playlets. Some Coasters' records also deal with teen life, like the songs of Chuck Berry, the Everly Brothers, or Ricky Nelson, discussed later in this chapter. Of these, "Yakety Yak" (p1 r1, 1958)—about household chores and teenage disputes with parents—and "Charlie Brown" (p2 r2, 1959)—about a kid who always gets in trouble at school— were the most popular. Mostly, however, the playlets dealt with topics in black culture and were directed at a black audience (even if they also became popular with white audiences). Original Coasters member Carl Gardner has marveled at how two white songwriters so expertly captured aspects of black culture. Leiber and Stoller responded, "We thought we were black—we were wrong, but that's what we thought." The producers had considerable control over their records with the Coasters, though group members were free to change things or reject entire numbers they didn't like. Nevertheless, many aspects of the arrangements were composed in advance. Stoller, who was trained as a classical composer, even wrote out many of the saxophone lines played by Atlantic session man King Curtis that became closely associated with hits like "Yakety Yak," "Charlie Brown," and "Along Came Jones" (p9 r14, 1959).

"Smokey Joe's Cafe" and "Down in Mexico" are early examples of playlets by the Coasters. "Smokey Joe's Cafe" was recorded when the Coasters were still the Robins, and was initially released on Spark in 1955. After Leiber and Stoller signed with Atlantic, the song was rereleased on the Atlantic subsidiary Atco and rose to number ten on the rhythm and blues charts (but only as far as number seventy-nine on the pop charts). The lyrics proceed in an AABA formal pattern: two verses develop the story, a bridge brings the action to a climax, and a return of the verse forms a kind of epilogue. In this case, the singer is sitting in Smokey Joe's Cafe when a sexy woman sits next to him and starts to flirt. Other patrons warn him about the woman's jealous boyfriend just as the boyfriend emerges from the

The Coasters were important collaborators with Leiber and Stoller. This team produced a number of hits, including the playlets "Smokey Joe's Cafe" (when the Coasters were still the Robins) and "Down in Mexico."

Listening Guide

Get Music ⑤ **wwnorton.com/studyspace**

The Coasters, "Down in Mexico" Atco 6064

Words and music by Jerry Leiber and Mike Stoller, produced by Leiber and Stoller. Reached #8 on the *Billboard* R&B "Most Played in Juke Boxes" chart in 1956.

FORM: AABA form. Each 16-bar verse is divided into an 8-bar section with lyrics that change from verse to verse, and a refrain that begins with the lyrics "He wears a red bandana" (most refrains are not as lengthy as this one). The bridge repeats a 2-bar section eight times, building to the song's comic punchline. Note the dramatic introduction and the spoken fade-out, both of which heighten the comedy of this classic playlet.

TIME SIGNATURE: 4/4. There are three distinct Latin-tinged feels on this track, one with the first half of the verse, another with the second half of the verse (refrain), and a third with the bridge. These changes of feel are unusual in pop music of the time, and reinforce the influence of Broadway stage numbers, in which such changes are common.

INSTRUMENTATION: Piano, bass, electric guitar, nylon-string guitar, percussion, lead and backup vocals. Mike Stoller plays piano on this (and most) Coasters tracks. Famous jazz guitarist Barney Kessel plays guitar on this track.

0:00–0:21	**Introduction**, 6 mm., 2 mm.	Rubato (sax and guitar), and then 4 mm. in time to begin sultry Latin feel.
0:21–0:57	**A-Verse 1 w/refrain**, 16 mm., 8 mm. verse + 8 mm. refrain	The verse uses the sultry Latin feel, while the refrain uses a brighter Latin feel employing nylon-string guitar and castanets, "Down in . . ."
0:57–1:32	**A-Verse 2 w/refrain**,	As before, "The first time . . ."
1:32–2:06	**B-Bridge**, 16 mm., eight 2 mm. phrases	Employing a more violent Latin feel to suggest a sensual dance show, building to the song's dynamic high point, "All of a sudden . . ."
2:06–3:13	**A-Verse 3 w/refrain**, 16 mm.	As before, then fade on intro material, "If you're . . ."

kitchen, wielding a knife and telling the singer to finish his meal and get out. In the last verse the singer explains that he'll never go into that café again. "Down in Mexico" reached number eight on the rhythm and blues charts in 1956 but missed the pop charts entirely. This song takes the barroom action south of the border; in the first two verses, we hear about a "honky tonk, down in Mexico." A guy named Joe who works at the bar "wears a red bandana" and "plays a blues piana." The bridge narrates how a scantily clad dancer enters the bar to the accompaniment of Joe's piano playing; she grabs the singer and dances with him, doing "a dance I never saw before." The last verse advises listeners to visit the bar if they're ever in the neighborhood. Both of these songs are clear extensions of the hokum blues discussed in Chapter 1 in connection with Big Joe Turner's "Shake, Rattle, and Roll," complete with themes of seduction that were hardly the kind of thing that would sell to white listeners in the mid-1950s. Leiber and Stoller's production makes the south-of-the-border theme more vivid through the use of Mexican-sounding nylon-string guitars and percussion. The bridge is sung to music the dancer might have performed to, a kind of Latin striptease with emphasis on the conga drums.

In composing playlets such as "Smokey Joe's Cafe" and "Down in Mexico," Leiber and Stoller drew from a broad range of musical styles, often blending these within a single track. This type of comingling also appeared in their work with other groups. In 1959 they recorded "There Goes My Baby" with the Drifters (featuring Ben E. King) and the song's arrangement employed the orchestra in a manner reminiscent of classical music. Such stylistic blending prompted Atlantic's Jerry Wexler to remark that "There Goes My Baby" sounded like a radio stuck between two stations. This combination of easygoing rhythm and blues with orchestral backing would soon be dubbed "sweet soul" and will be discussed later.

Producers in the Brill Building: The Rise of the Girl Groups. By the late 1950s Leiber and Stoller's approach to record production had spread throughout the music business. At Aldon Music, the songwriting teams of Neil Sedaka and Howie Greenfield and Carole King and Gerry Goffin began making demonstration records (demos) of their songs, which were sometimes released without being rerecorded. Like Leiber and Stoller, other Brill Building songwriting teams such as Cynthia Weil and Barry Mann and Jeff Berry and Ellie Greenwich were increasingly working in the studio supervising the recording process. By the early 1960s, these producers were directing many female vocal groups, often referred to as "girl groups." The Chantels, Shirelles, Crystals, Chiffons, Cookies, Dixie Cups, and Ronettes were among the many girl groups that appeared during the first half of the 1960s. These groups were mostly comprised of black teenagers with little professional experience. (There were some exceptions; Claudine Clark was a singer who had an undergraduate degree in music composition and wrote much of her own music.) A few groups included one male (the Exciters) or were made up of white teens (the Angels). Like the teen idols discussed earlier, girl groups provided the performance and image to go with a song. Unlike the teen idols, however, most girl group vocalists were strong singers. Still, in most cases the producer made crucial musical decisions at the session; as a result, the performing talent was almost completely interchangeable. Girls were regularly changed out between recordings and tours and sometimes, as in the case of the Crystals, the entire group could be replaced.

Female singers had not been completely absent from teen pop before the girl groups. Connie Francis enjoyed a string of thirty-nine hit records between 1958 and 1964 (including Neil Sedaka and Howie Greenfield's "Stupid Cupid," which hit number fourteen in 1958), while Connie Stevens ("Kookie, Kookie [Lend Me Your Comb]"; p4, 1959) and Annette Funicello ("Tall Paul"; p7, 1959) also had Top 10 hits. These singers were more or less the female counterparts to the male teen idols. After 1960, many female solo singers such as Little Eva ("The Loco-Motion"; p1 r1, 1962), Mary Wells ("My Guy"; p1 r1, 1964), and Leslie Gore ("It's My Party"; p1 r1, 1963) fit well into the girl-group stylistic category, since most of their records featured backup vocals and thus differed from girl-group records only in terms of image. This easy crossing of the stylistic border between teen-idol and girl-group music underscores the principal similarity between the styles: the Brill Building approach.

More than any other style of music discussed in this chapter, girl-group music was dominated by the industry's drive to control the music. There was no way a performer could rock the boat since so little depended on her. The creative control had shifted from the performer (who, to the public at least, still seemed to be important) to the producers and songwriters (who worked behind the scenes with multiple groups, often having more than one record on the charts at the same time). This system was tremendously successful. Girl groups were responsible for dozens of hit records between 1960 and 1965, including the Shirelles' "Will You Love Me Tomorrow" (p1 r1, 1960) and "Soldier Boy" (p1 r3, 1962), the Crystals' "He's a Rebel" (p1 r2, 1962), the Chiffons' "He's So Fine" (p1 r1, 1963) and "One Fine Day" (p5 r6, 1963), the Angels' "My Boyfriend's Back" (p1 r2, 1963), and the Dixie Cups' "Chapel of Love" (p1, 1964). The combination of mostly African-American singers and accessible pop music also helped the girl group movement achieve consistent crossover success between the pop and rhythm and blues charts.

In spite of the artists' lack of control, girl-group records represented some of the most ambitious and socially conscious pop music during this time. One of the first records to approach a subject that might have been considered provocative was the Shirelles' "Will You Love Me Tomorrow." Produced and written by Aldon's team of King and Goffin, this song dealt with a topic many teenage girls were likely to face: whether or not to engage in sexual intimacy. While such a topic seems mild by today's standards, in 1960—just as payola and the struggle against the negative influences of rock and roll were beginning to subside—lyrics dealing with teenage sex posed a commercial risk. But Carole King, a young female herself, was especially dedicated to the song, at one point taking the mallets and playing the tympani part when the professional percussionist could not get it just the way she

The Brill Building approach to music-making involved songwriting teams including Gerry Goffin (left) and Carole King (right). Strongly influenced by Leiber and Stoller, King and Goffin also exerted a great deal of control over the production of their songs.

wanted. Becoming a number one hit that further fueled the public's enthusiasm for girl-group music, the song addressed the topic with enough sensitivity to quell any parental fears.

Phil Spector and the Wall of Sound. Phil Spector was the most ambitious producer of the early 1960s and the most important producer of girl-group pop. While still a teenager in Los Angeles, he had a number one hit as both a performer and songwriter with the Teddy Bears in 1958 (r10). The idea for the song, "To Know Him Is to Love Him," is reported to have come from the inscription on Spector's father's gravestone. Having tasted national success but being unable to repeat it with subsequent releases, Spector began to work under Leiber and Stoller, helping at sessions and learning how to produce records. More than any other producer during the early 1960s, Spector demanded total control of the recording process. He wanted his records to have a signature sound. While it took him a while to achieve such control, when he did, he developed an approach to production that he called the "Wall of Sound." Most groups, of course, have a distinct sonic identity, often resulting from the singing voices involved. But for Spector, the production was the star of the record, not the group. His trademark sound came from several sources. He often recorded an enormous number of instruments in a relatively small space. Several guitars, pianos, basses, and drum sets could be crammed into one room at Gold Star Studios in Los Angeles. The sound from one instrument would spill into the microphone of the next, and all of this would be mixed together into a monophonic backing track. Moreover, Spector's arrangements supported this wash of sound by including interesting cases of "doubling," a technique that requires two or more instruments (sometimes contrasting in sonic character) to play exactly the same notes, creating a novel combination of instrumental color. Finally, Spector relied on heavy amounts of reverb to thicken up the record's "sound" and blend the instruments and voices. Like the ingredients in a fine sauce, the idea was for a single sonic "taste" to emerge that could not easily be broken down into its component parts. Vocals were layered over this mono backing track, with strings added to finish it off.

The most important Wall of Sound hits are the Crystals' "Da Doo Ron Ron" (p3 r5, 1963) and "Then He Kissed Me" (p6 r8, 1963), featuring the lead vocals of Darlene Love, and the Ronettes' "Be My Baby" (p2 r4, 1963). Written with Jeff Barry and Ellie Greenwich, "Be My Baby" featured the distinctive voice of Ronnie Bennett (who would later become Ronnie Spector). As with almost all his Gold Star sessions, Spector utilized a cast of Los Angeles's top studio musicians, nicknamed the Wrecking Crew and often including drummer Hal Blaine, pianist Leon Russell, bassists Larry Knechtel and Carole Kaye, and guitarists Glen Campbell and Barney Kessel. The recording was done on a three-track machine that allowed each track to be recorded separately. The usual procedure was to record the guitars, basses, pianos, and percussion on the first track, all the vocals on the second track, and add the strings on the third track. This three-track version was then mixed down to the mono version that would appear on the record. By the time "Be My Baby" was recorded, Spector had developed a reputation as a perfectionist, asking for multiple playbacks and rerecording until the sound was exactly as he imagined it in his head. This method produced some tremendously successful records that were very expensive to make.

Phil Spector defined the role of the dominant producer. He ferociously controlled his music—both the songwriting and production. Spector was also an innovator in recording techniques. His "Wall of Sound" was built by packing many instruments into a small room and recording them as they all played together.

"Be My Baby" opens with a heavy drumbeat from Blaine, delivered with plenty of reverberation that establishes a bigness of aural space. Bennett delivers the first two lines of the verse to the accompaniment of the rhythm section. At the lyrics "So won't you say you love me," the background vocals enter with the low saxophone, building to the chorus ("Be my baby"), in which the sound opens up as Bennett's lead vocal is set in call-and-response to the backup vocals and the drum beat changes to create a sense of greater forward drive. After a return to the verse, the second chorus adds another brick to the Wall of Sound by bringing in the strings, which then perform the melody for the abbreviated third verse. After this, the entire ensemble plays out two statements of the chorus, interrupted only by Blaine's drumbeat from the introduction, before beginning the fade-out. The form is simple and the song is short (less than three minutes). But somehow the track created an aural impression of grandness of scale that made it stand out from other songs on the radio.

In addition to their great popularity, Wall of Sound records like "Be My Baby" made an enormous impression on music industry professionals. Spector referred to these singles as "teenage symphonies" and comparisons to great classical composers and conductors abounded. As a producer, he was characterized as an eccentric genius who followed nothing but his own artistic impulses in creating innovative and ambitious records. Some characterized him as a Wagner-like figure (a reference to the German opera composer, Richard Wagner). The fact that Spector had blended instruments into a single timbral entity made the records almost impossible to cover and added to the mystery of his technique. In the face of the British invasion, Spector continued to have hits, though by the end of 1964 the girl-group sound in which he played such a crucial role began to fade. However Spector had yet

Listening Guide

The Ronettes, "Be My Baby" Phillies 116

Words and music by Phil Spector, Ellie Greenwich, and Jeff Barry, produced by Phil Spector. Reached #2 on the *Billboard* "Hot 100" chart and #4 on the "Hot R&B Singles" chart in 1963.

FORM: Contrasting verse-chorus. Note how verse 1 builds, starting with only the lead vocal for the first 8 bars, then adding backup vocals and saxes for the second 8 bars, and finally bringing all the instruments and vocals in for the chorus, which is clearly the "hook"—the part of the song that sticks in the listener's memory. Verse 2 pulls back again, but not all the way back to the level of verse 1, before building to the chorus. The orchestral strings take the melody in the instrumental verse, though only the first 8 bars are used before breaking into the chorus again. Just when it seems like there's not much more the tune can do, Spector brings back the catchy drum intro and launches once more into the chorus before the track fades out.

TIME SIGNATURE: 4/4. Note the way hand claps and percussion are used to build excitement and drive toward the chorus.

INSTRUMENTATION: Piano, bass, electric guitar, drums, horns, orchestral strings, percussion, hand claps, lead and backup vocals.

0:00–0:08	**Introduction**, 4 mm.	2 mm. drum intro and then 2 mm. in time. Note the heavy reverb on the drums.
0:08–0:37	**Verse 1**, 16 mm.	Solo vocal in first 8 mm., then backup vocals; saxes added in second 8 mm., "The night we met . . ."
0:37–0:52	**Chorus**, 8 mm.	Lead and backup vocals, this is the song's hook, "Be my baby."
0:52–1:22	**Verse 2**, 16 mm.	Mostly as before, though first 8 mm. are fuller than before, "I'll make you happy . . ."
1:22–1:37	**Chorus**, 8 mm.	As before, "Be my baby . . ."
1:37–1:52	**Instrumental Verse** (partial), 8 mm.	Violins play first half of melody with vocal backups.
1:52–2:07	**Chorus**, 8 mm.	As before, "Be my baby . . ."
2:07–2:10	**Reprise of intro**, 2 mm.	Drum intro returns to relaunch the chorus.
2:10–2:25	**Chorus**, 8 mm.	As before, with lead vocals improvising over top.
2:25–2:36	**Chorus**, 8 mm.	As before, with fade-out.

another production innovation up his sleeve and the Righteous Brothers' "You've Lost That Lovin' Feelin'," written by Barry Mann, Cynthia Weil, and Spector, was the result. Topping the pop charts in early 1965 (r2), the record was longer and more musically ambitious than anything Spector had tried to that point. After two statements of the verse and chorus sections, the music moves into a bridge section with a contrasting rhythmic feel. It was considered unwise to change the feel of a tune like this because delaying the return of the chorus could prevent listeners from remembering it. Mann, Weil, and Spector may have had similar middle sections from Coasters records in mind when they wrote this song, and the gamble paid off as the record became enormously successful.

Girl-group pop in the early 1960s might be thought of as a study in opposites. It was blatantly commercial: the songs were formulaic and written by pros who tried almost cynically to project a kind of "wholesome" teen lifestyle. But in the hands of producers such as Carole King and Phil Spector, girl-group records became the most artistically ambitious music that rock and roll had yet produced. As innocent and frivolous as some of these records seemed at the time, many would have a lasting impact on the music that followed. The ambitious experimentation that became so characteristic of psychedelic rock of the later 1960s can be traced directly back to groups like the Shirelles and the Ronettes, and we will pick up this story in the chapters that follow.

SWEET SOUL ON THE RISE

Sam Cooke Turns to Pop. In the late 1950s, a new and softer approach to black pop emerged that turned out to have tremendous crossover potential. Working with the Drifters and Ben E. King, Leiber and Stoller produced a long series of hits in a style that came to be called "sweet soul." In addition to the rhythm and blues and rock and roll artists we have discussed thus far, other black singers had already appeared regularly on the pop charts since the mid-1950s. Nat King Cole scored a number of soft-pop hits, including "Send for Me" (p6 r1, 1957) and "Looking Back" (p5 r2, 1958). Johnny Mathis was also a familiar artist on the pop Top 40, with such releases as "It's Not for Me to Say" (p5, 1957), "Chances Are" (p1 r12, 1957), and "Misty" (p12 r10, 1959). Neither of these singers were rock and rollers, since they tended to record easy-listening pop ballads that were similar to other mainstream-pop

Sam Cooke at a recording session. Like many artists, including Ray Charles, Cooke was strongly influenced by gospel. Cooke combined this sensibility with a sweet soul style to create his own sound. After a string of hits, including "You Send Me," Cooke's career came to a tragic end when he was murdered at a motel in 1964.

song stylists such as Al Martino, Eddie Fisher, and Dean Martin. It would also be difficult to find much rhythm and blues influence in their music.

Singing in a light pop style that *did* have marked elements of black music, however, was Sam Cooke, who placed twenty-nine singles in the pop Top 40 between 1957 and 1965, including "You Send Me" (p1 r1, 1957), "Chain Gang" (p2 r2, 1960), "Twistin' the Night Away" (p9 r1, 1962), and "Another Saturday Night" (p10 r1, 1963). Cooke came to the pop side of the business from gospel, where he had sung with the Soul Stirrers. In many ways, Cooke's transition from gospel to pop was preceded by Ray Charles, who had a number two rhythm and blues hit in 1955 by setting a gospel tune to secular lyrics with "I Got a Woman." Charles went on to have a number of important hits outside of rhythm and blues, surprising many in the music business with pop and country and western influenced records such as "Georgia on My Mind" (p1 r3, 1960), "Hit the Road Jack" (p1 r1, 1961), and "I Can't Stop Loving You" (p1 r1, 1962). With the success of "I Got a Woman," record companies began to consider gospel artists as potential rhythm and blues hit-makers. These artists were deeply conflicted about turning to pop, since gospel was "the Lord's music," and many considered pop the Devil's music. Cooke's first record was released under the name Dale Cooke, to test his marketability without adversely affecting his gospel reputation. What Cooke brought to pop from gospel was a clear tenor voice and a penchant for frequent melodic embellishment that often sounded improvisatory.

The Drifters and Ben E. King. As one of the most successful groups on the Atlantic roster, during the 1950s the Drifters recorded many important examples of "sweet soul." At first featuring Clyde McPhatter, the group scored a series of rhythm and blues hits in the mid-1950s. But by 1958, the Drifters were floundering and Atlantic was reluctant to let the group dissolve since the name had become strongly associated with a string of hits. Manager George Treadwell found another vocal group, the Crowns, to take over as the Drifters. In fact, the Drifters and the Crowns appeared together on the same bill at the Apollo theatre in Harlem one evening in 1958, after which the Crowns became the Drifters. To rebuild the group's career, Atlantic brought in Leiber and Stoller. "There Goes My Baby" (p1 r2, 1959) was the first fruit of this new combination, and it was followed by a string of hits, including "Save the Last Dance for Me" (p1 r1, 1960) with Ben E. King singing lead, and "Up on the Roof" (p5 r4, 1962) and "On Broadway" (p9 r7, 1963) with Rudy Lewis singing lead ("On Broadway" features an uncredited electric guitar solo by Phil Spector). Atlantic staff producer Bert Berns took over from Leiber and Stoller in 1963. His "Under the Boardwalk" reached number four pop in 1964 with Johnny Moore on lead vocals (r1).

The influence of Cooke's singing can be found throughout Ben E. King's performance on "There Goes My Baby." While the song was written by King (aka Benjamin Nelson), it is credited to Benjamin Nelson, Lover Patterson, George Treadwell, Jerry Leiber, and Mike Stoller. With the deals that were typically made on publishing rights, it is possible that everyone credited was not involved in the song's composition but were included as compensation for their services. At any rate, it is certain that the lead singer is Ben E. King and the record hit number one on the rhythm and blues charts (number two on the pop charts) in the summer of 1959. As mentioned earlier, fellow producer Jerry Wexler was initially so confused by the

Listening Guide

Get Music ⓢ **wwnorton.com/studyspace**

The Drifters, "There Goes My Baby" Atlantic 2025

Words and music by Benjamin Nelson, Lover Patterson, and George Treadwell, produced by Jerry Leiber and Mike Stoller. Released in 1959 as a single. Reached #1 on the *Billboard* "Hot R&B Sides" chart and #2 on the "Hot 100" chart in 1959.

FORM: Simple verse-chorus. The same 8-bar pattern is used for the entire song, underpinning the introduction, verses, and chorus. The song begins typically enough, with a doo-wop inflected vocal intro, two verses, and a chorus. Verse 4 introduces what sounds like an improvised verse over a melodic figure in the cellos that might have been borrowed from a classical composer (Stoller has suggested the line resembles Russian composer Rimsky-Korsakov). The rest of the song continues to create this impression of improvising over the repeated 8-bar progression, with the background vocals from the introduction returning, as well as the chorus, before the song fades out.

TIME SIGNATURE: 12/8.

INSTRUMENTATION: Acoustic guitar, electric guitar, bass, tympani, orchestral strings, lead and backup vocals.

0:00–0:15	**Introduction**, 8 mm.	Doo-wop vocals led by bass voice.
0:15–0:30	**Verse 1**, 8 mm.	Lead vocal enters, along with backing string melody, "There goes my baby . . ."
0:30–0:45	**Verse 2**, 8 mm.	String melody continues, backup vocals enter, "I broke her heart . . ."
0:45–0:59	**Chorus**, 8 mm.	Main melody sung in backup vocals, with lead vocal improvising over top, "There goes my baby . . ."
0:59–1:14	**Verse 4**, 8 mm.	Classical-style cellos enter, improvised lead vocal melody, tympani can be heard clearly in this section, "I want to know . . ."
1:14–1:29	**Verse 5**, 8 mm.	Cellos continue, backup vocals added, "I wonder why . . ."
1:29–1:44	**Verse 6**, 8 mm.	String melody replaces cellos, no backup vocals, "I was going to tell her . . ."
1:44–1:59	**Verse/Intro**, 8 mm.	String melody continues, backup vocals reenter, "Where am I . . ."
1:59–2:08	**Chorus**, 8 mm.	Backup vocals take melody as before, lead vocal improvises over top, "There goes my baby . . ."

sound of the record that he thought it sounded like a radio stuck between two different stations. This comes from the fact that orchestral strings had not been used on rhythm and blues records much before this song was released, and the classically oriented strings combined with a relatively square-cut doo-wop introduction would have seemed incongruous to many listeners.

The track begins with a male vocal-harmony passage led by bassist Elsbeary Hobbs, who sings a pattern outlining a chord progression common to much doo-wop. But set against this are tympani, followed by an ascending flourish from the strings (four violins and a cello, according to Mike Stoller). Finally King enters with the chorus, as his melody is accompanied by the rest of the Drifters and a counter melody played by the violins. When King gets to the verse lyrics, "I want to know, did she love me," the strings introduce a melodic figure with resonances of nineteenth-century orchestral music in a call-and-response exchange that sounds like it could have come from the gospel tradition. This track encapsulates the eclectic musical influences that fed Leiber and Stoller's songwriting and producing. It is unlikely that many other producers could have gotten away with releasing such a record at the time, but by 1959 Leiber and Stoller had an established record of success, giving them the influence they needed to get the track issued.

Ben E. King was fired from the Drifters in May 1960, reportedly because he complained to Treadwell that the members of the group were not being paid enough to live on, despite their chart success. Leiber and Stoller quickly stepped in and offered to produce King as a solo act for Atlantic. At the first session King recorded four tracks, "Spanish Harlem," "First Taste of Love," "Young Boy Blues," and at the last minute, a song King had begun writing himself called "Stand by Me." Out of this first session, both "Spanish Harlem" (p10 r15, 1961) and "Stand by Me" (p4 r1, 1961) reached the pop Top 10, initiating a series of five Top 40 hits for King in the 1961–63 period. (Illustrating the interconnectedness of figures and styles in the early 1960s, "Spanish Harlem" was written by Jerry Leiber and Phil Spector because Mike Stoller was out of town one weekend.) Taken together, the music of the Drifters and Ben E. King established sweet soul as a style characterized by a fluid lead vocal melody often supported by doo-wop backup vocals, counter melodies in the strings, and a rhythm section laying down a medium-tempo beat, sometimes influenced by Latin music (remember that Harry Belafonte had just had several hits employing a calypso sound).

After the first few successful records from the Drifters, other performers had hits with similarly styled releases. Jerry Butler scored with "He Will Break Your Heart" (p7 r1, 1960), and Chuck Jackson hit with "Any Day Now (My Wild Beautiful Bird)" (p23 r2, 1962). While the string of hits from the Drifters and Ben E. King was mostly over by the end of 1964, other artists took some of the elements of sweet soul into the British invasion years and beyond. Pop song-stylist Dionne Warwick was first noticed by composer Burt Bacharach while singing backup at a Drifters session. She became the most important performer of songs by Burt Bacharach and Hal David, hitting the charts in 1964 with "Anyone Who Had a Heart" (p8 r6) and "Walk On By" (p6 r1)—two of many hits that would follow. Motown artists were also influenced by sweet soul, while rhythm and blues singers with a more strongly pronounced gospel element—such as Solomon Burke, Otis Redding, and Wilson Pickett—emerged early in the 1960s and paved the way for soul music later in the decade. Motown and southern soul are covered in Chapter 6.

ROCKABILLY POPSTERS

While Brill Building pop tended to dominate pop music in the early 1960s, other styles also vied for attention. We have already seen how folk defined itself in opposition to the commercialism of Brill Building offerings, even if its careful construction and marketing of its anticommercial image did parallel teen pop. And while rockabilly is not usually associated closely with Brill Building pop, perhaps because the style is seen to have its roots in the South, its development after the first wave was very much influenced by Brill Building practices. The wilder music of early Elvis, Carl Perkins, and Jerry Lee Lewis became the sweeter country-inflected pop of the Everly Brothers, Roy Orbison, and Ricky Nelson. The development of rockabilly, however, does not fit into neat chronological divisions, with significant overlap between the first-wave artists and their successors. By 1959, Presley, Perkins, Lewis, and Buddy Holly were no longer playing a role in rockabilly. However, the Everlys and Nelson continued to develop without losing a step on the pop charts, and Roy Orbison was just beginning to make his mark in 1960. So, there was a dovetailing between these two groups of musicians, as well as a stylistic tendency of the second group of artists (the Everlys, Nelson, and Orbison) to soften the rockabilly sound by incorporating a more marked pop component, under the general influence of the Brill Building approach. After 1958, and perhaps in reaction to the controversy surrounding first-wave performers due to the payola scandal, this second group of rockabilly popsters seemed eager to please a teen audience without offending parents or other authorities.

The Everly Brothers. Coming from a strong background in the traditional country music of the southeast—their father Ike was a professional musician who had the brothers performing together from an early age—the Everly Brothers' easygoing rockabilly sound emerged in 1957 when their first single, "Bye Bye Love," raced up all three charts. Like Carl Perkins's "Blue Suede Shoes" and Elvis Presley's "Heartbreak Hotel," "Bye Bye Love" reached the Top 10 on each chart, hitting number one on the country and western charts, number two on the pop charts, and number five on the rhythm and blues charts. The duo had signed with Columbia in 1955 but were dropped after only one release and subsequently rejected by a number of labels. In 1957, their manager Wesley Rose (an important song publisher in Nashville whose father had managed Hank Williams) convinced Archie Bleyer at the New York–based independent Cadence to sign the brothers, even though he had declined to do so the previous year. After their hit with "Bye Bye Love," the Everlys went on to score fifteen additional Top 40 hit singles on Cadence through 1960, and seven more through 1964 after moving to Warner Brothers.

Don and Phil Everly each wrote songs that became hits: Don wrote "('Til) I Kissed You" (p4 r22 c8, 1959), "Cathy's Clown" (p1 r1, 1960), and "So Sad (to Watch Good Love Go Bad)" (p7 r16, 1960), while Phil wrote "When Will I Be Loved" (p8, 1960). But in the first few years of their success, the Everlys depended on the well-crafted songs of Boudleaux and Felice Bryant and the backup of top Nashville studio musicians under the direction of Bleyer. The Everly Brothers released a consistent stream of hits under this system, two of which went to number one on all three of the most important charts ("Wake Up, Little Susie" and "All I

Have to Do Is Dream" in 1957), while "Bird Dog" hit number two on the rhythm and blues chart in 1958 and reached the top slot on the two others. A country influence is readily evident in the earlier hits, where the energetic strumming on jumbo acoustic guitars by both brothers provides the rhythmic drive. Both "Bye Bye Love" and "Wake Up, Little Susie" reveal the influence of rhythm and blues in their respective guitar introductions, played here—as in much Everly Brothers music—on the steel-string acoustic guitar. The lyrics address teenage love life, the best example being "Wake Up, Little Susie," which deals with a young couple who go to a drive-in and fall asleep during the movie. Waking up after the film has ended, they worry that their reputations will be shot because their parents will suspect them of engaging in sexual activity.

The most distinctive feature of the Everly Brothers' music is the duet singing of Don and Phil. Much like the "brother duets" popular in Bluegrass music, their songs are often sung in harmony throughout, their voices tending toward the high end of the male vocal range and using a relatively straight tone, free of vibrato. Arguably their best duet singing occurs on "All I Have to Do Is Dream," a soft ballad that the brothers treat with a gentle touch, blending their voices in close-knit harmony in a very controlled manner. This high, light vocal quality gives their music its distinctive sound, and was very influential on later artists, especially Simon and Garfunkel, the Hollies, and the Beatles, who covered several Everly Brothers

Listening Guide

Get Music Ⓢ wwnorton.com/studyspace

The Everly Brothers, "All I Have to Do Is Dream" Cadence 1348

Words and music by Boudleaux Bryant, produced by Archie Bleyer. Reached #1 on *Billboard* pop, country and western, and rhythm and blues charts in 1958. In mid-1958 there were two active *Billboard* charts ("Disc Jockey" and "Sales") in each of the three major markets (Pop, R&B, and C&W). This single went to #1 on all six of these charts.

FORM: AABA, with partial reprise. The "Dream" refrain from the introduction returns just before the repeat of the bridge and then again at the end as the song fades.

TIME SIGNATURE: 4/4, with a slightly Latin feel.

INSTRUMENTATION: Electric guitars, acoustic guitar, acoustic bass, drums, and two-part harmony vocal throughout.

0:00–0:12	**Introduction**, 4 mm.	Guitar chord, and then vocals enter, "Dream . . ."
0:12–0:30	**A-Verse**, 8 mm.	"When I want you . . ."
0:30–0:49	**A-Verse**, 8 mm.	"When I feel blue . . ."
0:49–1:07	**B-Bridge**, 8 mm.	"I can make you mine . . ."
1:07–1:31	**A-Verse**, 10 mm. (8 mm. + 2 mm. drawn from intro)	"I need you so . . ."
1:31–1:49	**B-Bridge**, 8 mm.	"I can make you mine . . ."
1:49–2:18	**A-Verse**, 8 mm. and fade on intro	"I need you so . . ."

songs in their early years. The Everlys' tendency toward a softer style brought a more pronounced mainstream-pop influence to rockabilly. Unlike the recordings that Jerry Lee Lewis was making for Sun at about the time of the Everlys' first chart success and much more like the teen-idol music discussed above, this music is neither dangerous nor out of control.

Roy Orbison. Hailing from Wink, Texas, Roy Orbison toured the west Texas region with the Wink Westerners before ending up at the University of North Texas (called North Texas State at the time) as a fellow student of Pat Boone. Orbison's first release, "Ooby Dooby," was written by two of his North Texas school buddies and was chosen because it was a crowd favorite with Orbison's band. The song was initially recorded in Fort Worth by Columbia (which rejected it) and then again by Norman Petty in Clovis (this second version was released on Je-Wel). On the advice of Johnny Cash, who Orbison met when Cash was touring west Texas in

Listening Guide

Get Music ⑤ **wwnorton.com/studyspace**

Roy Orbison, "Only the Lonely (Know How I Feel)" Monument 421

Words and music by Roy Orbison and Joe Melson, produced by Fred Foster. Released in 1961 as a single and on the album *Lonely and Blue*. Reached #2 on the *Billboard* "Hot 100" chart and #14 on the "Hot R&B Sides" chart.

FORM: This song has an interesting structure derived from AABA form. The first 11-bar verse takes the place of the first two A-section verses usually found in AABA forms, and is followed by an 8-bar B-section bridge, before a return to the A-section verse, here 6 bars in length. The first 11-bar verse is tricky to count, since Orbison flips the regular accent on beat one over to beat three to create bars of 2/4 time. If you keep counting in four, however, everything will work out, though you may feel you are off for a couple of measures. A 10-bar interlude connects the two presentations of this special AABA-derived form, and this music is taken directly from the introduction. The second time through, the structure is similar to the first time except that the end of the bridge is much more dramatic, and the return to the verse is shorter and more melodically and lyrically connected to the bridge.

TIME SIGNATURE: This song is 4/4 throughout, though there are measures of 2/4 created in the verse sections. Challenge yourself to hear the measures of 2/4 and create a metric scheme that maps the entire verse section.

INSTRUMENTATION: Piano, bass, electric guitar, acoustic guitar, orchestral strings, vibraphone, lead and backup vocals.

0:00–0:21	**Introduction**, 10 mm.	Doo-wop style backup vocals, "Dum dum dum . . ."
0:21–0:43	**Verse 1**, 11 mm.	Lead vocal enters, backups continue, "Only the lonely . . ."
0:43–0:59	**Bridge**, 8 mm.	Dramatic solo vocal with stop-time string orchestra and vibraphone chords to add musical emphasis, "There goes my baby . . ."
0:59–1:11	**Verse**, 6 mm.	Added string melody in dialogue with lead vocal, "But only the lonely . . ."
1:11–1:30	**Interlude**, 10 mm.	Repeat of introduction, "Dum dum dum . . ."
1:30–1:52	**Verse 2**, 11 mm.	As before, "Only the lonely . . ."
1:52–2:14	**Bridge**, 8 mm.	Solo vocal with stop-time chords as before, but now driving to the song's dramatic high point on highest vocal notes, "Maybe tomorrow . . ."
2:14–2:24	**Verse**, 4 mm.	Tempo resumes to end, "If your lonely heart breaks . . ."

Roy Orbison in concert. While usually associated with rockabilly, Orbison's music spans a range of influences and styles: country and western ("Ooby Dooby" and "Rockhouse"), doo-wop (his trademark use of falsetto), pure pop ballads ("Running Scared" and "Crying"), and rhythm and blues ("Candy Man" and "Mean Woman Blues").

1955, Orbison sent the record to Sam Phillips at Sun, who subsequently rerecorded and released it in 1956. None of Orbison's four Sun releases were significant hits ("Ooby Dooby" reached number 59), nor were the songs he did in the late 1950s for RCA with Chet Atkins producing. Orbison then signed with a new independent label, Monument, and released "Only the Lonely (Know How I Feel)," which rose as high as number two on the pop chart in 1960 (r14). He followed with a string of nineteen hit records for Monument through 1965, including "Running Scared" (p1, 1961), "Crying" (p2, 1961), "Dream Baby (How Long Must I Dream)" (p4, 1962), "In Dreams" (p7, 1963), and his biggest hit, "Oh, Pretty Woman," which occupied the number one slot for three weeks in the fall of 1964 at the height of the British invasion.

Like Buddy Holly, Orbison wrote most of his own material and his music incorporates a wide range of styles. Orbison's "Ooby Dooby" and "Rockhouse" singles for Sun are squarely in the up-tempo, country-influenced rockabilly style of Presley and Perkins. With the Monument releases, however, his west Texas roots in country and western are less perceptible, replaced with a haunting ballad singing style that features both Elvis-like low chest singing and frequent, almost operatic passages in which Orbison flips into his **falsetto** voice. The verses of "Oh, Pretty Woman"—beginning "Pretty woman, walkin' down the street"—present an example of the lower, Presleyesque delivery; the "mercy" and growl that follow are reminiscent of Presley's mannerisms in "Don't Be Cruel." The stop-time sections of "Only the

Lonely (Know How I Feel)" are a good example of Orbison's characteristic falsetto; in the second verse, after delivering a pair of lines in his chest voice and beginning with the lyrics "maybe tomorrow," Orbison builds to the song's expressive climax on the words "but that's the chance you gotta take." His trademark use of falsetto is an adaptation of doo-wop practice, and the backup vocals—"dum dum dum dum de doo wah"—are clearly drawn from doo-wop and help make the stylistic derivation clear. Orbison's next two hits, "Blue Angel" (p9 r23, 1960) and "I'm Hurtin'" (p27, 1960), follow the same general pattern, using the standard pop practice of succeeding a hit with another, very similar record. By contrast, "Runnin' Scared" and "Crying," are pure pop ballads without a hint of Presley leads or doo-wop backups. Orbison's delivery is very similar in these songs, building to a dramatic climax in each case. Orbison's vocal style influenced several later rockers, including Bruce Springsteen, and his songs have been covered in well-known versions by artists as diverse as Linda Ronstadt ("Blue Bayou"; p3 c2, 1977) and Van Halen ("Oh, Pretty Woman"; p12, 1982).

Ricky Nelson. Ricky Nelson's music from 1957–64 draws together a number of themes that have been discussed thus far. The son of bandleader Ozzie Nelson and singer Harriet Hilliard, Ricky played himself in the Ozzie and Harriet radio show *The Adventures of Ozzie and Harriet* from 1949, moving with the show to television in 1952. Inspired by his girlfriend's enthusiasm for Elvis, seventeen-year-old Nelson's character on the television show boasted that he was also making a record. Behind the cameras, Nelson's father Ozzie was quickly convinced of the commercial possibilities of Ricky singing rock. Growing up in a family of professional musicians, Nelson had a knack for singing from the very start of his career. His first single was a cover version of Fats Domino's "I'm Walkin'," which went to number four in 1957 (r10), followed by the B-side "A Teenager's Romance," which climbed to the number two slot. Suspecting that there would be problems collecting royalties from the Verve label on which these hits appeared, Ozzie signed Ricky to the Los Angeles–based Imperial (Fats Domino's label). Starting with "Be Bop Baby" (p3 r5, 1957), Nelson scored a series of twenty-six Top 40 singles for Imperial through 1962, and a few more after switching to Decca in 1963. Nelson's good looks and clean-cut image made him one of the first teen idols.

Musically, Nelson's records are well crafted, although he did not write his own music and depended on songwriters for material, especially Baker Knight, Johnny Burnette, and Dorsey Burnette. Nelson's music is clearly patterned after that of Elvis Presley. He even used some of the same musicians on his records that Elvis did during his RCA period, with guitarist James Burton featured on lead guitar in most cases (Burton would later play in Presley's band). Presley's influence is clear on "Stood Up" (p2 r4 c8, 1957), "Believe What You Say" (p4 r6 c10, 1958), and "Just a Little Too Much" (p9, 1959), songs that sound like Elvis's up-tempo rockers on RCA like "Too Much," "All Shook Up," and "Teddy Bear," all of which preceded Nelson's first hit for Imperial. Other influences are clearly audible in Nelson's music, too. Gene Vincent's "Be Bop a Lula" may have been the initial inspiration for "Be-Bop Baby," though Nelson's record is bouncier and has none of Vincent's swagger. Nelson's "Waitin' in School" (p18 r12 c12, 1958), which deals with going through the school day in anticipation of dancing later, seems inspired by Chuck Berry's "School Day"; the lyrics and vocal delivery on the chorus of "Waitin' in

School" ("one-two, buckle my shoe, three-four, get out on the floor") are also reminiscent of Bill Haley's "Rock Around the Clock." The lyrics to "It's Late" (p9 r30, 1959) describe how the singer gets in trouble for bringing his girlfriend home too late and parallel the Everly Brothers' "Wake Up, Little Susie." Far from being overly derivative, however, Ricky Nelson's music emerges as a rich product of its time. Stylistically, Nelson combines the pop rockabilly approach of the Everly Brothers with the good-boy image of Pat Boone to imitate the music of Elvis Presley.

In the development of rockabilly music during the early 1960s, we can clearly see the influence of Brill Building practice, especially in regard to the rise of teen idols. But there is also a distinct connection with the first wave of rock and roll. The songs of the Everly Brothers and Ricky Nelson were as much continuations of Elvis and Carl Perkins as they were parallels to Frankie Avalon and Fabian. Unlike the teen idols, however, rockabilly artists sometimes wrote their own music, though they often depended on professional songwriters for hits. As we will see in Chapter 8, these later rockabilly artists were a more controlled and polite first wave of southern rock, filtering the original rockabilly sound through a Brill Building sensibility.

SURFIN' USA: IT'S JUST GOOD, CLEAN, WHITE-SUBURBAN FUN

The Beach Boys, Jan and Dean, and Vocal Surf Music. Aside from a handful of labels that were based in Los Angeles (majors MGM and Capitol and indies Modern, Imperial, and Specialty), most of the rock music business in the first half of the 1960s was located east of the Mississippi (primarily in New York and Philadelphia). Elvis and a few other teen idols were in Hollywood making movies, and Ricky Nelson was in southern California, but they were in many ways a long way from the pop-music action. *American Bandstand* was broadcast from Philadelphia and many of the important songwriters and producers worked from the Brill Building in Manhattan. This may explain why the influences that came together in the Beach Boys' music seem so eclectic. Growing up in suburban Los Angeles in the late 1950s, this quintet of three brothers, a cousin, and a high school friend were influenced by black doo-wop groups, mainstream white vocal groups like the Four Freshmen, Chuck Berry's driving rock and roll, and Phil Spector's Wall of Sound. Along with their fellow Los Angelenos Jan and Dean, the Beach Boys created a style of music that seemed devoted to the ideal teenage world of summer fun: surf music.

The Beach Boys first enjoyed success in late 1961 with a regional hit single, "Surfin'," written by group leader Brian Wilson and released on the small Candix label. The group signed with Capitol in 1962 and released a series of Top 40 hits—twenty-six by the end of the decade—including "Surfin' Safari" (p14, 1962), "Surfin' U.S.A." (p3 r20, 1963), "Surfer Girl" (p7 r18, 1963), "Be True to Your School" (p6 r27, 1963), and "Fun, Fun, Fun" (p5, 1964). While the British invasion was taking American pop by storm in the first half of 1964, the Beach Boys enjoyed their first number one hit, "I Get Around," the B-side of which, "Don't Worry Baby," rose as high as number twenty-four. The tremendous popularity of the Beatles only made Wilson and the Beach Boys work that much harder. We will

The Beach Boys—(from left) Dennis Wilson, Al Jardine, Carl Wilson, Brian Wilson, and Mike Love. While the Beach Boys' music seemed like simple, catchy pop, their harmonies and arrangements were very complex. Influenced by Phil Spector, Brian Wilson wrote and produced many of the Beach Boys' songs, and was an innovator of recording techniques.

take up that aspect of the Beach Boys in Chapter 5, but note that in the period between the Beatles' arrival in the United States in early 1964 and the psychedelic summer of 1967, the Beach Boys had fourteen Top 40 singles, ten of which were in the Top 10 and two of which hit number one.

Until 1964, the Beach Boys' music held fairly close to the same surf-music formula that was also followed by Jan and Dean. Song lyrics are usually about three topics: cars, girls, and surfing. At times lighthearted (as in Jan and Dean's 1964 number-three hit, "Little Old Lady from Pasadena," which tells the story of a hot-rod granny), the lyrics hardly ever deal with adult sexuality. The vocals seem to draw in equal parts from the doo-wop, girl-group, and glee-club traditions, with some perceptible vocal jazz elements. The instrumental accompaniments lean heavily on Chuck Berry's music. In fact, "Surfin' U.S.A." is an obvious reworking of Berry's "Sweet Little Sixteen," and Berry sued the Beach Boys for copyright infringement (modern copies of this song list the songwriters as Berry and Wilson). Nevertheless, the song is a good example of the band's early surf style. Wilson's new lyrics list all the hot surf spots in southern California, while the back-up vocals alternate between "ooo" and "inside, outside, U.S.A.," all sung in multivoice harmony. Wilson's ringing falsetto on "everybody's gone surfin'" provides the song's hook, while the instrumental solos provide a slice of early 1960s beach music, featuring a very "electronic" organ followed by a clean, Berryesque electric guitar solo soaked in electronic reverb.

In addition to using Berry as a model, Brian Wilson and the Beach Boys drew

Listening Guide   Get Music Ⓢ wwnorton.com/studyspace

The Beach Boys, "Surfin' U.S.A." Capital 4932

Words and music by Brian Wilson and Chuck Berry, produced by Nik Venet. Based on Chuck Berry's "Sweet Little Sixteen." Reached #3 on the *Billboard* "Hot 100" chart and #20 on the "Hot R&B Singles" chart in 1963.

FORM: Simple verse form. Each verse ends with the refrain "surfin' U.S.A.," though verses 2 and 4 feature the high falsetto "everybody's gone surfin'," making these verses seem to function like choruses, even though they are not actually choruses. The song ends with an instrumental verse shared by organ and guitar; the refrain here is sung as in verses 2 and 4, with a tag made up of four repetitions of the refrain.

TIME SIGNATURE: 4/4, with stops during verses 1 and 3. Note the constant bass drum during stops.

INSTRUMENTATION: Electric guitars, bass, drums, organ, lead and backup vocals.

0:00–0:03	**Introduction**, 4 mm.	Chuck Berry–style guitar intro, note the heavy reverb.
0:03–0:27	**Verse 1 w/refrain**, 16 mm.	Lead vocal with "oo" backups; note the stop time with bass drum beats that continue, "If everybody had an ocean . . ."
0:27–0:50	**Verse 2 w/refrain**, 16 mm.	Backup vocals sing lyrics as lead vocal continues, band plays in regular time to add rhythmic drive, "You can catch 'em at Del Mar . . ."
0:50–1:15	**Verse 3 w/refrain**, 16 mm.	As verse 1, in stop time, "We'll all be plannin' out a route . . ."
1:15–1:39	**Verse 4 w/refrain**, 16 mm.	As verse 2, regular time, "At Haggarty's and Swami's . . ."
1:39–2:04	**Instrumental Verse w/ refrain**, 16 mm.	Organ solo, guitar solo, and then sung refrain.
2:04–2:24	**Tag (refrain)**, 16 mm.	Repeat of refrain and fade.

heavily upon the music and production techniques of Phil Spector. While the band was initially assigned a producer in what was then typical music-business fashion, Brian soon demanded that he produce the records. A good example of the audible connection between the Beach Boys and Spector can be found in the Wilson-produced "Don't Worry Baby." Describing the first time he heard "Be My Baby" on the radio, Wilson recalls that while he was fascinated by the first verse, he was so captivated by the chorus that he had to pull his car over to avoid an accident. His enthusiasm for the Ronettes/Spector record was so great that, together with Los

Angeles disc jockey Roger Christian (who is mostly responsible for the lyrics), he wrote a song especially for the Ronettes to record. When Spector rejected "Don't Worry Baby," Wilson and the Beach Boys recorded it. Wilson's song is modeled closely on "Be My Baby," featuring a similar form and series of chord progressions. The similarity can be heard right from the start, as the tune begins with a drum-beat strongly reminiscent of the Spector tune. This beat is played by drummer Hal Blaine, who had performed the instrumental accompaniment for "Be My Baby" with other members of the Wrecking Crew. After Wilson sings the first two lines of the verse, the backup vocals enter on the third line at the lyrics "but she looks in my eyes," building the texture to drive toward the chorus, where Wilson's voice and

Sound Check

Artist	Kingston Trio	Coasters	The Ronettes
Title	Tom Dooley	Down in Mexico	Be My Baby
Chart peak	p1, r9 1959	r8 1956	p2, r4 1963
Form	Simple verse-chorus	AABA	Contrasting verse-chorus
Rhythm	12/8	4/4	4/4
Instrumentation	Electric guitar Acoustic bass Lead vocal Background vocal Banjo	Electric guitar Nylon-string guitar Bass Drums Lead vocal Background vocal Piano Percussion	Electric guitar Bass Drums Lead vocal Background vocal Piano Horns Orchestral strings Percussion Hand claps
Comments	Form begins with chorus Spoken introduction Music has changing dynamics, getting louder and softer throughout	A dramatic form called a "playlet" Three different Latin-tinged rhythmic feels No repeat of the AABA	Heavy reverb throughout the track Dense orchestration Reprise of introduction at the end

the backup vocals work together in a call-and-response relationship. All of this is in direct imitation of "Be My Baby."

But there are also some notable differences between the songs. For example, "Don't Worry Baby" does not use strings and features male voices. Rather than dealing with romantic longing as in "Be My Baby," Christian's lyrics describe the singer's reluctant involvement in a drag race. As Wilson tells the story, he was concerned he would never be able to equal Spector's achievement and his wife reassured him with the phrase, "Don't worry, baby." Perhaps the drag race described in "Don't Worry Baby" is a metaphor for Wilson's sense of competition with Spector. In any case, "Don't Worry Baby" is closely related to "Be My Baby."

The Drifters	The Everly Brothers	Roy Orbison	Beach Boys
There Goes My Baby	All I Have to Do Is Dream	Only the Lonely (Know How I Feel)	Surfin' U.S.A.
p2, r1 1959	p1, r1, c1 1958	p2 1960	p3, r20 1963
Simple verse-chorus	AABA	AABA (modified)	Simple verse
12/8	4/4	4/4 (2/4)	4/4
Electric guitar Acoustic guitar Bass Lead vocal Background vocal Orchestral strings Tympani	Electric guitar Acoustic guitar Acoustic bass Drums Vocal duet	Electric guitar Acoustic guitar Bass Drums Lead Vocal Background vocal Piano Strings Vibraphone	Electric guitar Acoustic bass Drums Lead vocal Background vocal Organ
Note the lack of a drum set Doo Wop vocals in chorus Prominent strings	Two-part vocal harmony throughout the song Partial reprise of AABA form, repeating B and A sections only Slight Latin feel to rhythm	Doo Wop style backing vocals Stop-time chords in bridge Dramatic high vocals in second bridge	Chuck Berry-style introduction Note the difference between a refrain (included) and a chorus (not included) Intricate backing vocals

Despite these formulaic early singles, the Beach Boys were also capable of great musical subtlety and sophistication. The slow ballads "Surfer Girl" and "In My Room" are elegant Wilson compositions that, despite their teen themes, are compositionally innovative and reveal the group's prowess as a vocal ensemble. Although their vocal performances were astounding, perhaps the most important elements in the Beach Boys' success were the writing and production of Brian Wilson. Strongly influenced by Phil Spector's most ambitious records, Wilson worked to create the biggest recorded sound for the band that he could muster, increasingly emphasizing innovation. His records with the Beach Boys are a clear continuation of the ambitious producer story this chapter has traced, though his most creative and ambitious work was yet to come.

Jan and Dean, Dick Dale, and Duane Eddy. Jan and Dean also had a series of surf-music hits during the early 1960s with songs like "Little Old Lady from Pasadena" (p3, 1964), "Surf City" (written with Brian Wilson, p1 r3, 1963), "Honolulu Lulu" (p11, 1963), "Drag City" (p10, 1963), and "Dead Man's Curve" (p8, 1964). In the early years of surf music, Jan and Dean worked closely with the Beach Boys until their respective record companies objected to this practice. And while the Beach Boys and Jan and Dean were placing one single after another on the Top 40 charts, another group of southern California surf records was focused almost exclusively on instrumental music featuring the guitar. Dick Dale and the Del-Tones were pioneers in this style of guitar-based surf music and spent the autumn of 1961 (the season of the first Beach Boys single) at the lower reaches of the national pop charts. While only one of the Beach Boys (Dennis Wilson) ever spent any time surfing, Dale's music grew straight out of surf culture; Dale recalls that it was normal for him to come in from the beach, dry off, and step directly onstage to play. Dick Dale and the Del-tones' "Misirlou" (1962) features his trademark rapid tremolo picking on the guitar set to a tune that had been a Greek pop standard in the 1940s. His most commercially popular single was "Let's Go Tripping," which hit number sixty in 1961. Dale's tendency to slide his hand down the guitar strings (from high to low) while picking rapidly created an effect he thought sounded like a wave crashing around a surfer. That trademark sound can be heard in many of the surf hits of the time, including the Chantay's instrumental hit, "Pipeline" (p4 r11, 1963), the Duals' "Stick Shift" (p25, 1961), and the Surfaris' "Wipe Out" (p2 r10, 1963). While Dale and the surfers developed a particular form of guitar-band instrumental, in many ways these groups were building on the success of guitarist Duane Eddy, whose "Rebel Rouser" hit number six in 1958 (r8) and was followed by a series of instrumental hits through 1962. Eddy's distinctively twangy guitar records also inspired the Seattle-based Ventures, who hit number two with "Walk, Don't Run" in 1960 (r13). Driven by two guitars, bass, and drums, the group had placed five hits in the Top 40 by 1964. The instrumental records by Dale, Eddy, and the Ventures were considered a novelty, which indicates how much the music business had changed in the fifteen years since the end of World War II. Instrumental records had been quite popular during the Big Band Era, but the rise of the singers (led by Sinatra) had changed all that, and most rock and roll focused on vocal performances. With surf music as a major proponent of wordless songs, increased attention would be given to instrumental playing after 1964 as young guitarists inspired by electric blues and jazz made accomplished instrumental playing as much a feature of rock music as the vocals.

NARRATIVE LYRICS RUN AMOK: THE SPLATTER PLATTER

Connections across the Pop Spectrum. In this chapter we have discussed a lot of music in relative isolation. Therefore, it is important to realize that many of the most important artists and producers of this time worked together, across boundaries of race, region, gender, and style. To conclude, we will look closely at "Leader of the Pack," a song that brings together several of the threads we have followed in this chapter, and serves as an example of a "splatter platter." Splatter platters were popular songs from the period between 1959 and 1964 that dramatically portrayed teenage death.

In perhaps the first move that spelled the end of the the Brill Building domination of teen pop, Aldon Music was sold to Columbia Pictures-Screen Gems in the summer of 1963 (at about the same time that the Beatles were enjoying their first overwhelming success in England). Aldon founder Don Kirshner joined the corporation, running its Colpix label, while his associate Al Nevins was hired as a consultant (we will hear from Kirschner and some of his Brill Building colleagues again in Chapter 5). At about the same time, Leiber, Stoller, and George Goldner founded Red Bird Records (one reason that Leiber and Stoller turned production of the Drifters over to Bert Berns was to concentrate on developing the new label). Jeff Barry and Ellie Greenwich had begun writing and producing for Red Bird, having a number one hit in 1964 with the Dixie Cups' "Chapel of Love," a song they had written with Phil Spector and which he had recorded with both the Crystals and the Ronettes but never released. An old acquaintance of Greenwich's, George "Shadow" Morton, worked with Barry and Greenwich on a new single by the Shangri-Las, "Remember (Walkin' in the Sand)," which was released on Red Bird and rose to number thirteen in August of 1964. The trio then began writing the follow-up, "Leader of the Pack," produced by Barry and Morton.

In addition to serving as an interesting example of collaboration behind the scenes, "Leader of the Pack" was perhaps the most infamous of the splatter platters, a genre of records that were maudlin at best and downright tasteless at worst. Other famous splatter platters included Mark Dinning's "Teen Angel" (p1 r5, 1960), Ray Peterson's "Tell Laura I Love Her" (p7, 1960), the Everly Brothers' "Ebony Eyes" (p8, 1961), and J. Frank Wilson and the Cavaliers' "Last Kiss" (p2, 1964). True to the death-disk genre, "Leader of the Pack" chronicles the untimely demise of a teenager, in this case a motorcycle hoodlum named Johnny (paralleling Marlon Brando's character in *The Wild One*). Johnny's violent motorbike death is represented by taped crash sounds and screams, a feature that caused some consternation among parents. This Shangri-Las splatter platter is perhaps best viewed as a death-disk playlet. The involvement of Leiber and Stoller further underscores this. The verses set up the middle section, which provides the climax (the bike crash), and a final verse offers an epilogue. The sound-effect technique had also been employed in their first Coasters single, "Riot in Cell Block #9" (released as the Robins on Spark), which featured taped gunshots and police siren noises to represent the jailbreak. In a strange way, "Leader of the Pack" brings the Leiber and Stoller story back to where it began, incorporating a number of elements of their careers. "Leader

DEAD MAN'S CURVE
b/w THE NEW GIRL IN SCHOOL
JAN & DEAN
LIBERTY
#55672

JAN & DEAN FAN CLUB
1307 Brinkley
West Los Angeles, Calif.

The quintessential "splatter platter": Jan and Dean's "Dead Man's Curve." "Splatter platters" or "death disks" told the stories of teenagers meeting gruesome deaths, usually in a car or motorcycle crash. This record reveals the strong storytelling style of Leiber and Stoller.

of the Pack" would be among the last records to come out of the Brill Building establishment, since by 1964 the British invasion had arrived on American shores, causing yet another shake-up of the American popular-music business.

A far more tragic epilogue to the splatter-platter genre is the true story of Jan and Dean. In 1964 Jan and Dean also had a teenage tragedy hit, "Dead Man's Curve," which rose to number eight. The song chronicles a car crash on a stretch of road so treacherous that it had earned the nickname "dead man's curve." On April 19, 1966, Jan Berry was involved in an auto accident in which three passengers were killed and he was critically injured, effectively ending his career.

As mentioned at the beginning of this chapter, the period between the first wave of rock and roll and the arrival of the Beatles is viewed by some as a period of decline—a kind of "dark age" in rock history—while others see it as an important era filled with a lot of great music. For those who champion early 1960s pop, the British invasion was an unfortunate turn of events that snuffed out a number of pop styles prematurely. For those who view the early 1960s as dark days, Brill Building pop was rock and roll without its vitality, cynically neutered for crass commercial purposes. Whatever position one takes, it is clear that these years saw the music business gain control of a youth market that was cultivated during the first wave. Almost no aspect of pop during the early 1960s was completely immune from the influence of Brill Building practices, which were themselves merely a return to the practices that had dominated mainstream pop before rock emerged. If teens generally thought the new, more controlled pop constituted a decline, they certainly did not abandon pop music as a result. With business booming, it must have been enormously frustrating to the music-business establishment to face another serious challenge to their control of youth music: just when they thought they had it all figured out, a band arrived from England in February 1964 and radically changed the business again.

FURTHER READING

Alan Betrock, *Girl Groups: The Story of a Sound* (Delilah Books, 1982).

Hal Blaine with David Goggin, *Hal Blaine and the Wrecking Crew: The Story of the World's Most Recorded Musician* (MixBooks, 1993).

Robert Cantwell, *When We Were Good: The Folk Revival* (Harvard University Press, 1996).

Ron Cohen, *Rainbow Quest: The Folk Music Revival and American Society, 1940–1970* (University of Massachusetts Press, 2002).

Ken Emerson, *Always Magic in the Air: The Bump and Brilliance of the Brill Building Era* (Penguin Books, 2005).

Peter Guralnick, *Dream Boogie: The Triumph of Sam Cooke* (Little, Brown, and Company, 2005).

John A. Jackson, *American Bandstand: Dick Clark and the Making of a Rock 'n' Roll Empire* (Oxford University Press, 1997).

Mark Ribowsky, *He's a Rebel: The Truth about Phil Spector—Rock and Roll's Legendary Madman* (E. P. Dutton, 1989).

Ronnie Spector with Vince Waldron, *Be My Baby* (HarperCollins, 1990).

Jacqueline Warwick, *Girl Groups, Girl Culture: Popular Music and Identity in the 1960s* (Routledge, 2007).

Timothy White, *The Nearest Faraway Place: Brian Wilson, The Beach Boys, and the Southern California Experience* (Henry Holt, 1994).

Brian Wilson with Todd Gold, *Wouldn't It Be Nice? My Own Story* (HarperCollins, 1991).

Ⓢ VISIT STUDYSPACE AT WWNORTON.COM/STUDYSPACE

Access free review material such as:

- music links
- performer info
- practice quizzes
- outlines
- interactive listening guide software

THE 1960s

Although the 1960s in America began with great hope, it was a decade that saw tremendous turbulence and war. The true spirit of the time was reflected in the rise and fall of President John F. Kennedy. Some historians say the sixties ethos began with Kennedy's election—that his youthfulness and passion for grand ideas epitomized the growing influence of youth culture. Others say the sixties truly began with Kennedy's assassination in 1963, and the resulting despair and conspiracy theories foreshadowing the many social movements that were deeply critical of government and traditional economic, social, and religious institutions. Wherever one places the beginning of the 1960s, it is clear that both themes are present in these chaotic years: youth culture presented itself more forcefully than ever, and social movements became more vigorous, critical, and violent. The music of this time—revealing and heightening these trends—provided the appropriate soundtrack. The world was exploding, and rock musicians were listening more closely than ever.

Among the issues that divided Americans, none loomed larger than the Vietnam War and the civil rights movement. Although the struggle for the rights of African Americans began when the first blacks were brought to America (1619) and continued through the landmark desegregation case, *Brown v. Board of Education of Topeka, Kansas*, the intensity and organization of the movement increased greatly in the 1960s. To protest the racial segregation that lingered after *Brown*, four young African American students "sat in" at a segregated lunch counter in 1960 at Woolworth's in Greensboro, North Carolina. Their protest set off many more across the country and caused Woolworth's to integrate its lunch counters. The movement for African American civil rights continued in many locales, with major protests in Birmingham and Montgomery, Alabama.

A watershed moment in the movement came on August 28, 1963, when 250,000 Americans—black and white—took part in the "March on Washington." At this historic event, Martin Luther King, Jr. delivered his "I Have a Dream" speech, which vocalized the movement's goals and spirit to all Americans. Following the March, Congress passed the Civil Rights Act (1964), making discrimination based on race illegal. Despite this, racial tensions remained high in some big cities: Race riots erupted in the Watts neighborhood of Los Angeles in 1965, in Newark and Detroit in 1967, and in many cities fol-

As the decade rolled on, the movement became more militant, and earlier calls for integration and nonviolence gave way to "Black Power"—promoted by the Black Panthers, among others.

The antiwar movement paralleled the civil rights movement. By mid-decade, America had combat troops in Vietnam and the number of American casualties began to increase. Many young Americans questioned the wisdom of the war, and organized, especially on college campuses. Students—white and black, rich and poor—"sat in" and burned their draft cards; some even escaped to Canada to avoid the war. Like civil rights protests, antiwar demonstrations could also turn violent, as happened at the 1968 Democratic National Convention in Chicago. In 1970, four students were killed at Kent State University in Ohio, and two more at Jackson State College in Mississippi.

African-American students were particularly active in initial public acts connected to the civil rights movement during the early 1960s. Here, a group of students demand service by "sitting in" at a Woolworth counter in Little Rock, Arkansas in 1963.

In addition to the civil rights and antiwar movements, many other movements first appeared on the radar of national awareness in the 1960s. The feminist movement was nurtured significantly by Betty Friedan's 1963 best-selling book *The Feminine Mystique*, which argued that women were constrained by the traditional role of homemaker. In 1966, the National Organization of Women (NOW) was founded with Friedan as its first president. Environmentalism grew when Rachel Carson's *Silent Spring* (1962) drew the country's attention to the dangers resulting from the indiscriminate and persistent use of pesticides such as DDT. Similarly, the consumer protection movement got its spark from Ralph Nader's 1965 book *Unsafe at Any Speed*, which accused automobile companies of placing

Anti-Vietnam war protesters taunt military police during a demonstration at the Pentagon in Washington, D.C., October 21, 1967. Throughout the 1960s antiwar sentiment increased, especially among students, as more and more young American soldiers died in battle.

4

STEREO

CAPITOL FULL
DIMENSIONAL

MEET
THE **BEATLES!**

The First Album by England's Phenomenal Pop Combo

Capitol
RECORDS

HIGH FIDELITY

THE BEATLES AND THE BRITISH INVASION

The early 1960s offered a wide variety of musical styles to American youth, from the simple teenybopper love songs of the teen idols to the more worldly traditionalism and social consciousness of the folk revival. In the music-stylistic space between these opposing poles were girl-group music, rockabilly, surf music, and sweet soul. In this context, four young men from Liverpool, England, took the American music business by storm. On February 9, 1964, the Beatles appeared on Ed Sullivan's Sunday evening variety show, just as Elvis Presley had done eight years earlier in 1956. The Beatles reached a record-breaking 73 million viewers, making them a household name practically overnight. This performance was so popular that it was reported later that the crime rate in the United States went down during the time the show was on the air.

The Beatles' success created a fad, and during most of 1964 American fans had a voracious appetite for music performed by young men with British accents, long hair, and matching suits. This "British invasion" of American pop, and the enormous success of the Beatles in particular, altered the music business in several significant ways, affecting both musical style and music-business practice. The Beatles first became popular in the UK, and the British popular-music scene during the late 1950s and early '60s was also transformed by the music and musicians that would invade the colonies only slightly later. The story of the British invasion is therefore not one, but rather two interdependent stories: the first is a chronicle of British pop before 1964 and British musicians' fascination with American pop, country, jazz, and rhythm and blues; the second is an account of how British music strongly affected American pop after the arrival of the Beatles.

This famous album was almost never released in the United States. Capitol Records, the American subsidiary of the British label EMI, was confident that a British act could never sell enough records in the United States to be profitable. After declining to release the British hit singles "Love Me Do," "Please Please Me," and "She Loves You" in the States, however, Capitol finally released "I Want to Hold Your Hand" in the last week of 1963. By early 1964, the single had gone to number one on U.S. charts. At one point in April 1964 the top five slots of the *Billboard* "Hot 100" were taken by Beatles songs, three of which were on independent labels. In the midst of this "Beatlemania," Capitol quickly put together an album for American release, combining tracks from the first two British albums with both sides of the "I Want to Hold Your Hand" single. The resulting album, *Meet the Beatles!*, was the first Beatles album most American fans owned, though it differs somewhat from the similar British release, *With the Beatles*. Capitol continued carving up Beatles albums through the first few years of the band's career, creating several American albums that have no direct British counterparts, such as *The Beatles' Second Album* (1964), *Beatles VI* (1965), and *Yesterday and Today* (1966).

BRITISH POP IN THE LATE 1950S AND EARLY 1960S

The Music Business in the UK. Prior to 1964 American listeners viewed Britain as a secondary force in popular music. Likewise, listeners in the UK consumed a lot of American music, importing far more popular music than it exported. A comparison of the pop hits in Britain during the late 1950s and early '60s with those in the United States reveals that many of the same records, performed in many cases by white American artists, were popular in both countries. British artists were far more likely to achieve success at home than in the States, with occasional exceptions. Orchestra leader Mantovani, for instance, placed twenty-six albums in the American Top 40 between 1955 and 1963, and two singles in the U.S. pop Top 40—the movie themes from *Around the World in Eighty Days* (p12, 1957) and *Exodus* (p31, 1961)—but this was a level of American success unmatched by other British artists. This American dominance in popular music was largely a product of the differences between British and American society. After the end of World War II in 1945, there was tremendous enthusiasm in Britain for American popular culture. American armed forces had taken their culture overseas with them during the war, and many Britons had developed a taste for American pop. Many areas in Britain, and London especially, were devastated by German bombing and the postwar years were marked by struggle and rebuilding in the UK. Many Britons looked to America as a country full of hope and confidence, affluent and unburdened by the scars of war or the weight of history and tradition. When rock and roll began to emerge in the United States, teens in Britain enthusiastically embraced the new style. The idea of the "teenager" was seen as an American innovation. To many young people in Britain, teens in the United States led lives filled with rock and roll, dancing, cars, and drive-in movies. In the sometimes dreary rebuilding years of the 1950s, British teens found such images enormously attractive and rock and roll became the music of teenage rebellion.

Big companies influenced the music business in Britain much more than in the United States, and this affected the way rock and roll was understood by listeners in the UK. Britain had four major record labels—EMI, Decca, Pye, and Philips—and two radio stations—the BBC and Radio Luxembourg. These major labels licensed music from American majors and indies for release in the UK, Decca and EMI being the most active. The BBC was government-owned and featured three channels, only one of which played rock and roll. Beginning in 1958, the BBC's two-hour radio show *Saturday Club* (hosted by Brian Matthew) became an important weekly source of rock and roll music and information. Radio Luxembourg was a commercial station broadcast from the European continent. Rock and roll was mostly played on shows financed by the major labels, which used these broadcasts to promote their own records. Unlike the United States, Britain had no independent radio stations before 1964, and very few successful independent labels.

Running an indie label in the UK was a tough business: since radio access was controlled by the government or wealthy major labels, an independent stood little chance of ever getting a record played. While rock and roll records that appeared on the American pop charts were mostly available in stores, rhythm and blues was much more difficult to find, as was country and western music. Information about such music was even scarcer, though newspapers such as *Melody Maker*, *New Musical Express*, and *Record Mirror* increasingly devoted attention to rock and roll. Movies became an important resource for young people interested in rock and roll; films made to capitalize on the first wave that featured performances (the Freed movies and *The Girl Can't Help It*) and Elvis films were very popular. British tours by performers such as Bill Haley, Buddy Holly, and the Everly Brothers were important events for young rock and roll fans as well, giving them a chance to see some of their favorite artists perform in person.

These rock and roll enthusiasts were not the first to seek out American pop music. The British had a long-standing infatuation with American folk and jazz that dated back to before World War II. After 1945, both of these styles experienced a resurgence in the UK and, in many ways, the British infatuation with rock and roll was a continuation of this interest in earlier American forms. Traditional jazz ("trad"), which stuck very close to the early twentieth-century New Orleans style, was championed by bandleader Ken Colyer and was later broadened to include other jazz styles by Chris Barber, Kenny Ball, and Acker Bilk. Barber's band featured banjo player Tony Donegan, who later began to use the first name "Lonnie." Donegan recorded a version of the traditional folk song "Rock Island Line" in a new style called "skiffle" that blended folk music with an up-tempo rhythmic feel and American textual themes. Credited to Lonnie Donegan and His Skiffle Group (Donegan on vocals and guitar, Barber on bass, and Beryl Bryden on washboard), the single rose to the number eight slot on the UK charts in 1956, igniting a pop craze for skiffle music. Parallel to the folk boom that took hold in the United States slightly later, this tuneful yet easy-to-play music encouraged the participation of many British teenagers. "Rock Island Line" crossed the Atlantic to hit number eight on the U.S. pop charts in 1956. Donegan followed up this success by placing thirty-one hits on the UK charts by 1962, including a version of "Tom Dooley," which rose to number three in the UK in 1958. By the late 1950s, however, the skiffle fad had been replaced by a preference for trad on the British charts, with Ball, Barber, and Bilk each scoring a series of hits. Some of these even crossed the Atlantic, such as Barber's "Petite Fleur" (p5 uk3, 1959), Ball's "Midnight in Moscow" (uk2, 1961; p2, 1962), and Bilk's "Stranger on the Shore" (uk2, 1961; p1 r7, 1962).

The most pressing challenge facing the UK music business in the late 1950s and early 1960s, however, was not how to place more British records on the American charts. It was how to place more domestic records on the British charts which, despite the success of homegrown artists like Donegan, Barber, Ball, and Bilk, were still dominated by Americans. British companies had already begun to produce teen-idol singers modeled on Elvis Presley. The first was Decca's Tommy Steele, who hit in 1956 with "Rock with the Caveman" (uk13) and followed later the same year with the number-one British hit, "Singin' the Blues," and sixteen more hits through 1961. The most successful British rocker was EMI's Cliff Richard. From 1958 to 1963, Richard scored twenty-seven UK hit singles. His backup band, the Shadows, was the English equivalent of the Ventures and placed a series of instrumental hits on the UK charts, beginning with "Apache" (uk1, 1960). For all the domestic success that Richard and the Shadows enjoyed, however, only one record crossed the Atlantic before 1964: "Living Doll," which went to number thirty on the U.S. charts in 1959. Like Bob Marcucci's star-making machinery in Philadel-

Regarded as the most important figure in the late-1950s skiffle movement in Britain, Lonnie Donegan and his band blended American folk music with a traditional jazz beat. This photo shows Donegan (second from left) playing banjo while other group members play stand-up bass, tambourine, and the type of hollow-body electric guitar commonly used in jazz.

phia discussed in Chapter 3, London's Larry Parnes managed a stable of teen idols. Building on his success managing Tommy Steele, Parnes developed Marty Wilde, Billy Fury, Georgie Fame, and Joe Brown, each of whom had a series of hits in the UK. Despite the increased success of British artists, in 1962 the UK charts were still full of Americans: four Elvis Presley records hit number one, along with one each by Ray Charles and B. Bumble and the Stingers. The turnaround for British performers would occur in 1963 with the emergence of what Britons called the "beat boom"—a style led by a group from Liverpool.

THE BEATLES AS STUDENTS OF AMERICAN POP, 1960–1963

Formation and First Gigs. The Beatles formed in Liverpool in 1957, playing as a skiffle band and calling themselves the Quarry Men, then moving on to rock and roll as the popularity of skiffle waned. John Lennon was born in 1940 and Paul McCartney in 1942, so they were fifteen and thirteen years old, respectively, when rock and roll broke out on both sides of the Atlantic. They were among the first generation of musicians for whom rock was the music of their youth. Elvis Presley, by contrast, was fifteen in 1950 and twenty-one when he hit nationally in 1956. Coming along a few years after the first wave, young British musicians learned to play by imitating these older American rock and rollers, and the music of the first wave left an indelible imprint on British rock in the 1960s. It is not surprising that the first recording of the Beatles from 1958 (as the Quarry Men and now including a fifteen-year-old George Harrison on lead guitar) features Buddy Holly's "That'll Be the Day," performed in close imitation of Holly's record. The group also recorded an original song that emulated Holly's style, written by Harrison and McCartney, called "In Spite of All the Danger."

After performing locally with some success and winning a talent contest under the name Johnny and the Moondogs, in 1960 Lennon, McCartney, and Harrison auditioned for manager Larry Parnes. Parnes decided not to sign them as a feature act, but to use the group (now known as the Silver Beetles, after Holly's Crickets) to support one of his singers (Johnny Gentle) on a brief tour of Scotland. Earlier that year Lennon's art-college buddy Stuart Sutcliffe had joined the band on bass, and by summer Pete Best had joined on drums. It was this lineup, with Lennon, McCartney, and Harrison all playing guitar and singing, that later set out to play a four-month stint in the red-light district of Hamburg, Germany.

Hamburg and Liverpool (1960–1962). Between August 1960 and May 1962 the group traveled to Hamburg for three extended stays (playing 106, 92, and 48 nights) and then returned for two shorter periods in late 1962. The Beatles' first regular gig in Hamburg was at the small Indra Club, and they later moved to the larger Kaiserkeller. The group had been booked through agent Allan Williams, who had already sent another Liverpool band, Derry and the Seniors, to Hamburg. Other bands in the city at the time included the Jets, from London, and Liverpudlians Rory Storm and the Hurricanes, featuring drummer Ringo Starr. The Beatles played six-hour sets in which they were constantly being prompted to "make a show." In order to fill the time, the group learned every song they could find, especially high-energy rock and roll numbers that excited German patrons. During their second stint in Hamburg, at the Top Ten Club, the band played from 7 P.M. until 2 A.M. with a fifteen-minute break each hour. Conditions improved greatly by the time of their third visit, when they played the Star Club, at one point sharing the bill with Little Richard. These long nights in tough German bars refined the Beatles' performance skills, making professionals out of the aspiring rock and rollers. The Beatles also became regulars at Liverpool's Cavern Club during this period. Their first appearance was in February 1961, two months after their first stay in Hamburg and only a few weeks after a tremendously successful dance gig at the Litherland Town Hall in Liverpool. Arranged by Cavern Club DJ Bob Wooler, the band played almost 300 shows at the Cavern through early 1962. Many of these were lunchtime affairs, with the crowd and the band eating during the performance. Between shows at the Cavern and stints in Hamburg, the Beatles were performing frequently and continually developing their skills while building an enthusiastic following.

There were advantages and disadvantages to being a Liverpool group. An important advantage was that the city was a seaport, and seamen who traveled the Atlantic regularly brought back American records. This gave the young Beatles greater expo-

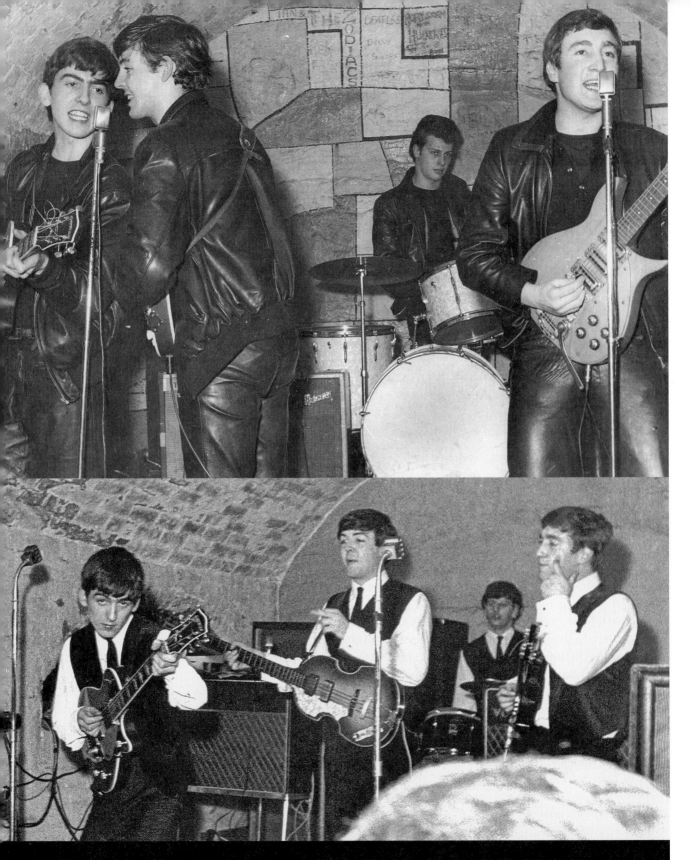

Before they became worldwide stars, the Beatles regularly played the Cavern Club in their hometown of Liverpool. The top photo shows the band at the Cavern in 1961, clad in leather and with Pete Best on drums. The bottom image shows them in 1963 with Ringo Starr on drums and wearing the matching suits suggested by manager Brian Epstein.

sure to American pop than they might have had even in London. That exposure continued in Hamburg (also a port city) and added to the band's knowledge of American pop, rhythm and blues, and country and western music. The major disadvantage to being based in Liverpool was that the entire British music business was centered in London. It was very difficult for groups outside of the capitol to gain acceptance by the most important players in the business, especially bands from the more working-class north.

In November 1961, Brian Epstein first saw the Beatles perform at the Cavern. Epstein was running a family-owned record store and discovered the group partly through customers' requests for a rocked-up version of "My Bonnie Lies Over the Ocean" (1961) performed by Tony Sheridan (backed by the Beatles), a record that had been a hit in Germany. Epstein soon became the Beatles' manager, and immediately set to work on cleaning up the band's stage appearance. In addition to their new "Beatle haircuts" the band also donned matching tailored suits. Epstein's efforts to change the group's image and his efforts at promotion helped the group get better jobs for more money. Epstein then set his sights on a recording contract. Using his contacts inside the British record industry, he was able to secure a recording audition at Decca's London studios. Based on this fifteen-song session (January 1, 1962) and after months of consideration, Decca's Dick Rowe chose to sign Brian Poole and the Tremeloes rather than the Beatles. The Beatles were allowed to keep the demo tape, however, and while the group was in Hamburg in early May 1962, Epstein made the rounds of record companies in London. After being turned down by several labels, Epstein was introduced to George Martin, then serving as A&R man for a small EMI label called Parlophone. Martin heard promise in the Decca tape and set up an EMI recording audition for the group in June 1962. By September, he was producing the group's first release for Parlophone, Lennon and McCartney's "Love Me Do." The Hurricanes' Ringo Starr had joined the band in August (replacing Best), but Martin was wary of Starr's amateurish playing at the audition and hired a session drummer for the recording date. Martin also had the group record "How Do You Do It?" written by Mitch Murray, although the band successfully lobbied to release an original song as the first single. "Love Me Do" rose to number seventeen on the UK charts by late 1962, and in 1963, "How Do You Do It?" hit number one when it was released by another Epstein-managed Liverpool group, Gerry and the Pacemakers.

By the end of 1962, the Beatles had done what no Liverpool band had done before: gone to London, signed a recording contract, and placed a single on the UK charts. As a result, more bands from Liverpool, Manchester, and Birmingham made their way south and were welcomed by record companies eager to capitalize on the success of the "Mersey Beat" (pop music originating in the mid-1960s around Liverpool and northwest England).

BEATLE INFLUENCES

A survey of the songs the Beatles played during the Hamburg and Liverpool period provides valuable insight into their influences and allows us to trace their development as songwriters. Young songwriters often learn their craft by modeling new songs on ones they know. Live recordings provide documentation of what the Beatles played during those years, songs that likely served as models for their later hits. Perhaps the richest source for this repertoire are tapes the band made for a variety of BBC radio broadcasts, including Brian Matthew's *Saturday Club*, in the first years of their British success (1963–65). *The Beatles Live at the BBC* reveals the extent of the band's fascination with American rock and roll. The tapes feature four Elvis Presley covers, including McCartney performing a close copy of "That's All Right (Mama)," and nine Chuck Berry covers, including Lennon singing the lyrically sophisticated "Memphis." Among the other first-wave rockers, Little Richard and Carl Perkins are also represented multiple times. The band also shows an appreciation for Leiber and Stoller's Coasters records, as well as Phil Spector's "To Know Him Is to Love Him." The first of the *Anthology* CD sets, released in 1995, provides five selections from the band's audition tape for Decca (including two Coasters tunes) and an excerpt from Ray Charles's "Hallelujah I Love Her So" recorded at the Cavern Club. Finally, their first two British albums, *Please Please Me* and *With the Beatles* (both 1963), contain several cover versions, including girl-group numbers ("Chains" and "Baby It's You"), Motown tracks ("You Really Got a Hold on Me," "Please Mr. Postman," and "Money"), and a movie theme ("A Taste of Honey"). Based on these early recordings, it is clear that Lennon and McCartney were experienced students of American pop by the time they entered the EMI Abbey Road studios with Martin to make their first hit record in fall 1962.

BEATLEMANIA, 1963–1966

Success in England. The success of "Love Me Do" was a sign of things to come for the Beatles, but nobody expected the level of success the group achieved in the UK in 1963, which spread to the rest of the world the next year. They began the year by recording and touring in support of their first album, *Please Please Me*. By August, they had three more hit singles in the UK—"Please Please Me" (uk2), "From Me to You" (uk1), and "She Loves You" (uk1)—as well as a chart-topping album. That summer, the British press coined the term "Beatlemania" to describe the tremendous excitement created among fans at the band's live performances. The group's breakthrough in Britain occurred in mid-October when they performed on *Sunday Night at the London Palladium*, a national television broadcast similar to Ed Sullivan's *Toast of the Town*. This was followed in early November by another high-profile television appearance on the *Royal Variety Performance* in the presence of the Queen Mother, Princess Margaret, and Lord Snowdon. By late November the group's second album, *With the Beatles*, entered the UK charts at number two on its way to the top spot (which it held until the end of April 1964). In December, "I Want to Hold Your Hand" hit number one on the UK charts, where it replaced "She Loves You" and became the band's fourth consecutive hit. In late December *The Times'* music critic William Mann named Lennon and McCartney the "outstanding English composers of 1963."

The Beatles' tremendous success opened the British popular-music business to dozens of other groups. Most of the number one hits on the UK charts in 1963 were by domestic artists, many of whom made their debuts that year. If the first goal of the British music business had been to place more homegrown acts on the UK charts, 1963 had been an important year. Despite Beatlemania and all that followed in its wake, however, none of this success and excitement made any impact across the Atlantic. Capitol Records, EMI's American subsidiary, declined the right to issue the first Beatles hits in the United States. George Martin was forced to license these singles to American indies—"Please Please Me" and "From Me to You" appeared on Vee Jay, while "She Loves You" was released by Swan. None of the three records had much chart impact. As strange as it seems today, Capitol was reluctant because they were sure that the Beatles would fail in the United States. This was logic based on experience: most British artists, even Cliff Richard, had been unable to establish themselves as consistent hit-makers in America. In fact, the Beatles were so afraid of failing in America that they told Brian Epstein they did not want to go to the United States until they had a number one hit there. Despite their reluctance, Epstein tried to get the band booked in the United States. In November 1963 he visited New York and worked out a deal for three appearances on Ed Sullivan's variety show in February 1964. Sullivan had agreed that the Beatles would get top billing on the show, so Epstein and Martin were able to convince Capitol to release "I Want to Hold Your Hand" in late December 1963. By the beginning of February 1964 the single had hit number one in the the United States, just in time for the first Sullivan performance on February 9.

The American Experience. With the breakthrough success of the first Sullivan appearance (see p. 159), the Beatles became the hottest act in the American entertainment business almost overnight. Still, everyone involved with the band expected that their success might dry up just as quickly as it had appeared, as had happened with the first wave of rock and roll. Laboring under the idea that they had to make the most of their brief moment of opportunity, the Beatles worked at a furious pace, touring and recording almost without a break. The result was one of the most impressive runs of hit records ever posted in popular music. Of course, success had not come to the group as easily as it seemed to Americans in 1964. Few fans knew of the long, grueling hours in Hamburg or the many shows at the Cavern and across Britain that had filled the previous four years. The Beatles followed the success of "I Want to Hold Your Hand" with more than thirty Top 40 U.S. hits through 1966 (including the records that had been rejected by Capitol), with twelve going to number one, including "Can't Buy Me Love" (1964), "A Hard Day's Night" (1964), "Ticket to Ride" (1965), "Help!" (1965), and "Paperback Writer" (1966). The week after the first Sullivan show, *Meet the Beatles!* hit the top of the American album charts, staying at number one for almost three months, only ceding its spot to *The Beatles' Second Album*. All the group's studio albums would go to number one in both the UK and the United States, although the U.S. albums often featured different titles and songs than the British releases. In July 1964, the band was featured in their first full-length movie, *A Hard Day's Night*, and followed up with *Help!* in August 1965. Both were tremendous box-office successes, taking advantage of a lucrative market for teen movies that had been established by Alan Freed, Elvis, and others.

Things turned sour for the band in 1966 when controversy erupted in the

THE BEATLES ON SULLIVAN

by Tim Riley

By early 1964, Beatlemania had seduced Britain and Europe, but American success was still elusive. Capitol Records had rejected "Please Please Me," "From Me To You," and "She Loves You," and was about to snub "I Want to Hold Your Hand," when manager Brian Epstein intervened. Tired of the runaround, Epstein called Capitol president Dave Dexter, who confessed he hadn't heard these silly Beatles. Dexter agreed to listen, and quickly overruled his underlings (and his wife) in November 1963. Epstein thanked him and demanded a $40,000 promotional campaign as

he played his trump: Ed Sullivan had booked the band for three consecutive weeks in February 1964. Epstein wanted a hit record for their arrival. Dexter, who admired Epstein's gumption as much as the prime-time booking, agreed to the purse, and the stars quickly aligned.

On February 9, 1964, alongside the Broadway cast of *Oliver!*, comedian Frank Gorshin, and Olympian Terry McDermott, the Beatles played five numbers, starting with "All My Loving," "Till There Was You," and their first U.S. number one, "I Want to Hold Your Hand." For viewers, time froze: it had been seven years since Elvis Presley had graced this same stage, but it must have felt like forever for fans of rock and roll. With "She Loves You" and "I Saw Her Standing There" especially, rock and roll cracked open again—the music sounded bigger, more provocative, and more pressing than ever. In their Sullivan debut, the Beatles reframed all of rock and roll history up to that point, and hinted at a thousand enticing new directions.

The overpowering immediacy of the Beatles' impact was a key part of their appeal, and largely ironic. What seemed fresh and spontaneous to Americans was actually

a polished act of songs and quips refined throughout 1963. Stories of Britain's peculiar Beatlemania phenomenon had trickled in via Jack Paar and Walter Cronkite—the Beatles were news fluff ("mop-tops" with "screaming girls") even before their songs began playing on Top 40 radio over Christmas and the New Year.

Early 1964 was not, however, what many historians routinely call a "fallow" period for rock and roll. In fact, John, Paul, George, and Ringo saw themselves as participants, not saviors; the Beatles symbolized less a resurgence of rock and roll than an argument for its ongoing richness. The week "I Want to Hold Your Hand" reached number one, it ranked just above the Trashmen's "Bird Is the Word," and the Kingsmen's "Louie Louie," both absurdist juggernauts. If anything, the Beatles somehow made sense of such inanity, or at least lent it new context and bearing.

The Sullivan audience, and fans who picked up Capitol's *Meet the Beatles!* (compiled from UK singles and their second album), heard a galloping embrace of American styles, from swooning doo-wop ("This Boy") to rakish rhythm and blues ("I Saw Her Standing There," their first in Chuck Berry's "classic" mode). Alongside their Little Richard and Carl Perkins covers, they slung Motown (Barrett Strong's "Money" and Smokey Robinson's "You've Really Got a Hold On Me"), girl groups (The Marvelettes' "Please Mr. Postman" and the Shirelles' "Boys") and soul that threw off giddy, intractable sparks (the Isley Brothers' "Twist and Shout"). The Beatles were already tinkering with the style of rock—exploiting new cracks in the sound, writing songs that implied even more than they entertained (the gigantically coy understatement of "I Want to Hold Your Hand," for example). Performing with supernatural self-confidence to the largest TV audience before or since, at least half the fun was watching the Beatles light their sonic firecrackers right in Sullivan's staid living room, his embalmed gaze acquiring the look of a catatonic Tin Pan Alley. "So you think America bounced back after the war, do ya?" their British attitude chided, while outmaneuvering the witless Yanks at their own game.

The Beatles played right into Sullivan's variety-show format while transcending it. Their first number, a jaunty original ("All My Loving"), was followed by bassist Paul McCartney singing "Till There was You," from 1960's Broadway hit *The Music Man*. How could a band so hip get away with such hokey sentimentality? (The arrangement, complete with flamenco acoustic guitar, was lifted off Peggy Lee's 1958 *Latin ala Lee!* album, not remotely rock and roll.) Elvis sang gooey ballads, but that was almost the only rule he didn't break. The Beatles delivered this "girly" stuff with relish, as if scribbling love notes between tossing cherry bombs.

Many had thought rock and roll was dead. Not only was it proven to be a vital, healthy style, but the Beatles abruptly redeemed it—"the biggest long-shot of all the biggest long-shots in the history of the world," says critic Richard Meltzer. That this renewal came as an import from Britain made it irresistible. It gave the Beatles their halo effect. Rock's second act began on a familiar stage with a transformational new context: these British youths, brash yet appealing, completely new yet instantly recognizable, held up an astonishing cultural mirror to Americans. Their command of rock and roll made it seem like they'd always known us, grinning strangers who had cracked our aesthetic DNA and were suddenly, inexplicably, lifelong friends.

Tim Riley, editor of the Riley Rock Index (www.rileyrockindex.com), is the author of Tell Me Why: A Beatles Commentary; Lennon: The Man, the Myth, the Music—The Definitive Life; *and a contributor to NPR.*

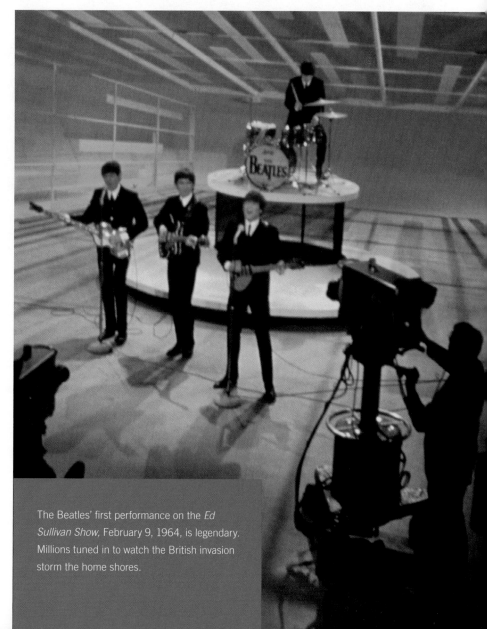

The Beatles' first performance on the *Ed Sullivan Show*, February 9, 1964, is legendary. Millions tuned in to watch the British invasion storm the home shores.

Viewing Rock

After the establishment of rock films during the late 1950s, the Beatles were perfectly poised to release a movie upon their rise to international stardom in early 1964. The result was *A Hard Day's Night*, a film directed by Richard Lester, released in both the UK and the U.S. later that summer. *A Hard Day's Night* featured the Beatles playing themselves, and furthered stereotypes of the band including their childish nature, a rock-like unreliability, and the group's knack

for exposing a cultural gap between rock listeners and an older generation. The action of the film is based entirely on the Beatles in the context of Beatlemania. In public, the group is constantly chased by rabid female fans (1).

In private, group members playfully disrespect the authority of their managers and handlers. And on stage, the band performs perfectly to audiences full of screaming female fans. As a vehicle for promoting the group's international stardom, this film certainly blurred the lines between reality, fiction, and corporate marketing. Although Beatles songs are used throughout the film soundtrack, the songs are not integrated into the plot, there are limited instances of the group actually miming performance, and all performances are lip-synched. One performance occurs early in the film on a train, when a card game inexplicably turns into a musical rendition of "I Should Have Known Better" (2).

The plot of the film, which involves losing and finding Ringo, leads up to a musical performance on a television variety show. The last ten minutes of the film consist of a mini-Beatles concert, providing the perspective of the production crew, as if the film audience was present at the filming of the final television special (3) and (4).

Even though it was a thinly veiled promotion tool with little-to-no plot value, *A Hard Day's Night* still stands up as an interesting film. It places the Beatles in the context of Beatlemania (even if on the terms of the filmmakers), allows us to see them in a quintessentially British environment, and provides several noteworthy video performances.

United States over remarks that John Lennon had made in a UK interview. Asked about the role religion played in the lives of British youth, Lennon replied that "Christianity will go," and that in British society the Beatles were more popular than Jesus Christ. These comments were made in the context of a larger debate in the UK about youth and the church—prompted in part by the changes brought by the Roman Catholic church through the Vatican II reforms. Lennon's words were taken out of context by American reporters and he was cast as having claimed that the Beatles were more important than Jesus. An uproar in the American South resulted, with Beatles records and other merchandise being burned in large bonfires

Listening Guide   Get Music ⑤ wwnorton.com/studyspace

The Beatles, "I Want to Hold Your Hand" Parlophone R-5084 (UK), Capital 5112 (U.S.)

Words and music by John Lennon and Paul McCartney, produced by George Martin. Reached #1 in UK charts in late 1963 and #1 on the *Billboard* "Hot 100" in early 1964.

FORM: AABA, with partial reprise. The bridge and verse sections are repeated after the complete verse-verse-bridge-verse structure has been presented. Each verse ends in a 4-bar refrain, employing the song's title in the lyrics and featuring two-part vocal harmony; the previous bars in the verse are sung in two-part unison. Note that the first bridge is sung in unison (except at the very end), while the repeated bridge is sung in two-part harmony. The introduction is built from the last 4 bars of the bridge, while the song's ending is created by tagging the last bars of the refrain.

TIME SIGNATURE: 4/4. This lighthearted, driving pop feel with accents on beats 2 and 4, was called "Mersey beat" in the UK.

INSTRUMENTATION: Electric guitars, bass, drums, hand claps, and two-part lead vocal (with sections in unison and in harmony).

0:00–0:08	**Introduction**, 4 mm.	Instrumental with lots of driving rhythm guitar, derived from bridge.
0:08–0:29	**A-Verse w/refrain**, 12 mm.	Mostly unison vocals, hand claps enter, "Oh yeah I'll tell you . . ."
0:29–0:51	**A-Verse w/refrain**, 12 mm.	As before, "Oh please, say to me . . ."
0:51–1:11	**B-Bridge**, 11 mm.	Unison until end, quieter to provide contrast, but building at end, "And when I touch you . . ."
1:11–1:33	**A-Verse w/refrain**, 12 mm.	As before, hand claps return, "Oh you got that somethin' . . ."
1:34–1:54	**B-Bridge**, 11 mm.	New two-part harmony vocals, quiet until the end as before, "And when I touch . . ."
1:54–2:22	**A-Verse** with tag, 15 mm.	As before, three bars added at ending, "Yeah you got that . . ."

in major cities. The Ku Klux Klan threatened violence at Beatles concerts and the band began to fear for their lives. As a result of this controversy, and the toll taken by constant work, the Beatles played their last public concert at San Francisco's Candlestick Park on August 29, 1966.

The Beatles' Music Develops: From Craftsmen to Artists. A clear development can be heard in the Beatles' music during the 1964–66 period. Early on the band seemed content to imitate U.S. models, combining diverse but nonetheless identifiable elements from earlier American music. This derivative music often took

American pop of the late 1950s and early '60s, blended it with some hallmark stylistic elements, and sold it back to Americans as British pop. The sources employed by the group tell us that much of the Beatles' music extends American traditions, and these surprising juxtapositions begin to mark the distinctive ways the band reinterpreted American rock and roll. The Beatles' first American hit, "I Want to Hold Your Hand," is a good example. The driving guitars, playing Chuck Berry–like chords in the low register, recall "Johnny B. Goode" or "Roll Over Beethoven," while the hand claps could have come from girl-group tunes of the early 1960s (such as "My Boyfriend's Back"). The duet singing in the song's bridge is reminiscent of the Everly Brothers, while the "ooo's" that became one of the Beatles' trademarks are lifted directly from Little Richard. The form of the song is AABA with abbreviated reprise—a structural design common in the music of Tin Pan Alley.

Much of the Beatles' music recorded in 1963–64 relies heavily on reworking a limited number of musical elements, most of which can be traced back to the band's earlier music. The group can hardly be faulted for this, since they anticipated their success would be fleeting and wrote and recorded quickly. In this context, it is impressive how much variety they achieved early on. The practice of producing songs according to a "formula" is an aspect of the craft of songwriting. Brill Building songwriters worked in precisely the same manner, as had the Tin Pan Alley songsmiths before them. Another approach employed by the Beatles is usually associated with classical-music composers from the nineteenth and twentieth centuries. Composers such as Beethoven, Brahms, or Schoenberg never solved the same musical problem in precisely the same way. Rather than finding a formula, these composers sought novel solutions for each piece of music. For the purposes of this discussion, we can therefore place craft and art in opposition and reveal something crucial about the Beatles' music and its effect on popular music. From 1964 to 1966, the Beatles increasingly moved away from the formulaic approach to songwriting and toward the artistic one. This transition began in very small ways, but by the time the band entered the studio in early 1966 for the sessions that produced *Revolver*, they had begun experimenting with studio effects, stylistic juxtapositions, and novel timbral and structural elements.

"Tomorrow Never Knows" is a good example of how far the Beatles had come in just over two years. The song is in simple verse form, built on a single 8-measure structure played nine times with no chorus. Lennon draws his lyrics from the *Tibetan Book of the Dead*, an ancient spiritual text that offers advice to those who will soon die (Lennon found the verses adapted in Timothy Leary's *The Psychedelic Experience*). The music creates a kind of static meditative drone, using a repetitive drumbeat and a limited number of chords. The strange sounds that occur throughout the work and especially during the instrumental verse include repeating fragments of prerecorded material created by looping a small piece of tape. These tape loops were manipulated to suggest an otherworldly sonic landscape and mixed into the final recording in real time. Because of the randomness of this procedure, the same result cannot have been easily duplicated either in the studio or in live performance. "Tomorrow Never Knows" is a one-time solution to the challenges presented by the ideas behind this particular track: the band did not repeat this exact approach in subsequent tracks (though other tape techniques were often employed). In this way, "Tomorrow Never Knows" is more art than craft.

Listening Guide

Get Music ⓢ wwnorton.com/studyspace

The Beatles, "Tomorrow Never Knows" Parlophone PMC-7009 (UK), Capital T-2576 (U.S.)

Words and music by John Lennon and Paul McCartney, produced by George Martin. Included on the album *Revolver*, which rose to #1 on the U.S. and UK album charts in 1966.

FORM: Simple verse, with each verse built on the same 8-bar structure. The droning of the bass makes the harmonic dimension of the music sound static, suggesting the influence of Indian music, while the tape loops, backward guitar, and processed lead vocals create an otherworldly atmosphere.

TIME SIGNATURE: 4/4. Notice the constant repeated notes in the bass, which interact with the repeated drum pattern, creating a rhythmic feel that seems unrelenting.

INSTRUMENTATION: Bass, sitar, drums, organ, backward guitar, tape loops, piano (at end), and electronically processed lead vocal.

0:00–0:12	**Introduction**, 4 mm.	Opens with sitar, then other instruments and tape loops enter. Note persistent but catchy drumbeat and drone bass.
0:12–0:26	**Verse 1**, 8 mm.	Vocals enter, tape loops slip in and out, "Turn off your mind . . ."
0:26–0:42	**Verse 2**, 8 mm.	As before, "Lay down all thoughts . . ."
0:42–0:56	**Verse 3**, 8 mm.	As before, "That you may see . . . "
0:56–1:12	**Instrumental Verse**, 8 mm.	Tape loops and then backward guitar prominently featured.
1:12–1:27	**Instrumental Verse**, 8 mm.	Continues loops and backward guitar.
1:27–1:42	**Verse 4**, 8 mm.	Vocals return, as before, "That love is all . . ."
1:42–1:57	**Verse 5**, 8 mm.	As before, "That ignorance and hate . . ."
1:57–2:13	**Verse 6**, 8 mm.	As before, "But listen to the color . . ."
2:13–2:55	**Verse 7 w/ tag and fade**, 20 mm.+	Fades out with piano, "Or play the game . . ."

The Growing Importance of Lyrics. The Beatles' tendencies toward a more artistic approach are also evident in their song lyrics. The words for "She Loves You," "I Want to Hold Your Hand," and "A Hard Day's Night" typify the band's early lyrics in their dedication to teenage love, and are no more suggestive than the songs by contemporary teen idols. The lyrics for songs like "Help!" and "Norwegian Wood," however, are far more unconventional. In "Help!" Lennon confesses that he has lost his confidence and needs to be reassured, looking back on his youth, when his own naïveté provided a self-confidence that maturity has stripped away. The story of "Norwegian Wood" concerns a one-night stand that leaves the singer sexually frustrated. In a surprising turn (like the one found in Chuck Berry's "Memphis") the singer then burns the apartment down, sarcastically admiring the quality of the wood as it goes up in flames. Most of the more ambitious lyrics came from Lennon, though McCartney's "Eleanor Rigby" paints a dark picture of alienation, perhaps influenced by the existentialist German students the band befriended in Hamburg. McCartney would follow this song with "She's Leaving Home" on *Sgt. Pepper's Lonely Hearts Club Band* (1967), proving any characterization of Lennon as the "lyric man" and McCartney as the "music man" to be overly facile and misleading. The Beatles' fascination with increasingly complex lyrics led them to print the complete lyrics on the album sleeve of *Sgt. Pepper*, a move that was uncommon among pop acts but has since become standard. The band's focus on lyrics was clearly influenced by folk music, especially the music of Bob Dylan. Dylan, whom the band met in 1964, was the first to challenge Lennon and McCartney to move past teenage love tunes. The folksinger is also perhaps responsible for introducing the Beatles to marijuana (though this claim has been disputed)—an event that would have tremendous influence on pop culture by 1967.

Developing Greater Stylistic Range. The Beatles' early songs incorporated American styles such as rhythm and blues, country and western, and girl group pop, but this began to change in 1965. The easiest way to observe this expansion of range is by looking at instrumentation. On *Help!* (1965), for example, Lennon's "You've Got to Hide Your Love Away" incorporates a flute and is clearly influenced by Dylan and the folk revival, while McCartney's "Yesterday" features string accompaniment that evokes German classicism. On *Rubber Soul* the folk influence became even more pronounced, with Harrison introducing a sitar into the band's sound on "Norwegian Wood." *Revolver* ranged even more widely, from McCartney's "Eleanor Rigby" to Lennon's "Tomorrow Never Knows" and from the children's song "Yellow Submarine" to the show-band horns of "Got to Get You into My Life." Being the most successful band in the world brought with it a certain freedom not usually extended to young pop musicians, and the Beatles were able to experiment much more than other bands. In taking advantage of this opportunity, they established a model for the rock musician as recording artist. The Beatles' progression from craft to art in this period marks a shift to greater seriousness and self-consciousness among rock musicians and their listeners, paving the way for something that would have seemed like an oxymoron earlier in the decade: rock culture. The next stage of the band's career, when the group's ambition extended even further, will be taken up in our discussion of psychedelia in Chapter 7.

THE BRITISH INVADE

Haircuts, Accents, and Guitars. In the wake of the Beatles' overwhelming American success in early 1964, a number of British bands flooded the U.S. charts. After the Beatles, the most prominent band was the Rolling Stones, a group that positioned itself as the bad boys of the British invasion. If the Beatles were charming, cute, and friendly, the Stones were sensual, dangerous, and often rude—in short, they were the anti-Beatles. In reality, the Stones and the Beatles were good friends and the individual members of these groups shared more similarities than differences. Other British bands of the time can be roughly divided into Beatles-type and Stones-type groups. Beatles-type bands such as Gerry and the Pacemakers and the Dave Clark Five were more pop and vocally oriented, while Stones-type groups like the Animals and the Yardbirds were more blues oriented. This split did not apply to all popular British bands in the United States, and bands such as the Who and the Kinks do not fit well into either category.

The term "British invasion" refers to UK groups who played guitars and, initially, wore long hair. Stylistically, there is a broad range of music within the British invasion, so while the term is useful as a general stylistic marker (these bands did have a number of things in common musically), it is most useful in terms of marketing and image. As discussed later in this chapter, the British invasion was clearly a fad at first. It hardly seemed to matter whether the music was influenced by the slick production of Motown or the direct expressiveness of Chess recordings. Initially, the Beatles and the British-invasion bands that followed in their wake drew a large portion of their audience from teenagers who, just a few years earlier, were listening to the teen idols of the early 1960s.

Gerry and the Pacemakers, the Dave Clark Five, and Other Beatles-type Bands. In retrospect we can see that the Beatles' success overshadows that of almost every other British band in the 1960s, but this was less obvious at the time. In the UK, Gerry and the Pacemakers were nearly as popular as the Beatles. The Pacemakers followed their 1964 number one, "How Do You Do It?" with two more chart-topping British singles that year: "I Like It" and "You'll Never Walk Alone." While the band eventually scored seven Top 40 hits in the United States through

1966, with "Don't Let the Sun Catch You Crying" rising as high as number four in summer 1964, they were never as popular in America as they were in Britain. London's Dave Clark Five was a Beatles-type band that fared better in the United States, with seven Top 40 American hits in 1964 alone, and nearly as many in 1965, including "Glad All Over" (p6 uk1, 1964) and "Over and Over" (p1 uk45, 1965). The success of the Dave Clark Five led some in the business to predict that they would topple the Beatles. (By the end of the 1964, however, the Beatles had nineteen Top 40 hits.) Two other Liverpool bands, Billy J. Kramer and the Dakotas and the Searchers, also did well in the United States, respectively placing four and five singles in the Top 40 in 1964. The fact that the music business was on the lookout for the next big thing while the Beatles were enjoying their first success reveals how widely rock music, or at least particular rock acts, were still viewed as passing fads. Many music business professionals at the time saw all these bands as pretty much the same act. In many ways, these professionals were right.

Herman's Hermits, Freddy and the Dreamers, and the Hollies. A second wave of Beatles-type Manchester bands began to hit U.S. shores in 1965. They were led by Herman's Hermits, whose "I'm Into Something Good" went to number thirteen in late 1964. The group followed this success with seventeen more Top 40 hits through 1968, including "Mrs. Brown You've Got a Lovely Daughter" (p1, 1965), "I'm Henry VIII, I Am" (p1, 1965), and "Listen People" (p3, 1966). The boyish good looks of singer Peter Noone made him an immediate teen heartthrob just when the Beatles were moving away from their mop top haircuts and pop image. Another Manchester group, Freddie and the Dreamers, topped the U.S. charts early in 1965 with "I'm Telling You Now," following with three more Top 40 hits that year. Singer Freddie Garrity took a cue from the Beatles' flair for comedy by performing a silly dance while singing "Do the Freddie" (p18, 1965). The Hollies also found popularity in America with the "Manchester sound," placing six hits in the U.S. Top 40, including "Bus Stop" (p5, 1966). The Hollies' music emphasized and expanded the precise harmony singing heard on many Beatles records, a feature that their lead vocalist, Graham Nash, would further develop with the group Crosby, Stills, and Nash at the end of the decade.

THE ROLLING STONES AND THE BRITISH BLUES REVIVAL

Bad Boys, Blues, and Rhythm and Blues. Following the lead of the Rolling Stones another group of British bands projected a more brash, nonconformist, and rebellious image. These groups depended less on the vocal- and song-oriented pop styles of the late '50s and early '60s. Instead, they drew on the 1950s Chicago electric blues tradition, featuring slide guitar, harmonica, and styles of vocal delivery that were indebted to Muddy Waters, Elmore James, and Little Walter. These blues-oriented bands emerged from a blues revival scene in the UK that flourished during the early 1960s and gained popularity in the United States after the Beatles broke into the American market. Despite the differences in musical style between the Beatles- and Stones-type bands, they were all packaged in the matching suits and haircuts ushered in by Beatlemania—even if some groups loosened their ties a bit more or lost parts of their outfits from time to time.

Blues Enthusiasts. The UK blues revival was mostly centered in London, and was fueled by the same British enthusiasm for American folk styles that had launched trad and skiffle. The catalysts for this scene were guitarist Alexis Korner and harmonica player Cyril Davies, who began playing blues during breaks at performances of Chris Barber's trad band. Korner and Davies soon began regular blues sessions in London's Marquee Club (which Barber owned) and later in the Ealing Club. Aspiring blues musicians would generally play cover versions of American electric blues, trying to emulate the sounds on the records as closely as possible. Recordings from 1962 of the Korner-Davies group, Blues Incorporated, demonstrate how faithful these cover versions were. American blues records were not easy to find in the UK, and the scarcity of these recordings led to trading and borrowing among members of the London-based blues culture—which further reinforced the subculture aspects of the UK blues revival. Many important musicians in the history of rock came up through the London blues scene, including John Mayall, Steve Winwood, Eric Clapton, Jack Bruce, and John McLaughlin. Among those who attended Davies and Korner's jam sessions were a pair of teenagers from London's Dartford suburb, guitarist Keith Richards and singer Mick Jagger. Hailing from Newcastle, the Animals were another blues-based band that enjoyed success in the UK and United States. Fronted by the powerful blues singing of Eric Burdon, the group initially played clubs in the north of England and even did a two-month stint at Hamburg's Star Club before moving to London in early 1964. The Animals got a crucial break when they were chosen to play on a UK tour featuring Chuck Berry as headliner. Figuring that they needed to make a strong musical impression on this important tour, the band closed their set with a slow traditional American folk-blues number, "House of the Rising Sun," calculating that it would be unwise to try to outrock Chuck Berry. Produced by Mickey Most (who would also produce Herman's Hermits), the single hit number six in the UK and number seven in the United States during the summer of 1964. The group followed with a string of international Most-produced hits, including a cover of Nina Simone's "Don't Let Me Be Misunderstood" (p15 uk3, 1965), Barry Mann and Cynthia Weil's "We've Gotta Get Out of This Place" (p13 uk2, 1965), and "It's My Life" (p23 uk7, 1965). After switching to producer Tom Wilson, the band continued to enjoy hit singles, including the traditional prison blues song "Inside Looking Out" (p34 uk12, 1966) and the Gerry Goffin–Carole King song "Don't Bring Me Down" (p12 uk6, 1966). By September the original Animals lineup had dissolved, although Burdon continued with new musicians as Eric Burdon and the Animals, while bassist Chas Chandler went on to manage Jimi Hendrix.

The Rolling Stones. While our current image of the Rolling Stones tends to focus on Jagger and Richards, in its first years the group was led by guitarist Brian Jones, a talented and dedicated student of American blues. The Rolling Stones were formed by Jones (and modeled after Blues Incorporated) to cover American blues records in the clubs of the London underground blues scene. Jagger and Richards were also enthusiastic fans of Chuck Berry, although this music was viewed with some suspi-

Listening Guide

The Animals, "House of the Rising Sun" Columbia OB 7301 (UK), London 45-LON 9766 (U.S.)

Also known as "Rising Sun Blues," the music and text of this song are based on a traditional ballad, which dates back at least to the early nineteenth century. Early recordings exist by Clarence "Tom" Ashley (1932) and Leadbelly (1948). The Animals version was arranged by Alan Price and produced by Mickie Most. It reached #1 on the U.S. *Billboard* "Hot 100" and UK *Record Retailer* charts in 1964.

FORM: Simple verse.

TIME SIGNATURE: 6/8. Throughout the song each chord change is held for two "big" beats.

INSTRUMENTATION: Electric guitar, bass guitar, drums, electric organ, lead vocals.

0:00–0:11	**Introduction**, 8 mm.	Featuring the guitar and bass, the introduction comes from the last eight measures of the verse structure.
0:11–0:46	**Verse 1,** 22 mm.	Each verse consists of a pattern of chords that seems to continually rise and then stabilize twice, forming two phrases. The first phrase is eight measures ("There is a house . . .") and the second fourteen measures ("It's been the ruin . . ."). Note how the second phrase seems to "skip" two measures, beginning the eight-measure instrumental interlude and introduction music two measures early.

cion by dedicated blues aficionados like Jones. The group got its start in July 1962 filling in for Blues Incorporated at the Marquee and later played regularly at the Ealing Club. By January 1963 bassist Bill Wyman and drummer Charlie Watts had joined forces with Jones, Jagger, Richards, and pianist Ian Stewart. Excitement for the band's live performances started to build when they established a regular weekly gig at the Richmond Crawdaddy Club in February. The club's manager, Giorgio Gomelsky, managed the group during its early days and helped the Stones build a strong following at the Crawdaddy. In May 1963, Andrew Loog Oldham and Eric Easton took over management of the band. Easton was experienced in the recording industry and Oldham had worked as a publicist for Larry Parnes and Brian Epstein (he had helped promote Gerry and the Pacemakers and Billy J. Kramer).

The Stones turned toward a more mainstream, pop-oriented style in the wake of the Beatles' first UK success in mid-1963. The two groups knew one another and were friendly, although the Beatles were by far the more successful and experienced group. The Stones recorded for Decca and were signed by Dick Rowe, "the man who turned down the Beatles." Before they were signed, Rowe was judging a talent contest in Liverpool on a panel that included George Harrison. After apologizing

Get Music ⓢ wwnorton.com/studyspace

Time	Section	Description
0:46–1:20	**Verse 2**, 22 mm.	The story of the song recalls a myth of gambling and prostitution in New Orleans, showing the Animals' interest in American folklore.
1:20–1:53	**Verse 3**, 22 mm.	This verse emphasizes the difficulty of a gambler's lifestyle, reflecting on (and arguably glorifying) an unstable upbringing.
1:53–2:27	**Verse (Instrumental)**, 22 mm.	Solo section featuring the organ playing of Alan Price.
2:27–3:00	**Verse 4**, 22 mm.	A confessional verse, during which the protagonist takes on a type of religious fervor. Is this an invitation to the "House," or an admonition to stay away?
3:00–3:34	**Verse 5**, 22 mm.	Note the intensity created by the strumming guitar at the opening of the verse, which parallels the decision to return to New Orleans in the text.
3:34–4:04	**Verse 6**, 22 mm.	The repeated lyrics from verse 1 help to depict circularity in both the gambling lifestyle, to which addicts return again and again, and a cycle of abuse that passes from parents to their children. Note the intensity of the music at the end. As a song in simple verse form, the growing dynamic levels help to define the action.
4:04–4:30	**Postlude**, 16 mm.	Just after the most intense part of the song, the postlude helps to "wind down" the intensity level almost to a halt.

to Harrison about not signing the Beatles, he asked whether Harrison knew any up-and-coming groups. Harrison enthusiastically endorsed the Stones and Rowe immediately sought them out at the Crawdaddy. Oldham and Easton negotiated an unprecedented deal with Decca, specifying that while the label would have exclusive rights to distribute the band's recordings, the Stones would retain ownership of their recordings. Oldham got the idea of retaining these rights from a conversation with Phil Spector when the American producer was in the UK. Although he had no experience in the recording studio, Oldham immediately assumed the additional role of producer for the band. With Oldham in charge of the group's recording sessions, the Rolling Stones relied on engineers for technical support and enjoyed extensive creative freedom in the studio. This led to the group cultivating a rough sound on record, which matched their brash style of performance.

Initially, the Stones did not write their own music. Their first single was a cover version of Chuck Berry's "Come On" (uk21, 1963) and their third was a cover of Buddy Holly's "Not Fade Away" (uk3, 1964). The band's second single was a song Lennon and McCartney wrote for them, "I Wanna Be Your Man" (uk12, 1963), which both groups recorded. (Comparing the two versions reveals an interesting

The pandemonium of rock shows could sometimes turn violent. This photo shows a Zurich crowd getting out of hand in April 1967 at a Rolling Stones concert. Considering the manic quality of many of these events, it seems remarkable that such chaos did not break out more often.

contrast between these two bands in their early years: the Stones version shows much more of a blues influence, with a loose arrangement that prominently features the slide guitar, and the Beatles' version is tightly arranged and focuses on the vocals.) Quickly understanding the financial advantages that writing music could provide, Oldham decided that Jagger and Richards, who had become the leaders of the group, should try their hand at songwriting, reportedly locking them in a room until they wrote a song. "The Last Time" was the first of many Jagger-Richards hits, reaching number one in the UK in 1965 (p9). The budding songwriting team also had an international hit in 1964 with Marianne Faithfull's recording of "As Tears Go By" (p22 uk9). While the Stones would increasingly record more Jagger-Richards songs, their first six albums contain more cover versions than originals, and reveal the band's dedication to American rhythm and blues artists such as Muddy Waters, Jimmy Reed, and Bo Diddley, among others. Two early hit singles show the band's range of influences: "It's All Over Now" (p26 uk1, 1964) was originally recorded by African-American vocalist Bobby Womack, and the Stones give it a country and western feel, while Chicago bluesman Willie Dixon's "Little Red Rooster" (uk1, 1964) is a slow blues tune.

The Stones enjoyed great popularity in the UK in late 1963 and through 1964 but this success did not extend to the United States, where the Beatles, Gerry and the Pacemakers, and the Dave Clark Five were much more warmly received. Late in 1964 things began to improve, with "Time Is on My Side" hitting number six in the United States and "The Last Time" reaching number nine in spring 1965 (r19). The Stones' slow start in the United States was partly due to the group's bad-boy image. Oldham had bought the Stones matching outfits when he took over, but the band soon lost or hopelessly soiled parts of these stage clothes—and not entirely by accident. The Stones rode to fame in the UK as the antithesis of the Beatles,

Listening Guide   Get Music Ⓢ wwnorton.com/studyspace

The Rolling Stones, "(I Can't Get No) Satisfaction"
Decca F12220 (UK), London 45-LON 9766 (U.S.)

Words and music by Mick Jagger and Keith Richards, produced by Andrew Loog Oldham. Reached #1 on the U.S. *Billboard* "Hot 100" and UK *Record Retailer* charts in 1965.

FORM: Contrasting verse-chorus. Each chorus is followed by two measures that repeat the opening riff and lead back to the next verse, except at the end, where this riff is used to create the ending of the song. Note that the song features a reprise of the introduction at the end, similarly to The Ronettes' "Be My Baby" (see Listening Guide in Chapter 3).

TIME SIGNATURE: 4/4 throughout, with each beat punctuated by a snare hit.

INSTRUMENTATION: Electric and acoustic guitars, bass guitar, tambourine, drums, lead and backing vocals.

0:00–0:15	**Introduction**, 8 mm.	Focused on the main riff of the chorus. Note the way the instruments enter one at a time in this order: electric guitar, bass, drums, acoustic guitar, and tambourine.
0:15–0:42	**Chorus**, 16 mm.	The multi-section chorus begins with an calm 8-measure statement, and is followed by two shorter four-measure group vocal sections ("Cause I try . . ." followed by "I can't get no . . .").
0:42–1:16	**Verse 1**, 18 mm.	"When I'm driving in my car. . . ." Each multi-section verse begins with ten measures explaining a frustrating situation, followed by two four-measure refrains ("I can't get no . . ." followed by "No, no, no . . .")
1:16–1:42	**Chorus**, 16 mm.	The chorus section seems to project less energy in this song, which is the opposite of its usual role. This is especially evident at the beginning of each chorus, when the intensity drops.
1:42–2:15	**Verse 2**, 18 mm.	"When I'm watching my TV . . ."
2:15–2:43	**Chorus**, 16 mm.	Notice how Jagger changes the lyrics from "satisfaction" to "girl reaction."
2:43–3:16	**Verse 3**, 18 mm.	"When I'm riding 'round the world . . ."
3:16–	**Postlude**, 16 mm.	This repeated section reveals the rhythm and blues influence on the Stones. Jagger improvises over the main riff, accelerating the intensity while the song fades out.

sporting scruffier clothing, longer hair, and rebellious attitudes that shocked adults. This, of course, was the key to the Stones' appeal for many young people in Britain. That appeal would soon spread to the United States, starting with an American tour in late 1964 which generated several stories portraying the band as rock and roll troublemakers.

The Stones solidified their image as rock's bad boys with the single "(I Can't Get No) Satisfaction," which, driven by Richards's fuzz-guitar introduction, hit number one in the United States and the UK in summer 1965 (r19). Although the song's lyrics clearly express a general dissatisfaction with the superficiality of daily life, a rumor circulated that the topic of the song was masturbation, perhaps owing to the last verse, which refers to menstruation and a resultant sexual frustration. Jagger and Richards did little to calm the storm over the record, since the rumor fit well into the anti-Beatles image the band was now cultivating. What could be better, after all, than a thin, swaggering Mick Jagger singing a song about something many American kids and their parents regarded—publicly at least—as a forbidden pleasure? The Stones followed with "Get Off of My Cloud" (p1 uk1, 1965), "As Tears Go By" (p6, 1966), "19th Nervous Breakdown" (p2 uk2, 1966), and "Paint It Black" (p1 uk1, 1966). As the group's popularity rose in the United States, they appeared on American television and toured with increasing success. Unfortunately, as an outgrowth of the band's rebellious image, their shows were often marked by fan riots and police interventions. After experiencing what was becoming the standard fan mania during the band's first appearance on his show in 1965, Ed Sullivan vowed the Stones would never return. By 1967, however, Sullivan had changed his mind, but in a situation reminiscent of Elvis Presley's appearances, the group was asked to change the chorus of "Let's Spend the Night Together" to "let's spend some time together." Jagger did not change the lyric, but rather mumbled it.

The Stones and the Blues Tradition. Considering the importance of blues music for the Stones, it is somewhat surprising that the majority of 12-bar blues in their mid-1960s repertoire consists of cover versions. ("19th Nervous Breakdown," which does employ the twelve-bar pattern, is one important exception.) Jagger-Richards originals tend to be influenced more by Chuck Berry and Motown than by Muddy Waters or Howlin' Wolf. This may reflect Jagger's opinion, expressed during the band's first years of success, that the idea of a blues song being written by a white Brit was preposterous. Whatever the reason, "Satisfaction" illustrates an approach used often by Jagger and Richards. The strong riff and Jagger's improvisation during the song's final seconds are clearly reminiscent of the blues, but the song's complex form is more indebted to non-blues popular styles. While the Beatles employed mostly AABA forms of Brill Building pop, Jagger and Richards preferred the contrasting verse-chorus form found in Chuck Berry and Buddy Holly's music. "Satisfaction" is the same contrasting verse-chorus form as Holly's "That'll Be the Day" and Berry's "Rock and Roll Music."

This photo from January 1965 shows Keith Relf, the lead singer of the Yardbirds, playing blues harmonica with Paul Samwell-Smith and Chris Dreja (background) during a gig at Woolwich.

By the summer of 1967, the original Animals lineup had dissolved and lead singer Eric Burdon forged ahead with a new band. The concert advertised on this poster featured Burdon, 1950s legend Chuck Berry—showing the continuing connection between classic rock and roll and the British invasion—and the Steve Miller Band, who would enjoy considerable success in the 1970s.

The Yardbirds and Other UK Blues Revivalists. When the Stones gave up their regular date at the Crawdaddy Club in Richmond in 1963, the Yardbirds took their place, and also took on Gomelsky as a manager. The group initially consisted of Keith Relf on vocals and harmonica, Paul Samwell-Smith on bass, Jim McCarty on drums, and Chris Dreja and Tony Topham on guitar, but Topham was soon replaced by lead guitarist Eric Clapton. Clapton earned his nickname "Slowhand" during these early years because he often broke guitar strings and had to change them onstage, as audience members joked with him about it by providing slow applause. Initially, the group was even more devoted to the blues tradition than the Stones had been, and Clapton was especially uncompromising in his resistance to pop music at the time. The Yardbirds developed long, improvisatory passages at the end of songs that they called "rave-ups"; these emphasized the instrumental prowess of band members (Clapton especially) and were forerunners to the instrumental jam sessions that would characterize much rock music later in the decade. An example of this can be heard at the end of the band's version of Howlin' Wolf's "Smokestack Lightning," recorded at the Marquee and released on the album *Five Live Yardbirds* in December 1964.

Gomelsky had hopes that the Yardbirds could follow the Stones' model as hitmakers, but the band's first two UK singles performed disappointingly: "I Wish You Would" failed to chart and "Good Morning Little Schoolgirl" rose only as high as number forty-four. Deciding that the group needed a sure-fire pop hit, Gomelsky (who was not only managing but also producing the band, with Samwell-Smith acting as musical director), acquired songwriter Graham Gouldman's "For Your Love" for the Yardbirds. The verses of the tune primarily use studio musicians, with the band playing as a whole only during the middle bridge section. While session musicians often played on pop records, this concession was more than Clapton could bear. After "For Your Love" was finished the guitarist left the Yardbirds to join John Mayall and the Bluesbreakers. The Yardbirds' single rose to number six in the United States and number three in the UK in the first half of 1965. Jeff Beck replaced Clapton on lead guitar and his more experimental nature can be heard on the group's follow-up single, "Heart Full of Soul" (p9 uk2, 1965). Beck uses a fuzztone to create the tune's distinctive guitar **lick**, a technique Keith Richards would use on "Satisfaction." ("Heart Full of Soul" was recorded on April 20, 1965, while "Satisfaction" was recorded three weeks later on May 12, 1965.) "Heart Full of Soul," also written by Gouldman, reached number nine in the United States and number two in the UK in the summer of 1965.

While Clapton felt the band had not remained true to its blues roots, the other members of the Yardbirds might not have agreed. The band was especially excited to record their first original single, "Shapes of Things" (p3 uk11, 1966), at the Chess studios in Chicago, where they also recorded a cover of Bo Diddley's "I'm a Man." At Sam Phillips's new recording studio (the successor to Sun Studios) in Memphis, the Yardbirds recorded a version of "Train Kept a Rollin'," a Memphis rockabilly track most often associated with the Johnny Burnette Rock and Roll Trio version of 1956. In spring 1966, Simon Napier-Bell and Paul Samwell-Smith took over production duties from Gomelsky, resulting in the band's last hit single, "Over, Under, Sideways, Down" (p13 uk10). In June, Samwell-Smith left the band to devote himself to producing, and session guitarist Jimmy Page was brought in. Page initially played bass, but by the fall Dreja switched to bass, leaving Beck and Page to share the lead-guitar spot. In October, Beck left the Yardbirds, going on to form the Jeff Beck Group, while Page, Dreja, Relf, and McCarty kept the Yardbirds alive until the summer of 1968, when they disbanded. Page formed a new group to fulfill the remaining dates the Yardbirds had booked: Led Zeppelin.

Not all the blues-based bands playing the London clubs achieved chart success. Perhaps the busiest band on the London scene was Georgie Fame and the Blue Flames—which at various times featured guitarist John McLaughlin and drum-

Led by brothers Ray and Dave Davies, the Kinks blended elements of the Beatles and the Rolling Stones. This photo from December 1965 shows Dave Davies (left), Pete Quaife (back), Mick Avory (front), and Ray Davies (right) performing on television.

Listening Guide   Get Music ⓢ wwnorton.com/studyspace

The Kinks, "You Really Got Me" Pye 7N 15673 (UK), Reprise 0306 (U.S.)

Words and music by Ray Davies, produced by Shel Talmy. Reached #1 on the UK *Record Retailer* and #7 on the *Billboard* "Hot 100" in the United States in 1964.

FORM: Simple verse form, with repeated 20-bar verses built on a two-chord pattern that is repeated progressively higher on the guitar providing a sense of growing tonal intensification as the verse proceeds. This two-chord pattern is not transposed during the guitar solo, and a comparison of that partial verse with the other complete ones highlights this tonal difference.

TIME SIGNATURE: 4/4. Note the use of repeated piano chords and tambourine to underscore the beat and its division in two parts (simple time).

INSTRUMENTATION: Electric guitars, piano, bass, drums, tambourine, lead and backup vocals. While this track is professionally produced, the backup vocals give it a wild and almost amateurish quality, an impression reinforced by the manic but relatively primitive guitar solo.

0:00–0:07	**Introduction**, 4 mm.	Starts with 1-bar guitar figure played twice, then band enters. Note the distorted tone in the guitar.
0:07–0:42	**Verse 1 w/refrain**, 20 mm.	Vocals enter. Note how the verse builds, first with solo vocal, then with added piano, then with added backup vocals, also getting increasingly louder to drive to the refrain, "Girl, you really got me . . ."
0:42–1:17	**Verse 2 w/refrain**, 20 mm.	As before, "See, don't ever set . . ."
1:17–1:34	**Instrumental verse** (partial), 10 mm.	Guitar solo as the music breaks into a controlled frenzy.
1:34–2:12	**Verse 2 w/refrain**, 20 mm.	Repeats lyrics of second verse, last two bars changed to create ending.

mer Mitch Mitchell, who would later play with Jimi Hendrix. Fame, who was born Clive Powell but renamed by Larry Parnes in the early 1960s, scored several UK hits, including two number ones: "Yeh Yeh" (p21) in 1965 and "Get Away" in 1966. Other bands on the scene included the Graham Bond Organization, featuring Jack Bruce, future Cream drummer Ginger Baker, and McLaughlin; and Zoot Money's Big Roll Band, featuring future Police guitarist Andy Summers. The Spencer Davis Group, with organist Steve Winwood, scored two chart-topping UK hits, "Keep On Runnin'" (1965) and "Somebody Help Me" (1966), before hitting internationally with "Gimme Some Lovin'" (p7 uk2, 1966) and "I'm a Man" (p10 uk9, 1967).

The Who were embraced by the British Mod movement in the mid-1960s. This live shot from a March 1966 television shoot shows the snappy fashion so typical of Mods. Band members are (from left to right) John Entwhistle, Roger Daltrey, Keith Moon, and Pete Townshend.

The Kinks and the Who: Raw Power and Ambitious Lyrics. The Beatles- and Stones-type labels obviously cannot be applied to all British bands from the 1960s. The most important among the bands that defy such strict categorization are the Kinks and the Who. The Kinks emerged from the same rhythm and blues roots as the Stones-type groups but performed mostly with package tours that featured more pop-oriented acts. The Who claimed no real roots in the blues but played the London rhythm and blues clubs regularly. Like the Beatles, both bands depended on members' strong songwriting for their best material (Ray Davies for the Kinks and Pete Townshend for the Who); and like the Stones, both groups emphasized the raw power and rhythmic drive of American rhythm and blues.

Formed in 1963, the Kinks featured brothers Ray and Dave Davies on guitar and vocals, with Peter Quaife on bass and Mick Avory on drums. Both Davies brothers had played in various blues-oriented groups around London, while Avory had been one of the first drummers for the Rolling Stones. The Kinks benefited early on from an aggressive management team and the production talents of Australian Shel Talmy. The band's first two singles, released in the first half of 1964, did not chart. Their third single, "You Really Got Me," went to number one in the UK and number seven in the United States in fall 1964. The Kinks' aggressive pop approach can be heard in the opening guitar chords of "You Really Got Me," and in the wild guitar solo in the middle of the track. A series of original songs followed, including "All Day and All of the Night" (p7 uk2, 1964), "Tired of Waiting for You" (p6 uk1, 1965), and "Till the End of

Sound Check

Artist	The Beatles	The Beatles	The Rolling Stones	
Title	I Want to Hold Your Hand	Tomorrow Never Knows	(I Can't Get No) Satisfaction	
Chart peak	p1, uk1 1964	1966	p1, uk1 1965	
Form	AABA	Simple verse	Contrasting verse-chorus	
Rhythm	4/4	4/4	4/4	
Instrumentation	Electric guitar Bass Drums Two-part lead vocal Hand claps	Backward guitar Bass Drums Lead vocal Piano Organ Sitar Tape loops	Electric guitar Acoustic guitar Bass Drums Lead vocal Background vocal Tambourine	
Comments	Each verse ends in a 4-bar refrain Two-part vocal alternate between unison (or singing the same thing) and harmony Mersey Beat: Emphasis in beats two and four (listen in handclaps)	Atmosphere created by droning bass, tape loops, sitar, and processed lead vocals Influence of Indian music Guitar sound created by playing recorded guitar backwards	Two-measure riff is the basis for the song's musical structure Instruments enter one at a time Chorus has multiple sections	

the Day" (p50 uk6, 1965). As the Beatles grew more serious and ambitious with their lyrics in 1965, so did Davies: his "A Well-Respected Man" (p13, 1965) and "Dedicated Follower of Fashion" (p36 uk4, 1966) offered clever and biting critiques of 1960s culture.

Initially formed in 1962 as the Detours, the Who combined the guitar playing and songwriting of Pete Townshend with the singing of Roger Daltrey, the assertive bass playing of John Entwistle, and the manic drumming of Keith Moon. Although they eventually became one of the most important bands in the history of rock music, the Who did not exert much influence in America until the late 1960s. Their series of UK hit singles during the mid-1960s never made the U.S. Top 40, and the band's success was restricted to Britain until the release of "I Can See for Miles," which went to number nine in the United States in the fall of 1967. Like the Kinks,

The Animals	The Kinks
House of the Rising Sun	You Really Got Me
p1, uk1 1965	p7, uk1 1964
Simple verse	Simple verse
6/8	4/4
Electric guitar Bass Drums Lead vocal Organ	Electric guitar Bass Drums Lead Vocal Background vocals Piano Tambourine
Odd, 22-measure verse structure (8 + 14) The song becomes more intense throughout, echoing the story Based on a traditional American ballad	Two-measure riff is the basis for the song's musical structure Frenzied guitar solo Amateurish background vocals

the Who's early singles were produced by Shel Talmy. Their first single, "I Am the Face," was released under the name the High Numbers in summer 1964 and failed to chart. In 1965, now performing as the Who and recording Townshend's songs, the band scored a series of top UK hits, including "I Can't Explain" (uk8, 1965), "Anyway, Anyhow, Anywhere" (uk10, 1965), "My Generation" (uk2, 1965), "Substitute" (uk5, 1966), "I'm a Boy" (uk2, 1966), and "Happy Jack" (uk3, 1966; p24, 1967). Appearing every Tuesday for six months at the Marquee Club during 1964–65, the group billed its music as "maximum R&B" and quickly became popular among the Mod subculture in London.

The Mod movement never made it to the United States, although "the Mods" were a significant faction within the London youth culture of the mid-1960s. Mods listened to American rhythm and blues and Jamaican ska and Blue Beat, dressed in very particular ways, worked but disdained advancement, often rode motorscooters, and danced late into the night—frequently under the influence of amphetamines—at select London clubs such as the Scene. Mods often conflicted with "rockers," who rode motorcycles and wore leather jackets after the style of Marlon Brando in *The Wild One* (1953). The animosity between these two factions was serious enough for riots to break out, with mods and rockers fighting openly in the streets of Brighton, a quiet seaside resort town, in the summer of 1964. The mod scene and lifestyle is captured in the Who's 1973 album *Quadrophenia*, a concept album in which the Brighton Beach rumble plays a crucial role, and in the 1979 movie of the same name. By the late 1960s, Townshend's songwriting had become increasingly ambitious, and this progression through *Tommy* and on to *Quadrophenia* will be taken up in Chapter 8.

THE MOP TOPS THREATEN THE BIG WIGS

The rise of the Beatles transformed popular music in at least two significant ways. First, it opened doors for British acts within the UK, allowing British artists to reclaim their own popular-music charts and reap the benefits of domestic success. This revitalized British popular music in a fundamental way. Second, the success of the Beatles in America—and indeed, the world—opened new opportunities for British acts outside the UK. Considering the broad stylistic range of the British bands that succeeded in the United States in the wake of the Beatlemania, it is clear that for many young Americans the British invasion was as much about fashion as it was about music. Strictly in terms of musical style, a Beatles concert and a Yardbirds concert were quite different. But in the eyes of the American fans, the groups were part of the same trend. The British invasion was initially a fad in which music was only one factor. For our purposes, distinguishing between pop-oriented (Beatles-style) groups and blues-oriented (Stones-style) groups helps to organize the music of the British invasion along music-stylistic lines that can be placed within the broader context of music before 1964 and after 1966. The most important aspect of the British invasion is that it established a more equal footing within American popular music for U.S. and British artists. The musical cross-fertilization between the United States and the UK has been a prominent feature of popular music in both countries ever since.

Rock historians often emphasize the impact of the Beatles on the American scene in early 1964 and the subsequent flood of British bands. While it is clear that the UK bands pushed many American groups off the charts, the 1964 *Billboard* pop charts show that domestic music continued to enjoy success even after the British arrived, including records by Phil Spector, the Beach Boys, and a host of Motown artists. While the dividing line of February 1964 is convenient for articulating changes within popular music at the time, it is only a rough boundary. In the next chapter we will see how American musicians reacted to the Brits and what the American music business did to gain back its lost market share.

FURTHER READING

Tony Bacon, *London Live* (Miller-Freeman Books, 1999).

Walter Everett, *The Beatles as Musicians:* Revolver *through the* Anthology (Oxford University Press, 1998).

Walter Everett, *The Beatles as Musicians: The Quarry Men through* Rubber Soul (Oxford University Press, 2001).

Dave McAleer, *The Fab British Rock 'n' Roll Invasion of 1964* (St. Martin's Press, 1994).

Barry Miles, *The British Invasion: The Music, The Times, The Era* (Sterling, 2009).

Philip Norman, *The Stones* (Penguin, 1993).

Philip Norman, *Shout! The Beatles in Their Generation* (Simon & Schuster, 2006).

James E. Perone, *Mods, Rockers, and the Music of the British Invasion* (Praeger, 2008).

Roberta Freund Schwartz, *How Britain Got the Blues: The Transmission and Reception of American Blues Style in the United Kingdom* (Ashgate, 2007).

Harry Shapiro, *Alexis Korner: The Biography* (Bloomsbury, 1996).

Gordon Thompson, *Please, Please Me: Sixties British Pop, Inside Out* (Oxford, 2008).

Bill Wyman with Ray Coleman, *Stone Alone: The Story of a Rock 'n' Roll Band* (Da Capo, 1997)

VISIT STUDYSPACE AT WWNORTON.COM/STUDYSPACE

Access free review material such as:

- music links
- performer info
- practice quizzes
- outlines
- interactive listening guide software

COLUMBIA

45
RPM

THE
BYRDS

4-43271
RZSP 72245
2:18

MR. TAMBOURINE MAN
B. Dylan
Produced by Terry Melcher
® "COLUMBIA 🅜 MARCAS REG PRINTED IN USA

AMERICAN RESPONSES

The reaction of American teenagers to the music of the Beatles in early 1964 is easy to document. Although the term "Beatlemania" had been coined in the UK in 1963 to describe the reaction of British fans to the Beatles' music, it is an even more apt description of the reaction in the United States. Chapter 4 described the enormous commercial success enjoyed by the Beatles, the Rolling Stones, and a host of other British groups during 1964–66. This chapter will focus on the response of American musicians and the American popular music business to the competition offered by the Brits, showing that this reaction was not nearly as immediate as the one found among fans. In fact, British bands did not erase all American pop acts from the charts, and many groups who had hit records during 1963 continued to have success, seemingly undiminished by the enormous popularity of the Beatles and other British groups. Phil Spector, the Beach Boys, the Four Seasons, and most artists on the Motown label, for instance, vied neck-and-neck with the foreign invaders for top chart positions and radio airtime.

By the summer of 1965, new musical styles in American pop were emerging as a result of the cross-fertilization of American styles with the Mersey beat. Folk rock is perhaps the most obvious example. Led by the Byrds and Bob Dylan, folk rock took the easy strumming-and-singing texture of folk and added electric guitars, bass, drums, and (occasionally) keyboards to create an American music-stylistic reaction to the British invasion. It is easy to see how and why this happened. Many young American musicians had learned to accompany themselves (usually on guitar) during the folk revival. Moreover, during their early years on the charts the Beatles were essentially a guitar-oriented vocal group. Many performers who sang and harmonized about social injustice to the accompaniment of the acoustic guitar or banjo made an easy transition to the electric guitar and bass. Emulating the Beatles' and Stones' guitar-dominated sound, a slew of garage bands formed across the country, most with only minimal musical skills that tended not to impede their enthusiasm.

The Byrds' distinctive version of Bob Dylan's "Mr. Tambourine Man," frequently cited as the first folk-rock hit, was part of an American response to the British invasion. While the Byrds were steeped in the music of the American folk revival, they were also influenced by the Beatles' early music. After seeing *A Hard Day's Night*, the group added an electric twelve-string guitar to their already refined vocal harmonies, blending the Beatles, Dylan, the Kingston Trio, and a touch of surf music to create a trans-Atlantic number one hit in the summer of 1965. Although the Byrds played as a band on subsequent releases, the only member of the group to play an instrument on this first single was Roger McGuinn, who played the electric twelve-string. With the Byrds providing the vocals and McGuinn adding his jingle-jangle guitar sound, the rest of the music was performed by Los Angeles studio musicians—a group of top professionals who went by the nickname "The Wrecking Crew."

New York was the center of the American pop music scene in the early 1960s, but after 1964, much of the most popular new music emerged from Los Angeles (on New York–based record labels). Many folk rockers made their way from New York's Greenwich Village to Los Angeles, and by 1965 the Hollywood-based television industry was becoming a factor in the music business with several pop-music variety shows aimed at America's teens. These included a show hosted by Paul Revere and the Raiders, who underlined the idea of an American response by donning Revolutionary War costumes. The American response was heightened in 1966, when the industry put forward its most direct answer to the Beatles: the Monkees. The music business may have been surprised in 1964 by the overwhelming success of the Brits, but by mid-1965 American bands were again scoring significant chart successes by imitating British bands and adapting tried-and-true music-business practices.

FOLK ROCK

Dylan Plugs In. In December 1960, a young folksinger arrived in New York from Minnesota, where he had been playing gigs in folk clubs and coffeehouses. Within a few months, Bob Dylan was performing in Greenwich Village and becoming increasingly active in the city's burgeoning folk scene. By the beginning of 1964, he was among the most respected young folksingers in the United States. Dylan was not particularly well known outside the folk community, since the general pop audience associated "folk" with the music of the Kingston Trio or Peter, Paul, and Mary. Some pop listeners might have known that Dylan wrote "Blowin' in the Wind" and "Don't Think Twice It's Alright" (both hits in 1963 for Peter, Paul, and Mary), but most would not have heard Dylan's own versions, which appear on his second album, *The Freewheelin' Bob Dylan* (p22 uk16, 1963). Like many folk artists, he enjoyed success mostly on the album charts and only had the occasional hit single. Dylan's popularity, fueled by appearances in folk clubs and on college campuses, was greater in the UK than in the United States. By 1964 his albums *The Times They Are A-Changin'* (p20 uk20, 1964) and *Another Side of Bob Dylan* (p43, uk8 1964) did well enough on both sides of the Atlantic to make him one of the most emulated folksingers of this period.

Dylan was a skilled performer and an even more accomplished songwriter. It was common for folksingers to write their own music, often creating new songs from tunes drawn or adapted from traditional folk melodies. Dylan's idol Woody Guthrie frequently reworked familiar music with new lyrics that chronicled social injustice. Dylan initially followed this model, creating topical songs such as "Blowin' in the Wind," which addressed civil rights, and "Masters of War," which challenged the Vietnam conflict. Dylan's songs, however, became increasingly focused on his own feelings and attempts to understand the world. Early songs such as "Girl from the North Country" and "Don't Think Twice It's Alright" display his exceptional gifts as a songwriter. The personal lyrics of these songs are crafted with the painstaking aesthetic attitude more common among poets than musicians.

After an enormously successful tour of the UK in 1965 (documented in the D.A. Pennebaker film *Don't Look Back*), Dylan made a break with the folk tradition that would have tremendous consequences for popular music. Contrary to the folk revival orthodoxy, he had long been interested in using electric instruments in his music and a few sessions for his second album had been recorded with what was essentially a rock band; he even tried out a version of "That's All Right (Mama)." Dylan was not satisfied with the results of these sessions and only one of the resulting tracks was used on the album ("Corrina, Corrina"). (Another of these songs, "Mixed Up Confusion," became his first single, but it did not chart when released in 1962.) Dylan's interest in rock instrumentation was also evident on his album *Bringin' It All Back Home* (p6 uk1, 1965), half of which used electric instruments, including his first hit single, "Subterranean Homesick Blues" (p39 uk9, 1965). The folk community did not express an overwhelmingly negative reaction to Dylan's electrified music when the album was released perhaps because of the strong acoustic-based material. However, when he played the Newport Folk Festival in July 1965 an enormous controversy began. As a headliner, Dylan was one of the most sought after artists at the festival. The festival program only allotted Dylan a short set, and he performed three electric numbers ("Maggie's Farm," "Like a Rolling Stone," and "Phantom Engineer") backed by the Paul Butterfield Blues Band. When he left the stage after only a few songs, the crowd heckled Master of Ceremonies Peter Yarrow (of Peter, Paul, and Mary) until Dylan came back out. As an encore, Dylan performed acoustic versions of "Mr. Tambourine Man" and "It's All Over Now Baby Blue." Despite the positive reaction to his acoustic material, Dylan's electric numbers met with resistance among the more traditionally minded folkies in attendance. Many senior members of the folk establishment who had strongly supported Dylan up to this point (including Pete Seeger) felt betrayed by his turn to electric instruments. Dylan's insistence upon performing nontopical material with a rock band, made him the target of very strong criticism within folk circles.

Bob Dylan first made his name as a folksinger, strongly influenced by the music and image of Woody Guthrie. As a folk revivalist who addressed issues of social, economic, and political injustice, Dylan developed a reputation for delivering "finger-wagging songs" that brought attention to such issues. In this picture, a young Dylan is shown performing at a voter registration drive in 1963.

Listening Guide

Get Music ⑤ **wwnorton.com/studyspace**

Bob Dylan, "Positively 4th Street" Columbia 43389

Words and music by Bob Dylan, produced by Bob Johnston. Rose to #7 on the *Billboard* "Hot 100" (uk8) in the fall of 1965.

FORM: Simple verse. Like many Dylan songs, this song has a lot of lyrics. In this case, Dylan delivers 12 verses over the same 8-bar structure, without much change in the accompaniment. In contrast to the technique of building an arrangement by adding instruments or vocal parts as the song progresses, this track remains static, leaving the listener to focus on the lyrics.

TIME SIGNATURE: 4/4. Note the finger cymbals on beat four of each measure.

INSTRUMENTATION: Piano, organ, electric guitars, drums, finger cymbals, lead vocal. Pay particular attention to Al Kooper's organ playing, which came to be much imitated despite Kooper's insistence that he was not really an organist.

0:00–0:09	**Introduction**, 4 mm.	Organ melody featured.
0:09–0:26	**Verse 1**, 8 mm.	Vocals enter, organ adds melodic interest, while the other instruments keep a low profile, supporting the vocal, "You got a lot of nerve . . ."
0:26–0:44	**Verse 2**, 8 mm.	As before, "You got a lot of nerve . . ."
0:44–1:01	**Verse 3**, 8 mm.	As before, "You say I let you down . . ."
1:01–1:19	**Verse 4**, 8 mm.	As before, "You say you lost your faith . . ."
1:19–1:36	**Verse 5**, 8 mm.	As before, "I know the reason . . ."
1:36–1:53	**Verse 6**, 8 mm.	As before, "Do you take me . . ."
1:54–2:11	**Verse 7**, 8 mm.	As before, "You seen me on the street . . ."
2:11–2:28	**Verse 8**, 8 mm.	As before, "When you know . . ."
2:28–2:46	**Verse 9**, 8 mm.	As before, "Now I don't feel . . ."
2:46–3:03	**Verse 10**, 8 mm.	As before, guitar and piano get a little busier, but not much, "And now I know . . ."
3:03–3:21	**Verse 11**, 8 mm.	As before, "I wish that for just one . . ."
3:21–3:38	**Verse 12**, 8 mm.	As before, "I wish that for just one . . ."
3:38–3:51	**Instrumental Verse** (partial), 4 mm.+	Organ featured again, as track fades out.

A week before the 1965 festival, Columbia Records released Dylan's single "Like a Rolling Stone," one of the three electric songs he performed at Newport. It was his most popular song as a performer, and rose to number two in the United States (uk4) in the summer and fall of 1965. He followed with the album *Highway 61 Revisited* (p3 uk4, 1965) and the angry hit single, "Positively 4th Street" (p7 uk8, 1965). The folk music establishment continued to react negatively to Dylan's use of electric instruments, and he felt betrayed by their response. As a traditional folksinger, he had written songs like "Masters of War," which attacked those who exploited others to gain unfair social or economic advantage. Dylan referred to such tunes as "finger pointing" songs, and after his 1965 Newport performance he used "Positively 4th Street" to point his finger at the folk establishment he felt had unfairly criticized him. The fervor of Dylan's obsession on this issue can be seen in the song's structure, which is a simple verse form employing twelve verses. After a short four-measure introduction, Dylan plows away at verse after verse, all based on the same eight-measure harmonic pattern. The song concludes with part of a thirteenth time through the chord progression, with vocals absent and the focus on Al Kooper's organ part, until the song fades out.

Dylan followed up with the single "Rainy Day Women Nos. 12 and 35" (p2 uk7, 1966), which drew on the double meaning of the word "stoned." On one hand, Dylan spoke of criticism, but the not-so-veiled other meaning was a reference to his growing interest in recreational drugs. Later that year he recorded his landmark album *Blonde on Blonde* (p9 uk3) using most of the Hawks (later known as the Band), along with session musicians from Nashville. In July 1966 Dylan was almost killed in a motorcycle accident in upstate New York and his injuries kept him out of the spotlight for months afterward. Even while Dylan was out of commission, his records continued to influence other musicians, and his lyrics were especially important. Dylan's songs showed that pop music could address serious social issues rather than just teenage romance or frivolous concerns, and this became a model for many other songwriters. While the folk traditionalists may have believed his music had become too commercial, it was Dylan who arguably changed the mainstream approach to rock by infusing his lyrical and musical sophistication and wit.

The Byrds and the Jingle-Jangle of the Electric Twelve-String Guitar.
Dylan's importance in the rise of American folk rock is evident in the fact that the first international number one folk-rock single was a song he wrote. In the summer of 1965, the Byrds' recording of "Mr. Tambourine Man" hit the top of both the U.S. and UK charts. The Byrds formed in Los Angeles in 1964. The band's leading members had been active in the folk music scene for several years. Roger McGuinn had studied folk music as a teenager

Bob Dylan shocked the folk establishment by shifting his focus to nontopical songs backed by an electric band in 1965. Dylan appears here on July 25, 1965, with his Fender Stratocaster electric guitar at the Newport Folk Festival, a performance that is legendary for the manner in which Dylan challenged the expectations of the folk revival audience.

at Chicago's Old Town School of Folk Music before working as an accompanist for the Limelighters and the Chad Mitchell Trio. He was also part of the early 1960s music scene in New York's Greenwich Village, playing in folk clubs by night while working as a Brill Building songwriter for Bobby Darin during the day. In 1964, he went to Los Angeles for a stint at the Troubadour Club, where he played sets mixing folk numbers with Beatles songs. At the Troubadour McGuinn met songwriter and singer Gene Clark, who had been a member of the commercialized folk revival group the New Christy Minstrels, and they began writing songs together. Soon singer-guitarist David Crosby joined the group and bluegrass mandolin player Chris Hillman was recruited to play bass, while Michael Clarke joined on drums. The band rehearsed under the direction of manager Jim Dickson, who taped the rehearsals and insisted that the group to listen to themselves. Surviving tapes from that period document the band's progression from a folk vocal-harmony act to a rock band. The distinct jingle-jangle guitar sound played a key role in that development, inspired by a viewing of *A Hard Day's Night*, during which band members noticed that George Harrison was playing an electric twelve-string guitar. The instrument was not widely used in pop at that time and Harrison was playing the second one ever made. McGuinn traded in his acoustic twelve-string for a Rickenbacker electric twelve, and the distinctive sound of that guitar, heard on the introduction to "Mr. Tambourine Man," became a Byrds hallmark.

The Byrds initially made their mark with rock versions of folk songs. The group's first album, *Mr. Tambourine Man* (p6 uk7, 1965), featured three additional Dylan covers, including "All I Really Want to Do," which hit number four in the UK but stalled at number forty in the United States when a version by Cher went to number fifteen. The Byrds' second number one U.S. hit, "Turn, Turn, Turn" (uk26, 1966), was a version of a Pete Seeger song that McGuinn had played on a Judy Collins album years before. The album that contained this single, also called *Turn, Turn, Turn* (p17 uk11, 1966), included other Dylan covers and Byrds originals, mostly written by Gene Clark. When Dylan met with success performing rock versions of his own songs, the Byrds were forced to rely on their own songwriting, and Clark, McGuinn, and Crosby wrote the band's next hit, "Eight Miles High" (p14 uk24, 1966). The guitar introduction invokes jazz, employing a melodic figure borrowed from legendary saxophonist John Coltrane's "India." The lyrics refer both to the cruising altitude of a transatlantic jet (actually six miles high) and to drugs, and when an American radio tip sheet listed it as a "drug song" in summer 1966, stations immediately stopped playing it.

The Byrds, Dylan, the Beach Boys, and the Music Business.

The Byrds' recording of "Mr. Tambourine Man" represents a point of convergence for several elements of the music business that are often thought of as mutually exclusive. The seriousness of the Byrds' brand of folk rock seemed to set this music apart from manufactured Brill Building music and carefree surf songs. On this first hit single, however, separating the authenticity of folk music (Dylan especially) from the calculated aspects of teen pop is more difficult than might be expected. All the members of the Byrds do not actually play on this record: McGuinn plays the electric twelve-string guitar and he and David Crosby sing, but the rest of the music is provided by the Wrecking Crew—a loose group of studio musicians who played on many Los Angeles–based hits (the Byrds played on their own records after this).

The Byrds are joined onstage by a harmonica-playing Bob Dylan. Note that Roger McGuinn (right) is playing his signature Rickenbacker electric twelve-string guitar, while David Crosby (left) plays a Gretsch Tennessean similar to the one George Harrison used on *Beatles for Sale.*

Listening Guide

Get Music ⓢ **wwnorton.com/studyspace**

The Byrds, "Mr. Tambourine Man" Columbia 43271

Words and music by Bob Dylan, produced by Terry Melcher. Rose to #1 on the *Billboard* "Hot 100" (uk7) in the summer of 1965.

FORM: Contrasting verse-chorus, beginning with the chorus. Dylan's original alternates the chorus with multiple verses, but the Byrds use only one of the original verses. The resulting form looks a little strange, but the band had to fit the arrangement into the two-minute format of AM radio at the time.

TIME SIGNATURE: 4/4, with a feel borrowed from "Don't Worry Baby."

INSTRUMENTATION: Electric 12-string guitar, electric 6-string guitar, bass, drums, solo and duet vocals.

0:00–0:08	**Introduction**, 4 mm.	Electric 12-string begins with a lick inspired by J. S. Bach, then sliding bass enters, followed by the entire band.
0:08–0:41	**Chorus**, 17 mm.	Duet vocals, then 2-bar link to verse; note the jingle-jangle picking on the electric 12-string guitar, "Hey Mr. Tambourine Man . . ."
0:41–1:30	**Verse**, 25 mm.	Solo vocal; note the short, sharp chords played high on a second electric guitar, "Take me for a trip . . ."
1:30–2:00	**Chorus**, 15 mm.	Duet vocals as before; "Hey Mr. Tambourine Man . . ."
2:00–2:15	**Coda**, 6 mm. and fade	Music is the same as in the introduction.

Wrecking Crew musicians had provided the musical backing for the Beach Boys' "Don't Worry Baby," and they used the same rhythmic feel to back the Byrds' "Mr. Tambourine Man" at the suggestion of producer Terry Melcher. Thus, "Mr. Tambourine Man" brings together the folk revival (Dylan's song), girl groups (Phil Spector), surf music (The Beach Boys) and, with the use of the electric twelve-string inspired by *A Hard Day's Night*, the British invasion as well.

The Byrds adapted the tune from an acoustic folk version that Dylan had decided not to release. As the Listening Guide shows, the song is in a contrasting verse-chorus form. The Byrds use only one of Dylan's three verses to keep the song at the two-minute length typical of pop singles in 1965. The odd number of measures in the verse and chorus arise because these sections are expanded (and in the case of the second chorus, contracted) from what would typically be sixteen-measure sections. As you listen, see if you can detect where the extra measures are added or dropped (this is especially obvious in the verse section).

Modeling themselves on the Everly Brothers, Paul Simon (left) and Art Garfunkel (right) enjoyed modest success in the late 1950s as Tom and Jerry. When folk rock became popular in mid-1965, electric guitar, bass, and drums were added to an earlier recording to create the duo's first hit single, "The Sounds of Silence."

Simon and Garfunkel Go Electric. Perhaps no song better illustrates the transformation of folk into folk rock than Simon and Garfunkel's "The Sounds of Silence" (p1, 1965). Paul Simon and Art Garfunkel began their professional careers as high school students in the late 1950s under the name Tom and Jerry. Modeling their act on the Everly Brothers, Tom and Jerry had a minor hit in late 1957/early 1958 with "Hey Schoolgirl," and even appeared on *American Bandstand*. The pair turned to folk in the early 1960s, recording the album *Wednesday Morning, 3 A.M.* (1964). When the album sold poorly, the pair went their separate ways. Simon went to London to perform solo and Garfunkel went to graduate school. After "Mr. Tambourine Man" and "Like a Rolling Stone" became hits for the Byrds and Bob Dylan, somebody at Columbia Records remembered the Simon and Garfunkel album. Without their knowledge, Tom Wilson, who had produced Dylan's albums and *Wednesday Morning, 3 A.M.*, was brought in to augment the acoustic version of "The Sounds of Silence" that appears on the album—the same master tape was used—with jangly guitar, electric bass, and drums in the style of the Byrds. The resultant folk-rock single topped the charts in the United States in January 1966. Simon rushed home from the UK and the duo released an album, *Sounds of Silence* (p21 uk13, 1966), to capitalize on their newfound and unexpected success as rock stars. Subsequent singles, "Homeward Bound" (p5 uk9, 1966), "I Am a Rock" (p3 uk17, 1966), and "Hazy Shade of Winter" (p13, 1966) continued in the folk-rock style. By late 1966, however, the album *Parsley, Sage, Rosemary and Thyme* (p4), which contains the delicate "Scarborough Fair/

Canticle" (p11, 1968) made it clear that the duo were still pursuing traditional folk revival material. Later in the 1960s, Simon and Garfunkel would enjoy their greatest commercial and aesthetic success with *Bookends* (p1 uk1, 1968), the single "Mrs. Robinson" (p1 uk4, 1968) from the soundtrack to the film *The Graduate*, and *Bridge Over Troubled Water* (p1 uk1, 1970).

California Dreamin': Barry McGuire, the Turtles, and the Mamas and the Papas.

While many of the first folk-rock records simply set preexisting folk songs to a rock beat and instrumentation, new songs were soon written specifically as folk-rock numbers. Perhaps the first of these—aside from those Dylan wrote and recorded after he went electric—was P. F. Sloan's "Eve of Destruction." Recorded by Barry McGuire, another former member of the New Christy Minstrels who had made his way to Los Angeles from Greenwich Village, this song ascended to number one on the U.S. charts (uk3) in fall 1965. Producer Lou Adler had given Sloan the task of writing a batch of Dylan-like songs, and the songwriter did his best to mimic the earnest sense of social protest found in much folk.

Meanwhile, groups continued to cover Dylan songs with hopes of scoring folk-rock hits as the Byrds had done. The Los Angeles–based Turtles worked this trick successfully with "It Ain't Me Babe" (p8, 1965) before moving on to a more mainstream pop style and a series of non-Dylan hits including "Happy Together" (p1 uk12, 1967). The Turtles' arrangements often showcased the polished dual lead vocals of Howard Kaylan and Mark Volman, who went on to work with Frank Zappa and the Mothers of Invention and later performed as the duo Phlorescent Leech (Flo) and Eddie.

Formed in New York in 1965, the Mamas and the Papas also followed the folk migration westward and moved from Greenwich Village to Los Angeles, where they first enjoyed commercial success in the wake of Dylan, the Byrds, and Simon and Garfunkel. Three of the group members had worked previously in vocally oriented

Updating the polished folk approach of Peter, Paul, and Mary with a folk-rock beat, the Mamas and the Papas focused on sophisticated vocal arrangements by John Phillips (second from left).

pop or folk acts. Led by singer/songwriter/arranger John Phillips and including Michelle Phillips, Denny Doherty, and Cass Elliot, the group showcased John Phillips's sophisticated four-part vocal arrangements. The group's sound was influenced by the close harmony singing found in early 1960s folk (especially Peter, Paul, and Mary) and doo-wop (they had a hit with a cover of the 5 Royales' "Dedicated to the One I Love"), and these distinctive vocals were often accompanied by a rock rhythm section of drums, electric bass, guitars, and keyboards. The Mamas and the Papas had nine hit singles, most written by John Phillips, including "California Dreamin'" (p4 uk23, 1966), "Monday Monday" (p1 uk3, 1966), "I Saw Her Again" (p5 uk11, 1966), and the autobiographical "Creeque Alley" (p5, 1967), the lyrics of which mention both Roger McGuinn and Barry McGuire. This run made the quartet one of the most successful acts of the era.

AMERICAN POP ON BOTH COASTS

L.A.: Spector and His Legacy. Phil Spector was another American record producer and songwriter that had tremendous success in the Beatles' wake. Spector was a favorite of the Fab Four, to the extent that he flew with the band from London to New York on February 7, 1964. However, he was yet to experience some of his greatest successes when the Beatles stormed the U.S. charts. The Crystals' "Doo Doo Ron Ron" (p3 r5 uk5, 1963) and "Then He Kissed Me" (p6 r8 uk2, 1963), and the Ronettes' "Be My Baby" (p2 r4 uk4, 1963), were all Spector-produced hits in the months before the Fab Four landed. After the onset of the British Invasion, Spector produced one of his most enduring songs, the Righteous Brothers' "You've Lost That Lovin' Feeling," which went to number one in both the United States and the UK in early 1965, and hit number three on the U.S. rhythm and blues charts. The group followed with "Unchained Melody" (p4 r6 uk14, 1965) and "Ebb Tide" (p5 r13 uk48, 1966) before Spector began to lose his hit-making touch. During this time, Spector could have produced the Young Rascals and the Lovin' Spoonful, but he declined offers from both bands. Instead, he pinned everything on what he hoped would be his greatest record yet, Tina Turner's "River Deep, Mountain High." Written by Spector with Jeff Barry and Ellie Greenwich, the song failed in the United States, rising only as high as number eighty-six in mid-1966. The record did hit number three in the UK (mostly through airplay on pirate stations), but Spector was crushed by the failure in America and retired from the music business. He would return to producing a few years later, enjoying the success of several Beatles-related projects in the early 1970s, including number one albums for the Beatles (*Let It Be*, 1970), George Harrison (*All Things Must Pass*, 1970), and John Lennon (*Imagine*, 1971).

The Beach Boys: Brian Stays Home. Like Spector, the Beach Boys continued to produce hits in 1965 and 1966. In 1964 the group released "Fun, Fun, Fun," which reached number five in the United States during the height of Beatlemania. That summer, the Beach Boys had their first number one U.S. hit (uk7), "I Get Around," while the world was also celebrating *A Hard Day's Night*. Contending with the Beatles' success was tougher for the Beach Boys than most other American pop

The Beach Boys Pet Sounds

Sloop John B./Caroline No
Wouldn't It Be Nice/You Still Believe In Me
That's Not Me/Don't Talk (Put Your Head on My Shoulder)
I'm Waiting For The Day/Let's Go Away For Awhile
God Only Knows/I Know There's An Answer/Here Today
I Just Wasn't Made For These Times/Pet Sounds

In late 1964, Brian Wilson (second from left) decided not to tour with the Beach Boys, opting to stay at home working on new material while the band hit the road. By the time *Pet Sounds* was recorded, Brian was working long hours in the studio experimenting with new sounds, some of which he considered his "pet" sounds.

acts, however, because both groups were signed to Capitol Records. This meant that the Beach Boys had to fight for the attention of both pop listeners and their record company. In December 1964, the band's music began to change when songwriter and producer Brian Wilson decided to stop touring. Instead, he stayed in California writing new music and recording backing tracks. During breaks from touring, the other band members added vocal tracks that Wilson had carefully worked out for them. On the road, Glen Campbell and then Bruce Johnston replaced Brian, so he could focus entirely on making records.

The Beach Boys' next two albums, *The Beach Boys Today!* (p4, 1965) and *Summer Days (and Summer Nights!!)* (p2, 1965) reflected Wilson's increasingly sophisticated approach to songwriting, arranging, and production. "Help Me Rhonda" (p1 uk27, 1965) and especially "California Girls" (p3 uk26, 1965) began to explore more complicated musical structures and employed a broader palette of instrumentation, including orchestral instruments.

After *Beach Boys' Party!* (p6 uk3, 1966), a quickly recorded and informal taping of the band jamming and singing with friends (which produced the hit single "Barbara Ann" (p2 uk3, 1966)), Brian set to work on a much more musically ambitious project. Named after some of his favorite studio sounds, *Pet Sounds* (p10 uk2, 1966) set a new standard for record production and musical sophistication within rock music. On the single released in advance of the album, "Sloop John B." (p3 uk2, 1966), you can hear the clear combination of Spector's Wall of Sound with Wilson's

Listening Guide

Get Music ⑤ wwnorton.com/studyspace

The Beach Boys, "California Girls" Capital 5464

Words and music by Brian Wilson, produced by Brian Wilson. Rose to #3 on the *Billboard* Pop charts in fall 1965 (uk26).

FORM: Contrasting verse-chorus, with a 10-bar intro leading into a 2-bar vamp that prepares the arrival of the first-verse vocals. The verse and chorus are both 8 bars in length. Wilson builds his arrangement by employing solo lead vocals in the first two verses, then introducing a call-and-response scheme in the harmony vocals of the chorus, and using doo-wop inspired backup vocals in the third and fourth verses. As Phil Spector does in "Be My Baby," Wilson uses a short instrumental break late in the song to allow a fresh return of the chorus: a brief 2-bar organ and glockenspiel passage based on the "Happy Trails" bass line that prepares the way for the song's hook, "I wish they all could be . . . ."

TIME SIGNATURE: 4/4 (with a shuffle). Note that the repeated figure in the bass sounds like the old cowboy song, "Happy Trails," giving the track a bouncy, easygoing rhythmic feel.

INSTRUMENTATION: Electric 12-string guitar, organ, bass, drums, glockenspiel, horns, percussion, lead and backup vocals.

0:00–0:26	**Introduction**, 12 mm.	10 mm. intro using harp and 12-string guitar, then bass and cymbals, and then horns, followed by a 2-mm. lead-in to verse 1 using the "Happy Trails" bass line.
0:26–0:43	**Verse 1**, 8 mm.	Solo lead vocal enters, "Well, east coast girls . . ."
0:43–0:59	**Verse 2**, 8 mm.	As before, "The midwest farmers' daughters . . ."
0:59–1:16	**Chorus**, 8 mm.	Arrangement gets fuller and louder, with call-and-answer harmony vocals, "I wish they all could be . . ."
1:16–1:32	**Verse 3**, 8 mm.	Doo-wop vocals, lightly doubled by horns, now backup solo lead vocal, "The west coast . . ."
1:32–1:49	**Verse 4**, 8 mm.	Texture continues as in verse 3, "I've been all 'round . . ."
1:49–2:06	**Chorus**, 8 mm.	Louder, fuller, with call-and-answer vocals, as before.
2:06–2:27	**Coda**, 10 mm. and fade	2 mm. interlude drawn from intro, and then 4 mm. drawn from chorus repeated as track fades.

lush vocal-harmony arrangements. The echo-drenched harp introduction of the first track, "Wouldn't It Be Nice," announces that what follows moves beyond the surf music that had brought the band its early success. "God Only Knows," which Paul McCartney once called the perfect rock song, is the best illustration of how far Wilson's music had come during this period. Although not as commercially successful as previous Beach Boys' albums, *Pet Sounds* would become one of the most influential records of the 1960s, prodding the Beatles to experiment more radically while recording *Sgt. Pepper's Lonely Hearts Club Band*. In Chapter 7 we will return to the friendly competition that developed between the bands, and consider the Beach Boys' music after *Pet Sounds*.

Sonny and Cher: Dylan Meets the Wall of Sound.

By the mid-1960s Sonny Bono had been working in the music scene around Los Angeles for a decade. A sometime songwriter, he worked at Specialty Records and was designated to deal with Little Richard when the singer decided to give up rock and roll for the ministry. Bono eventually began handling promotion for Phil Spector's Philles label and became one of the producer's most trusted aides. Present at many of the important Los Angeles recording sessions at Gold Star Studios, Bono often sang backup or played percussion on tracks, and thus had ample opportunity to soak up Spector's methods in the studio. He frequently brought his girlfriend, Cher (Cherilyn La Piere), to sing backup. A failed Spector project that attempted to cash in on Beatlemania had Cher singing a song called "Ringo I Love You" under the name Bonnie Jo Mason. Sonny and Cher began performing together in 1963 under the name Caesar and Cleo and released three singles that did not chart. In late 1964, Sonny produced and wrote "Baby Don't Go" and "Just You," and both singles enjoyed regional success in Southern California in the first half of 1965. When the Byrds' "Mr. Tambourine Man" became a hit, Sonny produced a Cher cover of Dylan's "All I Really Want to Do"—which eclipsed the Byrds' version— and wrote and produced the duo's signature song, "I Got You, Babe." In fall 1965, "I Got You, Babe" hit number one on both the U.S. and UK charts (r19). Although the couple got their start by capitalizing on the folk rock boom, Sonny and Cher's later recordings moved into a more traditional brand of pop, including the Bono-written song "The Beat Goes On" (p6 uk29, 1967).

While Bono extended the Spector legacy through his productions, he and Cher also made a significant impact on hippie fashion. The pair wore deliberately outlandish clothes, both onstage and off, which drew nearly as much comment as their music. A few years later Sonny and Cher hosted a very successful network television variety show, but during the 1965–67 period they were considered subversive by establishment culture. They were frequently refused accommodation at hotels in the United States and abroad because of their appearance. Sonny's "Laugh at Me" (1966) is a response to a specific incident when he was ridiculed for his clothing and haircut at one of the couple's favorite restaurants. While this became a common experience for hippies a few years later, in the rebellious spirit of rock and roll, Sonny and Cher were among the first to insist that they had the right to dress any way they chose.

Musically, Sonny and Cher drew upon the legacy of Phil Spector to create lush pop arrangements. They were also known for a flamboyant style of dress, and were pioneers of hippie fashion.

Johnny Rivers's first album was recorded live, and its success prompted him to release a string of live albums during the 1960s—an unusual practice for pop music during that time. In 1966, Rivers released his famous song "Secret Agent Man."

Gary Lewis and the Playboys and Johnny Rivers. Gary Lewis and the Playboys, led by the son of comedian Jerry Lewis, was another Los Angeles group that enjoyed tremendous chart success. Like Ricky Nelson, Gary started as an actor in family projects, and had appeared in his father's 1957 film *Rock-a-Bye Baby.* By 1964 he formed a band that was booked as regular entertainment at Disneyland and earned a cameo appearance in the Raquel Welch film *A Swingin' Summer.* The group's first hit was "This Diamond Ring" (p1, 1965), which Lewis performed with his father in the film *The Family Jewels.* The song was produced by veteran Snuff Garrett and featured arrangements by Wrecking Crew pianist Leon Russell (the song was cowritten by Al Kooper, who played on Dylan's "Like a Rolling Stone" and "Positively 4th Street"). Gary Lewis and the Playboys followed with eleven more U.S. hits including "Count Me In" (p2, 1965), "Save Your Heart for Me" (p2, 1965), "She's Just My Style" (p3, 1965)—clearly influenced by the Beach Boys' records of the same period—and "Green Grass" (p8, 1966). Lewis and the band broke up when he was drafted into the U.S. Army in 1967.

Like Sonny Bono, Johnny Rivers had been in the music business for several years before he scored a hit record. Born John Ramistella, he took the stage name Rivers on the advice of Alan Freed in 1958. That same year, Ricky Nelson recorded Rivers's "I'll Make Believe," though it proved unpopular. After playing with Louis Prima's band in Las Vegas and Lake Tahoe, Rivers made his way to Los Angeles, where he established himself as a live act. He became a regular at the Whiskey-a-Go-Go, where he played mostly rock oldies and drew a star-studded crowd. His popularity at the Whiskey led to a contract with Imperial Records. Rivers was signed by Lou Adler, who made the strange but inspired decision to record a live album, *Johnny Rivers at the Whiskey-a-Go-Go,* which went to number twelve on the U.S. album charts. His first two hit singles were covers of Chuck Berry tunes, "Memphis" (p2, 1964) and "Maybelline" (p12, 1964). Rivers placed eleven more singles in the U.S. Top 40 during the 1960s and released eight Top 40 albums. Although not aligned with the folk movement, Rivers also experimented with folk rock. In 1965, before the Byrds or Dylan had hit with folk rock, Rivers released covers of the Weavers's "Midnight Special" (which became the theme song of the early 1970s music-variety show of the same name), and the Kingston Trio's "Where Have All the Flowers Gone." In late 1966, his ballad "Poor Side of Town," written with Adler, hit number one in the United States, although Rivers is perhaps best known for the song "Secret Agent Man" (p3) released earlier that year. "Secret Agent Man" was written in part by P. F. Sloan ("Eve of Destruction") and became the theme song of a popular television spy program. In 1966, Rivers started his own label, Soul City, signing songwriter Jimmie Webb and singing group the Fifth Dimension. He produced the Fifth Dimension's version of Webb's "Up, Up, and Away," which won multiple Grammy awards in 1967.

Meanwhile Back in New York: The Lovin' Spoonful and the Rascals.

There was a steady migration of folk musicians from Greenwich Village to Southern California in 1964 and 1965. Most of the folkies who headed west did so because they felt neglected by record labels in New York. Ironically, many of the Los Angeles acts who signed recording contracts in summer 1965 (when the folk-rock style emerged) were signed by New York–based labels. The Byrds, for instance, were on Columbia, and Sonny and Cher were on Atlantic. One Greenwich Village folkie who stayed in New York was John Sebastian, who had played on several folk albums (including an early version of Dylan's "Subterranean Homesick Blues") and performed with the Even Dozen Jug Band. Sebastian met guitarist Zal Yanovsky at a recording session and, inspired by the Beatles, they formed the Lovin' Spoonful with bassist Steve Boone and drummer Joe Butler. The new band became a popular attraction at the Night Owl Coffee House in Greenwich Village, but was not signed by a major New York label. Instead, the newly formed independent Kama Sutra Records released "Do You Believe in Magic" in summer 1965, and the single rose to number nine on the U.S. charts. This easygoing melodic hit was followed by a string of catchy, playful, and mostly upbeat hit singles written by Sebastian and produced by Erik Jacobsen, including "Daydream" (p2 uk2, 1966), "Did You Ever Have to Make Up Your Mind" (p2, 1966), and "Summer in the City" (p1 uk8, 1966).

Formed in New York in early 1964 but emerging from rhythm and blues clubs rather than the Greenwich Village folk scene, the Young Rascals (later simply the "Rascals") are better seen as precursors to British blues bands like the Spencer Davis Group than as an answer to the Beatles. Nevertheless, they caught the attention of New York promoter Sid Bernstein, who became their manager, booking them as the opening act for the Beatles' 1965 performance at Shea

Lovin' Spoonful vocalist and guitarist John Sebastian in a 1966 photo. Based out of New York, the Lovin' Spoonful created pop music that was indebted to their folk revival roots. Here, Sebastian is seen performing on the autoharp, an instrument associated more with folk than with rock.

Emerging in the mid-1960s, the Young Rascals developed a reputation for a hard-driving, rhythm and blues–inspired approach to rock. The New York group's aggressive sound was driven by Felix Cavaliere on the Hammond organ and drummer Dino Danelli.

Stadium. The group was led by the funky Hammond organ of Felix Cavaliere and the soulful vocals of Eddie Brigati, and backed by Gene Cornish's guitar and Dino Danelli's drums. The Rascals first hit with a note-for-note cover of the Olympics' 1965 rhythm and blues hit, "Good Lovin'," which went to number one on the U.S. charts in spring 1966. Allowed to produce themselves with oversight from Atlantic's experienced house producers, the band followed with a series of rhythm and blues–inspired hits written by Cavaliere and Brigati, including "I've Been Lonely Too Long" (p16, 1967), "Groovin'" (p1 r3 uk8, 1967), "How Can I Be Sure" (p4, 1967), "A Beautiful Morning" (p3, 1968), and "People Got to Be Free" (p1 r14, 1968).

The Old Guard Hangs On: New York. By mid-1963, Don Kirschner had left New York's Brill Building for the Los Angeles–based Colpix label. Brill Building veterans Leiber and Stoller continued to place hit records on the pop charts through 1965 on their newly formed Red Bird label. The Ad Libs' "The Boy from New York

City," for instance, hit number eight in the first half of 1965 (r6), while Red Bird releases such as the Dixie Cups' "Chapel of Love" and the Shangri-Las' "Leader of the Pack" also enjoyed chart success. When Leiber and Stoller formed Red Bird, they turned production of the Drifters over to Bert Berns. In 1965, Berns formed Bang! Records with his bosses from Atlantic, Ahmet and Neshui Ertegun and Jerry Wexler. In the fall of 1965, Berns produced an Indiana-based band, the McCoys, doing a version of a 1964 Atlantic release called "My Girl Sloopy." This cover version reached the top of the *Billboard* "Hot 100" (uk5) in October 1965. The McCoys followed with two more Top 40 hits for Bang!: "Fever" (p7 uk44, 1965) and "Come On Let's Go" (p22, 1966). Berns had the most success with singer-songwriter Neil Diamond, who began his hit-making career on Bang!, scoring first with "Cherry, Cherry" (p6, 1966), and following with eight more hits before leaving the label. Diamond also worked as a Brill Building songwriter, and wrote several hit songs for the Monkees, including "I'm a Believer."

The Four Seasons, featuring lead vocalist Frankie Valli, was another New York–based act that didn't seem to be affected by the British invasion. The group's first success came in 1962 with successive crossover number one singles produced by Bob Crewe, "Sherry" and "Big Girls Don't Cry." The Four Seasons would release twenty-five more U.S. Top 40 hits during the 1960s, including "Walk Like a Man" (p1 r3, 1963), "Rag Doll" (p1, 1964), "Let's Hang On" (p4, 1965), and "Workin' My Way Back to You" (p9 uk50, 1966) (the last was recorded under the name the Wonder Who?). In early February 1964, "Dawn (Go Away)" rose to the top of the *Billboard* chart in the United States alongside the Beatles' "She Loves You" and "I Want to Hold Your Hand." The Four Seasons recorded for Vee Jay, which had also released the Beatles' first album (in the months before Beatlemania), and the label released a double album late in 1964 called *The Beatles vs. the Four Seasons*, which was a rerelease of *Introducing the Beatles* combined with a Four Seasons greatest hits compilation. The Four Seasons' doo-wop vocal style was very different from the music of the Beatles and other British invasion groups, however. Nevertheless, combining these records in a single package shows Vee Jay's confidence that the same group of listeners would be interested in both groups. Despite the success of the Four Seasons and a handful of other New York–based groups, the British invasion and the changes it caused in American rock, marked the end of New York's domination of pop during the early 1960s.

GARAGE BANDS: NO EXPERIENCE NECESSARY

From the Northwest: Garage Bands, the Kingsmen, and "Louie Louie." Almost immediately after the Beatles landed in the United States, bands comprised of male teenagers with more enthusiasm than musical training sprang up across the country. These bands gained regional popularity playing at dances and clubs, and local record labels attempted to cash in by releasing records for small markets. These "local hero" bands often rehearsed in basements or garages on inexpensive instruments, and their records were frequently recorded on very simple equipment. Like

TOP 40: MORE HITS MORE OFTEN

by Ben Fong-Torres

It's hard to imagine, but there was a time, not long ago, when radio was declared dead. In the early 1950s, television was taking over as the most popular form of entertainment for Americans. Radio's network stars fled for the greener pastures of TV land—even if it was still black and white. Goodbye, Red Skelton; hello, red ink.

Radio networks indeed had problems, but independent stations—the great majority of license holders—fought back by focusing on local listeners and advertisers. They hired announcers who could relate to listeners in ways that a Jack

Benny or Marshall Matt Dillon never could. Market research showed that music was a major reason listeners used the radio, and stations began to program records. Radio survived. But it didn't really explode until rock and roll and the Top 40 format came along.

The format came first. In the early 1950s, a young man named Todd Storz was running KOWH, a small station in Omaha, Nebraska, that his father had purchased. He had replaced the network programming on KOWH with music and disc jockeys, and following such countdown shows as *Your Hit Parade*, gave the top ten songs heavy airplay. In a 1957 article in *Television* magazine, "The Storz Bombshell," Storz explained his formula. "I became convinced that people demand their favorites over and over while in the Army during the Second World War," he said. "I remember vividly what used to happen in restaurants here in the States. The customers would throw their nickels into the jukebox and come up repeatedly with the same tune."

At another of his father's stations—WTIX in New Orleans—Storz heard about rival WDSU's "Top 20 on 1280" show. Radio historian Richard Fatherley, a former

Storz employee, recalls: "He (Storz) added 20 titles, upstaged WDSU by one hour, and went on for an hour after the other show had ended." Thus, he had a forty-song playlist. Another broadcaster often credited with pioneering the format is Gordon McLendon, who operated stations in Texas. McLendon, Fatherley notes, has conceded that Storz was first. But McLendon is credited with labeling the format "Top 40." By 1953, McLendon's Dallas station, KLIF, "burst into national prominence with its formula of music and news plus razzle-dazzle promotion," according to a broadcasting magazine. Edd Routt, a former McLendon employee, explained that "disc jockeys were selected for their sexiness, their voice, their ability to communicate excitement. Basic service consisted of time and temperature checks. Any idea of doing anything more than entertain the listener was out of the question." The listener, back then, was adult; the music, pop. Before rock, it was Perry Como and Patti Page; Nat "King" Cole and Doris Day; Les Paul and Mary Ford.

And then came rock and roll. It was perfect for Top 40, and vice versa. Combined with new technology—in the 1950s, that meant the portable, transistor radio—rock and roll and the top 40 format opened the floodgates to a new audience: teenagers. Music, and the medium, would never be the same. Disc jockeys became local stars, and some gained even greater fame by doing local versions of *American Bandstand*. But Top 40 did more than rock. Dedicated to playing the top-selling songs of the day, these stations amounted to democratic jukeboxes. Rock and pop shared airtime with rhythm and blues, country and western, folk and novelty tunes, and jazz and blues records that sold enough copies to hit the charts.

Top 40 itself hit the top of the radio ratings in many markets. Around the country, jingles identified stations as "Color Radio" or "Boss Radio." DJs—invariably men—were "Good Guys," "Swingin' Gentlemen," or "Boss Jocks." Stations fought one another for Beatles interviews, for star DJs, and for ratings and revenue. In the late 1960s, they began fighting upstart stations on the FM band, which offered better audio fidelity, and "free-form" formats that rendered Top 40, with its jingles, screaming DJs, and tight playlists, somehow passé.

But Top 40 carried on. Ironically, as a popular format, Top 40 lasted just about forty years. But by the mid-'90s, industry publications had turned to other labels—like CHR, or "contemporary hit radio"—and many stations had zeroed in on one specific area of music. There was dance, "light rock" and "smooth jazz," along with the old standby, R&B. Hip-hop further fragmented the format. Like rock itself, Top 40 was declared dead more than once. But it still exists—if not in name,

As Top 40 radio became increasingly popular, its disc jockeys became increasingly influential. As a high-profile DJ in New York, "Murray the K" Kaufman whipped up enthusiasm for the Beatles and their music in early 1964.

then in concept. Wherever a station plays the hits of the day on a regular basis, and plays them with energy, though maybe without the jingles, newscasts, and stunts from yesteryear, it's Top 40.

Ben Fong-Torres is the author of The Hits Just Keep on Coming: The History of Top 40 Radio *and six other books. He is a columnist at the* San Francisco Chronicle, *and published his most recent book* Eagles: Taking It to the Limit *in October 2011.*

the doo-wop groups of the preceding years, garage bands often had only one hit, and many of these were songs that only achieved regional popularity. When a garage band did have more than one hit, the music almost always became more refined as the band migrated away from the charming but amateurish sound of their first success. There are hundreds of garage-band singles from the 1960s, records that have spawned an entire culture of collectors. Much of this interest grew out of a collection assembled in the early 1970s by writer and guitarist Lenny Kaye. Called *Nuggets*, this compilation brought together rare recordings that collectively told a story of a thriving rock underground during the 1960s. Many bands of the early punk movement took their inspiration from the rough-and-tumble, amateurish character of these 1960s garage bands.

The first important national garage-band hit was the Kingsmen's "Louie Louie." This song was a live staple for many early garage bands in the Pacific Northwest. The Kingsmen's recording went to number two on the *Billboard* "Hot 100" at the same time Beatlemania was reaching a fever pitch in the United States (r1). The song was written by Richard Berry and originally recorded in 1956 as a calypso-flavored rhythm and blues tune. The Kingsmen's version was recorded for $50 in a small studio in Portland, Oregon. This rendition is notably amateurish: at one point vocalist Jack Ely comes in at the wrong place and abruptly corrects himself. The song's difficult-to-discern lyrics led to a rumor that it contained foul language. At one point in early 1964, the governor of Indiana declared "Louie Louie" to be pornographic and called for an FCC investigation. In fact, the lyrics did not contain any profanity or overt sexual references, and the FCC ultimately concluded that the lyrics were indecipherable. Even though another Portland group, Paul Revere and

Hailing from Portland, Oregon, the Kingsmen rose to national attention in 1963 with "Louie Louie." Though the song was famously rumored to contain obscene language, an FCC investigation pronounced the passage in question to be unintelligible.

Listening Guide

Get Music ⓢ **wwnorton.com/studyspace**

The Kingsmen, "Louie Louie" Wand 14

Words and music by Richard Berry, produced by Ken Chase and Jerry Dennon. Reached #2 on the *Billboard* "Hot 100" (r1 uk26) in late 1963.

FORM: Simple verse-chorus, with the entire song built on the famous four-chord sequence that opens the song. In the first half of the song, the choruses precede the verses, but after the guitar solo, the order is flipped and verse 3 precedes the final chorus. The guitar solo was likely meant to be 16 bars in length (twice that of a verse or chorus). When the vocal enters at the end of these 16 measures, however, singer Jack Ely stops abruptly as if he's made a mistake, and then starts again two bars later. This "mistake" was left in the released version, and creates a section of 18 bars. The final chorus is extended by five bars, with the last of these extra measures simply being the last chord of the song.

TIME SIGNATURE: 4/4.

INSTRUMENTATION: Electric piano, electric guitar, bass, drums, and lead vocals.

0:00–0:08	**Introduction**, 4 mm.	The famous four-chord sequence is played on the electric piano, then the band joins in.
0:08–0:24	**Chorus**, 8 mm.	Lead vocal enters. Note the cross between blues and Jamaican singing styles. "Louie, Louie . . ."
0:24–0:40	**Verse 1**, 8 mm.	Lead vocal continues, as music remains the same. The lyrics are hard to decipher at times. "A fine little . . ."
0:40–0:55	**Chorus**, 8 mm.	As before. "Louie, Louie . . ."
0:55–1:11	**Verse 2**, 8 mm.	As in verse 1, hard-to-discern lyrics could be selectively interpreted as profanity. "Three nights . . ."
1:11–1:27	**Chorus**, 8 mm.	As before, with an increase in energy leading into the guitar solo. "Louie, Louie . . ."
1:27–2:02	**Guitar solo**, 18 mm.	Blues-based guitar solo for 16 measures, followed by 2 bars that prepare the next verse.
2:02–2:17	**Verse 3**, 8 mm.	As in the previous verses, though lyrics are here even more garbled. "See Jamaica . . ."
2:17–2:41	**Chorus**, 13 mm.	One last time through the chorus, with a 4-bar extension and a final chord stretching the section to 13 measures. "Louie, Louie . . ."

Garage rock emerged in the wake of the Beatles when amateurish bands across the United States began recording singles, some of which achieved regional and national popularity. The compilation *Nuggets*, first released in 1972, documented the garage rock movement for the emerging punk generation.

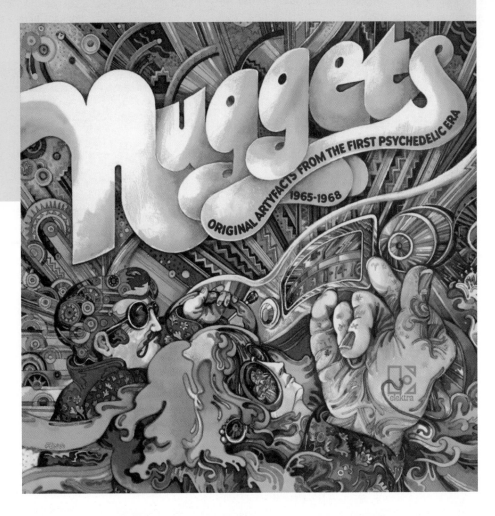

the Raiders, recorded their version of "Louie Louie" soon after and in the same studio, it was the Kingsmen's version that took off, as controversy stoked the curiosity of young listeners across the country.

After the success of the Kingsmen in 1964, record companies licensed records by many unknown American bands and in the summer of 1965, a series of mostly one-time garage-band Top 40 hits appeared on the U.S. pop charts. Among these groups and their hits were: Cannibal and the Headhunters, "Land of 1000 Dances" (p30, 1965); the Count Five, "Psychotic Reaction" (p5, 1966); ? & the Mysterians, "96 Tears" (p1, 1966); the Seeds, "Pushin' Too Hard" (p36, 1966); Shadows of Knight, "Gloria" (p10, 1966); the Standells, "Dirty Water" (p11, 1966); and the Syndicate of Sound, "Little Girl" (p8, 1967). Some bands followed up with additional hits. Tommy James and the Shondells initially recorded their version of the Jeff Barry and Ellie Greenwich song "Hanky Panky" in 1963 at a studio in their hometown of Niles, Michigan. A few years later a Pittsburgh DJ began playing it, and the song took off. Released on Roulette, it rose to number one in the second half of 1966. James then formed a new bunch of Shondells and followed with thirteen Top 40 hits over the next few years, including "Mony Mony" (p3, 1968), "Crimson and Clover" (p1, 1968), and "Crystal Blue Persuasion" (p2, 1969). Dallas-based Sam the Sham & the Pharaohs hit nationally with "Wooly Bully" (p2, 1965) and followed with five more hits through 1967, including "Little Red Riding Hood" (p2, 1966).

TV ROCK: THE INDUSTRY TRIES TO TAKE CONTROL ONCE MORE

One If by Land, Two If by Sea: Paul Revere and the Raiders. Part of the Pacific Northwest garage-band scene in the early 1960s, Paul Revere and the Raiders had initially formed in Idaho and made their commercial mark mid-decade after relocating to Los Angeles. After their single "Like, Long Hair" hit number thirty-nine on the national charts in 1961, the group moved to Portland, Oregon. When their version of "Louie Louie" failed to break out of the regional market, lead singer Mark Lindsay and organist Paul Revere parted ways. Revere and Lindsay would later rejoin and, with the help of *American Bandstand* impresario Dick Clark, Paul Revere and the Raiders debuted in 1965 as musical hosts of Clark's

Paul Revere & the Raiders (from left to right): Drake Levin, Phil Volk, Mark Lindsay, Mike Smith, Paul Revere) on a television set. As the house band for Dick Clark's *Where the Action Is*, the Raiders grew out of the garage band movement to help define the growing presence of rock on television in the mid-1960s.

new rock variety show on CBS, *Where the Action Is*. Clark's show was launched in response to ABC's *Shindig*, which had debuted earlier that year under the production of Jack Good, who had produced similar shows in the UK. NBC also joined the TV-rock race with *Hullabaloo*. Together, these three shows targeted America's teenagers, providing wide exposure for British invasion and American acts. Regular television exposure on *Where the Action Is*, combined with a Columbia Records recording contract and the production talents of Terry Melcher (who was also producing the Byrds), helped Paul Revere and the Raiders score a series of hit singles on the American charts. They became the most successful of all the garage bands, scoring hits with "Just Like Me" (p11, 1966), "Kicks" (p4, 1966), "Hungry" (p6, 1966), and "Good Thing" (p4, 1966). "The Great Airplane Strike" (p20, 1966) marked the first Paul Revere and the Raiders single written by members of the group (Lindsay and Melcher). The band continued to enjoy chart success through the rest of the decade, scoring their first number one hit with "Indian Reservation" in 1971.

A Collision of the Old and New: The Monkees' Tale. No group benefited more from television exposure than America's most commercially successful answer to the Beatles: the Monkees. Initially, the Monkees were formed as a band to make records in support of a weekly television series. The brainchild of television producer

Listening Guide

The Monkees, "Last Train to Clarksville" Colgems 1001

Words and music by Tommy Boyce and Bobby Hart, produced by Tommy Boyce and Bobby Hart. Rose to #1 on the *Billboard* "Hot 100" chart in fall 1966 (uk23, early 1967).

FORM: Modified simple verse, with verses of different lengths and two interludes not derived from the verses. While the first verse is 14 bars in length, the second is 2 measures longer, owing to a closing line that extends the verse, "and I don't know . . . ." The third verse is like the first, except that it is preceded by the 2-bar guitar figure from the introduction, while the fourth verse is like the second, with the extra concluding bars. The last verse repeats the lyrics of the first, while using the ending of the second. In the middle of all this, two instrumental interludes are inserted. These interludes are actually based on similar material, but differ enough to sound new when they appear in the arrangement.

TIME SIGNATURE: 2/4, with a hint of a country two-step feel, which is a lively one-two, one-two rhythm.

INSTRUMENTATION: Electric guitars, acoustic guitar, bass, drums, tambourine, lead and backup vocals. Note that the guitar lick employed here seems influenced by similar figures in the Beatles' "Ticket to Ride," "Day Tripper," and "I Feel Fine." Note as well that the background vocals imitate a train whistle in various ways throughout the track, picking up on the song's title.

0:00–0:10   **Introduction**, 8 mm., 2 mm.   Beatles-style guitar lick played (w/bass and tambourine) 4 times.

Modeled on the witty and fun-loving Beatles of *A Hard Day's Night* and *Help!*, the Monkees were originally formed as an acting troupe, with the music intended to help promote their weekly television show. Written by professional songwriters and using a studio band, the music proved much more popular than the producers anticipated, and the band enjoyed a string of hit singles and albums.

0:10–0:27	**Verse 1**, 14 mm. (last 2 mm. truncated)	Lead vocal enters, "Take the last . . ."
0:27–0:47	**Verse 2**, 16 mm.	As verse 1 (with 2 mm. ending added), train-whistle background vocals added, "'Cause I'm leaving . . ."
0:47–1:08	**Verse 3**, 18 mm.	4 mm. of guitar from intro, then 14 mm. verse, lead vocal with train-whistle backup vocals, "Take the last . . ."
1:08–1:18	**Interlude 1**, 8 mm.	Vocal melody without words, quieter, pulsating bass guitar.
1:18–1:38	**Verse 4**, 16 mm.	As in verse 2, new train-whistle backup vocals, "Take the last . . ."
1:38–1:57	**Interlude 2**, 16 mm.	No vocal melody, based on the harmonies from interlude 1 but louder and brighter, verse 4 backup vocals enter toward end of this section.
1:57–2:17	**Verse 1**, 16 mm.	Same lyrics as verse 1, same ending as verse 2, "Take the last . . ."
2:17–2:42	**Coda**, 20 mm.	Repetition of same four-measure phrase, with Beatles-inspired guitar lick and another variation of the train-whistle backup vocals.

Bert Rafelson and media executive Bob Schneider, *The Monkees* was a clear response to the Beatles' *A Hard Day's Night* and *Help!* Its intent was to reproduce the spirit of fun and wit that Richard Lester had captured with these two Beatles films. In forming the band, Rafelson and Schneider sought four unknowns who could be trained primarily as an on-camera acting team, but could also play music. In August 1965, auditions were held and eventually four young men who had never worked together were selected. Guitarist and songwriter Michael Nesmith had played professionally in Texas and the Los Angeles folk clubs, while Peter Tork had been part of the Greenwich Village folk scene. Davy Jones and Mickey Dolenz both had professional backgrounds in acting, Dolenz as star of the TV series *Circus Boy*, and Jones as a star of the musical *Oliver!* in London and New York (Jones performed in a selection from the show on the same Ed Sullivan broadcast that featured the Beatles' debut).

Sound Check

Artist	Bob Dylan	The Byrds	The Beach Boys	
Title	Positively 4th Street	Mr. Tambourine Man	California Girls	
Chart peak	p7 1965	p6 1965	p3 1965	
Form	Simple verse	Contrasting verse-chorus	Contrasting verse-chorus	
Rhythm	4/4	4/4	12/8	
Instrumentation	Electric guitar Bass Drums Lead vocal Piano Organ	Electric guitar (12-string) Electric guitar Bass Drums Lead vocal Background vocal	Electric guitar (12-string) Bass Drums Lead vocal Background vocal Organ Percussion Glockenspiel	
Comments	Finger cymbals played on beat four of each measure Organ featured throughout Repetitive 8-bar verse puts the focus on lyrics	Uses only one verse from the Dylan original Guitar enters first, followed by bass and then the full band 12-string guitar has a "jangly" sound often associated with the Byrds	Ambitious instrumentation and arrangement for a rock group Full doo-wop background vocals Short interlude at the end, followed by a return to the chorus	

Since Rafelson and Schneider were mainly concerned with the success of the television show, not the records that might be released by the band, they focused the group's efforts on building their rapport and acting skills. As a result, the musical aspect of the group's training was neglected and when the show was ready to begin production, Rafelson and Schneider needed songs. They turned to the songwriting-production team of Tommy Boyce and Bobby Hart (who had auditioned to become band members themselves), and to former Brill Building publisher Don Kirschner, who had relocated to Los Angeles. The Monkees' music was created according to a distinctively old-school music-business procedure: songs were written by professionals (Boyce and Hart, Goffin and King, Neil Diamond), backing tracks were performed by studio musicians, and the records were produced by Boyce and Hart. Initially, the Monkees did little more than sing on their records, and when word of this leaked out, many in the rock community used the information to discredit the

The Kingsmen	The Monkees
Louie Louie	Last Train to Clarksville
p2, r1 1963	p1 1966
Simple verse-chorus	Simple verse (modified)
4/4	2/4
Electric guitar Bass Drums Lead vocal Electric piano	Electric guitar Acoustic guitar Bass Drums Lead vocal Tambourine
Four-chord riff defines the musical structure Extended guitar solo may have been a mistake Unintelligible lyrics	Clear Beatles influence Backing vocal imitate a train whistle Verse is modified with slightly different lengths and interludes

group. None of this affected the band's popularity, however. While Rafelson and Schneider may have hoped their series would be a hit (which it was), they could not have imagined how successful the music would be. After the show debuted on NBC in fall 1966, the Monkees' "Last Train to Clarksville" rose to the top of the U.S. charts. Soon the success spread to Britain, when "I'm a Believer" went to number one in the States and the UK at the end of 1966. The Monkees followed with "A Little Bit Me, a Little Bit You" (p2 uk3, 1967), "Pleasant Valley Sunday" (p3 uk11, 1967), and "Valleri" (p3 uk12, 1968). The band's first four albums went to number one in the United States and placed in the UK top five. The first two Monkees albums together occupied the U.S. top slot for thirty-one consecutive weeks from late 1966 through the summer of 1967.

While the Monkees were clearly modeled on the Beatles, their music was produced according to the established Brill Building pattern, and this association has led many to dismiss the Monkees' hits. With the exception of guitarist Michael Nesmith, the Monkees did not play on their early records, and Mickey Dolenz or Davy Jones mostly sang songs written by professional songwriters to the accompaniment of studio musicians. "Last Train to Clarksville," however, gives some indication of the kinds of musical complexities that often resided behind the band's bubblegum image. This song is generally in simple verse form, presenting a series of five verses (the fifth repeats the lyrics of the first) with no real chorus. These verses are built on a sixteen-measure pattern, although the first and third verses come to only fourteen measures, owing to the truncation of what would have been the final two measures. Musical contrast is provided by two interludes, the first featuring a wordless vocal melody sung on the syllable "dooo." The second interlude is based on the first, but now guitar **arpeggios** and high background vocals rework the musical material and expand it to encompass sixteen measures.

The Monkees themselves soon came to resent the entertainment-business machine. This was especially true of Nesmith, who felt that the band should be able to write its own material and perform on recordings. This struggle clearly illustrates how the new approach to popular music initiated by the Beatles conflicted with the older approach represented by the Brill Building. Taking their cue from the Beatles, the Monkees wanted to exercise control over the music they recorded. Eventually the band did gain control, although its popularity quickly slipped away. The fact that the Monkees did not initially play on their own records does not set them apart from most Beach Boys records or the Byrds' "Mr. Tambourine Man." Rather, the Monkees' eagerness to play and write is an indication of how deeply the idea that band members should exert greater control had infiltrated rock record production.

In the mid-1960s, there was a clear division in the rock market between young teens who listened to the pop-oriented music of the Monkees and older teens who were drawn to the increasingly more serious-minded and self-conscious rock of the Beatles. Music aimed at younger listeners was called "bubblegum" or "teenybopper" music, and continued to be played on AM radio stations nationwide. After the Monkees, Don Kirschner went on to promote a group made up of cartoon characters that also had a TV show, the Archies. After hitting number twenty-two in the United States with "Bang Shang a Lang" in 1968, the fictitious Archies (whose music was written by Jeff Barry and played by studio musicians) had a chart-topping hit in America and the UK with "Sugar Sugar" (1969). Other make-believe bands directed at young teens populated television in the late 1960s, including the Banana

Splits (characters in fuzzy costumes) and Lancelot Link and the Evolution Revolution (a band of chimpanzees). Even episodes of the Hanna-Barbera cartoon *Scooby-Doo Where Are You!* featured obligatory chase scenes to the accompaniment of pop tunes. By the early 1970s, the Partridge Family would become America's foremost make-believe television band, with David Cassidy (Keith Partridge) sharing space in teen magazines with Bobby Sherman and members of the *Brady Bunch.*

While the younger teens listened to bubblegum pop, their older brothers and sisters were turning to psychedelia—a style of music that eschewed singles in favor of albums and was more likely to be heard on FM instead of AM radio. We will turn to psychedelia in Chapter 7. In the next chapter we explore the rise of soul music in the 1960s and the story of an American company that benefited from the British invasion: Motown.

FURTHER READING

Glenn A. Baker with Tom Czarnota and Peter Hogan, *Monkeemania: The True Story of the Monkees* (Plexus Publishing, 1997).

Sonny Bono, *And the Beat Goes On* (Pocket Books, 1991).

Marc Eliot, *Paul Simon: A Life* (Wiley, 2010).

Clinton Heylin, *Bob Dylan: The Recording Sessions, 1960–1994* (St. Martin's, 1997).

Dave Laing, Karl Dallas, Robin Denselow, and Robert Shelton, *The Electric Music: The Story of Folk into Rock* (Methuen, 1975).

Michelle Phillips, *California Dreamin': The True Story of the Mamas and the Papas* (Warner Books, 1986).

Johnny Rogan, *Timeless Flight Revisited: The Sequel* (Rogan House, 1998).

Andrew Sandoval, *The Monkees: The Day-By-Day Story of the 60s TV Pop Sensation* (Thunder Bay, 2005).

Robert Shelton, *No Direction Home: The Life and Music of Bob Dylan* (Da Capo, 2003).

Ritchie Unterberger, *Urban Spacemen and Wayfaring Strangers: Overlooked Innovators and Eccentric Visionaries of '60s Rock* (Backbeat Books, 2000).

Richie Unterberger, *Turn! Turn! Turn! The '60s Folk-Rock Revolution* (Backbeat Books, 2002).

Sean Wilentz, *Bob Dylan in America* (Doubleday, 2010).

VISIT STUDYSPACE AT WWNORTON.COM/STUDYSPACE

Access free review material such as:

- music links
- performer info
- practice quizzes
- outlines
- interactive listening guide software

DANCING IN THE STREET
MARTHA & THE VANDELLAS

MOTOWN POP AND SOUTHERN SOUL

Until the early 1960s, many African-American musicians were blocked from mainstream success by white artists covering their records. The majority of African-American recording artists were signed to independent labels, and the popularity of their recordings could easily be eclipsed by major label versions. Moreover, British invasion bands took much of their early inspiration from African-American popular music. While some black artists from the early 1960s remarked that the British invasion had a disastrous effect on the girl group movement and sweet soul, by 1965 the situation in the youth-music market had significantly improved for black artists hoping for mainstream hits. Between 1964 and 1970, music by black musicians from regional centers, such as Detroit, Memphis, Muscle Shoals (Alabama), and Atlanta, made an impact on the pop charts. Some black pop was certainly pushed off the charts by the British invasion, but a wealth of new music by African-American performers flourished during this period. Among the most important developments was the music that came out of Motown Records—an independent company whose most important era of success parallels that of the Beatles—and the emergence of southern soul from Memphis. Other legendary performers also established themselves during the 1960s, including James Brown, who had his first success as early as 1956. However, the question we explore in this chapter is not whether black popular music was shoved aside by the British invasion and the American response to it. It is, instead, a question that involves race in a new way: Can one form of this new black popular music be considered "blacker" than another? The American rock press that emerged in the mid-1960s often cast Motown as black pop music that made too many concessions to white sensibilities—that sold out its blackness to make money in the white market. These same

While Motown was best known in the 1960s for its politely restrained pop music, Martha and the Vandellas represented the more soulful side of the Detroit-based label. Lead singer Martha Reeves (center) was a secretary at Motown before being tapped at the last minute to replace Mary Wells for a recording session. "Dancing in the Street" is probably the group's best-known record, and this Holland-Dozier-Holland–produced single rose as high as number two on the *Billboard* "Hot 100" in the summer of 1964. Martha and the Vandellas' style displays more gospel influence than that of their Motown rivals the Supremes, though the looser quality of their music did not translate into considerations of image. As exemplified in this "picture record," the dress and image projected by Motown and its artists was usually polished and controlled, regardless of the musical style explored in the recording. Here, Reeves and company wear evening dresses, presenting an image of sophistication and elegance. One could imagine them performing for the president or the Queen of England as easily as in front of 10,000 screaming teenagers.

writers portray southern soul as music that makes no excuses for its blackness and stays closer to its origins in black culture. This adds a new dimension to the issues of race that played an important role in previous chapters. Here we will consider not only questions of black and white, but also the question of black and blacker. Can such distinctions within black music be valid? After white audiences accepted African-American performers into the mainstream, perceptions of racial authenticity became extremely important to the reception of black pop for both listeners and industry professionals. This was also a time when crossover became so prevalent that between December 1963 and January 1965 *Billboard* stopped tracking R&B charts separately. On one hand, this integration was an encouraging sign. However, with no discreet barometer for an artist's popularity with black audiences, artists that did not have much crossover potential lost an important mechanism for showcasing their popularity. We begin our study of black pop with Motown—a label that enjoyed enormous commercial success in the 1960s.

BERRY GORDY, JR. AND BLACK MUSIC FOR WHITE AUDIENCES

Go Where the Money Is: White Kids and Disposable Income. In the years after World War II, Berry Gordy, Jr., a professional boxer in the Detroit area, worked for his father's construction company, owned a record store, and worked on the Ford assembly line. He spent a lot of time in Detroit's jazz clubs, although his experience with the record store taught him that—financially, at least—jazz was not the key to success in the music business. Gordy began writing songs for fellow Detroiter and former boxer, singer Jackie Wilson, who was looking for material to record. Working with his sister Gwen Gordy and Roquel "Billy" Davis (a.k.a. Tyran Carlo), Gordy wrote several songs that became hits for Wilson, including "Reet Petite" (1957), "Lonely Teardrops" (p7 r1, 1958), and "That's Why (I Love You So)" (p13 r2, 1959). Gordy also wrote and produced songs for other Detroit singers and musicians, leasing these recordings to labels in New York and Chicago. In 1959, Gordy formed Motown records with a loan from his family trust. His first hit record for Motown was Barrett Strong's "Money (That's What I Want)" (p23 r2), a song he had also leased to his sister's record company, Anna Records.

During his first few years in business, Gordy often modeled his releases on already successful records. The Marvelettes' "Please Mr. Postman" (p1 r1, 1961) resembles the girl-group hits of the Brill Building, while the grittier "Do You Love Me" (p3 r1, 1962) by the Contours is similar to the Isley Brothers' style of the early '60s. Gordy knew that there was enormous commercial potential in producing records that could cross over from the rhythm and blues charts onto the pop charts. Adopting Chuck Berry's strategy to prevent covers of his songs by white artists, Gordy decided to make Motown singles acceptable to white listeners in their original versions. In the early 1960s, this meant making records that would appeal to white teenagers. This interest in accommodating white tastes aligned closely with Gordy's roots in the black middle class and the emerging Civil Rights movement. On one hand, Gordy certainly wanted white listeners to buy his music. But this should not be confused with "selling out," as Gordy had been raised in a culture of African Americans that dressed well, had social ambition, and were financially successful. Despite this crossover potential, in the early years the label's success was primarily in the rhythm and blues market. In fact, throughout the 1960s Motown releases frequently charted higher on the rhythm and blues charts than the pop charts. While the first target audience may have been white teens, Gordy soon set his sights on the older middle-class audiences who frequented upscale supper clubs.

Adapting the Brill Building Production Model.
Motown was groundbreaking in many ways, but Gordy's production method was derived from Brill Building practices. He gave songwriting and production duties to a collection of specialized individuals and teams, using a model that had been established by Leiber and Stoller a few years earlier. From 1960 to 1964, Gordy, William "Mickey" Stevenson, and William "Smokey" Robinson handled many of the songwriting and production duties. The first consistently successful Motown group was the Miracles, fronted by Robinson as lead vocalist. Gordy and Robinson wrote the first Miracles hit, "Shop Around" (p2 r1, 1960), while Robinson wrote and produced the group's "You've Really Got a Hold on Me" (p8 r1, 1962). Robinson was among Motown's most successful producers, handling songwriting and production for singer Mary Wells, whose string of hits included "The One Who Really Loves You" (p8 r2, 1962), "You Beat Me to the Punch" (p9 r1, 1962), "Two Lovers" (p7 r1, 1962), and "My Guy" (p1, 1964). The years between 1964 and 1967 at Motown were dominated by the tremendous success of the Brian Holland, Lamont Dozier, and Eddie Holland team. "H-D-H" were responsible for a string of hits by the Supremes, the Four Tops, and Martha and the Vandellas, among others. H-D-H left Motown and stopped producing music in late 1967 over a royalty dispute. The dissatisfaction of the H-D-H team with Gordy's controlling interest in Motown echoed a common complaint about the company through the years. Yet, no one could deny that, no matter how questionable his business practices, Gordy had the rare ability to facilitate the creation of enormously popular music. Following the departure of H-D-H, Norman Whitfield emerged as the label's most successful producer with a series of singles by the Temptations through the early 1970s. In the late 1960s the team of Valerie Ashford and Nick Simpson also had tremendous success at Motown, beginning with a series of Marvin Gaye and Tammi Terrell duets, and Frank Wilson collaborated with the Supremes and the Four Tops.

The Studio, the Band, and Quality Control.
Through most of the 1960s, Motown productions were recorded in the company studio at 2648 West Grand Boulevard in Detroit—called "Hitsville, USA." This studio, and several other offices in converted houses on the same block, made up the business headquarters for the company. The studio was open and busy around the clock, as artists and producers moved in and out working on various releases. Like Phil Spector in Los Angeles, Motown producers had a gifted and experienced group of studio musicians to help them craft their arrangements. Drawn from Detroit's lively jazz scene, these players were adept at creating their parts on the spot, often without the benefit of scored-out parts or even a completed formal design. The musicians might receive only a general idea of the chords and rhythms the producers had in mind. Many musicians were employed at Motown sessions throughout the decade, but the key

The Funk Brothers: Behind the Scenes

The 2003 documentary film *Standing in the Shadows of Motown* chronicles the contributions of the studio musicians behind the Motown sound. Most listeners tend to focus their attention on singers, and perhaps songwriters or producers. Few are aware of the crucial role that backup musicians play on a given record. Candid and intelligent interviews with surviving Motown studio musicians bring these players out of the shadows and into the spotlight.

players were pianist Earl Van Dyke, drummer Benny Benjamin, and electric bassist James Jamerson. One key to the "Motown Sound" was that most of the records featured this studio band, referred to as the Funk Brothers.

Gordy promoted competition within the ranks of Motown performers, songwriters, and producers. Once a week, he gathered the staff together for "quality control" meetings, which served as the final test for each song, its arrangement, and its recorded sound. A number of freshly recorded potential releases were presented for Motown employees, and sometimes members of the community, to vote on which songs would be released that week. These meetings generally proved to be a good barometer of a song's potential success, although the initial vote occasionally went against a now-classic song. Perhaps the most famous example is Marvin Gaye's version of "I Heard It through the Grapevine" in 1967. Only after Gladys Knight and the Pips recorded a new version of the song, which climbed to the top of the charts in late 1967 (p2 r1), did local disc jockeys begin to play Gaye's recording. Realizing that quality control had made a rare mistake, Gordy eventually released Gaye's version of "Grapevine" as a single in 1968, which sold several million copies and went to number one on both the "Hot 100" and the "Best Selling Rhythm & Blues Singles" charts.

Artist Development and Professional Choreography. According to Gordy's philosophy, Motown artists had to project an image of class and sophistication. He wanted the dance movements that accompanied singing in live performance to be refined and graceful, so he hired former Broadway choreographer Cholly

Motown's founder Berry Gordy, seated left, maintained strong influence and control over the artists on his record label. Here, he sits with the Supremes—Mary Wilson and Diana Ross to his left and Florence Ballard seated behind—discussing an upcoming performance. Gordy employed a large staff to help manage and perfect the Motown sound and image.

The Supremes were known as much for their elegant style as for their ubiquitous records during the mid-1960s. Here, the trio performs "I Hear a Symphony" wearing stunning green gowns with an orchestra in 1965 on the NBC television program *Hullabaloo!*

Atkins, who carefully honed every onstage movement and dance step. For what Motown performers playfully called "the charm school," Gordy hired Maxine Powell, who had run a finishing school within Detroit's black community since the early 1950s. Powell was charged with teaching both women and men how to move and speak with grace. Gordy's goal was to prepare his acts for the highest echelons of success in the music business and to book his best acts into elegant supper clubs such as the Copacabana in New York or the big hotel stages of Las Vegas. In light of these ambitious goals, Powell told her charges that she was preparing them to perform and socialize in two places: the White House and Buckingham Palace.

THE MOTOWN ARTISTS

The Supremes. The Supremes were the quintessential Motown girl group from the mid to late 1960s. Working out of the Phil Spector and Brill Building traditions at the beginning of the 1960s, the Supremes extended the girl-group format to the highest reaches of commercial success. The group formed in Detroit in 1959, when Diana Ross, Mary Wilson, Florence Ballard, and Betty McGlown started a quartet called the Primettes—a sister group to the Primes (later known as the Temptations). McGlown soon left the group, and the remaining trio hung around the Motown headquarters hoping to sing backup and convince Gordy to sign them (he once told them to go home and finish school). They were eventually signed, though their first singles were so unsuccessful that other Motown artists jokingly called them the "no-hit Supremes." Holland-Dozier-Holland took over production and songwriting duties for the group, and they hit in 1964 with "Where Did Our Love Go?" (p1). Although Ballard was considered the most accomplished singer, H-D-H experimented during the sessions for this single with both Wilson's and Ross's voices, deciding that Ross's was the more evocative. Once they found the formula, the team chalked up a string of five consecutive number one pop hits, following up with "Baby Love" (1964), "Come See about Me" (r3, 1964), "Stop! In the Name of Love" (r2, 1965), and "Back in My Arms Again" (r1, 1965). Showing the perceived interchangeability of Motown artists in groups like the Supremes, Ballard was asked to leave the group in 1967 after a series of personal issues, and was replaced by Cindy Birdsong. The group continued its success with "Reflections" (p2 r4, 1967) and, after the departure of H-D-H, "Love Child" (p1 r2, 1968). Ross left the

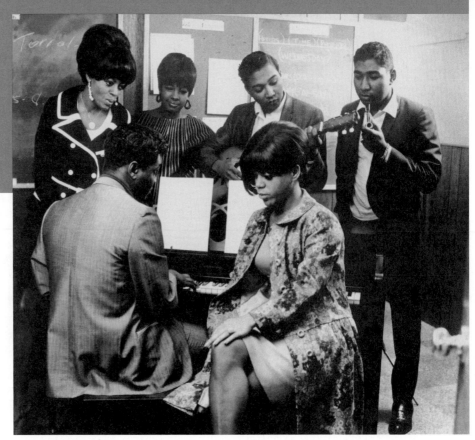

group in late 1969 to focus on her solo career. "Someday We'll Be Together" (p1 r1, 1969), an ironic title in retrospect, was her last hit single with the group, which had changed its name to Diana Ross and the Supremes amidst Ross's growing stature as the leader of the group. Ross became a very successful solo artist, and was replaced in the Supremes by Jean Terrell as the group went on to score several more pop hits in the 1970s, including "Stoned Love" (p7 r1, 1970).

The Supremes and Holland-Dozier-Holland. From 1964 to 1967, the teaming of the Supremes with Holland-Dozier-Holland produced a series of hit singles that made H-D-H one of the most successful writing and production teams in popular music and placed the Supremes among the top recording artists of the decade. A number one hit in the fall of 1964, "Baby Love" is a prime example of a Supremes hit written and produced by H-D-H during the mid-1960s.

The track begins with an introduction that features a series of pulsating piano chords accompanied by drums. Notice that the rhythm of the piano and drums is supported by what sound like handclaps or marching. This sound was produced by slapping together wooden two-by-fours, making the song's beat unmistakable. Also present is the sound of the vibraphone (or "vibes"), a percussion instrument similar to the xylophone but featuring a sustained sound with vibrato. Notice from the Listening Guide that the song is a simple verse form. The repeated verses are performed with little change in the accompaniment, which includes electric guitar and bass after the introduction. The other Supremes provide backup vocals as Ross works her way through seven verses. There are a few twists to the arrangement: in the third verse, a saxophone takes over for the lead vocal for the last eight measures,

Listening Guide

Get Music ⑤ wwnorton.com/studyspace

The Supremes, "Baby Love" Motown 1066

Words and music by Brian Holland, Lamont Dozier, and Edward Holland, Jr., produced by Brian Holland and Lamont Dozier. Reached #1 on the *Billboard* "Hot 100" chart in the fall of 1964. (Note that the *Billboard* R&B charts did not run from December 1963 to late January 1965.)

FORM: Simple verse. A 12-bar verse structure is repeated relatively unchanged throughout. The only significant alterations are in verse 3, where the saxophones take over the melody after four bars, and in verse 5, which introduces a change of key via a 2-bar transition. The arrangement builds by adding instruments: the guitar enters in verse 2, as do call-and-response phrases between the lead and backup vocals, and saxophones are added in verse 3. The change of key gives the song a lift after verse 4. The song structure is nevertheless very simple, relying heavily on the vocal performance of Diana Ross.

TIME SIGNATURE: 4/4 (shuffle in four). Note how the sounds of feet stomping on boards pound out the beat throughout the song.

INSTRUMENTATION: Piano, vibes, electric guitar, bass, drums, saxes, foot stomping, lead and backing vocals.

0:00–0:09	**Introduction**, 5 mm.	Stomping boards, vibes, piano, and drums prepare the way for the vocals.
0:09–0:30	**Verse 1**, 12 mm.	Vocals enter, and Ross sings solo with only a little backup. "Ooo, baby love . . ."
0:30–0:51	**Verse 2**, 12 mm.	Add guitar, as backup vocals add call and response to second half of verse. "'Cause baby love . . ."
0:51–1:13	**Verse 3**, 12 mm.	4 mm. of vocals with sax backup, and then saxes take melody, "Need ya . . ."
1:13–1:34	**Verse 4**, 12 mm.	As verse 3, without the saxes, "Baby love . . ."
1:34–1:58	**Verse 5**, 14 mm.	2 mm. key change peps up arrangement and then the regular 12 mm. verse follows, as the saxes return. "Need to hold you . . ."
1:58–2:20	**Verse 6**, 12 mm.	As verse 5, ". . . of me my love . . ."
2:20–2:40	**Verse 7**, 12 mm.	Fade out on second half of verse, "'Til it's hurtin' me . . ."

making the vocal return for verse 4 sound fresher than it might otherwise. Verse 5 introduces a change of key (up a half-step from D-flat to D) that also propels the song forward. The pronounced rhythmic stomping in this tune is a continuation from the previous single, "Where Did Our Love Go?," as is the repetition of the word "baby"—showing that H-D-H were trying to repeat a winning formula with this second single.

Martha and the Vandellas. Formed in Detroit in 1962 by former members of the Del-Phis, who had recorded for Chess Records, Martha and the Vandellas was another important Motown girl group. Martha Reeves was performing in a Detroit club when she was spotted by Motown producer Mickey Stevenson, who hired her not as a singer but as his secretary. When the backup singers hired for a Marvin Gaye recording session failed to show up for one session, Reeves and her friends provided backup vocals on "Stubborn Kind of Fellow" (p46 r8, 1962), impressing Gordy enough that he had them record "I'll Have to Let Him Go" (which did not chart) as Martha and the Vandellas. By early 1963, the group consisted of Reeves on lead vocals, backed by Rosalyn Ashford and Annette Beard (Betty Kelly replaced Beard in 1964). The group had its first hit during the winter of 1963, when the Holland-Dozier-Holland–produced "Come and Get These Memories" hit number twenty-nine on the *Billboard* "Hot 100" (r6). After their first hit with H-D-H, the group followed up with "Heat Wave" (p4 r1, 1963) and "Quicksand" (p8, 1963) before Mickey Stevenson took over production duties for what would become the group's most successful and best known single, "Dancing in the Street" (p2, 1964). Martha and the Vandellas continued their success through 1967 with singles produced by H-D-H, including "Nowhere to Run" (p8 r5, 1965) and "Jimmy Mack" (p10 r1, 1967). Despite their popularity, the group certainly suffered because of the Supremes' success and the attention Motown gave to cultivating Diana Ross. Moreover, roots in gospel and rhythm and blues were more apparent in the recordings of Martha and the Vandellas than those of the Supremes, who sounded somewhat controlled by comparison. This was largely due to Martha Reeves's full-throated, soulful vocal style, which paralleled southern soul and set the stage for Aretha Franklin later in the decade.

The Temptations. A typical Motown guy group known for their athletic choreographed dance moves, the Temptations were among the label's top acts between 1964 and 1972. The group formed in 1961 in Detroit when Otis Williams, Melvin Franklin, and Al Bryant of the Distants joined forces with Eddie Kendricks and Paul Williams (no relation to Otis) of the Primes. In 1963, after a few unsuccessful releases for Motown, Bryant left the group and David Ruffin joined, completing the classic Temptations lineup that would remain intact until 1968. The group hit the pop charts in early 1964 (when the Beatles were making their first splash), with "The Way You Do the Things You Do" (p11), a tune written and produced by Robinson that showcased Kendricks's high tenor lead vocal. This catchy track is an example of the early Temptations style, and highlights Robinson's clever approach to writing lyrics. While lines such as "You got a smile so bright, you know you could've been a candle" may sound a bit corny in isolation, when combined with Robinson's sunny music, they come to life in a distinctive and broadly appealing way. On the basis of this song's success, subsequent Temptations releases were produced by Robinson, including "My Girl" (p1 r1, 1965) and "Get Ready" (p29 r1, 1965). Perhaps disappointed that Robinson could not duplicate the enormous success of "My Girl," Gordy gave Norman Whitfield a chance to produce the group in 1966. Beginning with "Ain't Too Proud to Beg" (p13 r1, 1966), he delivered a string of hits for the group, including "I Know I'm Losing You" (p8 r1, 1966) and "You're My Everything" (p6 r3, 1967).

THE 'TEMPTATION WALK'

THE DANCE CRAZE SWEEPING THE COUNTRY
— AS DEMONSTRATED BY —

THE TEMPTATIONS
GORDY RECORDING ARTISTS

The seven basic steps of the "Temptation Walk," a prancing, high-stepping routine created by the sensational Temptations, is shown here.

The Temptations were one of Motown's most consistently successful groups. They were known for their smooth singing style—drawing strongly on the doo-wop tradition—and their tightly choreographed dance steps.

Listening Guide   Get Music ⓢ wwnorton.com/studyspace

The Temptations, "The Way You Do the Things You Do"
Gordy 7028

Words and music by William "Smokey" Robinson and Robert Rogers, produced by Smokey Robinson. Reached #11 on the *Billboard* "Hot 100" chart in 1964.

FORM: Simple verse. After an introduction based on a two-chord vamp, the first two verses follow the same lengthy structure: a 16-bar section that leads into a 4-bar refrain and then a 3-bar ending subsection (based on the two-chord vamp from the introduction). This extended structure is truncated after the second verse, first in an 8-bar instrumental verse, then in the third verse, which pares the structure down to 12 mm. Robinson builds the arrangement by adding horns in verse 2, changing key for the saxophone solo, and scoring the horns in a higher register in verse 3.

TIME SIGNATURE: 4/4 (shuffle in four).

INSTRUMENTATION: Electric guitar, piano, bass, drums, horns, lead and backup vocals.

0:00–0:08	**Introduction**, 4 mm.	Two-chord vamp featuring guitar with treble tone.
0:08–0:53	**Verse 1 w/refrain**, 23 mm.	Harmony vocals take first part of each phrase ("You got a smile so bright . . ."), which is answered by Kendricks's high tenor ("You know you could have been . . .").
0:53–1:37	**Verse 2 w/refrain**, 23 mm.	Vocals continue call and response, though now the harmony parts add some supporting "ooo's" derived from doo-wop. Horns are added. "As pretty as you are . . ."
1:37–1:52	**Instrumental Verse** (partial), 8 mm.	Verse is shortened, change of key, sax solo.
1:52–2:16	**Verse 3 w/refrain** (partial), 12 mm.	Horns are higher than before, and this gives the song an increased intensity, "You made my life so rich . . ."
2:16–2:38	**Coda**, 12 mm.	Vamp on chords from introduction, lead vocal improvises over repeated backup vocals.

The Four Tops. Formed in 1954 by Levi Stubbs, Obie Benson, Lawrence Payton, and Duke Fakir, the Four Tops were older and more experienced than most Motown groups of the mid-1960s. The group was originally signed to Chicago's Chess Records, but moved to Motown in 1964 and recorded a jazz album for Gordy's Workshop Jazz label. They were soon teamed up with Holland-Dozier-Holland, who had begun working with the Supremes a few months earlier. Led by the vocals of Stubbs, the Four Tops were in many ways the male counterparts of the Supremes, enjoying a string of H-D-H–produced hits, including "Baby

I Need Your Loving" (p11, 1964), "I Can't Help Myself (Sugar Pie, Honey Bunch)" (p1 r1, 1965), "It's the Same Old Song" (p5 r2, 1965), "Reach Out I'll Be There" (p1 r1, 1966), and "Standing in the Shadows of Love" (p6 r2, 1966). Like the music of the Supremes, most of the Four Tops' songs have a pronounced pop orientation, with frequent use of orchestral strings and other instrumentation drawn from classical music. "Reach Out I'll Be There" illustrates this blend of rhythm and blues and classical music in the use of winds in its orchestral introduction and its harmonic progressions, combined with a strong beat and soulful vocals.

Marvin Gaye and Stevie Wonder. Motown was also home to many important solo singers during the 1960s, including Mary Wells, Kim Weston, and Brenda Holloway. Two of the company's most important solo vocalists were Marvin Gaye and Stevie Wonder (known for much of the decade as "Little" Stevie Wonder). Originally, Gaye sought a career as a pop crooner in the vein of Frank Sinatra or Nat "King" Cole, but he found the Motown environment more suitable to creating dance-oriented R&B hits. In 1962 he had a hit with "Stubborn Kind of Fellow," and continued this success through the decade with sixteen more singles in the pop Top 40, and another ten duets with Mary Wells, Tammi Terrell, and Kim Weston. Gaye worked with most of the Motown producers, recording upbeat soul hits like "Pride and Joy" (p10 r2, 1963) with Mickey Stevenson, pop hits like "How Sweet It Is to Be Loved by You" (p6 r4, 1965) with Holland-Dozier-Holland, and "Ain't That Peculiar" (p8 r1, 1965) with Smokey Robinson. He also recorded classic duets like "Ain't Nothing Like the Real Thing" (p8 r1, 1968), sung with Tammi Terrell and produced by Ashford and Simpson. In 1968, Gaye continued his solo success with the Norman Whitfield and Barrett Strong song "I Heard It through the Grapevine." By the end of the decade, he was also writing and producing for other artists, and the Originals, a male vocal quartet, became his charges in the studio. The combination produced the hits "Baby I'm for Real" (p14 r1, 1969) and "The Bells" (p12 r4, 1970).

Stevie Wonder followed a path similar to Marvin Gaye's. Signed to Motown in 1961 at the age of eleven, Wonder was blind from birth and promoted as a musical prodigy in the manner of Ray Charles. At the age of thirteen, he scored a surprise number one hit on both the pop and rhythm and blues charts with "Fingertips, pt. 2" (1963). The record captures an impromptu moment during a live Motown Revue concert when Wonder launches into an extended improvisation without warning (bass player Larry Moses can be heard asking "What key? What key?"). The spontaneous and exuberant quality of that moment transferred well to vinyl, and Motown ended up with one of its most successful releases up to that time. After this initial success, Wonder floundered a bit—his voice changed and Motown seemed unsure how to advance his career. By early 1966, however, his "Uptight (Everything's Alright)" hit number three on the pop charts (r1), beginning a string of hits that included "I Was Made to Love Her" (p2 r1, 1967), "For Once in My Life" (p2 r2, 1968), and "My Cherie Amour" (p4 r4, 1969), with Wonder earning partial songwriting credit for each. In 1970, he produced "Signed, Sealed, Delivered, I'm Yours" (p3 r1), helping Motown to make the transition out of the 1960s. The music of Gaye and Wonder, and their role as producers, will be considered further in Chapter 9.

Assimilation, Motown, and the Civil Rights Movement. The enormous crossover appeal of Motown's records and artists in the mid-1960s, combined with Gordy's desire to appeal to white audiences, has frequently prompted criticisms that Motown sold out to white America. The rock-oriented music press never gave Motown pop much credit, and the black community frequently complained that Gordy hired too many white executives. In defense of the label, even if this is so, black American listeners never really tuned Motown out. In fact, even if the pop charts are not taken into account, Motown remains one of the most important and successful rhythm and blues labels of the 1960s. Considerations of musical style aside, the carefully choreographed movements and the charm-school training may be the most important signals of an assimilationist attitude on Gordy's part—the idea that blacks can or should assimilate into the larger American population (while retaining a strong sense of heritage). This perception of Motown as pandering to the white public was complicated by the company's middle-class origins. Who is to say, for example, that black listeners didn't like the white music of the pop charts? For many who oppose the idea of refined black pop, the African-American music that began coming out of the South—and Memphis especially—in the mid-1960s can be seen as a counter-example. This southern soul music, some would argue, was actually much more in touch with its own roots in black culture. Whatever position you take, Berry Gordy was a pivotal figure in the development of black pop music, and his success inspired and served as a model for many African-American musicians in the 1970s, including George Clinton and Gamble and Huff.

ATLANTIC, STAX, AND SOUTHERN SOUL

Atlantic in the Early 1960s. Motown was not the only label with crossover hits in the 1960s. As discussed at the end of Chapter 3, New York–based Atlantic Records enjoyed considerable success in the early 1960s with hits from the Drifters, the Coasters, and Ben E. King. During this period, the highly produced and often relaxed style of sweet soul was the most public face of the label's activity. Later in the decade, Atlantic invested heavily in a new stylistic direction—a harder-edged brand of black pop that became known as southern soul.

Along with the label's cofounder Ahmet Ertegun, producer Jerry Wexler was responsible for much of Atlantic's success in the late 1950s. With the emergence of other producers at the label, most notably Leiber and Stoller, Wexler soon found himself focused on directing the label's business affairs. His interest in producing was rekindled, however, when Atlantic signed gospel-influenced singer Solomon Burke in 1961. Working with Bert Berns, Wexler produced a series of successful singles for Burke, including "If You Need Me" (p37 r2, 1963), "Everybody Needs Somebody to Love" (p58, 1964), "Got to Get You off My Mind" (p22 r1, 1965), and "Tonight's the Night" (p28 r2, 1965).

There is an important stylistic difference between sweet and southern soul: sweet soul tends to be more restrained. The Drifters' "Under the Boardwalk" and Ben E. King's "Stand by Me" are examples of sweet soul from the early 1960s. Southern soul incorporates enthusiastic emotional expression, often associated with gospel music. As was apparent in the reception of southern soul as it emerged in the mid-1960s, expectations of both black and white listeners often perceived the pronounced gospel influence in southern soul as truer to the African-American heritage than softer, more pop-oriented styles of black music. Wexler was quick to hear this quality and realize the potential for sales in the mainstream market. While black listeners were searching for music that expressed a growing consciousness of racial identity in the context of the Civil Rights movement, white listeners were fascinated with "real" black culture and wanted to hear unadulterated sounds from the South. Wexler played a crucial role in developing southern soul throughout the decade, either by signing artists directly to Atlantic or licensing their recordings from other, smaller labels.

Soulsville, USA: The Memphis Connection.

Larger record companies often licensed recordings from smaller labels, pressing new copies or simply distributing a record for smaller companies. This was a mutually beneficial relationship: it relieved the smaller company of the significant financial commitment of pressing large numbers of records while providing access to markets that would otherwise be out of reach. Larger companies benefited from sharing in the profits of records that were proven regional hits, and were often more innovative than those produced within an established company. Atlantic and Memphis-based Stax formed a very successful partnership through this type of agreement. Founded in 1960 by Jim Stewart and his sister Estelle Axton, Stax Records came to the attention of Atlantic's Jerry Wexler with the single "Cause I Love You." Written by Memphis DJ Rufus Thomas and sung as a duet with his daughter Carla, it became a regional hit in the South. Atlantic leased the national rights to the record, and then secured the rights to "Gee Whiz," a second single written and sung by Carla Thomas, which rose to number ten on the *Billboard* "Hot 100" chart and number five on the "Hot R&B Sides" in early 1961. With right of first refusal on the Stax catalog, Atlantic scored success on both the pop and R&B charts with several Stax singles, including the instrumentals "Last Night" (p3 r2, 1961) by the Mar-Keys and "Green Onions" (p3 r1, 1962) by Booker T. & the MG's, as well as Rufus Thomas's dance hit "Walkin' the Dog" (p10 r5, 1963). The leasing of rights worked out well for both labels, and led to a closer relationship between them.

In the early 1960s, Stax was a much smaller operation than Motown. Like Motown, however, Stax often depended on its studio band, Booker T. & the MG's, to pull together backing tracks on the spot, often without music or prepared arrangements. The band's membership changed a bit, but by the time of the classic recordings by Otis Redding, Wilson Pickett, and Sam and Dave in the mid-1960s, the core members of the band were: Booker T. Jones on organ, Steve Cropper on guitar, Donald "Duck" Dunn on bass, Al Jackson, Jr. on drums, Andrew Love on saxophone, and Wayne Jackson on trumpet. Unlike Motown, where roles were mostly kept distinct, production duties and credits at Stax were shared among the studio musicians, Stewart, and other singers and producers present at the sessions. Cropper worked closely with Otis Redding, cowriting songs and playing the role of producer at many sessions. The closest thing Stax had to the songwriting and production specialists at Motown was the team of David Porter and Isaac Hayes. Porter and Hayes wrote and produced material for the Astors, Carla Thomas, and the Soul Children, but their greatest success was with Sam and Dave. Stax sessions were often less regimented than Motown sessions might have been, with studio musicians filling whatever role was needed in a given situation. Despite the differences between Stax and Motown, the Hitsville and "Soulsville" approaches were quite similar. In reality, at both companies, music often emerged spontaneously during recording sessions. This was not as common at the larger companies located in New York and Los Angeles.

Otis Redding and Stax.

One of the most important Stax artists during the 1960s was Otis Redding, who recorded for the company's Volt label. As early as 1963,

Redding released "These Arms of Mine," which scored moderately on the R&B charts (r20). A series of crossover hits followed during 1965, including "Mr. Pitiful" (p41 r10), "I've Been Loving You Too Long" (p21 r2), and "Respect" (p35 r4). Redding's success brought the "Stax sound" to a national audience. His gospel-influenced vocals, combined with the driving accompaniment of Booker T. & the MG's, produced a style of southern soul that seemed less polished but more heartfelt and urgent than the slicker records coming out of Motown. Redding followed up his earlier chart success with "Try a Little Tenderness" (p25 r4, 1966) and "Sittin' on the Dock of the Bay" (p1 r1, 1968), which became a hit after after he was killed in a plane crash in December 1967. Before his tragic death, Redding made significant inroads with the hippie rockers when he appeared (backed by Booker T. & the MG's) at the Monterey Pop Festival in spring 1967. Although present day audiences might not consider it strange for a southern-based rhythm and blues singer to perform at a mainstream pop festival in northern California, at the time the band was extremely apprehensive. As it turned out, the flower children who attended the festival warmly embraced Redding and his music, encouraging white audiences to further explore the southern soul movement.

Wilson Pickett and the Muscle Shoals Sound.

After singing with a Detroit-based vocal group called the Falcons, Wilson Pickett came to the attention of Jerry Wexler in 1963 under unlikely circumstances. Pickett had sung on the original demo recording from which Wexler, Bert Berns, and Solomon Burke worked while recording "If You Need Me." In a strange error of omission, Atlantic bought the rights to the song but not the original demo, and Pickett's version, released on the Double L label, competed directly on the rhythm and blues charts with Burke's recording. In 1964, Pickett came to Atlantic looking for a record deal, and Wexler was happy to sign him as a solo act. After a few unsuccessful releases produced by Berns and recorded in New York, Wexler decided to take Pickett to the Stax studios, where he hoped to capture something of the more relaxed quality heard in Otis Redding's music. During the recording sessions for Pickett's "In the Midnight Hour," Wexler described to the musicians a dance he had seen in New York featuring a movement that seemed to delay beats two and four until the last possible moment. Trying to imitate this movement musically, the band discovered a "delayed backbeat" feel that became a regular element in the southern soul sound. Recorded in May 1965, "In the Midnight Hour" hit number one on the rhythm and blues charts and number twenty three on

This poster advertises three Redding performances at the Fillmore (San Francisco) in 1966, each night with a different local band opening—including the Grateful Dead!

Listening Guide

Get Music ⑤ wwnorton.com/studyspace

Wilson Pickett, "In the Midnight Hour" Atlantic 2289

Words and music by Wilson Pickett and Steve Cropper, produced by Jerry Wexler. Rose to #23 on the *Billboard* "Hot 100" chart and #1 on the *Billboard* "Top Selling Rhythm and Blues Singles" chart in the summer of 1965.

FORM: Simple verse, with an instrumental interlude. After an instrumental introduction featuring the horns, the band falls into a repeated figure, often called a "vamp." In this case, the vamp is made up of two chords played over one measure, and this measure is repeated. Two 17-bar verses featuring Pickett's lead vocal are followed by an instrumental interlude with the horns playing over new material based on the intro vamp. Pickett's vocals then return, and he delivers only the first part of a verse before seeming to improvise over the intro vamp as the song fades out.

TIME SIGNATURE: 4/4, with an accent on the second beat of each measure that is so late it is almost out of time. This is the Stax "delayed backbeat."

INSTRUMENTATION: Electric guitars, bass, drums, horns, lead vocals.

0:00–0:13	**Introduction**, 6 mm.	A 4 mm. harmonized line in horns leads into the 2 mm. vamp.
0:13–0:50	**Verse 1**, 17 mm.	Vocals enter. Note the low horn (baritone sax) that helps to propel the song's groove, and how the rhythm guitar and snare drum lock in on beats two and four. "I'm gonna wait . . ."
0:50–1:27	**Verse 2**, 17 mm.	As before, but horns added to the first part of the verse. "I'm gonna wait . . ."
1:27–1:44	**Instrumental Interlude**, 23 mm.	Horns play over a new melody loosely based on the introduction.
1:44–2:31	**Verse** (partial), 20 mm.	Pickett seems to start a final verse as the horns play a new line underneath, but the vamp continues without changing in the usual place, as Pickett improvises and the song fades out. "I'm gonna wait . . ."

the pop charts around the time that Bob Dylan and the Byrds were introducing listeners to folk rock.

Presumably to maintain his label's sonic identity, Stax founder Jim Stewart then began denying outside productions in the Stax studio. Wexler's response was to take Pickett to Muscle Shoals, Alabama. Atlantic had distributed the 1965 hit "Hold What You've Got" (p5 r2), recorded at Fame Studios by Dial Records artist Joe Tex.

Wexler had also recently licensed Percy Sledge's "When a Man Loves a Woman," which also had crossover success in spring 1966. The song had been recorded at a small studio called Quinvy in the Muscle Shoals area, but Wexler's contact Rick Hall owned and operated Fame Studios. Impressed by Sledge's record even before it became a hit, Wexler brought Pickett to Fame to record. Pickett recorded some of his best-known tracks at the studio, including "Land of 1000 Dances" (p6 r1, 1966), "Mustang Sally" (p26 r6, 1966), and "Funky Broadway" (p8 r1, 1967).

Like Memphis and Detroit, Muscle Shoals had a core of fine studio musicians, the most important of whom were guitarist Jimmy Johnson, keyboardist Spooner Oldham, and drummer Roger Hawkins. The success of "When a Man Loves a Woman" and Pickett's hits was attributed by many in the music business to the "Muscle Shoals sound," which made the area a popular place to record.

Sam and Dave, Porter and Hayes. A second part of Wexler's response to being shut out of the Stax studio was to offer the vocal duo Sam and Dave to Stax "on loan." They would remain under contract to Atlantic but Stewart maintained creative control over the duo, making records with them as if they were Stax artists. Stewart teamed Sam and Dave with Stax songwriters David Porter and Isaac Hayes, and the team produced a series of successful singles, starting with "You Don't Know Like I Know" (r7) in early 1966, and crossing over to the pop charts in mid-1966 with "Hold On, I'm Comin'" (p21 r1). Sam and Dave's best-known song is "Soul Man," which hit number two on the pop charts and number one on the rhythm and blues charts in fall 1967. In 1979 the song achieved even wider popularity with a cover version by the Blues Brothers (led by *Saturday Night Live* comedians John Belushi and Dan Aykroyd), who were in part modeled on Sam and Dave. Working in tandem with successful Stax artists like Otis Redding and Booker T. & the MG's, Sam and Dave brought soul music to a national audience through their hit records and energetic stage performances.

The Stax Sound. Because so much southern soul was recorded in Memphis and Muscle Shoals, the genre is strongly associated with Stax. Musicians from some southern labels clearly attempted to imitate the style and sound of the first hits by Otis Redding, Wilson Pickett, and Sam and Dave that were recorded at Stax. Other southern soul, such as Al Green's music for Memphis-based Hi Records, shares sonic elements with the stereotypical Stax sound: a prominent organ, distinctive horn arrangements that became associated with Memphis, a funky bass, and a clean, biting guitar sound. Yet, within the style of southern soul, Green's music differs sharply from anything released by Stax during the 1960s, mainly in Green's high, falsetto vocal delivery. Wilson Pickett's "In the Midnight Hour," released by Atlantic and recorded at Stax, is representative of the Stax sound. The track begins with a four-measure introduction featuring horns, followed by two measures of a simple two-chord pattern that forms the basis for the tune. Between the horn intro and the entrance of Pickett's voice, listen to the character of the rhythmic feel: notice that the guitar and snare drum play together on beats 2 and 4, which occur so late that they are almost out of time. (This is the delayed backbeat rhythm mentioned above.) Comparing "In the Midnight Hour" to the Supremes' "Baby Love" clarifies the differences between stereotypical music from Stax and Motown during the mid-1960s. Both songs are in simple verse form and use instrumental introductions and interludes featuring horns to create a sense of formal variety. Typical of the Stax sound, however, there are no backup vocals on the Pickett track, making his vocal delivery the focus of the song. Pickett's performance makes it seem as if his vocalizing is spontaneous and only loosely planned, leaving the listener to imagine that another performance could differ greatly.

Aretha Franklin. Known as the Queen of Soul, Aretha Franklin was born in Memphis, raised in Detroit, and recorded most of her hits in New York. Of all the artists Jerry Wexler brought to Atlantic, Franklin enjoyed the greatest success on both the pop and rhythm and blues charts, despite her relatively late arrival on the southern soul scene.

Franklin is the daughter of the Reverend C. L. Franklin, who led one of the most prominent African-American congregations in the United States at New Bethel Baptist Church in Detroit. C. L. Franklin was known throughout the country for his rousing sermons, which were regularly broadcast on the radio and released on record. Aretha grew up hearing some of the best gospel singers in the world at close range. She credits Clara Ward's performance of "Peace in the Valley" at a Franklin family funeral with inspiring her to devote herself to a career as a singer. When she turned eighteen and with her father's blessing, Franklin left Detroit for New York to pursue a singing career. In the early 1960s she was signed to Columbia Records, and released several records of traditional pop songs in a mainstream setting. These early records did not make much of a commercial impact. When the Columbia contract expired in 1966, Wexler moved in, trying to get Stax to sign Franklin, but eventually signing her directly to Atlantic. In early 1967, in the wake of his fallout with Stax, Wexler brought Franklin to Fame Studios to record her first tracks for Atlantic.

The sessions at Fame started well. The first track completed was the hit "I Never Loved a Man (The Way I Love You)" (p37 r9, 1967), which abandoned the supper-club, easy-jazz character of Franklin's Columbia work to showcase the gospel roots of her singing. After completing this first track, however, the session fell apart when a dispute broke out between Franklin's husband and somebody else in the studio. Soon thereafter Franklin and Wexler were back in New York working on more tracks with the Muscle Shoals rhythm section, who had been flown in without Rick Hall's knowledge. These and later New York sessions—southern soul recorded in the Big Apple—produced a series of hits for Franklin, including a reworking of Otis Redding's "Respect" (p1 r1, 1967), as well as "Baby I Love You" (p4 r1, 1967), "(You Make Me Feel Like) A Natural Woman" (p2 r2, 1967), "Chain of Fools" (p2 r1, 1968), and "Think" (p7 r1, 1968). "Respect" illustrates the power of Aretha Franklin's soul music from the late 1960s. By changing the perspective of the song from male to female, she turned Redding's arguably sexist rant into a feminist anthem. Her performance of "Respect" is so powerful that, although Redding wrote it and recorded it first, Franklin's performance has become the cultural standard.

Motown, Atlantic, Stax, and Issues of Blackness. Rock critics have often characterized the southern soul of Stax and Atlantic as being truer to black culture than the productions of Motown, which, despite its tremendous success, is often cast as a kind of sellout to the white market. The wide scope of black culture explored in the musical output of these two companies, however, shows a broad range of African-American experience in the United States after World War II. Furthermore, no company makes records unless it believes they will sell. Motown, Stax,

Like many rhythm and blues singers, Aretha Franklin was strongly influenced by gospel music. Pictured here is one of her first-ever recordings, a 1962 live performance at her father's church in Detroit. This album featured sermons from her father, C. L. Franklin, and music from Sammie Bryant, another prominent gospel artist. Franklin never totally abandoned gospel. Her best-selling album was *Amazing Grace* (1972), which featured "Precious Lord" and "Never Grow Old," two songs also featured on this record.

ARETHA FRANKLIN

THERE IS A FOUNTAIN FILLED WITH BLOOD

PRECIOUS LORD Part 1

PRECIOUS LORD Part 2

YOU GROW CLOSER

NEVER GROW OLD

SAMMIE BRYANT

THE ANGELS KEEP WATCHING OVER ME

THE LAST MILE

REV. C. L. FRANKLIN

THE LORD WILL MAKE A WAY Part 1

THE LORD WILL MAKE A WAY Part 2

TRYING TO GET HOME Part 1

TRYING TO GET HOME Part 2

SPIRITUALS RECORDED DURING SERVICE AT
NEW BETHEL BAPTIST CHURCH—DETROIT, MICH.

REV. C. L. FRANKLIN, PASTOR

and Atlantic were simply directing their music to different areas of the marketplace. If we compare the Supremes' "Baby Love" and Wilson Pickett's "In the Midnight Hour," the sonic contrast between the two labels is clear—the Supremes track is much more polished in the traditional music-business sense: it focuses on the song and the vocals, and never makes too much of its blackness. If Martha and the Vandellas' "Heat Wave" or "Dancing in the Street" is brought into the discussion, however, the differences between the two companies are harder to discern. The same can be said of Carla Thomas's music on Stax, which often sounds more gentle than stereotypical southern soul. Further confounding the typical distinctions between Motown and Stax/Atlantic is that Motown was owned and run by black Americans. Until the mid-1960s, almost everybody involved with Motown was black and by the end of the decade it was among the country's top black-owned businesses. Stax and Atlantic, on the other hand, both had white owners, and most of their records had white producers. Both the Stax and Motown bands were integrated. Booker T. & the MG's was comprised of two white performers (Cropper and Dunn) and two black performers (Jones and Jackson), and Motown's Funk Brothers employed white guitarists Joe Messina and Dennis Coffey. To further confuse stereotypes of race and southern soul, almost everyone aside from the singers at Muscle Shoals was white. This raises many questions for consideration: What makes music sound black or white? What is it in the music that makes it "sound black"? Can white musicians

Aretha Franklin in a recording session at Fame Studios in Muscle Shoals, Alabama, 1967. After recording smooth pop songs for Columbia, Franklin signed with Atlantic. Jerry Wexler encouraged her to be more expressive, drawing on the passion of gospel. The session pictured here was Franklin's first for Atlantic, and it yielded some of her biggest hits, including "I've Never Loved a Man (The Way I Love You)." While other hits, like "Respect," were recorded in New York, Franklin and Wexler continued to pursue the "southern sound" that first surfaced in Muscle Shoals.

Listening Guide

Get Music Ⓢ **wwnorton.com/studyspace**

Aretha Franklin, "Respect" Atlantic 2403

Words and music by Otis Redding, produced by Jerry Wexler. Reached #1 on the *Billboard* "Hot 100" and "Top Selling R&B Singles" charts.

FORM: Modified simple verse. Beginning with a 4-bar introduction, this track continues by presenting three very similar 10-bar verses. It then moves into an 8-bar instrumental bridge, which provides a brief contrast before returning to the fourth verse. Perhaps the most notable formal feature of this track is the coda, which begins with Franklin's famous passage ("R E S P E C T"). As distinctive as these measures are, they really only help launch the song's ending and are built on the same two-chord vamp that is used for the entire coda and fade-out.

TIME SIGNATURE: 4/4. This is Wexler's attempt to capture the Stax rhythmic feel in Atlantic's New York studios.

INSTRUMENTATION: Electric guitar, organ, piano, bass, drums, tambourine, horns, lead and backup vocals. Note that while Franklin's lead vocals are much more relaxed than most other female lead singers of the 1960s, the backup vocals are more restrained, in the girl-group tradition.

0:00–0:09	**Introduction**, 4 mm.	Horns and guitar play in call and response.
0:09–0:30	**Verse 1**, 10 mm.	Vocals enter. Note the backup vocals, which blend girl-group support with a strong gospel element. "What you want . . ."
0:30–0:51	**Verse 2**, 10 mm.	As before. Note that the guitar and snare are not locked in with the same precision as "In the Midnight Hour," and that the low notes in the piano here take over the role played by the baritone sax in the Pickett song. "I ain't gonna do you wrong . . ."
0:51–1:12	**Verse 3**, 10 mm.	As before, "I'm about to give ya . . ."
1:12–1:28	**Instrumental Bridge**, 8 mm.	Sax solo offers contrasting material in a new key.
1:28–1:50	**Verse 4**, 10 mm.	As before and back in the original key, though harmonic shift back is somewhat awkward. "Your kisses are . . ."
1:50–2:22	**Coda**, 16 mm.	Famous "R E S P E C T" stop-time passage, and then vamp, as Stax-style baritone sax enters just as the song fades out.

play black music and do some black artists play music that is somehow "less black"? Does it matter who owns the record company or supervises the sessions in this regard? Is Stax really "blacker" than Motown? Effective arguments have been made on both sides of this issue. What do you think?

1968: A Pivotal Year for Black Popular Music. On April 4, 1968, the Reverend Dr. Martin Luther King, Jr. was assassinated on the balcony of his Memphis hotel room. It would be difficult to exaggerate the importance of this event for race relations in America at the end of the 1960s. King had been an important leader in the civil rights movement, and he was perhaps the most respected and widely known advocate for racial equality in the United States. King's approach to social protest was markedly nonviolent. The reaction to his death, however, led to an escalation of protest violence that had begun months earlier in black neighborhoods in some of the country's major cities (including Detroit).

King's death had a palpable impact on black music. It hit especially hard at Stax, which was plagued with business problems and was located only minutes away from the hotel where Dr. King was killed. In late 1967, Atlantic had been sold to Warner Brothers–Seven Arts, leaving Stax with a six-month option to continue or terminate its distribution agreement with Atlantic. During the sale, Jim Stewart learned that the agreement he had signed with Atlantic some years before was not a simple distribution contract. The Atlantic attorneys had inserted a clause assigning ownership of the master tapes for all Stax recordings to Atlantic. Stewart was also reminded that Sam and Dave were on loan to Stax, and if the contract were not renewed they would revert to Atlantic. With the death of his best artist, Otis Redding, in late 1967, Stewart was left with few choices. Disgusted with the Atlantic negotiations, he and his sister eventually opted to sell the company to Gulf and Western, a conglomerate that once produced metal bumpers. Stax continued as a very different company under the leadership of Al Bell and Detroit-based record producer Don Dixon, who once competed with Berry Gordy for the local Detroit market. The label was soon back on the charts with Johnnie Taylor's "Who's Makin' Love" (p5 r1, 1968), but the original community of Stax musicians, writers, and producers began to pull apart.

In July 1967, a series of riots broke out in Detroit, which made many at Motown uncomfortable about working in the city's downtown area. By April 1968, Holland-Dozier-Holland had departed and Norman Whitfield was the label's most successful writer and producer. Berry Gordy was set on moving the label to Los Angeles in order to become more involved with the film industry, and he turned over much of the day-to-day operation to others. In the wake of King's death, Motown records began to deal more directly with issues facing black America: the Supremes' "Love Child" (p1 r2, 1968), for instance, confronts the realities of urban life from the perspective of an illegitimate child, a growing issue in the black community. By the early 1970s, Whitfield and the Temptations, Marvin Gaye, and Stevie Wonder would all focus on issues in black urban life in unmistakable terms. Examples of later Motown recordings in the 1970s will be discussed in Chapter 9.

JAMES BROWN: ON THE WAY TO FUNK

From Doo-Wop to Soul. In light of his tremendous importance and stylistic distinctiveness during the 1960s, it is strange to think that James Brown started his career as a stand-in for Little Richard. Born in South Carolina and raised in southern Georgia, Brown had gained some regional attention in the mid-1950s as a mem-

HOT PANTS MAKE YOU SURE OF YOURSELF!

by Gutherie Ramsey

"Let's keep it real!" At face value those words, taken from the lyrics of James Brown's 1971 hit single "Hot Pants," make little political or practical sense. Yet I seemed to focus in on them when, after learning of Brown's passing on Christmas morning 2006, I decided to marinate in a CD collection of his greatest hits throughout the night. Not that the man couldn't be lyrically profound; "Say It Loud, I'm Black and I'm Proud" became the anthem for social equities across the board and around the globe, yet he was equally known for good-time lyrics that simply celebrated life. But

truly, it was his music—pared down ostinato bass patterns, syncopated guitars, and interlocking horn lines that worked as the mortar in the soundscape—that captivated our minds and our dancing feet. Add in a scream, a shout, or other oral nonsensical declamations like neck bones, candied yams, and a camel walk, and you have the recipe for a funk revolution. For legions of listeners, this was how good music was supposed to be.

At times his music made a real difference. Mid-1960s America was a kettle, and its contents were on a high boil. On the one hand, black performers were defining the very essence of American popular music, enjoying unprecedented prestige, influence, and financial rewards. But on the other hand, America was still living the nightmare of its quasi-apartheid state: many African Americans were stuck in low-paying jobs and living segregated existences in schools, churches, and neighborhoods. There was a general sense that America had come to a crossroads, and that change had better come—and soon. On April 4, 1968, when a gunshot ended the life of civil rights leader Martin Luther King Jr. in Memphis it silenced one of the most audible

proponents of that change, and the kettle finally blew its top. Civil unrest swept like a tidal wave across the land: Chicago, Detroit, and Washington, D.C. all experienced the force of raw frustrations that had been simmering for years. Inner-city neighborhoods burned, businesses were destroyed and lives were lost.

The day after King's assassination on April 5, James Brown was scheduled to play a concert in Boston, which city officials were threatening to cancel for fear of the type of violent outbreaks ravaging other cities. Boston had already seen hints of unrest as teenagers had roamed the streets of Roxbury that evening in protest for the slain leader. But a greater fear was that if the concert were canceled, the city could go up like tinder, and the already palpable racial tension could turn into violence. Mayor Kevin White and his advisors had to act fast. After meeting with Brown, they decided that not only would the show go on, but it would be televised as well.

The plan worked.

Although the Boston Garden's capacity was 14,000, only 2,000 loyal revelers attended, and many more could view the show at home on WGBH. The evening began with Mayor White greeting the crowd and

his city and then Brown, who had already earned the title "The Hardest Working Brother in Show Business," came on stage and gave the performance of a lifetime. He was in his most rare form that night, giving what one witness called a "million-watt performance." Existing grainy, black and white footage shows the entertainer wooing and subduing his audience with the genius of his many talents.

It was, indeed, a spectacle. Decked out in a tailored suit, Brown's hair flipped dramatically from side-to-side, his arms, legs, and torso performed a litany of dance steps from "the James Brown" to the mashed potato and the camel walk, one of many African American social dances that mimicked the movements of animals. (Some of his protégé Michael Jackson's dance moves, in particular the "moonwalk," owed a strong debt to Brown's camel walk.) The crowd roared its approval as the band played the smash hit "There Was a Time," and Brown chanted line after line of call-and-response with his band mates and the cheering crowd. Even when enthusiasm threatened to escalate into unruly behavior, Brown was able to get the party back on track, on the "good foot" as one of his songs suggests. This was sanctified theater, indeed.

James Brown performing in Boston after the assassination of Martin Luther King, Jr. Boston's mayor, Kevin White (pictured in center image), allowed the concert to be televised, and many credit White and Brown with keeping the peace in Boston while other cities were engulfed in riots.

That night Brown showed why he was affectionately known as "The Godfather of Soul." As one of the most important American musicians of the late twentieth century, he used his considerable power to influence the country's political and civil life, not just that evening, but on many other occasions. Part preacher and teacher, part magician and shaman, that night James Brown taught America that "the funk" could cure all ills.

Guthrie P. Ramsey, Jr. (University of Pennsylvania) is the author of Race Music: Black Cultures from Bebop to Hip-Hop. *He is also a founding member of the jazz band Dr. Guy's MusiQology, and composes and arranges the band's music.*

Viewing Rock

Dance variety shows were extremely popular during the 1950s and 1960s. In addition to dances performed by a studio full of teens, many of these programs contained feature performances, during which a popular group would appear on the show and lip-synch to their latest hit record. *American Bandstand* is the most famous of these programs, but there were dozens of other local and regional dance programs. Among their many television appearances during the

mid-1960s, the Detroit-based Temptations appeared several times on the local, Windsor, Ontario program *Swingin' Time*. One of the most compelling of these appearances

is a 1966 performance of the group's 1965 hit "My Girl." The performance style of the Temptations offers and example of a typical rhythm and blues vocal group, in which choreography and physical movement are the vital elements. The group appears with a single lead singer, in this case David Ruffin, staged to the viewer's right, while the remaining four members form a collective backup group on the left of the screen. Echoing their vocal roles, Ruffin is able to move freely, while the group must remain synchronized. Although it is hard to know the origin of the choreography, it was most likely developed by group member Paul Williams and Motown staff choreographer Cholly Atkins. Some of the moves are literal readings of the lyrics, such as "I've got sunshine" (1) and "when it's cold outside" (2). Other steps are more abstract. As per the vocal roles, the camera often focuses on Ruffin depicting the lead vocal line (3). All the while, it is important to remember that the group is performing for a studio full of dancing teenagers, who are often visible in the broadcast (4). Performances such as "My Girl" were extremely popular during the earliest decades of rock, offering artists the opportunity to show physical depictions of their music and giving listeners entrée to dance around the living room.

ber of the Fabulous Flames. At a show just before Little Richard hit with "Tutti Frutti," Brown and his group delivered an uninvited, impromptu performance that impressed Richard's manager, Clint Brantley. Brantley booked the Flames for a series of performances across the South. When "Tutti Frutti" became a hit, Richard left Georgia to capitalize on his success, and Brown stepped in to perform as Little Richard for a series of appearances that Brantley had already scheduled. James Brown and the Fabulous Flames enjoyed moderate success with Brown's impassioned delivery on "Please Please Please" (r6, 1956), his first record released by the

Listening Guide

Get Music ⑤ wwnorton.com/studyspace

James Brown, "Papa's Got a Brand New Bag, Pt. 1" King 5999

Words and music by James Brown, produced by James Brown. Rose to #1 on the *Billboard* "Top Selling Rhythm and Blues Singles" chart and #8 on the *Billboard* "Hot 100" chart in fall 1965.

FORM: Simple verse with bridge. The 12-bar verses return without alterations (except for new lyrics), and are based on the 12-bar blues structure. The 8-bar bridge enters after two verses, which might indicate an AABA form, especially since a verse returns right after the bridge. However the bridge is static, vamping on a single chord and not driving toward the return of the verse as in an AABA form. The structure of this song is perhaps best understood as a verse-verse-bridge structure that is repeated, with the bridge serving as the ending while the song fades. The form of this track is closest to a simple verse form, though one might also see it as a hybrid of simple verse and AABA forms.

TIME SIGNATURE: 4/4. Note the precise interplay between the instruments and how they work together to project an intricate rhythmic background over which Brown delivers his lead vocal.

INSTRUMENTATION: Electric guitar, bass, drums, horns, and lead vocal.

0:00–0:26	**Verse 1**, 12 mm.	After opening upbeat chord, vocal enters and verse locks in based on the 12-bar blues, "Come here sisters . . ."
0:26–0:48	**Verse 2**, 12 mm.	As before. Note the use of the baritone sax, playing the same role here as it does in Pickett's "In the Midnight Hour." Similarly, the rhythm guitar and snare are locked in on beats two and four throughout. "Come down brother . . ."
0:48–1:03	**Bridge**, 8 mm.	Lead vocals over vamp on single chord, with horn backups. "He did the jerk . . ."
1:03–1:26	**Verse 3**, 12 mm.	As before, "Come down sister . . ."
1:26–1:48	**Verse 4**, 12 mm.	As before, "Oh and father . . ."
1:48–2:06	**Coda** (Bridge), 8 mm. +	Based on single-chord vamp from bridge and then fade out, "c'mon, hey hey . . ."

Cincinnati-based King Records, run by Syd Nathan. King would release all but a handful of Brown's records until Brown signed with Polydor in 1971. Brown hit again in 1958 with "Try Me," his first number one rhythm and blues hit, which also enjoyed moderate crossover appeal (p48).

Brown's early hits remained within the stylistic range of 1950s doo-wop, as he sang lead vocal supported by the backup vocals of the other Flames. With "Think" (p33 r7, 1960), however, Brown began to develop the soul style for which he would become so well known. The song's tight accompaniment features horns and a driving rhythm section. While much pop music of the time focused on lyrics, harmony, and background vocals, Brown's aggressive singing and the rhythmic groove created to support it are the clear focal points of the music.

By the early 1960s, Brown was known on the R&B circuit for his stage show, which featured athletic dancing and a famous closing routine in which he was led off stage exhausted, only to vault back into the spotlight with fresh energy. Hoping to capture on record the excitement of James Brown and the Fabulous Flames in concert, Brown and manager Ben Bart decided to release a live album recorded during a 1962 performance at the Apollo Theater in New York. Except for jazz, folk, and classical, albums were not the focus of record sales in the early 1960s. Despite

Sound Check

Artist	The Temptations	The Supremes	Wilson Pickett
Title	The Way You Do the Things You Do	Baby Love	In the Midnight Hour
Chart peak	p11 1964	p1 1964	p23, r1 1965
Form	Simple verse	Simple verse	Simple verse
Rhythm	12/8	12/8	4/4
Instrumentation	Electric guitar Bass Drums Lead vocal Background vocal Piano Horns	Electric guitar Bass Drums Lead vocal Background vocal Piano Saxes Stomping boards	Electric guitar Bass Drums Lead vocal Horns
Comments	Structure based on a two-chord vamp 4-bar refrain: "Well, you could have been . . ." Horns added in verse 2	Stomping on boards used in introduction to establish beat Key change in verse 5 Arrangement builds by adding instruments: guitar and backing vocal (verse 2), saxes (verse 3)	Instrumental interlude that features a horn melody Low, baritone saxophone propels the groove Listen for the delayed second beat of each measure

this, Brown's *The James Brown Show* (now called *Live at the Apollo*) went to number two on the pop album charts in the summer of 1963, showcasing both his energetic performance and stylistic range. While "Think" had already anticipated Brown's turn toward a domination by tight rhythmic grooves, "Out of Sight" (p24, 1964) went even further in this direction, introducing the hard-driving soul style that continued with "Papa's Got a Brand New Bag, Pt. 1" (p8 r1, 1965), "I Got You (I Feel Good)" (p3 r1, 1965), "It's a Man's Man's Man's World" (p8 r1, 1966), and "Cold Sweat, Pt. 1" (p7 r1, 1967).

Unlike most of the other artists in this chapter, James Brown exerted almost total control over his music from the beginning of his career. He wrote and produced most of his hits and after the death of King Records' Syd Nathan and his manager Ben Bart in 1968, he also made most of his own business decisions.

	Aretha Franklin	James Brown
	Respect	Papa's Got a Brand New Bag, Pt. 1
	p1, r1 1967	p8, r1 1965
	Simple verse (modified)	Simple verse (modified)
	4/4	4/4
	Electric guitar Bass Drums Lead vocal Background vocal Organ Piano Tambourine	Electric guitar Bass Drums Lead vocal Horns
	Famous R-E-S-P-E-C-T line comes in the coda Based on a two-chord vamp Backing vocals from the girl group tradition	Bridge added to simple verse form 12-bar blues Intricate rhythmic background

James Brown, live at the Apollo. Brown worked with top-notch musicians and rehearsed them tirelessly. His live shows were equally tiring, with Brown passionately dancing, belting out lyrics, and directing the band. His performances at New York's Apollo Theater have become legendary.

Brown uniquely combined an aggressive style of vocal and dance performance, songwriting and production skills, and astute business acumen. In his artistic and musical independence, he parallels Brian Wilson, Bob Dylan, and the Beatles, who also took significant control over their music and careers during the 1960s. As a bandleader, Brown hired great musicians and rehearsed them vigorously. He even fined players who made mistakes during performances. Although some of his musicians found this work environment too difficult, Brown's rigorous approach produced some of the best ensemble playing in popular music during the 1960s and 1970s.

"Papa's Got a Brand New Bag, Pt. 1" is an example of the instrumental precision achieved in performances by James Brown and the Famous Flames. The track opens with a sustained chord, and soon falls into the first verse (the verses employ the 12-bar blues structure). Listen to how the ensemble works together rhythmically to create the groove that drives the song. The stops at the end of the verses help distinguish this track from a Stax arrangement, and exhibit the cohesiveness of Brown's band. The form of the song mixes verses with a bridge, which is sung once and then used as the basis for the vamp in the coda. Note the absence of background vocals—a feature that helps distinguish Brown's approach from that of Motown and highlights the contrast with his music in the 1950s, which often featured doo-wop backup vocals.

Black Pride and the Birth of Funk. After the assassination of Martin Luther King, Jr., James Brown and his music were increasingly valued within the black community for his apparent racial pride. To many, Brown's hard-edged musical style, political lyrics, and outward interest in arranging his own affairs seemed uncompromised in comparison to the necessary concessions made by Motown and

Atlantic artists to appeal to white audiences. While this perception was not entirely accurate, Brown was counted among the most important figures in black popular music when "Say It Loud, I'm Black and I'm Proud" (p10 r1) climbed the charts in the fall of 1968. Brown's music would soon turn toward funk, making him one of the principal influences on 1970s black pop. We will continue our consideration of Brown and his influence on funk in Chapter 9, and the issues of race addressed in this chapter will return in our discussions of the rise of black pop, disco, and the emergence of rap.

FURTHER READING

Rob Bowman, *Soulsville, U.S.A.: The Story of Stax Records* (Schirmer, 2006).

James Brown, with Bruce Tucker, *James Brown, the Godfather of Soul* (Da Capo, 2003).

Gerald Early, *One Nation Under a Groove: Motown and American Culture* (University of Michigan Press, 2004).

Jon Hartley Fox, *King of the Queen City: The Story of King Records* (University of Illinois Press, 2009).

Nelson George, *Where Did Our Love Go? The Rise and Fall of the Motown Sound* (University of Illinois Press, 2007).

Berry Gordy, *To Be Loved: The Music, the Magic, and the Memories of Motown* (Warner Books, 1994).

Peter Guralnick, *Sweet Soul Music: Rhythm and Blues and the Southern Dream of Freedom* (Back Bay, 1999).

Brian Ward, *Just My Soul Responding: Rhythm and Blues, Black Consciousness, and Race Relations* (University of California Press, 1998).

Jerry Wexler and David Ritz, *Rhythm and the Blues* (St. Martin's, 1994)

Otis Williams, with Patricia Romanowski, *Temptations* (Cooper Square, 2002).

Ⓢ VISIT STUDYSPACE AT WWNORTON.COM/STUDYSPACE

Access free review material such as:

- music links
- performer info
- practice quizzes
- outlines
- interactive listening guide software

CHAPTER 7

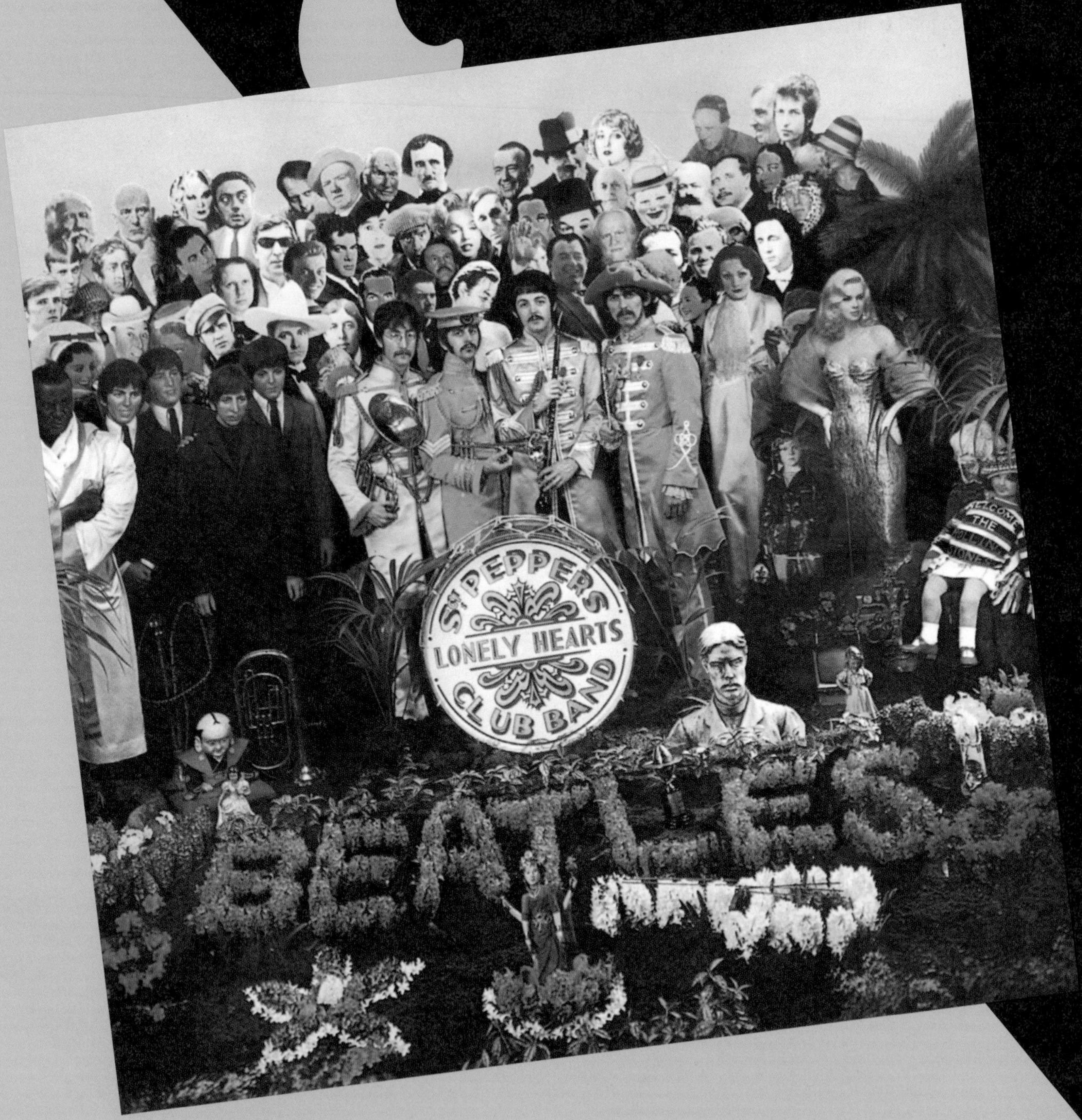

PSYCHEDELIA

June, July, and August of 1967 are frequently referred to as the Summer of Love, a time when Scott McKenzie's "San Francisco (Be Sure to Wear Flowers in Your Hair)" played on radios across the United States and England. The song, written by John Phillips of the Mamas and the Papas, celebrates the emerging hippie culture and flower power movement centered in San Francisco. At the same time in London, the Beatles released *Sgt. Pepper's Lonely Hearts Club Band*— perhaps the most important album in the history of rock music. The summer of 1967 also saw an American guitarist fronting a British band and emerging as an international sensation at a rock festival in Monterey, California. When Jimi Hendrix set his guitar aflame at the climax of his virtuosic and outrageous performance, it was an important signal that rock music was heading down a new path in 1967: "psychedelia." Psychedelic music and culture began in the regional underground scenes of London and San Francisco in the 1950s and were well established by the end of 1965. Thus, the Summer of Love does not mark the beginning of psychedelia per se, but rather its breakthrough into mainstream popular culture.

In early 1966 only hints of psychedelic music were found on the records of major rock artists. Instead, relatively unknown musicians were developing the new style. Some of these bands became commercially successful (the Grateful Dead, Pink Floyd, Jefferson Airplane), though others did not (Soft Machine, Tomorrow, the Charlatans). Psychedelia emerged from its origins in the London and San Francisco underground movements (consisting of regional bands, clubs, shops, and newspapers) into mainstream pop culture and became a pervasive influence on rock culture by the end of the 1960s. It is important to examine the development of psychedelic music on two fronts, exploring the underground scenes in London and San Francisco and considering how this music infiltrated the pop charts. But before we trace its history, we need to define it: What is psychedelia and what makes music psychedelic?

Many critics cite the Beatles' *Sgt. Pepper's Lonely Hearts Club Band* (1967) as the most influential album ever made. After more than a decade of rock's most popular music originating from singles, *Sgt. Pepper* made the album into an art form. The Beatles conceived of this album as a complete artistic production rather than a string of stand-alone songs. Albums of this type were later called "concept albums." Musically, the songs on *Sgt. Pepper* are wide-ranging, drawing on rhythm and blues, Indian music, and even brass bands, while employing groundbreaking recording techniques. Lyrically—and visually, considering its packaging—the album tells the story of a fictional band. Reinforcing the growing importance of the text, the Beatles' chose to print the song lyrics on the album jacket. Although the album did not contain a hit single, *Sgt. Pepper* was extremely popular, influencing many artists working in a wide variety of styles.

DRUGS AND THE QUEST FOR HIGHER CONSCIOUSNESS

The Doors of Perception: Ken Kesey, Timothy Leary, and LSD. The psychedelic movement was concerned with exploring new ways of experiencing the world. Young adults in the mid-1960s felt that the cultural values of the 1950s were too focused on being "normal," and they challenged these values by seeking out alternative approaches to life and culture. Influenced by the civil rights movement and a growing public resistance to the Vietnam War, many young people in the 1960s were suspicious of institutions in American life: government, schools, churches, big business, the military, and the police. Teens in the 1950s were the first to experience a youth culture that could be clearly distinguished from adult culture, but the counterculture that emerged in the 1960s was much more assertive in this separation.

Drugs generally—but marijuana and LSD especially—played a central role in the new worldview many young people were seeking. Led by author Ken Kesey and ex-Harvard professor Timothy Leary, two older men who had publicly rejected "the establishment," many young people came to see hallucinogenic drugs as essential to unlocking "the doors of perception" (a reference to Aldous Huxley's essay of the same name, in which the author describes his experience with the hallucinogenic drug mescaline). Leary's advice to "turn on, tune in, and drop out" became a slogan of the counterculture, as many young adults earnestly explored drug use, radical philosophy, and Eastern religion.

LSD (lysergic acid diethylamide) was developed accidentally by Swiss scientist Albert Hoffmann in 1943 while he was working on a cure for migraine headaches. Along with mescaline, LSD was tested by the CIA during the 1950s as a truth serum and was considered as a potential treatment for alcoholism. LSD was also used recreationally by a relatively small group of people in the United States and the UK. The young adults who discovered it in the mid to late 1960s thought LSD allowed the user to suppress the false and misleading modes of understanding imposed by school and society and to perceive the world and life itself as they really were. "Dropping acid" supposedly allowed one to see new possibilities, opening the mind to new knowledge and modes of understanding. In short, LSD was viewed as a kind of magic drug that led to a "higher consciousness" that had previously been available only to mystics and visionaries.

A Journey to the East. Until the summer of 1967, most counterculture activity was restricted to large cities like New York, San Francisco, and London, and to college campuses. In many ways the psychedelic counterculture grew directly out of the folk revival. As discussed in Chapter 5, the Byrds' "Eight Miles High" hit the U.S. charts in 1966 and was one of the first public signs that drug use was becoming a central part of rock music and youth culture. The unlikely blend of Eastern spirituality and drug use that "Eight Miles High" evoked had been advocated by Timothy Leary in his 1964 book *The Psychedelic Experience*. Cowritten with Harvard colleagues Ralph Metzner and Richard Alpert (who would later change his name to Ram Dass and play an important role in popularizing Eastern religion among the hippies), the book offered a guide to acid use based on the ancient

Tibetan Book of the Dead. Interest in Eastern philosophy was further reinforced by the Beatles, who became students of transcendental meditation with the Maharishi Mahesh Yogi around the time that they released *Sgt. Pepper's Lonely Hearts Club Band*. While drug use is not part of the practice of yoga in most Eastern traditions, it became linked with Eastern religion and higher consciousness in the eyes of the burgeoning hippie culture. As Eastern gurus sought truth through spiritual discipline, the hippies sought truth through the use of LSD. Taken together, these sometimes contradictory approaches were at the heart of a burgeoning 1960s counterculture—a hippie worldview committed to cultural change. And music was at the center of this lifestyle.

Two Psychedelic Approaches to Music. There are two general ways music might reflect a growing interest in higher consciousness. The first is to use music to enhance a drug trip. According to this approach, the focus is the drug experience itself, and the music is a soundtrack that may provoke a response with novel and unfamiliar sounds, but does not provide a trip itself. We will encounter instances of this tendency in our discussions of both the San Francisco and London underground scenes and groups like the Grateful Dead and Pink Floyd. A second approach is to understand the music as the trip. In this case, the artist must craft music that acts as an aesthetic drug, taking the listener on an aural journey that may or may not be enhanced by the use of drugs. This approach is demonstrated by the music of the Doors and the Beatles, discussed below. In both instances, the trip and the quest for higher consciousness are essential, and in this context musicians became more experimental and ambitious about writing, performing, and recording music. For music to enhance or provide a trip, however, it had to move beyond the two- or three-minute radio format that was standard for AM radio in the mid-1960s.

PSYCHEDELIC AMBITION: THE BEACH BOYS AND THE BEATLES

Two Bands, One Label. The cultural rise of psychedelia coincided with a tendency toward more ambitious approaches to rock songwriting, arranging, and recording. For example, once firmly within the domain of teen interests, the music of both the Beatles and the Beach Boys became increasingly complicated as the '60s progressed. Lyrics addressed more serious topics, a wider range of instrumentation was used, harmonic language became more innovative, standard formal types were often modified or abandoned, and more time was taken in the studio to record tracks that were often not reproducible in live performance. The Beatles gradually moved away from the model of professional craftsmen (best exemplified by the Brill Building songwriters) and toward a more self-consciously "artistic" stance (akin to that of a classical-music composer or artist). With the Beach Boys, a quest to match and surpass the accomplishments of Phil Spector seemed to drive Brian Wilson to an increasingly experimental approach. In the United States the Beatles and the Beach Boys were on the same record label, Capitol. This meant that they not only competed for the public's attention but also for the attention of their own record

The Beatles were leaders in the popularization of Eastern religion during the psychedelic era. Band members are pictured here with their wives, Mike Love from the Beach Boys, and many others at the Rishikesh in India with the Maharishi Mahesh Yogi in March 1968.

company. The combined effect of the increased artistic ambitions of both bands and a commercial rivalry produced a sequence of records that exhibit the transformation of rock from dance music to listening music.

We have already considered the Beatles' music through *Revolver* and the Beach Boys' music through *Pet Sounds* (Chapters 4 and 5). Here we consider how these bands influenced and even inspired one another. Brian Wilson has remarked, for instance, that he admired the way the songs on *Rubber Soul* all worked together as an album. This inspired Wilson to think of *Pet Sounds* as an album of related songs. Paul McCartney remembers that he listened to *Pet Sounds* constantly after its release, admiring the production and songwriting. With *Revolver*, and especially "Tomorrow Never Knows," the Beatles pushed the limits of studio experimentation, producing a track that many consider the introduction of psychedelia into the mainstream.

"Good Vibrations." Not to be outdone by the ambition of "Tomorrow Never Knows," Wilson and the Beach Boys released "Good Vibrations" (p1 uk1, 1966)—a single that consumed more studio time and budget allocation than any other pop single ever had before. Wilson called it his "pocket symphony," and many consider this single to be his finest achievement. As the Listening Guide shows, "Good Vibrations" begins by using a contrasting verse-chorus approach. But after the second time through the chorus, the track continues with a sequence of three sections of new material. In a sense, "Good Vibrations" takes the listener on a "trip," through unfamiliar musical territory. Each section of the song was recorded separately and spliced together later, cutting and pasting tape with scotch tape and a razor blade. Each of the three sections introduces new musical material. Section 1 employs a tack piano (an upright piano with tacks stuck in the hammers to create a sharper attack), a Jew's harp (a small instru-

Rising Rock Ambitions

Beatles, *Rubber Soul* (late 1965)

Beach Boys, *Pet Sounds* (early to mid-1966)

Beatles, *Revolver* (late summer 1966), "Tomorrow Never Knows"

Beach Boys, "Good Vibrations" (late 1966)

Beatles, "Penny Lane/Strawberry Fields Forever" (early 1967)

Beach Boys, *SMiLE* (late 1966/early 1967; not released)

Beatles, *Sgt. Pepper's Lonely Hearts Club Band* (June 1, 1967)

Beach Boys, *Smiley Smile* (August 1967)

Listening Guide

Get Music ⓢ **wwnorton.com/studyspace**

The Beach Boys, "Good Vibrations" Capital 5676

Words and music by Brian Wilson and Mike Love, produced by Brian Wilson. Reached #1 on the *Billboard* "Hot 100" chart in late 1966 (uk1).

FORM: The first half of the song uses contrasting verse-chorus form, which breaks off after the second statement of the chorus (1:41). At that point, a series of three sections begin, the last of which uses music from the chorus to help round the song off as it fades out. Taken as a whole, the song does not fit neatly into any conventional pop formal pattern, except in the most general sense that contrasting material often follows the second statement of the chorus.

TIME SIGNATURE: 4/4.

INSTRUMENTATION: Organ, guitar, bass, drums, woodwinds, cellos, slide theremin, bass harmonica, Jew's harp, tambourine, sleigh bells, maracas, lead and backing vocals.

0:00–0:25	**Verse 1**, 16 mm. (8 mm. phrase with repeat)	Lead vocals enter immediately, note repeated chords in the organ, orchestral-style drumming, and subtle use of woodwinds in second 8 mm. "I love the colorful clothes . . ."
0:25–0:50	**Chorus**, 16 mm. (four 4 mm. phrases)	Multipart vocals in counterpoint, note entrance of cellos low in the texture and theremin melody on the top. "I'm pickin' up . . ."
0:50–1:15	**Verse 2**, 16 mm.	As before. Note that verse is quieter than chorus—this dynamic contrast can be heard clearly in this shift back to the verse. "Changed my mind . . ."
1:15–1:41	**Chorus**, 16 mm.	As before, end leads into section 1. "I'm pickin' up . . ."
1:41–2:13	**Section 1**, 20 mm.	New music. Piano, bass harmonica, sleigh bells, Jew's harp enter, "Excitations . . ." Listen for tape splice to section 2.
2:13–2:57	**Section 2**, 24 mm.	More new music, quieter now, starting with organ and ending with vocal "ah." Listen again for tape splice into section 3. "Gotta keep . . ."
2:57–3:35	**Section 3**, 22 mm.	Based on chorus, with new vocal counterpoint. Starts louder, gets quieter and then louder again before fade-out. "I'm pickin' up . . ."

ment held against the teeth or lips and plucked with the fingers), bass harmonica and sleigh bells in addition to voices, bass, tambourine, and organ. The splice into Section 2 can be heard clearly, as the music immediately gets quieter, starting only with a low organ and percussion. After the vocals, a higher organ, and bass enter,

Most of the Beach Boys' creative songwriting and production came from Brian Wilson (pictured here in the studio, 1966). Like his hero Phil Spector, Wilson demanded total control of the musical production and experimented with nontraditional instruments and recording technology. Wilson was constantly pushing himself to outdo the Beatles and their legendary producer, George Martin.

the passage works its way toward a beautiful harmony on "ah" to end the section (listen carefully for the echo as the vocals die out). The third section then begins as if it might be another chorus, only to introduce a new three-part vocal passage before resuming the chorus music for the fade-out. While "Good Vibrations" starts out as a contrasting verse-chorus form, the addition of these three sections and the way they introduce new sounds and material represented an important departure for pop music. Wilson spent a great deal of time experimenting with the order of these sections before arriving at the final version. Capitol later released some of the alternate versions and studio rehearsals of "Good Vibrations" and these tapes illustrate the centrality of studio techniques and the sense of experimentation in the creation of this song. The rehearsal tapes reveal how diligently Wilson worked at finding the precise instrumental sounds he employed, providing a rare glimpse of his working method. "Good Vibrations" marked a high point in the musical ambition of the Beach Boys that they would never again equal.

Sgt. Pepper's Lonely Hearts Club Band. After the release of *Revolver*, the Beatles abandoned touring and devoted their energies to recording. There were several reasons for this drastic change. Some of the group's recent songs were nearly impossible to perform live as a quartet, and fan noise made performances generally unpleasant. In the wake of the controversy surrounding John Lennon's remarks about Christianity, live appearances had also become too dangerous. Perhaps more importantly, working on recordings that the group knew did not need to be reproduced in a live setting allowed for an immense amount of freedom in the recording studio, satisfying the creative ambitions of an emerging psychedelic movement.

In the fall of 1966 the Beatles began working on *Sgt. Pepper's Lonely Hearts Club Band*, seeking to use the full resources of a recording studio and London's musical community. At first, the idea was to unite all the songs on the album around a central theme—their memories of growing up in Liverpool. But by early 1967, EMI was eager to at least release a single, since the label knew it was never good for a pop act—even the Beatles—to be away from the pop charts for too long. The band's next release was a double-A-sided single of "Penny Lane" and "Strawberry Fields Forever." The lyrics to "Penny Lane" describe a variety of scenes that McCartney felt captured a cross-section of everyday life in his hometown, while "Strawberry Fields Forever" recalls a neighborhood park where Lennon played as a child.

The group's growing musical ambitions can be heard in the piccolo trumpet solo in "Penny Lane," inspired by a Bach concerto McCartney heard while they were working on the track. "Strawberry Fields Forever" is more adventurous in terms of recording. It uses a wide variety of sounds including cellos, inside-the-piano playing, reversed-tape, and the Mellotron, an early **sampling** keyboard that uses taped sounds to create orchestral strings, choral voices, and an ensemble of recorders (simple wooden flutes). This keyboard can be heard at the very beginning of the song using its recorder-ensemble setting. The final version of "Strawberry Fields Forever" is actually a spliced together combination of two versions that had been recorded at different tempos and in different keys. Producer George Martin varied the tape speed so the recordings could be joined without the listener noticing the splice. "Strawberry Fields Forever" also includes a novel feature: after the song fades at the end, there is a moment of silence and then a brief passage of new music fades back in. This must have surprised disc jockeys the first time they played the song: just as the jock talked over the end of the song, the music marched back in!

The idea of creating an album based on childhood in Liverpool was dropped when the "Penny Lane"/"Strawberry Fields Forever" single was released. Paul McCartney then hit on the idea of the Beatles assuming the role of the fictional Sgt. Pepper's Lonely Hearts Club Band. The album would be a recorded performance of various acts, hosted by the made-up band. Thus, the album begins with "Sgt. Pepper's Lonely Hearts Club Band," in which the group introduces itself and announces singer "Billy Shears" (played by Ringo) to sing "With a Little Help from My Friends." The plan breaks down after these first tracks, however, returning only at the very end with a reprise of the first track before "A Day in the Life" concludes the album. Because of the Sgt. Pepper idea, the fact that there were no gaps between songs, and the way the album packaging participates in the charade (the original album came in a gatefold cover, complete with pictures of the band dressed in uniform), *Sgt. Pepper's Lonely Hearts Club Band* is often cited as rock's first "concept album"—an album that is organized around some central idea or story. John Lennon resisted thinking of *Sgt. Pepper* this way, claiming that his songs could have appeared on any Beatles album. However, Lennon's objections did little to discourage rock fans from lauding, and musicians from imitating, this aspect of *Sgt. Pepper*, and in the wake of its release concept albums seemed to pop up everywhere.

Sgt. Pepper's Lonely Hearts Club Band is one of the most important albums in the history of rock music. In the weeks after its release, most of the important figures in rock music and millions of listeners were listening to it carefully. There are many aspects of the album that marked a fundamental change in rock music. In addition to the elaborate photographs intimately bound up with the "concept," the complete lyrics were printed on the album cover, signaling that they were central to the experience and perhaps worth reading on their own. Stylistically the album ranges widely, bringing together British music hall, Indian music, chamber music, and rock and roll. The use of techniques borrowed from avant-garde music is central to "Being for the Benefit of Mr. Kite," which uses taped organ sounds randomly assembled to create a kaleidoscopic aural background. "A Day in the Life" also incorporates experimental techniques with two passages in which the orchestral string players start from a low note on their instrument and gradually play higher notes until given a cue to play an E-major chord closest to wherever they happen to end. Such chance techniques, called "aleatoric" in classical music, were very much a part of avant-garde music in the 1960s. The Beatles were well aware of the connection, as they included avant-garde composer Karlheinz Stockhausen on the cover of the album. The use of such techniques further underscores the seriousness with which the Beatles now approached their music.

Perhaps one of the most important and influential aspects of *Sgt. Pepper* is that it created a new focus on the album as opposed to the single. In the years following *Sgt. Pepper*, single-oriented pop would be directed at a teen audience via AM radio, and album-oriented rock (AOR) would be directed at older teens and college-age listeners on FM. While the Beatles would continue to have hit singles after *Sgt. Pepper*, the new album-as-basic-unit idea served as a model for rock for several decades after 1967.

Listening Guide

The Beatles, "A Day in the Life" Parlophone PMC-7027 (UK), Capital MAS-2653 (U.S.)

Words and music by John Lennon and Paul McCartney, produced by George Martin. Included on the album *Sgt. Pepper's Lonely Hearts Club Band*, which hit #1 on the *Billboard* "Top LPs" chart in the summer of 1967 (uk1).

FORM: Compound ABA form, with both the A and B sections using a simple verse scheme. The A section is an incomplete song by John Lennon, while the B section is an incomplete song by Paul McCartney. The two songs are stitched together by an interlude that leads from the A section to the B section, and by a bridge that returns to the A section. In the interlude, the Beatles employ the strings in an avant-garde manner, creating a strange growing rush of sound that is repeated at the end of the song.

TIME SIGNATURE: 4/4 in both sections.

INSTRUMENTATION: Acoustic guitar, piano, bass, drums, maracas, strings, brass, alarm clock, lead vocal.

A	0:00–0:12	**Introduction**, 8 mm.	Strummed acoustic guitar, with bass, drums, and percussion joining in second 4 mm.
	0:12–0:44	**Verse 1**, 20 mm.	Vocal (Lennon) enters. Note the echo on the voice. Starts with guitar, piano, and maracas only. "I read the news . . ."
	0:44–1:11	**Verse 2**, 20 mm.	As before. Drums enter, played in an orchestral manner, with a lot of fills in dialogue with vocal line. "He blew his mind . . ."

Collapse and Retreat: *SMiLE* **and** *Smiley Smile.* While the Beatles were recording "Penny Lane" and "Strawberry Fields Forever," Brian Wilson was at work on perhaps the most famous album never released. Working from the idea that laughter and "good vibes" were what made the world a better place, Wilson planned to call his new concept album *SMiLE*. After a planned release date of December 1966 was missed, he continued working through the first months of 1967 before eventually abandoning the project, with more than 70 percent of the album finished according to some reports. The Beach Boys did release *Smiley Smile* (p41 uk9, 1967), a significantly different album from what *SMiLE* would have been (and turned out to be). In the years since, many myths about *SMiLE* have arisen. Some writers speculate that it would have been Wilson's masterpiece, while others claim that his high intake of drugs left him confused and unable to manage the complexity of the music. Scholars now have a good idea of how the album might have sounded from studio material released by Capitol in the 1990s and from bootleg recordings. One track was released at the time and provides a sample of the original *SMiLE*. Much like "Good Vibrations," "Heroes and Villains" is a product of the recording studio, with sepa-

		Get Music ⓢ wwnorton.com/studyspace	
	1:11–1:41	**Verse 3**, 19 mm.	As in verse 2, but last measures overlap with beginning of interlude, "I saw a film . . ."
	1:41–2:16	**Interlude**, 23 mm.	Orchestral sound builds up, creating an enormous crescendo that cuts off abruptly, forming a transition to the second big section. "I'd love to turn you on . . ."
B	2:16–2:21	**Introduction**, 4 mm.	Repeated chords on acoustic piano help establish a quieter contrasting mood. Note the alarm clock.
	2:21–2:36	**B Verse 1**, 9 mm.	Vocal (McCartney) enters. Note how little reverb there is on the vocal. Bass plays a happy walking line on the second half, "Woke up . . ."
	2:36–2:49	**B Verse 2**, 9 mm.	As before, "Found my coat . . ."
	2:49–3:18	**Bridge**, 20 mm.	10 mm. phrase occurs twice, sung by Lennon and soaked in reverb. Note the ominous orchestral backdrop.
A'	3:18–3:46	**Verse 4**, 19 mm.	As in verse 3 of the A section, with last measures overlapping with ending section. "I read the news . . ."
	3:46–4:57	**Interlude** as ending, 24 mm.	Orchestral crescendo as in the previous occurrence of the interlude, but with a giant chord played on the piano to end at 4:21. This chord is sustained for almost 40 seconds using electronic means to keep the sound audible.

rately recorded and highly produced sections spliced together to create a sequence of musical episodes. While a version was released officially during the summer of 1967 (p14 uk8), several alternate versions released later exist that are much more experimental—one runs over ten minutes. Wilson's rerecorded version from 2004 maintains the spirit of the original, although his vocal energy is less active, and the musical tracks betray a twenty-first century sheen.

Since it was abandoned *SMiLE* has achieved considerable status, so it may seem surprising that the project created controversy within the band when Wilson was working on it. The other Beach Boys spent a lot of time on the road performing the band's earlier hits. When they encountered Brian's newest music in late 1966, they thought it would never be popular with fans. To a certain extent this was true: *Pet Sounds* had not sold as well as previous albums. On *Smiley Smile* and subsequent albums through the rest of the decade, the Beach Boys made an effort to simplify their sound, although the group never again achieved the kind of commercial success they had enjoyed in the mid-1960s. Wilson was still writing for the band and performing on the recordings, but the albums were now listed as "produced by the Beach Boys."

And in the End: The Beatles after *Sgt. Pepper.* John Lennon may have insisted that *Sgt. Pepper* was not a concept album, but much of what the Beatles did after *Sgt. Pepper* was driven by organizing themes, often dreamed up by Paul McCartney. *Magical Mystery Tour*, for instance, was built around the concept of the band traveling the English countryside by bus, making a movie as they went. In early 1968, the band traveled to India to study meditation at the ashram of the Maharishi Mahesh Yogi and brought back dozens of songs, many of which would appear on *The Beatles* (often called the "White Album"). The band was also approached about making an animated film that would use them as characters in a surrealist adventure in Pepperland. The result, *Yellow Submarine*, could be described as a kind of psychedelic *A Hard Day's Night*. After this, McCartney devised a plan to make a documentary film of the Beatles writing, rehearsing, and recording an album, concluding with a performance of the finished music. The "Get Back" project went badly, with producer George Martin walking out (he was replaced by Phil Spector), and the camera frequently captured arguments among band members. The film and album were scrapped and the Beatles reunited with Martin to record what would become their last studio album, *Abbey Road* (1969). The film and studio tracks from "Get Back" were later salvaged and released as *Let It Be* in 1970. (In 2003, the Beatles rereleased these same recordings as *Let It Be Naked*, which erased much of Spector's production to return the music to a more elemental and raw sound.)

The period after *Sgt. Pepper* also saw major changes in the business side of the Beatles: in the summer 1967, their manager Brian Epstein died of a drug overdose. The band eventually decided to take over their business affairs themselves, renting offices and forming Apple Records (the Beach Boys formed Brother Records at about the same time). Apple was launched with much fanfare: the Beatles would not only run their own careers but would also promote the work of deserving artists who might otherwise be turned away by mainstream commercial backers. It was based on a generous idea, but Apple was soon losing money and professionals had to be called in to stem the losses and reorganize the group's finances. By

In the late 1960s, the Beatles' interest in the culture of India translated into using the Indian sitar on several tracks. Here George Harrison plays sitar for the Maharishi as John Lennon and Ringo Starr look on.

late 1969 all four Beatles were ready to disband, and in April 1970, the Beatles officially broke up. In the years that followed, each band member went on to a successful solo career.

Despite some failed projects and the Apple fiasco, the Beatles' success never lagged during the 1967–70 period: every album and single they released placed high on the pop charts, most at number one in both the United States and the UK. In many ways, the band's later music would prove to be more influential for future rock musicians than their early releases. In terms of the development of psychedelic music, the friendly competition between the Beach Boys and the Beatles had important consequences. The ways these bands applied themselves to developing the stylistic, timbral, and compositional range of rock music was a model for other groups. *Pet Sounds*, "Good Vibrations," "Strawberry Fields Forever," and *Sgt. Pepper* demonstrated that rock could stand on its own as music and be taken seriously. Rock music was no longer simply dance music about teen romance. Because these bands were so successful, Capitol and EMI gave them a certain freedom to experiment. When these experiments produced hit singles and albums, other groups were given greater license as well.

THE SAN FRANCISCO SCENE AND HAIGHT-ASHBURY

Between the summers of 1966 and 1967, the Beatles and the Beach Boys were dominating American rock with increasingly ambitious music, but a local psychedelic scene had been developing since mid-1965 in San Francisco. One of the first important signs to the greater public that something new was burgeoning in the city was the Human Be-In, held in Golden Gate Park in January 1967. Posters advertising the event called it a "gathering of the tribes," and it brought together thousands of hippies from northern California for a day of poetry, spirituality, and music provided by local bands such as Quicksilver Messenger Service and Jefferson Airplane. The Be-In drew media attention to San Francisco's growing hippie culture and within a few months the event was imitated in New York and Los Angeles. A local San Francisco bus-tour company began offering a "Hippie Hop Tour." In many ways the San Francisco psychedelic scene grew out of the area's Beat movement of the late '50s and early '60s—with gatherings at Lawrence Ferlinghetti's City Lights Bookstore in North Beach, this bohemian scene celebrated the poetry of Allen Ginsberg and the prose of Jack Kerouac. Ginsberg and fellow Beats Michael McClure and Gary Snyder mentored the emerging hippie movement, even helping to organize the Human Be-In. Despite the many parallels between the Beats and the hippies, however, there were also significant differences, the most crucial being music: the jazz of be-bop musicians Charlie Parker and Dizzy Gillespie was the choice of most Beats, while hippies favored the music of the Rolling Stones, Bob Dylan, and the Beatles.

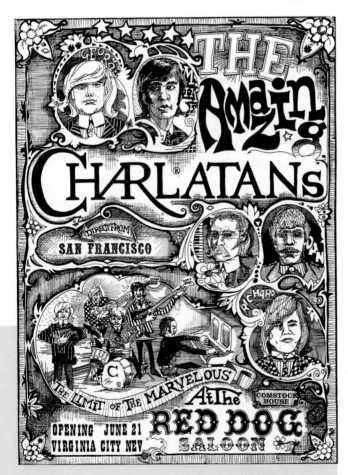

This poster announces a series of shows by San Francisco's Charlatans at the Red Dog Saloon in Virginia City, Nevada. These shows took place in June 1965, two years before psychedelia went mainstream during the Summer of Love in 1967.

The Red Dog, the Family Dog, and Kesey's Acid Tests. During the mid-1960s, counterculture scenes developed rapidly in many areas of the United States, with important bands, newspapers, and clubs emerging in New York, Detroit, Los Angeles, and northern California. San Francisco, and the old Victorian neighborhood of Haight-Ashbury especially, soon became the center of the American psychedelic scene. However the first stirrings of psychedelia actually took place in Virginia City, Nevada, at a restored western-style bar called the Red Dog Saloon. In June 1965, San Francisco musicians the Charlatans became the house band at the Red Dog. Evenings of free-form music-making and acid tripping increasingly drew young people out to Virginia City for psychedelic happenings that would serve as the model for later ones in the Bay Area. By the fall of 1965, a group of friends calling themselves the Family Dog began organizing psychedelic dances at local San Francisco ballrooms. The first was held in October at the Longshoremen's Hall under the title "A Tribute to Dr. Strange" and featured the Charlatans, the newly formed Jefferson Airplane, and the Great Society. The second dance, "A Tribute to Sparkle Plenty," was held several days later with the Charlatans and the Lovin' Spoonful (a New York band).

Around the time of the psychedelic dances, novelist Ken Kesey organized a series of events that he called "acid tests." Since 1964 Kesey and a band of vigorously bohemian friends who called themselves the Merry Pranksters had been traveling the country in a brightly painted schoolbus emblazoned with the destination

This multicolor bus was used by Ken Kesey and his Merry Pranksters to take their acid tests on the road. The destination sign on the front of the bus read simply: Further.

FURTHUR. Like Timothy Leary, Kesey celebrated the liberating effects of LSD and wanted to share the drug as broadly as he could. But Kesey was not seeking spiritual wisdom through methods of quiet contemplation and revelation. Instead, he and the Pranksters wanted to provide an environment rich in unpredictable stimulation to those who paid a dollar to enter the acid tests and experience LSD. In addition to a dose of the drug, participants were treated to light and slide shows, bizarre sound effects, and rock music, all in hopes of intensifying the effects of the acid. Kesey first offered his acid tests to the public in November 1965 in Santa Cruz and they quickly caught on. In January 1966, 2,400 people attended one of Kesey's acid tests at San Francisco's Fillmore Auditorium. The house band for the evening was a group called the Grateful Dead, who had recently changed their name from the Warlocks.

It Takes a Village to Raise a Ruckus: Concerts, News, the Psychedelic Shop, and FM Radio.

The multiple-bill dances combined with the unpredictable and multimedia aspects of Kesey's acid tests became the model for psychedelic events in San Francisco for the next few years. Soon psychedelic evenings of LSD and rock music were a regular feature in the Bay Area. Promoter Bill Graham began organizing shows at the Fillmore while Chet Helms promoted shows at the Avalon Ballroom. Ron and Jay Thelin opened the Psychedelic Shop in the Haight-Ashbury district to meet the countercultural needs of the hippies, and local bands rented large Victorian houses in the neighborhood that also served as rehearsal spaces. (The Grateful Dead lived at 710 Ashbury.) By September 1966, the *San Francisco Oracle* joined the *Berkeley Barb* as the area's most important counterculture newspaper, and they were joined by *Rolling Stone* magazine in November 1967. While many outside the hippie subculture may have first learned about it in 1967 with news of the Human Be-In and the summer of love, the hippie underground in San Francisco was already firmly established in the fall of 1966.

One place where psychedelic music was absent, however, was on the radio.

Pop music radio was still entirely on the AM dial and oriented toward short hit singles. Clearly the new, lengthier psychedelic rock would not fit that format. The FM dial had been available for some years and mostly featured public-service programming—university lectures, classical music concerts, and foreign-language shows. Many radios did not even have an FM dial. San Francisco radio veteran Tom Donahue, a member of the psychedelic scene, became disgruntled with the AM radio business and developed a new, free-form approach to programming. His format featured longer tracks placed back-to-back with more freedom given to the disc jockey and less in-your-face between-song chatter. Donahue's wife Rachel reports that he phoned a number of FM stations in the local phone book until he found one where telephone service had been disconnected. Figuring that any radio station that could not pay its phone bill might be receptive to new ideas, Donahue eventually came to terms with KMPX-FM. Starting with an evening slot in April 1967, Donahue and a growing staff soon took over the full day's programming, mostly playing records from their own collections. While Donahue was not the first to launch a free-form FM radio show—a New York station had briefly run one in 1966 and another DJ had tried one at KMPX just a month before Donahue went on the air—he was the first person to make the format successful. Within months he was also running a station in Los Angeles, and FM rock stations popped up across the country in the wake of the breakthrough of psychedelia in the summer of 1967.

A San Francisco Timeline

June 1965: Charlatans begin at Red Dog Saloon

October 1965: Family Dog's "A Tribute to Dr. Strange," Longshoremen's Hall, Charlatans, Great Society, Jefferson Airplane

October 1965: Family Dog's "A Tribute to Sparkle Plenty," Charlatans, Lovin' Spoonful

November 1965: Kesey's first public acid test

December 1965: Acid test draws 400 in San Jose after Rolling Stones concert

January 1966: Acid test at the Fillmore Auditorium draws 2,400, Grateful Dead

January 1966: Three-evening Trips Festival, Longshoremen's Hall, Grateful Dead, Big Brother

Early to mid-1966: Psychedelic Shop opens

September 1966: First issue of *Oracle*

January 1967: Human Be-In draws 20,000, Quicksilver, Jefferson Airplane, Big Brother

April 1967: KMPX-FM goes on the air

November 1967: First issue of *Rolling Stone*

The Grateful Dead. Music was at the center of San Francisco psychedelia, and the group at the center of psychedelic music in the Bay Area was the Grateful Dead. The band had its roots in the folk movement of the early 1960s. Guitarist Jerry Garcia started out as a folk, bluegrass, and jug-band musician, playing traditional music on guitar and banjo. Like many young American musicians of his generation, he was introduced to American electric blues by the Rolling Stones. By the spring of 1965, Garcia was playing a combination of blues covers, folk-based traditional songs, and original music with the Warlocks. Based in the Bay Area, the Warlocks also included Ron "Pigpen" McKernan (organ, harmonica), Bob Weir (guitar), Bill Kreutzmann (drums), and eventually Phil Lesh (bass). The band soon changed its name to the Grateful Dead and, as the house band for the Kesey acid tests, began to develop a highly improvisational approach in which single songs could last longer than most albums. While the group's free-form style worked well in the context of the acid tests and in subsequent performances at the Fillmore and Avalon, capturing it in the recording studio posed significant difficulties. Signed by MGM in 1966, the band and the label parted ways after several months without a record ever being released. The band then signed

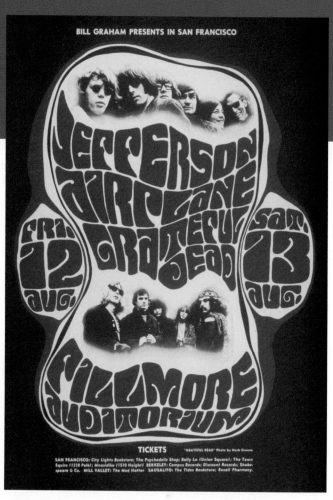

with Warner Brothers and in March 1967 it released a debut album, *The Grateful Dead*, containing short tunes that give no real indication of the improvisatory nature of the band's live shows.

The group's second album, *Anthem of the Sun* (1968), did not solve the problem of how to record a representative portrayal of their live act, but it provided an important instance of the band's improvisational bent. Made up of segments drawn from live and studio recordings, the album consists of two sides that were each assembled via multiple tapes in real time. Just as the Beatles had mixed tape loops in real time on "Tomorrow Never Knows," Garcia and Lesh "mixed" each side of their album on the fly with a considerable amount of studio improvisation subject to the element of chance. According to Garcia, the album was mixed with the goal of intensifying the acid experience. Lesh, a former composition student, was familiar with electronic avant-garde music, and has remarked how impressed the band was when they heard "Tomorrow Never Knows." The parallels between Lennon's lyrics (drawn from Leary's *The Psychedelic Experience*, which counsels one during an acid trip) and the psychedelic aesthetic of *Anthem of the Sun*, combined with the similarities in the manipulation of taped sounds, make the Grateful Dead album a clear extension of the Beatles track. The Dead had still not captured their live show on record, however, although the 1970 album *Live/Dead* would go a good way toward achieving that. *Live/Dead* was recorded before a group of friends live in the studio, and it contains a twenty-five-minute version of "Dark Star," a song written with poet Robert Hunter (a friend of Garcia's from his army days) that had become a staple of the band's live set. This track is representative of the band's extended improvised instrumental solos, which frequently occur over simple chord progressions and feature the use of modal scales (as opposed to the more common major and minor scales), as might be found in jazz of about the same period. Released later in 1970, *Working Man's Dead* and *American Beauty* return to shorter, more country- and folk-oriented tracks, and taken with *Live/Dead*, form a trio of albums that launched the Grateful Dead as one of the most successful live bands in the 1970s and '80s. While they struggled at times to create commercial recordings in the studio, during the 1970s their fans began a long-standing tradition of recording live concerts. Subverting conventional methods of studio recordings, Grateful Dead fans have always felt more connected to this form of listening, as evidenced by the vast networks trading these "bootleg" recordings, and the prominence of many noncommercial live recordings.

Jefferson Airplane. Formed by singer Marty Balin and guitarist Paul Kantner in mid-1965, Jefferson Airplane established themselves on the San Francisco scene slightly earlier than the Dead. Formed to play in Balin's Matrix club, the band's performance at the club opening in August 1965 garnered a positive review from *San Francisco Chronicle* critic Ralph Gleason (who was to mentor young editor Jann Wenner in the early years of *Rolling Stone*) and led to a recording deal with RCA. Along with original members Jorma Kaukonen (guitar) and Signe Anderson (vocals), bassist Jack Cassady and drummer Spencer Dryden rounded out the band lineup that recorded *Jefferson Airplane Takes Off*. Recorded in late 1965, it was not released until late 1966. By October 1966, however, Anderson had been replaced by Grace Slick, who had been a member of another San Francisco group, the Great Society. Slick brought two songs with her, both of which became hit singles: "Somebody to Love" (p5, 1967) and "White Rabbit" (p8, 1967). Jefferson Airplane's second album, *Surrealistic Pillow* (1967), which contained both of these songs, featured Slick and rose to number three on the American album charts. This

Listening Guide

Get Music Ⓢ wwnorton.com/studyspace

Jefferson Airplane, "White Rabbit" RCA Victor 47-9248

Words and music by Grace Slick, produced by Rick Jarrard. Reached #8 on the *Billboard* "Hot 100" chart in the summer of 1967.

FORM: AABA form, with the last verse expanded to create a musical climax. The entire piece builds gradually, beginning quietly and ending loudly.

TIME SIGNATURE: 4/4, with the drums suggesting a Spanish flavor in imitation of a bolero rhythm.

INSTRUMENTATION: Electric guitars, bass, drums, lead vocals.

0:00–0:28	**Introduction**, 12 mm.	Bass guitar and snare drum suggest "bolero" rhythm, as the guitar enters with winding lines that evoke Spanish music.
0:28–0:55	**A-Verse**, 12 mm.	Vocals enter quietly, with only bass, guitar, and snare drum accompaniment. "One pill makes you . . ."
0:55–1:23	**A-Verse**, 12 mm.	Just a little louder and more forceful, "And if you go . . ."
1:23–1:42	**B-Bridge**, 8 mm.	Second guitar now enters, drums go into a more traditional rock beat, and the music gains intensity, getting markedly louder. "When men on . . ."
1:42–2:27	**A-Verse** (expanded), 21 mm.	Vocal now much more forceful, as rhythm in the accompaniment gets much more insistent, driving toward the climax at the end. "Go ask Alice . . ."

lineup subsequently recorded a series of successful and often innovative albums, including *After Bathing at Baxter's* (p17, 1967), *Crown of Creation* (p6, 1968), the live *Bless Its Pointed Little Head* (p17 uk38, 1969), and the politically inspired *Volunteers* (p13 uk34, 1969), all of which became staples of late 1960s progressive FM radio. The group's early influences were American folk and blues, but elements of modal jazz and Indian music can be found throughout their music, especially in their extended instrumental solos.

The single "White Rabbit" shows how Jefferson Airplane was able to blend musical ambition with the AM single format. The song is in AABA form, with an introduction. The first two verses are followed by a bridge and then an expanded verse, which also includes a dramatic ending. The lyrics of the song refer to Lewis Carroll's *Alice in Wonderland* stories, although the clear reference in lines like "feed your head" is to the use of psychedelic drugs. Slick's surreal images resonate with those of many other psychedelic songwriters, especially John Lennon, whose "Lucy in the Sky with Diamonds" was also inspired in part by *Alice in Wonderland*. Jefferson Airplane modeled the music in "White Rabbit" on the Spanish bolero, heard especially in Kaukonen's Spanish-sounding guitar lines in the introduction. Slick recalls listening to the Miles Davis and Gil Evans orchestral jazz album *Sketches of Spain* for inspiration, but the overall dynamic shape of the piece closely resembles a well-known orchestral work by the French composer Maurice Ravel entitled *Boléro* (1927–28). Often used by music educators to illustrate the wide variety of tone colors available to the master orchestrator, Ravel's *Boléro* employs a single Spanish-tinged melody that is repeated several times, but contextualized differently at each repetition to exploit the full range of available orchestral colors. More important to our discussion of "White Rabbit," however, *Boléro* is constructed as a single long crescendo—it continually and gradually builds toward its violent musical climax. This is precisely what "White Rabbit" does, although on a more compressed time scale (the Ravel piece lasts almost fifteen minutes). As with the Grateful Dead's *Anthem of the Sun* and the Beatles' "Tomorrow Never Knows," we again find a song dealing with the acid experience and employing ambitious techniques borrowed from classical music. In the case of "White Rabbit," however, the classical music involved is not avant-garde music, but early twentieth-century orchestral music.

Big Brother and the Holding Company and Janis Joplin.
Like the Grateful Dead and Jefferson Airplane, Big Brother and the Holding Company experimented with classical and avant-garde music. At one point the band regularly performed a version of Edvard Grieg's "Hall of the Mountain King" from the play *Peer Gynt*, and contemplated an experimental piece called "Bacon," which would last as long as it took to fry a plate of bacon on stage. The band enjoyed its greatest acclaim and success, however, backing up singer Janis Joplin on electric blues numbers. Joplin had left her hometown of Port Arthur, Texas, in the early 1960s to sing in Austin night clubs. By mid-decade she had made her way to San Francisco, where she sang for a brief period before giving up music to return to Port Arthur. Big Brother and the Holding Company was formed in part by concert promoter Chet Helms who convinced her to return to San Francisco to join the band. The band's self-titled first album was released in the fall of 1967. Their second album, *Cheap Thrills*, became an enormous commercial success, hitting number one on the U.S. album charts in the fall of 1968 while the single "Piece of My Heart" rose to number twelve. Joplin

Before embarking on a solo career, Janis Joplin sang for Big Brother and the Holding Company, an important group in the emerging psychedelic scene of San Francisco. This cover to their 1967 album *Cheap Thrills*, portrays the songs and the band in cartoon form, including the band's cover versions of George and Ira Gershwin's "Summertime" and Big Mama Thornton's "Ball and Chain."

Janis Joplin (left) singing with her group Big Brother and the Holding Company at a 1967 concert at Winterland in San Francisco. Joplin's aggressive, passionate blues style drew inspiration from singers like Bessie Smith and Ma Rainey. Their hard lives proved a model for Joplin, who died of a drug overdose in 1970, just months before her album *Pearl* was released and quickly climbed the charts to number one.

soon left Big Brother to embark on a solo career, and by the fall of 1969 her debut album, *I Got Dem Ol' Kozmic Blues Again Mama!*, went to number five on the U.S. pop chart. Throughout her adult life Joplin struggled with drug and alcohol abuse and on October 4, 1970, she was found in a hotel room dead from an overdose. Her posthumously released album *Pearl* became her most popular release, rising to number one in early 1971, while her version of Kris Kristofferson's "Me and Bobby McGee" hit the top of the U.S. singles charts. Joplin's powerful blues style and hard-living image were reminiscent of the earlier blues singers like Ma Rainey, Bessie Smith, and Big Mama Thornton whom she emulated. She was a central figure in the Haight-Ashbury scene leading up to the summer of 1967 and her blues-based singing style offers an important example of the connection between psychedelia and African-American music. The musicians in Big Brother were more in step with other aspects of the psychedelic aesthetic, and while acknowledging the importance of blues in their music, also stressed how they were striving to find something new—a style they called "blues in Technicolor."

Country Joe and the Fish. Led by singer-guitarist Joe McDonald from Washington, D.C. and Barry "The Fish" Melton from New York, Country Joe and the Fish were active in radical politics in Berkeley, California. While the politics of the Berkeley radicals and the counterculture of the San Francisco hippies are typically thought of as different aspects of the same local scene, the two communities often had difficulty agreeing on issues of cultural and political change. Music was important to both groups, but to many of the radicals, the hippies seemed spacey and generally detached from the political issues that most concerned them. To many hippies, the radicals seemed too intense and hung up on political action. Country Joe and the Fish were something of a bridge between the two communities. In 1965, for instance, the band issued an extended-play (EP) recording that was included in an issue of *Rag Baby*, a radical magazine founded by McDonald that circulated in the San Francisco area. Two years later, the band released a markedly psychedelic debut album, *Electric Music for the Mind and Body* (p39, 1967). While this album clearly displays the band's origins in acoustic blues and folk, it is most noteworthy for its many moments influenced by the band's use of LSD. The atmospheric and experimental "Section 43" is the best example of this. According to band accounts, the entire record was designed, like the Grateful Dead's *Anthem of the Sun*, to enhance the listener's acid trip. The group's next album, *I-Feel-Like-I'm-Fixin'-to-Die* (p67, 1968), featured the title song, originally recorded in 1965 as an outspoken denouncement of the Vietnam War, and the "Fish Cheer," which the band made famous by inserting the word "fuck" in place of "Fish" at live performances, most notably at Woodstock. While *Together* (p23, 1968) brought the group's greatest commercial success, it already marked the musical decline of the band.

THE LONDON SCENE

The Rise of the British Underground. In 1965, while the Grateful Dead were turning to electric blues and Jefferson Airplane were rehearsing for their debut performance, Beat poet Allen Ginsberg was in London helping bookstore owner

Barry Miles organize a poetry reading that featured several American and European Beats, including Lawrence Ferlinghetti and Gregory Corso. Convinced that Miles's Better Books was far too small to contain the crowd they were hoping to draw, the organizers rented the Royal Albert Hall. In June 1965, "Poets of the World/Poets of Our Time" drew over 5,000 people—many under the influence of pot or acid—and inaugurated the London psychedelic underground. The following September, British researcher Michael Hollingshead (who had introduced Timothy Leary to LSD), opened the World Psychedelic Center in London, which would soon become the English center for psychedelic music and culture.

Drugs were not entirely new to rock culture in the UK. The Beatles had been introduced to marijuana in late 1964, and John Lennon and George Harrison had already experienced LSD in the spring of 1965 (it was secretly slipped into their coffee after dinner at the home of an acquaintance). But similar to San Francisco, a community of young people in London was beginning to form around drugs, Eastern philosophy, radical politics, and experimental music. By the end of January 1966, a series of weekly events called the Spontaneous Underground were initiated that combined poetry, music, and avant-garde performance art. Held in the Marquee Club on Sundays, these events were akin to Kesey's acid tests, although on a smaller scale. In February, a bookstore and gallery called the Indica was launched by Barry Miles, John Dunbar (the husband of Marianne Faithfull), and Peter Asher (of the musical duo Peter and Gordon and brother of Paul McCartney's girlfriend, Jane). The Indica, similar to the Psychedelic Shop, specialized in counterculture items, and it was here that John Lennon first encountered *The Psychedelic Experience*. Unlike the San Francisco scene, the London underground boasted a kind of counter-cultural night school where students could study topics such as housing problems, race relations, mental health, and law. Called the London Free School, it began to hold meetings in March 1966.

Underground Clubs in Swinging London.
In April 1966, just as the London psychedelic scene was gaining momentum and remained unknown to anyone outside of it, *Time* magazine ran a cover story on "Swinging London," focusing on what the editors in New York perceived as a refreshing urban lifestyle filled with glamorous nightspots attended by hip stars adorned in daring and colorful fashions. The summer of 1966 saw young tourists flocking to London to catch some of the excitement, but the psychedelic scene developed mostly out of their sight. In October, the *International Times* began publication, providing the burgeoning scene with a newspaper devoted to its concerns, and before the end of the year the UFO Club was established. Unlike the Fillmore or the Avalon in San Francisco, the UFO

In the spring of 1966, *Time* magazine proclaimed London "the swinging city." But while tourists and the media were focused on Swinging London, a psychedelic underground was developing in the British capital, mostly out of view of anyone except those in the know.

was more of an organization than a place. UFO evenings occurred in a spot that was an Irish pub during the rest of the week. When using that bar became a problem, the UFO simply relocated. While other clubs also featured psychedelic music (even some of the same bands, such as Pink Floyd, Soft Machine, Tomorrow, and the Crazy World of Arthur Brown), for most of 1967, the UFO was the most prominent gathering of the psychedelic underground in London. Larger events occurred during this period as well. In late April 1967 an evening of psychedelia brought 10,000 London hippies together. Called "The 14-Hour Technicolor Dream," the all-night event was held at Alexandra Palace, a Victorian palace overlooking London. Avant-garde happenings (one supervised by Yoko Ono), a light show, and a long roster of bands were meant to intensify the chemically enhanced experiences of those in attendance. A month later Pink Floyd sponsored a similar event, "Games for May," which was held in Queen Elizabeth Hall, and in July, a "Love-In" back at Alexandra Palace featured Pink Floyd, Tomorrow, the Crazy World of Arthur Brown, and the Animals. By August, when

the Middle Earth Club was established for evenings similar to those hosted by the UFO, little about psychedelia was underground anymore: in the wake of *Sgt. Pepper's Lonely Hearts Club Band*, it seemed that psychedelia was everywhere.

A London Timeline

June 1965: "Poets of the World/Poets of Our Time," Royal Albert Hall

September 1965: Michael Hollingshead opens World Psychedelic Center

January 30, 1966: Spontaneous Underground weekly events begin (Marquee Club)

February 1966: Indica Bookshop and Gallery opens

March 1966: London Free School is launched

April 1966: *Time* cover story on Swinging London

October 1966: *International Times* begins publication

December 1966: UFO evenings begin

April 1967: "The 14-Hour Technicolor Dream," Alexandra Palace

May 1967: "Games for May," Pink Floyd, Queen Elizabeth Hall

July 1967: "Love-In," Pink Floyd, Tomorrow, the Animals, Arthur Brown, Alexandra Palace

August 1967: Middle Earth evenings begin

Musical Notes from the Underground: Pink Floyd, Soft Machine, and Tomorrow.

There were generally two types of bands on the London scene during the 1966–69 period: those who enjoyed commercial success (the Beatles, the Stones, Cream, Jimi Hendrix, Donovan), and those whose success was limited to the London underground. The first band to make its name on the underground scene formed in 1965 and took its name from American bluesmen Pink Anderson and Floyd Council. Initially calling themselves the Pink Floyd Sound, then simply Pink Floyd, the band became regulars at Spontaneous Underground events, and later at the UFO Club.

The band took its name from the blues, but much of its approach was more indebted to avant-garde art music. The group's extended improvisations would often dispense with chord patterns and scales and wander into exploratory noise-making, produced by playing their instruments in unconventional ways or feeding their electric guitars and keyboards through tape-echo devices. While leader and guitarist Syd Barrett, bassist Roger Waters, organist Richard Wright, and drummer Nick Mason could play songs like "Interstellar Overdrive" for half an hour, they also had a pair of radio-friendly hit singles in mid-1967, written by Barrett. "Arnold Layne," a song about a transvestite who steals women's clothing off other people's clotheslines at night—which somehow avoided being banned by the BBC—reached number twenty on the UK charts. The follow-up, "See Emily Play," hit number six. The band refused to play these songs live, however, preferring to perform their extended

Like San Francisco, London had a strong psychedelic scene that remained underground until mid-1967. The UFO Club—less an actual place than an organization—hosted many important bands of the era. This 1967 poster advertises a Pink Floyd concert (they were regulars at the UFO) and reveals a clear artistic connection with the rock posters of the Fillmore in San Francisco.

improvisations instead. Pink Floyd's first album, *Piper at the Gates of Dawn* (uk6, 1967), was recorded around the same time and at the same Abbey Road facility as the Beatles' *Sgt. Pepper* (Paul McCartney is reported to have visited at least one of the sessions). Barrett, however, soon began to show signs of mental illness, and during an American tour in 1967, he became unable to perform reliably. Guitarist and Barrett friend David Gilmour was brought in to cover, but eventually replaced Barrett entirely. In light of the tremendous success the band enjoyed worldwide in the 1970s (discussed in Chapter 8), it is surprising that their success before *The Dark Side of the Moon* (1973) was limited to the UK. The group scored a string of hit albums in Britain, including *A Saucerful of Secrets* (uk9, 1968), *More* (uk9, 1969), *Ummagumma* (p74 uk5, 1969), and *Atom Heart Mother* (p55 uk1, 1970), but they could never break the Top 40 of the album charts in the States. Their concert performances in London during 1966–68, often accompanied by elaborate light shows and played for audiences tripping on acid, made them one of the most important bands in the London psychedelic underground.

Soft Machine also performed regularly for the UFO Club and other psychedelic events in London. They blended a passion for experimental weirdness with a penchant for the free jazz of Ornette Coleman and John Coltrane. Unlike Pink Floyd, the group never had a hit single and had only modest success with their albums. *The Soft Machine*, a 1968 U.S.-only release, did not chart (the band was touring America at the time, opening for Jimi Hendrix). In 1966–68, the band alternated short song-like sections with avant-garde improvisations. After this, in a series of numbered albums (*Volume Two*, *Third*, *Fourth*, etc.), the band tended toward jazz fusion and became pioneers of the British jazz fusion called Canterbury progressive rock. Tomorrow was another band that became regulars at UFO events and around the London scene. Featuring guitarist Steve Howe (who would later play in the progressive rock band Yes) and vocalist Keith West, the band released a pair of singles that were popular around London but failed to chart. One of these, "My White Bicycle," exhibits many of the psychedelic features found on other records: backward tape sounds, exotic Eastern-sounding melodies, and simple pop lyrics.

The Rolling Stones: Psychedelic Rhythm and Blues?
While Pink Floyd, Soft Machine, and Tomorrow were important components of the burgeoning London psychedelic scene in 1966–67, other British bands and artists enjoyed a much higher profile, especially after June 1967. First among these was certainly the Beatles. The Rolling Stones also continued to score hit singles and albums throughout the second half of the 1960s. New bands such as Cream, the Jimi Hendrix Experience, and

Traffic emerged in the months leading up to the Summer of Love, building on the Stones' passion for electric blues. Folksinger Donovan Leitch also turned to flower power and provided a lighter take on British psychedelia.

By late 1966, Brian Jones's contribution to the Rolling Stones' music had diminished considerably, and the Jagger-Richards songwriting partnership began to dominate the band's music. Their seventh album, *Aftermath*, was the first to contain only Jagger-Richards songs, securing their role as group leaders. Despite their well-established position as one of rock music's leading bands, however, the Stones remained junior colleagues of the Beatles, which was evident in the second half of 1967, as the band prepared *Their Satanic Majesties Request* in response to *Sgt. Pepper*. Jagger had been present at sessions for *Sgt. Pepper* and appeared with the Beatles on their worldwide broadcast of "All You Need Is Love" in July 1967. Jagger had also accompanied the Beatles when they traveled to Wales to study with the Maharishi later that summer. The summer and fall of 1967 had been difficult for Jones, Jagger, and Richards. Each was convicted on drug possession charges and faced the possibility of serving a prison sentence. The single "We Love You" was the band's way of thanking fans for their support during the trials. It hit number eight in the UK in the fall of 1967 and provided a somewhat darker echo of the Beatles' "All You Need Is Love." Released in December 1967, *Their Satanic Majesties Request* (p2 uk3) featured a holographic cover image of the band dressed in wizard outfits—if the Beatles were a happy-go-lucky brass band, the Stones would pose as menacing magi of the occult. The single "She's a Rainbow" illustrates the *Sgt. Pepper* influence on the Stones: the tune employs orchestral instruments and a classical-sounding piano figure that recurs frequently, each time breaking the steady beat of the music.

This album remains a source of disagreement among rock writers. Some consider it to be the Rolling Stones' low point—a project that fails by attempting to imitate the Beatles too closely. Others think it is an interesting and perhaps necessary step in the band's development. Most writers agree, however, that the Rolling Stones came into their own as a band when they stopped worrying about what the Beatles were doing and turned back to their rhythm and blues roots. The hard-driving rhythm of "Jumpin' Jack Flash" (p3 uk1, 1968) gives the first indication of this new stylistic orientation, and the band's next album, *Beggar's Banquet* (p5 uk3, 1968), confirmed it. As discussed in Chapter 4, the Stones' manager Andrew Loog Oldham had marketed the band as bad boys beginning in 1964. By the end of 1967, Oldham was no longer managing the group, but this did not keep the Stones from amplifying the outlaw image that had been crystallized by the scandal over "(I Can't Get No) Satisfaction." In the wake of their widely publicized legal issues, and at a time when the counterculture shifted to include the riots and antiwar protests of 1968, the Stones' "Street Fighting Man" was banned from the radio because authorities thought it might fuel violence. When Jagger adopted the role of Lucifer to sing "Sympathy for the Devil" in 1968, it was clear the band's involvement with flower power was over.

Cream: British Blues on Acid with Pop on the Side. The first rock band to be billed as a "supergroup" was formed in July 1966 when Eric Clapton (formerly of the Yardbirds), bassist Jack Bruce, and drummer Ginger Baker formed Cream. Individually they had played in British blues bands with Alexis Korner,

Listening Guide   Get Music ⓢ wwnorton.com/studyspace

Cream, "Sunshine of Your Love" Polydor 56286 (UK), ATCO 45-6544 (U.S.)

Words and music by Eric Clapton, Jack Bruce, and Pete Brown, produced by Felix Pappalardi. Reached #5 on the *Billboard* "Hot 100" chart in early 1968 (uk25).

FORM: Simple verse, with each verse employing the same 24-bar pattern, created by doubling each measure in the standard 12-bar blues structure so that each single measure becomes two measures. The song draws on the "lick blues" tradition of building a tune around a repeating riff or lick. Note the expansion of the 24-bar pattern that occurs in the last verse.

TIME SIGNATURE: 4/4.

INSTRUMENTATION: Electric guitar, bass, drums, and lead vocal.

0:00–0:16	**Introduction**, 8 mm.	2 mm. riff stated four times in guitar and bass. Note that the drum part employs no cymbals.
0:16–1:06	**Verse 1**, 24 mm.	Vocal enters as riff continues. Clapton and Bruce trade off singing vocal phrases. "It's gettin' near dawn . . ."
1:06–2:00	**Verse 2**, 26 mm.	A 2 mm. link precedes a repetition of the 24-mm. verse. Vocal trade-off continues and the verse is performed as before. "I'm with you my love . . ."
2:00–2:50	**Instr. Verse**, 24 mm.	Clapton blues-based guitar solo. After laying off the cymbals in the previous verses, Baker employs them heavily now.
2:50–4:08	**Verse 3**, 32 mm. and fade-out	This last verse is much more forceful, owing to the now copious use of cymbals carried over from the solo. The verse proceeds as before until "I've been waiting so long," where the 24 mm. structure is expanded by repeating this line to create a dramatic ending before the fade-out. "I'm with you my love . . ."

John Mayall, and Graham Bond, and the initial idea was that the trio would focus on traditional blues. The band eventually covered several traditional blues numbers, including Robert Johnson's "Crossroads" and Muddy Waters's "Rollin' and Tumblin'." But Clapton had helped develop the instrumental "rave-up" sections that had been a feature of the Yardbirds' live shows, and these became an important element in Cream's blues adaptations. The live version of Willie Dixon's "Spoonful" found on *Wheels of Fire* (1968) is typical. It includes a lengthy instrumental rave-up and runs to almost seventeen minutes. While the focus of the music was often on Clapton's guitar playing, Bruce and Baker were also accomplished players who would solo from time to time. Baker's drum solo on "Toad," for example, became a model for many rock drummers. Clapton was widely celebrated in England as guitar "god," and helped popularize distortion and the wah-wah pedal among guitarists. Although the blues were a central element in Cream's music, the band also had a knack for pop singles, demonstrated by the success of "I Feel Free" (uk11, 1966) and "Strange Brew" (uk17, 1967) in the first year of their career.

Initially, the band's success was greater in the UK where the band members were already well known. *Fresh Cream*, the group's first album, hit number six on the UK charts at the beginning of 1967. In the wake of the Summer of Love, the new passion for trippy music sent *Disraeli Gears* to number four on the U.S. charts (uk5) in the fall, and *Wheels of Fire* rose to number one (uk3) a year later. Whereas the focus of the Beatles' and Beach Boys' music was on expanding the limits of rock songwriting and recording techniques, Cream relied more on virtuosic playing. Cream's penchant for instrumental soloing parallels that of the San Francisco bands, many of whom were inspired by the Rolling Stones' and Yardbirds' adaptations of American electric blues. While the San Francisco guitarists were known more for the bands they played in, Clapton and Hendrix became famous as individuals, ushering in the idea of the "guitar hero." For all the excitement generated by Cream, the band stayed together for only about two years. In November 1968, the band performed a farewell concert in London's Royal Albert Hall. All three members went on to solo careers, although Clapton was the most successful, scoring hit singles and albums in the 1970s, '80s, and '90s.

Cream—(from left) Ginger Baker (drums), Jack Bruce (bass), and Eric Clapton (guitar)—performing at Royal Albert Hall during their farewell appearance in November 1968. Strongly influenced by the blues, Cream showcased the virtuosic instrumental solos of Clapton (formerly of the Yardbirds), the soulful vocals of Bruce, and the powerful drumming of Baker.

Cream's Blues Adaptations. One of Cream's best-known tracks is "Sunshine of Your Love," written by Clapton, Bruce, and lyricist Pete Brown (p5 uk25, 1968). The song is built around a central guitar figure (sometimes called a "riff" or "lick") that is repeated in the guitar and bass throughout much of the song. (The technique of building a blues number around a central riff is common in American electric blues.) In "Sunshine of Your Love," this central riff is combined with the 12-bar blues structure to create verses that repeat throughout the tune according to the simple verse formal design. The 12-bar pattern is doubled to twenty-four measures, although the proportions remain the same—the first 4-bar phrase is now 8 bars, and the second and third phrases are expanded in the same manner. The third phrase departs somewhat from the standard blues version, but is clearly derived from that pattern. By modifying elements within the 12-bar blues structural framework, Cream creates an original blues-rock song that builds on and expands traditional blues techniques and patterns.

The Jimi Hendrix Experience: Psychedelic Blues Meets the Avant-garde.
Seattle-born Jimi Hendrix is one of the most influential guitarists in the history of rock music. Hendrix spent the first half of the 1960s (with the exception of a short term of service in the U.S. Army) playing in various bands, including stints with Little Richard and the Isley Brothers. In 1964 he moved to New York, where he worked with soul singer Curtis Knight before forming his own band, Jimmy James and the Blue Flames. In July 1966, Animals bassist Chas Chandler saw Hendrix's act at Café Wha? in Greenwich Village and offered to manage the guitarist. Chandler brought Hendrix to London in September, where he formed the Jimi Hendrix Experience with Hendrix, drummer Mitch Mitchell, and bassist Noel Redding. Despite being an American, Hendrix first made his mark on the London psychedelic scene. By early 1967, the Experience's rendition of "Hey Joe" was number six on the UK charts, followed by "Purple Haze" (uk3) in May. The band's first album, *Are You Experienced?* (p5 uk2, 1967), was a tremendous success in the UK during the second half of 1967. It rose to the number two spot behind *Sgt. Pepper*. Hendrix's success in the United States followed his appearance at the Monterey International Pop Festival in the summer of 1967 (see below). His first album was not released in the United States until August, and while it did well, "Purple Haze" reached only number sixty-five and "Foxey Lady" stalled at number sixty-seven on the American singles charts. By early 1968 *Axis: Bold as Love* was at number three in the United States (uk5), and the band followed up with *Electric Ladyland* (p1 uk6, 1968) and the compilation *Smash Hits* (uk4, 1968; p6, 1969). In the summer of 1969, just weeks before his legendary Woodstock performance,

Jimi Hendrix was an innovative and explosive rock guitarist. His music displays a strong blues influence mixed with psychedelic elements and catchy lyrics and melodies. Hendrix used his guitar to produce a wide range of sounds, including his signature fuzz and feedback. His stage shows were exciting, improvisational, and often destructive.

Listening Guide

Get Music ⑨ **wwnorton.com/studyspace**

The Jimi Hendrix Experience, "Purple Haze" Reprise 0597 (U.S.), Track 604001 (UK)

Words and music by Jimi Hendrix, produced by Chas Chandler. Reached #65 on the *Billboard* "Hot 100" in 1967 (uk3). Contained on the album *Are You Experienced?*, which rose to #2 in the UK and #5 in the United States.

FORM: Simple verse, with contrasting instrumental bridge. The introduction plays an important role in the track, and it returns after the instrumental bridge, serving to relaunch the tune. The practice of using an instrumental bridge and returning to the introduction to set up the last verse are features that will become commonplace in later rock music.

TIME SIGNATURE: 4/4.

INSTRUMENTATION: Electric guitars, bass, drums, lead vocal, and extra spoken voices.

0:00–0:32	**Introduction**, 14 mm.	The first 2 mm. introduce the famous dissonant riff in the guitar and bass, followed by 8 mm. of blues-based melodic phrases on the guitar. The introduction concludes by setting up the chord progression that will follow in the verse.
0:32–0:52	**Verse 1**, 9 mm.	Vocal enters. Note call and response between the vocal ("S'cuse me") and the lead guitar at the end of the verse. "Purple haze all in my brain . . ."
0:52–1:12	**Verse 2**, 12 mm.	The first 9 mm. are as before, but then a 3-mm. transition ("Help me") leads into the guitar solo. "Purple haze all around . . ."
1:12–1:35	**Instrumental Bridge**, 8 mm.	Guitar solo. While based on the blues, this solo also invokes sitar-like lines. Note speaking voices in the background.
1:35–1:53	**Return of Introduction**, 8 mm.	A repetition of the melody from the intro.
1:53–2:12	**Verse 3**, 9 mm.	As before, "Purple haze all in my eyes . . ."
2:12–2:49	**Coda**, 17 mm. and fade	Music is drawn from the instrumental bridge.

the Experience parted ways after Hendrix began to explore different material more based in blues. For the next year, Hendrix performed and recorded widely with many different musicians, including the group Band of Gypsys. On September 18, 1970, Jimi Hendrix died of a drug overdose, cutting short a career of less than four years in the mainstream spotlight.

"Purple Haze" and "Foxey Lady" from *Are You Experienced?* are good examples of Hendrix's distinctive blend of blues and pop. Both tracks employ chord progressions and melodic materials derived from electric blues to form effective pop "hooks." In "Purple Haze," the line, "S'cuse me while I kiss the sky," is followed by a catchy response in the guitar, just as the titular line "foxey lady!" is answered in a parallel manner by the guitar.

There are many examples of Hendrix's experimental music. "If 6 Was 9," from *Axis: Bold as Love,* runs more than five minutes, with three minutes of instrumental playing featuring novel guitar sound effects and some counterculture narration. Perhaps Hendrix's most ambitious experimental track, "1983 (A Merman I Should Turn to Be)" from *Electric Ladyland,* clocks in at just under fourteen minutes. After about four minutes of the song proper (which is filled with backward tape effects), the band launches into a series of loose atmospheric instrumental sections that allow Hendrix, Mitchell, and Redding ample opportunity to shine

After achieving success with the Experience in the UK, Jimi Hendrix made his mark on the American psychedelic scene by setting his guitar on fire during this performance in the summer of 1967 at the Monterey Pop Festival.

individually before ending with a reprise of the song. Immediately following the track is the short electronic piece, "Moon, Turn the Tides . . . gently gently away," which adds a clear avant-garde final touch to "1983." Hendrix's experimentation in the recording studio (he often worked very closely with engineer Eddie Kramer) clearly extends the work done by others, especially the Beatles and the Beach Boys. His virtuosity as a guitarist served as a model for many important rock musicians who followed, and his sonic innovations employing feedback and the vibrato bar on the electric guitar were much imitated. His performances were flamboyant and often sexually suggestive or physically destructive—setting the guitar on fire or otherwise destroying it—and became the stuff of rock legend.

Traffic and Van Morrison. At the beginning of 1967, the Spencer Davis Group was enjoying great success. In the previous six months the band had two top ten singles in both the United States and the UK. During that time, however, rumors had also circulated that eighteen-year-old Stevie Winwood would leave the group. The tremendous success of the Spencer Davis Group brought with it musical limitations that Winwood was eager to abandon in favor of exploring more "musicianly" concerns. Winwood quit the band and formed Traffic in April 1967 with drummer Jim Capaldi, guitarist Dave Mason, and flutist/saxophonist Chris Wood. The band's first single, "Paper Sun" (p94 uk5) was released in May 1967 and captured the whimsical character of emerging British flower power with its opening measures of sitar and upbeat vocal melody. The band's next single, "Hole in My Shoe" did even better, going to number two in the UK. By

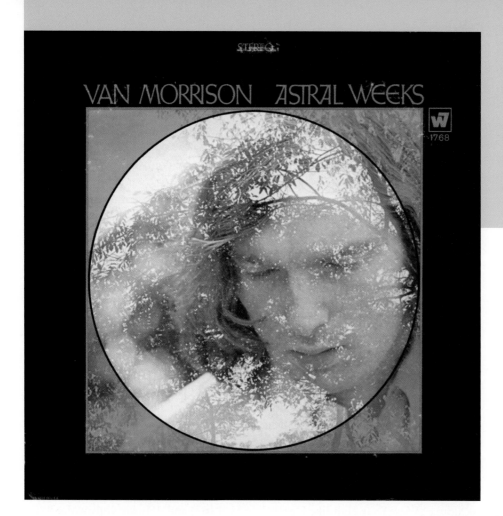

the end of 1967, the band had released its first album, *Mr. Fantasy*, which rose to number eight in the UK. With their second album, *Traffic* (p17 uk9, 1968), the group finally scored success in the United States, which increased with the release of *Last Exit* (p19, 1969). While the Spencer Davis Group had been rooted securely in rhythm and blues, Traffic experimented with a broad range of styles. Tracks from the first album blend psychedelic pop and blues ("Heaven Is in Your Mind") with Latin rhythms ("Dealer"), classical instrumentation ("No Face, No Name, No Number"), and jazz soloing ("Coloured Rain"). The group disbanded in early 1969 and Winwood went on to play with Clapton and Baker in Blind Faith before reforming Traffic with Wood and Capaldi in early 1970 (Traffic's music from the 1970s is discussed in the next chapter).

Irish singer-songwriter Van Morrison first hit the charts as a member of the band Them, whose "Baby Please Don't Go" (uk10, 1964) and "Here Comes the Night" (p24 uk2, 1965) enjoyed success in the UK. The band's recording of "Gloria"—the B-side of "Baby Please Don't Go"—became a garage-band classic and was covered most famously by Patti Smith (1976). By 1967, Morrison had set out on a solo career, and this move was given a substantial boost by the commercial success of "Brown Eyed Girl" (p10) a song that has been a staple of American radio ever since. As catchy as his hit songs could be, Morrison also had a more experimental side, which showed itself clearly on the 1968 album *Astral Weeks*. Recorded in New York in less than two days, the album's raw looseness influenced many later singer-songwriters, though it was more a critical than a commercial success. The tracks on *Astral Weeks* bring together a wide variety of styles, including acoustic folk music, jazz, classical, and rhythm and blues, and many of the tracks were recorded with top-notch studio players improvising in support of Morrison. This highly improvised dimension of the music has a certain aleatoric (chance) quality that was popular in both jazz and avant-garde performances of the 1960s. There are also connections to the experimental aspects of performances by Pink Floyd or the aleatoric studio practices found on the Grateful Dead's *Anthem of the Sun*. The music is loose and improvisatory, but rarely dissonant or angular—it is impressionistic, jazzy, and filled with a sense of poetic mysticism. Morrison went on to be an important singer-songwriter in the 1970s, and we will consider his music further in Chapter 8.

Donovan and Psychedelic Folk. Born Donovan Philips Leitch, Donovan first attracted international attention as a traditional folksinger and songwriter with his 1965 hit single "Catch the Wind" (p23 uk4). Much like the music of Bob Dylan, Donovan's early folk music was strongly influenced by Woody Guthrie. As folk rock developed in mid-1965, Donovan adapted his music to the new style by using electric guitars, keyboards, bass, and drums in his arrangements. Among the many studio musicians who played on Donovan's recordings were future Led Zeppelin members Jimmy Page and John Paul Jones. Donovan enjoyed a series of hit singles in the UK and United States, including "Sunshine Superman" (p1 uk2, 1966) and "Mellow Yellow" (p2, 1966; uk8, 1967). When psychedelia and flower power emerged from regional underground scenes into mainstream culture in 1967, Donovan's gentle melodic sense, eclectic stylistic range, and often mystical lyrics made him a leading figure for hippie pacifism. His success continued with more hit singles including "Wear Your Hair like Heaven" (p23, 1967) and "Hurdy Gurdy Man" (p5 uk4, 1968), the second of which features the playing not only of Page and Jones but also future Led Zeppelin drummer John Bonham. With "Atlantis" (uk23, 1968; p7, 1969), Donovan reached the edge of counterculture utopianism, reciting the tale of the lost continent in a manner suggesting that its lost wisdom might help rebuild Western culture. The song concludes with a long sing-along section similar to the end of the Beatles' "Hey Jude." Donovan remained active in the 1970s, releasing albums such as *Cosmic Wheels* (p25 uk15, 1973) and providing music for films, including Franco Zeffirelli's *Brother Sun, Sister Moon* (1973).

LOS ANGELES AND NEW YORK

The Byrds and Buffalo Springfield. The most important psychedelic subcultures were based in San Francisco and London, but other American cities also participated in the growth of the psychedelic movement. Along with the Mamas and the Papas and the Beach Boys, the Byrds were among the most successful bands to come out of Los Angeles in the mid-1960s. After the controversy over "Eight Miles High" in the summer of 1966, the group released *Fifth Dimension* (p24 uk27, 1966), which contained "Eight Miles High" and "Mr. Spaceman" (p36, 1966), the band's first attempt to mix rock with country music. While this was more the exception than the rule for the Byrds in 1966, by 1968 they had released *Sweetheart* *of the Rodeo*, often cited as a pivotal album in the development of country rock. By the end of 1967 David Crosby had left the group to join Hollies vocalist Graham Nash and guitarist Stephen Stills. Stills had enjoyed moderate success with Buffalo Springfield, whose single "For What It's Worth" (the chorus of which, "Stop children. What's that sound?" inspires this textbook's title) had hit number seven on the U.S. charts in early 1967. Crosby, Stills, and Nash (sometimes joined by ex-Buffalo Springfield guitarist Neil Young) became one of the first supergroups of the 1970s. Their music will be considered in Chapter 8. As these established artists were heading off in new musical directions, other musicians were emerging from the Los Angeles scene.

The Doors and Jim Morrison: Turning to the Dark Side. The Doors were formed in Los Angeles in 1965 by singer and lyricist Jim Morrison and keyboardist Ray Manzarek, taking their name from eighteenth-century British poet William Blake (via Aldous Huxley's book *The Doors of Perception*). Rounding out the lineup were guitarist Robbie Krieger and drummer Jon Densmore. The Doors first attracted attention with their hit single "Light My Fire" (p1 uk49, 1967). The foursome produced an often-moody brand of late 1960s blues-based psychedelia with a tendency to linger over the darker aspects of emotional life, perhaps best exemplified by "The End," a dramatic and shocking piece in which Morrison recites and then shouts his Oedipal desires. If most psychedelia in 1967 seemed to focus on the positive side of drug use—the path to higher consciousness and liberation—the Doors seemed determined to explore avenues opened up by the "bad trip," beginning with the first track on the first album, "Break on Through." Morrison's lyrics are filled with grotesque and unsettling images of alienation and repression, and his onstage antics took to a new level the bad-boy, nonconformist, overtly sexual image cultivated by Elvis Presley and Mick Jagger. With the band's third album, *Waiting for the Sun* (p1 uk16, 1968), Morrison introduced an alter ego, the Lizard King. The idea of a rock singer assuming an onstage persona would influence many other performers, including Alice Cooper, David Bowie, Peter Gabriel, and Madonna. While the group's music became increasingly refined over the course of the six studio albums from *The Doors* (p1, 1967) to *L.A. Woman* (p9 uk26, 1971), their style remained relatively stable as the band produced several hit singles, including "Hello, I Love You" (p1 uk15, 1968), "Touch Me" (p3, 1969), and "Love Her Madly" (p11, 1971). *L.A. Woman*, however, would be their last album, as Morrison died under mysterious circumstances in 1971.

The Doors' Jim Morrison during a 1968 television performance in Copenhagen, Denmark. Unlike many in the psychedelic scene, Morrison chose to explore the darker side of life, exemplified by the lyrics to "The End" and "Break on Through."

Love, Iron Butterfly, and Vanilla Fudge. Formed in 1965 by singer and guitarist Arthur Lee, Love played an important role in the Los Angeles psychedelic scene, although they never achieved the level of success enjoyed by groups like the Byrds or the Doors. Love was actually signed to Elektra before the Doors, and recommended the Doors to the record label. Love's first single, "My Little Red Book" (1966), was a rock cover version of a Burt Bacharach and Hal David song, and much of the group's other early music shows strong Byrds and Rolling Stones influences. In the wake of *Sgt. Pepper,* Love released their third and most celebrated album, *Forever Changes* (1967), which featured ambitious tracks, at times employing orchestral accompaniment, heady lyrics, and dense vocal harmonies.

As dark as the Doors could get, the heaviest band of the late 1960s was Iron Butterfly. Formed in San Diego in 1966 they bounded onto the scene with their second album, *In-a-Gadda-Da-Vida,* which hit number four in the United States during the summer of 1968. The seventeen-minute title track to this album is filled with extended organ, guitar, bass, and drum solos that would serve as the model for almost every live rock show in the following few years. The song's heavy, menacing opening riff and references to classical organ music (perhaps purposefully overdone for a melodramatic effect similar to a bad horror movie), established some of the characteristics that would develop into the early heavy metal music of Black Sabbath, Deep Purple, and even Led Zeppelin (see Chapter 8).

Back in New York, Vanilla Fudge developed a reputation for taking simple pop songs and turning them into elaborate and often lengthy cover versions. "You Keep Me Hangin' On" (p6 uk18, 1967) is a representative example: the band takes a two-minute song by the Supremes and Holland-Dozier-Holland and turns it into a five-minute psychedelic movement complete with dramatic dynamic shifts and sitar lines. The musical ambition exemplified by these psychedelic-symphonic cover versions made Vanilla Fudge, like many other groups discussed in this chapter, a significant, early influence for many of the progressive rock bands that would emerge in the 1970s.

Upstate Americana: Dylan and the Band. Just as the Byrds were turning to country music, Bob Dylan made a similar turn in his music. Sidelined by a motorcycle crash in 1966, Dylan retreated to Woodstock, New York, where he continued his recording work with the Band. Drummer Levon Helm (the lone American), guitarist Robbie Robertson, bassist Rick Danko, pianist Richard Manuel, and organist Garth Hudson (all Canadian) had played the Ontario bar circuit behind rockabilly singer Ronnie Hawkins in the early 1960s and, without Helm, backed Dylan on his world tour in 1965 and 1966. The extensive sessions from this period between Dylan and the Band were released in 1975 as *The Basement Tapes* (p7 uk8). Albums released by these musicians in 1968, the Band's *Music from Big Pink* (p30) and Dylan's *John Wesley Harding* (p2 uk1), were collaborations that became important records for the emergence of country rock. It might seem strange that a band mostly made up of Canadians could play such a central role in redefining American rock, but the members of the Band were experienced students of rural American musical styles. Just as it took a loose collection of British bands to introduce many Americans to their own electric blues during the mid-1960s, a group of Canadians helped introduce American audiences to musical Americana during the latter part of the decade.

A WOODSTOCK NATION:
FESTIVALS, AUDIENCES, AND RADIO

Do You Know the Way to Monterey? Large, open-air music festivals became an important element of rock culture for the first time in the late 1960s. In the spring of 1967, John Phillips of the Mamas and the Papas and record-company executive Lou Adler organized the Monterey International Pop Festival, modeling it on the already established Monterey Jazz Festival. Monterey Pop was the first important international rock festival and it brought together bands from San Francisco, Los Angeles, and London to perform on June 16–18 at the Monterey County Fairgrounds in California. Jefferson Airplane, the Grateful Dead, Big Brother and the Holding Company, the Byrds, the Mamas and the Papas, the Animals, the Who, and many others played for free, receiving only travel expenses. Jimi Hendrix's appearance introduced him to musicians and businessmen in the United States and was crucial to his subsequent success. The Mamas and the Papas performed for the last time in their original lineup. The Beach Boys' decision not to play was widely thought to have hurt their reputation within the burgeoning counterculture. Otis Redding, backed by Booker T. & the MG's, wowed the hippie audience with the Stax brand of southern soul. While attendance figures for any outdoor event often vary widely, most responsible accounts agree that between 55,000 and 90,000 people attended the festival. In many ways, Monterey was simply an extension of the regular hippie concert events in San Francisco that began in 1965. While the San Francisco events featured mostly local and regional acts, the Monterey Festival placed a broad range of international acts on the same bill. This provided a model for the open-air rock festival that would be followed by major concert events staged in Newport (1968 and 1969), Miami (1968), Toronto (1969), Atlanta (1969), Denver (1969), and many other locales.

LIVE FROM... WOODSTOCK

by Graeme Boone

They say that if you remember the 1960s, you weren't there. But one of the greatest here-and-now moments in American history took place on Max Yasgur's farm in Bethel, New York, from August 16 to 18, 1969: the Woodstock Festival. Officially called the "Woodstock Music and Art Fair, An Aquarian Exposition," it drew half a million fans to 600 acres of rolling countryside for three days of music, community, and sheer psychedelic ecstasy.

In the months leading up to the festival, "Are you going?" seemed a universal question among the hip tribes, but no one knew what to expect, because Woodstock was a risky bet on unknowable odds. Could the East Coast counterculture

really pull off a West Coast–style "happening" on such a massive scale? A horde of fans bet that it could, and they were right. For a moment, the counterculture became the culture, and the diverse strands of '60s radicalism seemed to fuse together, with all varieties of celebration and rebellion converging in a great river—not of violence and destruction, but rather of celebration and sharing.

In February 1969, when planning for this huge event began, the logistics quickly grew into an unprecedented complexity. Organizers Michael Lang, Joel Rosenman, and Artie Kornfield probably never would have continued if they had realized how difficult their task was going to be. But they soldiered on toward their dream as obstacles arose over and over again. Negotiations proceeded fitfully and at astronomic expense over the dizzying array of utilities, services, and infrastructure, all of which had to be brought in or constructed on the spot; public opposition proliferated; and permission to use the site was denied just a month before the festival, so another venue had to be located. During the festival itself, catastrophe loomed at every moment: mind-boggling traffic jams;

a complete breakdown of ticket-taking; thunderstorms and rivers of mud; bad drugs and bad trips; food, sanitation, and medical crises; and other logistical nightmares of every

Richie Havens performing at Woodstock. Although the event was dominated by rock-oriented groups, Havens was the festival's first act. Due in part to travel delays and scheduling issues, Havens kept the large crowd captivated for several hours with a stunning solo performance.

No one anticipated the huge crowd that descended on Bethel, New York, for the Woodstock Music and Art Festival (1969). More than 400,000 people attended, sharing peace, love, drugs, and music, and getting soaked by rain. The Who, Sly and the Family Stone, Richie Havens, Santana (above), and Jimi Hendrix provided just some of the standout musical performances.

description. The governor of New York declared it a disaster area, and emergency help was provided from all directions, ranging from local stores and medical services to the National Guard and the Army. But for the fans, such realities paled before the triumphal Woodstock vision of peace and harmony in action and adversity, soaring on a flying carpet of sex, drugs, and rock and roll.

One of the many uncertainties about the festival was whether musical groups would actually agree to participate. Many bands initially refused to play or demanded stiff fees, and even after the festival began there were holes and question marks in the three-day schedule. Scheduling problems were exacerbated by the fifty-mile traffic jams that made it necessary to fly every band in and out by helicopter. Ultimately, the majority of those who were invited did play,

and they represented a remarkable cross-section of the late-1960s counterculture in music. On the first day, folk and acoustic performers were highlighted in a set that included Richie Havens, Country Joe McDonald, John Sebastian, Sweetwater, the Incredible String Band, Bert Sommer, Tim Hardin, Ravi Shankar, Melanie, Arlo Guthrie, and Joan Baez, as well as a spiritual lecture from Swami Satchidananda. The second day highlighted psychedelic, hard, and blues rock, with Quill, Keef Hartley, Santana, Canned Heat, Mountain, Creedence Clearwater Revival, the Grateful Dead, Janis Joplin, Sly Stone, the Who, and Jefferson Airplane. The lineup for the third day was even more eclectic, featuring Joe Cocker, Country Joe and the Fish, Alvin Lee, the Band, Blood Sweat & Tears, Johnny Winter, Paul Butterfield, Crosby Stills Nash & Young, and Sha Na Na. Jimi Hendrix was given

the supreme position of closing out the Festival; but by that time, 8:30 a.m. on Monday morning, most of the fans had already left for the long trek home.

The release of a film documentary in 1970 and a two-album LP in 1971 helped to transform Woodstock from a fleeting experience into a classic document of late '60s culture. While lacking the enveloping tribulations and epiphanies of those three days, the documentary and album do provide a vivid account of the music, which still sounds fresh today. And some of the performances—notably Jimi Hendrix's rendition of the "Star Spangled Banner," which went relatively unnoticed at the time—are now counted among the finest in '60s rock.

Graeme Boone (The Ohio State Univerity) is coeditor, with John Covach, of Understanding Rock *(Oxford University Press, 1997).*

As rock became oriented toward more ambitious, lengthy performances in the late 1960s, documentary films provided an appropriate forum to display visual performances. Among the most important rock documentaries from this time is *Woodstock*, a film released in 1970 depicting the famous August 1969 festival in upstate New York. Of the many iconic performances associated with *Woodstock*, perhaps the most famous is that of Jimi Hendrix, which occurred at

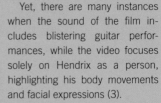

mances of the Hendrix segment have also been released independently of the larger film.) Hendrix's appearance in the "director's cut" begins with a rendition of "Voodoo Chile (A Slight Return)," which segues into his famous rendition of "The Star-Spangled Banner," and then transitions into "Purple Haze." In some instances, Hendrix is shown as a guitar virtuoso, performing tricks such as placing his right hand over top of the strings or playing the instrument with his teeth (1 and 2).

Yet, there are many instances when the sound of the film includes blistering guitar performances, while the video focuses solely on Hendrix as a person, highlighting his body movements and facial expressions (3).

This is especially evident during the rendition of "The Star-Spangled Banner," when the pink, white, and turquoise of Hendrix's outfit form an interesting correlation to the red, white, and blue of the American flag. In the context of the film, however, Hendrix's performance is used to signal the aftermath of the three-day festival, showing various efforts to clean up the mess of more than half-a-million hippies camping on the mud-soaked farmland (4).

the end of the festival and also serves as the finale to the film. Performing on Monday morning after much of the crowd has dispersed, Hendrix led a makeshift group called Gypsy Suns and Rainbows. Much of the footage focuses on Hendrix performing without accompaniment. (Complete performances of the Hendrix segment have also

As more than half of the crowd had left before this performance, the video footage is an important record of Hendrix's historic part of this program exhibiting the growing importance of documentary films in the reception of rock during the 1970s.

Monterey Pop was filmed by D. A. Pennebaker, and the release of the *Monterey Pop* film in December 1968 (as well as a not-very-representative album) further added to the importance of the festival.

Good Trip, Bad Trip: Woodstock and Altamont. If Monterey marked the beginning of the era of large outdoor rock festivals, Woodstock was its peak. Held on a large patch of farmland in Bethel, New York, from August 15–17, 1969, the

Woodstock Music and Art Festival drew at least 400,000 hippies. The roadways in upstate New York were so unexpectedly crowded that many had to be closed to avoid large-scale regional gridlock. Tickets had been offered for sale in advance, but most fans turned up at the event expecting to get in for free. The meager security forces were overwhelmed—all in the spirit of hippie fellowship—and most people ended up crashing the event without paying. In addition, heavy rain stopped the show and created muddy conditions and other issues. Despite these potentially devastating financial and logistical setbacks, the event was tremendously successful, turning the festival's slogan, "Three Days of Peace and Music," into an ideal that represented the power and influence of the hippie counterculture. Many important American and British bands performed (the Grateful Dead, Jimi Hendrix, Jefferson Airplane, Janis Joplin, the Who), while performances by Santana; Crosby, Stills, and Nash; Joe Cocker; and Sly and the Family Stone effectively introduced these acts to a much wider audience. The 1970 release of Michael Wadleigh's documentary film, *Woodstock*, and a multidisc live album helped make the event a financial success and, like the Monterey film and album, added to the event's significance.

After large-scale gatherings in Monterey and Woodstock, the era symbolically ended on December 6, 1969, with a festival organized by the Rolling Stones at the Altamont Speedway in Livermore, California. The original plan was that the Grateful Dead would sneak the Stones into San Francisco's Golden Gate Park for a free surprise show for the hippie faithful. The Stones saw the show as a way to thank loyal fans and announced the concert at a press conference a few days beforehand. The original plans were canceled when San Francisco city officials got word of the event, but a venue was located out of town at an old racetrack. Two decisions seem to have led to the disaster that followed: the Stones employed a motorcycle gang, the Hells Angels, to provide security; and they waited until nightfall to begin their portion of the show, leaving an open spot in the day's

The 1969 Rolling Stones free concert at the Altamont speedway ended in disaster when a fan was stabbed to death by the Hells Angels security detail. Here, an all-nude fan enjoys wine from a bottle, providing a glimpse of possible reasons for the concert's later chaos.

program that left concertgoers with nothing to do. The Stones waited until dark because they had planned a light show and were filming a movie, later released as *Gimme Shelter* in 1970. The Hells Angels were without some of their senior members, and a few confrontations got out of control, with fans being beaten if they got too close to the stage (Jefferson Airplane's Marty Balin was knocked out cold at one point). When Meridith Hunter, an eighteen-year-old black fan, pulled

Sound Check

Artist	The Beach Boys	The Beatles	Jefferson Airplane
Title	Good Vibrations	A Day in the Life	White Rabbit
Chart peak	p1 1966	1967	p8 1967
Form	Contrasting verse-chorus Three new sections	Compound ABA	AABA
Rhythm	4/4	4/4	4/4
Instrumentation	Electric guitar Bass Drums Lead vocal Background vocal Organ Winds Cellos Theremin Bass harmonica Jew's harp Tambourine Sleigh bells Maracas	Acoustic guitar Bass Drums Two lead vocals Piano Strings Brass Maracas Alarm clock	Electric guitar Bass Drums Lead vocal
Comments	Unconventional formal design "Space age" Theremin sound on chorus Form achieved by splicing together tape from different performances	Two separate songs stitched together with an interlude Interlude is avant-garde string performance, starting with lowest note and ending with highest Reverb used to depict a dream state	Bolero rhythm Last verse expanded to create a musical climax *Alice in Wonderland* theme

a gun at the front of the stage, he was beaten to death—the events were captured on film and took place in front of the band's eyes as they tried to perform. Many writers have since pointed out that the sometimes haphazard organization of these events meant it was only a matter of time before something tragic occurred. Nevertheless, Hunter's murder has caused many to view Altamont as the event that marked the end of the hippie era.

Cream	The Jimi Hendrix Experience
Sunshine of Your Love	Purple Haze
p5 1968	p65 1967
Simple verse	Simple verse (modified)
4/4	4/4
Electric guitar Bass Drums Two lead vocals	Electric guitar Bass Drums Lead vocal Spoken voices
12-bar blues doubled to make 24 measures for each verse (with some extensions) Two-measure riff Lead vocals trade between Jack Bruce and Eric Clapton	Introduction music also serves as basis for the bridge Virtuosic blues-based guitar throughout Extra spoken vocals add to the psychedelic aura

Festivals in the UK and Europe. As Monterey had expanded on Family Dog events and outdoor gatherings like the Human Be-In, so too did the August 1967 Festival of Flower Children at Woburn Abbey expand the 14-Hour Technicolor Dream for British hippies. This three-day outdoor event included performances by Jimi Hendrix, Tomorrow, the Jeff Beck Group, and the Small Faces, among others. (The Duchess of Bedford attended, mistakenly believing it would be a flower show.) Rock acts also appeared on the bill of the National Jazz and Blues Festival, an annual event that had begun in 1961. In August 1967 the festival was held in Windsor and included Cream, Tomorrow, Donovan, and the Crazy World of Arthur Brown. Other large-scale concerts followed in France, Italy, and Switzerland. The most important later British festivals were held in London's Hyde Park in July 1969 (organized by the Rolling Stones to honor the recently deceased Brian Jones), and the Isle of Wight Festival in August 1970. The Isle of Wight festivals began in 1968, when about 10,000 people enjoyed a one-day bill that included the Crazy World of Arthur Brown and Jefferson Airplane. The 1969 festival was a far more ambitious enterprise: expanded to two days and including Bob Dylan and the Band on a roster along with the Who, the Moody Blues, and the Nice, it drew about 150,000 attendees. Conservative estimates place the attendance of the enormous 1970 Isle of Wight Festival at 500,000, and this festival remains among the largest ever to take place in Great Britain. The program included a mix of established artists and emerging acts that would make their name in the years that immediately followed. The Doors, Donovan, and Jimi Hendrix (in his last public performance) were joined by Emerson, Lake & Palmer, Jethro Tull, and Chicago.

The Fracturing of the American Radio Audience: AM versus FM. Psychedelic music was never meant to appeal to young teens or preteens. Like folk, it was music targeted at college-age listeners. With the development of free-form FM radio in 1967 and its spread to radio markets across the country, an important distinction between single-oriented AM pop and album-oriented FM rock began to develop: younger listeners tended toward the AM dial while their older siblings listened to FM. By the end of the decade, the free-form format was becoming somewhat more organized, and by the mid-1970s the increasing constraints of the album-oriented rock (AOR) format sparked great debate within the rock community. In the late 1960s, however, it was possible to tune in an AM station and hear the Monkees, the Fifth Dimension, the Association, and many other hit-oriented artists, while the FM dial might play longer album tracks by groups that did not have hit singles. There was some crossover: the Doors' "Light My Fire" charted as a pop single, for instance, in an edited version that removed much of the instrumental soloing from the center section.

This separation by age group within the rock market foreshadowed the even greater fragmentation of that market in the 1970s, even among FM rock stations. As we will see in Chapter 8, rock music in the 1970s took the psychedelic era as a point of departure, taking musical features that coexisted within psychedelia and separating them out for further development. It is to this expansion and fragmentation of psychedelia that we turn next.

FURTHER READING

Nick Bromell, *Tomorrow Never Knows: Rock and Psychedelics in the 1960s* (University of Chicago Press, 2002).

Ray Coleman, *Clapton! An Authorized Biography* (Pan Books, 1995).

Jim DeRogatis, *Kaleidoscope Eyes: Psychedelic Rock from the '60s to the '90s* (Citadel Press, 1996).

James Henke and Parke Puterbaugh, eds., *I Want to Take You Higher: The Psychedelic Era 1965–1969* (Chronicle Books, 1997).

Michael Hicks, *Sixties Rock: Garage, Psychedelic, and Other Satisfactions* (University of Illinois Press, 2000).

Jerry Hopkins and Daniel Sugerman, *No One Here Gets Out Alive* (Grand Central Publishing, 2006).

Timothy Leary, Ralph Metzner, and Richard Alpert, *The Psychedelic Experience: A Manual Based on the Tibetan Book of the Dead* [1964] (Citadel Press, 2000).

Ray Manzarek, *Light My Fire: My Life with the Doors* (Century, 1998).

John McDermott with Eddie Kramer, *Hendrix: Setting the Record Straight* (Warner Books, 1992).

Gene Sculatti and Davin Seay, *San Francisco Nights: The Psychedelic Music Trip, 1965–68* (St. Martin's Press, 1985).

Joel Selvin, *Summer of Love: The Inside Story of LSD, Rock and Roll, Free Love, and High Times in the Wild West* (Cooper Square Press, 1999).

Grace Slick with Andrea Cagan, *Somebody to Love? A Rock-and-Roll Memoir* (Warner Books, 1998).

Derek Taylor, *It Was Twenty Years Ago Today* (Simon and Schuster, 1987).

Chris Welch with Steve Winwood, *Steve Winwood: Roll with It* (Perigee, 1990).

Tom Wolfe, *The Electric Kool-Aid Acid Test* (Picador, 2008).

(S) VISIT STUDYSPACE AT WWNORTON.COM/STUDYSPACE

Access free review material such as:

- music links
- performer info
- practice quizzes
- outlines
- interactive listening guide software

By the early 1970s, the counterculture of the late 1960s had become mainstream. The peace signs, long hair, tie dye, incense, and hippie values that had been found mostly on college campuses, were now popular in middle-class suburbs and shopping malls across the country. This commodification of counterculture might have been a signal that some of the problems that had divided America in the 1960s were "solved" in the 1970s. However, people continued to question these solutions and expose new problems that kept the country in a state of turmoil throughout the decade.

In the first years of the 1970s, Richard Nixon reached an agreement with the North Vietnamese, effectively ending the Vietnam War, which had been one of the most divisive issues of the 1960s. Though its real horrors were over, the scars from Vietnam ran deep. Many called it the first war America lost and questioned the government's attention to "the people" in matters of policy. This skepticism exploded in 1974, when a Republican break-in to the Democratic offices at the Watergate office complex in Washington, D.C., was covered up by members of the Nixon White House. As a result of the ensuing scandal, Nixon became the first president in history to resign his position.

Jimmy Carter promised America a brighter future and was elected in 1976, but his presidency was plagued with problems. In the last few years of the decade, the American economy was stagnant and inflation was high, a situation so pronounced that economists coined a new term to describe it: "stagflation." Part of the problem was a fuel shortage, leading to long lines at gas stations and a general sense of an "energy crisis." Nuclear power seemed to offer a viable alternative, but a 1979 accident at the Three Mile Island nuclear power plant in Harrisburg, Pennsylvania, raised public fears about the safety of such facilities. Finally, a political revolution in Iran resulted in the taking of American hostages—a situation that gave more than a hint of political problems to come in the Middle East.

As mentioned above, the hippie values of the 1960s became mainstream in the 1970s. Feminism became known as "women's liberation"—or simply "women's lib"—in popular culture. Gloria Steinem established *Ms.* magazine in 1972, providing a high-profile media forum for feminist issues. In a long-running series of advertisements beginning in 1969, Virginia Slims promoted a cigarette made especially for women with the slogan, "You've come a long way, baby." Women's lib also found its way into sports and mainstream music. Tennis pro Bobby Riggs challenged Billie Jean King to a "Battle of the Sexes" match in 1973, claiming that a man could easily beat a woman (he lost), and in 1972 Helen Reddy won a Grammy for the feminist anthem, "I Am Woman."

Advocates for gay rights also became more visible in pop culture. After the 1969 "Stonewall Riots" erupted in reaction to a police raid on a New York City gay club, the movement organized and worked to change state laws prohibiting homosexual activity. An important step forward occurred when the American Psychological Association removed homosexuality from its list of diseases in 1973.

Television began to reflect these social and cultural changes. *All in the Family* debuted in 1971 and addressed many of the burning issues of the time. Set in the home of a working-class New York City family, the show's central character was

Tennis star and vocal advocate for women's rights Billie Jean King after defeating Bobby Riggs in 1973. King was the first sports star of the "Women's Lib" movement, showing that it had become part of the mainstream.

All in the Family was one of television's most popular shows in the 1970s. Archie Bunker (Carroll O'Connor) constantly battled cultural changes of the time. Here he spars with his liberal son-in-law Michael (Rob Reiner) and daughter Gloria (Sally Struthers), as his wife Edith (Jean Stapleton) looks on.

(whom he called "Meathead"), his women's lib–inspired daughter Gloria, and even his bighearted but somewhat dim-witted wife Edith. Archie sometimes tangled with neighbor George Jefferson on issues of race.

Maude, whose central character was a strong-willed woman who had also traded barbs with Archie.

The show that best captured the growing sense that women could make careers for themselves without the support of a husband was *The Mary Tyler Moore Show*. From its first episode in 1970, the show consistently dealt with issues that women faced in the workplace, though these were usually handled in a lighthearted manner. By mid-decade, *Chico and the Man* was raising the country's awareness of Hispanic life, making television programming more diverse than it had ever been.

The 1970s also saw the rise of rock-music television, a step forward from 1960s teen-oriented shows such as *American Bandstand*. Brill Building mogul Don Kirshner produced a new series in 1972, *In Concert* (later called *Rock Concert*), that featured live performances by leading rock bands and artists. *The Midnight Special* debuted the next year, featuring famous radio disc jockey Wolfman Jack. R&B found a television home on Don Cornelius's *Soul Train*, which broke through in 1971 and continued until 2006. By the late 1970s, *Saturday Night Live* would become the premiere live showcase for rock groups, with many launching their careers in America there.

FM radio grew into big business, and the album-oriented rock (AOR) format dominated, often with two or three stations in each city fighting for listeners (and advertising revenue). As FM developed, AM radio was increasingly the home of pre-teen pop, oldies, and what was left of traditional network-style programming. As the decade progressed, FM rock radio became more tightly formatted, allowing the disc jockeys less control over what was played and reducing their influence on music and culture.

Outer space remained a fascination for American moviegoers, though it now had a definite hippie tinge. When George Lucas's *Star Wars* appeared in 1977, record crowds flocked to see Luke Skywalker fight totalitarianism in a galaxy far, far away. At the climactic moment of the movie, when Skywalker must destroy the evil Death Star, he hears the voice of his guru, Obi Wan Kenobi, telling him to "use the force." Skywalker turns off his high-tech equipment, plugs into the cosmic oneness, and fires the shot that saves his people.

Throughout the 1970s, blacks struggled with whites, men struggled with women, and gays struggled with straights. However, these groups were standing closer to each other than ever before. If the '60s was about the problems of segregation (or division), the '70s was about the problems of diversity. As we will see, this diversity was reflected in the music of the time. Folk and progressive rock, disco and punk, rhythm and blues, and funk all fought for—and received—attention. Every social group, it seemed, had a band. And every band had an audience.

THE GROWING ROCK MONSTER

The late 1960s provided fertile ground for rock musicians of the 1970s. Most of the styles we will explore in this chapter grew out of new developments in rock from the late 1960s. We will witness elements that coexisted within psychedelia splinter into more distinct styles during the 1970s. In general, the first half of the 1970s was characterized by bands who continued the ambitious experiments of the late 1960s, testing the boundaries of what might be considered rock. In the second half of the decade, the business of rock music grew dramatically, transforming into a large industry run by corporate conglomerates with interests outside of music. It is not difficult to interpret a correlation between the stylistic changes in rock during the second half of the 1970s and corporate expansion. Accordingly, those who disdain "corporate rock" feel that music after the late 1960s became progressively corrupted by big money and even bigger egos, all motivated by the corporate bottom line. In spite of this, the music of many of the bands that critics tended to hate in the 1970s—Led Zeppelin, Bad Company, Boston, Kansas, and Foreigner—became the core of the "classic rock" radio format that developed throughout the 1980s.

There are some central issues to consider when studying rock in the 1970s, including corporate rock as a form of corruption, the celebration and subsequent emergence of punk and new wave from the underground, and the emergence of classic rock on modern FM radio and cable television since about 1990. This chapter will explore rock music in the first half of the 1970s with a focus on how this music developed out of psychedelic music. The evolution of each style is traced from its 1960s roots through its development during the 1970s. Later chapters will continue the discussion: Chapter 9 examines black pop, disco, and reggae during the same period, and Chapter 10 focuses on the later 1970s, charting the expansion of the music business and examining the development of punk and new wave. After reading these chapters, you will have the background to consider whether either interpretation of corporate influence on rock should be revised, incorporated into another view, or abandoned entirely.

The cover of Led Zeppelin's untitled fourth album, often called *Zoso* (1971). This album contains one of the band's best known songs, "Stairway to Heaven." This song, the album, and the group that produced them represent one answer to a central musical and stylistic question in the early 1970s: How would musicians after psychedelia incorporate, extend, or reject "the hippie aesthetic"? Led Zeppelin chose to combine the "hippie aesthetic" with elements of electric and acoustic blues, as well as folk music.

THE HIPPIE AESTHETIC

Psychedelic Legacies. Among the most important changes in the 1966–69 period were the shifts of focus in rock music from the single to the album, and from dancing to listening music. While hit singles did not disappear entirely—in fact, some psychedelic groups had successful single releases—there was a growing sense that singles were a different part of the business. After *Sgt. Pepper's Lonely Hearts Club Band*, many artists were fixated on creating albums that provided a musically provocative listening experience. Moreover, musicians expanded rock's stylistic range by incorporating elements of classical music, electronic music, and jazz, and became increasingly dependent on the recording studio as a creative tool, producing records that were difficult to reproduce live.

Some of the main tenets of the late 1960s revolution in rock continued in the early 1970s, while others were questioned. A focus on musical and technological craft, combined with a distinctly artistic approach to music-making (even among groups who cultivated a no-nonsense, hard-rocking image), led to an aesthetic approach we will call the "hippie aesthetic," or the aesthetic of ambition. According to this set of principles, a rock musician is an artist who has a responsibility to produce sophisticated music using whatever means are at his or her disposal, and rock music should stand up to repeated listening and the lyrics should deal with important issues or themes. Instrumental virtuosity became especially valued in this era. Fans voted in annual music magazine polls to select performers in categories like Best Guitarist, Best Keyboardist, Best Drummer, Best Bassist, and Best Vocalist, in addition to typical categories like Best Album and Best New Act. Such polls were already common in jazz publications, which greatly valued musical virtuosity and improvisatory fluency, and in teenage magazines that valued popularity. Now rock musicians and their fans began using performance ability and musical ambition as indicators of musical importance.

The hippie aesthetic is central to understanding the connections among a wide variety of 1970s rock styles. Using this framework, we can see that artists as diverse as Yes, the Eagles, the Allman Brothers Band, Steely Dan, and even Alice Cooper share elements of a common musical approach. This approach helps clarify that much of the rock music created during the 1970s had important ties to psychedelia. Aspects of the hippie aesthetic continued to influence a wide variety of artists well into the 1980s, including those who seemed to be soundly rejecting it. For now, we will consider how this approach influenced a popular style of blues-based rock in the early 1970s in the UK.

BLUES-BASED BRITISH ROCK

The Rolling Stones, Cream, and the Yardbirds. Blues-based rock music coming out of Britain in the 1970s was an important extension of earlier blues-influenced rock. Blues music, especially the Chicago electric blues of musicians like Muddy Waters and Howlin' Wolf, was central to much rock music of the 1960s, especially in the UK. As discussed in Chapter 5, groups like the Rolling Stones brought this

style back to America, or perhaps more specifically, they introduced blues to white American teenagers. In the wake of the Stones came the Yardbirds, a group which at various points featured Eric Clapton, Jeff Beck, and Jimmy Page. In the early 1970s, British bands like Deep Purple, Led Zeppelin, and Black Sabbath built on this stylistic foundation established by the Stones, the Yardbirds, and Cream. The Stones themselves enjoyed tremendous commercial success during this period by returning to their blues roots after a brief foray into psychedelia. Albums such as *Sticky Fingers* (p1 uk1, 1971), *Exile on Main Street* (p1 uk1, 1972), and *Goat's Head Soup* (p1 uk1, 1973) were wildly popular on both sides of the Atlantic, bringing the Stones out of the Beatles' shadow and positioning them as one of the most important groups to make the transition from the 1960s to the 1970s. Yardbirds alumni also remained active: Clapton continued as a solo artist after his stints with Cream and Derek and the Dominoes, emerging with the hit single, "I Shot the Sheriff" (p1 uk9, 1974), and Jeff Beck led a succession of bands, including the Jeff Beck Group and Beck, Bogert & Appice, that tended toward a jazz-fusion approach. Mixing blues roots with psychedelic sounds and heavy rock volume, Jimmy Page played an important role in continuing the guitar virtuosity and showmanship standards set by Clapton and Hendrix during the 1960s. Drafted into the Yardbirds toward the end of the band's career, Page was the only band member left by 1969. In order to fulfill a series of performance obligations, Page called on bassist John Paul Jones, a seasoned session musician, and two newcomers: vocalist Robert Plant and drummer John Bonham. After working for a short time under the name the New Yardbirds, the band changed their name to Led Zeppelin.

Led Zeppelin: Blues, Folk, and Psychedelia Take the Next Step. With a string of eight number one albums in the UK and six number ones in the United States, Led Zeppelin was among the most successful new British groups of the 1970s. Page cowrote most of the group's music (often with Robert Plant providing the lyrics) and, deeply devoted to the album format, the band was resistant to releasing tracks as singles. When Page first approached Plant about forming a band, he described his vision as a blend of traditional electric blues, acoustic folk, and a fair amount of experimentation. Over the years, listeners and critics have focused on

the heavier elements of the group's music, forgetting other aspects of their catalog. For example, a blend between electric and acoustic instrumentation is clear on the group's first two albums, *Led Zeppelin* (p10 uk6, 1969) and *Led Zeppelin II* (p1 uk1, 1970). On the first record, "Babe I'm Gonna Leave You" is a reflection of the band's acoustic tendencies, while "Good Times, Bad Times" shows off a harder edge. The more psychedelic side comes out in "Dazed and Confused," a staple of the band's live shows that featured Page playing his guitar with a violin bow. A blend of the harder elements and psychedelia can also be found in "Whole Lotta Love."

This blend of acoustic, blues, and psychedelic elements can also be found in what is arguably Led Zeppelin's best-known track, "Stairway to Heaven," from their fourth, untitled album (p2 uk1, 1972). The song begins with an acoustic guitar passage and introduces a chorus of recorders followed by Robert Plant's vocals. This texture continues for the first two minutes of the song. As the arrangement slowly builds, electric twelve-string guitar, electric piano, bass, and drums are added. The final section of the song moves into heavy rock, featuring a blues-influenced electric guitar solo from Page and Plant's distinctive high wailing vocals. The lyrics to "Stairway to Heaven" deal with the topic of spiritual enlightenment, a perennial concern among hippies of the late 1960s, and a recurrent theme in 1970s rock. The band would later return to themes of spirituality and the wisdom of the ancients and the East, most famously in "Kashmir" from *Physical Graffiti* (p1 uk1, 1975).

Led Zeppelin lyrics often focus on sexual themes as well. Plant's swaggering on "Whole Lotta Love" and "Black Dog" take the playful hokum blues lyrics of songs like "Shake, Rattle, and Roll" beyond metaphor, making direct references to sexuality. Page produced all of the band's albums and was especially masterful at creating a thick sonic palette by double-tracking vocals, creating deep reverb for Bonham's drum tracks, and layering electric guitars—adding one after another, each playing distinct parts. Led Zeppelin continued to perform widely throughout the 1970s, releasing albums such as *Houses of the Holy* (p1 uk1, 1973), *Presence* (p1 uk1, 1976), and *In Through the Out Door* (p1 uk1, 1979). The group disbanded after the tragic alcohol-related death of John Bonham in September 1980.

As we saw in our discussion of Cream's "Sunshine of Your Love" in Chapter 7, adapting blues practices to rock often resulted in tracks that strayed far from the aesthetic of traditional blues. Led Zeppelin's 1969 track "Whole Lotta Love" provides another chance to see this transformation at work and gives a sense of how British bands combined the blues with other elements. Originally credited to Jimmy Page and Robert Plant, the song is an adaptation of a Willie Dixon number called "You Need Love." (After some legal wrangling, it is now credited to Dixon and all four members of Led Zeppelin.) While blues is clearly a central component of "Whole Lotta Love," elements of psychedelia, and features that anticipate later 1970s rock can be found in the song. It begins as a simple verse-chorus form, presenting two verse-chorus pairs based on the same music after the brief guitar-riff introduction. A long central section follows—longer, in fact, than all the music that precedes it. This section uses panning across the stereo spectrum to make it seem as if the sound is swirling in circles. Vocal moaning from Plant creates a distinctively psychedelic flavor, while Page's aggressive guitar solo continues the psychedelic blues-rock virtuosity associated with Eric Clapton and Jimi Hendrix. The song then returns to the verse-chorus pair, presented a third time with only slight alterations. The track ends with a coda, which moves from a free-form Plant vocal phrase (a kind of vocal

Listening Guide

Get Music wwnorton.com/studyspace

Led Zeppelin, "Whole Lotta Love" Atlantic 2690

Words and music by Jimmy Page, Robert Plant, John Paul Jones, John Bonham, and Willie Dixon; produced by Jimmy Page. Released as a single that rose to #4 on the *Billboard* "Hot 100" chart in late 1969.

FORM: Compound AABA. The A sections follow simple verse-chorus form, with verse and chorus based on the same musical material. An extended central section forms the B section, leading to a return of the A section and a coda, which begins with a vocal "cadenza" in free time before the riff kicks back in and the song fades out.

TIME SIGNATURE: 4/4.

INSTRUMENTATION: Electric guitars, bass, drums, lead and backup vocals.

	0:00–0:11	**Introduction**, 4 mm.	Begins with guitar alone, playing 2-bar blues-derived riff. Bass joins for the second time through this riff.
A	0:11–0:35	**Verse 1**, 9 mm.	Lead vocal enters, riff continues in guitar and bass. "You need coolin' . . ."
	0:35–0:47	**Chorus**, 4 mm.	Drums enter, as backup vocals provide vocal hook. Note sliding guitar effect in call-and-response to vocal. "Got a whole lotta love . . ."
A	0:47–1:10	**Verse 2**, 9 mm.	As before, except that drums now continue from previous section. "You been learnin'. . ."
	1:10–1:21	**Chorus**, 4 mm.	As before, but the fourth bar of the chorus serves as the first bar of the central section that follows.
B	1:21–3:22	**Central Section**, 45 mm.	39 bars of spacey psychedelia. Drums keep a light beat, as guitar sounds and vocal wails move from side to side, amid avant-garde sound effects. An aggressive 6-bar guitar break concludes this section.
A	3:22–3:50	**Verse 3**, 11 mm.	As in verse 2, but extended by 2 bars at the end. "You've been coolin' . . ."
	3:50–4:00	**Chorus**, 4 mm.	As before. "Got a whole lotta love . . ."
	4:00–5:30	**Coda**, 24 mm.	Vocal "cadenza" in free time begins this final section, and then the song's riff returns as Plant improvises vocally and the song fades out.

"cadenza" in which the music stops and Plant provides a solo flourish), to a return of the tune's guitar riff and fade-out.

The overall formal structure of "Whole Lotta Love" follows a pattern that became common among rock bands in the 1970s. After two verse-chorus pairs, a contrasting section occurs: this section might be a guitar, sax, or keyboard solo over the verse material, or it may consist of entirely new material. A return to the verse-chorus pair or the verse often concludes this pattern. If the verse-chorus pairs are thought of as A sections and the contrasting section is considered the B section, a large-scale AABA pattern emerges. When an AABA section is made up of verse-chorus components, the term "compound AABA" is used (reserving "AABA" for the song forms discussed earlier). "Whole Lotta Love" provides a bridge from the 1960s into the 1970s, with its blues roots, psychedelic central section, aggressive guitar virtuosity, and use of compound AABA form. The combination of elements looks both forward and backward in the development of rock.

Deep Purple: Blues, Classical, and Psychedelia. Like Led Zeppelin, Deep Purple had its origins in late 1960s rock. Formed in London in 1968, the group had a number four U.S. hit single that year with a version of Joe South's "Hush." From its inception, the band mixed blues-based rock with classical music, releasing one of the first albums to combine a rock band with a symphony orchestra, *Concerto for Group and Orchestra* (uk26, 1969). After three relatively unsuccessful albums ("Hush" notwithstanding), founding members Jon Lord (keyboards), Ritchie Blackmore (guitar), and Ian Paice (drums) replaced original singer Rod Evans and bassist Nick Simper with singer Ian Gillan and bassist Roger Glover. This lineup stormed the rock charts in the first half of the 1970s. *Deep Purple in Rock* went to number four in the UK in 1970, followed by *Fireball* (p32 uk1, 1971) and *Machine Head* (p7 uk1, 1971), albums that showed increasing popularity in the United States. *Machine Head* contains "Smoke on the Water" and "Highway Star," two songs that have become staples of rock radio.

"Highway Star" is often cited as one of the songs that most influenced the development of heavy metal in the late 1970s and early 1980s, but in the context of the hippie legacy, it illustrates how Deep Purple blended rock music and classical idioms. The song features two long instrumental sections—one each for guitar and keyboard solos. Both solos make use of harmonic and melodic practices more often associated with the European baroque music of Bach and Vivaldi than with the blues of Muddy Waters or Elmore James. While the earlier *Concerto for Group and Orchestra* had merely juxtaposed the band with a classical orchestra, here classical music compositional techniques are integrated much more effectively (though no orchestra is used). Another track from *Machine Head*, "Lazy," is a blend between psychedelic trippiness and blues-rock style. The track begins with a moody organ solo, which seems to combine church music, blues, and a bit of *Phantom of the Opera*–style organ playing. Both Lord and Blackmore provide blues-oriented solos, and Gillan delivers falsetto screams, which became common in rock singing during the late '70s and early '80s. (Gillan's vocal style also became well known in the context of musical theater through his performance as Jesus on the 1970 Tim Rice/Andrew Lloyd Webber concept album, *Jesus Christ Superstar*.) The classic lineup folded by 1974, and singer David Coverdale and bassist Glenn Hughes joined the band for several albums, most notably *Burn* (p9 uk3, 1974).

Deep Purple's Ritchie Blackmore in concert. Deep Purple was innovative in mixing its blues-based rock with classical music. Like Led Zeppelin, the band focused on instrumental solos, often displaying strong blues and classical influences.

By the end of the decade, members had formed other bands, including Rainbow (Blackmore), Whitesnake (Coverdale), and Gillan (Gillian).

Black Sabbath: British Rock Meets Boris Karloff and the Gothic Beginnings of Metal. Consisting of guitarist Tony Iommi, bassist Geezer Butler, drummer Bill Ward, and singer John "Ozzy" Osbourne, Black Sabbath began as a blues band in the late 1960s, but quickly turned to the darker elements of rock. Early on, the band changed its name from "Earth" to "Black Sabbath," after a Boris Karloff horror movie. "Black Sabbath," the first track on their first album, *Black Sabbath* (p23 uk8, 1970), begins with the tolling of distant church bells, followed by a sinister riff using the musical interval of the tritone, a dissonant and unstable combination of notes known among classical-music aficionados for its association with Satan. The band's next album, *Paranoid* (p12 uk1, 1970), contains "Iron Man," which begins with the low-pitched tolling of guitars to accompany Osbourne's distorted voice intoning "I am Iron Man." Instrumentally, Black Sabbath songs often convey a dark texture because the guitar, bass, and vocals all perform variants of the same riff simultaneously ("Iron Man" is a good example of this). Despite these gothic touches, however, Black Sabbath's music is mostly based on blues riffs and common rock structures. The group's first four albums, including *Master of Reality* (p8 uk5, 1971) and *Black Sabbath, Vol. 4* (p13 uk8, 1972), were great commercial successes and laid the foundation for the use of music and images that would become central to the emergence of heavy metal a few years later. By the end of the decade, the original lineup parted ways and Ozzy went on to a solo career as one of the most prominent practitioners of heavy metal in the 1980s and 1990s.

AMERICAN BLUES ROCK AND SOUTHERN ROCK

Southern Rock: The Allman Brothers Band, Lynyrd Skynyrd, and the Charlie Daniels Band. The influence of 1960s British blues rock was not restricted to UK bands. Many aspiring young rockers from the United States were drawn to electric blues in the 1960s, and by the early 1970s a strong blues influence could be

Listening Guide

The Allman Brothers Band, "Whipping Post" Capricorn 2476-124

Words and music by Gregg Allman, produced by Adrian Barber. Contained on *The Allman Brothers Band*, released in 1969. A much longer version that represents the development of this song in a live context is included on *At Fillmore East* (1971).

FORM: Contrasting verse-chorus. Each verse consists of two 4-bar phrases over the same repeating 2-bar chord progression, followed by a 2-bar buildup to the chorus. Each chorus consists of three 1-bar phrases followed by a stop-time phrase, and then a bar of instrumental response that echoes the vocal. Note the instrumental interlude that follows the second instrumental verse. It creates a passage that dramatically builds up to the final statement of the chorus in an almost symphonic manner, using an ascending scale and stop-time lead-guitar blasts. Also note how the final chord shows some of the band's jazz influences.

TIME SIGNATURE: 12/8, with sections in 11/8 as indicated. In this case, 11/8 can be counted as 1 & uh, 2 & uh, 3 & uh, 4 &, as if it were 12/8 with the last element lopped off. It is also possible to count this song in 6/8, in which case all measure numbers below can simply be doubled and the 11/8 sections would be counted as a measure of 6/8 followed by a measure of 5/8.

INSTRUMENTATION: Two electric guitars, bass, organ, drums (featuring two drummers), and lead vocals.

0:00–0:26	**Introduction**, 8 mm. (in 11/8 time)	This section begins with the bass, adding drums, guitars, and organ one by one to provide a gradual buildup that leads to the first verse.

Brothers Gregg (organ) and Duane (guitar) Allman shown together on stage. Duane was a popular studio musician before devoting his full energies to the Allman Brothers Band. He played on important recordings in Muscle Shoals, Alabama. Gregg's bluesy lead vocals and organ playing were key elements of the band's sound, which blended rock virtuosity, a rhythm and blues sensibility, and psychedelic elements to create southern rock.

Get Music ⓢ wwnorton.com/studyspace

0:26–1:04	**Verse 1**, 10 mm. (in 12/8)	Lead vocal enters singing two 4-bar phrases and then a 2-bar phrase that leads to the chorus. "I've been run down . . ."
1:04–1:38	**Chorus**, 9 mm.	Music gets louder and more dramatic as 1-bar vocal phrase is repeated, leading to stop-time climax. Guitars then echo vocal phrase, and then lead into a 4-bar transition in 11/8 based on the introduction. ". . . tied to the whipping post . . ."
1:38–2:07	**Instrumental Verse**, 8 mm.	Guitar solo over the first 8 bars of the verse.
2:07–2:45	**Verse 2**, 10 mm.	As in verse 1. "My friends tell me . . ."
2:45–3:19	**Chorus**, 9 mm.	As before, once again leading to a guitar solo. ". . . tied to the whipping post . . ."
3:19–3:49	**Instrumental Verse**, 8 mm.	A second guitar solo, structured just like the first one.
3:49–4:31	**Interlude**, 10 mm.	This instrumental buildup consists of 4 bars of an ascending scale that leads to 4 bars of dramatic stop-time. The music then stops, as Allman introduces the 2-bar buildup to the chorus found in the previous verses ("Sometimes I feel"), which drives headlong into the final statement of the chorus.
4:31–5:18	**Chorus**, 5 mm.	As before, but with more energy and a tremendous sense of arrival. The final echo of the vocal presented previously by the guitars is replaced with a gentle and mysterious jazz-influenced ending. ". . . tied to the whipping post . . ."

heard in rock associated with the American South. During the late 1960s, Nashville-born guitarist Duane Allman became a studio favorite of Rick Hall at Fame Studios in Muscle Shoals, adding his blues-drenched playing to numerous sessions for Hall and Atlantic's Jerry Wexler, including Wilson Pickett's version of the Beatles' "Hey Jude" (p23 r13, 1968). Through his playing at Muscle Shoals, Allman came to the attention of Phil Walden, who had managed several southern rhythm and blues singers during the 1960s, including Otis Redding. By the end of the decade, Walden was managing Allman, and the young guitarist formed the Allman Brothers Band. By 1969, Allman had enlisted bassist Barry Oakley, guitarist Dickey Betts, and drummers Jai Johnny Johnson ("Jaimoe") and Butch Trucks. Duane's brother Gregg was the last to join, and his blues-influenced vocals and organ playing rounded out the group. Walden, who founded Capricorn Recording Studios in Macon, Georgia, signed the band to his label. In short order, the Allman Brothers Band became the most important band playing "southern rock."

The Allman Brothers Band drew their influences from the blues and rhythm and blues that they heard growing up in the South, and the British blues rockers of the 1960s. Their live shows featured extended improvised solos, a practice drawn from San Francisco psychedelia. Like Led Zeppelin and Deep Purple, the Allman Brothers Band developed and extended methods of blending blues and rock that began in the 1960s, and the embrace of both their musical and cultural heritage served as a model for many other southern bands. After modest commercial success with their first two studio albums, the Allman Brothers released a double live album, *At Fillmore East*, which rose to number thirteen in the United States in 1971. The album contains the band's signature song from their first studio album, "Whipping Post," written by Gregg Allman and perhaps the best example of the band's strong blues influences and penchant for extended soloing.

Despite the death of Duane Allman in a 1971 motorcycle accident, the band's next album, *Eat a Peach*, hit number four on the U.S. album charts in early 1972. Slightly more than a year after Allman's death, Oakley was killed in a similar accident. Now depending much more on Betts, the group also added Lamar Williams on bass and Chuck Leavell on piano. The album *Brothers and Sisters* hit number one in the United States in the fall of 1973, and yielded the hit single "Ramblin' Man" (p2). This Dickey Betts track brings the band's country influences to the fore. Much of the band's early music was produced by veteran engineer and producer Tom Dowd, who had worked on recordings for Atlantic (including sessions at Stax and Muscle Shoals) since the early 1950s.

Among other rock groups from the South, perhaps the greatest beneficiaries of the Allmans' success were a group of rockers from Florida that named their band after a high school teacher. Like the Allman Brothers, Walden and Capricorn also courted Lynyrd Skynyrd. Figuring that they might get more attention from a label that did not already have a southern rock band, however, Skynyrd signed with Al Kooper's label, Sounds of the South, based in Atlanta. Several years after the Allman Brothers had made their mark nationally, Lynyrd Skynyrd released a series of successful albums, beginning with *Pronouced Leh-nerd Skin-nerd* (p27, 1973) and peaking with *Street Survivors* (p5 uk13, 1977). Kooper was a veteran in the recording studio who had played organ on most of the Dylan sessions from 1965 to 1966. As a result of his experience, Skynyrd's tracks were somewhat more radio-friendly than those of the Allmans. Skynyrd also associated itself with the South much more directly than the Allman Brothers Band. Lynyrd Skynrd's songs provided images of everyday life in the South, and they scored hits with "Sweet Home Alabama" (p8, 1974), "Saturday Night Special" (p27, 1975), and "What's Your Name?" (p13, 1977). The song "Free Bird" has been a staple of rock radio playlists since its release on the live album, *One More from the Road* (p9 uk17, 1976). A plane crash in late 1977 killed singer Ronnie Van Zant and two other band members—Steve and Cassie Gaines—only days after the release of *Street Survivors*. While this tragic event raised the band's profile and prompted radio stations to play more of their older music, the remaining members found it difficult to go on and split up soon after, although the band eventually regrouped years later.

Another important southern rock artist was guitarist, singer, and fiddle player Charlie Daniels. Daniels started as a studio musician in Nashville, playing on a wide variety of records (including Dylan sessions in the late 1960s), and formed his own band in the early 1970s. He had five Top 40 albums between 1975 and 1982, including *Million Mile Reflections* (p5 c1, 1979) and *Full Moon* (p11 c5, 1980). "The Devil Went Down to Georgia" (p3 c1 uk14, 1979), a song about a young fiddler making a deal with the devil, became his trademark. Daniels's style is sometimes thought of as more country than rock, although he moved in southern rock circles during the 1970s. His early music shows strong connections to the hippie movement and since he was an older musician, members of the other southern rock bands looked upon him as a mentor.

Although the three bands discussed above were wildly popular at the time, the connotations associated with the term "southern rock" can be misleading. This label stemmed partly from writers in the North and on the West Coast describing bands from the South. A "southern rock" category allowed music executives to market this music through connections with stereotypical images of the South fostered by northern media outlets (hard-drinking men, pickup trucks with gun racks, and Confederate flags). These southern musicians were certainly proud of their geographical heritage, and often embraced this label, even if they felt conflicted about being identified with the politics of the old South. Some of these artists were extremely progressive in their political views, accepting of racial integration, and were more closely aligned with the legacy of psychedelia. As we see and hear in the images and music of these groups, southern culture is more complex than the simple stereotypes conjured by the label "southern rock."

Texas and South of the Border: Santana and ZZ Top.

As we have seen, the term southern rock usually referred to bands from the southeastern United States who emerged in the wake of the Allman Brothers Band. But the influence of electric blues extended further, and can be heard clearly in the music of Texas-based ZZ Top and the Mexican-influenced sounds of Santana. Led by Mexican-born guitarist Carlos Santana and featuring the organ playing and singing of Greg Rolie (who would later form Journey), Santana emerged from the San Francisco psychedelic scene in 1969. The band's success was fueled in part by their inspired performance at Woodstock. *Santana* (p4 r13, 1969) featured the band's trademark blend of jazz- and blues-influenced improvisation set to the accompaniment of Latin rhythms and percussion. "Evil Ways" (p9, 1970), the band's first hit, is an example of Santana's style from the early 1970s. The group built on the success of its first album with *Abraxas* (p1 r3 uk7, 1970), which contained "Black Magic Woman" (p4, 1970) and "Oye Como Va" (p13, 1971). Later albums included *Santana III* (p1 r5 uk6, 1971) and *Caravanserai* (p8 r6 uk6, 1972). If Duane Allman was the South's answer to Eric Clapton, Carlos Santana's smooth soulful playing was the Latino response to the electric blues explosion of the 1960s.

ZZ Top became a staple of rock radio by the end of the 1970s and enjoyed success into the 1980s. In the early 1970s, however, Texas electric blues was not yet an influential force, and guitarist Billy Gibbons, bassist Dusty Hill, and drummer Frank Beard struggled for recognition. While *ZZ Top's First Album* (1971) did not chart, *Tres Hombres* fared much better, hitting number eight on the U.S. charts in 1973. *Fandango!* (p10, 1975) contained the track "Tush" (p20, 1975), an up-

Led by virtuoso guitarist Carlos Santana (pictured here), Santana took influences from psychedelia (their performance at Woodstock is legendary) and combined them with Latin rhythms and percussion. Carlos Santana's improvisations put him in the same league as guitar greats Duane Allman, Jimi Hendrix, Eric Clapton, and Jimmy Page.

Listening Guide Get Music Ⓢ wwnorton.com/studyspace

Santana, "Evil Ways" Columbia 4-45069

Words and music by Sonny Henry, produced by Brent Dangerfield and Santana. The song reached #9 on the *Billboard* "Hot 100" chart in early 1970.

FORM: Simple verse, based on a two-chord vamp that remains constant except for the last bars of each verse. Each verse is based on a 16-measure structure, though the last measures can be repeated to create an 18-bar verse, as in verses 1 and 3. The solos are built on the two-chord vamp and unfold in 4-bar units. Note that the organ solo is 24 bars in length, which is simply six times through the 4-bar unit. Heading into the third verse, the band plays a 4-bar interlude that sets the scene for this final verse and closes out the organ solo.

TIME SIGNATURE: 4/4, with a strong emphasis on Latin rhythms, especially during the guitar solo at the end.

INSTRUMENTATION: Electric guitar, Hammond organ, bass, drums, various Latin percussion, lead and background vocals

0:00–0:18	**Introduction**, 8 mm.	After a brief lead-in from the drums, the entire band enters with the two-chord vamp that forms the basis for the song.
0:18–0:54	**Verse 1**, 18 mm.	Vocals enter, sung mostly in unison by multiple voices. The 16-bar structure is extended by two measures to create an 18-bar section. "You got to change . . ."
0:54–1:27	**Verse 2**, 16 mm.	Very similar to verse 1, except that the section is not extended by 2 bars and is thus 16 bars in length. "When I come home . . ."
1:27–2:17	**Organ solo**, 24 mm.	Solo begins slowly, developing more activity and energy as it unfolds, leading to a climax in the closing measures.
2:17–2:25	**Interlude**, 4 mm.	Band comes together on the two-chord vamp to mark the end of the organ solo and the beginning of verse 3.
2:25–3:01	**Verse 3**, 18mm.	Similar to verse 2, except that the 2-bar extension at the end serves to launch the guitar solo. "When I come home . . ."
3:01–3:54	**Guitar solo**, 24 mm. + fade	High-energy guitar solo, as the rhythm section becomes much more active and drives the music forward before the song eventually fades out.

tempo 12-bar blues tune. While Santana's music is often referred to as "Latin rock," and ZZ Top is considered Texas blues, neither is typically thought of as southern rock (much less country rock). Stylistically, however, the music of both bands is similar to that of the southern rock bands. Santana most closely parallels the Allman Brothers with an emphasis on improvisation, while the tighter arrangements in ZZ Top's music are more similar to Lynyrd Skynyrd. The key element in the music of both groups is a significant stylistic debt to the electric blues.

American Bands: Steppenwolf, Three Dog Night, Grand Funk Railroad, and Aerosmith. The musical impact of the blues in American rock in the early 1970s was not restricted to the South. Bands such as Steppenwolf, Grand Funk Railroad, and Aerosmith were all influenced strongly by the blues tradition. German-born singer and guitarist John Kay spent time in many of the important musical hot spots of the 1960s. He visited the folk scene in New York, experienced San Francisco psychedelia, and hung around Los Angeles in the months before Love and the Doors burst onto the scene. Together with organist Goldy McJohn and drummer Jerry Edmunton—whom he had worked with in Canada—Kay formed Steppenwolf (named after the Hermann Hesse novel) in Los Angeles in 1967. The band's first album, *Steppenwolf* (p6, 1968), contained the hit single "Born to Be Wild" (p2 uk30, 1968), and "Magic Carpet Ride" (p3, 1968) was released on the next album, *Steppenwolf the Second* (p3, 1969). Either single can be taken as representative of Steppenwolf's approach to blues rock: Kay's gruff vocals are supported by driving guitars and drums, with McJohn's distorted organ often coming to the front of the texture. The band continued into the 1970s but disbanded after a special concert played on Valentine's Day in 1972. Three Dog Night was also based in Los Angeles, and Brian Wilson produced their early music. The group's blue-eyed soul featured three lead singers, and focused on the song and vocals with an AM-friendly approach. The band had a series of hit records, many written by songwriters who would later establish themselves as performers. Successful singles included Harry Nilsson's "One" (p5, 1969), Laura Nyro's "Eli's Coming" (p10, 1969), and Randy Newman's "Mama Told Me (Not to Come)" (p1 uk3, 1970). Often overlooked by rock writers, Three Dog Night enjoyed enormous success until their breakup in the mid-1970s.

Hailing from Flint, Michigan, Grand Funk Railroad also had roots in 1960s pop. As members of Terry Knight and the Pack, guitarist and vocalist Mark Farner and drummer and vocalist Don Brewer had a minor hit in 1967 with "I (Who Have Nothing)" (p46). Soon they brought in bassist Mel Schacher to form Grand Funk Railroad, and Knight managed the new band. The group enjoyed success almost immediately, as *On Time* hit number twenty-seven on the U.S. charts in 1969, and the band's next nine albums charted in the *Billboard* Top 10. Among these, *We're an American Band* (p2, 1973) was the most successful, and the single of the same name went to number one in 1973. The band followed with *Shinin' On* (p5, 1974), which contained a version of Little Eva's 1962 hit "The Loco-Motion" (p1, 1974), and they later released a version of the old rhythm and blues number "Some Kind of Wonderful" (p3, 1975). Grand Funk's music is deeply rooted in 1960s soul, and Farner's singing shows these influences at almost every point. The band's sustained success during the early 1970s made them one of the most popular acts in rock music at the time.

Although their first album, *Aerosmith* (1973), did not chart and the track "Dream On" rose only as high as number fifty-nine in the U.S. charts, Aerosmith's music became much more popular by the middle of the decade. Led by singer Stephen Tyler and guitarist Joe Perry, the Boston-based band was often compared to the Rolling Stones. Tyler's appearance and stage performance style were reminiscent of Mick Jagger, and Perry's stoic, tough-guy demeanor paralleled that of Keith Richards. With the success of *Toys in the Attic* (p11, 1975) and *Rocks* (p3, 1976) the group's music saturated American FM radio with songs such as "Same Old Song and Dance" (1974), "Train Kept a Rollin' " (1974), "Sweet Emotion" (p36, 1975)

LED ZEPPELIN IN CONCERT, 1970–79

by Susan Fast

Led Zeppelin's studio recordings are innovative and awe-inspiring, but they tell only part of the band's story. For Led Zep fans in the 1970s, live shows were considered the "real deal," and there is little question that the concert setting highlighted much of what has become legendary about this group. Until recently, there was only one official live concert release, the 1976 documentary film *The Song Remains the Same* (also released as a double live album). This film captures Zeppelin in concert at Madison Square Garden on their 1973 tour, at the height of their domination of record charts and concert stages around the

world. It is a fascinating document, not just for the music, but also for the famous "fantasy sequences" in which Page, Plant, and Jones are depicted as protagonists in different fictional quest narratives. But the quality of the performance fails to capture how great they really were in concert. For years, committed fans circulated bootleg recordings of particularly renowned Zeppelin concerts, and *The Song Remains the Same* simply paled in comparison. In 2003, some of these recordings were remastered and officially released as a two-DVD set (*Led Zeppelin*) and on the CD *How the West Was Won*. These recordings provide an accurate and easily accessible snapshot of the band's concert legacy.

Led Zeppelin's concerts were marathons: three-hour shows were not unusual and the increased length of individual songs, filled with extended improvisation, is a Led Zeppelin trademark that signals the band's much-revered penchant for taking musical risks.

Their 1970 gig at the Royal Albert Hall ranks as one of the best representations of the band's musical capabilities. Long virtuosic guitar solos by Page, sometimes brilliant and sometimes slightly off the mark,

are moments in which expressiveness overtakes technique, usually to great effect. Aside from guitar solos, improvisation also included full-out jams by the band on old blues and pop songs, and musical ideas worked out on the spot. Page referred to the combination of precision and risk taking as the "tight but loose" factor of the band. Robert Plant's vocals are in peak form at this show, and the overwhelming power of his voice reaches above the excessive volume of the instruments. The performance of "How Many More Times" brings all these elements together: listen to the incredible driving energy of the riff, played by Page, Jones, and Bonham for large stretches of the song; the improvised exchanges between Page and Plant; and the lengthy blues-based improvisations toward the end of the song.

Bonham's drum solo—the core of the song "Moby Dick"—is already a feature in this early concert, and it remained a central component of their live shows. Much of what is "heavy" about Zeppelin's sound comes from Bonham, an astonishingly powerful drummer who was also agile and capable of very subtle gestures. Another important element of the live shows was Page's use of the violin bow to play his guitar during "Dazed and Confused." The purpose of this was to explore new and interesting timbres on the electric guitar. The technique became strongly associated with Page's image as a kind of musical wizard.

A few features crucial to the later Led Zeppelin concert experience are not yet present in the Royal Albert Hall show. As with other rock bands, when they moved into stadiums and played to much larger crowds, the band exaggerated its visual gestures so the audience could see them. Page started wearing custom-made suits—one of them black with stars and planets, another featuring dragons, and a white silk suit emblazoned with red poppies—that furthered the magical aura around him. He also began to cultivate a grander kind of showmanship, duck-walking across the stage and throwing his left hand up triumphantly after laying down a riff. These gestures became more "wizardly" and emphatic when Page played the theremin, a simple electronic instrument used to recreate the experimental middle section of "Whole Lotta Love" in concert. Plant began to bare his chest in a display of virility, like many rockers in the 1970s. The band rarely used pyrotechnics, which they felt would detract from the "pure" presentation of the music, but Bonham did set his gong on fire at the end of the concert. The muscial and visual sparring between Page and Plant was a constant feature of the shows, Page often playing licks on his guitar that Plant would respond to or imitate. Theirs was one of many displays of intimacy between singer and guitarist that have become hallmarks of rock music.

Jimmy Page of Led Zeppelin performing at the Los Angeles Forum in June 1977. Zeppelin's concerts were lengthy affairs, which gave them time to display their improvisational creativity. Page is shown here playing the solo in "Dazed and Confused" with a violin bow.

Page played the acoustic instrumental "White Summer" at the Royal Albert Hall, but the band would subsequently perform an entire acoustic set. While the band became legendary for the raw and excessive power and volume of their music (some have claimed them as the progenitors of heavy metal), they also produced a great deal of acoustic music. This is especially evident on their third album, and their acoustic songs were showcased in a separate section of their concerts. The acoustic set demonstrated an important element of the band's musical ability: they were flexible and multifaceted musicians. Heavy rock bands have used acoustic performances to prove their versatility ever since.

Susan Fast (McMaster University, Ontario) is the author of In the Houses of the Holy: Led Zeppelin and the Power of Rock Music *(Oxford University Press).*

and "Walk This Way" (p10, rereleased in 1976). Aerosmith's success has continued into the present, and "Walk This Way" helped rap cross over to the rock audience in the mid-1980s, which will be considered in Chapter 11.

Taken together, American blues rockers from the Allman Brothers to Aerosmith balanced their British counterparts. Stylistically, both American and British groups extended the blues rock of the 1960s into the 1970s and forged a mainstream rock style that enjoyed tremendous commercial success. Most of these groups subscribed to the hippie aesthetic that developed in the psychedelic era: some bands blended in classical, folk, or country elements, while others focused on virtuosic soloing influenced by blues and jazz. The blues tradition was just one influence on 1970s rock, and for British progressive bands the traditions and practices of classical music played a greater role.

PROGRESSIVE ROCK: BIG IDEAS AND HIGH AMBITION

Philosophical Lyrics and Concept Albums. Following the release of *Sgt. Pepper's Lonely Hearts Club Band*, many bands on both sides of the Atlantic recorded concept albums. A heightened sense of concept, however, became the hallmark of a new type of "progressive rock" that emerged from the UK. The idea of turning an album into a self-contained artistic statement was already a few years old by the 1970s, but progressive rock bands turned the practice into an obsession within rock music. These groups also took a cue from *Sgt. Pepper* in lavishing attention on album covers. The bizarre covers Hipgnosis designed for Pink Floyd and Roger Dean's fantasy landscapes for Yes, for example, are integral to the album-listening experience. These new concept albums also featured lyrics dealing with philosophical issues such as religion and spirituality, politics and power, the forward march of technology, and existential angst. Some fans devoted to the emotional aspects of rock were repelled by such ambitious topics in the context of the hippie aesthetic, and critics often dismissed progressive rock as pretentious. Yet, these elaborately packaged concept albums were clearly an extension of the idea that music should provide a trip. Progressive rockers may have taken themselves and their music very seriously, but the style was a logical development of the increasingly lofty ambitions that rock had adopted over the course of the 1960s. Contrasts between the rise of progressive rock and the singer-songwriter movement, which embraced a return to simplicity (detailed later in the chapter), show two different manifestations of the hippie aesthetic during the 1970s.

The Use of Classical Music with Rock. A primary element of British progressive rock in the 1970s was the clear and self-conscious use of classical music. The Beatles were the most obvious source of this practice, although many other psychedelic groups employed elements drawn from classical music (as we saw in Chapter 7). For example, Procol Harum's best-known track, "A Whiter Shade of Pale" (p5 uk1, 1967), combines the feel of Percy Sledge's "When a Man Loves a Woman" with a chord progression drawn from a cantata by J. S. Bach. Among the earliest attempts to blend classical music into a concept album is the Moody Blues' *Days of Future Passed* (p3 uk27, 1967). The band already had a hit single with "Go Now" (p10 uk1, 1965) when their label, Decca, asked them to record a rock version of Dvořák's *New World Symphony* as a demonstration record to help sell stereo units. Instead the group came up with a song suite, and a professional arranger was brought in to compose the orchestral interludes between tracks, eventually creating *Days of Future Passed*. The Moody Blues went on to place a string of albums high on the charts, including *A Question of Balance* (p3 uk1, 1970), *Every Good Boy Deserves Favor* (p2 uk1, 1971), and *Seventh Sojourn* (p1 uk5, 1972).

The Who: Townshend's Big Projects. Although they are not usually considered a progressive rock band, the Who were tremendously influential in the development of rock ambition at the end of the 1960s. Comprised of guitarist Pete Townshend, vocalist Roger Daltrey, bassist John Entwistle, and drummer Keith Moon, the band was managed by Kit Lambert, the son of a well-known classical-music composer in Britain. The younger Lambert was well acquainted with the structure of classical music, and encouraged Townshend to borrow classical-music ideas in his writing for the Who. Townshend's first attempts were relatively short pieces, "A Quick One While He's Away" (1966) and "Rael" (1968). These laid the groundwork for a much larger work, *Tommy* (p4 uk2, 1969). *Tommy* tells the story of a deaf, dumb, and blind boy who gains spiritual enlightenment through playing pinball. When Tommy is cured of his handicaps, he is cast as a guru, possessing the great wisdom of the ages. The story is a parable about the superficiality of much hippie spirituality. When Tommy tells his followers that to gain spiritual insight they will need to renounce smoking pot and drinking, mute their senses, and play pinball, the crowd soundly rejects him. Through *Tommy*, Townshend sent a message that spiritual pursuits require effort and sacrifice. Ironically, many of the hippies who were the intended targets of this album never understood its message. Musically, Townshend employed a variety of recurring material that is reintroduced during important moments of the album, a practice that occurs often in opera.

The Who followed *Tommy* with two more concept albums, *Who's Next* (p4 uk1, 1971) and *Quadrophenia* (p2 uk2, 1973). *Who's Next* began as a project called *Lifehouse*, which sought to merge the band and its listeners through a series of concert experiences that would be captured on record. When this didn't work out, the band recorded much of the music as the *Who's Next* collection. With *Quadrophenia*, Townshend returned to his Mod past, crafting a story about a young Mod seeking meaning in his life. The Who had continued success throughout the 1970s, although they moved away from large conceptual projects.

The Who continued their success throughout the 1970s, with their music becoming increasingly complex and conceptual. Guitarist and songwriter Pete Townshend used elements of classical music and opera to create concept albums like *Tommy* (1969), *Who's Next* (1971), and *Quadrophenia* (1973). Here Townshend demonstrates his athletic style of guitar performance.

In the Beginning: King Crimson and Emerson, Lake & Palmer. While the Beatles, the Moody Blues, Procol Harum, and the Who were clear influences on 1970s progressive rock, the album that created the stylistic template for the progressive rock that followed was King Crimson's *In the Court of the Crimson King* (p28 uk5, 1969). The band was led by guitarist Robert Fripp, who was joined by bassist and vocalist Greg Lake, drummer Michael Giles, and multi-instrumentalist Ian McDonald on keyboards and woodwinds. King Crimson blended the harder, more dissonant aspects of twentieth-century music, the softer more consonant elements of nineteenth-century classical music, and a modern jazz influence into a rock context. The group's first album opens with "21st Century Schizoid Man," which features Lake belting out aggressive vocals and a virtuosic middle section filled with odd rhythmic syncopations and angular melodic riffs. The group endured a number of personnel changes, although the lineup that settled in for several albums in the early 1970s, featuring Fripp with drummer Bill Bruford, bassist and vocalist John Wetton, and violinist David Cross, produced some of the band's finest music, including *Larks' Tongues in Aspic* (p61 uk20, 1973) and *Red* (p66 uk45, 1974).

King Crimson enjoyed far less commercial success than the bands centered on multi-keyboardist Keith Emerson. As early as 1967, Emerson was well known on the London scene as a member of the Nice, which enjoyed two hit albums in Britain, *The Nice* (uk3, 1969) and *Five Bridges Suite* (uk2, 1970). During his time with the Nice, Emerson built a reputation for virtuosic playing and destroying (or seeming to destroy) keyboards during shows—an idea he got from Jimi Hendrix (the Nice toured with the Jimi Hendrix Experience in the late '60s). Emerson also became known for his clever rock adaptations of classical-music favorites. While touring the United States with King Crimson during late 1969, Emerson and Lake decided to form their own band together, drawing in Carl Palmer, who had played drums with Arthur Brown. Emerson, Lake & Palmer ("ELP") picked up where the Nice had left off, and the band's self-titled debut album rose to number four in the UK in 1970 (p18). For their second album, the band considered releasing a double album consisting of one record of original material and a second containing a live version of nineteenth-century Russian composer Modest Mussorgsky's piano suite, *Pictures at an Exhibition*. The dual-release plan was scrapped and the albums were released separately as *Tarkus* (p9 uk1, 1971) and *Pictures at an Exhibition* (p10 uk3, 1971). These two records illustrate the two key characteristics of ELP's approach to progressive rock. The original music on *Tarkus* features long tracks that alternate lyrical songs with Emerson's versatile playing on organ, piano, and synthesizer. *Pictures* provides an example of the band reworking classical music, dropping some parts and adding newly composed ones, to produce a new work in its own right. The band followed up with *Trilogy* (p5 uk2, 1972) and *Brain Salad Surgery* (p11 uk2, 1973) and remained successful on both sides of the Atlantic through the 1970s.

Hippie Spirituality: Jethro Tull and Yes. Just as *Tommy* had touched on the role of spirituality in hippie culture, Jethro Tull and Yes focused their most ambitious works on religious institutions and traditions. Unlike most other progressive rock bands, Jethro Tull began as a blues band. On early albums such as *Stand Up* (p20 uk1, 1969), group leader Ian Anderson played more harmonica than his trademark flute (in addition to singing lead vocals). By the beginning of the 1970s, however, Anderson became increasingly focused on issues of spirituality, and like Townshend, was highly suspicious of religious and political institutions. The first album to express these ideas was *Aqualung* (p7 uk4, 1971), which deals with society's treatment of the poor and is, in part, a bitter indictment of the Church of England. The band's next album, *Thick as a Brick* (p1 uk5, 1972), is an attack on bourgeois values, while *A Passion Play* (p1 uk13, 1973) takes on the topic of life after death and reincarnation. While *Aqualung* is divided into separate tracks, the other albums are divided only by the obligatory break required to turn the record over and are essentially single tracks of about forty minutes' length. The band's personnel shifted over the decade, although the lineup of Anderson, Martin Barre (guitar), John Evans (keyboards), Barrie Barlow (drums), and Jeffrey Hammond (bass) played on most of the more conceptual albums.

Led by singer and flautist Ian Anderson (shown here), Jethro Tull emerged as one of the top progressive rock bands of the early 1970s. The group had formed as a blues outfit, and those influences can be heard in their later music, especially the long instrumental solos on *Thick as a Brick* (1972) and *A Passion Play* (1973).

Led by vocalist Jon Anderson (no relation to Ian), Yes was also concerned with issues of spirituality inspired by the hippie mélange of Eastern religious ideas. Although the group had released three albums, *Fragile* (p4 uk7, 1971) marks the first release by the band's definitive lineup, consisting of Anderson, guitarist Steve Howe, bassist Chris Squire, drummer Bill Bruford, and multi-keyboardist Rick Wakeman. In terms of instrumental prowess, Yes was perhaps the most accomplished group in all of progressive rock, with Howe, Squire, Wakeman, and Bruford consistently winning awards for their playing in magazine polls on both sides of the Atlantic. While spiritual themes can be found on *Fragile*, they are much more obvious on *Close to the Edge* (p3 uk4, 1972). Based in part on Hermann Hesse's novel *Siddhartha*, the eighteen-minute title track is inspired by the quest for spiritual wisdom with very little of the caustic critique found in the music of Jethro Tull. (If any band from the 1970s perfectly captures the naïve and hopeful innocence of psychedelia, it is Yes.) The concept for the band's follow-up, *Tales from Topographic Oceans* (p6 uk1, 1973), was inspired by Eastern scripture (drawn from a footnote in Paramahansa Yogananda's *Autobiography of a Yogi*, a hippie favorite) and consists of four tracks on two albums. After the release of *Tales*, Wakeman left to pursue a solo career and the band drafted Swiss keyboardist Patrick Moraz for *Relayer* (p5 uk4,

Designed by graphic artist Roger Dean, the cover to Yes's *Tales from Topographic Oceans* (1973) provides an example of a progressive rock album cover that was designed to be part of the listening experience.

1974), featuring the epic track "The Gates of Delirium," inspired by Leo Tolstoy's *War and Peace*. The band's heady blend of instrumental virtuosity and spiritual subject matter proved to be a winning combination. Together with ELP and Jethro Tull, Yes was one of the most commercially successful rock bands during the first half of the 1970s.

Symphonic Expansion. Most progressive rock bands were eager to integrate classical-music influences to create longer, more intricate musical arrangements, but the elements of these more symphonic rock tracks are drawn from common pop-music forms. Yes's "Roundabout" illustrates how a long track—it is almost nine minutes—can be constructed out of shorter, more familiar components. The piece uses the same compound AABA form that we saw in Led Zeppelin's "Whole Lotta Love."

Listening Guide

Yes, "Roundabout" Atlantic 2854

Words and music by Jon Anderson and Steve Howe, produced by Yes and Eddie Offord. Reached #13 on the *Billboard* "Hot 100" chart in early 1972.

FORM: Compound AABA form. The A sections consist of verse and bridge sections, but no chorus. The B section falls into three parts: new verses based on a repeating riff, a return of the introduction and bridge section, and a series of solos on the organ and guitar. Note how the return of the introduction (marked by asterisks) restarts the song—a formal strategy that became common in the 1970s, especially in longer and more complicated songs.

TIME SIGNATURE: Mostly in 4/4, with measures of 2/4 and 3/4 occurring along the way.

INSTRUMENTATION: Acoustic and electric guitars, bass, organ, piano, synthesizer, mellotron, drums, percussion, lead and backup vocals.

*	0:00–0:44	**Introduction**	Rubato, acoustic guitar free rhythm, punctuated by tape effect created by playing tape-recorded grand-piano bass notes backward.
A	0:44–1:18	**Verse 1**, 20 mm.	Entire band plays 8 bars to prepare for the entrance of lead vocals, which then present a 2-bar verse. "I'll be the roundabout . . ."
	1:18–1:45	**Verse 2**, 16 mm.	4 bars now prepare the return of the vocals, which present the 12-bar verse as before, but with backup vocals added and leading to the bridge. "The music dance . . ."
	1:45–2:15	**Bridge**, 18 mm.	Starts with guitar, high hat, and vocal only, then organ and finally bass enter. "In and around the lake . . ."

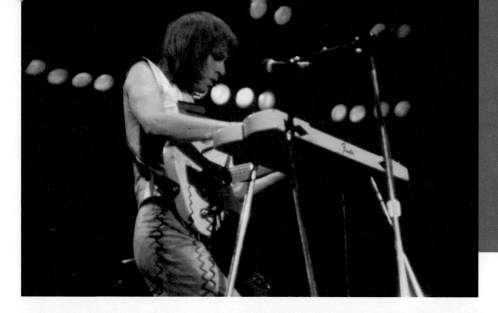

Get Music ⑤ wwnorton.com/studyspace

A	2:15–2:49	**Verse 3**, 20 mm.	8 bars prepare vocal return, then the 12 mm. verse as before with slight changes in instrumentation. Note the use of synthesizer here, as well as the new fast melodic figure that occurs just before the singing returns. "I will remember . . ."
	2:49–3:25	**Bridge**, 21 mm.	As before, without staggered entrance in bass and drums, but adds new backup vocal part. Fast melodic figure returns to create transition to middle section. "In and around the lake . . ."
B	3:25–4:57	**Middle section**, 50 mm.	Twelve times through a 4-bar phrase based on a riff in the bass and guitar. Choral vocals present melody, with some instrumental interludes along the way. The end of the section reintroduces the verse melody to transition back to the introduction. "Along the drifting cloud . . ."
*	4:57–5:50	**Reprise of Introduction and bridge**	Rubato during intro and then 9 bars that reinterpret the music from the bridge. "In and around the lake . . ."
	5:50–7:05	**Instrumental solos**, 45 mm.	The organ and guitar alternate solos based on music drawn from the bridge. An ascending scale passage creates a transition to the return of the verse.
A	7:05–7:26	**Verse 4**, 12 mm.	The verse returns varied somewhat, but using the lyrics from verse 1. "I'll be the roundabout . . ."
	7:26–7:53	**Bridge**, 17 mm.	The fullest presentation of the bridge so far, leading directly into the coda. "In and around the lake . . ."
	7:53–8:30	**Coda**, 20 mm.	Layered harmony vocals over a strummed acoustic guitar, as the song ends with a guitar phrase drawn from the end of the introduction.

"Roundabout" is filled with many musical features that show classical-music influences, including the idea of reusing melodic material in new ways, which is a central feature of much classical music. The piece also incorporates a number of inventive rhythmic ideas. Notice how the bridge sections cannot be counted according to a simple four-beat pattern. This kind of rhythmic patterning (called "changing meter") is standard in much twentieth-century classical music and some jazz, but is not often a feature in earlier rock (the Beatles' "All You Need Is Love" is a notable exception—try it using three- and four-beat counting). A similar use of changing meter can be heard in in the Allman Brothers' "Whipping Post."

With its formal patterning drawn from simpler pop forms and its manipulation of melodic and rhythmic material drawn from classical music, "Roundabout" demonstrates how progressive rock depended on both pop and classical traditions. While formal patterns within progressive rock vary considerably, the pattern found in "Roundabout" recurs regularly (although with some variation) in Yes's music from the 1970s. The Listening Guide also shows that the track is separated into two big parts, marked by the classical guitar introduction and its return at 4:57 (shown by asterisks). This division does not however line up with the AABA form, revealing a formal structure that is operating on multiple levels (two in this case), another feature common in classical music.

Bizarre Tales and Progressive-Rock Theater: Genesis and Pink Floyd.

During the first half of the 1970s, Genesis was among the most creative and bizarre bands in progressive rock. The band included singer Peter Gabriel, drummer and backup vocalist Phil Collins, Michael Rutherford on bass, Steve Hackett on guitar, and Tony Banks on keyboards. Musically, Genesis focused on lengthy, carefully worked out arrangements, while Gabriel's lyrics spun fantastic tales that delivered stinging, if sometimes obscure, criticisms of British life and values. Onstage, while the other band members were absorbed in their playing, Gabriel acted these stories out. Using costumes and props to create a new kind of rock theater, Genesis extended the rock-opera ambitions of the concept album into the concert hall. For example, during live performances of "The Musical Box" from *Nursery Cryme* (1971), Gabriel donned a mask to help him act out the role of a reincarnated spirit who has aged seventy years and built up decades of unsatisfied sexual longing. *Foxtrot* (uk12, 1972), includes the twenty-minute track "Supper's Ready," live performances of which featured Gabriel in the role of the returning Messiah, lifting him from the stage via wires to increase the effect of divine presence. In *The Lamb Lies Down on Broadway* (p41 uk10, 1974), much as in Jethro Tull's *A Passion Play*, we follow the main character, Rael (like the Who piece mentioned above), after death and before rebirth. Gabriel's costumes for performances of *The Lamb* became so elaborate that he sometimes found it difficult to hold the microphone close enough to his mouth to sing.

Gabriel's penchant for the bizarre was paralleled by Roger Waters's fascination with madness—which is evident on many Pink Floyd albums from the 1970s. After their success on the London psychedelic scene late in the 1960s, Pink Floyd—featuring Waters on bass and vocals, Rick Wright on keyboards, Nick Mason on drums, and guitarist David Gilmour—scored a series of successful albums in the UK, including *Ummagumma* (uk5, 1969), *Atom Heart Mother* (uk1, 1970), and *Meddle* (uk3, 1971). True to the psychedelic ethos, these albums were markedly

experimental, depending more on interesting electronic timbres and compositional devices than instrumental virtuosity. *The Dark Side of the Moon* (pl uk2, 1973) firmly established the band in the United States: the album was enormously successful and many of its tracks have been staples of FM rock radio since its release. Barrett was forced to leave the group in the late 1960s by the onset of mental illness, and Waters seemed obsessed with Barrett's illness and the death of his own father during World War II. Many Pink Floyd lyrics can be traced to these two themes: *Wish You Were Here* (pl uk1, 1975), for instance, directly deals with Barrett's madness, especially in the track "Shine On You Crazy Diamond." While Genesis made Peter Gabriel the focus of its live show, Pink Floyd chose to extend the idea of the psychedelic light show to include a variety of elaborate stage effects, such as a crashing airplane and a flying pig. The complex stage show for the band's two-record concept album *The Wall* (pl uk3, 1979) featured a wall being slowly built onstage between the band and the audience, and projected animations (akin to the famous album art) by artist Gerald Scarfe.

Impressive lighting and prop effects were a part of almost all progressive rock shows, although some bands took this idea farther than others. Concept albums and rock operas first developed in the late 1960s, as did the notion of addressing important and serious-minded issues. Progressive rock in the 1970s extended and refined these psychedelic tendencies, and had roots that extend as far back as the playlets of Leiber and Stoller. Of all the music of the 1970s, progressive rock was

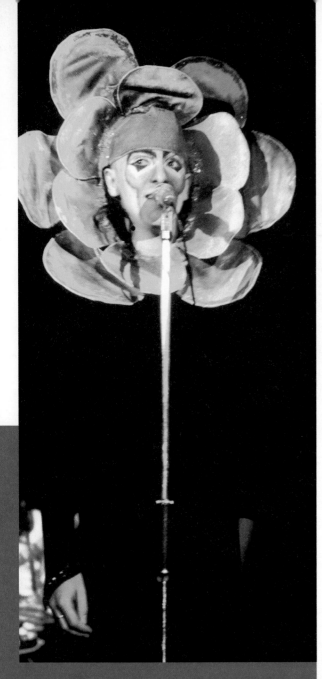

In the early days of Genesis, lead singer Peter Gabriel hit on the idea of donning costumes for performances of the band's lengthy numbers. Here Gabriel is shown performing the "Willow Farm" section from the ambitious "Supper's Ready," an epic that engages in sexuality and surrealistic images, and ends with the Second Coming. It is one of the group's signature tracks from the early 1970s and was often the climax of their live shows.

most faithful to the hippie aesthetic, making it the prime target against which punk rebelled later in the decade (more about that in Chapter 10).

JAZZ-ROCK FUSION AND JAZZ-INFLUENCED ROCK

Jazz and the Studio Musician. As rock musicians became increasingly ambitious about their music, they also focused more on achieving technical mastery on their instruments. Jazz, in particular, provided a model that many musicians embraced. For decades, jazz had been revered for the musical prowess of its players, with artists such as Charlie Parker, Dizzy Gillespie, John Coltrane, and Art Tatum setting high standards with their technical and aesthetic achievements. As solos assumed a more central role in rock music, it was natural that many artists would look to jazz as a source for new ideas. Jazz players had been involved in popular music for years, and it is a style that encourages musicians to develop their improvisatory skills. In addition to playing clubs at night, many jazz artists made a living by playing at pop recording sessions by day. The Funk Brothers who played the Motown sessions, for instance, were all gifted and experienced jazz players, as were Los Angeles studio musicians like guitarist Barney Kessel, who played on everything from Phil Spector records to those by the Monkees. In the 1970s, the "studio musician" came to mean a player who was fluent in all styles, could read music well, and could be counted on to play expertly in any musical situation. Many of the studio musicians came from the jazz tradition. Jazz-schooled players such as drummer Steve Gadd, bassist Tony Levin, and guitarists Lee Ritenour and Larry Carlton played on many rock records and their high level of professionalism served as a model for many aspiring rock musicians.

Jazz-Rock Fusion: Miles and Beyond. Already one of the most important figures in jazz during the late 1960s, trumpeter Miles Davis began noticing that the extended jams of Cream and Hendrix were not all that different from what a lot of jazz players were doing. What impressed Davis most, however, was that rock audiences would sit and listen to this kind of music. Jazz audiences were generally much smaller than those for even a moderately well attended rock show, and Davis decided that he wanted to play for festival-sized crowds. He began experimenting in live performance and in the recording studio with jazz musicians whom he thought could fuse rock with jazz, including guitarist John McLaughlin, keyboardists Joseph Zawinul, Chick Corea, and Herbie Hancock, and saxophonist Wayne Shorter. The most famous result of these experimentations was the double album *Bitches Brew*, which rose to number thirty-five on the U.S. album charts in 1970 (r4), and introduced rock audiences to jazz-rock fusion.

Following the success of *Bitches Brew*, and with a rising appreciation for technical virtuosity triggered by the progressive rock bands, members of Davis's band formed their own groups and enjoyed commercial success on the pop album charts. John McLaughlin formed the Mahavishnu Orchestra, bringing rock, jazz, and Eastern mysticism together on the debut album *Inner Mounting Flame* (1972) and subsequently enjoyed moderate success with *Birds of Fire* (p15, 1973). Herbie Hancock hit with *Head Hunters* (p13 r2, 1974), while Chick Corea's band, Return to Forever, appeared on the album charts several times with *Romantic Warrior* (p35 r23, 1976), which owed a clear debt to progressive rock. Shorter and Zawinul formed Weather Report and scored later in the decade with *Heavy Weather* (p30 r33, 1977). Violinist Jean-Luc Ponty left McLaughlin's band to pursue a solo career and released *Enigmatic Ocean* (p35, 1977). Taken together these fusion bands were only moderately successful in pop terms, but compared with typical jazz sales and audiences they were enormously popular. Instrumental music had not enjoyed such commercial success since the days of the big bands.

Frank Zappa: Satire and Complexity. Beginning with the Mothers of Invention's *Freak Out!* (1966), Frank Zappa's music blended satire, compositional sophistication, and musical virtuosity that at times pressed the bounds of good taste. Zappa's penchant for cynicism can be seen in the 1968 album sending up *Sgt. Pepper* called *We're Only in It for the Money* (p30). After the moderate success of *Money*, Zappa, with the support of a long line of band members, chalked up

Pictured here during a 1973 concert in Copenhagen, Miles Davis was the most influential artist of the jazz-rock style. Although Davis was a key player in jazz from the late 1940s, in the late 1960s he began to incorporate funk and rock influences, drawing inspiration from the music of Jimi Hendrix, James Brown, and Sly and the Family Stone. Davis's album *Bitches Brew* (1970) was very influential in jazz-rock fusion and included many artists who formed important fusion groups. Among these were Chick Corea of Return to Forever, John McLaughlin of the Mahavishnu Orchestra, and Joseph Zawinul and Wayne Shorter of Weather Report.

eight more Top 40 albums in the United States. His most successful album in the UK was *Hot Rats* (uk9), while *Apostrophe* (p10, 1974) was his biggest American success. "I'm the Slime" from *Overnite Sensation* (p32, 1973) displays Zappa's blend of jazz-fusion style playing with cartoonish vocals and satirical lyrics that offer a critique of television. Although Zappa clearly took his music-making seriously, he was vigilant in deflating any effort to interpret his music according to the usual categories, insisting that he didn't care whether it was "commercial," "artistic," or "relevant." Zappa also composed a number of pieces for small and large ensembles (or adapted rock band pieces) that are best classified as twentieth-century classical music, despite often-goofy titles such as "Mo and Herb's Vacation."

Low Sparks and Pretzel Logic: Traffic and Steely Dan. The second incarnation of the British group Traffic flourished in the 1970s on the jazz-rock scene, which was dominated by American acts. After their hiatus in the late 1960s, Steve Winwood (keyboards and vocals), Jim Capaldi (drums), and Chris Wood (flute and sax) teamed up again to release *John Barleycorn Must Die* (p11 uk5, 1970). Capaldi soon left and the band released its signature album of the 1970s, *The Low Spark of High-Heeled Boys* (p7, 1971) with drummer Jim Gordon, bassist Rick Grech, and percussionist Reebop Kwaku-Baah. The title track provides a good example of how Traffic blended Winwood's bluesy vocals with Wood's Coltrane-inspired sax soloing. After more personnel changes, the band released more successful albums, including *Shoot Out at the Fantasy Factory* (p6, 1973) and *When the Eagle Flies* (p9 uk31, 1974). Winwood left the band in 1975 to embark on a successful solo career.

Back in the United States, Steely Dan emerged with their debut album *Can't Buy a Thrill* (p17, 1972), which contained two hits, "Do It Again" (p6, 1972) and "Reelin' in the Years" (p11, 1972). Led by Donald Fagen (keyboard and vocals) and Walter Becker (bass and guitar), the band's initial lineup also included guitar-

Featuring Walter Becker (bass and guitar, second from left) and Donald Fagen (vocals and piano, right), Steely Dan used jazz elements and virtuoso studio musicians to create a winning jazz-rock sound. Every one of their seven albums in the 1970s charted in the *Billboard* Top 40. Although they did perform concerts, Becker and Fagan focused their attention on the studio, where they wrote carefully organized arrangements punctuated with improvised solo sections.

ist Jeff "Skunk" Baxter. After some initial success as a traditional touring band, Becker and Fagen began to focus on recording, using studio musicians to provide the instrumental tracks and virtuosic solos. For much of Steely Dan's late work, the band's only regular members were Fagen and Becker. Perhaps the best album showing this arrangement at work is *Aja* (p3 uk5, 1977), which included three hit singles: "Peg" (p11, 1977), "Deacon Blues" (p19, 1978), and "Josie" (p26, 1978). Steely Dan arrangements, like those of Zappa and other jazz rockers, were often written out before recording began. Solos, however, were left open and became showcases for the some of the best studio musicians in the business. In "Peg," for example, the horns and rhythm section play mostly worked-out parts while Jay Graydon's guitar solo was improvised live in the studio. Steely Dan placed seven albums in the American Top 40 during the 1970s, in addition to scoring ten Top 40 singles.

Horn Bands: Blood, Sweat & Tears and Chicago.
The music of Miles Davis, Frank Zappa, Traffic, and Steely Dan often relied on horns to provide a jazz element, but two bands from the early 1970s are most often identified as the jazz-rock "horn bands": Blood, Sweat & Tears and Chicago. After playing sessions with Bob Dylan and before he became Lynyrd Skynyrd's producer, keyboardist Al Kooper formed Blood, Sweat & Tears, releasing *Child Is Father to the Man*, which hit number forty in the UK in 1968 (p47). Kooper soon left the band and teamed with guitarists Michael Bloomfield and Stephen Stills to record *Super Session* (p12, 1968). With Kooper's departure from Blood, Sweat & Tears, singer David Clayton-Thomas joined and the group enjoyed enormous success in the United States with its next album, *Blood, Sweat & Tears* (p1 r15 uk15, 1969), which contained three hit singles—"You've Made Me So Very Happy" (p2, 1969), "Spinning Wheel" (p2, 1969), and "And When I Die" (p2, 1969). The album also won the Grammy Award for Album of the Year in 1970. Their follow-up *Blood, Sweat & Tears 3* (p1 uk14, 1970) contained Goffin and King's "Hi-De-Ho" (p14, 1970) and Clayton-Thomas's own "Lucretia MacEvil" (p29, 1970). Their use of a small horn section was certainly nothing new in the history of rhythm and blues or pop: Stax and Motown arrangements often used horns to "sweeten" the accompaniment. But Blood, Sweat & Tears made the horns more central to the arrangements, even providing instrumental showcases for both solo and ensemble playing that were influenced by the big band tradition in jazz. An example of this is the group's arrangement of the Rolling Stones' "Sympathy for the Devil," which Blood, Sweat & Tears titled "Symphony for the Devil/Sympathy for the Devil." Similar to a Vanilla Fudge symphonic-psychedelic cover version, Blood, Sweat & Tears created an almost eight-minute epic out of the Stones tune, including long instrumental passages that employ both traditional jazz and avant-garde practices. Although their most popular music was released at the beginning of the decade, Blood, Sweat & Tears continued to release successful music until the middle of the 1970s.

Another band to place increased focus on a horn section was Chicago. Beginning with their debut album, *Chicago Transit Authority* (p17 uk9, 1969), the band released thirteen Top 40 albums in the United States during the 1970s (five in the UK) and five of these went to number one. The band also scored twenty-two Top 40 singles (three in the UK) with its blend of melodic pop vocals and sophisticated, horn-dominated accompaniments. "If You Leave Me Now" rose to number

one in both the U.S. and UK charts in 1976, and is a good example of the band's softer side. "Does Anybody Really Know What Time It Is?" (p7, 1970) from their first album features the singing of keyboardist Robert Lamm and demonstrates how they blended Beatles-influenced pop with jazz-influenced horn arrangements. The track begins with an instrumental introduction focusing on rhythmic ensemble playing and breaks into a brief trumpet solo from Lee Loughnane. The horns then retreat to the accompaniment as Lamm delivers the verses and chorus, supported by Beatle-esque backup vocals. A final flourish at the end is provided by a jazzy trombone lick courtesy of James Pankow.

As popular as jazz rock was during the 1970s, it was also the source of enormous controversy within the jazz community, especially later in the decade. Some jazz musicians and fans welcomed the blending of rock and jazz elements, but many traditionalists hated it, labeling the style a sell-out to the pop-music industry. Some rock purists also rejected jazz rock because it seemed too concerned with instrumental virtuosity and lacked the visceral punch that they felt was essential to rock. Similarly, these same rock purists often rejected progressive rock as too complex and pretentious, while most classical-music listeners found progressive styles too pop-oriented to be taken seriously. Thus, jazz rock and progressive rock often found themselves in an in-between situation with some listeners—"neither fish nor fowl," stylistically speaking.

GLAM ROCK AND ROCK THEATER: SHOCKING CHARACTERS

Dressing Up and Acting Out. In our discussion of Genesis, we touched on Peter Gabriel's use of costumes, makeup, and props in performance and linked this to Pink Floyd's growing fascination with highly visual stage shows. In the early 1970s, big rock shows were mostly staged in arenas and stadiums rather than theaters and ballrooms, as they had been in the late 1960s. This led to a growth in production standards across the rock-music industry. Increasingly, audiences expected a show with professional stage lights and some kind of special effects. Genesis and Pink

Floyd stand out in the context of many bands that offered elaborate extra-musical excitement. Amid this new attention to the more theatrical elements of rock performance, it was perhaps inevitable that certain artists would come to specialize in portraying fictional characters onstage. In the 1970s two of the most important figures in this regard were David Bowie and Alice Cooper. Both adopted distinct onstage personas that most audiences understood as characters they were portraying. The roots of this practice go back to the Beatles and the "concept" of the Beatles portraying the Lonely Hearts Club Band. With the growth of the theatrical side of the concert business in the 1970s, it became possible to put on and tour a sophisticated show with elaborate props and effects—a kind of rock theater with increasingly higher production values.

Ziggy Played Guitar: David Bowie. A style of theatrical rock called "glam rock" was particularly important in the United Kingdom in the early 1970s. Popular glam rock groups, such as T. Rex and Mott the Hoople, dressed in androgynous clothing and sang songs that often discussed the aspects of glam culture, including themes of science fiction, alienation, and typical characters associated with the glam scene. Of all the British glam stars who stormed the UK charts, however, the most important was David Bowie. His first important success in the UK came with the single "Space Oddity" (uk5, 1969; p15, 1973), a song inspired by the Stanley Kubrick film adaptation of Arthur C. Clarke's *2001: A Space Odyssey.*

By the early 1970s, Bowie had formed the Spiders from Mars, a band with shifting personnel that featured Mick Ronson on guitar. He also created the character of Ziggy Stardust for the album *The Rise and Fall of Ziggy Stardust and the Spiders from Mars* (uk5, 1972), which contained "Suffragette City" (uk10, 1972). The release of *Aladdin Sane* (p17 uk1, 1973) and *Pin-Ups* (p23 uk1, 1973) reinforced Bowie's stature in the UK, while helping him become the only UK glam artist to achieve significant success in the United States. The album that made Bowie's reputation in America was *David Live* (p8 uk2, 1974), which featured a generous selection of songs from earlier albums that had topped the charts in the UK. The success of *Young Americans* (p9 uk2, 1975), which contained the single "Fame" (p1 uk17, 1975), and *Station to Station* (p3 uk5, 1976) solidified Bowie's star status in America.

David Bowie performing in 1973 as his alter ego, Ziggy Stardust. Like Alice Cooper and Peter Gabriel, Bowie pushed the boundaries of sexual and gender identity, although in a more mysterious, fashion-conscious manner. Ziggy Stardust emerged on the album *The Rise and Fall of Ziggy Stardust and the Spiders from Mars* (1972), and Bowie continued to reinvent the character throughout the decade.

Alice Cooper performances shocked many audiences during the 1970s, as the band developed a reputation for being dangerous, dark, and irreverent. Cooper is shown here dressed in black leather holding a large snake, only one of his many shocking stage antics.

Alice Cooper: Welcome to My Nightmare. It is perhaps a measure of how far hippie androgyny had developed by the early 1970s that a band of hard-drinking, tough-looking rock and rollers could have a front man whose named Alice. On stage, Vincent Furnier became Alice Cooper and led his audiences into the darkest parts of the imagination, often ending the show in a gruesome way. On different tours, Cooper was hanged, executed in an electric chair, and beheaded by a guillotine. His obsession with such ghoulish topics was influenced by his admiration for Jim Morrison, who befriended the young Cooper in the late 1960s. After two commercially unsuccessful records produced by Frank Zappa and released on Zappa's label, Cooper and his band released *Love It to Death* (p35, 1971), which contained the single "I'm Eighteen" (p21, 1971), an almost gothic study in teenage depression and anger. Bob Ezrin (who later produced *The Wall*) produced this album and continued to work with the group. Cooper enjoyed rising success with *Killer* (p21 uk27, 1971); *School's Out* (p2 uk4, 1972), which contained the single "School's Out" (p7 uk1, 1972); and *Billion Dollar Babies*, which hit number one on both sides of the Atlantic in 1973. Cooper's often-dramatic music had just enough self-satire in it to keep things from getting too heavy. For example, in "Be My Lover," Cooper and the band go into the kind of bump-and-grind ending found in strip clubs, prefaced by an "oh" spoken in the manner of movie sex goddess Mae West. By the middle of the decade the original band had split up and Cooper went solo, enjoying more success with *Welcome to My Nightmare* (p5 uk19, 1975).

It is important to recognize the similarities and differences between Bowie and Cooper. Each adopted a stage persona that was based in fantasy and both pushed the boundaries of sexual and gender identities. But while Cooper enjoyed his greatest commercial success in the UK when glam was at its peak, he did not share Bowie's interest in the world of urbane fashion. Bowie also tended to change characters, while Cooper stuck with his Alice character for his entire career. Despite their differences, Cooper and Bowie shared a common aesthetic goal that had its roots in psychedelia: making the music a trip—even if the trip ended up being weird, campy, or ghoulish.

KISS and Makeup. Taking the theatrical element even further, all four member of KISS—bassist Gene Simmons, drummer Peter Criss, and guitarists Paul Stanley and Ace Frehley—cast themselves as distinct characters onstage, rather than only the lead singer donning makeup and costumes. The band wore elaborate face makeup that kept their countenances secret for years. From the beginning, KISS provided a bombastic live show using lights, flames, and explosions to create a high-energy rock spectacle. Stylistically, KISS was essentially a blues-rock band. "Rock and Roll All Nite" illustrates their approach, blending verses not unlike those of Bad Company or Foghat with an anthemic sing-along chorus that works well as the song's hook. The group's first few albums—*KISS* (p87, 1974), *Hotter Than Hell* (p100, 1974), and *Dressed to Kill* (p32, 1975)—did not do particularly well. When the band released a live version of "Rock and Roll All Nite," however, it went to number twelve in the United States (1975) and prepared the way for the success of *Destroyer* (p1 uk22, 1976). The live album *Alive* (p9, 1975) contained songs from their earlier albums, which saw increased sales and playing time on rock radio. By the end of the decade, KISS had masterfully exploited the marketing opportunities provided by their success, starring in their own feature film and even selling action figures.

THE SINGER-SONGWRITERS

The Importance of Being Earnest. The singer-songwriter style of the 1970s arose in part from the folk revival of the 1960s, and from the acoustic music of the Beatles. When Bob Dylan delivered a song from behind his acoustic guitar, or Paul McCartney sang while at the piano, it was understood that each was sincerely expressing the results of his own personal reflection. The singer-songwriter movement was especially appealing to audiences that had left college and moved into adulthood. In a famous 1976 *New York* magazine article, writer Tom Wolfe referred to the 1970s as the "Me Decade," which is particularly fitting in the context of the "self"-oriented singer-songwriter movement. The singer-songwriters stood as the direct antithesis to Bowie and Cooper: rather than playing characters, these artists seemed to reveal their unmediated personal perspectives. Much of this, it is important to understand, is only an ideal. No matter how authentic a performance or recording seems, show-business concerns for projecting the proper image almost always mediate it. The aural impression of sincerity and intimacy created by most singer-songwriter records was achieved by placing the singer front and center, with the accompaniment in a secondary and supporting role. In the 1970s, Dylan continued his career as a singer-songwriter, as did John Lennon. Lennon enjoyed several hit singles and albums in the first half of the decade, perhaps most notably *Imagine* (p1 uk1, 1971), which featured a title single that went to number three in United States. In the case of both these artists, the focus was always the singer and the song.

1960s Connections: James Taylor, Carole King, and Paul Simon. One of the important new singer-songwriters to emerge out of the late 1960s was James Taylor. Taylor was among the first acts signed to the Beatles' record label, Apple, in 1968. His debut on Apple, *James Taylor* (1968), did not chart, although it contained "Carolina in My Mind," which would become internationally popular over time. Taylor soon signed to Warner, and hit in 1970 with "Fire and Rain" (p3 uk4) and *Sweet Baby James* (p3 uk6, 1970), which established his popularity on both sides of the Atlantic. He enjoyed continued success with albums like *Mud Slide Slim* (p2 uk4, 1971) and *One Man Dog* (p4 uk27, 1972). Taylor's single "You've Got a Friend" (p1 uk4, 1971) was written by a familiar name in American popular music, Carole King. By the end of the 1960s, King had decided to step out from behind the scenes, becoming one of the most important and influential female artists of the 1970s. She scored a string of successful albums, beginning with *Tapestry* (p1 uk4, 1970), which contained the hit "It's Too Late" (p1 uk6, 1971) as well as her own version of "You've Got a Friend" and a reinterpretation of "Will You Love Me Tomorrow?" Later King albums included *Music* (p1 uk18, 1972) and *Rhymes and Reasons* (p2, 1972).

Another familiar name among the singer-songwriters was Paul Simon. In the wake of his tremendous run of hit records with Art Garfunkel, Simon decided to strike out on his own, updating his 1960s approach and releasing *Paul Simon* (p4 uk1, 1972). The album contained "Mother and Child Reunion" (p4 uk5, 1972)—a song that featured Jamaican musicians before reggae was well known. He often employed studio musicians to play on his tracks and expanded the singer-songwriter style. Simon increasingly incorporated jazz elements in his music with a series of albums and singles including *There Goes Rhymin' Simon* (p2 uk4, 1973), "Kodachrome" (p2, 1973), *Still Crazy After All These Years* (p1 uk6, 1975), and "50 Ways to Leave Your Lover" (p1 uk23, 1975). A clear example of this is "Still Crazy After All These Years." The lyrics reflect on meeting an old lover by chance and reassessing the course his life has taken. The backup playing is subdued but sophisticated during the verses, while the middle section features a soaring and melodic jazz-tinged saxophone solo.

American Poets Society. Carly Simon (no relation to Paul) first came to the attention of most rock listeners with "That's the Way I Always Heard It Should Be" (p10, 1971) and "Anticipation" (p13, 1971). Similar to the music of Carole King, Simon's confessional songs focus on her vocals, piano, acoustic guitar, and strings.

In the 1970s, singer-songwriters often focused on social issues. This poster advertises a concert to benefit the liberal Democrat George McGovern's 1972 campaign for president.

Listening Guide   Get Music ⓢ wwnorton.com/studyspace

Carole King, "You've Got a Friend" Ode SP-77009

Words and music by Carole King, produced by Lou Adler. Contained on *Tapestry* (1970).

FORM: Compound AABA form. The A section is based on contrasting verse-chorus form, and consists of a 16-bar verse and a 14-bar chorus. The 10-bar bridge section is followed by a partial return of the A section, consisting of only the chorus. The song ends with a quiet coda.

TIME SIGNATURE: 4/4.

INSTRUMENTATION: Acoustic piano, acoustic bass, acoustic guitar, congas, string quartet, lead and backup vocals.

	0:00–0:12	**Introduction**, 4 mm.	Solo acoustic piano sets the intimate tone of the song.
A	0:12–0:58	**Verse 1**, 16 mm.	Vocal enters, as piano continues but with the support of the acoustic bass. "When you're down . . ."
	0:58–1:49	**Chorus**, 18 mm.	Congas and harmony vocal are added. James Taylor's acoustic guitar playing can just barely be heard in the background. The chorus consists of 14 bars, to which 4 bars are added, drawn directly from the additional introduction. "You just call . . ."
A	1:49–2:34	**Verse 2**, 16 mm.	As before, but now with acoustic guitar continuing and string quartet added. "If the sky . . ."
	2:34–3:13	**Chorus**, 14 mm.	All instruments continue, as harmony vocal and congas return. "You just call . . ."
B	3:13–3:42	**Bridge**, 10 mm.	Same instrumentation as verse 2, "Now ain't it good . . ."
A'	3:42–4:21	**Chorus**, 14 mm.	As in the first chorus, as string quartet drops out until the very end. Note how the guitar gets busy toward the end. "You just call . . ."
	4:21–5:05	**Coda**, 15 mm.	Repeat of vamp drawn from first 2 bars of the introduction, with King improvising vocal lines on top. "You've got a friend . . ."

Simon's lyrics frequently discuss life changes facing the post-college generation. Her album *No Secrets* (p1 uk3, 1973) stands as the peak of her popular appeal, and contains the single "You're So Vain" (p1 uk3, 1972). The song features backup vocals by Mick Jagger and was rumored to refer to Simon's romantic relationship with Jagger, actor Warren Beatty, or many other dominant male characters in her life at the time. After nearly 40 years of remaining secretive about the subject of the song, in 2010 Simon revealed "You're So Vain" was written about music executive

David Geffen. Harry Chapin was another important singer-songwriter from the period. His "Taxi" (p24, 1972) and "Cat's in the Cradle" (p1 1974) both reflect on life's twists and turns while highlighting his emotive baritone voice and acoustic guitar. Don McLean also used piano, acoustic guitar, and nostalgic lyrics to create music aligned with this movement. His "American Pie" (p1 uk2, 1972) attempts to summarize the previous two decades of rock and roll history, while his song "Vincent" (p12 uk1, 1972) offers a portrait of the painter Vincent Van Gogh. Jim Croce was at the height of his popularity in 1973 when he was killed in an airplane crash. His song "Bad, Bad Leroy Brown" (p1, 1973) was at the top of the U.S. charts at the time of the accident. The release a few months later of his "Time in a Bottle" (p1, 1974), a reflection on the unwelcome approach of death, recorded just months before the crash, gave the song an eerie poignancy.

Elton John, pictured here in a 1975 concert, was the most successful singer-songwriter of the early 1970s. He blended folk and rhythm and blues influences (he performed on the black dance show *Soul Train*) with some of David Bowie's glam-rock sensibility. John's worldwide popularity continues to this day.

British Singer-Songwriters: Van Morrison, Cat Stevens, and Elton John. The singer-songwriter style was not restricted to Americans, as Van Morrison, Cat Stevens, and Elton John all enjoyed considerable success during the early and mid-1970s. Morrison continued his 1960s success into the new decade, bringing his blend of jazz and rhythm and blues influences to albums like *Moondance* (p29 uk32, 1970) and *Tupelo Honey* (p29, 1971). Cat Stevens first stormed the U.S. charts with his single "Peace Train" (p7, 1971). A string of successful albums made him a regular on the charts on both sides of the Atlantic, including *Teaser and the Firecat* (p2 uk3, 1971), *Catch Bull at Four* (p1 uk2, 1972), and *Buddha and the Chocolate Box* (p2 uk3, 1974). Perhaps the most successful of the singer-songwriters was Elton John. John was introduced to American audiences with the single "Your Song" (p8 uk7, 1971), and followed with a series of hugely successful albums: *Honky Chateau* (p1 uk2, 1972), *Don't Shoot Me I'm Only the Piano Player* (p1 uk1, 1973), *Goodbye Yellow Brick Road* (p1 uk1, 1973), and *Caribou* (p1 uk1, 1974). He wrote most of his songs with lyricist Bernie Taupin, forming a songwriting team that rivaled the success of Lennon and McCartney. Taupin's images are clever and compelling, and John's melodic-harmonic sense draws on a wide range of influences. Except for the fact that John performs the tunes, the partnership is strongly reminiscent of the Tin Pan Alley and Brill Building songwriting teams of previous decades, owing to the fact that they wrote their respective parts completely separately. John began employing a backup band in the early 1970s (most often drummer Nigel Olsson, bassist Dee Murray, and guitarist Davey Johnstone) and the idea of the singer-songwriter as front man became the model for many others later

With music ranging from folk to avant-garde rock to jazz, Joni Mitchell (pictured here in a 1974 concert) is probably the most musically eclectic and experimental singer-songwriter of the decade. She combined her own strong songwriting skills with a unique style of acoustic guitar performance and several very talented backup bands.

in the decade. Elton John's move into rock prepared the way for the next batch of harder-rocking singer-songwriters, including Billy Joel, Bob Seger, and Bruce Springsteen (discussed in Chapter 10).

Canadian Voices: Joni Mitchell and Neil Young. Joni Mitchell's music in the 1960s was very much indebted to the folk revival, and like Paul Simon, she began experimenting with the use of jazz in the 1970s. Mitchell first climbed the pop charts as a songwriter when Judy Collins recorded "Both Sides Now" (p8 uk14, 1968). Mitchell's albums, including *Ladies of the Canyon* (p27 uk8, 1970) and *Blue* (p15 uk3, 1972) did not achieve popularity to match their critical success. Her music developed further into the mid-1970s, as she made a practice of using very talented and sometimes well-known musicians to back her. *Court and Spark* (p2 uk14, 1974), which contained the single "Help Me" (p7), was her biggest commercial success and featured the playing of Tom Scott's LA Express. A year later she experimented with new, sometimes avant-garde stylistic territory with *The Hissing of Summer Lawns* (p4 uk14, 1975), and later explored esoteric jazz with *Mingus* (p17 uk24, 1979). Mitchell was probably the most musically eclectic and experimental singer-songwriter of the decade, and her influence extended directly into the Lilith Fair movement of the 1990s (discussed in Chapter 13).

Also with roots in the 1960s, Neil Young enjoyed success as a member of Buffalo Springfield, and in his on-again, off-again relationship with Crosby, Stills, and Nash. As a solo artist, Young placed a string of albums high on the charts. He began the 1970s with *After the Gold Rush* (p8 uk7, 1970), containing "Southern Man," a song that directly confronted slavery and the question of reparations. The track never charted, but received enough airplay that Lynyrd Skynyrd felt they had to answer it in the lyrics to "Sweet Home Alabama" (the entire second verse responds to Young's sharp criticism of racism in the South). Young enjoyed his greatest commercial and critical success with *Harvest* (p1 uk1, 1972), which featured the hit "Heart of Gold" (p1 uk10). Performing in a style in which voices are often pretty and controlled, Young's singing voice is frequently thin, somewhat out of tune, and seemingly unsure. But like Bob Dylan, Young showed that in the rock context imperfect vocal qualities could be deeply expressive and evocative.

COUNTRY ROCK

The Gift to Be Simple. Like the singer-songwriter movement, the country-rock style that emerged in the early 1970s was in many ways the result of a reaction against the growing excesses of psychedelic rock. The impulse that made rock listeners interested in blues or folk also attracted many rockers to country music. The apparent simplicity of country music seemed more honest and authentic to the American experience than most pop music. As we saw in Chapter 1, this was partly because the genre projected a perception that it was down-home music. Nashville and Bakersfield, California, became destinations for many rock musicians to connect with the country side of the music business. The Byrds were among the first rockers to record in Nashville in the new country rock style. By 1968, most of the original Byrds had left the band and Roger McGuinn brought guitarist Gram Parsons on board. Parsons knew the country style well, and this is evident in the band's influential *Sweetheart of the Rodeo* (1968). Bob Dylan also headed to Nashville to record *Nashville Skyline* (p3 uk1, 1969) during this period, which contains a duet version of "Girl from the North Country" sung with Johnny Cash.

Now out of the Byrds, David Crosby teamed up with the Buffalo Springfield's Stephen Stills and the Hollies' Graham Nash to record *Crosby Stills and Nash* (p6 uk25, 1969). Their next album, *Déjà Vu* (p1 uk5, 1970), included Neil Young (who had been in Buffalo Springfield with Stills), followed by the live album, *Four Way Street* (p1 uk5, 1971). Crosby, Stills, and Nash (with or without Young) blended the folk rock of the Byrds with touches of jazz, country, and blues. "Suite: Judy Blue Eyes" (p21, 1969) provides a good example of the band's blend of acoustic and electric instruments, close vocal harmony, and catchy pop songwriting. The family narrative of "Teach Your Children" (p16, 1970) (in addition to a prominent pedal steel guitar performed by Jerry Garcia) also shows strong connections to country music.

While working with Dylan in upstate New York, the Band recorded its first album, *Music from Big Pink* (p30, 1968). Led by drummer Levon Helm and guitarist Robbie Robertson, this group of mostly Canadian musicians had a deep love for the music of the American South, including country music. A series of successful albums, including *The Band* (p9 uk25, 1970), *Cahoots* (p21, 1971), and *Rock of Ages* (p6, 1972), established them among American listeners. Their first single was "The Weight" (uk21, 1968), a great example of a song that went largely unnoticed in the U.S. at the time of release, but has since become a fixture in the standard rock repertoire. The group's next release, "Up on Cripple Creek" (p25, 1970), had as its B-side "The Night They Drove Old Dixie Down." "Dixie" chronicles the fall of the South during the Civil War and draws on both folk and country styles.

Poor Boys Make Good: Creedence Clearwater Revival. Most listeners in the late 1960s were surprised to learn that the band made up of brothers John and Tom

Fogerty on guitar, Stu Cook on bass, and Doug Clifford on drums were from the San Francisco Bay area. Their music was an eclectic blend: stylistically they had a country sound, John Fogerty sang like a rhythm and blues vocalist, and they came from the home of psychedelia. Recording for the small Fantasy label, Creedence Clearwater Revival (CCR) placed a long string of singles on the charts, beginning with "Suzie Q" (p11, 1968), and extended their success to Britain with "Proud Mary" (p2 uk8, 1969) and "Bad Moon Rising" (p2 uk1, 1969). John Fogerty wrote most of the band's music, delivering commercially successful albums like *Green River* (p1 uk20, 1969), *Willy and the Poor Boys* (p3 uk10, 1970), and *Cosmo's Factory* (p1 uk1, 1970). The hippie component was not entirely missing from CCR's music. *Willy and the Poor Boys* showed the influence of *Sgt. Pepper*, as the members of CCR became the jug band pictured on the cover and named in the title. From the first track, "Down on the Corner," to "Poor Boy Shuffle" and "Fortunate Son," the tracks seem to be generated from the central "concept" of the album. Yet, much like the Canadian members of the Band, the southern themes of this music aligned CCR most closely with country rock.

The Avocado Mafia. By the early 1970s, Los Angeles, Woodstock, and San Francisco became centers for country rock in the United States. In southern California, the Eagles were the leading band working in this style. Guitarist Glenn Frey and drummer Don Henley got to know one another while playing in the touring band for singer Linda Ronstadt. After recording Ronstadt's *Silk Purse* (1970), Frey and Henley were hired as backup players. Soon bassist Randy Meisner joined the band, and for one gig at least, guitarist Bernie Leadon joined the Ronstadt show. The foursome quickly decided to strike out on their own, leaving Ronstadt and recording their debut album—ironically in London and not sunny California—under the production of Glyn Johns. This album, called *Eagles* (p22, 1972), was followed by a country-rock concept album about the Old West called *Desperado* (p41, 1973). Guitarist Don Felder joined the group after the second album, and they subsequently released *On the Border* (p17 uk28, 1974) and *One of These Nights* (p1 uk8, 1975). Beginning with "Take It Easy" (p12, 1972), the band placed eight singles in the American Top 40 by 1975, including "Best of My Love" (p1, 1974) and "One of These Nights" (p1, 1975). By mid-decade, Leadon was replaced by ex–James Gang guitarist Joe Walsh, and the band moved away from its country rock sound to become even bigger stars.

The Eagles' "Take It Easy." The Eagles brought together many elements of previous rock styles, and their first hit "Take It Easy" is a good example of the group's country-rock approach. The first seventeen seconds of the tune tell the listener a lot about where the band is coming from musically. Opening with big, brilliant electric guitar chords reminiscent of folk rock, another electric guitar soon enters with a lick that is meant to imitate the sound of the steel guitar, characteristic of country music. As the song continues and the lead vocal enters, Glenn Frey sings with a southern accent. When the backup vocals enter, they show a marked Beatles and Beach Boys influence (notice how the harmonies are set high in the male voice register). In the second verse, a high harmony is added to make it a duet, much in the style of the Everly Brothers. The guitar continues to emulate a steel guitar during the solo, and banjo is added in the accompaniment to reinforce the country connection. In the third verse, a new vocal part is added above the lead vocal to create interest and keep the arrangement fresh. In the coda the banjo comes to the front of the mix, and the band showcases their harmony vocals. The song is in simple verse form—there is no clear chorus or bridge—but the verse structure is more complicated than is usual for a simple verse form. In this case, it consists of three 8-bar sections to total 24 bars. Notice that only the first two 8-bar sections are used in the instrumental verse.

This chapter has followed the development of several rock styles of the first half of the 1970s, tracing their roots in the psychedelic era. Surveying the music of the first half of the 1970s, it is clear that aspects of psychedelia became the impetus for the formation of new styles. Country rock focused on the integration of country music into rock, for instance, while progressive rock refined the use of classical music, and jazz rock experimented with infusing jazz into the rock tradition. The close connections found in rock music between 1966 and 1976 might raise ques-

Sound Check

Artist	Led Zeppelin	The Allman Brothers Band	Santana
Title	Whole Lotta Love	Whipping Post	Evil Ways
Chart peak	p4 1969	1969	p9 1970
Form	Compound AABA	Contrasting verse-chorus	Simple verse
Rhythm	4/4	12/8 (11/8)	4/4
Instrumentation	Electric guitar Bass Drums Lead vocal Background vocal	Electric guitar Bass Two drum kits Lead vocals Organ	Electric guitar Bass Drums Lead vocal Background vocal Organ Latin percussion
Comments	Riff-based Psychedelic central section Vocal cadenza	Jazz influence Rhythmic fluctuation Dramatic build to final chorus	Two-chord vamp Emphasis on Latin rhythms Lengthy organ and guitar solos

The Eagles, live at Wembley Stadium, London, July 1975. The whole band is pictured here: (left to right) Randy Meisner (bass), Glenn Frey (electric guitar), Don Henley (drums), Bernie Leadon (banjo), and Don Felder (acoustic guitar). The Eagles were the leaders of the California country-rock scene and placed eight singles in the U.S. Top 40 by 1975.

Yes	Carole King	The Eagles
Roundabout	You've Got a Friend	Take it Easy
p13 1972	1970	p12 1972
Compound AABA	Compound AABA	Simple verse
4/4 (2/4 and 3/4)	4/4	4/4
Electric guitar Acoustic guitar Bass Drums Lead vocal Background vocal Organ Piano Synthesizer Mellotron Aux. percussion	Acoustic guitar Acoustic bass Piano Lead vocal Background vocal Conga String quartet	Electric guitar Bass Drums Lead vocal Background vocal Acoustic guitar Banjo
Extended B section Extended instrumental solos Layered harmony vocals	No drum kit or electric instruments Intimate tone Close vocal harmony	Country mood Active banjo Extended vamp at the end

Listening Guide

The Eagles, "Take It Easy" Asylum 11005

Words and music by Jackson Browne and Glenn Frey, produced by Glyn Johns. Reached #12 on the *Billboard* "Hot 100" chart in the summer of 1972.

FORM: Simple verse form. The verse structure is complicated, with three distinct 8-bar phrases. The middle phrase sounds like it might be a chorus, and the last phrase has a refrain. The song cycles through the verse four times, with the third time (instrumental verse) consisting of only two repetitions of the verse.

TIME SIGNATURE: 4/4.

INSTRUMENTATION: Acoustic and electric guitars, bass, banjo, drums, lead and backup vocals.

0:00–0:17	**Introduction**, 10 mm.	8 bars of big-sounding guitars, then 2 bars with the entire band, setting the country-flavored mood of the song.
0:17–0:58	**Verse 1**, 24 mm. (8 + 8 + 8)	Lead vocal enters, joined by rich vocal harmonies in the second 8-bar phrase. "Well I'm runnin' . . ."
0:58–1:44	**Verse 2**, 26 mm.	2-bar country guitar riff from introduction is followed by the 24-bar verse, performed mostly as in verse 1, with the addition of a second backup vocal part in the first and third 8-bar phrases. "Well I'm standin' . . ."
1:44–2:13	**Instrumental verse**, 16 mm.	Guitar solo based on first two phrases of the verse. Note the addition of banjo to the accompaniment.
2:13–2:55	**Verse 3**, 24 mm.	As before, but with the addition of even more backup vocals. The banjo continues in the background. "Well I'm runnin' . . ."
2:55–3:31	**coda**, 19 mm.	10 Bars of vamp with choral vocals on top and the banjo moving to the front of the mix, then a new 9-bar melody based on the verse that ends with a surprise chord.

tions about the usefulness of these stylistic divisions. It is probably best to view the music discussed in Chapters 7 and 8 as more unified than divided, and to look for connections between stylistic categories. What the music shares is a seemingly necessary reaction to the hippie aesthetic, and until about 1975 there was nothing to deter the idea that rock music would continue to develop the subgenres that emerged under the banner of psychedelia. However, three things happened in the mid-1970s that changed the course of rock history: (1) corporate conglomerates became involved in the music business, (2) the punk movement began to emerge from the underground, and (3) disco music produced to accompany dancing at large-scale clubs became widely popular. These issues will enter our narrative in the next two chapters.

FURTHER READING

Mark Blake, *Comfortably Numb: The Inside Story of Pink Floyd* (Da Capo, 2008).

Hank Bordowitz, *Bad Moon Rising: The Unofficial History of Creedence Clearwater Revival* (Schirmer, 1998).

Marley Brandt, *Southern Rockers: The Roots and Legacy of Southern Rock* (Billboard Books, 1999).

Henry Edwards and Tony Zanetta, *Stardust: The David Bowie Story* (McGraw-Hill, 1986).

John Einarson, *Desperados: The Roots of Country Rock* (Cooper Square Press, 2001).

Susan Fast, *In the Houses of the Holy: Led Zeppelin and the Power of Rock Music* (Oxford University Press, 2001).

Edward Macan, *Rocking the Classics: English Progressive Rock and the Counterculture* (Oxford, 1997).

Dave Marsh, *Before I Get Old: The Story of the Who* (St. Martin's, 1983).

Barry Miles, *Zappa: A Biography* (Grove Press, 2005).

Stuart Nicholson, *Jazz Rock: A History* (Schirmer, 1998).

Philip Norman, *Sir Elton: The Definitive Biography* (Carroll & Graf, 2001).

Keith Richards, *Life* (Little, Brown & Company, 2010).

Marc Shapiro, *The Long Run: The Story of the Eagles* (Omnibus, 1995).

Paul Stump, *The Music's All That Matters: A History of Progressive Rock* (Quartet Books, 1997).

Brian Sweet, *Steely Dan: Reelin' in the Years* (Omnibus, 2000).

Sheila Weller, *Girls Like Us: Carole King, Joni Mitchell, Carly Simon—and the Journey of a Generation* (Washington Square Press, 2008).

Dave Zimmer, *Crosby, Stills, and Nash: The Authorized Biography* (Da Capo, 2000).

VISIT STUDYSPACE AT WWNORTON.COM/STUDYSPACE

Access free review material such as:

- music links
- performer info
- practice quizzes
- outlines
- interactive listening guide software

CHAPTER 9

BLACK POP, REGGAE, AND THE RISE OF DISCO

When rock and roll emerged in the mid-1950s, it was controversial for a number of reasons. One of the ways rock and roll challenged white middle-class values was in its blending of rhythm and blues and country and western. For many in America, the increased emphasis on musical elements clearly drawn from black music elicited the strongest reaction.

Early rock and roll, it is often claimed, acted as a force for breaking down racial and cultural barriers in the 1950s. In the context of rock's early history, it is ironic that by the end of the 1970s fans of mainstream rock were overwhelmingly white, as were most of the musicians and others involved with making, performing, and selling rock. While in marketing terms black pop existed in a separate category from rock, there were many important similarities between the genres. Black pop in the 1970s deserves a much fuller treatment than can be provided here—one that sets this music primarily in the larger context of the African-American pop traditions. We will consider this music in terms of how it relates to the history of rock. In the context of the 1970s, we will also explore how black pop in the 1970s inspired disco.

BLACK POP IN THE 1970S

Sly and the Family Stone: Sly Crosses Over. It is difficult to exaggerate the influence of Sly and the Family Stone on the course of black pop at the end of the 1960s. The changes brought about by Sly's music inspired an entire generation of funk and pop, ranging from groups like the Temptations to the Jackson 5 and the Osmonds. Beginning with "Dance to the Music," which went to number eight on the pop charts (r9, 1968), Sly and the Family Stone topped the charts with a series of crossover hit singles, including number one hits on both the pop and rhythm and

Released in 1970, Marvin Gaye's *What's Going On* signaled an important change in direction for Motown. Departing from the traditional Motown formula, which featured singles over albums, it was a concept album. Gaye's songs are linked together, flowing seamlessly from one to the next, creating the feeling of a larger, complete artistic work. Diverging from the traditional Motown stance against controversy, Gaye focused his lyrics on important social issues like the Vietnam War ("What's Going On" and "What's Happening Brother"), the environment ("Mercy Mercy Me [The Ecology]"), and urban blight ("Inner City Blues [Make Me Wanna Holler]"). While certainly popular and influential in its own time, *What's Going On* is often cited by industry professionals as one of the most important albums ever made.

Listening Guide

Get Music ⑤ wwnorton.com/studyspace

Sly and the Family Stone, "Thank You (Falettinme Be Mice Elf Agin)" Epic 10555

Words and music by Sylvester Stewart, produced by Sly Stone. Hit #1 on the *Billboard* "Hot 100" and "Best Selling Soul Singles" chart in 1970.

FORM: Simple verse-chorus. The entire song is based on the groove laid down in the introduction. Twice in the song the bass drops out to create an instrumental interlude after each chorus, allowing the bass to reenter sounding fresh. After the third verse-chorus pair, a contrasting verse occurs, providing further contrast.

TIME SIGNATURE: 4/4.

INSTRUMENTATION: Electric guitars, bass, drums, horns, and vocals.

0:00–0:18	**Introduction**, 8 mm.	Groove established first with guitar, bass, and high-hat only, with drums and horns entering for second 4 bars.
0:18–0:54	**Verse 1**, 16 mm.	Unison vocals, music continues as in introduction. "Lookin' at the devil . . ."
0:54–1:12	**Chorus**, 8 mm.	Harmony added to vocal part. "Thank you . . ."
1:12–1:21	**Interlude**, 4 mm.	Bass drops out and leaves guitar and drums only.
1:21–1:57	**Verse 2**, 16 mm.	As before, but with horns fading in and out to create a train-whistle effect. "Stiff all in the collar . . ."
1:57–2:15	**Chorus**, 8 mm.	As before, with horn line added. "Thank you . . ."
2:15–2:24	**Interlude**, 4 mm.	As before.
2:24–3:01	**Verse 3**, 16 mm.	As in verse 2, with slightly busier accompaniment filling in the spaces between vocal phrases. "Dance to the music . . ."
3:01–3:19	**Chorus**, 8 mm.	As before, with horns. "Thank you . . ."
3:19–3:37	**Contrasting Verse**, 8 mm.	A new verse is presented over the same music. Note the treble tone of the vocals, which adds timbral contrast. "Flamin' eyes . . ."
3:37–3:55	**Chorus**, 8 mm.	As before, with horns. "Thank you . . ."
3:55–4:13	**Chorus**, 8 mm.	As before, with horns.
4:13–4:32	**Chorus**, 8 mm.	As before and fade-out.

blues charts: "Everyday People" (1969), "Thank You (Falettinme Be Mice Elf Agin)" (1970), and "Family Affair" (1971).

Sly Stone (Sylvester Stewart) was born in Texas but moved to the San Francisco area as a child. During the mid-1960s he was a disc jockey and record producer, working with artists including the Beau Brummels and the Great Society (the band Grace Slick left to join Jefferson Airplane). In 1967, Sly and the Family Stone began playing in the Bay Area and circulating in the San Francisco psychedelic music scene. Bassist Larry Graham, drummer Gregg Errico, and guitarist Freddie Stone laid down a rhythmic backdrop strongly influenced by James Brown's bands, and Sly and his sister Rose Stone Banks provided the catchy vocals and solid keyboard playing (topped off by the trumpet and sax playing of Cynthia Robinson and Jerry Martini). The band stood out not only for its distinctive blend of white and black musical styles, but also because it was one of the few racially and sexually integrated bands of the era. Early Family Stone tracks are optimistic and dance-oriented, such as "Stand" (1969) and "I Want to Take You Higher (1969). "Thank You (Falettinme Be Mice Elf Agin)" is representative of the group's musical approach. The entire song is built over a repeating riff in the bass, which established the song's rhythmic feel or "groove." It is the catchiness of this groove that is central to the song's effectiveness, which can be said for much of the Family Stone's music.

With the 1971 album *There's a Riot Goin' On* (p1 r1 uk31), the band's music began to adopt a more militant stance, at times focusing on controversial racial and political issues. The next album, *Fresh* (1973), which contains the hit single "If You Want Me to Stay" (p12 r3), would prove to be the last major commercial success for the group. By 1973, the overwhelming crossover appeal of the band was already much imitated among black artists. From the beginning, CBS subsidiary Epic Records had marketed the band as if they were a rock act, emphasizing both singles and albums, and creating a hybrid category of "psychedelic soul." This cross between San Francisco hippie culture and heavy funk music helped introduce a new style of African-American pop music that drew upon the crossover success of Motown and southern soul acts during the mid-1960s.

In Sly's Wake: Ohio Players, Kool and the Gang, and Earth, Wind, and Fire. The funk element of the Family Stone's music paved the way for many dance-oriented African-American groups in the early 1970s. Hailing from Dayton, the Ohio Players began as Robert Ward and the Untouchables in 1959. Over the course of the 1960s, the band—subsequently called the Ohio Untouchables and then the Ohio Players—released a series of singles without much commercial success. In 1973, their novelty number, "Funky Worm," hit number one on the rhythm and blues charts and rose as high as number fifteen on the pop charts. The Ohio Players followed up with a string of number one rhythm and blues albums, all of which placed high on the pop charts as well, including *Skin Tight* (p11, 1974), *Fire* (p1, 1975), *Honey* (p2, 1975), and *Contradiction* (p12, 1976). The band is perhaps best known for the singles "Fire" (p1 r1, 1974) and "Love Rollercoaster" (p1 r1, 1975), both of which incorporated funk musical elements, such as heavy riff-bass and sing-along refrains.

Another Sly-influenced band was Kool and the Gang, who started out as the Jazziacs and developed their musical skills in Jersey City, New Jersey. By the late 1960s, the group had turned from jazz to a more commercial sound, enjoying modest success on the soul charts with singles like "Let the Music Take Your Mind" (r19, 1970) and "Funky Man" (r16, 1970). The band emerged as an important crossover act in 1973 with the album *Wild and Peaceful*, which developed the pop funk of Sly Stone and hit number six on the *Billboard* "Soul LPs" chart (p33), while spawning three crossover hit singles, "Funky Stuff" (p29 r5), "Jungle Boogie" (p4 r2), and "Hollywood Swinging" (p6 r1). Both the Ohio Players and Kool and the Gang built on Sly's blending of funky rhythms with catchy vocal hooks. While the Ohio Players' popularity peaked in 1975 with "Love Rollercoaster," Kool and the Gang would enjoy even greater success after disco became popular, hitting with "Ladies'

Kool and the Gang, shown here in live performance. The group first achieved popularity as a funk band strongly influenced by Sly and the Family Stone. As the '70s wore on, however, their sound became smoother and they became major players in disco, scoring hits with "Ladies' Night" and "Celebration."

Night" (p8 r1 uk9, 1979) and "Celebration" (p1 r1 uk7, 1980), two songs that have since become popular staples of the party-band repertoire.

Maurice White was a studio drummer at Chess Records during the mid-1960s, and he performed on recordings by many Chess artists. In 1966, White joined the Ramsey Lewis Trio, a group that had formerly been a fixture of the Chicago jazz scene, but had begun exploring more pop-oriented instrumental tracks, including "Wade in the Water" (1966). In 1969, White moved to Los Angeles and formed Earth, Wind, and Fire, soon adding lead singer Philip Bailey to the lineup. Operating with a large, shifting cast of top performers during the 1970s, Earth, Wind, and Fire scored a series of crossover hits with catchy pop hooks and sophisticated horn arrangements. "Shining Star" (p1 r1, 1975) is a prime example of the band's approach. The tune begins with a hard-driving funk groove in the style of Sly and the Family Stone, setting up vocals that alternate sophisticated vocal harmonies with gritty solo singing, all complemented by rhythmic horn shots and held down by a catchy chorus.

The Rock Connection: Tower of Power and War. The Oakland-based band Tower of Power were also part of the Bay Area hippie scene, counting among their first important supporters Fillmore concert promoter Bill Graham and record producer David Rubinson. A band comprising white, Latino, and black musicians, Tower of Power was celebrated for their hard-driving funk grooves and the high caliber of their horn section, which often performed on other artists' records, including Elton John, the Rolling Stones, and Rod Stewart. Recording for Warner Brothers, the band had a series of moderately successful albums during the first half of the 1970s, including *Bump City* (r16, 1972), *Tower of Power* (r11, 1973), and *Back to Oakland* (r13, 1974), almost always finding more success on the soul charts than they did in the pop market.

Another notable rock connection in 1970s black pop came via Eric Burdon, who was lead singer for the Animals. While Burdon was a major player in the British invasion, the members of War were based in the Los Angeles rhythm and blues circuit during the 1960s. As the Nightriders, they had been hired to back up Deacon Jones, a famous football player who made a failed attempt to build a new career in music. While backing Jones, the band was spotted by Burdon, Danish harmonica player Lee Oskar, and producer Jerry Goldstein. With Burdon and Oskar, War recorded *Eric Burdon Declares War*, which hit number eighteen on the pop album charts in 1970 and contained the number three pop single "Spill the Wine" (1970). Burdon soon left the group, although this did nothing to weaken their popularity. War's *All Day Music* (p16 r6, 1971) began a string of highly successful albums and singles for the group, who often blended Latin styles with their rhythm and blues roots. *The World Is a Ghetto* (p1 r1, 1973) was the band's most commercially successful album, containing the crossover hit singles "The World Is a Ghetto" (p7 r3, 1972) and "Cisco Kid" (p2 r5, 1973). War's 1975 single "Low Rider" (p7 r1 uk12) is probably their most enduring track, and has come to symbolize the large, often-customized automobiles of the mid-1970s.

Motown in the 1970s.

Motown was quick to absorb the changes in black pop that characterized the late 1960s. According to the Temptations' Otis Williams, "Cloud Nine" (p6 r2 uk15, 1968) was recorded as a direct response to the Family Stone's "Dance to the Music." The Temptations had recently suffered the departure of lead singer David Ruffin, who was replaced by Dennis Edwards in the summer of 1968. Now sharing the songwriting duties with Motown veteran Barrett Strong, Norman Whitfield's production style created a more aggressive, groove-oriented, and psychedelic sound for the Temptations. This new stylistic turn would prove even more successful with "I Can't Get Next to You," which hit the number one slot on both the *Billboard* "Hot 100" and the recently renamed "Best Selling Soul Singles" chart during the summer of 1969 (uk13). A string of funk-oriented hits continued with "Psychedelic Shack" (p7 r2 uk33, 1970) and "Ball of Confusion" (p3 r2 uk7, 1970) were followed by the gentle lyricism of "Just My Imagination (Running Away with Me)," which topped both the pop and R&B charts in the spring of 1971 (uk8). In the context of psychedelic soul, the throwback style of "Just My Imagination" shows how much Motown's sonic palette had grown since the mid-1960s. Whitfield and the Temptations addressed more serious social issues with "Papa Was a Rolling Stone" (p1 r5 uk14, 1972). A dramatic and atmospheric track focusing on problems within black urban life, it features a haunting string arrangement by Motown arranger Paul Riser and ranks as Whitfield's finest achievement as a producer. Like the Family Stone's "Thank You," "Papa Was a Rolling Stone" is built over a single repeated bass line, extending to almost seven minutes.

As a new Motown group in the 1970s, the Commodores were among the most commercially successful black pop bands of the decade. The group started in 1968 as a party band in Tuskegee, Alabama, where the members met as freshmen at the prestigious Tuskegee Institute. In 1971, the band was signed to Motown and opened for the Jackson 5 (see below), who were at the peak of their popularity. The Commodores' earliest roots in funk can be heard in tracks such as "Brick House" (p5 r4 uk32, 1977), but it was the band's ballads, written by singer Lionel Richie, that yielded the greatest commercial success. "Easy" (p4 r1 uk9, 1977) and "Three Times a Lady" (p1 r1 uk1, 1978) illustrate the Commodores' smooth, pop-ballad style, featuring Ritchie's polished lead vocals and refined and tasteful horn arrangements.

Listening Guide

Get Music Ⓢ **wwnorton.com/studyspace**

The Temptations, "Papa Was a Rolling Stone" Gordy 7121F

Words and music by Norman Whitfield and Barrett Strong, produced by Norman Whitfield. Hit #1 on the *Billboard* "Hot 100" chart in 1972, and #5 on the "Best Selling Soul Singles" chart (uk14).

FORM: Simple verse-chorus. Like Sly Stone's "Thank You (Falettinme Be Mice Elf Agin)," the entire song is built over the same repeating bass line. Perhaps the most striking feature of this track is its drama and scope, running to almost seven minutes, employing orchestral strings, harp, and jazz trumpet to establish a menacing atmosphere.

TIME SIGNATURE: 4/4.

INSTRUMENTATION: Electric guitars (one with wah-wah), electric piano, bass, drums, hand claps, trumpet, orchestral strings, harp.

0:00–1:57	**Introduction**, 60 mm.	Lengthy and atmospheric introduction, beginning with bass and high-hat, but then adding orchestral strings, wah-wah guitar, jazzy trumpet improvisation, hand claps, and harp.
1:57–2:28	**Verse 1**, 16 mm.	Lead vocal enters, counterpointed by bluesy guitar lines and wah-wah guitar. "It was the third . . ."
2:28–3:00	**Chorus**, 16 mm.	Choral vocals share melody with lead vocal. Note the double-time hand claps that begin with the second 8-bar phrase. "Papa was a rolling stone . . ."
3:00–3:31	**Interlude**, 16 mm.	Jazzy trumpet and wah-wah guitar return, along with orchestral strings.
3:31–4:03	**Verse 2**, 16 mm.	Melody now traded between singers, "Hey mama . . ."
4:03–4:35	**Chorus**, 16 mm.	As before, but hand claps begin immediately, doubled by the wah-wah guitar. "Papa was a rolling stone . . ."
4:35–4:59	**Interlude**, 12 mm.	Trumpet returns, now with pronounced echo effect and supported by electric piano, bass, and drums, and wah-wah guitar.
4:59–5:30	**Verse 3**, 16 mm.	This verse mostly features the high tenor voice of Damon Harris. "Hey mama . . ."
5:30–6:02	**Chorus**, 16 mm.	As before, but without hand claps. "Papa was a rolling stone . . ."
6:02–6:18	**Chorus**, 8 mm.	Hand claps kick in with partial repeat of the chorus.
6:18–6:52	**Coda**, 16 mm.	Strings enter as vocals fade and double-time hand claps continue, then track fades out.

The Jackson 5 performing on television (Michael is holding the microphone in the foreground). While Marvin Gaye and Stevie Wonder were demanding control over their music, the Jackson 5 developed in the traditional Motown mold: Berry Gordy controlled most aspects of their sound, style, and look. The group's tight arrangements and short, catchy songs, combined with Michael Jackson's powerful voice and charismatic performances, made the brothers enormously successful worldwide.

By the early 1970s, Motown was mostly run from Los Angeles, since Berry Gordy had left Detroit to pursue a broader range of possibilities for his company in southern California. While many consider the 1960s to be the "golden age" of Motown, Gordy's label continued to record an impressive roster of successful artists. For example, Diana Ross continued her hit making as a solo artist, though no longer at quite the level she had achieved with the Supremes. Ross also made the move into film after Motown moved to Los Angeles, receiving an Oscar nomination for her portrayal of jazz singer Billie Holiday in the 1972 film *Lady Sings the Blues.*

Many still-successful Motown artists from the mid-1960s appealed to an older generation, and the label expanded its presence in the teen market during the early 1970s with a group of brothers from Gary, Indiana. The Jackson 5, featuring the high prepubescent vocals of younger brother Michael, scored a string of top bubblegum hits, starting with "I Want You Back" (p1 r1 uk2, 1969) and continuing with "ABC" (p1 r1 uk8, 1970), "The Love You Save" (p1 r1 uk7, 1970), and "I'll Be There" (p1 r1 uk4, 1970)—all of which hit number one on both the pop and rhythm and blues singles charts. The funk-oriented dance music of the Jackson 5, and the group's Technicolor psychedelic wardrobe, showed how Motown reacted to the crossover success of Sly and the Family Stone. The Jackson 5 as a group, and Michael as a solo artist, placed over a dozen more hits on the charts before leaving Motown for Epic in the mid-1970s. In the second half of the decade, the Jacksons (as they were now called, since Gordy owned the Jackson 5 name), continued to enjoy success, and Michael began a solo career that made him one of the most successful artists in the history of popular music.

Motown Matures: Stevie and Marvin. As Berry Gordy was setting up shop on the West Coast during the early 1970s, two Motown artists in particular were allotted freedom to work outside of the traditional system. One of the most successful African-American male vocalists of the 1960s who had married into the Gordy family, Marvin Gaye experimented as a songwriter and producer by helping to create music for the Originals, whose "Baby, I'm for Real" and "The Bells" achieved notable popularity. With his 1971 album *What's Going On*, Gaye produced one of the first concept albums in black pop, reflecting yet another link with rock-music practice while remaining faithful to his Motown roots. Containing the crossover hit singles "What's Goin' On" (p2 r1), "Mercy Mercy Me (The Ecology)" (p4 r1), and "Inner City Blues (Make Me Wanna Holler)" (p9 r1), Gaye's album confronted problems of black urban life, issues of environmentalism in modern society, and questioned the U.S. presence in Vietnam. In the wake of his success with *What's Going On*, Marvin Gaye continued to be a fixture of black pop with his albums *Let's Get It On* (p2 r1, 1973) and hits such as "Trouble Man" (p7 r4, 1972) and "Got to Give It Up, Pt. 1" (p1 r1 uk7, 1977).

After his twenty-first birthday in early 1971, Stevie Wonder was also given complete artistic control over his records and produced a series of albums that each cohered in a similar manner to album-oriented rock. Unlike any other Motown artist of the time, Wonder often wrote, produced, and played many of the instruments on his albums. While Wonder was a leading force in African-American dance music and balladry, his experiments with new sounds and timbres (including extensive use of the synthesizer) and studio techniques were highly indebted to rock. Blending cutting edge aspects of rock and rhythm and blues, his complex arrangements, inventive musical material, intense vocal style, and topical lyrics were among the most original of the decade.

Wonder's albums showed the effects of his self-produced approach beginning with *Music of My Mind* (p21 r6, 1972) and *Talking Book* (p3 r1 uk16, 1972). Throughout the remainder of the decade he continued to release chart-topping albums which explored a variety of musical styles and ambitious approaches, including on *Innervisions* (p4 r1 uk8, 1973), *Fulfillingness' First Finale* (p1 r1 uk5, 1974), *Songs in the Key of Life* (p1 r1 uk2, 1976), and *Journey through the Secret Life of Plants* (p4 r4 uk8, 1979). "Living for the City" (p8 r1 uk15, 1973), from *Innervisions*, demonstrates these traits in Wonder's music. The track tells the tale of a poor, black country youth whose family scrimps and saves to send him to the city to seek his fortune. He is duped into carrying drugs and summarily convicted and jailed. In the last verse, Wonder's gravelly voice testifies to the suffering undergone by this young man and his family. The full version of the track (there is a shorter radio edit) provides a spoken vignette over Wonder's synthesizer accompaniment, telling of the

Stevie Wonder, one of Motown's most successful artists, in performance. In the 1960s Wonder was a staple of Motown's lineup of pop stars. He broke with Motown tradition in the 1970s and took total control of his music—writing, producing, and playing a variety of instruments. Wonder combined the driving, danceable funk of Sly and the Family Stone with Marvin Gaye's social consciousness to create albums of lasting influence, including *Music of My Mind* (1972), *Talking Book* (1972), and *Songs in the Key of Life* (1976).

youth's arrival, duping, arrest, and conviction. The song's tone is not confrontational, and seems to indict society at large rather than pit black society against the white power structure. It is easy to see in this track a general thematic kinship with "Papa Was a Rolling Stone," *What's Going On*, and *There's a Riot Goin' On*. In its extended length (over seven minutes) and with its harmonic and melodic sophistication, "Living for the City" even shows a connection to progressive rock. The relationship of Wonder's music to white rock in the 1970s was strong: he received a significant amount of rock-radio airplay, reviews of his work appeared in rock magazines, and his records sold well among rock-oriented listeners.

Listening Guide

Stevie Wonder, "Living for the City" Tamla 326L

Words and music by Stevie Wonder, produced by Stevie Wonder. An edited single version (Tamla 54343F) rose to #1 on the *Billboard* "Hot Soul Singles" chart and #8 on the "Hot 100" in 1973 (uk15).

FORM: Modified compound AABA. The A sections are made up of two verses and one instrumental bridge each. The verse contains the "Livin' just enough for the city" refrain, while the instrumental bridges make clear references to classical music through their use of more complicated harmony, melody, and rhythm. The B section is not really a musical section, but rather a mini-drama that has some musical accompaniment. The compound AABA form is modified in the use of a third A section before the B section (though this A section is itself a modified version). The repetitions of the bridge section at the end of the track help create a strong sense of ending and are not exceptional in such larger forms. The closest formal comparison among the pieces we have studied would be "Roundabout" by Yes.

TIME SIGNATURE: 4/4 in the 12-bar verses, with a 9-bar section made up of 6 bars of 3/4, one of 2/4, and then 2 bars of 4/4 used in the instrumental bridges.

INSTRUMENTATION: The rhythm section is made up of synthesizer bass, electric piano, hand claps, and drums. Wonder's lead vocal is featured with sparing use of backup vocals, and multiple synthesizers are employed to lend a symphonic quality to the track. All instruments on this track are played by Wonder.

	0:00–0:11	**Introduction**, 4 mm.	Electric piano and synthesizer bass establish the song's basic chord progression.
A	0:11–0:40	**Verse 1**, 12 mm.	Lead vocals added, along with bass drum. "A boy is born . . ."
	0:40–1:09	**Verse 2**, 12 mm.	Drumbeat kicks in. "His father works . . ."
	1:09–1:26	**Bridge**, 9 mm.	Synthesizers enter, playing a classical-sounding passage with lead vocal on the syllable "la." Time signature changes to 3/4, with the final bar in 2/4 before returning to 4/4.
A	1:26–1:56	**Verse 3**, 12 mm.	As before, though the vocal may now be a little more urgent. "His sister's black . . ."

The Philadelphia Sound: Gamble and Huff. The concept of the independent record producer, who worked as a creative intermediary between artists and record companies, was important in black pop as early as the late 1950s. During the second half of the 1960s, Kenny Gamble and Leon Huff were independent producers in Philadelphia, writing songs and producing records for the rhythm and blues market. They released some of these records themselves, such as the Intruders' "(We'll Be) United" (r14, 1966), which appeared on the Gamble label. Other records were released through major labels, including Archie Bell's "I Can't Stop Dancin'" (p9 r5, 1968) and Wilson Pickett's "Don't Let the Green Grass Fool You" (p17 r2,

Get Music Ⓢ **wwnorton.com/studyspace**

	1:56–2:30	**Verse 4**, 14 mm.	As before, with new synthesizer line added. Two extra bars are added to end of verse. "Her brother's smart . . ."
	2:30–2:47	**Bridge**, 9 mm.	As before.
A'	2:47–3:56	**Vamp**, 28 mm.	A vamp drawn from the verse is played as Wonder provides vocal improvisations supported by gospel-flavored backup vocals and hand claps. Synthesizer lines weave in and out, and synthesizer bass gets busier.
	3:56–4:13	**Bridge**, 9 mm.	As before, and then vamp and fade create transition.
B	4:13–5:19	**Central Drama**	"Bus for New York City . . ." with spoken dialogue portraying story of deception, arrest, trial, and prison. The music continues to play underneath, and then breaks down to synthesizer incidental music (with some drumming), and verse music fades back in.
A	5:19–5:47	**Verse 5**, 12 mm.	Lead vocals become bitter and gruff, backup vocals added, as synthesizer lines continue to weave in and out. "His hair is long . . ."
	5:47–6:21	**Verse 6**, 14 mm.	Lead vocals are still gruff, as second vocal part is added and synthesizers play in harmony. Two bars added to end of verse as music seems to break down briefly. "I hope you hear . . ."
	6:21–6:38	**Bridge**, 9 mm.	As before, but now with more elaborate counterpoint in the synthesizer part.
	6:38–6:54	**Bridge**, 9 mm.	Repeat of previous 9 bars.
	6:54–7:24	**Bridge**, 16 mm.	As before, but here extended to create majestic ending. Note that this section is all in 3/4, with no time signature change at the end as in previous statements.

Debuting nationally in 1971, *Soul Train* was a dance-party television show that celebrated black music and culture and provided important performance opportunities for some of the decade's top black pop singers and bands, including soul artists produced by Gamble and Huff and Thom Bell. Like *American Bandstand* had done years earlier, *Soul Train* featured both dancing and in-person performances, all under the magisterial supervision of host Don Cornelius.

1971), both of which appeared on Atlantic. Independents like Atlantic, Motown, and Stax had dominated black music sales during the 1960s, and major labels began to take note of the potential for increased sales in the new "soul" market in the early 1970s. In 1971, CBS reacted to this market potential by providing the money for Gamble and Huff to establish their own label, Philadelphia International, devoted specifically to their records but distributed through the well-established CBS network.

Philadelphia International became quickly known as the home of the "Philadelphia sound," a style that blended lyric vocals and a driving rhythm section with elegant string arrangements. In 1972, the label began a series of hit releases that put them on top of the charts through the end of the decade. Some acts had one or two hit singles, such as Billy Paul, MFSB, the Three Degrees, McFadden and Whitehead, and Lou Rawls. But Gamble and Huff's most consistently successful acts were Harold Melvin and the Blue Notes (featuring Teddy Pendergrass), whose hits were often limited to the rhythm and blues charts, and the O'Jays, whose singles regularly crossed over to the pop charts.

The O'Jays' "Back Stabbers" (p3 r1 uk14, 1972) is a representative example of the Philadelphia sound. After a dramatic solo piano opening, a Latin-flavored groove begins, which is then overlaid with strings and brass. As the O'Jays enter singing the hook-oriented chorus, it is easy to hear the Motown influence of the Temptations or the Four Tops. A happy, up-tempo groove is also central to "Love Train," which hit number one on both the "Hot 100" and soul charts in 1973 (uk9), and may be the best-known Gamble and Huff song. A major part of the success of Gamble and Huff productions was their house band, Mother Father Sister Brother (MFSB). MFSB had a hit of their own when they provided the theme music to *Soul Train*, a television show devoted to black pop hosted by Don Cornelius. This song, "TSOP (The Sound of Philadelphia)," hit number one on both pop and rhythm and blues charts in 1974 (uk22).

Thom Bell, the Spinners, and the Stylistics. Thom Bell was another important purveyor of the Philadelphia sound, producing artists for Gamble and Huff in addition to his own freelance work for other labels. Bell had notable success with the Spinners who had a history in Detroit going back to the late 1950s and had been signed to Motown in the 1960s. Though the group had scored a handful of hits for Motown, including "It's a Shame" (p14 r4 uk20, 1970), they left the company in 1972 and were picked up by Atlantic. With Bell producing them, the group stormed the charts with a string of records that helped to establish the Philadelphia sound, including "I'll Be Around" (p3 r1, 1972), "Could It Be I'm Falling in Love" (p4 r1 uk11, 1972), "They Just Can't Stop It (The Games People Play)" (p5 r1, 1975), and "The Rubberband Man" (p2 r1 uk16, 1976). Bell had similar results with the Stylistics, a Philadelphia group signed to Avco Records. Along with lyricist Linda Creed, Bell wrote many of the Stylistics' hits, including "Betcha by Golly, Wow" (p3 r2 uk13, 1972) and "You Make Me Feel Brand New" (p2 r5 uk2, 1974). With both groups he continued to work in the polished Philadelphia style, emphasizing upbeat themes and elegant string arrangements.

"Blaxploitation": Isaac Hayes and Curtis Mayfield.
Drawing on the increasingly cinematic sound of African-American pop music in the 1970s, a new genre of film (with supporting soundtracks) rose to prominence at the beginning of the 1970s—a genre often called "blaxploitation." Arguably the first of these films was Melvin Van Peebles's 1971 independent feature *Sweet Sweetback's Baadasssss Song*, which offered a rare African-American perspective on urban life. *Sweet Sweetback's* was made entirely outside the usual Hollywood establishment, and the film's unexpected success tipped the major studios off to the realization that there was money to be made in movies that cast strong main characters in tough urban situations. Musically, *Sweet Sweetback's* featured a soundtrack on Stax by Earth, Wind, and Fire, recorded just after the group moved to Los Angeles. Blaxploitation films and soundtracks were closely linked, and many of these films, often stereotyped today as campy black-oriented action films, are now best remembered for their music.

In 1971, *Shaft* became the first widely popular blaxploitation movie, and Isaac Hayes's music for the film earned him an Oscar. Hayes had been part of a team at Stax with David Porter during the 1960s, writing and producing a series of hits for Sam and Dave. After the sale of the company (as discussed in Chapter 6), the opportunity arose for Hayes to record as a solo artist. His first album, *Hot Buttered Soul* (p8 r1, 1969), was the first in a series of seven number one Hayes albums to appear on the soul album charts. Hayes also crossed over to the pop charts with "The Theme from *Shaft*" (p1 r2 uk4, 1971) and the accompanying soundtrack album. His ultra-cool vocal delivery on this track—part spoken and part sung—served as a model for many black artists. The text of the song is concerned with the stereotypical "private dick that's a sex machine to all the chicks," and the accompaniment prominently features the wah-wah effect on the electric guitar. The wah-wah had been a staple in rock music since psychedelic guitarists such as Jimi Hendrix and Eric Clapton popularized the sound in the late 1960s. As early as 1968, "Cloud Nine" introduced the wah-wah as a part of Motown's psychedelic soul, and Family Stone singles such as "Family Affair" relied heavily on this sound. While many examples exist, "The Theme from *Shaft*" has become especially associated with the rhythmic sound of the wah-wah guitar in black pop.

Like Hayes, Curtis Mayfield also had deep roots in 1960s rhythm and blues. Throughout the decade he had been a member of the Chicago-based vocal group, the Impressions, who scored a long series of rhythm and blues hits, including crossovers such as "It's All Right" (p4 r1, 1963), "People Get Ready" (p14 r3, 1965), and

WATTSTAX: "BLACK WOODSTOCK" AND THE LEGENDARY FILM IT INSPIRED

by Rob Bowman

The story of Stax Records is chock full of glorious moments, but perhaps none was as grand or ambitious as the Wattstax concert. It was the crowning moment in the label's post-Atlantic period when, under the leadership of co-owner Al Bell, the company was growing in a number of new directions. Bell had established a West Coast office in Los Angeles headed by Forest Hamilton, the son of jazz drummer Chico Hamilton. Stax West was conceived with a mandate that included the promotion and marketing of existing Stax products, the ferreting out of untapped regional talent and the establishment of Stax within Hollywood's motion-picture and television industries.

According to John KaSandra, one of Stax's West Coast–based artists, Wattstax began in March of 1972 when "I came down [to the L.A. office] with an idea that we'd have a black Woodstock." Seven years earlier, to the chanting of "burn, baby, burn," a sizable section of the predominantly black Watts neighborhood of Los Angeles had been destroyed by fire during the first of the 1960s race riots (referred to as rebellions within the community). The Watts Summer Festival had been established to commemorate the rebellions and raise money for the ailing community. It was Hamilton's idea that Stax should be involved in the 1972 Festival for promotional purposes, and he had not forgotten KaSandra's "black Woodstock" idea.

On August 20, 1972, that notion blossomed into an epic one-day festival at the Los Angeles Coliseum. The day opened with Reverend Jesse Jackson leading the audience in a proclamation of the black litany, "I Am Somebody," followed by Kim Weston singing the black national anthem, "Lift Every Voice and Sing." It closed with Isaac Hayes as Black Moses embodying the strength, beauty, and spirituality of contemporary black culture. In between, virtually every major artist signed to Stax performed, including the Staple Singers, Rufus and Carla Thomas, Albert King, and the Bar-Kays. All the artists played for free, and the Schlitz Beer Company helped underwrite production expenses. The event drew more than 100,000 people, making it one of the largest gathering of African Americans at the time, and undoubtedly one of the pinnacle events in black culture of the early 1970s.

The day itself proved to be unremittingly glorious. The capacity audience paid a dollar apiece (all proceeds went to charities in Watts) to spend seven hours in the warm California sun listening to a stunning array of gospel, blues, jazz, and funk. Stax artists Melvin Van Peebles, KaSandra, Rev. Jackson, Billy

Eckstine, and William Bell handled the MC chores alongside movie stars Fred Williamson and Richard Roundtree.

While Wattstax was clearly an event with large-scale political and sociological overtones, it was also a marketing coup. More than six months after the actual concert, the Stax Organization was still producing and promoting a variety of Wattstax-related products. A double album featuring most of the live performances shipped in early 1973. Several months later, a second double album of Wattstax performances was issued. But by far the most important product to come in the wake of the concert was the documentary film *Wattstax: The Living Word*, which premiered in Los Angeles in February 1973.

Wattstax became much more than a string of great concert performances. Under the guidance of award-winning director Mel Stuart, the film remains one of the finest examples of the use of music—and its visual aspect—as a form of profound social commentary. In addition to the concert material, Stuart, with the aid of assistant director and Stax marketing executive Larry Shaw, shot substantial footage within the Watts community. This material was deftly intercut with a biting monologue by comedian Richard Pryor. The combination helped dramatize certain realities of contemporary African-American life and the crucial role that music played within it.

The film unfolds in a series of brilliantly edited chapters, with songs such as Little Milton's "Walking the Back Streets and Crying," Luther Ingram's "(If Loving You is Wrong) I Don't Want to Be Right," and Albert King's "I'll Play the Blues for You"

setting the stage for impromptu meditations on themes such as religion, the blues, black pride, love, and race relations. Reinforced visually and verbally by the community footage and various "man-on-the-street" interviews, each song seems to capture a different aspect of the Watts neighborhood and, more generally, of the African-American

experience. Pryor's hilarious Greek chorus–like monologues further cement these connections, creating a tapestry that is—like the festival that inspired it—both multilayered and incredibly rich.

Rob Bowman (York University, Toronto) is the author of Soulsville, U.S.A.: The Story of Stax Records.

Virtually all of the major artists on Stax Records performed at the Wattstax Festival, including the Staple Singers (bottom) and Issac Hayes (top). Hayes, composer of the soundtrack to the wildly successful film *Shaft*, closed the show in front of approximately 100,000 screaming fans.

Curtis Mayfield performing on television. Although Mayfield started his career as a songwriter and singer for the rhythm and blues group the Impressions, he struck out on his own at the beginning of the 1970s, forging a successful solo career. Much of Mayfield's music tackled social issues with an optimistic outlook. His soundtrack to the 1972 film *Superfly* contained some of Mayfield's biggest hits, including "Superfly" and "Freddie's Dead."

"We're a Winner" (p14 r1, 1968). Inspired by Hayes's success with *Shaft*, Mayfield enthusiastically accepted the challenge of writing music for the 1972 film *Superfly*. His high tenor voice soars above the rhythmic wah-wah guitar and elegant strings on "Freddie's Dead" (p4 r2, 1972), showing the influence of Hayes and Stone alongside the smooth production values of Philadelphia and Motown. Mayfield followed with the title track "Superfly" (p8 r5, 1972), a song that reveals his funk influences. To white audiences of the early 1970s, Mayfield was a voice for the problems of black urban life. He performed frequently on prime time network television shows and became a cultural ambassador to the white community.

JAMES BROWN, GEORGE CLINTON, AND PARLIAMENT/FUNKADELIC

Soul Brother Number 1. In the first half of the 1970s, funk was closely associated with black culture in the minds of both black and white listeners. Much of the success of funk before the 1970s can be attributed to the work of James Brown. As discussed in Chapter 6, Brown's career began in the 1950s and by the mid-1960s, his groove-oriented soul made him one of the most important figures in black pop. Brown's success in both the mainstream and soul markets continued into the first half of the 1970s, with hits such as "Get Up (I Feel Like Being a) Sex Machine (Part 1)" (p15 r2, 1970), "Super Bad" (p13 r1, 1970), and "Hot Pants" (p15 r1, 1971). After the 1968 assassination of Martin Luther King, Jr., Brown became an important voice within the black community, encouraging black pride. Although it became an anthem of Black Power, the 1968 song "Say It Loud, I'm Black and I'm Proud" was a top ten hit on the pop charts. Brown also made statements against drug abuse with songs like "King Heroin" (p40 r6, 1972) and "Public Enemy #1" (a B-side from 1972), both of which contain strong antidrug messages and are delivered more like sermons than songs. Many of his 1970s tracks put more emphasis on the rhythmic interlocking of guitar, bass, and drums than his '60s records had, although horns still played an important role in these later tracks. Brown's music influenced and served as a model for many of the acts discussed already in this chapter. Sly Stone, Stevie Wonder, and Norman Whitfield all drew on Brown's characteristic emphasis on the rhythmic groove and tight ensemble playing as well as his flamboyant approach to live performance.

Mothership Connections: George Clinton and Company. Despite James Brown's influence on a wide range of black pop bands and artists, it was an ambitious musician and songwriter from Detroit, George Clinton, who is most closely associated with the extensive development of funk in the 1970s. Beginning in the late 1960s, Clinton combined the approaches of James Brown and Berry Gordy to establish one of the most successful music-business operations in the second half of the 1970s. Originally from New Jersey, Clinton moved to Detroit during the Motown boom of the 1960s. He sang, wrote, and produced songs for a vocal group called the Parliaments, who performed in the manner of the Temptations or Four Tops. Although he worked for a short time as a songwriter at Motown, Clinton

Parliament in concert. George Clinton was strongly influenced by James Brown's high musical standards. In fact, many of Clinton's musicians had come directly from Brown's band, including bassist Bootsy Collins, saxophonist Maceo Parker, and trombonist Fred Wesley. Clinton, however, drew influence for his stage shows from rock bands like KISS (who were also on the Casablanca label). His shows had an otherworldly, comic-book feel, with a spaceship—"the mothership"—landing on stage, ready to take the band away.

Listening Guide

Parliament, "Tear the Roof Off the Sucker (Give Up the Funk)" Casablanca NB 856

Words and music by George Clinton, Bootsy Collins, and Jerome Brailey, produced by George Clinton. Rose to #5 on the *Billboard* "Hot Soul Singles" chart and #15 on the "Hot 100" chart in 1976.

FORM: Modified contrasting verse-chorus. This track employs two choruses rather than a verse and chorus, and each uses music that is different enough for it to be considered contrasting. The form is built up generally through an alternation of these two choruses. The first time through, chorus 2 is expanded, creating an 8-bar interlude. The second time through this interlude itself is expanded by four measures. The third time through presents the most extensive expansion: chorus 1 is repeated once and then chorus 2 occurs seven times. The track ends with a fourth time through chorus 1 and chorus 2, returning them to the texture and length found at the beginning of the tune.

TIME SIGNATURE: 4/4. Note especially how bass and electric guitar weave often complicated rhythmic patterns against the more straightforward patterns in the drums.

INSTRUMENTATION: Drums, bass, and guitar form rhythmic background throughout. Horns employed for emphasis and embellishment, and vocals throughout are sung in a choral, sing-along style. Note the use of synthetic orchestral strings, a keyboard sound more often associated with mainstream rock and disco.

0:00–0:19	**Introduction**, 8 mm.	Low male voice intones "Tear the roof off the mutha . . ." to the accompaniment of the drums, and then to the rest of the band.
0:19–0:37	**Chorus 1**, 8 mm.	Choral, sing-along vocals; note syncopated bass line and sustained keyboard chords. "You've got a real type of thang . . ."

also collaborated with Motown's cross-town rivals Golden World and Revilot, the latter releasing the Parliament's number three rhythm and blues hit "(I Wanna) Testify" in 1967 (p20). Due to a dispute over the name of the group, Clinton began recording with his backing musicians under the name Funkadelic to avoid legal complications. When the legal wrangling ended, Clinton used both group names for contracts with different record companies. Parliament's first record was released on Holland-Dozier-Holland's label Invictus. Funkadelic records were first released on the Detroit-based funk label Westbound then, beginning in 1976, on Warner Brothers. From the beginning, Parliament was considered the more commercial act, while Funkadelic was more avowedly experimental. The first few Funkadelic albums blend heavy psychedelic rock with soul, showing such diverse influences as Jimi Hendrix, Sly Stone, Miles Davis, and James Brown. The group also developed a reputation for dressing outrageously during performances, as well as for wild onstage antics.

Get Music ⑤ wwnorton.com/studyspace

0:37–0:56	**Chorus 2**, 8 mm.	Choral vocals continue, but notice change in bass line and keyboard part, and sparer texture in the rhythm section. "We want the funk . . ."
0:56–1:14	**Interlude**, 8 mm.	This section employs the music from chorus 2. "La la la . . ."
1:14–1:33	**Chorus 1**, 8 mm.	As before, but now with bass voice at the front of the mix. "You've got a real type of thang . . ."
1:33–1:51	**Chorus 2**, 8 mm.	As before. "We want the funk . . ."
1:51–2:09	**Interlude**, 8 mm.	As before. "La la la . . ."
2:09–2:19	**Interlude extension**, 4 mm.	New vocal added over same music, as sustained keyboard chord returns. "We gotta turn this mutha out . . ."
2:19–2:54	**Chorus 1**, 16 mm.	Length is doubled by repetition of 8-bar section, "You've got a real type of thang . . ."
2:54–3:30	**Chorus 2**, 16 mm.	Length is also doubled here, as the texture builds up by adding layers, "We want the funk . . ."
3:30–5:00	**Chorus 2**, 40 mm.	Extension here comprises five times through the 8-bar pattern, beginning by returning to a simpler texture and then building up again, adding the material from the interlude extension. "We want the funk . . ."
5:00–5:18	**Interlude**, 8 mm.	"La la la . . ." Note that chorus 1 melody enters early.
5:18–5:35	**Chorus 1**, 8 mm.	As at the beginning, "You've got a real type of thang . . ."
5:35–5:44	**Chorus 2**, 8 mm.	As at the beginning, with fade-out. "We want the funk . . ."

By 1974, Clinton had convinced Neil Bogart of Casablanca Records to sign Parliament, and the band released *Up for the Down Stroke* (r17, 1974), the first in a series of successful releases for Clinton and crew under the Parliament moniker. The next year, Clinton exposed his political side with the release *Chocolate City* (r18, 1975), which contained a title track that empowered citizens of black ghettoes or "chocolate cities" (focusing on Washington, D.C.) and reminding the white establishment "we're gaining on ya." The band's important breakthrough record was *Mothership Connection* (p13 r4, 1976), which contained the hit "Tear the Roof Off the Sucker (Give Up the Funk)" (p15 r5). For the tour to support this album, Clinton developed an elaborate stage show that featured a spaceship descending onto the stage, from which he would emerge as a character called Dr. Funkenstein. Casablanca was to fund this elaborate show, and considering that Bogart also had KISS on his label, it is no surprise that he supported the idea. *Mothership Connection* brought a surreal quality to Parliament shows and albums, and Clinton liked to emphasize this aspect of the music. He borrowed and adapted considerably from audacious rock acts such as Alice Cooper and Genesis. Subsequent albums such as *The Clones of Dr. Funkenstein* (p20 r3, 1976) and *Funkentelechy vs. the Placebo Syndrome* (p13 r2, 1977) continued to develop the concept-album idea, bringing funk to the masses along with a healthy dose of irony and humor. During the string of successful Parliament albums in the later 1970s, Funkadelic was also releasing albums that enjoyed considerable success on the rhythm and blues charts. *One Nation under a Groove*, for instance, went to number one on the rhythm and blues charts in 1978 and *Uncle Jam Wants You* hit number two in 1979.

Clinton led the songwriting and producing on these records, which used a large stable of musicians that included many who had previously played in James Brown's bands, such as sax player Maceo Parker, trombonist Fred Wesley, and bassist Bootsy Collins. Because of his success with Parliament and Funkadelic after 1975, Clinton was able to negotiate deals for other artists within his "Parliafunkadelicment Thang" collective, and albums were released by Bootsy's Rubber Band (led by bassist Collins), the Horny Horns (the horn section), the Brides of Dr. Funkenstein (female backup singers), and Parlet (more female backup singers), among others. By building on the examples set by Brown and Gordy, George Clinton became one of the most influential figures in black pop during the second half of the 1970s as both a performer and businessperson, and he has remained the prime exponent of funk in the years since.

Average White Band: The Funk Band That Did Get Airplay on White Rock Radio.
Despite the popularity of Parliament and Funkadelic among black listeners and the positions on the pop charts earned by some of their albums, white rock listeners heard very little Parliament or Funkadelic on the radio. Ironically, the funk band that many rock listeners would have known best was a group from Scotland called the Average White Band. Their first American album, *AWB*, hit number one on both the pop and soul charts in fall 1974 (uk6), propelling the single "Pick Up the Pieces" to number one on the pop singles chart (r5 uk6). *Cut the Cake* (p4 r1, 1975) and *Soul Searching* (p9 r2, 1976) also did well and received significant airplay on rock radio. It is some measure of how far apart white and black audiences had grown that many white listeners who enjoyed the Average White Band had little awareness of funk in the first half of the 1970s. This lack of familiarity with funk—

and with black pop generally—would contribute significantly to the furor that later developed in the rock community over the rise of disco.

REGGAE COMES ASHORE

New Orleans and New York. During the 1970s the Jamaican form of popular music called reggae entered the mainstream in the United States and Britain. Reggae had roots in American rock and rhythm and blues, and produced aftershocks in many later pop styles, especially punk and rap. Jamaican music has played at least a peripheral role in mainstream popular music in the United States since the 1940s and 1950s. In Chapter 3, we mentioned the late 1950s craze for calypso music, the popularity of songs such as "Jamaican Farewell," and the fact that the Kingston Trio took its name from a town in Jamaica. As a result of British imperialism, the music of Jamaica also played an important part in the popular culture of the UK, especially after World War II. While many Americans enjoyed Jamaican music during the late 1950s, however, Jamaicans were also listening to American pop. For years, Jamaican radio stations had been quite conservative, based on the model of the BBC. But when portable radios become more affordable, Jamaicans tuned in to American radio stations, especially those broadcasting from New Orleans and Florida. As a consequence, many Jamaicans developed a taste for artists such as Fats Domino and the rolling feel of New Orleans–based rhythm and blues.

The scarcity of American rhythm and blues records on the island led to the appearance of the "sound system man"—an entrepreneur who assembled a powerful sound system on the back of a truck and drove it from town to town, stopping to play records for public gatherings. Competition soon arose among these mobile music promoters, leading some to scratch the labels off their records so that competitors would not know the identity of the artist. It also led sound system men to begin featuring disc jockeys who would talk over records, often inventing rhyming verses to display their cleverness and verbal dexterity.

In the early 1960s, a Jamaican form of popular music called "ska" emerged, which emphasized an upbeat tempo reminiscent of American rhythm and blues and featuring offbeat "skank" rhythm pattern. As the 1960s progressed, ska was replaced by a newer style called "rock steady," which was popular from about 1966 to 1968. Reggae developed out of this second style. The leaders of the reggae movement in the 1970s had backgrounds in Jamaican pop that stretched back into the early 1960s. The most important figure among these musicians was Bob Marley. With Peter Tosh and Bunny Livingston, Marley had been a member of a vocal trio in the 1960s called the Wailers. The Wailers were signed by Jamaican producer Lee "Scratch" Perry, who recorded the group backed by his band, the Upsetters. The Wailers' records did well regionally, and Perry convinced them that they needed to play instruments to be successful. In 1970, Marley and the Wailers released their first recordings in Jamaica.

At about the same time, Chris Blackwell established Island Records in the UK featuring recording artists such as Free, Traffic, and Cat Stevens. In addition to these mainstream artists, Blackwell also released Jamaican records to the British market. The demand for such records was stronger in England than it was in Amer-

ica, largely because there was a large Jamaican population living in the UK, and they were eager to hear music from home. The homesick Jamaicans enjoyed the music, but so did British kids, and the availability of reggae in the UK influenced many English musicians who would later end up in punk and new wave bands. Blackwell signed the Wailers to Island and advanced them enough money to record an album. In the spring of 1973, *Catch a Fire* was released internationally on Island, followed by *Burnin'* at the end of the year. "Get Up, Stand Up" appeared on the second of these records, and exemplifies Bob Marley's approach to reggae. Like much funk-influenced rhythm and blues of the early 1970s, the track is built on a bass and drum groove that remains steady throughout the tune and demonstrates the reggae rhythmic feel that emphasizes the upbeats. While the verse and chorus are built on different bass lines, they are similar, and contrast is provided by the use of group vocals on the chorus and solo vocals during the verses. Showing the development from ska, which was often called "rude boy" music because of its youth-oriented subject matter, the focus in "Get Up, Stand Up" is more topical, as the lyrics advocate political freedom.

While Marley and the Wailers were popular among reggae fans, their music remained mostly underground until the mid-1970s. Two events helped bring a broader audience to reggae after this time. The first was the independent film *The Harder They Come*, which chronicled the rise and fall of a fictional pop singer in Jamaica. Released in the United States in 1973, the movie became a cult hit. A soundtrack album was released by Island and featured tracks by Jimmy Cliff (who had starred in the movie) and other Jamaican artists, including Toots and the Maytals. Reggae also garnered attention with the successful Eric Clapton cover of Marley's "I Shot the Sheriff," which had originally appeared on Marley's *Burnin'*. Clapton's version topped the U.S. pop charts during the summer of 1974 (r33 uk9) and Clapton fans soon sought out Marley's music. About this time, both Tosh and Livingston left the Wailers to pursue solo careers, but Marley's career was the one that really took off. A year later, *Burnin'* surfaced for the first time on the *Billboard* album charts (two years after it was originally released), sparking a wave of hits in

Listening Guide

Get Music ⊕ wwnorton.com/studyspace

Bob Marley and the Wailers, "Get Up, Stand Up"
Island ILPS 9256 [Tuff Gong 422-846 200-4]

Words and music by Bob Marley and Peter Tosh, produced by Chris Blackwell and the Wailers. Contained on *Burnin'*, which was released in 1973.

FORM: Contrasting verse-chorus, with verse and chorus based on similar but distinct bass lines. Choruses and verses alternate regularly with no interludes in between. Like "Papa Was a Rolling Stone" and "Thank You (Falettinme Be Mice Elf Agin)," this track is driven by the bass part and drumbeat, even if it does not use the same bass line all the way through.

TIME SIGNATURE: 4/4. Note how every second measure features a stress on beat 3. This is sometimes referred to as the "one-drop" rhythm.

INSTRUMENTATION: Electric guitar, clavinet (an electric keyboard similar to a harpsichord, but sounding more like an electric guitar), electric piano, bass, drums, percussion, lead and backup vocals.

0:00–0:08	**Introduction**, 4 mm.	After drum lead-in, clavinet, guitar, bass, and drums enter, setting up entrance of the voices.
0:08–0:32	**Chorus**, 16 mm.	Unison, sing-along vocal melody. "Get up, stand up. . ."
0:32–0:57	**Verse 1**, 16 mm.	Lead vocal takes over; note the change in the line played by the bass and guitar. "Preacher man . . ."
0:57–1:21	**Chorus**, 16 mm.	Choral vocals return. Note the percussion in the background. "Get up, stand up . . ."
1:21–1:46	**Verse 2**, 16 mm.	Lead vocal takes over again. Note wah-wah guitar lines in background. "Most people think . . ."
1:46–2:11	**Chorus**, 16 mm.	Choral vocals return, but now Marley improvises over the melody. "Get up, stand up . . ."
2:11–2:35	**Verse 3**, 16 mm.	New lead singer, Peter Tosh, changes the melody somewhat. "We're sick and tired . . ."
2:35–3:00	**Chorus**, 16 mm.	Choral vocals return, and both Marley and Tosh improvise over the melody. "Get up, stand up . . ."
3:00–3:13	**Chorus**, 8 mm.	As before, as song fades out.

the both the pop and soul markets that peaked in the U.S. with *Rastaman Vibration* (p8 rl1 uk15, 1976) and *Exodus* (p20 rl5 uk8, 1977). By the end of the decade, Marley was revered as a musician, cultural hero, and fighter for political and social justice. His albums sold well, especially in the UK, and he played to sold-out audiences around the world. Late in the 1970s, Marley developed cancer and in 1981 he died at the age of thirty-six. After his death, both Tosh and Livingston (as Bunny Wailer) continued their solo careers, and Marley's son Ziggy enjoyed success with his band, the Melody Makers.

As a crossover form of music that grew out of the African diaspora, reggae is similar in many ways to 1970s black pop. Although not a style of black pop in the strict sense, reggae can be seen as a parallel consequence of crossover during the 1950s and 1960s. When 1950s rock and roll and electric blues went out of style in the United States, it continued to develop in the UK, returning to the States—with a distinctive accent—via the Beatles and the Rolling Stones. New Orleans rhythm and blues and 1960s soul had a similar effect in Jamaica, returning to the mainland transformed into reggae.

THE RISE OF DISCO

I Should Be Dancin': A New Dance Craze. In the late 1970s, dance-oriented "disco" music became extremely popular in the United States. Like many forms of music that suddenly achieve mainstream popularity, disco had a long history as an underground style. The popularity of disco, beginning largely in 1977, can be attributed to an interest in enjoying music through physical movement (dancing) rather than cerebrally (stationary listening). By the mid-1970s, rock had become music that was meant primarily for listening. Although people could dance along with much rock music, and many did, dancing was not the driving force behind 1970s rock. In rock clubs and bars, live bands were considered preferable to disc jockeys, who were thought to be budget alternatives to live music. Within black pop, however, dancing was still a central element. Early in the 1970s, dancers visited small clubs that specialized in spinning dance records late into the night. According to many accounts, this practice first began to grow within urban gay communities, especially in New York at small dance clubs like 12 West, The 10th Floor, the Loft, and Paradise Garage. Until it hit the mainstream in 1977, disco was mostly an underground style that occasionally popped up into greater visibility. Among the first hits to arise from the disco subculture were George McCrae's "Rock Your Baby" (p1 r1, 1974) and Van McCoy's "The Hustle" (p1 r1 uk3, 1975). These songs blended a direct dance beat with a catchy pop hook that is repeated frequently. Barry White's Love Unlimited Orchestra also scored with "Love's Theme" (p1 r10 uk10, 1973), which added lush strings to the disco mix. A series of early hits came from Florida's KC and the Sunshine Band, including "That's the Way I Like It" (p1 r1 uk4, 1975). Rock listeners would have known all of these songs, but viewed them as novelty tunes rather than serious threats to the rock world order. Moreover, many disc jockeys created special extended versions of dance songs, which were not available to the record-buying public.

Disco emerged onto the national scene in 1977 with the release of *Saturday Night Fever*, a film starring John Travolta. A gifted dancer, Travolta became the model for the macho disco dancer, establishing a markedly heterosexual context for disco. The soundtrack to *Saturday Night Fever* featured tracks by the Bee Gees that became disco staples: "Stayin' Alive" (p1 r4 uk4, 1978) and "Night Fever"

(p1 r8 uk1, 1978) both topped the pop charts and fueled a craze for disco music. Amid the excitement of Travolta, *Saturday Night Fever*, and the Bee Gees, many hippies cut their hair, put on sleek polyester shirts, and headed out to dance clubs. Suddenly many major artists were turning out disco-flavored tracks: rockers Rod Stewart ("Do You Think I'm Sexy?"), the Rolling Stones ("Miss You"), and even KISS ("I Was Made for Loving You") jumped on the disco bandwagon. Disco versions of well-known songs began popping up, including a popular disco version of the first movement of Beethoven's Fifth Symphony! Extended disco mixes started selling over the counter in significant numbers.

The Return of the Producers. By the mid-1970s, the music industry had given over much of the production authority in rock to the musicians themselves. Bands used producers to help run recording sessions, but often retained a significant amount of say in how the record sounded. The popularity of disco represents a return to the authority of producers. Disco records were made according to the Brill Building or Motown models, with producers and engineers taking a central role in the creative process. Two of the most important producers in commercial disco were Jacques Morali and Giorgio Moroder, who both produced American acts using a European style of disco (often called Eurodisco). Eurodisco differed from the underground dance music of urban clubs in America because it was more rhythmically precise and not as funk-based. Along with the Bee Gees, one of the first disco acts to emerge in the mainstream was the Village People, a group whose music often exemplifies Eurodisco. Assembled by producer Jacques Morali as a kind of "gay Monkees," the group specialized in songs that took a playful slant on life in the gay underground, with references that most listeners missed entirely. The group's 1978 hit "YMCA" (p2 r32 uk16) depicts the YMCA as a place to meet young gay men. Even today, this song is regularly played at sporting events, with crowds getting up and dancing to the chorus, most of them unaware of the song's original context. By contrast, it would be difficult to mistake what Donna Summer was singing about on "Love to Love You Baby" (p2 r3 uk4, 1976). Produced by Munich-based Moroder and Pete Bellotte, Summer moans and groans her way through a seventeen-minute extended mix that underscores the sensual aspects of disco dancing. After disco broke into the mainstream, Summer became one of its biggest stars, hitting the top of the charts with "Hot Stuff" (p1 r3 uk11, 1979) and "Bad Girls" (p1 r1 uk14, 1979), both contained on the album *Bad Girls*, which could be considered a disco concept album. Michael Jackson also took advantage of the disco craze in 1979, releasing the album *Off the Wall*, which contained the hit "Don't Stop 'Til You Get Enough" (p1 r1 uk3). *Off the Wall* began Jackson's collaboration with producer Quincy Jones—a partnership that would enjoy overwhelming success in the 1980s.

Sound Check

Artist	Sly and the Family Stone	The Temptations	Stevie Wonder
Title	Thank You (Falettinme Be Mice Elf Agin)	Papa Was a Rolling Stone	Living for the City
Chart peak	p1, r1 1970	p1, r5 1972	p8, r1 1973
Form	Simple verse-chorus	Simple verse-chorus	Compound AABA (modified)
Rhythm	4/4	4/4	4/4 (3/4, 2/4)
Instrumentation	Bass Drums Group vocal Horns	Electric guitar Bass Drums Lead vocal Background vocal Electric piano Trumpet Harp Strings Handclaps	Synthesized bass Drums Lead vocal Background vocal Electric piano
Comments	Riff-based Slightly altered "contrasting verse" Mostly group vocals	Riff-based Expansive drama and scope Alternation between lead singers and group vocals	All instruments performed by Wonder AABA form augmented by improvised vocal section (A') Central drama (B section) offers a contrast

DISCO AND THE HIPPIES

Disco Sucks? The rise of disco after the release of *Saturday Night Fever* caused a violent reaction within parts of the rock-music community. Perhaps the clearest instance of this can be seen in the anti-disco rally held by Chicago rock DJ Steve Dahl in 1979 before a White Sox baseball game. Dahl arranged to have a large crate of disco records placed in the outfield and ceremoniously blown up. The resulting rioting was so extreme that the scheduled baseball game had to be called off. This hatred of disco was widespread among rock fans, who popularized the slogan "disco sucks." There are many misconceptions about the source of this hostility toward disco. A common fallacy is that rockers were reacting against the origins of disco in the gay community. There may be some truth in this, but remember that most

Parliament	Bob Marley and the Wailers	Donna Summer
Tear the Roof Off the Sucker (Give Up the Funk)	Get Up, Stand Up	Bad Girls
p15, r5 1976	1973	p1, r1 1979
Contrasting verse-chorus (modified)	Contrasting verse-chorus	Contrasting verse-chorus (modified)
4/4	4/4	4/4
Electric guitar Bass Drums Group vocal Horns Synthetic strings	Electric guitar Bass Drums Lead vocal Background vocal Clavinet Electric piano Percussion	Electric guitar Bass Drums Lead vocal Background vocal Piano Horns Percussion
Two separate chorus sections, but no verse Bass and guitar weave complicated patterns against strict drums Choral, sing-along vocals	Riff-based Emphasis throughout on beat three ("one-drop" rhythm) Verse and chorus built on different (but similar) bass lines	Disco beat featuring bass drum on every beat Each verse has two parts Girl-group style background vocal

Listening Guide

Donna Summer, "Bad Girls" Casablanca 988

Words and music by Donna Summer, Eddie Hokenson, Bruce Soldano, and Joe Esposito, produced by Giorgio Moroder and Pete Bellotte. Rose to #1 on both the *Billboard* "Hot 100" and "Best Selling Soul Singles" charts in 1979 (uk14).

FORM: Modified contrasting verse-chorus, but with the chorus preceding the verse. Each statement of the chorus is preceded by an instrumental interlude featuring a melody in the horns. The verses that follow the chorus are split into two 8-bar subsections. Note that again we see a song restart through a return to the introduction, as in "Purple Haze" and "Roundabout."

TIME SIGNATURE: 4/4. Note the strong disco beat provided by emphasizing the regular groove and mixing the bass drum, high-hat, and snare forward throughout.

INSTRUMENTATION: The rhythm section is made up of drums, bass, guitar, and piano, with horns used in the traditional rhythm and blues manner. Summer's lead vocal is supported by female backups, and miscellaneous percussion is used throughout (the whistles are the most noticeable of these).

0:00–0:32	**Introduction**, 16 mm.	Texture builds up gradually, with 8 bars of groove played by guitars and drums only. The next 8 bars add horns, whistles, and "toot, toot."
0:32–0:40	**Interlude**, 4 mm.	Melody presented in the horns.
0:40–0:56	**Chorus**, 8 mm.	Lead vocal with rhythm section only. "Bad girls . . ."
0:56–1:11	**Verse**, pt. 1, 8 mm.	Girl-group style backup vocals are added at the ends of phrases, "See them out on the street . . ."

Donna Summer, shown here in concert in 1979, was one of disco's biggest stars. Her hits "Love to Love You Baby," "Hot Stuff," and "Bad Girls" are disco classics. Summer's music exemplifies the style of Eurodisco.

1:11–1:28	**Verse**, pt. 2, 8 mm.	Horn hits are added in, "You ask yourself . . ."
1:28–1:36	**Interlude**, 4 mm.	Uses horn line from last 4 mm. of introduction.
1:36–1:52	**Chorus**, 8 mm.	This time backup vocals echo Summer, "Bad girls . . ."
1:52–2:08	**Verse**, pt. 1, 8 mm.	As before. "Friday night and the strip is hot . . ."
2:08–2:24	**Verse**, pt. 2, 8 mm.	As before. "Now don't you ask yourself . . ."
2:24–2:32	**Interlude**, 4 mm.	As before.
2:32–2:48	**Chorus**, 8 mm.	Changed to include taunt from backup vocals. Note new guitar line in the background. "Bad girl, such a naughty bad girl . . ."
2:48–3:04	**Verse**, pt. 1, 8 mm.	As before, but guitar continues. "You and me, we're both the same . . ."
3:04–3:19	**Verse**, pt. 2, 8 mm.	Guitar solo emerges from the background to take the melody previously handled by the lead vocals.
3:19–3:59	**Reprise of Introduction**, 20 mm.	Varied and expanded to encompass four 8-bar sections based on introduction material and Summer speaking and singing ("Hey mister . . .") over groove.
3:59–4:14	**Interlude**, 8 mm.	Expanded to 8 bars and emerges directly out of reprised introduction, as "Hey mister . . ." in vocals returns.
4:14–4:54	**Chorus and ending**, 20 mm.	8-bar chorus is followed by 8-bar return to interlude material that immediately preceded it, though the horn melody continues throughout this section. The backup vocals add a 4-bar ending.

rock fans had no idea that disco originated in gay night spots. For most American listeners, disco originated in the very heterosexual context of John Travolta and *Saturday Night Fever*. Moreover, rock fans had traditionally tolerated many different forms of androgyny without a similar reaction, and by the end of the decade many rock musicians happily admitted nonheterosexual orientations. Another specious explanation is that disco was largely music that facilitated meeting members of the opposite sex at bars for quick, one-night stands, and rockers were offended by this blatant promiscuity. Sexual practices may have been different within disco culture, but it is difficult to square such puritanical attitudes with rock and roll since swaggering braggadocio was hardly foreign to rock culture.

In retrospect, there are several more plausible reasons why rock fans hated disco with such a passion. One important explanation requires us to question the ways in which disco was viewed as a threat within the rock community. In many ways, disco stood in direct confrontation to the hippie aesthetic that had been developing in

Taking advantage of many rock fans' hatred for disco, Chicago disc jockey Steve Dahl arranged a Disco Demolition Night between games of a Tigers–White Sox doubleheader. When disco records were blown up on the field, the resulting riot caused the second game to be canceled by the umpires, who declared the field unfit for play.

rock music since the mid-1960s. Disco was not about listening to music but dancing to it. Instead of being concerned with important spiritual or social issues, disco was about fun. And perhaps most important to the musicians involved, disco was not about the specific artists but about the beat in general—which was sometimes provided by a machine. It took the production authority away from the artist and returned it to the producer. In fact, disco threatened the very foundation of the rock subculture since *Sgt. Pepper's Lonely Hearts Club Band* had made rock a more serious-minded, "listening" music. While homophobia and racism may have played a small role in how some rock fans reacted to disco, more often, these fans rejected the anti-hippie aesthetic of disco. In other words, this was a reaction against a genre that catered to the tastes of the mainstream. Thus, the "disco sucks" movement is an early instance of what we will later call "rockism," a belief that some forms of popular music are less important because of a perceived lack of authenticity. Strangely enough, disco was united with the emerging punk movement in its rejection of the hippie aesthetic. Many rock fans, whether they could articulate it precisely or not, sensed that their approach to music was under attack from the widespread popularity of disco and punk. As things turned out, neither disco nor punk displaced rock. Both did have a marked effect on rock, however, and in the next chapter we chart punk's assault on "corporate rock" and, more importantly, on the hippie aesthetic.

FURTHER READING

Lloyd Bradley, *This Is Reggae Music: The Story of Jamaica's Music* (Grove Press, 2000).

Anne Danielsen, *Presence and Pleasure: The Funk Grooves of James Brown and Parliament* (Wesleyan University Press, 2006).

Alice Echols, *Hot Stuff: Disco and the Remaking of American Culture* (W. W. Norton, 2011).

Nelson George, *The Death of Rhythm and Blues* (Penguin, 2004).

John Jackson, *A House on Fire: The Rise and Fall of Philadelphia Soul* (Oxford University Press, 2004).

Arthur Kempton, *Boogaloo: The Quintessence of American Popular Music* (University of Michigan Press, 2005).

Dave Thompson, *Funk* (Backbeat Books, 2001).

Michael Veal, *Dub: Soundscapes and Shattered Songs in Jamaican Reggae* (Wesleyan University Press, 2007).

Rickey Vincent, *Funk: The Music, the Rhythm, and the Power of the One* (St. Martin's Griffin, 1996).

Timothy White, *Catch a Fire: The Life of Bob Marley* (Henry Holt, 2000).

VISIT STUDYSPACE AT WWNORTON.COM/STUDYSPACE

Access free review material such as:

- music links
- performer info
- practice quizzes
- outlines
- interactive listening guide software

CHAPTER 10

The Clash

LONDON
CALLING

MAINSTREAM ROCK, PUNK, AND NEW WAVE

I n many ways, the spirit of psychedelic music continued well into the 1970s. By the middle of the decade, various manifestations of hippie rock had become the status quo. Punk and new wave also began to challenge mainstream rock's commercial domination. Rock music had become big business, and some critics and fans argued that this was beginning to have a negative effect on the musical substance of rock. According to this view, which was based on a growing need for authenticity in rock, musicians were designing their music for the greatest popular appeal rather than as sincere musical expressions.

While the first half of the 1970s was mostly a time of emerging new styles that developed aspects of psychedelic music, the second half can be seen largely as a consolidation of earlier styles. Commercial rock continued to develop in the mainstream, while the punk movement flourished in underground scenes in New York and London, eventually emerging into the mainstream in the form of new wave. Punk and new wave both positioned themselves in opposition to mainstream rock: they rejected the highly produced and sophisticated sounds of hippie bands in favor of simplicity, which they believed had been central to pre-hippie rock. In order to understand what the punks were rebelling against we must explore how the rock music business grew over the course of the 1970s.

MAINSTREAM ROCK: 1975–1980

FM Radio Goes from Late 1960s Free Form to AOR. The radio industry saw tremendous growth in the 1970s. By the beginning of the decade, FM stations were broadcasting rock music and focusing on album cuts, following the model established by Tom Donahue in San Francisco. This format developed into what is now called "album-oriented rock," or AOR. The change was accompanied by a decrease in the freedom of disc jockeys to choose their own music. By the end of the decade,

The cover of the Clash's *London Calling* (1980), illustrates that punk was about rebellion: political, social, and musical. Government and traditional moral values were the focus of punk's political and social attacks, while disco and concert rock were the focus of its musical attacks. *London Calling* was a landmark punk album, and the Clash's first success in the United States. Punk started in the New York underground, and later developed and gathered steam in London. With the success of the Sex Pistols, the Clash, the Buzzcocks, and others, punk soon broke into the mainstream in both the UK and the U.S. The movement culminated in new wave, which many saw as a more radio-friendly version of punk.

most AOR stations were heavily formatted, with program directors or consultants programming the music. By this time, extended tracks and rock symphonies were no longer considered "radio friendly." Moving toward the commercial tendencies of AM, programmers felt that long rock songs did not leave enough time for commercials or prompted listeners to change the station. Musicians and record companies understood that there was an ideal length for an FM radio track (about four to five minutes), and bands that did not conform would have a hard time breaking into the growing AOR market.

Young people were increasingly tuning in to these stations, which translated into growing sources of advertising revenue. Since listeners tuned in for free, commercial radio stations had to look to advertising to provide profits. In general, advertising rates are based on how many people are expected to listen to a station, and radio stations do extensive research to determine listener demographics. As AOR radio grew, this information figured heavily into how much stations could charge their advertisers, and since the kind of music played on the station directly influenced who listened, advertising concerns often affected what music was programmed. When rock radio became increasingly profitable in the mid-1970s, major corporations invested in the music business, buying radio stations. Because the corporations were only interested in the financial bottom line, and programming decisions were made to

Listening Guide

Peter Frampton, "Show Me the Way" (Live) A&M 1795

Words and music by Peter Frampton, produced by Peter Frampton. As a single, the song hit #6 on the *Billboard* "Hot 100" chart in 1976. The song was also released on the album *Frampton Comes Alive!,* which topped the "Top LPs & Tape" chart.

FORM: Contrasting verse-chorus. The verses consist of an 8-bar phrase, its repetition, and a 4-bar phrase that leads to the chorus, and the chorus is based on a contrasting 4-bar phrase that occurs two to four times. Note the false ending at 3:49, probably provided to fool the audience into thinking the song was ending so as to charge back into the chorus by surprise. Since this version is taken from a live recording, timings may differ among CD reissues.

TIME SIGNATURE: 4/4.

INSTRUMENTATION: Acoustic guitar, electric guitar, bass, drums, lead and backup vocals.

0:00–0:33	**Introduction**, 16 mm.	Strummed acoustic guitar opens the song as the band comes in after first 4 bars, first in stop time and then in regular time. Note the use of the voice box on the lead guitar, which makes the guitar seem to speak.
0:33–1:09	**Verse 1**, 20 mm.	Lead vocal enters with two 8-bar phrases, followed by 4 bars that drive toward the chorus. "I wonder how . . ."

maximize profits, there was a growing perception that AOR had abandoned the rebelliousness once central to the rock movement, and it was often called "corporate rock" by its detractors.

Show Me the Way: The Advent of the "Big Album." Corporations that prompted concern among mainstream rock's critics were not restricted to radio. Fueled by the steady growth of hippie culture, the entire record business experienced a transformation during the 1970s. The psychedelic rock culture celebrated at Woodstock in the summer of 1969 had become the hippie rock culture that flourished across the country in the first few years of the 1970s. By the middle of the decade, it became clear that more money could be made in rock music than anybody had ever imagined.

A significant factor in this realization was the emergence of the "big album." Generally, before the mid-1970s most bands and their record labels would be thrilled if an album sold 500,000 copies, achieving what the Record Industry of America (RIAA) called a "Gold" album award. However, as more records began to achieve this level, the RIAA launched a "Platinum" award for sales of a million copies. A good example of a million-selling album from the 1970s is Peter Frampton's live album *Frampton Comes Alive!* (1976). Frampton had been a member of

		Get Music ⑤ **wwnorton.com/studyspace**
1:09–1:30	**Chorus**, 12 mm.	Backup vocals enter to sing two 4-bar phrases, followed by a 4-bar transition drawn from the introduction, again featuring voice-box lead guitar. "I want you . . ."
1:30–2:07	**Verse 2**, 20 mm.	As before, "Well I can see no reason . . ."
2:07–2:29	**Chorus**, 12 mm.	As before, but now the 4-bar phrase is sung three times and then goes right into the guitar solo. "I want you . . ."
2:29–2:58	**Instrumental Verse**, 16 mm.	Twice through the 8-bar phrase, featuring a solo on the voice-box lead guitar.
2:58–3:20	**Verse 3**, 12 mm.	Only once through the 8-bar phrase, then to the 4-bar phrase leading to the chorus. The sung verse is shortened here because we have just heard an instrumental verse and a full sung verse following that might become too repetitive. "I wonder if . . ."
3:20–3:49	**Chorus**, 16 mm.	As before, but four times through the 4-bar phrase. "I want you . . ."
3:49–3:56	**False Ending**, 4 mm.	Song sounds as if it will end, but comes charging back.
3:56–4:18	**Chorus**, 12 mm.	As before, but three times through the 4-bar phrase. "I want you . . ."
4:18–4:32	**Coda**, 5 mm.	Once through the 4-bar progression from the introduction, plus one last bar on the final chord, provide the real ending for the tune.

Shown playing his trusty Les Paul Custom guitar, Peter Frampton enjoyed spectacular commercial success in the mid-1970s. Frampton was the poster boy for the "big album" and "corporate rock." His album *Frampton Comes Alive!* set a benchmark by selling over 13 million copies, while he consistently played to huge, sell-out crowds.

Humble Pie but left to go solo after the *Rockin' the Fillmore* album in 1971. Stylistically, Frampton's music exemplified approachable, middle-of-the-road rock from the period that focused on his guitar solos and melodic songwriting. After releasing four moderately successful solo albums, *Frampton Comes Alive!* was a blockbuster hit, reaching number one on the U.S. album charts (uk6) and producing the singles "Show Me the Way" (p6 uk10), "Baby, I Love Your Way" (p12 uk43), and "Do You Feel Like We Do" (p10 uk39).

The substantial financial returns of albums such as *Frampton Comes Alive!* helped transform the record business into an attractive possibility for investment. Large multinational corporations with no previous experience in music—Phillips Petroleum, for instance—bought up record labels in hopes of cashing in on the "big album." The concert circuit had also changed, as venues became larger and national and international tours became the norm for bands signed to major labels. Theaters and ballrooms were too small for major acts so shows moved into stadiums and sports arenas, and attendance records were regularly broken. Important benchmarks of the rock live circuit were the scope of and venues played in tours by the Rolling Stones in 1969 and 1972, and Bob Dylan's return to live touring with the Band in 1974. The growth in record and concert revenues meant musicians began to enjoy the fruits of increased profits, leading to the use of private jets, long stays in expensive recording studios, and the ingestion of significant quantities of expensive—and illegal—drugs. A stereotypical look at the excesses of the rock touring circuit in the mid-1970s is depicted in the unreleased (but widely available) documentary *Cocksucker Blues*, which follows the Stones on their 1972 tour of America.

Life's Been Good to Me So Far: More Big Albums. Among the albums that followed *Frampton Comes Alive!* in the big money sweepstakes was the Eagles' *Hotel California*, which hit number one in the United States (uk2) in early 1977 and included three hit songs: "New Kid in Town" (p1 uk20), "Hotel California" (p1 uk8), and "Life in the Fast Lane" (p11). Guitarist Joe Walsh replaced Bernie Leadon on this album, and the band abandoned their easygoing country rock approach for a harder rocking, more mainstream style. The Eagles followed with *The Long Run* (p1, uk4), which was among the top albums of 1979.

While Frampton and the Eagles produced hit albums during this period, Fleetwood Mac soon took the big album phenomenon even further. Fleetwood Mac had started out as a British blues band in the late 1960s, led by guitarist Peter Green and including guitarist Jeremy Spencer, drummer Mick Fleetwood, and bassist John McVie. The band enjoyed some success in England with *Peter Green's Fleetwood Mac* (uk10, 1968) and a number one single the same year with "Albatross." By 1971 Green and Spencer had left the group and keyboardist and vocalist Christine McVie had joined, followed shortly thereafter by guitarist and vocalist Lindsay Buckingham and singer Stevie Nicks. The style of the revamped lineup changed significantly, focusing on mainstream rock and ballads led by Buckingham, Nicks, and Christine McVie, the group's newcomers and principal songwriters. The new quintet released *Fleetwood Mac* in 1975, which slowly rose up the *Billboard* album chart, reaching number one in the United States in 1976. The album contained several popular singles, including "Rhiannon" (p11) and "Say You Love Me" (p11 uk40). *Rumours*, the group's next release, was even more successful. It spent thirty-one weeks at number one on the *Billboard* charts in 1977 and contained the hit tracks "Go Your Own Way" (10p), "Dreams" (1p), and "Don't Stop" (p3). No album had ever sold so many copies and dominated pop music in this way. Fleetwood Mac would never duplicate the success of *Rumours*, though they continued to release successful albums into the 1980s, including *Tusk* (p4 uk1, 1979), *Mirage* (p1 uk5, 1982), and *Tango in the Night* (p7 uk1, 1987).

One effect of the quest for the mega-hit album within the recording industry was to encourage a conservative attitude. In looking for the next Frampton, Eagles, or Fleetwood Mac, record companies were less willing to take chances bands that might be interesting but were likely to sell only 350,000 records—a figure that had been acceptable only a few years before. Every new band was an entry in the big-album lottery, and record company staff increasingly seemed to ask themselves: Why waste a chance on a group that can't win? When modern critics lament the

Fleetwood Mac's Stevie Nicks (left) and Lindsay Buckingham (right). Building on the success of other "big albums" like *Frampton Comes Alive!*, Fleetwood Mac's *Rumours* stayed on the *Billboard* charts for thirty-one weeks in 1977, helping to make the band one of the most popular groups of the 1970s.

late 1970s, it is often because they feel that record companies killed the spirit of rock music when they became obsessed with the big album. This is undoubtedly the period when corporate interests became interested in music as a way to make money, with little regard for how the music sounded or what it stood for, so long as the financial benefits could be realized.

Maintaining Previous Approaches: It's Still Rock and Roll to Me. In Chapter 8, we saw how the wide range of rock styles in the 1970s emerged from the primordial rock soup of psychedelia. Rock in the early 1970s was teeming with competing stylistic approaches that are relatively easy to distinguish from one another. By mid-decade, however, these styles began to blend, reducing the usefulness of the old stylistic labels. Instead, mainstream rock moved back toward a more unified style in which elements of earlier styles could be easily detected but combinations of features were less predictable. This "evening out" of the earlier styles is sometimes attributed to the conservative attitude that became pervasive in the record company decision-making processes, a charge leveled by critics of banal "corporate rock." While we saw early 1970s rock through the lens of stylistic expansion, mainstream rock in the second half of the decade will be viewed in this chapter as a process of stylistic consolidation. It is important to understand how mainstream rock continued and *extended* earlier styles, while also pulling together elements that had previously been used to *distinguish among* styles.

Like Fleetwood Mac, many groups that were active in the early 1970s became more popular later in the decade, creating a strong relationship among earlier styles. This situation was new to rock music: rock musicians could sustain active careers as they approached middle age. The Rolling Stones, for example, continued active recording and touring schedules in the second half of the 1970s, hiring in ex-Faces guitarist Ron Wood to replace Mick Taylor and releasing *Black and Blue* (p1 uk2, 1976), *Some Girls* (p1 uk2, 1978), and *Emotional Rescue* (p1 uk1, 1980). Only a few years after the breakup of the Beatles, Paul McCartney formed Wings with his wife Linda, guitarist Denny Laine, and drummer Denny Seiwell. Considering the popularity of the front man, it was no surprise when the band's first album, *Red Rose Speedway*, hit number one on the U.S. charts (uk5) in 1973, and the ballad "My Love" topped the American singles charts (uk9). Wings' most successful album, commercially and aesthetically, was *Band on the Run* (p1 uk1, 1974), on which McCartney successfully updated his style to create an album of well-crafted tracks. Wings continued to enjoy success with a string of chart-topping albums and singles before the group disbanded in 1981. Unlike the Stones and McCartney, who had maintained popularity since the early 1960s, the Steve Miller Band enjoyed much more success in the 1970s than they ever had in the 1960s. Beginning with *The Joker* (p2, 1973), which contained an eponymous number one single, Miller and company were regular entrants on the American album and singles charts. *Fly Like an Eagle* (p3 uk11, 1976) is perhaps the band's best-known album, containing the tracks "Fly Like an Eagle" (p2), "Rock 'n' Me" (p1 uk11), and "Take the Money and Run" (p11). In all of these cases, artists that were popular (or active) in the 1960s extended their careers into the late 1970s while maintaining the essence of their musical style.

In addition to bands with roots in the 1960s, many groups that first achieved success in the early 1970s continued to build on their success during the remainder

Though successful in the first half of the decade with a harder, straight-ahead rock style, later in the 1970s the Doobie Brothers turned to a more laid back, jazz-influenced rock, with the help of lead singer and songwriter Michael McDonald and ex–Steely Dan guitarist Skunk Baxter (left).

of the decade. Faced with the departure of Tom Johnston due to illness, the Doobie Brothers brought pianist and singer Michael McDonald on board and adopted a stylistic approach that laid more emphasis on jazz influences. The resultant records *Takin' It to the Streets* (p8, 1976) and *Livin' on the Fault Line* (p10 uk25, 1977) reestablished the band, but *Minute by Minute* (p1, 1979) pushed the group to new levels of commercial success. The album contained the hit track "What a Fool Believes" (p14, 1979), which quickly became a staple of FM radio. KISS also reached its commercial peak in the U.S. during this same period with the live albums *Alive!* (p9, 1975), which contained the more popular live version of the single "Rock and Roll All Nite" (12p), and *Alive II* (p7, 1977) and the studio albums *Love Gun* (p4, 1977) and *Dynasty* (p9, 1979).

Rethinking Previous Approaches: New Arrivals in the Late 1970s. A number of mainstream bands that emerged in the second half of the 1970s also seemed to adopt features of earlier music, shaping them to fit the new, more restricted radio formats. The band Boston, for instance, blended blues rock with aspects of progressive rock to produce music that sold well and received generous radio play. Their first album, *Boston*, was released in early 1977 and quickly climbed to number three on the album charts (uk11). As a compact rock song with several highly organized instrumental sections, "More Than a Feeling" is representative of the group's approach. Boston's next album, *Don't Look Back* (p1 uk9, 1978) seemed to assure their continued success, but a dispute with their record label kept the highly anticipated *Third Stage* (1p) from being released until 1986.

If any late 1970s band showed that radio success could come from merging popular styles from the early 1970s, it was Foreigner. Formed by guitarist Mick Jones and featuring the lead vocals of Lou Gramm, the band's debut, *Foreigner* (p4, 1977), and the tracks "Feels Like the First Time" (p4) and "Cold as Ice" (p6) quickly established them with American audiences. The next album, *Double Vision* (p3, 1978), contained the hit singles "Hot Blooded" (p3) and "Double Vision" (p2). Gramm's vocal approach was clearly derived from an interest in rhythm and

Listening Guide

Get Music Ⓢ wwnorton.com/studyspace

Boston, "More Than a Feeling" Epic 50266

Words and music by Tom Scholz, produced by John Boylan and Tom Scholz. Reached #5 on the *Billboard* "Hot 100" chart in September 1976. Contained on the album *Boston*, which reached #3 on the *Billboard* "Top LPs & Tape" chart.

FORM: Compound AABA, with each A section based on contrasting verse-chorus form, while the bridge offers new material employing lead guitars playing in harmony. Note that the verse and chorus lengths are different in each presentation of the A section, giving some indication of the variety employed when these sections reappear.

TIME SIGNATURE: 4/4.

INSTRUMENTATION: Electric and acoustic guitars, bass, drums, handclaps, lead and backup vocals.

	0:00–0:18	**Introduction**, 6 mm.	Acoustic guitar fades in, as electric guitar and bass join in.
A	0:18–0:42	**Verse 1**, 11 mm.	Vocals and drums enter, music remains quiet, ending gets louder and transitions into chorus via lead guitar melody. "I looked out . . ."
	0:42–1:17	**Chorus**, 16 mm.	Louder, with backup vocals and hand claps added to create excitement. Again, ending provides a transition, this time back to the verse. "It's more than a feeling . . ."
A	1:17–1:51	**Verse 2**, 15 mm.	Quieter again, with 4 bars of interlude before singing returns. Transition to verse gets louder, as before. "So many people . . ."
	1:51–2:30	**Chorus**, 18 mm.	As before, but now a new transition leads to the instrumental bridge. "It's more than a feeling . . ."
B	2:30–2:55	**Instrumental Bridge**, 11 mm.	Melodic guitar solo featured, frequently doubled in harmony. The feel in this section is symphonic, similar to earlier progressive rock.
A	2:55–3:48	**Verse 3**, 24 mm.	Quieter again, with 4 bars of acoustic guitar preparing the introduction of the lead vocal. This time the verse is extended by repeating the end of the last phrase before beginning the transition to the chorus. "When I'm tired . . ."
	3:48–4:41	**Chorus**, 20 mm.	As before, and then fade out. "It's more than a feeling . . ."

blues, while Jones's blues-rock guitar hooks drove the songs forward. Differing from the traditional blues-rock approach, however, was the prominent use of keyboards, clearly influenced by progressive rockers like Yes and Emerson, Lake & Palmer, but pared down to radio-friendly dimensions.

Musicians who were active in other bands during the previous decade also formed many of the most popular new groups of the late 1970s. For example, each member of Foreigner, save Lou Gramm, had performed professionally before teaming up in the mid-1970s. Journey is another example of a new group formed by older members. Formerly of Santana, guitarist Neal Schon and organist Greg Rolie, teamed up with bassist Ross Valory (ex–Steve Miller) and drummer Aynsley Dunbar (ex-Zappa) to form the band's instrumental core. Journey experienced only moderate success until they added singer Steve Perry for their fourth album, *Infinity* (p21, 1978). The album contained such radio staples as "Lights" (a good example of the band's power ballad style) and "Feelin' That Way" (an example of their harder-rocking approach). With Perry's soaring tenor voice and the group's heavy, guitar-driven sound, Journey's style in many ways drew upon the legacy of progressive rock. As the decade closed, Journey's popularity grew, with *Departure* (p8, 1980) becoming the group's first Top-Ten album and *Escape* hitting the top spot in 1981.

Members of Journey had roots in the San Francisco and Los Angeles scenes of the late 1960s. When the band added lead singer Steve Perry in the late 1970s, their music developed a strong mainstream appeal, especially for female listeners. In this photo, Perry is shown with lead guitarist Neal Schon.

Listening Guide

Get Music ⓢ wwnorton.com/studyspace

Foreigner, "Feels Like the First Time" Atlantic 3394

Words and music by Mick Jones, produced by John Sinclair and Gary Lyons. Reached #4 on the *Billboard* "Hot 100" chart in the United States in mid-1977. Contained on the album *Foreigner*, which reached #4 on the *Billboard* "Top LPs & Tape" chart.

FORM: Modified compound AABA, with A sections based on contrasting verse-chorus form. The second A section includes a bridge, based on the chorus, inserted between the verse and the chorus. The last A section is abbreviated, using only the chorus section.

TIME SIGNATURE: 4/4, with bridge 1 in 2/2.

INSTRUMENTATION: Electric guitars, bass, drums, synthesizer, organ, lead and backup vocals.

	0:00–0:27	**Introduction**, 12 mm.	Begins with distorted guitar, then stop-time bass and drums enter, with sparkling progressive rock synthesizer above. Full band and drumbeat enter at m. 9.
A	0:27–1:02	**Verse 1**, 16 mm.	Vocals enter, as music builds from quiet to loud, first adding distorted guitars, and then backup vocals, as chords get higher and higher. "I would climb . . ."
	1:02–1:21	**Chorus**, 8 mm.	Loud, with choral vocals, with sparkling synthesizer on top. "It feels like . . ."
A	1:21–1:56	**Verse 2**, 16 mm.	As before, but now with rhythmic guitar underneath during the quiet part, and backup vocals entering earlier. "I have waited . . ."
	1:56–2:38	**Bridge 1**, 18 mm.	Change of meter to 2/2, change of key to minor, with classical-music references in the synthesizer part and in the accompanying harmony. "It feels like . . ."
	2:38–2:56	**Chorus**, 8 mm.	As before, but now with improvised lead vocals playing off the choral-vocal statement of the melody. "It feels like . . ."
B	2:56–3:14	**Bridge 2**, 8 mm.	Virtuosic guitar solo, with stop in the bass and drums, and improvised vocal interjections. "Open up the door . . ."
A'	3:14–3:32	**Chorus**, 8 mm.	As in the second statement of the chorus. "It feels like . . ."
	3:32–3:49	**Chorus**, 8 mm.+	Repeat of chorus and then fade out.

Emerging from Los Angeles and featuring the virtuosic guitar playing of Eddie Van Halen and the antics of singer David Lee Roth, the music of Van Halen provided a mainstream glimpse of the emerging California-based metal scene, which explored older forms of rock in extremely new ways. The band stormed the charts in the late 1970s with a style that blended hard-driving rock with blues-based vocals and futuristic guitar performance. Their album *Van Halen* (p19, 1978) contains a cover version of the Kinks' "You Really Got Me" (p36), and arguably their best-known track, "Runnin' with the Devil." Van Halen quickly became a radio favorite, and the albums *Van Halen II* (p6 uk23, 1979) and *Women and Children First* (p6 uk15, 1980) clearly established the band as one of the most promising new mainstream rock groups. In many ways, Van Halen's approach owes much to the earlier British blues rockers, especially Deep Purple, and we return to them in our discussion of heavy metal in Chapter 12.

Progressive Rock Revamped. For the most part, the progressive rock movement had expended its energies by mid-decade: King Crimson had broken up, Peter Gabriel had quit Genesis, and many of the other bands were winding down. Yes was the exception, as 1977's *Going for the One* went to number one on the U.S. and UK charts (in the same year that punk began to make its mark in Britain). In many ways, it fell to two American bands to revamp the progressive rock style for late-1970s radio: Kansas and Styx. Kansas enjoyed only moderate success until its fourth album, *Leftoverture* (p5, 1977), which contained the hit "Carry On Wayward Son" (p11). Powered by the songwriting of keyboardist Kerry Livgren and the singing of Steve Walsh, Kansas pruned away some of the extravagance associated with progressive rock, getting their tracks down to the four-minute range encouraged by radio. The band's most successful album was *Point of Know Return* (p4, 1978), which contained the ballad "Dust in the Wind" (p6). Like Kansas, Chicago's Styx recast progressive rock grandeur in a more economical manner. Although Styx often sung about progressive topics, such as space, the future, and science fiction, and the group created lengthy tracks, their music was not nearly as complex as the progressive rock of Yes or Genesis. After scoring a hit with "Lady" (p6, 1975), it was not until their seventh album that they had significant commercial success. *The Grand Illusion* rose to number six on the U.S. charts in 1977, containing "Come Sail Away" (p8), a track that blends Wakemanesque keyboards with a simpler pop-rock approach. Styx continued to enjoy hit albums into the 1980s with *Cornerstone* (p2, 1979), *Paradise Theater* (p1 uk8, 1981), and *Kilroy Was Here* (p3, 1983).

Perhaps the most enduring of the progressive rock–influenced bands to emerge in the second half of the 1970s was the Canadian power trio Rush. The band first made its mark in 1976 with its fourth release, the concept album *2112*, and followed with a string of records that were increasingly more popular. In 1980, *Permanent Waves* hit the number four spot in the United States (uk3) when most bands were turning away from ambitious concept albums. Because the band depended on Alex Lifeson's guitar playing rather than keyboards for its harmonic color, their sound avoided some of the classical pretension that generated so much criticism of the original progressive rock bands. Bassist Geddy Lee's high-pitched vocals were reminiscent of both Yes and Led Zeppelin. Neil Peart's virtuosic drumming and ambitiously poetic lyrics also made it clear that there was no return-to-simplicity to be found in Rush's music. The Canadian trio has remained commercially successful to the present day, with top-selling albums and sold-out tours, long after most other progressive bands had split.

North American acts were not the only ones reworking the progressive-rock

style. Electric Light Orchestra (ELO) was originally formed out of the ashes of the British psychedelic band the Move. Soon it became the vehicle for the singing and songwriting of guitarist Jeff Lynne, whose stylistic indebtedness to *Sgt. Pepper*–era Beatles is unmistakable. ELO took the idea of the rock band with chamber strings accompaniment, developed by the Beatles on tracks such as "Strawberry Fields Forever" and "I Am the Walrus," and made it their trademark. After moderate success in the UK during the first half of the decade, ELO broke through in the United States with their fifth album, the conceptually driven *Eldorado* (p16, 1975), which contained the hit "Can't Get It Out of My Head" (p9, 1975). The band followed with a series of hit singles, including "Evil Woman" (p10 uk10, 1976), "Telephone Line" (p7 uk8, 1977), and "Don't Bring Me Down" (p4 uk3, 1979).

The stylistically eclectic aspects of the late Beatles output and the later British progressive movement also inspired Queen. Featuring the singing of Freddie Mercury and the guitar of Brian May, the band scored its first success in the UK with *Queen II* (uk5, 1974). *Sheer Heart Attack* (p12 uk2, 1975) brought Queen to the attention of listeners in America, while *A Night at the Opera* (p4 uk1, 1976), featuring the extravagant "Bohemian Rhapsody" (p9 uk1), established the band as a cross between the glam aspects of David Bowie and the classical ambitions of progressive rockers. Queen continued their success into the late 1970s with *A Day at the Races* (p5 uk1, 1977) and *News of the World* (p4 uk3, 1977), the latter of which contained the anthemic one-two punch "We Will Rock You" and "We Are the Champions." More success followed in the early 1980s with the release of *The Game* (p1 uk1, 1980), which contained "Another One Bites the Dust" (p1 uk7). While many fans were convinced that he was gay, perhaps prompted by his use of flamboyant stage costumes, Mercury himself never fully disclosed his sexual orientation to the public. However his death from AIDS in 1991 raised public awareness of a disease that had been devastating the gay community for several years. As a prominent rock star, Mercury's death also forced many rock fans to confront sexual stereotypes, opening the door for many gay musicians to feel comfortable revealing their sexual orientation to the public.

Freddie Mercury of Queen, live in concert. Queen combined the "glam" tendencies of David Bowie with the scope of classical-influenced prog rock, exemplified in the ambitious song "Bohemian Rhapsody." Mercury died in 1991, a day after announcing he had AIDS—solidifying his position as an icon in the gay community.

Singers, Songwriters, and Bands. By the mid-1970s singer-songwriters were often fronting bands, keeping the intimate bond created by soul-searching lyrics but exploring harder rock styles in their music. In most cases this meant that the bands themselves, though now more prominent, were still not the focus of the act. The dean of American singer-songwriters, Bob Dylan, returned to touring in support of the hit album *Planet Waves* (p1 uk7, 1974). After a successful tour with the Band in 1974, Dylan released the stripped-down *Blood on the Tracks* (p1 uk4, 1975), which has since become a critical favorite. The end of 1975 saw Dylan back on the road with a large group of musicians that he called the Rolling Thunder Revue, followed by several more critically acclaimed albums, including *Desire* (p1 uk3, 1976) and *Street Legal* (p11 uk2, 1978). Famous for career shifts that confused and confounded his followers and critics, Dylan began espousing a relatively fundamentalist brand of Christianity in the late 1970s with *Slow Train Coming* (p3 uk2, 1979) and *Saved* (p24 uk3, 1980).

Elton John was another singer-songwriter who increasingly explored a rock band backing in the late 1970s, continuing his string of hit albums and singles. A cover version of "Lucy in the Sky with Diamonds" (p1 uk10, 1974) and his own "Philadelphia Freedom" (p1 uk12, 1975) both reached the top of the charts and his 1975 album *Captain Fantastic and the Brown Dirt Cowboy* (p1 uk2) was one of the top albums of the year. John's most popular song from the late 1970s was "Don't Go Breaking My Heart" (p1 uk1, 1976), a single recorded with singer Kiki Dee. As John explored rock and other popular forms less typical of singer-songwriters, Paul Simon's music in the late 1970s highlighted his interest in jazz, rhythm and blues, and gospel. His *Greatest Hits, etc.* (p18 uk6, 1977) blended a best-of package with new tracks, including "Slip Slidin' Away" (p5 uk36), in which jazz and gospel influences are pronounced. Simon then embarked on an album and movie, *One Trick Pony*, bringing on a band of studio pros including bassist Tony Levin, guitarist Eric Gale, pianist Richard Tee, and drummer Steve Gadd. While the movie received mixed reviews, the accompanying album *One Trick Pony* (p12 uk17, 1980) was the most musically complex of Simon's career. The album's single "Late in the Evening"

Pianist, singer, and songwriter Billy Joel illustrates the merging of piano-based singer-songwriter music and rock by performing while standing on top of his piano. Joel produced a string of popular songs and albums from the mid-1970s through the 1990s that centers on his strong piano playing and easy-to-follow, catchy lyrics.

(p6) is not representative of this complexity, but tracks like "Jonah" and "How the Heart Approaches What It Yearns" showcase Simon and his band at their most musically sophisticated.

By mid-decade other artists were building on the idea of the singer-songwriter fronting a band. Among these was Billy Joel, whose second album, *Piano Man* (p27, 1973), the title track of which went to number 25 on the pop chart and helped launch his career in early 1974. After several years of disappointing records, Joel released *The Stranger* (p2 uk25, 1977), which contained "Just the Way You Are" (p3 uk19), "Movin' Out" (p17), "Only the Good Die Young" (p24), and "She's Always a Woman" (p17). Joel continued this string of hit albums and singles into the 1980s. His *52nd Street* hit number one in 1978 (uk10), buoyed by the popularity of "My Life" (p3 uk12) and "Big Shot" (p14, 1979). Joel's music from this period incorporates his piano and vocals as the center of attention on both ballads and up-tempo rock songs backed by his band. With the arrival of new wave on the scene at the end of the decade, it was especially relevant when Joel released *Glass Houses* (p1 uk9, 1980), which engaged earlier rock and pop styles. A particularly strong connection with older music can be found in "It's Still Rock and Roll to Me" (p1 uk14), which discussed older forms and was musically modeled on late 1950s rock.

Jackson Browne was another singer-songwriter from the period whose music featured rock band accompaniment. Browne had been part of the early 1970s country-rock scene in southern California, and in addition to cowriting the Eagles' "Take It Easy," he scored a hit single with "Doctor My Eyes" (p8) in 1972. Browne released his most memorable music during the late 1970s, with a series of albums and singles that included *The Pretender* (p5 uk26, 1976), *Runnin' On Empty* (p3 uk28, 1978), and *Hold Out* (p1, 1980). Similarly, Detroit-native Bob Seger fronted a hard-rocking group called the Silver Bullet Band, but still fell squarely in the singer-songwriter mold of the late part of the 1970s. After nearly a decade of moderate success, Seger broke into the rock mainstream in 1977 with the album *Night Moves* (p8) and the singles "Night Moves" (p4) and "Mainstreet" (p24). For the remainder of the 1970s and well into the 1980s, Seger maintained a consistent style featuring folksy lyrics about everyday problems, distinctive gravelly vocals, and memorable rock hooks. A fixture of classic rock radio into the 1990s, later Seger "classics" included "Old Time Rock & Roll" (p28, 1979) and "Against the Wind" (p5, 1980).

Bruce Springsteen also emerged in the context of the late 1970s singer-songwriter movement. Backed by the E-Street Band, Springsteen established himself as an important new voice in rock music with his third album, *Born to Run* (p3 uk17, 1975). Much like the others discussed here, Springsteen wrote lyrics that were understood to be largely autobiographical and frequently confessional. He also embraced rock's past, and the single "Born to Run" (p23) seemed inspired equally by the narrative style of Bob Dylan, Phil Spector's Wall of Sound, and the energetic performance style of the Rolling Stones. Albums such as *Born to Run* and *Darkness on the Edge of Town* (p5 uk16, 1978) provided only a glimpse of Springsteen's future work (discussed in Chapter 11).

Form or Formula? We have stressed how mainstream (or "corporate") rock developed out of the music of the first half of the 1970s. In some cases, late-1970s mainstream rock streamlined musical elements, combining them to create new forms of stylistic synthesis. One way to examine how bands of the late 1970s recast music from earlier in the decade is through formal design. For example, the lengthiest tracks by earlier artists often employed multiple sections, organized so that at least a part of the music from early in a track would return later in the tune. In Chapter 8, we looked at Led Zeppelin's "Whole Lotta Love" and Yes's "Roundabout," noting that both employed a compound AABA formal scheme, with verses, choruses, or bridges used within the A sections. In this chapter, there are also several instances of AABA form that exhibit how groups in the last half of the decade compressed large-scale formal designs commonly associated with adventurous progressive music into the length of a radio-friendly single. Boston's "More Than a Feeling" squeezes a level of organizational complexity comparable to "Roundabout" into a track about half as long. The Boston track uses a compound AABA design, with a verse-chorus pair making up each A section and an instrumental guitar solo (actually two guitars playing in harmony) as the B section. Note that each verse and chorus varies in length, with no two being exactly the same. This creates a more complicated arrangement than simply repeating the material. Foreigner's "Feels Like the First Time" offers another interesting twist on the compound AABA design. It begins as if the A sections will consist of verse-chorus pairs like those found in the Boston track. However, in the second A section a bridge is inserted between verse two and the chorus. In a more conventional formal design, this bridge would occur after the second iteration of the chorus. "Feels Like the First Time" incorporates a second bridge in this spot, however, featuring a guitar solo. The final A section contains only a chorus, with no return to the verse, and the entire track clocks in at under four minutes—perfect for radio.

Instrumentation is another parameter that we may use to observe the ways rock from the late 1970s incorporates aspects of earlier rock. While both songs feature the distorted guitar sounds that are a central feature in blues-based rock (both American and British), there are a few progressive rock touches as well. With Foreigner, these are found mostly in the use of the high synthesizer arpeggios in the introduction and choruses, as well as in the synthesizer melody in the first chorus. In the Boston example, the harmony guitar parts throughout (and especially in the bridge) are carefully coordinated—"composed" in the classical sense—showing a concern for matching them with the parts being played by the other instruments. Both Boston and Foreigner condense qualities of earlier rock, blending them together and fitting them into shorter tracks. This can be seen as a culmination of earlier musical practices. However, it also shows how popular music often adheres to a constantly changing formula. The first interpretation suggests that late 1970s mainstream rock is a synthesis of earlier music, refining and recombining musical elements. The second interpretation suggests that the music was homogenized and simplified in order to reach the broadest possible audience.

THE ROOTS OF PUNK IN THE UNITED STATES, 1967–1975

Safety Pins and Leather. To an FM-rock radio listener in the 1970s, music did not change very drastically during the course of the decade. Many of the same bands remained popular, and most of the newer groups that emerged did not depart too radically from established acts. Listeners might have noticed that the playlists were becoming slightly more restricted, and certain albums were in heavy rotation, but there was not much else that signaled the big changes on the horizon for rock music. By the fall of 1977, however, American rock fans began to hear about a movement in the UK called "punk," spearheaded in large part by the Sex Pistols, whose outrageous antics were often the focus of news reports. Punk first rose to mainstream attention in the UK, where groups like the Sex Pistols, the Buzzcocks, and the Clash became popular in the later 1970s, placing singles and albums high on the British charts. However, because of the sometimes aggressive and dangerous images associated with punk, American record labels were quick to tone down the style, endorsing more fully a style they dubbed "new wave." Until the early 1980s, the mainstream American market barely registered the punk movement. Yet, punk actually had its most important roots in the American underground scenes of the 1960s in places such as the Pacific Northwest, Detroit, and New York. Like American rhythm and blues in the early 1960s, punk was exported from the United States to the UK, only to return and be reintroduced as new wave.

Punk Roots: The Velvet Underground, the Stooges, and the MC5. Between 1967 and 1975, when most of the rock world was focused on psychedelia and mainstream rock, punk was brewing underground. Among the most important early influences on this music was the Velvet Underground. The group emerged when Lou Reed, who had studied creative writing in college and then worked as a professional songwriter, and John Cale, who had studied avant-garde composition and was playing with a performance ensemble led by avant-garde composer LaMonte Young, came together in the mid-1960s. The Velvet Underground were closely associated with pop artist Andy Warhol, who had included the group in some of his pop-art happenings, including his *Exploding Plastic Inevitable* multimedia show that ran in various cities during 1966 and 1967. Warhol was among New York's leading young artists at the time, championing a style that adapted elements from everyday American culture, refocusing them in an artistic context. (You may be familiar with Warhol's multicolor prints of Campbell's Soup cans, Elvis, and Marilyn Monroe.) It is easy to see how pop music would fit into Warhol's project, and considering the experimental aspirations of Reed and Cale, Warhol was a valuable ally. Reed's lyrics focused on the darker side of urban life, while Cale was eager to employ avant-garde ideas in a pop context. With Reed on guitar and vocals, Cale on bass and viola, Sterling Morrison on guitar, and Maureen Tucker on drums, the band recorded *The Velvet Underground and Nico* in late 1966. The singer Nico was added at Warhol's insistence, and Warhol produced the album. In the summer of 1967, when much of rock culture was focused on the fantastic images of *Sgt. Pepper*, the Velvets' first album, containing tracks such as "Heroin" and "Venus in Furs," went largely unnoticed. The group split from Warhol soon thereafter and continued performing and recording until membership changes effectively ended their tenure. The band performed its last shows under the leadership of Reed at the Warhol hangout Max's Kansas City during the summer of 1970.

While the Velvets were experimenters obsessed with dark downtown reality, Detroit-based Iggy Pop made his mark in the late 1960s underground as an outrageous performer. Pop seemed to challenge the audience at every show, sometimes walking on the audience's hands and smearing peanut butter all over his body. The band's raw sound, characterized by loud guitars, heavy drumming, and Pop's screaming vocals, is best captured on its second release, *Fun House* (1970). Another Detroit band, the MC5, were also important to the later punk scene. The band's *Kick Out the Jams* (p30, 1969) is representative of the aggressive sound of the band, especially the title track, which contained profanities (anticipating the vulgarity of later punk). An element of confrontation in the music of all three of these bands provides evidence of a connection to the later punk movement. The Velvet Underground confronted sexual stereotypes, attitudes toward the use of hard drugs, and performance ability as a barometer of quality. The Stooges confronted

From left, Lou Reed, John Cale, and Nico of the Velvet Underground in concert. While hippies and "flower power" were dominating rock in the late 1960s, the Velvet Underground often looked at the darker side of life. Many of the creative artists of the punk and glam scenes—Patti Smith and David Bowie, among others—often cite the Velvet Underground as a major influence.

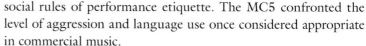

social rules of performance etiquette. The MC5 confronted the level of aggression and language use once considered appropriate in commercial music.

After Lou Reed left the Velvet Underground in 1970, the most important band on the New York underground scene was arguably the New York Dolls. Fronted by the flamboyant David Johansen, the band incorporated elements of British glam into their performances of gritty, hard-driving rock music. The Dolls used makeup and costumes, although they nevertheless projected an image of toughness, danger, and reckless disdain for convention that would become central to punk music. Their two albums, *The New York Dolls* (1973) and *Too Much Too Soon* (1974), sold poorly and the group never gained national popularity. Nevertheless, the band was an important step between the art-based experimental music of the Velvet Underground and the New York punk scene to follow. Alongside the New York Dolls, many others in New York began to develop an approach that drew on the underground music of the late 1960s.

New York Punk. In November 1973, poet Patti Smith teamed up with guitarist and rock critic Lenny Kaye. The two had performed together years before, with Smith usually reciting poetry while Kaye accompanied on guitar. Smith had already begun to develop a reputation as a poet, so initially these performances were less musical events than literary ones. But soon the duo added pianist Richard Sohl and by August 1974 had released "Hey Joe," a cover version of the song made famous by Jimi Hendrix. The Patti Smith Group, which eventually included Ivan Krahl on bass and Jay Dee Daugherty on drums, became the first band from the developing New York punk scene to sign a major-label record deal. Late in 1975 the band released *Horses*, which rose to number forty-seven on the American charts. The band's version of "Gloria" provides an example of how their numbers

Patti Smith in concert at CBGB in New York. Though Smith started her career as a poet, she formed a band, calling it the Patti Smith Group. Smith's group and Television (another punk band) began performing at CBGB in 1974 and the club quickly became the center of the U.S. punk rock scene. Smith's vocal style continued to be strongly influenced by poetic recitation.

would often unfold: Smith begins with a recitation that seems unrelated to the tune itself but eventually builds in intensity and winds its way to an energetic rendering of the chorus.

At about the same time Smith and Kaye were beginning to work together, school friends Richard Hell and Tom Verlaine formed Television. The two were interested in literature and had even published a collection of poetry under an assumed name. In early 1974 Hell and Verlaine began searching around New York for someplace their new band could perform. In March 1974, they landed a regular Sunday evening spot at a deserted bar in lower Manhattan called CBGB (the name is an acronym for Country, Bluegrass, and Blues). Shortly thereafter, Television and the Patti Smith Group were sharing the bill and attracting attention. CBGB became the home of the New York punk scene, joining a relocated Max's Kansas City as the most prominent clubs of the New York underground.

The Ramones was another seminal band to play these clubs in the mid-1970s. Playing under the stage names of Joey (vocals), Johnny (guitar), Dee Dee (bass), and Tommy (drums) Ramone, the Ramones produced a stripped-down, high-energy style of rock that focused on short, simple songs played very fast. The band signed with Sire Records—an important New York label—and released *Ramones* (1976), which contained "Blitzkrieg Bop." Because of the resurgence of interest in the Ramones' music years later, many are surprised to learn that the band never had any significant success in the United States. Despite the group's importance in the history of punk, no Ramones album ever reached the Top 40 of the *Billboard* album charts, even during the late 1970s when many of their CBGB colleagues were topping the charts. Perhaps owing to the Ramones musical style, the band's music was consistently received more warmly in the UK.

New York was by no means the only city in the United States to maintain a growing punk music scene. Cleveland, Detroit, Los Angeles, Boston, and many other towns saw a flourishing of this style and related fashion and art subcultures. Still, as home to bands such as the Dictators, Richard Hell and the Voidoids, the Dead Boys, the Cramps, and the Misfits, New York was the national center of the scene. During the late 1970s, the punk subculture became a national movement. Punks often dressed in radical clothing, including intentionally ripped jeans, leather jackets, and safety pins. Another important aspect of punk fashion was hairstyle, as punks experimented with outlandish hair color and often adopted the Mohawk. The overriding aesthetic of punk was strongly connected to the mantra "do it yourself" (or DIY). Punks often took on all aspects of musical production, including recording, distribution, album art, and concert promotion. Hence, a desire for professionalism was often avoided in favor of a product (album notes, concert flyers, sound recordings, etc.) that showed some evidence of being homemade. While this approach had obvious drawbacks in regard to maintaining quality, the punk aesthetic—much like the garage band movement of the 1960s—led many amateur musicians to experiment with rock music. In turn, many of these untrained musicians made an important impact in an area of rock that had expanded to an international audience. Although punk music was largely united by the DIY aesthetic, it was hardly a monolithic musical style. With artists ranging from the loud and fast Ramones to the extended instrumental jams of Television and the angular vocals of the Voidoids, American punk music was only united by what it *wasn't*, which was corporate rock.

THE RISE OF PUNK IN THE UK, 1974–1977

No Hope: Malcolm McLaren, British Punk, and the Sex Pistols. Unlike the situation in the United States, the rise of punk in the UK can be linked to specific socioeconomic circumstances. Britain in the mid-1970s was suffering a crushing economic recession. For Britain's youth, this meant jobs were hard to find, and those that were available offered no significant opportunity for advancement. Whether or not their feelings were justified by the country's economic troubles, many British teens were prone to despair. That despair soon turned into anger, and punk became the music that best represented this angry spirit. British manager and shop owner Malcolm McLaren became a central character in helping this socioeconomic frustration find its voice in punk music and culture in the UK. In the early 1970s, McLaren ran a clothing store in London called Let It Rock. He was interested in early rock and roll, and his shop specialized in biker jackets and other 1950s clothes. By 1973, McLaren relaunched his shop as Too Fast to Live, Too Young to Die and befriended members of the New York Dolls, who had wandered into the shop while in London to perform. McLaren provided matching red leather suits for the band, which they sported during performances in New York in early 1975. He was impressed by the underground punk scene in New York, and especially with Richard Hell's manic performing style and sense of punk fashion. McLaren helped manage the Dolls during the first months of 1975, but returned to London after the group dissolved amid bitter disputes among band members. McLaren then renamed his clothing shop Sex, specializing in leather clothing and fetish wear.

In the meantime, guitarist Steve Jones and drummer Paul Cook started a band, playing mostly on equipment that Jones had stolen from other London-based

Sid Vicious (left) and Johnny Rotten (right) of the Sex Pistols performing in 1978. The Sex Pistols were key members in the punk scenes in the UK and the United States. Their first single, "Anarchy in the UK," epitomizes their rebellious attitude, musically and socially.

groups. Soon Glen Matlock, who worked at Sex part-time, joined on bass followed by John Lydon, who used to hang around McLaren's shop and auditioned for the lead singer job by singing along to Alice Cooper's "School's Out" on the jukebox. The band pressured McLaren to manage them, and his first move was to change Lydon's name to Johnny Rotten. With McLaren now calling the shots, the Sex Pistols began playing gigs in late 1975 and by November 1976 they had signed with EMI, releasing their first single, "Anarchy in the UK" (uk34). In early December, the band filled in at the last minute for Queen on a British television show. Provoked by the host, they uttered a few forbidden words, causing a scandal and becoming notorious overnight. Embarrassed by their punk behavior, EMI dropped the band but paid their promised advance money, and McLaren quickly helped them sign to A&M. A&M then got cold feet and released the band as well, also paying off a healthy advance. The band then signed to Virgin Records. In other words, before their first album was released in late 1977, the Sex Pistols had already collected advances from three record companies, a fleecing of the music-business establishment that only enhanced their reputation as troublemakers. When *Never Mind the Bollocks, Here's the Sex Pistols* was released, it went straight to the number one slot in the UK. The band eventually placed seven singles in the UK Top 10 during the late 1970s, including the highly controversial "God Save the Queen," the cover of which featured a picture of the Queen with a safety pin through her face. The scandals surrounding the Sex Pistols lasted just over a year, and by early 1978 the band had broken up (with Sid Vicious replacing Matlock on bass during the final months). Although there was a related punk scene forming in the United States, the Sex Pistols were the catalyst for punk in the UK. In every spot the band played, it seemed, new punk bands would start up, inspired by the experience. McLaren, Rotten, and company made punk a dirty word—in the American music industry at least—and no label wanted to sign a new punk band if this meant they would go through what EMI and A&M had experienced with the Sex Pistols.

The Clash, the Buzzcocks, the Jam, and Siouxsie and the Banshees.
Based on the widespread popularity of the Sex Pistols, punk bands seemed to spring up all over England, giving British punk a greater stylistic range. Early in the history of British punk, for instance, a familiar relationship was forged between the Sex Pistols and the Clash. Managed by Bernard Rhodes, the Clash adapted a positioning strategy that had worked for the Rolling Stones: if the Sex Pistols were the nihilists of punk, the Clash would be its political protesters. Thus with Joe Strummer (vocals and guitar), Paul Simonen (bass), Mick Jones (guitar), and Tory Chimes (drums), the band released *The Clash* in April 1977 (uk12), which contained the single "White Riot" (uk38). After the demise of the Pistols and with Topper Headon on drums, the Clash did even better in late 1978 with *Give 'em Enough Rope* (uk2). In 1980, the band entered the American market with the release of *London Calling* (p27 uk9, 1980), which contained the radio favorite "Train in Vain (Stand by Me)" (p27). In addition to their political stance, it became evident by the turn of the 1980s that the Clash were interested in a wide range of musical styles. As the 1980 triple-album *Sandinista!* revealed, the group was comfortable incorporating American R&B, reggae and ska, and a varied assortment of other musical influences into their brand of UK punk.

Among the groups to emerge in the excitement caused by the success of the

The influence of the Sex Pistols was not restricted to male musicians. Fronted by Siouxsie Sioux (Susan Dallion), Siouxsie and the Banshees enjoyed success on the UK punk scene. The connections between the two bands were further reinforced when Sid Vicious left the Banshees and replaced original bassist Glen Matlock in the Sex Pistols.

Sex Pistols and the Clash, the Buzzcocks adopted a pop-influenced approach to punk. Led by Pete Shelley, the group released a series of successful albums, including *Another Music in a Different Kitchen* (uk15, 1978) and *Love Bites* (uk13, 1978). Similarly, the Jam drew their their distinctive look from mods and their musical influences from the mid-1960s Kinks and Who, even though these two groups had since embraced ambitious 1970s styles. Comprised of Paul Weller (guitar and vocals), Bruce Foxton (bass), and Rick Buckler (drums), the Jam signed with Polydor and released *In the City* (uk20) in May 1977. The band followed up later that year with *This Is the Modern World* (uk22), the title track of which demonstrates the band's blend of hard-driving rhythm with catchy pop hooks. The group's success built through the end of the decade and into the 1980s with the albums *All Mod Cons* (uk6, 1978), *Setting Sons* (uk4, 1979), and *Sound Affects* (uk2, 1980). The Jam grew to extreme popularity in the UK during the early 1980s, releasing four number one singles before disbanding in 1982.

Before joining the Sex Pistols, Sid Vicious had played drums for the debut concert of a band fronted by Siouxsie Sioux, who had created with bassist Steven Severin a group called Siouxsie and the Banshees. The band signed with Polydor and released "Hong Kong Garden" (uk7) in the fall of 1978, followed by *The Scream* (uk12, 1978), a dark, brooding album that contained a gothic cover of the Beatles' "Helter Skelter." The band enjoyed continued success into the 1980s with several albums and singles, the most popular of which was a cover version of "Dear Prudence" (uk3, 1983). Siouxsie was by no means the only woman in British punk in the late 1970s. X-Ray Spex, fronted by Poly Styrene, enjoyed brief success with *Germ Free Adolescents* (uk30, 1978) and the Slits, an all-female punk trio that opened for the Clash on their spring 1977 tour and released *Cut* (uk30) in September 1979.

The groups discussed here were quite successful in the British market during the late 1970s, but none enjoyed American success except the Clash, who broke into the American market in 1980. In general, British punk music did not make the Atlantic crossing until much later, when record aficionados became interested in the style. At the time, however, other British acts did become popular in America. Rather than "punk," these groups were categorized under a new label: "new wave."

Punk Poetics—Organization or Anarchy? Punk fashion attacked the status quo and punk lyrics often advocated social or political change. Morover, the sound of punk—which often featured difficult-to-discern vocals, sloppy distorted guitars, and loud drums—broadcast the movement's antagonistic stance toward author-

Listening Guide

Get Music ⑤ wwnorton.com/studyspace

The Sex Pistols, "Anarchy in the UK" EMI 2566

Words and music by Paul Cook, Steve Johns, Glen Matlock, and Johnny Rotten, produced by Chris Thomas and Bill Price. Reached #38 in the UK in late 1976. Contained on the album *Never Mind the Bollocks, Here's the Sex Pistols*, which went to #1 in the UK in late 1977.

FORM: Modified simple verse, with instrumental bridges inserted. Each verse ends with an 8-bar refrain.

TIME SIGNATURE: 4/4.

INSTRUMENTATION: Electric guitars, bass, drums, lead and backup vocals.

0:00–0:14	**Introduction**, 8 mm.	Music derived from the refrain sets the stage for the entrance of the vocals.
0:14–0:43	**Verse 1 w/refrain**, 16 mm.	Vocals enter, raw and urgent. "I am an antichrist . . ."
0:43–1:11	**Verse 2 w/refrain**, 16 mm.	As before, with no significant changes. "Anarchy for the UK . . ."
1:11–1:31	**Bridge 1**, 11 mm.	Simple guitar solo over new musical material. Note occasional rude vocal sounds throughout.
1:31–1:59	**Verse 3 w/refrain**, 16 mm.	As before, but now with repeated note on the guitar. "How many ways . . ."
1:59–2:14	**Bridge 2**, 8 mm.	New musical material, melodic but driving, as repeated note in guitar becomes sustained note, with feedback throughout the first half of the following verse.
2:14–2:42	**Verse 4 w/refrain**, 16 mm.	As before. "Is this the M.P.L.A. . . ."
2:42–2:57	**Refrain**, 8 mm.	Repeat of refrain to create ending. "I want to be . . ."
2:57–3:11	**Refrain**, 8 mm.	Repeat; note guitar licks in the background throughout the ending.
3:11–3:29	**Refrain**, 8 mm.	Repeat; ends with menacing vocal on the word "destroy" and guitar feedback.

ity. In spite of these seemingly out-of-control features, punk music is often fairly conventional in its structure. This is partly because of punk rock's "return-to-simplicity" aesthetic—the idea of eliminating the complexity and expansiveness that hippie rock had developed. For example, the Sex Pistols' first single, "Anarchy in the UK," provides an interesting example in terms of musical structure. Overall, the song employs a simple verse structure. Each verse is sixteen measures in length, with the last eight measures in each verse carrying the same lyrical refrain. This eight-bar refrain is repeated three times at the end of the track, creating a coda that drives home the song's catchiest line (its "hook"). The exceptions are the two bridges inserted along the way, the first between verses two and three, and the second between verses three and four. Ironically, the insertion of bridge sections into a typical formal design is similar to the Foreigner example explored earlier in this chapter. Unlike the bridge sections found in the Foreigner or Boston examples, however, this track features no elaborate guitar solos or synthesizer riffs. In fact, the return-to-simplicity approach is perhaps most obvious in the driving guitar, bass, and drums accompaniment and the self-consciously untrained and amateurish character of Johnny Rotten's singing. The fast tempo and driving, steady eighth notes in the guitar, bass, and drums are also clear features of early punk. The use of simple verse form—inserted bridges notwithstanding—links this music with early rock and rhythm and blues, as well as with much traditional folk music, and contrasts strongly with the examples from Yes, Boston, and Foreigner discussed earlier. While punk disrupted the rock status quo, the music itself had strong connections with earlier rock traditions and practices.

THE RISE OF NEW WAVE, 1977–1980

The Next Big Thing. As late as the fall of 1977, most mainstream rock fans in America were largely unaware of either British or American punk. CBGB was popular among some people in New York, but punk had virtually no presence on the increasingly restricted playlists of FM rock radio. In late 1977 and early 1978, the Sex Pistols toured the United States, but instead of playing rock clubs in the northeast and on the West Coast, the band toured the South—a move designed, it seemed, to invite trouble and provoke yet more headlines (which it did). In December 1977, Elvis Costello appeared on *Saturday Night Live* (filling in for the Sex Pistols, who had trouble getting into the country), marking a significant breakthrough for punk into the American mainstream. During the mid-1970s, rock magazines like *Rolling Stone, Crawdaddy,* and *Creem* were giving significant coverage to punk rock. Punk, however, had built a reputation for being dangerous and potentially embarrassing within the music business. For much of the commercial music business, relabeling punk as "new wave" was a solution to this problem. This new term tamed the more aggressive elements of punk, making it more of an artsy aesthetic statement than a statement of nihilism or protest. If punks were angry, new wavers were ironic. Punk's answer to frustration was to lash out, perhaps break a window and form a band. New wave's was to reflect on urban alienation, have a cup of coffee, and write a clever lyric. Since many of the CBGB bands had backgrounds in the arts, industry interest in new wave worked to their advantage. Blondie and Talking Heads, both regulars at CBGB, became stars under this banner, leaving the Ramones and the punks behind. Strangely enough, Television seemed as poised as any of the other CBGB bands to achieve broad commercial success, but Hell left the group in 1975 and Verlaine took over the band. Having signed with Elektra, the band's debut album, *Marquee Moon* (uk28), flopped in the United States in the first half of 1977. The next album, *Adventure* (uk7), was released in April 1978 and did no better in the States. It was a different story for the Patti Smith Group, who scored on both sides of the Atlantic with *Easter* (p20 uk16, 1978), which contained the hit single "Because the Night" (p13 uk5) (cowritten with Bruce Springsteen), and followed with *Wave* (p18 uk41, 1979).

CBGB Goes New Wave. In early 1978 Blondie had signed with Chrysalis, but it still seemed as if the band might be in for the same fate as Television—successful in England and unknown at home. Released in February 1978, Blondie's *Plastic Letters* (uk10) did well in the UK, in part on the strength of the hit singles "Denis" (uk2) and "(I'm Always Touched by Your) Presence, Dear" (uk10). But in the fall of that year, the band released *Parallel Lines* (p6 uk1, 1978), which contained a single that hit number one on both sides of the Atlantic, "Heart of Glass." Blondie followed with several smash hit singles in America, including "Call Me" (p1 uk1, 1980), "The Tide Is High" (p1 uk1, 1980), and "Rapture" (p5 uk1, 1981). In a few short years, Blondie had gone from a band many at CBGB thought were the least likely to make any headway in the business to the most successful of the lot. Moreover, modeling the industry change from punk to new wave, the musical style of each of Blondie's singles had little resemblance to American stereotypes of punk. This is especially evident in "Rapture," which is dance-oriented and even contains a rapped section that reveals a connection to the rising hip hop movement in New York.

Made up of students from the Rhode Island School of Design, Talking Heads was led by songwriter David Byrne, and featured Jerry Harrison (guitar), Chris Frantz (drums), and Tina Weymouth (bass and vocals). Talking Heads debuted at CBGB in May 1975, gaining recognition in New York almost immediately. Eventually the band signed with Sire and released *Talking Heads: 77* in September 1977. The track "Psycho Killer" provides an example of the early Talking Heads approach, with spare instrumental accompaniment and Byrne's spastic vocal delivery. The next album, *More Songs about Buildings and Food* (p29 uk21), was released in the summer of 1978 and enjoyed moderate success, although interest began to heat up consider-

Talking Heads at CBGB as a foursome (left to right: Jerry Harrison, David Byrne, Chris Frantz, and Tina Weymouth) in 1977. Like many so-called new wave groups that would follow, Talking Heads took punk's rebellion in a new, "artsy" direction. If punk turned passion into violence, new wave turned it into introspective vocals and more complex music.

ELVIS COSTELLO ON *SATURDAY NIGHT LIVE*

by Mark Spicer

Live television and rock music have often worked hand in hand to provide us with some of the most defining moments in the history of popular culture. Who can forget, for example, the Beatles' performance, live from Abbey Road, of their brand-new single "All You Need Is Love" as part of the *Our World* global television spectacular on June 25, 1967? The event single-handedly ushered in the Summer of Love and introduced some 400 million viewers worldwide to the

hip, new psychedelic fashions of swinging London. More recently, there was the infamous "wardrobe malfunction" at the Super Bowl half-time show on February 1, 2004, where a fleeting glimpse of Janet Jackson's bare breast during her dance routine with Justin Timberlake sparked an outcry. It resulted in stricter censorship laws that, for better or worse, have since affected all mainstream television and radio broadcasts in the United States.

Although the viewing audience was far more selective, Elvis Costello's December 17, 1977 performance on the NBC sketch-comedy show *Saturday Night Live* surely ranks as another of these defining moments. For more than thirty-five years, *SNL* has been well known for its cutting-edge comedy and biting political satire, serving as the launching pad for many of North America's most beloved superstar comedians. (Dan Aykroyd, Eddie Murphy, Adam Sandler, and Will Ferrell, to name but a few, all began their careers as members of the "Not Ready for Prime-Time Players," as the *SNL* cast is sometimes called.) Yet the show has always been as much about popular music as comedy, regularly featuring dead-on parodies of rock musicians

(such as John Belushi's and Gilda Radner's respective impersonations of Joe Cocker and Patti Smith during the show's early years) and inviting important new artists to perform as the weekly musical guest. The show often gave these artists—and the new styles they represented—their first real national exposure, much as the *Ed Sullivan Show* had done for pop and rock artists in the late 1950s and 1960s.

Such was the case with Costello's debut appearance on *SNL*, which, as it turned out, was also one of rock history's happy accidents. While punk rock was enjoying its peak in the UK in 1977, the style remained largely insular, with no British punk group able to crack the charts on the other side of the Atlantic. To capitalize on the growing buzz surrounding the new style, *SNL* producer Lorne Michaels had invited none other than the Sex Pistols—the notorious darlings of British punk—to perform on the show. But the Sex Pistols were unable to secure their work visas in time, so Costello and his back-up band the Attractions were brought in as last-minute replacements. It is customary for the musical guest on *SNL* to perform twice during the ninety-minute live broadcast,

and for their first number, Elvis and the Attractions played their UK top twenty single, the reggae-tinged "Watching the Detectives." What transpired during their second performance, however, is now legendary: after singing only a few bars of "Less Than Zero," Costello abruptly stopped the band, announcing "I'm sorry, ladies and gentlemen, there's no reason to do this song here." He then led the Attractions into a snarling rendition of his as-yet unreleased song, "Radio Radio," written as an angry reaction against mainstream radio stations in Britain, particularly the BBC, and their practice of banning punk songs with politically charged or unpatriotic lyrics (most famously, the Sex Pistols' "God Save the Queen"). Michaels was reportedly furious with Costello for changing the song without having first sought his approval, and he chased the band out of the studio, threatening that they would "never work on American television again."

For many American viewers this *SNL* performance by a gangly Buddy Holly look-alike was their first glimpse of the UK punk outrage that rock critics had been raving about for months. Although punk as a style would soon be on its way out, a whole "new wave" of British and American groups quickly emerged, following Costello's lead in their willful and ironic appropriation of past rock styles. Costello himself, of course, would go on to become one of rock's most eclectic and prolific chameleons, deftly changing styles from R&B to country to classical and everything in-between over the course of a remarkable career that is still going strong. Many rock fans, however, will always remember him most fondly for that moment in 1977 when he assumed the role of Britain's punk ambassador.

Mark Spicer is Associate Professor of Music at Hunter College and the Graduate Center, City University of New York, and coeditor (with John Covach) of Sounding Out Pop: Analytical Essays in Popular Music. *He is also a professional keyboardist and vocalist.*

ably when "Take Me to the River," written by R&B singer Al Green and guitarist Teenie Hodges, was released as a single in October (p26). The next two releases, *Fear of Music* (p21, 1979) and *Remain in Light* (p19 uk21, 1980), established the band as one of new wave's leading groups, especially since they were well liked by many music critics, who praised the intellectual and artsy character of Byrne's songs. Another important aspect of the recordings of Talking Heads was the production of Brian Eno, who had performed with Roxy Music during the early 1970s but had become an important voice in experimental approaches to recording rock music.

New Wave in the American Mainstream.

While New York was central to the development of American punk and new wave, many of the most successful of the new wave bands in the late 1970s did not arise out of CBGB or Max's Kansas City. The Boston-based Cars, led by guitarist and vocalist Ric Ocasek and drummer David Robinson, were among the first new wave bands to break onto the FM rock radio playlists. Signed to Elektra, the band's debut release, *The Cars* (p18, 1978), contained two tracks that got significant airplay on mainstream rock radio stations beginning in late 1978: "My Best Friend's Girl" (p35 uk3, 1978) and "Just What I Needed" (p27, 1978; uk17, 1979). The band followed with *Candy-O* (p3, 1979), which contained "Let's Go" (p14), and continued to top the charts well into the 1980s with perennial radio favorites such as "Shake it Up" (4p, 1981). The Cars were well versed in early rock styles, and these references pervaded their music, reinforcing cover art images redolent of the 1950s used on their albums.

Florida's Tom Petty and the Heartbreakers adapted the 1960s folk-rock style of Dylan and the Byrds, so much so that the Byrds' Roger McGuinn joked that the first time he heard "American Girl" from *Tom Petty and the Heartbreakers* (uk24, 1977), he thought it was one of his own songs. As new wave was gaining in popularity in the second half of 1978, Petty and company released *You're Gonna Get It* (p23), which contained "I Need to Know." When the band's label, Shelter, was sold, they ended up recording for MCA, releasing *Damn the Torpedoes* (p2, 1979), which rose to number two in the United States on the strength of several tracks, including "Don't Do Me Like That" (p10) and "Refugee" (p15, 1980), which became staples of FM rock radio. From a contemporary perspective, the Heartbreakers hardly seem like a new wave act. Yet, during the late 1970s the group was certainly marketed among the new wavers. Part of this connection was visual, as the group often donned the colorful suits and thin ties associated with new wave. Yet, there was also a sonic connection in the group's return to the 1950s roots of rock, which was at the heart of both punk and new wave.

Perhaps the most ironic of all new wave bands was Devo, led by brothers Bob and Mark Mothersbaugh. Using costumes, space-aged keyboard and guitar sounds, and alienated vocals, the band adopted the image of futuristic beings from 1950s science-fiction movies. The Ohio band's first album, *Q: Are We Not Men? A: We Are Devo!* (uk12, 1978), produced by Brian Eno, contained a mechanistic cover of "(I Can't Get No) Satisfaction" and their theme song "Jocko Homo." In spite of poor sales in America, this album became popular in England when released in September 1978. The band did not enjoy commercial success in the United States until *Freedom of Choice* (p22, 1980), which contained the single "Whip It" (p14). Devo's northern take on new wave was echoed from a southern perspective by the Georgia group the B-52s. Led by singer Fred Schneider and featuring singers Kate Pierson

Devo took new wave to the peak of irony, often employing high-tech sounds in their music and a 1950s space-movie look in their videos and live performances. Their robot-like version of the Rolling Stones' "(I Can't Get No) Satisfaction" and the pseudo-sexual "Whip It" epitomize the detached humor of the band's music and videos.

and Cindy Wilson, the band made its first significant showing in the UK with *The B-52s* (uk22, 1979), which contained "Rock Lobster," a track that has since become closely associated with the new wave movement. Performing at Max's in New York in 1978 and on *Saturday Night Live* in 1980 brought the band a national following, which led to broader commercial success with the release of *Wild Planet* (p18, uk18) in 1980. Like the Cars, the music of the B-52s was full of references to prepsyche-delic music, including frequent surf-style guitar riffs, a prominent electric organ sound popular in the mid-1960s, and vocals from Pierson and Wilson that played with girl group stereotypes. The group even recorded a cover of Petula Clark's "Downtown." As new wave icons, the B-52s did not achieve their greatest success until the late 1980s, after nearly more than a decade of recording and touring.

During the late 1970s The Knack was another popular new wave group that was calculating in the use of musical styles and images drawn from rock's history. Based in Los Angeles and led by guitarist Doug Feiger, the band signed with Capitol. The first album, *Get the Knack* (p1, 1979), was a smash hit and was supported by a hit single, "My Sharona" (p1 uk6). The front cover of the record featured the band in early 1960s Beatle-esque attire and the back cover was meant to suggest the Beatles' appearance on the *Ed Sullivan Show*. The group wore these same outfits in promotional videos and television performances. The band even had Capitol revert to using the same logo on the record labels as it had back in the mid-1960s. All this worked only briefly, as their next album, *But the Little Girls Understand* (p15, 1980), was the last Knack album to climb the charts.

British New Wavers in America. Besides the Sex Pistols and the Clash, most of the British punk bands that dominated the charts in England never made an impact in the United States. Those acts that fit the American new wave profile, however, did enjoy success. First among these was Elvis Costello. Signed with Stiff in the UK but distributed by Columbia in the United States, Costello's releases were among the first British new wave records to make the U.S. Top 40 in the first half of 1978. While *My Aim Is True* (p32 uk14, 1977) contained the ballad "Alison," Costello

Listening Guide

Get Music ⓢ wwnorton.com/studyspace

The Cars, "My Best Friend's Girl" Elektra 45537

Words and music by Ric Ocasek, produced by Roy Thomas Baker. Reached #35 on the *Billboard* "Hot 100" chart and #3 in the UK in mid-1978.

FORM: Compound AABA, with A sections based on contrasting verse-chorus form. The B section is instrumental, featuring a guitar solo and based on the music from the chorus.

TIME SIGNATURE: 4/4.

INSTRUMENTATION: Electric guitars, bass, synthesizer, organ, drums, handclaps, lead and backup vocals.

	0:00–0:16	**Introduction**, 8 mm.	Clean guitar for 4 bars, and then handclaps enter at 0:09.
A	0:16–0:48	**Verse 1**, 16 mm.	Vocals enter, with full band joining in after 4 bars, along with backup vocals. "You're always dancin' . . ."
	0:48–1:08	**Chorus**, 10 mm.	Choral vocals, as organ enters. Ends with 4 mm. rockabilly guitar that leads to next verse. "She's my best friend's . . ."
A	1:08–1:40	**Verse 2**, 16 mm.	As before, but now with "96 Tears" organ and lightly arpeggiated guitar in first half and rockabilly pattern in second half. "You got your nuclear boots . . ."
	1:40–2:00	**Chorus**, 10 mm.	As before, 4 mm. link leads to instrumental chorus this time. "She's my best friend's . . ."
B	2:00–2:20	**Instrumental Chorus**, 10 mm.	6-bar guitar melodic solo, then 4-bar link leads back to last verse.
A	2:20–2:51	**Verse 3**, 16 mm.	Repeat of verse 1 lyrics with verse 3 accompaniment.
	2:51–3:11	**Chorus**, 10 mm.	As before, 4 mm. link leads to coda.
	3:11–3:43	**Coda**, 10 mm.	New melody based on chorus with chords from verse. Synthesizer strings enter in the background at 3:19, and hand claps at 3:27, as fade-out begins, "My best friend's girlfriend."

became much better known for aggressive and clever attacks on the status quo. This was especially true after his performance on *Saturday Night Live* in late 1977. His second album, *This Year's Model* (p30 uk4, 1978)—recorded with a new backup band called the Attractions—contained "Pump It Up" (uk24), which is a good example of Costello's more raucous side, as is the single "Radio, Radio" (uk29, 1978). Elvis Costello and the Attractions followed with *Armed Forces* (p10 uk2,

1979), completing a trio of albums that would establish Costello as one of rock's most heralded songwriters.

The Police also debuted in America in the context of new wave. Their first album *Outlandos d'Amour* (p23) from early 1979 contained both "Roxanne" (p32 uk12) and "Can't Stand Losing You" (p42 uk2). Initially blending a strong reggae influence into their style, the Police became well known for the complex drumming of Stewart Copeland, the literary lyrics of Sting, and the atmospheric guitar of Andy Summers. A series of successful albums followed, including *Regatta de Blanc* (p25 uk1, 1979) and *Zenyatta Mondatta* (p5 uk1, 1980). Although Police songs from this period, such as "So Lonely" (uk6) and "Message in a Bottle" (uk1), are known well in the United States, the group did not achieve much success in the singles market until late 1980. The Police became one of the most important bands of the early 1980s, and will be discussed further in Chapter 11.

Pangs of Rock History? One aspect of new wave sets it apart from the hippie rock that preceded it: new wave bands had a clear fascination with earlier musical styles and—perhaps more important—with the visual images associated with those styles. Thus, it's Elvis Costello who wears horn-rimmed glasses like Buddy Holly, straight leg pants and short hair in an era of bellbottoms and shoulder-length hair. Why this dimension of new wave was important to these musicians and their fans is discussed below, but for now we will focus on the music itself. Spotting the references to rock history in the visual aspect of new wave is easy, but how can we hear stylistic references to earlier rock *in the music itself*? The Cars' "My Best Friend's Girl" offers an example rich in new wave references to past styles. Notice first the handclaps that enter during the introduction, reminiscent of early 1960s girl-group recordings ("My Boyfriend's Back") or early Beatles tracks ("I Want to Hold Your Hand"). The rockabilly guitar lick that occurs in the passages linking the choruses to the verses seem inspired by Carl Perkins, Elvis Presley, or Gene Vincent records from the late 1950s. The repeated organ chords that enter with the second verse bring to mind the mid-1960s garage-band sound. Ocasek's vocal delivery is full of vocal hiccups that imitate those of Buddy Holly and the naïve innocence of much teen music before the mid-1960s. These many references to pre-hippie rock are not particularly well reinforced by the form, which follows a compound AABA design not too different from Boston's "More Than a Feeling," employing verse-chorus pairs for A sections and a guitar solo for the bridge. Yet, the Cars material here is far simpler in its harmonic content than the harmonies in the Boston track, and all the sections are repeated without much structural change. Like much new wave, this song is less an attempt to duplicate earlier rock styles than an eclectic view of earlier rock taken in through a late 1970s "lens."

New wave's relationship to past rock-music styles is the key to understanding how it differentiated itself from mainstream rock. Rock music from psychedelia through late 1970s mainstream rock was founded on the hippie aesthetic: the idea that rock music should take the listener on a kind of trip and use all the possibilities of technology—in terms of both equipment and instrumental and compositional skill—to do so. Rock should deal with important issues, not teen love, and should reflect on man's place in the universe. New wave musicians moved away from these governing principles. They scaled back the musical complexities and shortened the tunes, returned to topics of teenage romance, and no longer paraded their musical prowess. Thus the music-stylistic and visual references in new wave were almost always to rock before *Sgt. Pepper*. The new wave haircuts, clothes, album art, music, and lyrics all seem to reject hippie culture and music. But in rejecting the hippie present, were new wavers advocating a return to rock's past? The answer is no; instead, new wave musicians were making ironic references to earlier music—they were not embracing past styles but rather using them to offer a critique of the present and a vision of the future.

Mainstream versus New Wave. One way to see the contrast between the mainstream rock and new wave approaches in the late 1970s is to compare bands and artists with obvious similarities but also with telling differences. American Gary Wright had been a member of Spooky Tooth (along with Mick Jones in his days before Foreigner), but set out on a solo career. He released *The Dream Weaver* (p7) in late 1975 and his music caught on in 1976 with two hit tracks, "Dream Weaver"

Sound Check

Artist	Peter Frampton	Boston	Foreigner
Title	Show Me the Way (Live)	More Than a Feeling	Feels Like the First Time
Chart peak	p6 1976	p5 1976	p4 1977
Form	Contrasting verse-chorus	Compound AABA	Compound AABA (modified)
Rhythm	4/4	4/4	4/4 (2/2)
Instrumentation	Electric guitar Acoustic guitar Bass Drums Lead vocal Background vocal	Electric guitar Acoustic guitar Bass Drums Lead vocal Background vocal Handclaps	Electric guitar Bass Drums Lead vocal Background vocal Synthesizer Organ
Comments	Voice box changes the sound of the lead guitar part Extended guitar solo False ending helps to regain listener attention	Each A section includes a verse and a chorus Vast dynamics, going from soft to loud Doubled guitar solo	Second A section modified by added bridge with references to classical music Second bridge features guitar solo Lyrics offer a thinly veiled commentary on "romance"

(p2) and "Love Is Alive" (p2). Englishman Gary Numan was originally a member of Tubeway Army, whose second album *Replicas* was number one in the UK in the summer of 1979 with the help of the hit single, "Are We 'Friends' Electric?" (uk1). Numan went solo as well, releasing *The Pleasure Principle* (p16 uk1) in September 1979, which contained the hit "Cars" (p9 uk1). Comparing "Dream Weaver" with "Cars" reveals that both tracks rely almost exclusively on synthesized sounds. Wright's warm timbres, saturated with reverb and echo, are similar to the broad textures used by progressive-rock keyboardists such as Rick Wakeman or Keith Emerson, while Numan's sounds are much harsher, creating a drier, more focused sound. Wright's vocals show a blues influence and Numan's are clipped and almost mechanical. Both Wright and Numan employ futuristic images on their respective album sleeves. Yet, Wright's future seems optimistic and utopian while Numan's seems cold and mechanical, dominated by machines. Despite similarities to "Dream Weaver," Numan's "Cars" makes its mark by rejecting the hippie dreams of fantastic

Sex Pistols	The Cars
Anarchy in the UK	My Best Friend's Girl
1977	p35 1978
Simple verse (modified)	Compound AABA
4/4	4/4
Electric guitar Bass Drums Lead vocal Background vocal	Electric guitar Bass Drums Lead vocal Background vocal Synthesizer Organ Handclaps
Form modified by inserted bridge sections Refrain at the end of each verse Intentional guitar feedback throughout the first half of verse 4	A sections based on contrasting verse-chorus Different musical styles highlighted in guitar (rockabilly) Handclaps reminiscent of girl groups

The music-stylistic contrast between Heart's Anne Wilson (left) and Blondie's Debbie Harry (right) are further underscored by these live images. Ever the rocker, Wilson belts out her vocal with a raised fist, while Harry flashes a coy and calculated shrug of her shoulder.

voyages into the bright technological future—Numan rejects the trip, or at least suggests a very different kind of trip.

Another comparison can be drawn between the music of Heart and Blondie. Led by sisters Anne and Nancy Wilson, Heart's debut album, *Dreamboat Annie* (p7, 1976), rose on the U.S. charts with the help of the tracks "Crazy on You" (p35) and "Magic Man" (9p). The group's music from the late 1970s has both a harder edge, in which Anne Wilson belts out her vocals with power and authority, and a softer, more acoustically oriented side, often showcasing Nancy's guitar. Anne Wilson adopted the stage persona of the tough, hard-driving woman. Her singing was often forceful and technically schooled, filled with bluesy melodic twists and turns. Debbie Harry (of Blondie), in contrast, had a vocal approach that was much more limited, far less free rhythmically, and devoid of any blues influence. This is immediately evident in comparing Heart's "Straight On" (15p, 1978) with Blondie's "Heart of Glass." Wilson belts out the vocals of "Straight On," performing forcefully often on the verge of screaming, featuring a noticeable thick vibrato. Harry's style is motivated by a rejection of hippie technical virtuosity. It is based on an amateurish quality common among many new wave performances. Harry's singing in this regard is similar to that of David Byrne and Ric Ocasek, neither of whom would be considered "polished" vocalists in a traditional sense. That was part of new wave's return-to-simplicity charm, and central to its rejection of rock's hippie legacy.

In the second half of the 1970s, mainstream rock continued many of the stylistic practices of the first half of the decade. It made adjustments in response to the tremendous growth of the record and radio businesses, as big albums came to dominate the charts and radio preferred shorter less expansive tracks. Fans of late 1970s rock argue that it was the culmination of hippie rock, while critics contend that it was cynically created to make as much money as possible for the corporations that came to dominate the music business during this time. Punk reacted against what it saw as an indulgent rock music industry, challenging its pomposity with a return to rock and roll basics. As powerful as the punk challenge was, however, it was commercially co-opted into a style called new wave. New wave kept much of punk's return-to-simplicity attitude and rejection of the hippie aesthetic. Yet, by the early 1980s, most new wave was incorporated within the mainstream rock playlists of FM radio, attesting to the influence of new wave, but also revealing underlying similarities between new wave and mainstream rock. When mainstream rock and new wave came together during the early 1980s, it seemed as if hippie rock had run its course and an era had ended. Although elements of the hippie aesthetic would reemerge innumerable times over the course of the 1980s and 1990s—especially in heavy metal and music videos—the era of ambitious rock devoted to the idea of music as a trip was over.

FURTHER READING

Victor Bockris, *Transformer: The Lou Reed Story* (Simon & Schuster, 1994).

Craig Bromberg, *The Wicked Ways of Malcolm McLaren* (Harper & Row, 1989).

Theo Cateforis, *Are We Not New Wave? Modern Pop at the Turn of the 1980s* (University of Michigan Press, 2011).

Jerome Davis, *Talking Heads* (Vintage, 1986).

Toby Goldstein, *Frozen Fire: The Story of the Cars* (Contemporary Books, 1985).

Debbie Harry, Chris Stein, and Victor Bockris, *Making Tracks: The Rise of Blondie* (Da Capo, 1998).

Clinton Heylin, *From the Velvets to the Voidoids: The Birth of American Punk Rock* (A Cappella, 2005).

Brian Hinton, *Let Them All Talk: The Music of Elvis Costello* (Sanctuary, 1999).

Glen Matlock with Pete Silverton, *I Was a Teenage Sex Pistol* (Omnibus, 1990).

Legs McNeil and Gillian McCain, *Please Kill Me: The Uncensored Oral History of Punk* (Penguin, 1996).

Thurston Moore and Byron Coley, *No Wave: Post Punk. Underground. New York. 1976–1980* (Abrams Image, 2008).

John Savage, *England's Dreaming: Anarchy, Sex Pistols, Punk Rock, and Beyond* (St. Martin's Griffin, 2002).

VISIT STUDYSPACE AT WWNORTON.COM/STUDYSPACE

Access free review material such as:
- music links
- performer info
- practice quizzes
- outlines
- interactive listening guide software

THE 1980s

The 1980s began with the defeat of incumbent president Jimmy Carter and the election of Ronald Reagan, a Hollywood actor turned politician. Reagan's presidency marked a new conservative attitude throughout much of the country and in popular culture. In his speeches and public remarks, Reagan evoked images of America's idyllic past, and his amiable, "grandfatherly" style helped many to regain their confidence in government after Watergate and the Iran hostage crisis.

Reagan's economic policy was driven by "supply-side economics"—lower taxes on wealthy Americans that would, arguably, inspire everyone to work harder (because they'd be keeping more income). His foreign policy embraced building up American military forces and weapons systems. Reagan believed that an arms race would cripple the Soviet Union (which he referred to as the "evil empire"), whose economy could not afford to keep pace with American advances. However, in the midst of this Cold War buildup, Mikhail Gorbachev became leader of the Communist Party in 1985, advocating policies of *glasnost* (openness) and *perestroika* (restructuring of Soviet government along Western lines). Historians differ on who gets credit for it, but in November 1989 (almost a year after Reagan left office), the Berlin Wall—a symbol of the division between the Soviet Union and the Western powers—fell, signaling an end to a cold war that had lasted almost half a century. By 1991, the Soviet Union had broken apart and the United States emerged as the world's leading superpower.

The 1980s also marked the emergence and growth of the AIDS epidemic, with more than 150,000 cases diagnosed and more than 90,000 AIDS-related deaths reported in the United States from 1981 to 1989.* AIDS was made most publicly visible by movie star Rock Hudson, who died from the disease in 1985. Hudson had been a leading man in romantic comedies for years, and his homosexuality came as a surprise to many of his fans. Despite the sensationalism following the disclosure of Hudson's sexuality, many Americans learned about AIDS for the first time, leading to an increased awareness of the disease and its seriousness. In 1991, Queen frontman Freddie Mercury succumbed to the disease, further raising the music world's awareness of AIDS.

The American economy grew in many ways during the 1980s, but no sector advanced as impressively and publicly as high tech. The space program had provided many spin-off benefits and technologies, and the development of ever-smaller,

*Statistics compiled from AVERT: www.avert.org/usa-statistics.htm

more powerful computers made it possible for home computers to be useful and affordable to most Americans. The earliest Apple computers from the mid-1970s were made from kits. By the early 1980s, however, Steve Jobs and Steve Wozniak were marketing a more refined home unit, while Microsoft founders Bill Gates and Paul Allen were offering the MS-DOS operating system for the IBM PC. In 1984, a now-famous commercial during the Super Bowl announced the arrival of the Macintosh computer, and by 1985, the first version of Windows was available for the PC. These years also marked the beginning of Inter-

net use by the general public; CompuServe offered home email in 1979 and real-time chat in 1980, and the number of users increased throughout the decade, though the real Internet explosion would not occur until the 1990s.

While many benefited from technologies developed by NASA, the space agency also experienced one of its greatest disasters in 1986. The space shuttle *Challenger* exploded minutes after taking off, killing all the astronauts aboard, including Christa McAuliffe. McAuliffe was a high school teacher who was making the journey in order to bring aspects of the space pro-

AIDS victims and activists in the March on Washington for Lesbian and Gay Rights, 1987. More than 150,000 cases of AIDS were diagnosed between 1981 and 1989. Many AIDS activists did not think the Reagan administration sufficiently supported their cause.

schoolchildren.

Another technology that experienced dramatic growth during the decade was cable television. By mid-decade, many American homes were wired to receive premium movies, news, and sports from channels like HBO, CNN, and ESPN. Most important for the history of rock music, MTV was launched, creating competition for FM radio, which had been the central way to expose the music to a large body of listeners. And just as it was forced to share its audience with a new kind of radio emerging on the AM band: talk radio. Taking advantage of the neglect into which many AM stations had fallen, entrepreneurial broadcasters such as Rush Limbaugh began offering hours of daily political and cultural commentary, sometimes from the left of the political spectrum, but most often from the right. Soon Limbaugh and others built up syndication networks, in a sense reinventing the radio networks of the '30s and '40s, as millions of listeners heard the same programming across

The Cosby Show was one of the most popular shows of the 1980s. It featured an upper-middle-class African-American family dealing not with issues of race, but usually with the more mundane problems of their school-age children. Here, Cliff Huxtable (Bill Cosby) and his son Theo (Malcolm-Jamal Warner) discuss marijuana found in Theo's school book.

11

I WANT MY MTV

During the late 1970s, rock became increasingly influenced by the idea of the smash album, and disco and punk challenged the rock status quo. Although it seemed as if these two styles would eclipse mainstream rock during the 1980s, neither punk nor disco became important in the 1980s pop music mainstream. Early in the decade, punk retreated into an underground scene, replaced in the limelight by new wave, which quickly blended into mainstream rock radio playlists. After reminding musicians that music was not only for listening but also for dancing, the craze for disco music ended almost as quickly as it had begun. Although punk and disco fell out of favor, the musical and cultural legacies of both of these styles continued into the 1980s.

Big changes were in store for rock music during the 1980s. Music Television (MTV) began to challenge radio as the most important medium for popular music, and heavy metal and rap emerged from the underground by the end of the decade. The rise of MTV led to the emergence of many visually oriented acts during the 1980s, and dance music eventually formed the core of early MTV programming. The decade also saw the continued development of mainstream rock and new wave, and punk fueled the development of hardcore and indie rock.

MTV IS ON THE AIR

The Roots of MTV in Promotional Video. Even though rock musicians had used short films and video performances to promote their music for decades, the idea of a television station devoted to nothing but promotional videos was not at all feasible until the 1980s. In fact, even in the early 1980s the idea seemed strange to many broadcasters. Rather than a music industry initiative, the emergence of MTV was closely aligned with the development of cable television. Initially, cable was seen as necessary in areas where antenna transmission was unsatisfactory. For people who lived in hilly or mountainous areas, for example, cable television provided a reliable

Soon after its release in 1982, Michael Jackson's *Thriller* became the best-selling album of all time. It contained several major hits, including "Billie Jean," "Beat It," and "Thriller." Jackson took full advantage of MTV to help promote his talents as both a musician and a performer. His innovative videos became instant classics. Jackson teamed up with film director John Landis to make the video for "Thriller," a short film featuring Jackson as a lovable boyfriend who turns into a gruesome monster. Despite the monster-movie aesthetic, the video provided Jackson ample time to show off his exquisite dancing. Jackson was one of the first performers in the MTV era to successfully combine hit music with artistic visuals.

way to deliver programming. Like any industry, cable television looked for ways to expand during the 1980s, even in areas where over-the-air transmission was perfectly viable. In order to develop new markets, cable had to offer something the networks and local stations could not, and at first the focus was on recent movies broadcast without commercial interruptions. Because there were no commercials, customers were required to pay for the service. Soon, cable channels such as Home Box Office (HBO) became quite successful, and cable providers looked for more specialty channels to add to their roster. Channels dedicated to sports, news, and weather were devised to bolster cable packages. MTV became the cable channel that focused on music.

Rock music was no newcomer to American television in the early 1980s. Going back to *American Bandstand* in the late 1950s, teenagers had proved that they would happily tune in to listen to new music and watch (often lip-synched) performances. The question for the people who developed MTV was not whether teens would tune in, but whether they would watch music television around the clock on a specialty channel. In the early days of planning MTV, two models were proposed. The first was to show nothing but promotional videos provided by the record companies at their expense. Critics of this approach pointed out that it would make MTV nothing more than an advertising mechanism for record labels. This critical faction, led by former Monkees guitarist Michael Nesmith, pushed for a more artistic approach. They argued that the videos should be experimental and innovative, not simply commercials. They saw great potential in music videos for expanding the artistic range of pop music by bringing filmmaking and music together in a symbiotic relationship. In the end, the corporate model was used, and it would be several years before artists explored the more creative aspects of music videos. On August 1,

MTV debuted on August 1, 1981, and its first video was, appropriately, "Video Killed the Radio Star" by the Buggles. The song and the visuals associated with it—exploding radios replaced by televisions—signaled the industry impact that MTV would have in the coming decades.

1981, MTV went on the air with the Buggles' "Video Killed the Radio Star," which followed in the tradition of the promotional videos of the 1960s.

On the Air, but Who's Watching? MTV faced enormous challenges in its earliest days, the first of which was having enough videos to fill the broadcasting hours. Videos had been growing in importance in Australia, New Zealand, and the United Kingdom, so many groups popular in these regions had material to offer. In the United States, videos had also appeared on shows such as *Saturday Night Live* and *Video Concert Hall* (on the USA network). However, MTV needed material to fill the cycle of an entire day. Initially, record companies were not entirely convinced that investing money in music videos would pay off in additional sales, and many of the first music videos were shot on shoestring budgets. One reason for the record companies' reservations was that cable television was not widely available in America in the first half of the 1980s. As viewers learned about the benefits of cable, however, more and more communities added the service, and by the end of the decade it was much more accessible. Initially, MTV had its biggest audience wherever HBO and other premium cable movie services had enjoyed success—mainly in the Midwest. Unlike HBO, MTV did sell advertising, so their programming choices were driven by this Midwest target audience, which consisted mainly of white teenagers. To appeal to these viewers, MTV played videos by mainstream rock artists who were, with only rare exceptions, white as well. However, as more new material was created in the early 1980s, dance-oriented styles also became central to the MTV lineup.

An important challenge to these stereotypes occurred in early 1983, with Michael Jackson's "Billie Jean." By some accounts, MTV refused to play Jackson's video because he was black (or because they believed their white viewers would not want to watch black artists). The legend in the music business is that Jackson's label, Epic, threatened to pull all of their artists off of MTV if the video was not aired, although this story has been disputed. Jackson's video first played on MTV in March 1983, and the enormous success of "Billie Jean" greatly increased the popularity of the network. Before long, record companies considered music videos to be crucial promotional tools for their artists, and MTV began to rival FM radio as the place to make or break hit records. With the struggle to represent nonwhite performers coupled with the growing importance of music videos, by the late 1980s MTV became a source of controversy in the rock community. Clearly, music videos privileged visual features over musical ones, and the look of an artist became paramount. Thus, MTV provided the perfect platform for artists who used the visual dimension as an important part of their act, while sometimes neglecting those who were not young, stylish, or physically attractive. For artists such as Michael Jackson and Madonna, who took full advantage of this new set of artistic and promotional tools, MTV allowed an entirely new way to project both music and image.

DANCE MUSIC OF THE 1980S

Music Video's New Elite: Michael Jackson and Madonna. As discussed in Chapter 9, Michael Jackson's career began during the early 1970s at Motown with the Jackson 5. Known for bubblegum pop hits, the group increasingly turned to

Madonna was one of the earliest dance-oriented artists from the United States to receive heavy exposure on MTV. Her music was influenced by her dance-club background and a close association with many of the most important instrumentalists and producers to work in the New York dance scene. Here, she dances and sings during a 1985 concert.

disco-oriented dance music in the mid-1970s, such as the popular "Dancing Machine" (p2 r1, 1974). Jackson left the group and Motown in 1975, signing to Epic Records as a solo artist. As disco increased in popularity during the late 1970s, Jackson teamed with veteran producer Quincy Jones to record the album *Off the Wall* (p3 r1 uk3, 1979), which contained four Top 10 pop hits. Jackson and Jones teamed again to record *Thriller* (p1 r1 uk1, 1982), which was released with enormous anticipation. Jackson was at the height of his fame, and the music video era, which suited him perfectly, was on an upswing. Thriller contained seven top ten singles, which included two number one crossover hits, "Billie Jean" and "Beat It." "The Girl Is Mine," a duet with Paul McCartney, hit number two on the pop charts. To date, *Thriller* is the best-selling album in the history of the music business, with more that 100 million copies sold. Jackson's next album, *Bad* (p1 r1 uk1, 1987), continued this success, containing four songs that hit the number one slot on both pop and rhythm and blues charts during 1987 and 1988: "Bad," "The Way You Make Me Feel," "I Just Can't Stop Loving You," and "The Man in the Mirror." Throughout this incredible run on the charts, Jackson not only sold tens of millions of records for Epic, but he also won numerous awards. He was arguably the biggest star in popular music during the 1980s and earned the title King of Pop. Jackson's music in the 1980s was almost always driven by a strong beat, showing not only his roots in 1970s black pop but also his experience with disco. "Billie Jean" is representative, beginning with a groove laid down in the bass and drums, which serves as the musical foundation for the song. Jackson's vocals project a sense of restrained emotional urgency during the verses, and the chorus provides the more open and catchy melodic hook. Jackson's famous high-voiced "ooo" can be heard scattered throughout the track, which features a Quincy Jones arrangement that builds continuously as the song unfolds.

Jackson was the perfect artist to take advantage of the emerging video age. As a performer, he continued the tradition of slick and sometimes athletic choreography made famous by the Temptations, updated with his silver glove and patented "Moonwalk" dance step. His video performances provided an opportunity to showcase his enormous dancing skill, making his videos stand out during the mid-1980s. Infusing unprecedented creative energy into his video productions, Jackson produced highly ambitious music videos. The first of these was the extended twelve-minute video for "Thriller," directed by Hollywood's John Landis and employing state-of-the-art special effects. The popularity of this video on MTV was buttressed by an hour-long documentary titled, *Making Michael Jackson's Thriller*, which aired nearly as frequently as the video itself.

Although Jackson's records after the mid-1970s no longer appeared on Motown, he continued Berry Gordy's practice of straddling the line between rhythm and blues and pop. Two of *Thriller*'s top hits featured white musicians who were well known to mainstream rock fans at the time. The duet with Paul McCartney, "The Girl Is Mine," paired Jackson with the most publicly visible Beatle, and Eddie Van Halen's guitar solo on "Beat It" brought a rising guitar icon into the picture. This was all smart business, and it certainly reflected Jackson's musical interests. Yet Jackson's crossover practices drew the ire of many critics who accused him of selling out his blackness. Of course, Jackson's close association with Motown during the first half of the 1970s made him an especially inviting target. Jackson, however, never backed down from his efforts to bridge the gaps he saw between white and black culture, and he continued to extend his musical range until the end of his career.

Like Michael Jackson, Madonna depended as much on the visual aspect of her music as the sonic dimension. She had worked as a professional dancer in New York, appearing at various points with the Pearl Lange and Alvin Ailey dance companies. Her first recordings enjoyed success within the New York dance-club scene, and she signed to Sire records, one of the most important labels to release New York–based new wave. Her 1984 debut album *Madonna* (p8 r20) contained two hit singles, "Borderline" (p10) and "Lucky Star" (p4 uk14), and the videos for these songs provided an early glimpse of one of the most controversial figures of the video age. By early 1985, Madonna's *Like a Virgin* (p1 r10 uk1) was climbing the pop album charts, while four singles from the album hit the top five, including "Like a Virgin" (p1 r9 uk3) and "Material Girl" (p2 uk3). *True Blue* did even better, reaching number one on the pop album charts in 1986 (uk1) and producing three number one pop singles that same year—"Live to Tell," "Papa Don't Preach," and "Open Your Heart."

Madonna benefitted from MTV exposure during the mid-1980s, using a combination of fashion, music, and dance to reach a new visually oriented audience. Here she performs in 1990 on her worldwide "Blonde Ambition" tour.

Listening Guide

Michael Jackson, "Billie Jean" Epic ES-823

Words and music by Michael Jackson, produced by Quincy Jones. Rose to #1 on the *Billboard* "Hot 100" and "Black Singles" charts, as well as on the UK charts, in 1983. Contained on the album *Thriller*, which also topped the album charts.

FORM: Simple verse-chorus. Most of the song is built over a repeating bass line (heard in the introduction) and a simple four-chord progression. Both the verse and the chorus use this material, making the form a simple verse-chorus type. This song also features a **"pre-chorus."** A pre-chorus is a section that is no longer the verse but not yet the chorus and functions as a way of intensifying the arrival of the chorus. In this case, the pre-chorus contrasts with the material used in the verse and chorus, making the form as a whole a simple verse-chorus with contrasting pre-chorus. The arrangement is constructed traditionally, adding new elements along the way and becoming increasingly busy as the song unfolds.

TIME SIGNATURE: 4/4.

INSTRUMENTATION: Drums, electronic percussion, synthesizers, electric piano, guitar, lead and backup vocals. Notice that all the voices are Jackson's and that he frequently doubles the melody an octave higher than the main voice.

0:00–0:28	**Introduction**, 14 mm.	10 mm. of drums and bass set up the song's groove, and then the synthesizer enters playing a repeating 4-chord pattern.
0:28–0:53	**Verse 1**, 12 mm.	Lead vocal enters; note the heavy reverb on Jackson's voice and the use of vocal octaves at the end, "She was more like a beauty queen . . ."

Like Jackson, Madonna's music is often driven by a dance beat, drawing from her dance-club background and a close association with many of the most important instrumentalists and producers to work in the New York dance scene. "Like a Virgin" provides an interesting comparison with Jackson's "Billie Jean." The tracks start out in a similar manner. Yet, while the repeating bass line in Jackson's song is somewhat menacing, the bass in Madonna's song is buoyant and celebratory. Madonna also seems to borrow Jackson's high-voiced "ooo" which can be heard in her chorus as "hey." "Like a Virgin" also betrays a dance-club influence in the layers of synthesizers that create an accompanimental backdrop for Madonna's singing. Later tracks expanded her stylistic range to include moodier songs such as "Papa Don't Preach" and sensual songs like "Justify My Love" (the video for which was banned on MTV). Madonna did not write or produce many of her early hits, but she began to take a more active role in the creative aspects of her music as her career developed, earning songwriter and production credits beginning with *True Blue* in 1986.

0:53–1:10	**Verse 2**, 8 mm.	As before, "She told me her name . . ."
1:10–1:26	**Pre-Chorus**, 8 mm.	Contrasting musical material, as arrangement builds through the addition of new synthesizer melody, electric piano, and splash cymbal. "People always told me . . ."
1:26–1:50	**Chorus**, 12 mm.	Harmony vocals enter. Note rhythmic octaves in the guitar, "Billie Jean is not my lover . . ."
1:50–2:15	**Verse 3**, 12 mm.	As before, with added string melody in the synthesizer part and more activity between voice parts, "For forty days . . ."
2:15–2:32	**Verse 4**, 8 mm.	As verse 3, "She told my baby . . ."
2:32–2:48	**Pre-Chorus**, 8 mm.	Builds as before, but now with new string melody, "People always told me . . ."
2:48–3:05	**Chorus**, 8 mm.	As before, but now with new string melody at end of phrase, "Billie Jean . . ."
3:05–3:28	**Chorus**, 12 mm.	Guitar line and synthesizer trumpet line are added.
3:28–3:54	**Interlude**, 12 mm.	Rhythmic guitar line highlighted, with vocals at end.
3:54–4:18	**Chorus**, 12 mm.	As before, but with guitar line mixed forward and more vocal interjections. "Billie Jean . . ."
4:18–4:50	**Coda**, 16 mm.	Various improvised singing along with harmony vocals as song fades out.

Madonna's albums and singles in the mid-1980s established her as one of the most important figures in pop music, and she remains among the most successful acts in the music business. She has continually challenged aspects of what she perceives to be some of society's most troubling issues and practices. Early on, her "boy toy" image cast her as a sex object, although this was done with great irony— Madonna put on the role of sex object in order to call it into question, and a link can be made to previous figures who adopted personae, such as Jim Morrison and David Bowie. In this way, Madonna has explored the boundaries of sexual conduct, racial issues, women's roles, and spirituality. Detractors have accused her of seeking publicity by titillating and shocking audiences, while her supporters have praised her methods of raising important social issues for debate. Whatever position you take on Madonna's place in popular culture, video images clearly played a central role in her music. Her videos are rich in symbolism and striking juxtapositions—a factor that has caused many academics to offer extended interpretations of their deeper meanings.

MOTOWN 25: CELEBRATION, NOSTALGIA, AND ACTUALITY

by Andrew Flory

On May 16, 1983, a two-hour television special aired on NBC entitled "Motown 25: Yesterday, Today, and Forever" that celebrated the music and historical achievements of Motown. With a reputation for creating world-famous stars, nearly 700 charting singles to its credit, and a history of successfully integrating black performers into the mainstream, there was much to admire in Motown's accomplishments during its first quarter-century. The Emmy-winning program

was primarily a tribute to Motown founder Berry Gordy, Jr., and it was produced in the style of an awards show. Hosted by comedian Richard Pryor, it featured musical performances, comedy sketches, and choreographed dance segments. The show made it clear that the company—now officially called Motown Industries—had changed dramatically over time, growing from a Detroit-based record company to a large-scale Los Angeles entertainment corporation that retained little of the character, sound, and personnel of its early years.

The most important performances on the program were by former Motown artists who had left the company for the greener pastures of major labels. Coming just weeks after the peak of "Sexual Healing," his first hit for Columbia, Marvin Gaye's performance included a monologue about black contributions to American culture (accompanied by his own piano playing), followed by his 1971 hit "What's Going On." The program's finale included a brief reunion of the Supremes, arguably the most popular Motown group of the 1960s, led by Diana Ross, who had left Motown for RCA Records two years earlier. In a bittersweet thank you

to Gordy, Ross acknowledged the many defections from the Motown stable, assuring the audience, "It's not about the people who leave Motown that's important, but it's about the people who come back, and tonight everybody came back."

One of the most notable performers who came back was Michael Jackson, whose appearance on "Motown 25" remains legendary in the annals of pop music. At the time of the broadcast, his second album for Epic Records, *Thriller*, was in the middle of a record yearlong run at the top of the *Billboard 200* album chart, and he was easily the most popular entertainer in the world. After a reunion of the Jackson 5, the anticipation of a modern-era Jackson song was incredible, extending far beyond the studio audience to include the millions of television viewers. *Thriller* was already a smash hit, but this was the first chance many of Jackson's fans had to see him perform this material live. He energetically paced the stage while reminiscing about the old days with Motown then, symbolically shedding his youthful past, declared his preference for "new songs" and launched into his current hit, "Billie Jean." It was not the vocal performance of this song that stunned the nation, for the television broadcast featured Jackson lip-synching to his well-known record. Instead, Jackson's physical presentation took the spotlight.

Donning his trademark sequined white glove and silver socks, his heavily choreographed introduction began with several highly stylized hip thrusts. While the audience screamed, Jackson's feet constantly moved as he kicked and spun freely, frenetically accompanying the song's controversial text about fathering an illegitimate child. It was not until the instrumental bridge, however, that Jackson made history by performing his signature dance move—the Moonwalk— for the first time. Perhaps more than any other appearance of his career, this five-minute performance helped to define Michael Jackson as the "King of Pop." But in many ways, it also helped to signify the end of the Motown era.

In hindsight, "Motown 25" was a deeply conflicted undertaking. Subtitled "Yesterday, Today, Forever," this special highlighted the nearly impossible task that Motown faced during the early 1980s: the need to celebrate the past while trying to remain vital in the present. This was a time of great nostalgic interest in early rhythm and blues, so there was real public interest in Motown's exploring its own history. However the company had grown and changed since the 1960s, and after focusing so much on the glory days, "Motown 25" did little to hide the bleak outlook of its present state. Fewer and fewer Motown acts were cracking the pop charts, and the departure of many of its most successful artists, songwriters, and producers meant the company's

music division was not the juggernaut it had once been. Two of the most successful Motown artists of the time, Lionel Richie and Rick James, did not even attend the live taping, allowing former Motown greats like Ross, Gaye, and Jackson to steal the show.

Although the program was ostensibly a tribute to the musical legacy of the company, the high production value of the show highlighted the fact that Motown was more interested in television and film production than music. Furthermore, the company's interest in producing music had drifted away from the styles that made it a household name during the 1960s and 1970s. The great Motown backing band the Funk Brothers had been largely forgotten after the company moved to Los Angeles in the 1970s, and "Motown 25" featured an awards show orchestra. The orchestra did little to recapture the early Motown sound while backing the performances of groups like the Four Tops, the Temptations, and the Miracles. In the end, the internal conflict among Motown's past, present, and future gave way in 1988, when Berry Gordy, Jr. made the first of several moves to sell the once fiercely independent company to a major corporate conglomerate. This signaled the end of what was arguably the most successful reign of black ownership in American music history to date.

Andrew Flory (Carleton College) is the author of I Hear a Symphony: Listening to the Music of Motown.

Although his album *Thriller* was a hit for Epic at the time, Michael Jackson agreed to perform on "Motown 25"—a tribute to the Jackson 5's longtime label. Jackson's performance at this event became legendary. It was here he first performed the "Moonwalk." Jackson brought down the house with this performance and further solidified his status as the world's most popular entertainer.

With the establishment of MTV in the early 1980s, music videos became an important way for performers to reach audiences visually. The video for Michael Jackson's "Thriller" was the most important music video of the early 1980s. A collaborative effort between Jackson and filmmaker John Landis, *Thriller* exceeded the scope of early music videos in length, depth, and creativity. Based loosely on Landis's film *An American Werewolf in London*, the fourteen-

movie with music by veteran film composer Elmer Bernstein. After being exposed to a full moon, Jackson's character transforms into a werewolf, using dramatic special effects more common in movies than in music videos (1).

The audience perspective then shifts to Jackson and the same girlfriend in the setting of a modern movie theater, revealing that the werewolf scene was actually a film-with-the-film (2).

After Jackson's date is frightened to the point of leaving the theater, the music of "Thriller" begins. Jackson presents the verses of the song in a famous two-minute sequence while walking down a dark street (3).

A spoken interlude by horror-film actor Vincent Price provides the backdrop for a scene reminiscent of *Night of the Living Dead*, where zombies rise out of their graves and surround Jackson and Ray. An extended dance interlude follows, in which Jackson, now in the form of a zombie himself, leads the group in a groundbreaking two-minute sequence choreographed by Jackson and Michael Peters (4).

As the best example of an early music video that highlights the artistic possibilities of the new form, *Thriller* had a dramatic effect on the creativity employed in music videos that followed.

minute *Thriller* begins by casting Jackson and an on-screen girlfriend (performed by Ola Ray) in the context of a 1950s horror

Dirty Minded? Prince and Janet Jackson. In addition to Michael Jackson and Madonna, Minneapolis-based Prince deserves credit for asserting racial difference and sexuality in the MTV lineup during the mid-1980s. Prince's video for "1999" actually predated "Billie Jean," and his practice of using blatant sexual images, both in his songs and live performance, goes back to the late 1970s, when Madonna was still in college. Born Prince Rogers Nelson, he was one of the most prolific artists of the 1980s, writing and producing a long string of hit records under his own name—often playing all the instruments on his records—and writing and producing other artists, such as the Time, Vanity 6, and Sheila E. Prince's musical roots were in the black pop and funk of the 1970s, and his careful control of both his music and

Madonna, "Like a Virgin" Sire 29210

Words and music by Billy Steinberg and Tom Kelly, produced by Nile Rodgers. Hit #1 on the *Billboard* "Hot 100" and #9 on *Billboard* "Hot Black Singles" charts in 1985 (uk3). Also contained on the album *Like a Virgin*, which went to #1 on the *Billboard* "Top Pop Albums" and #10 on the "Hot Black Albums" charts (uk1).

FORM: Compound AABA. The A sections are based primarily on simple verse-chorus form, except that the chorus is built on the first part of each verse only. The second part of each verse differs from the first in that its last 6 bars break off the pattern set by the first part, creating a section that functions similarly to the pre-chorus in "Billie Jean." The bridge presents contrasting material drawn from the last 6 bars of the second part of the verse, but developed and changed. The return of the final A section brings back only the second part of the verse, but the repetition of the chorus helps balance the end of the song.

TIME SIGNATURE: 4/4.

INSTRUMENTATION: Layers of synthesizers, drums, guitar, lead vocals.

	0:00–0:08	**Introduction**, 4 mm.	Synthesizer bass and drums begin, with synthesizer chords added in last 2 bars.
A	0:08–0:24	**Verse 1** (first part), 8 mm.	Vocals enter, as drumbeat locks in. "I made it through . . ."
	0:24–0:44	**Verse 1** (second part), 10 mm.	Note how the first 4 bars repeat the first part of the verse, but then add new material that propels the song toward the chorus. "I was beat . . ."
	0:44–1:00	**Chorus**, 8 mm.	Added synthesizer lines and rhythmic guitar. "Like a virgin . . ."
A	1:00–1:16	**Verse 2** (first part), 8 mm.	As before, with added synthesizer interjections. Note how this verse emerges directly out of the chorus. "Gonna give you . . ."
	1:16–1:36	**Verse 2** (second part), 10 mm.	As before, "You're so fine . . ."
	1:36–1:52	**Chorus**, 8 mm.	As before, but note Michael Jacksonesque high-voiced "hey." "Like a virgin . . ."
B	1:52–2:08	**Bridge**, 8 mm.	Material derived and developed from second part of verse, with vocals on "Whoa."
A	2:08–2:29	**Verse 3** (second part), 10 mm.	As verse 2, "You're so fine . . ."
	2:29–2:45	**Chorus**, 8 mm.	As before, with extra background parts added. "Like a virgin . . ."
	2:45–3:01	**Chorus**, 8 mm.	Repeat, but with a sensual vocal variation at the end.
	3:01–3:09	**Chorus**, 4 mm.	Repeat, with vocal improvisation as song fades out.

that of satellite projects is modeled on the practice of George Clinton, while his one-man-band approach is reminiscent of Stevie Wonder. Prince's first four albums did well in the rhythm and blues market, with both *Prince* (1979) and *Controversy* (1981) reaching number three and containing several singles that became especially popular on the *Billboard* "Hot Soul Singles" charts. During this early period Prince developed his image as a sexually charged and somewhat androgynous figure, and songs such as "Head" and "Jack U Off" provided ample opportunity for him to project this image in live performance.

While he had enjoyed modest crossover success earlier, the 1982 release of his album *1999* (p9 r4) made Prince a star in the pop world, fueled by the singles "1999" (p12 r4) and "Little Red Corvette" (p6 r15) and his exposure on MTV.

Like Marvin Gaye and Stevie Wonder before him, Prince had total control over his music (and, like Wonder, often played all the instruments). However, Prince demanded this arrangement from the beginning of his career. He combined Michael Jackson's crossover appeal with Madonna's blatant sexual imagery, and with this mixture scored hits throughout the 1980s and 1990s.

The title track finds Prince employing a synthesizer-heavy backdrop, driven hard by a strong beat in the drums. His technique of using different voices for each line in the verse goes back to doo-wop groups like Clyde McPhatter and the Drifters, but here the most immediate influences are probably Sly and the Family Stone or the Temptations. At the very end of "1999" you can hear the strong funk influences that support Prince's music.

In 1984, Prince released the semi-autobiographical feature film *Purple Rain*, which was greeted with critical acclaim and accompanied by a soundtrack album that quickly hit the top spot on both pop and rhythm and blues charts. Two singles from the album, "When Doves Cry" and "Let's Go Crazy," also went to number one on both singles charts. More hit albums and singles followed over the next few years, including *Around the World in a Day* (p1 r4, 1985), *Batman* (p1 r5 uk1, 1989), and *Diamonds and Pearls* (p3 r1, 1991), each of which sold more than two million copies. Prince's blending of the funk grooves and outrageous-ness of George Clinton with a strong pop sensibility made him one of the most influential artists of the decade, and among black artists he was rivaled only by Michael Jackson.

As Prince was developing his musical style in the late 1970s, Michael Jackson's younger sister Janet was a regular guest on the television sitcom *Good Times*. During the early 1980s, Janet released albums and singles on the side while continuing to act in television shows such as *Diff'rent Strokes* and *Fame*. In 1986, however, she teamed with the Minneapolis-based production and songwriting team of Jimmy Jam and Terry Lewis, two musicians who had been in the Prince-produced band, the Time. Under their direction, Janet's 1986 album *Control* shot to the top of the pop and rhythm and blues charts (uk8), contain-

Listening Guide

Get Music ⑤ **wwnorton.com/studyspace**

Prince, "1999" Warner Brothers GWB-0468

Words and music by Prince, produced by Prince. Originally released in late 1982, hitting #44 on the *Billboard* "Hot 100." Rereleased in summer 1983 (after the success of "Little Red Corvette"), it hit #12 on the *Billboard* "Hot 100" and #4 on the "Black Singles" charts. Contained on the album *1999*, which went to #9 on the *Billboard* "Top LPs and Tape" and #4 on the "Black LPs" charts in 1983.

FORM: Contrasting verse-chorus (with extended coda). Notice how extra measures are added to the end of each chorus: first 4 measures, then 8 measures, and then the final extended coda. It is also interesting to note that the repeating chord progression in the synthesizer part is based on the Mamas and the Papas' hit single "Monday, Monday."

TIME SIGNATURE: 4/4.

INSTRUMENTATION: Electric guitar, bass, drums, synthesizer, synthesized percussion, and lead all provided by Prince, plus female backup vocals.

0:00–0:50	**Introduction**, 16 mm.	Begins with electronically modified voice, as drumbeat enters, and then synthesizer.
0:50–1:22	**Verse 1**, 16 mm.	Vocal enters; notice exchange of voices, perhaps influenced by Sly or the Temptations. "I was dreaming when I wrote this . . ."
1:22–1:39	**Chorus**, 8 mm.	Harmony vocals, no extension added yet, "Two thousand zero zero . . ."
1:39–2:12	**Verse 2**, 16 mm.	As before but with new synthesizer and guitar lines, "I was dreaming when I wrote this . . ."
2:12–2:37	**Chorus**, 12 mm.	As before, but now extended by 4 mm., "Two thousand zero zero . . ."
2:37–3:10	**Verse 3**, 16 mm.	Now sung in harmony, with small variations in the accompaniment. "If you didn't come to party . . ."
3:10–3:25	**Chorus**, 8 mm.	As the first time, "Two thousand zero zero . . ."
3:25–3:58	**Chorus**, 16 mm.	As the second time, but now extended by 8 mm., with plenty of vocal improvisation.
3:58–4:13	**Chorus**, 8 mm.	One more time through the coda, before heading into the extended ending.
4:13–6:14	**Coda**, 60 mm.	Extension of chorus now becomes a lengthy coda. Note that the last 16 mm. are quieter, with a sudden stop in the last measure. The funk influence comes out especially in these last measures.

Often teaming with producers Jimmy Jam and Terry Lewis, Janet Jackson scored many Top 10 hits in the 1980s and 1990s. She often portrayed the image of a strong, powerful African-American woman, as on her albums *Control* (1986) and *Rhythm Nation 1814* (1989). Like Madonna, and her brother Michael, Jackson placed a heavy emphasis on dancing, often employing top choreographers to help plan her videos and concert performances.

ing six crossover hit singles. She projected an image of confidence and independence with *Control,* and the hard-driving beats behind this new music showed the influence of hip hop and funk. With the music of Jackson, Jam and Lewis became progenitors of a dance-based style of hip-hop and pop called New Jack Swing, which created dense, stark musical textures from drum machines and samples. The team of Jackson with Jam and Lewis followed with *Rhythm Nation 1814* (1989), which also topped both charts (uk4) and surpassed *Control* by producing seven singles to reach the top five of the "Hot 100." While *Rhythm Nation 1814* took on a more serious, socially conscious tone than its predecessor, the original plan had been for it to project a sexier and more seductive image for the singer. It would be her next release, *janet.* (pl rl uk1, 1993), that launched Jackson's more adult-oriented image. This was underscored by an infamous *Rolling Stone* cover photo released in September 1993 that featured a topless Jackson with her breasts covered only by a pair hands from an unseen person. Of the six hit singles on *janet.,* the chart-topping "That's the Way Loves Goes" illustrates the production approach taken by Jackson, Jam, and Lewis. In stark contrast to the choppy New Jack Swing of her previous albums, "That's the Way Love Goes" uses music sampled from the recording of James Brown's "Papa Don't Take No Mess," creating a more laid back and sultry sound. Throughout her career, video played a central role in Janet Jackson's musical presentation. As with her famous brother, dancing was as important as singing in Janet's performances (Paula Abdul choreographed many of Janet's early videos), and the musical dimension of her videos certainly takes a backseat to the visual one. As we have seen with both Madonna and Michael Jackson, during the early MTV era this balance was especially difficult for visually stimulating performers.

Brit Pop Hits MTV: Duran Duran and Culture Club.
Due to the shortage of usable videos in the early years of MTV, an entire crop of British pop acts received disproportionate airplay on MTV, prompting what many critics have called a "second British invasion." Bands and artists such as Bow Wow Wow, Adam and the Ants, A Flock of Seagulls, Howard Jones, Thomas Dolby, and ABC, who might otherwise have never cracked the American market, profited handsomely from the exposure their music received on MTV. Among the most successful of these groups was Duran Duran, whose synthesizer- and guitar-heavy new wave sound was driven by infectious dance beats. Their visual dimension was marked by a concern for style and rebellious elegance. The band first made its mark in the United States with *Rio*

(p6 uk2, 1982), containing "Hungry like the Wolf" (p3 uk5), and the video for this song went into regular MTV rotation. The success of *Rio* spurred American interest in the band's 1981 album, *Duran Duran* (p10, 1983), which had risen to number three in the UK when it was originally released. Appearing in late 1983, *Seven and the Ragged Tiger* (p8 uk1) continued Duran Duran's run on the international charts, spawning three Top 10 hits, including "The Reflex" (p1 uk1). Keeping in line with the band's reliance on MTV, the video for "The Reflex" was groundbreaking in its use of special effects, as it depicted a waterfall pouring over the audience of a Duran Duran concert.

Culture Club was another British group that exploited the visual side of their act through heavy exposure on MTV during the early 1980s. Singer George "Boy George" O'Dowd, who dressed in women's clothes and sported long dreadlocks, was the band's lead singer and most visible member. One of the group's first appearances on British television prompted one critic to write, "It's a bird, it's a bloke, it's Boy George." *Kissing to Be Clever* (p14 r24 uk5, 1982) featured three Top 10 hits, including the easygoing "Do You Really Want to Hurt Me" (p2 uk1), which was played heavily on both MTV and radio. The group's next album, *Colour by Numbers* (p2 r7 uk1, 1983), brought three more Top 10 hits, among them the ubiquitous "Karma Chameleon" (p1 uk1). Culture Club's music was unabashedly pop-oriented in the Brill Building sense: catchy tunes and hooks established a generally happy tone, while Boy George's fluid and laid-back singing style was influenced by black pop singers of the 1960s and 1970s. Moreover, while Boy George's looks may have seemed like a detriment, the cultural space between the UK and the American Midwest placed a comfortable distance between his obviously androgynous style and the often-conservative values of the American Heartland.

Thinking Person's MTV: Eurythmics and Tears for Fears.
Eurythmics took advantage of the synthesizer-pop sound that had emerged in the UK at the end of the 1970s and combined it with an innovative approach to music video. Combining the soul-influenced vocals of Annie Lennox, the synthesizer wizardry of David Stewart, and a penchant for intellectual experimentation, the duo released *Sweet Dreams (Are Made of This)* (p15 uk3, 1983), the title song of which hit number one in the United States (uk2). The song was supported by a surreal music video that featured a cow circling a boardroom table, several odd scenes in a pasture, and Stewart accompanying Lennox using a computer-turned-synthesizer. During a period in which many videos were relatively inane depictions of performance, the sophisticated "Sweet Dreams" video

The striking style of dress and soul-influenced vocals of Boy George helped Culture Club become popular in the U.S. market during the mid-1980s. Here, Boy George performs on stage in 1984 at London's Wembley Stadium.

Eurythmics (lead singer Annie Lennox and guitarist/keyboardist Dave Stewart) made their commercial mark by blending soul and synth pop with elements drawn from avant-garde art and literature. Lennox and Stewart are shown here during the filming of the video for "Missionary Man," a 1986 track that marked the band's move toward a more 1960s-influenced style.

became must-see MTV. Following with *Touch* (p7 uk1, 1984) and *Be Yourself Tonight* (p9 uk3, 1985), Eurythmics were able to remain successful in America through the mid-1980s. The group continued a string of successful albums and singles in Britain through the end of the decade before embarking on a long hiatus.

Influenced by the primal scream therapy of Arthur Janov, keyboardist Roland Orzabal and bassist Curt Smith called their UK-based band Tears for Fears. Basing their stylistic approach in British synthesizer-pop, the duo released its debut album, *The Hurting* (uk1), in 1983. The album barely created a ripple in the United States, but their follow-up, *Songs from the Big Chair* (p1 uk2, 1985), became an international sensation. Fueled by two number one American hits, "Everybody Wants to Rule the World" (uk2) and "Shout" (uk4), the record was also bolstered by heavy video rotation on MTV. In many ways, *Songs from the Big Chair* shows the more ambitious side of British pop from the 1980s: the lyrics deal with serious topics, the music is sometimes complicated, and tunes run into one another to create long tracks. Perhaps owing to their seriousness of purpose, the duo was not able to produce a timely third album, and while *The Seeds of Love* (p8 uk1, 1989) enjoyed success, it was the last big record for the band.

Girls Just Wanna Have Fun: The Go-Go's, Cyndi Lauper, and the Bangles.
The late 1970s had ushered in a new era for women in rock music, as artists such as Blondie, the B-52s, and Heart had all nurtured more aggressive and sensual female images. In the wake of this important line of female representation in rock, the Go-Go's became the first successful all-female new wave band. Fronted by singer Belinda Carlisle, the band's *Beauty and the Beat* hit the top of the U.S. charts in 1981, powered in part by the single "We Got the Beat" (p2), which offered a no-frills musical approach that featured a memorable sing-along chorus. The Go-Go's worked pre-hippie 1960s images to the hilt: the band name is derived from "go-go girls," while the *Beauty and the Beat* cover featured a shot of the band clad in bath towels, seemingly in the middle of a slumber party. Their success was fleeting, although Carlisle returned to the charts regularly as a solo artist. Her second album,

Cyndi Lauper, seen here in a 1986 concert, capitalized on woman-focused new wave groups like the Go-Go's and produced the girl-power rock anthem "Girls Just Want to Have Fun." Lauper projected an image of a strong and fiercely independent woman, and this was supported by her powerful voice, woman-focused lyrics, creative dress, and video production.

Heaven on Earth (p13 uk4, 1987), contained three hits including "Heaven Is a Place on Earth" (1987), which topped both the American and British charts.

Capitalizing on the girl-specific images of the Go-Go's, Cyndi Lauper emerged into the mainstream spotlight with the hit album *She's So Unusual* (p4 uk16, 1984), which featured a hit that could be considered an anthem for female power in rock, "Girls Just Want to Have Fun" (p2 uk2). The video for this song quickly became an MTV classic, featuring the energetic spirit of Lauper rebelling against the wishes of her parents. The album also included hits that showed other aspects of Lauper's musical personality. "Time after Time" (p1 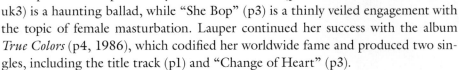 uk3) is a haunting ballad, while "She Bop" (p3) is a thinly veiled engagement with the topic of female masturbation. Lauper continued her success with the album *True Colors* (p4, 1986), which codified her worldwide fame and produced two singles, including the title track (p1) and "Change of Heart" (p3).

In the wake of the wild success of many female rock musicians, the Bangles emerged from California with *Different Light* (p2 uk3, 1986). The album was propelled up the charts by "Manic Monday" (p2 uk2, 1986), a song written by Prince, and the tongue-in-cheek "Walk like an Egyptian" (p1 uk3, 1986). Building on the long legacy of women in rock music provided by Heart, Fleetwood Mac, the Pretenders, the Talking Heads, and the Go-Go's, the Bangles coolly projected feminine identity into rock, blending the jingle-jangle of 1960s folk rock with smooth vocal harmonies.

THE NEW TRADITIONALISTS

No Irony, Just a Healthy Love for Earlier Styles. During the first years of new wave in the late 1970s, the fact that a band or artist made use of features associated with pre-hippie rock was enough to include them under a general banner of "new simplicity." The rejection of hippie values—even if only on the surface in some cases—was such an overriding characteristic that it tended to eclipse important differences within the first cluster of new wave bands. But as the 1980s began and hippie rock started to recede into history, it became increasingly clear that there were two distinct approaches to appropriating earlier rock music styles and features. The first was to employ these sounds and images in an ironic manner, not so much to endorse earlier rock as to reject the corporate rock of the 1970s—Devo offers the clearest example of this tendency. A second approach was to employ such sounds and images in earnest. That is, bands used elements of earlier rock music because they were genuinely interested in revisiting older styles. These bands and artists were not exploiting earlier music to create a pastiche but rather were "new traditionalists" concerned with returning rock to what they considered to be its core aesthetic values.

I Won't Back Down: Tom Petty, with and without the Heartbreakers.

Initially received in the context of new wave, during the early 1980s Tom Petty became more closely aligned with the new traditionalism approach. Ironically, Petty's music always had a strong connection to the 1960s, and he didn't change his style throughout the 1970s and 1980s. He hadn't come to new wave as much as new wave had come to him. As the 1980s began, however, Petty and the Heartbreakers continued their successful practice of blending jangly guitar sounds with catchy melodies and poetic lyrics. *Hard Promises* (p5, 1981) contained the radio favorite "The Waiting" (p19), while *Southern Accents* (p7, 1985) featured "Don't Come Around Here No More" (p13). Petty's music had tended to enjoy more success in the United States than in England, although his first solo album, *Full Moon Fever* (p3 uk8, 1989), cracked the UK Top 10, and produced the hits "Free Fallin'" (p7) and "I Won't Back Down" (p12) in the States. His position as keeper of the rock and roll flame was further solidified with the formation of the Traveling Wilburys in 1988, led by ex-Beatle George Harrison and including Petty, Bob Dylan, Roy Orbison, and Electric Light Orchestra front man Jeff Lynne. This all-star band released *Traveling Wilburys Volume 1* (p3, 1988), containing the single "Handle with Care" (p45). Displaying a Beatle-esque sense of humor—itself a throwback to those carefree mop-top days—the band named their second album *Traveling Wilburys Volume 3* (p11 uk14, 1990).

New Jersey Nostalgia: Bruce Springsteen and the E-Street Band.

Unlike Tom Petty, Bruce Springsteen was never lumped in with the new wavers of the 1970s. Springsteen's songs and fashion put him in the category of a colorful, New Jersey–based singer-songwriter who drew earnestly upon older traditions of rock. The dense, almost symphonic instrumentation of his third album with the E-Street Band, *Born to Run* (p3 uk17, 1975), showed more than a hint of Phil Spector's influence and its success marked Springsteen as an

Bruce Springsteen belts out "Born in the U.S.A." in Washington, D.C., the first stop on his 1986 concert tour. This song, although used briefly by Ronald Reagan in his 1984 campaign, was deeply critical of American involvement in Vietnam and the subsequent treatment of veterans after the war. Springsteen's music is marked by a big, seemingly traditional rock and roll sound combined with poetic, socially conscious lyrics reminiscent of Bob Dylan's.

Bruce Springsteen, "Born in the U.S.A." Columbia 04680

Words and music by Bruce Springsteen, produced by Bruce Springsteen, Jon Landau, Chuck Plotkin, and Steven Van Zandt. Rose to #9 on the *Billboard* "Hot 100" in 1984 (uk7). Contained on the album *Born in the U.S.A.*, which topped the pop album charts in the United States and the UK.

FORM: Simple verse-chorus. A 2-bar melodic figure permeates this track, which is further built on almost identical repeating 8-measure sections for both verse and chorus sections. After breaking the verse-chorus pattern after verse 3, notice how verses 4 and 5 also break off lyrically. The overall effect is to drive to verse 6 and toward the final statements of the chorus. Springsteen wants to parallel the sense of abandonment portrayed in the lyrics by allowing the music to wander somewhat. At certain points the song seems unsure of where it wants to go, but is nevertheless pushed forward by the nagging 2-bar melody.

TIME SIGNATURE: 4/4.

INSTRUMENTATION: Drums, guitar, bass, piano, synthesizers, lead vocal.

0:00–0:16	**Introduction**, 8mm.	Snare drum, piano, and synthesizer playing repeated 2 mm. melody.
0:16–0:33	**Verse 1**, 8 mm.	Vocal enters over this stark music of the intro, "Born down in a dead man's town . . ."
0:33–0:49	**Chorus**, 8 mm.	Lead vocal doubles the 2 mm. melody that has been repeating since the beginning of the song. "Born in the U.S.A. . . ."
0:49–1:05	**Verse 2**, 8 mm.	Guitars and bass enter and drums break into a beat, as the song gets louder and more intense. "Got in a little hometown jam . . ."
1:05–1:21	**Chorus**, 8 mm.	As before, but with new parts added in verse 2 continued. "Born in the U.S.A. . . ."
1:21–1:36	**Verse 3**, 8 mm.	As in verse 2, "Come back home to the refinery . . ."
1:36–1:52	**Interlude**, 8 mm.	Music continues without vocal melody, Springsteen improvises quietly in the background.
1:52–2:07	**Verse 4**, 8 mm.	Partial verse, as last phrase is broken off, "I had a brother . . ."
2:07–2:23	**Verse 5**, 8 mm.	Partial verse, broken off even sooner, "He had a woman . . ."
2:23–2:39	**Verse 6**, 8 mm.	Music goes back to spare texture of verse 1. "Down in the shadow . . ."
2:39–2:55	**Chorus**, 8 mm.	Spare, as in chorus 1. "Born in the U.S.A. . . ."
2:55–3:10	**Chorus**, 8 mm.	Music gets fuller again, as in chorus 2. "Born in the U.S.A. . . ."
3:10–4:28	**Coda**, 40 mm.	Vocal melody drops out, as Springsteen improvises and screams in the background. The music goes through the 8-bar pattern five times, with a dropout in the fourth one.

important force for the voice of rock traditionalists. Springsteen's greatest success would come in the 1980s, however, beginning with his fifth album, *The River* (p1 uk2, 1980), featuring the hit "Hungry Heart" (p5), and continuing with the more introspective and stripped-down *Nebraska* (p3 uk3, 1982). Springsteen's landmark release was 1984's *Born in the U.S.A.*, which topped the charts in both the United States and Britain and produced six Top 10 American hits, including "Glory Days" (p5 uk17) and "Born in the U.S.A." (p9 uk7). The boxed set *Live 1977–1985* (p1 uk4, 1986) was released at the height of Springsteen's popularity in the mid-1980s, introducing his many new fans to his older material and sparking renewed sales and radio play for his music from the 1970s. Springsteen followed up with *Tunnel of Love* (p1 uk1, 1987) and the simultaneous release of two albums in 1992: *Human Touch* (p2 uk1) and *Lucky Town* (p3 uk2).

Springsteen's image relied on the idea that he was the voice of that average working-class guy, and his lyrics reflected on common emotional and social problems. "Born in the U.S.A.," for instance, paints a vivid picture of the decay of American values in the industrial heartland, all seen from the perspective of someone who is powerless to effect change. (In a strange turn of events, "Born in the U.S.A." was mistakenly appropriated by Ronald Reagan's presidential campaign as a paean to traditional values and American pride, until Springsteen eventually asked them to stop using the song.) The song's form seems simple: it employs the same 8-bar progression and 2-bar melody, both of which are unrelentingly repeated. But formally, the song threatens to lose its way in the middle, as verses break off, incomplete. The constant repetition of the music, combined with the formal wandering of the song's midsection, creates a sense that the Vietnam veteran in the lyrics is not sure which way to turn. Throughout much of his career, Springsteen has projected an image reminiscent of a late 1950s or early 1960s white rock and roll singer, although the topicality of his lyrics hark back to Dylan in the 1960s.

Americana on Both Sides of the Pond: John Mellencamp and Dire Straits.

Emerging in 1979 with the radio hit "I Need a Lover" under the name John Cougar, John Mellencamp made his commercial and critical mark with his third album, *American Fool* (1982). The album topped the U.S. charts and contained the hits "Hurts So Good" (p2) and "Jack and Diane" (p1). Mellencamp followed up with *Scarecrow* (p2, 1985), featuring "Small Town" (p6). Like Springsteen's constant depiction of working-class New Jersey, Indiana-born Mellencamp embraced an image of a small-town Midwesterner. His songs show an interest in characters who are plainspoken, not fancy, and interested in social justice and emotional self-understanding. This homespun image was also projected musically through the use of traditional rock instrumentation and no-frills songwriting, making Mellencamp a foundational figure in the strain of new traditionalism commonly called Americana.

The English band Dire Straits, on the other hand, represented America through a much different lens. Led by singer-songwriter-guitarist Mark Knopfler, the band emerged during the first excitement of new wave in late 1978 with *Dire Straits* (p2 uk5), which featured the single "Sultans of Swing" (p4). The song celebrates the virtues of anonymous jazz virtuosos and features Knopfler's accomplished guitar playing, rendered without the usual amplifier distortion characteristic of 1970s mainstream rock. In the early 1980s, Dire Straits had markedly better luck in the UK than in America. The band's reemergence as international chart-toppers came with *Brothers in Arms* (p1 uk1, 1985), containing the hit "Money for Nothing" (p1 uk4). Sting (from the Police, discussed below) provided background vocals on the song and it was supported by an innovative music video that went into heavy rotation on MTV, despite its critique of that station. Like the other new traditionalists, Dire Straits employed a no-nonsense approach in their music, with a strong respect for older styles and a simpler, more transparent approach to production.

Keepers of the Wave: The Police and U2.
Another successful band to emerge into the rock mainstream from the new wave movement was the Police. Formed in England by Brits Andy Summers (guitar) and Sting (bass and vocals), and American Stewart Copeland (drums), the band's first hit single, "Roxanne" (p32 uk12, 1979), showed a strong reggae influence. Although the group's first album, *Outlandos d'Amour* (p23 uk7, 1979), picked up on the return-to-simplicity approach of punk, the group clearly were interested in creating sophisticated musical arrangements along with self-consciously poetic lyrics. The title of the band's fifth album, *Synchronicity* (p1 uk1, 1983), for instance, is drawn from the psychological writings of Carl Jung. The music of the Police dominated rock in the first half of the 1980s. Eight singles placed in the American Top 20 during that time, and while only one of these ever went to number one ("Every Breath You Take" in 1983), the band's music was a staple of FM rock radio. "Don't Stand So Close to Me" illustrates the band's musical approach. The music is spare and skillfully executed, creating a mysterious atmosphere to go with Sting's lyrics, which tell of a teacher's unhealthy romantic attraction to his young student. Andy Summers's guitar playing is more focused on creating washes of sound than soloing, and Copeland's drumming lays down an often complex rhythmic grid beneath the other instruments. There is a sense of agitation in this song that reflects the uneasiness of the teacher who, according to the lyrics, ends up being publicly accused.

As the Police's active career was coming to a close in the mid-1980s, Ireland's U2 was just getting started. The band's first five albums made good showings, includ-

Featuring bassist and lead singer Sting, guitarist Andy Summers, and drummer Stewart Copeland, the Police were one of the most popular rock bands of the 1980s. They combined the hard-driving guitar sound of punk, reggae's rhythmic complexity, and serious-minded lyrics to create eight Top 10 hits in the U.S. during the early 1980s.

Listening Guide

Get Music ⑤ wwnorton.com/studyspace

The Police, "Don't Stand So Close to Me" A&M AMS-7564

Words and music by Sting, produced by the Police and Nigel Gray. Rose to #1 on the UK charts and #10 on the *Billboard* "Hot 100" in the United States in 1981. Also contained on the album *Zenyatta Mondatta*, which also hit #1 in the UK and #5 in the United States.

FORM: Contrasting verse-chorus. Notice how each verse builds up a bit more, adding new parts with each occurrence—an arranging approach we have seen often. The timbre-rich instrumental verse thus arrives as a natural extension of this process. The lyrics describe a teacher who is attracted to an underage student. The agitation in the music, and perhaps the central instrumental verse, attempt to capture this sense of uneasiness.

TIME SIGNATURE: 4/4.

INSTRUMENTATION: Drums, bass, guitars, synthesizer, lead and backing vocals.

0:00–0:37	**Introduction**	Free-form synthesizer and guitar sounds establish a mysterious texture to open the track, and then drums usher in 4-bar reggae-inspired vamp as groove locks in.
0:37–1:04	**Verse 1**, 16 mm.	Lead vocal enters, accompanied by a quiet repeating guitar line, two-part harmony on second half of verse, "Young teacher . . ."
1:04–1:19	**Chorus**, 9 mm.	Harmony vocals, as music gets fuller and louder, "Don't stand so close . . ."
1:19–1:46	**Verse 2**, 16 mm.	As before, but sung higher and with added guitar parts. Harmony vocals on second half of verse are also sung higher, creating a sense that the song is getting more intense. "Her friends are so jealous . . ."
1:46–2:02	**Chorus**, 9 mm.	As before, "Don't stand so close . . ."
2:02–2:29	**Verse 3**, 16 mm.	As in verse 2, "Loose talk in the classroom . . ."
2:29–2:48	**Chorus**, 11 mm.	As before, "Don't stand so close . . ."
2:48–3:15	**Instrumental Verse**, 16 mm.	Synthesizer sweeps added. Are these sounds meant to capture the emotional confusion of the main character in the song?
3:15–3:29	**Chorus**, 8 mm.	As before, but with counter line added in vocals. "Don't stand so close . . ."
3:29–3:42	**Chorus**, 8 mm.	Repeated with counter line.
3:42–3:56	**Chorus**, 8 mm.	Repeated again as song fades out.

ing *War* (p12 uk1, 1983) and *The Unforgettable Fire* (p12 uk1, 1984). With 1987's *The Joshua Tree* (p1 uk1, 1987), however, U2 began a string of enormously successful albums that continues to the present day. U2 built on the sophisticated approach of the Police: both bands wrote simple songs but arranged them in innovative ways. Lead singer Bono's lyrics often strive for a poetic quality, while lead guitarist the Edge layers sound behind Bono's voice to create a rich backing texture. The band often composed their songs by improvising in the studio, then leaving producers such as Brian Eno and Daniel Lanois to collate and reassemble the most compelling material. "Pride (In the Name of Love)" illustrates some of the musical features of U2's music from the middle of the decade. The Edge plays repeated-note figures on the guitar, soaked in echo, that provide one of the band's most recognizable sonic signatures. During the verses, Bono delivers accounts of people who have given their lives in the name of love, including Dr. Martin Luther King, Jr., while his wailing on the chorus underscores the passion of the cause for which their lives were given. U2 has remained an important band to the present day, with a string of successful albums and sold-out tours, while Bono has become an outspoken advocate for humanitarian issues.

Old School Newcomers: AC/DC and Huey Lewis and the News. While older, more established bands continued to thrive and a host of new styles arrived on the scene, it was still possible for new acts to enjoy success playing music that seemed more suited to an earlier time. Neither AC/DC nor Huey Lewis was aligned with the new traditionalists or new wavers, and both of these groups harkened back to earlier music. Thus, these two vastly different groups offer an interesting comparison of bands that drew on earlier music in very different ways. The music of AC/DC is strongly influenced by the British blues rock of bands like Led Zeppelin and Deep Purple. This Australian group did not make its first important mark on the U.S. charts (and on American radio) until the 1970s were almost over. AC/DC had formed in 1973—during the salad days of British blues rock—and established

U2, "Pride (In the Name of Love)" Island 99704

Words and music by U2, produced by Brian Eno and Daniel Lanois. Single rose to #3 in the UK and #33 on the *Billboard* "Hot 100." Also contained on the album *The Unforgettable Fire*, which went to #1 in the UK and #13 in the United States in 1984.

FORM: Compound AABA. The A sections employ simple verse-chorus structure that is based on the same chord pattern, while the B section presents a new melody in the guitar, supported by a new chord progression, as well as a return to the introduction.

TIME SIGNATURE: 4/4.

INSTRUMENTATION: Electric guitars, bass, drums, lead and backing vocals. Notice the use of the repeated-note guitar sound throughout, and how avoiding that repeated-note sound in verses 2 and 3 adds excitement to its return.

	0:00–0:28	**Introduction**, 12 mm.	Rhythmic guitar with echo featured with drums before bass enters and song begins the repeated progression that will form the basis of the verse and chorus.
A	0:28–0:46	**Verse 1**, 8 mm.	Vocal enters over music established in the introduction, sung in the middle register. "One man come in the name of love . . ."
	0:46–1:04	**Chorus**, 8 mm.	Vocal continues over same music, but now sung higher and with more urgency. "In the name of love . . ."
A	1:04–1:23	**Verse 2**, 8 mm.	As before, but rhythmic guitar gives way to broad arpeggios to create a sense of contrast. "One man come on a barbed-wire fence . . ."
	1:23–1:41	**Chorus**, 8 mm.	As before, as rhythmic guitar returns, "In the name of love . . ."
B	1:41–1:58	**Bridge** (instrumental), 8 mm.	Contrasting music featuring a repeated guitar melody consisting of a three-note figure repeated as an echo, but in tempo.
	1:58–2:26	**Re-Intro**, 12 mm.	Same material as intro, last 4 mm. hummed. The technique of restarting a song by returning to the introduction can be traced back to "Purple Haze" and can be seen in much 1970s music.
A	2:26–2:44	**Verse 3**, 8 mm.	As in verse 2, with broad guitar arpeggios. "Early morning, April 4 . . ."
	2:44–3:02	**Chorus**, 8 mm.	As before, as rhythmic guitar returns. "In the name of love . . ."
	3:02–3:21	**Chorus**, 8 mm.	As before, but backup vocals add counter melody.
	3:21–3:47	**Coda**, 8 mm. + fade-out	Same material as verse, chorus, and intro, as Bono improvises on the song's melody.

themselves at home in Australia. But with the release of *Highway to Hell* (p17 uk8) in 1979, the band's music broke in the United States, driven by the powerful lead guitar playing of Angus Young and the raspy vocals of Bon Scott. Scott died tragically in 1980, and did not live to enjoy the band's American success. He was replaced by Brian Johnson, and the band did not skip a beat on the charts, as *Back in Black* (p4 uk1, 1980) and the rereleased *Dirty Deeds Done Dirt Cheap* (p3, 1981) further established AC/DC's position as old-school rockers and influenced the heavy metal bands that were beginning to assemble in places like Southern California.

Unlike AC/DC, who were earnestly interested in classic rock, Huey Lewis and the News made a trademark of being somewhat out of step with the times, perhaps best exemplified by their 1986 hit "Hip to Be Square" (p3). Veterans of the San Francisco rock scene of the 1970s, the band formed in 1980 and scored their first chart success in 1982 with "Do You Believe in Love" (p7 uk9). The albums *Sports* (1983) and *Fore!* (1986) topped the U.S. album charts and the song "The Power of Love" hit number one in 1985 after it appeared in the film *Back to the Future*. Huey Lewis and the News videos ran in regular rotation on MTV, and their songs became fixtures of FM rock radio. The easy-rockin', sunny, and wholesome feel of much of their music stood in stark contrast to some of the edgier music of the decade, and made them favorites for listeners who yearned for the days when pop music was more often fun than scandalous.

Blue-eyed Soul, '80s Style: Hall and Oates, George Michael, and Michael Bolton. A strain of traditionalism emerged in the 1980s among white artists who were strongly influenced by 1960s black pop styles. Daryl Hall and John Oates can probably claim the most direct connections to late 1960s and early 1970s rhythm and blues, since Hall grew up in Philadelphia and had worked with Leon Huff, Kenny Gamble, and Thom Bell. Hall and Oates's soul-drenched singing fueled their first American hits, "Sara Smile" (p4 r23, 1976) and "Rich Girl" (p1, 1977), and developed into a more mainstream sound with the release of *Private Eyes*. The

Hall and Oates found success throughout the 1980s performing a style of "blue-eyed" soul that drew from their connection to Philadelphia. Here, the duo performs in 1985 at New York's famous Apollo Theater.

George Michael and Andrew Ridgeley of Wham! in concert, 1984. Michael's singing had roots in 1960s rhythm and blues, and he enjoyed hits with Wham! ("Wake Me Up before You Go-Go" [1984]) and as a solo artist ("Faith" [1987]). Like Madonna, Boy George, and Prince, Wham! often projected images of androgyny, and became icons in the gay community.

album rose to number five on the U.S. charts in 1981 (r11 uk8), and contained two number one hits, "Private Eyes" and "I Can't Go for That." Hall and Oates later released *Big Bam Boom* (p5 uk28, 1984), which featured another number one hit, "Out of Touch," and established the duo as the most important American blue-eyed soul act of the early 1980s.

The British duo Wham! (George Michael and Andrew Ridgeley) were stylistically similar to Hall and Oates, and emerged at the height of Hall and Oates's popularity. Michael produced the albums and wrote much of the material, as Wham! scored first in the UK with *Fantastic* (uk1, 1983). The next year, the duo reached number one on both sides of the Atlantic with the aptly titled *Make It Big*, which had three U.S. number one hits—"Wake Me Up before You Go-Go" (uk1), "Careless Whisper" (r8 uk1), and "Everything She Wants" (r12)—and a single that rose to number three: "Freedom" (uk1). Despite the success of Wham!, Michael decided to go solo, releasing the chart-topping *Faith* (p1 r1 uk1, 1987), fueled by four number one hits and two top five hits in the United States, with three of these scoring in the British Top 10 as well. Michael's music, both with Wham! and as a solo act, is deeply indebted to the soulful singing of 1960s black pop, continuing a tradition established by earlier British singers such as Joe Cocker and Steve Winwood. In the wake of George Michael's international success, American Michael Bolton emerged with two moderately successful singles, "That's What Love Is All About" (p19, 1987) and a cover version of Otis Redding's classic "(Sittin' on) the Dock of the Bay" (p11, 1988). Bolton escorted blue-eyed soul into the 1990s with his *Soul Provider* (p3 uk4, 1990), which ascended the charts on both sides of the Atlantic powered by three Top 10 American hits, including "How Am I Supposed to Live without You" (p1 uk3). Bolton soon became one of the most successful singers of the first half of the 1990s, further reinforcing his strong debt to 1960s soul by covering Percy Sledge's "When a Man Loves a Woman" (p1 uk8, 1991). Unlike Wham! and Michael, however, Bolton never found success with African-American audiences, showing an interesting difference in reception between two of the most popular "blue eyed" soul singers during the 1980s.

PUNK GOES HARDCORE

Regional Hardcore. Thus far we have considered several forms of commercial rock in the 1980s. However, several underground movements were also thriving in the United States during this period. While MTV was popularizing dance music and the new traditionalists found solace in exploring older styles, the punk scene spawned a new generation of music that became known as hardcore. This new form of independent music was most closely associated with the Ramones and the UK punk bands, rather than the more conceptual music of first-wave New York punk bands such as Talking Heads or Blondie. Moreover, unlike the more accessible new wave styles that grew from punk and became commercially successful, hardcore continued the raw punk traditions of loud, fast, and aggressive music grounded in the DIY aesthetic. Hardcore bands were usually associated with a major city (or region) and released their music on independent labels. By the end of the 1980s, the hardcore movement had become a national underground movement, with a vast network of performance venues, record labels, and dedicated fans. Although hardcore punk never appeared on national charts, this music was responsible for the infrastructure that supported the alternative movement of the 1990s, which will be discussed in Chapter 12.

Los Angeles. One of the epicenters for hardcore music in the United States during the 1980s was Los Angeles. Chronicled in the historic Penelope Spheeris documentary *The Decline of Western Civilization* (1980), a growing discontent among the youth of Los Angeles translated perfectly into a hardcore scene. Although dozens of bands were important contributors to the independent punk-based music of Los Angeles, among the most important were Fear, X, the Germs, the Circle Jerks, and Black Flag. Formed in 1977, Fear was a fixture of the Los Angeles scene that, like so many hardcore bands, performed fast, loud, and distorted music to support the mostly screamed vocals of guitarist and singer Lee Ving. The group is perhaps best known for a 1981 performance on *Saturday Night Live* that went awry. Controversy resulted from several things that occurred on live television, which were perfectly representative of the hardcore scene. First, the group antagonized the New York–based studio audience by performing a song called "New York's Alright if You Like Saxophones," which discussed some of the less-appealing aspects of the Big Apple. Afterward, members of the band openly screamed "New York sucks." Second, the form of physical dancing enjoyed by the fans (called moshing or slam dancing) consisted of listeners running into one another and diving of off the stage, which was generally consensual among participants, but seemed chaotic and violent to observers. While these aspects of audience interaction and dancing were common in hardcore clubs, this display was frightening for a nationally televised program, and NBC faded to commercial during the musical performance.

Formed in 1976 by guitarist Greg Ginn, Black Flag was another seminal Los Angeles hardcore band. After several years of name and membership changes (the group's lineup was never stable), Black Flag slowly ingratiated itself to the Los Angeles scene through constant self-promotion and the formation of the SST record label, which became one of the most important independent companies associated with the hardcore movement. Beginning with the 1978 four-song EP, *Nervous Breakdown*, the music of Black Flag represented the burgeoning hardcore movement with rough production values, fast tempos, heavily distorted guitars, scream-ing vocals, and profane lyrics that exposed youthful alienation. Another feature of this release that became commonplace in hardcore was its brevity. The combined playing time of all four songs was just over five minutes, with the shortest song clocking in at fifty-five seconds. After several lead singer changes, the band settled on Henry Rollins, who became the longest-lasting vocalist for the group. The 1981 album *Damaged* is perhaps the best document of the Rollins-era incarnation of Black Flag, and has since become an icon of the Los Angeles hardcore movement of the early 1980s.

While Fear and Black Flag represented a stereotypical form of hardcore, with music that was loud, fast, and irreverent, the Minutemen, based in San Pedro (the port district of Los Angeles), offered a slightly different take on the movement. Consisting of guitarist and vocalist D. Boon, bassist Mike Watt, and drummer George Hurley, this trio performed music that was loud and fast, but lacked the distortion and anarchistic attitude of typical hardcore. Their slogan was "we jam econo." This mantra grew directly out of the DIY movement, signifying that the Minutemen were interested in shedding the excesses of corporate rock. Yet, "econo" also spoke to the group's interest in community and a back-to-basics philosophy that sometimes seemed closer to the hippie aesthetic than hardcore punk. Like other hardcore groups, the music of the Minutemen changed substantially in the mid-1980s, infusing a wider range of musical styles. An interesting take on the group's more developed sound can be found in the song "History Lesson, Part 2," from the 1984 double-album *Double Nickels on the Dime*. While the lyrics of this song recall the formation of the Los Angeles hardcore movement from the direct experience of the band, the musical accompaniment consists of a light, mid-tempo arrangement supporting a spoken-word vocal element.

D.C. Hardcore. In contrast to the Reagan administration that came to Washington, D.C. in 1980, the nation's capital became the center of an intense hardcore scene, fueled by bands such as Bad Brains, Teen Idles, and Minor Threat. While this music was often stylistically similar to hardcore found in other locales, the D.C. hard-core scene featured several unique aspects: doctrinaire attitudes toward substance abuse, racial tolerance, and a stance toward politics and government grounded in intellectual debate rather than anarchistic diatribes. Bad Brains, for example, was a hardcore group comprised entirely of African Americans who infused elements of funk and reggae into their music. Drawing on the close connection between British punk and West Indian forms, as found in the music of the Clash, the ethnic heritage of Bad Brains fit perfectly into the D.C. hardcore scene. The group was formed in 1977 and made an initial mark in Washington, but relocated to New York in the late 1970s amidst a growing anti-hardcore sentiment among club owners. After an ini-tial single release, "Pay to Cum" (1980), the group released a self-titled full-length record (1982), which became a foundational release of the hardcore movement.

Certainly the most important figure in the D.C. hardcore scene was guitarist, vocalist, songwriter, and label owner Ian MacKaye. MacKaye's first band was the short-lived Teen Idles, formed by MacKaye and drummer Jeff Nelson. Although the group was only active for a little more than a year, they released an extended-play album called *Minor Disturbance* (1981), the first offering by MacKaye and Nel-son's new label, Dischord. After the Teen Idles disbanded in 1980, MacKaye and

Nelson formed Minor Threat, which became arguably the most important group on the D.C. hardcore scene. In 1981, the band released *Minor Threat* and *In My Eyes*, two extended-play records that took musical cues from the same brand of UK punk rock that inspired Fear, Black Flag, and the Minutemen. However, MacKaye and company took a radically different social course than much of the punk rock that came before, swearing off drugs and alcohol and advocating a clean lifestyle. This philosophy was at the heart of the song "Straight Edge" (included on *Minor Threat*), which became the moniker for a new movement of unencumbered, drug-free hardcore musicians and fans. While Minor Threat was at the heart of D.C. hardcore until the group disbanded in 1983, the Dischord label became one of the most prominent independent companies of the hardcore movement. Sticking to a community-based philosophy of releasing no-frills music to fans at a reasonable price, the company had no connection to corporate interests.

Twin Cities Punk. In opposition to the movements in Los Angeles and Washington, D.C., which were closely related in style, a Minnesota-based strain of hardcore developed in the late 1970s that shied away from aggressive rants in favor of a melodic foundation, producing some of the most accessible music of the independent punk legacy. Two bands emerged in the early 1980s as representative of the Minnesota scene: the Replacements and Hüsker Dü. Fronted by singer, guitarist, and songwriter Paul Westerberg, the Replacements emerged in 1981. The group's first album, *Sorry Ma, Forgot to Take out the Trash* (1981), was released on the local Twin/Tone label, which became an important arbiter of Minnesota-based independent music. The music of the Replacements certainly had connections to the loud, fast, and distorted styles popular on the West Coast and in Washington and New York, but Westerberg's penchant for striking melodic and harmonic material set it apart. While most of the material recorded by Black Flag or Minor Threat was based on simple chord progressions and screamed melodies, the Replacements were quite ambitious in these areas, creating memorable melodic hooks in the context of hardcore punk. Also unlike many hardcore groups, the Replacements remained active throughout the decade, becoming more accessible to the average rock listener as the 1980s unfolded.

A good example of the typical Replacements style is the song "Color Me Impressed" from 1983. While it contains the fast, distorted, and sloppy style that many listeners might associate with punk rock, the compact song structure is deeply indebted to the pop tradition. Musical use and reuse in the song show Westerberg's highly economical songwriting, as verse and bridge sections appear in multiple contexts. Perhaps most importantly, the song is quite melodic and memorable, and contains a single chorus section, showing the band's ability to create a hook, but an unwillingness to repeat it throughout the song. Albums such as *Hootenanny* (1983) (which contains "Color Me Impressed") and *Let It Be* (1984), also released on Twin/Tone, included less screaming and more singing. Later albums, including *Tim* (1985) and *Pleased to Meet Me* (1987), were released on the major label Sire, which reflected the group's growing commercial appeal. Still, the Replacements never found success on the *Billboard* charts. In light of their connection to the punk movement, and the simultaneous rise of MTV, it is not surprising that the video for "Bastards of Young" (1985) consisted of nothing more than a live depiction of a stereo playing an album.

Hüsker Dü formed in St. Paul in 1979 in the wake of the growing Minnesota

Listening Guide

The Replacements, "Color Me Impressed" Twin/Tone 8332

Words and music by Paul Westerberg, produced by Paul Stark, Peter Jesperson, and the Replacements. Included on the 1983 album *Hootenanny*, which did not chart.

FORM: Contrasting verse-chorus, with instrumental bridge sections.

TIME SIGNATURE: 4/4.

INSTRUMENTATION: Drums, bass, guitar, and vocals.

0:00–0:11	**Introduction**, 8 mm.	A loud and fast rhythm guitar begins the tune. This might sound like punk rock, but listen to the speed at which the chords change (every two beats) and the melody created in the chords. Drums and bass enter at the end of the first chord cycle. The squeaking sound in the second half of this introduction is the sound of a guitarist sliding his pick against the guitar strings.
0:11–0:22	**Verse 1**, 8 mm.	The introduction becomes the basis for the verse sections. "Everybody at your party . . ."
0:22–0:33	**Interlude**, 8 mm.	The repeat of the introduction material (now called an interlude) creates an expectation of a scheme that will alternate between instrumental and sung sections. Notice how you can hear vocalist Paul Westerberg humming throughout this section, adding a bit of amateurism.
0:33–0:44	**Verse 2**, 8 mm.	The lyrics continue to describe the people at the "party" (or the people associated with the scene), a typical construction in later college and alternative rock. "Staying out late tonight . . ."

hardcore movement. Led by guitarist, vocalist, and songwriter Bob Mould, the group released several singles and albums beginning in 1981 before signing to SST records for the 1984 album *Zen Arcade*. Much like the Replacements, Hüsker Dü began exploring more accessible music in the mid-1980s, becoming popular with the growing college rock market. This was apparent in the group's choice to release a cover version of the Byrds' "Eight Miles High" as a single in 1984, but translated especially in the group's 1985 single "Makes No Sense at All," from the album *Flip Your Wig* (1985). Like the Replacements' "Bastards of Young," the music video was featured on MTV's alternative rock show "120 Minutes." In another con-

Time	Section	Description
0:44–0:55	**Instrumental Bridge**, 8 mm.	This section continues the alternating scheme between instrumental and vocal sections, but provides a different material from the verse/interlude. Notice how the mood of the chord progression is "darker" than the bright verse section.
0:55–1:07	**Verse 3**, 8 mm.	This verse makes a reference to drug use, which the group seemed to celebrate in their music. "Put the monkey on the mirror . . ."
1:07–1:17	**Chorus**, 8 mm.	Although not repeated, we should think of this section as a chorus. A common method of delivery in the very economical hardcore (and later indie) styles was to present a melodic chorus section only once, enticing the listener with the most appealing section but not repeating it too many times. "Can you stand me . . ."
1:17–1:28	**Instrumental Bridge**, 8 mm.	Another presentation of the contrasting bridge material. Listen to the vocal line Westerberg adds to this progression.
1:28–1:39	**Solo**, 8 mm.	The instrumental bridge becomes the basis for a short guitar solo by Bob Stinson.
1:39–1:50	**Verse 4**, 8 mm.	A varied repeat of verse 1, except now the party revelers *don't* look depressed. "Everybody at your party . . ."
1:50–2:01	**Interlude (with refrain)**, 8 mm.	The interlude and verse material is now repeated several times as a type of coda for the song, with the addition of the vocal refrain used at the end of each verse. "Color me impressed . . ."
2:01–2:12	**Interlude (with refrain)**, 8 mm.	Coda continues. "Color me impressed . . ."
2:12–2:24	**Interlude**, 4 mm.	The final tag section of the song. Notice how the first part of this section alludes to the chorus chord progression, creating a very subtle reprise before a typical chaotic rock ending.

nection to pre-punk popular culture, Hüsker Dü's video for "Makes No Sense at All" included an ironic punk version of "Love Is All Around," the theme from the 1970's sitcom *The Mary Tyler Moore Show*. In 1986, the group signed with Warner Brothers, releasing two more albums before disbanding a year later. Unlike the hardcore bands from Los Angeles and Washington, D.C., both the Replacements and Hüsker Dü showed a penchant for popular appeal, and eventually embraced a more approachable style, signing to major labels. Yet, all three of these scenes, as well as important hardcore music from Boston, San Francisco, and New York, continued the tradition of underground punk in the United States throughout the

1980s. These underground movements paved the way for the alternative movement that would enter the mainstream a decade later.

ADAPTING TO NEWER STYLES: OLDER MUSICIANS IN THE 1980S

The Dinosaurs Adapt. Even though the progressive rock style had died out by the end of the 1970s, the musicians associated with this movement remained active and in many cases enjoyed far more commercial success in the 1980s. By streamlining their sound and making it more accessible and radio friendly, members of Yes, Genesis, and Emerson, Lake & Palmer remained in the mainstream rock limelight with chart-topping albums and sold-out tours. While many had predicted the extinction of these progressive rock dinosaurs, the musicians instead adapted to changes in the pop climate and revitalized their careers. The success of these older musicians made it apparent that the rock mainstream was no longer confined to young artists, and that rock musicians could have careers that lasted decades.

Listening Guide

Peter Gabriel, "Sledgehammer" Geffen 28718

Words and music by Peter Gabriel, produced by Daniel Lanois and Peter Gabriel. Rose to #1 on the *Billboard* "Hot 100" in 1986 (uk4). Contained on the album *So*, which reached #2 in the States (uk1).

FORM: This track falls into two large sections, consisting of a contrasting verse-chorus form in the first half followed by a simple verse form in the second. The influence of southern soul is obvious throughout the track, and this two-part form may be modeled on tracks like Aretha Franklin's "Respect," which have a high-energy ending filled with vocal improvising. The lyrics mark the song as a tribute to hokum blues songs such as Big Joe Turner's "Shake, Rattle, and Roll."

TIME SIGNATURE: 4/4.

INSTRUMENTATION: Drums, bass, guitar, piano, synthesizers, brass, percussion, lead and backup vocals.

A	0:00–0:30	**Introduction**, 12 mm.	Rhythm and blues horns play a repeated melodic line, propelled by a driving beat.
	0:30–1:00	**Verse 1**, 12 mm.	Vocals enter, as the lyrical allusions remain fairly innocent. Organ comes in. "You could have a steam train . . ."
	1:00–1:20	**Verse 2**, 8 mm.	As before, the allusions get a little sexier. "You could have a big dipper . . ."

From Genesis to Corporation. When Peter Gabriel left Genesis in the middle of the 1970s, drummer Phil Collins took over the lead vocal duties, and initial predictions were that the group would probably lose some of its popularity. However, a series of albums in the early 1980s solidified the band's shift to a poppier style, as *Duke* (p11 uk1, 1980), *Abacab* (p7 uk1, 1981), and *Invisible Touch* (p3 uk1, 1986) went to the top of the charts, with the single "Invisible Touch" hitting the number one spot in the United States (uk15). At the same time, individual members of Genesis enjoyed success outside of the band. As a solo artist, Phil Collins released *Face Value* (p7 uk1) in 1981, which contained the single "In the Air Tonight" (p19 uk2)—a track that received significant radio play. Collins followed up in 1985 with *No Jacket Required*, which topped the charts in both the United States and the UK, producing the hits "One More Night" (p1 uk4) and "Sussudio" (p1 uk12). He scored again in 1989 with . . . *But Seriously* (p1 uk1), which contained "Another Day in Paradise" (p1 uk2). Collins's solo music eschewed the philosophical lyrics, sophisticated harmonies, and extended forms of earlier Genesis music in favor of direct lyrics, simple harmonies, and tight, radio-friendly arrangements. Collins was not the only member of Genesis to achieve popular success during the 1980s. Bassist Michael Rutherford led Mike + the Mechanics, whose first album did moderately well (p26, 1985) and produced two Top 10 hits, "Silent Running" and "All I Need

			Get Music ⓢ wwnorton.com/studyspace	
	1:20–1:40	**Chorus**, 8 mm.	Backup vocals are added, "I want to be your sledgehammer . . ."	
	1:40–1:51	**Interlude**, 4 mm.	Accompanimental groove continues.	
	1:51–2:11	**Verse 3**, 8 mm.	Horn line added, as lyrics push a little farther. "Show me 'round your fruit cage . . ."	
	2:11–2:31	**Chorus**, 8 mm.	As before, "I want to be . . ."	
	2:31–2:51	**Chorus**, 8 mm.	As before, "I'm gonna be . . ."	
	2:51–3:01	**Interlude**, 4 mm.	Creates transition to second section.	
B	3:01–3:21	**Verse**, 8 mm.	Spacey synthesizer melody, based on new musical material.	
	3:21–3:41	**Verse**, 8 mm.	Vocal enters, note the gospel-style call and response backup vocals, "I kicked the habit . . ."	
	3:41–4:00	**Verse**, 8 mm.	Vocal harmony added to lead vocal, "Show for me . . ."	
	4:00–4:21	**Verse**, 8 mm.	Lead vocal improvisation begins, as arrangement builds, "Show for me . . ."	
	4:21–4:40	**Verse**, 8 mm.	Vocal improvising continues, influenced by southern soul, as song seems to fade out. "Show for me . . ."	
	4:40–4:49	**Interlude**, 4 mm.	Drumbeat continues alone until snuffed out electronically.	

Is a Miracle" (p6, 1986). The next release, *The Living Years* (p13 uk2, 1988), did even better, producing the hit single "The Living Years" (p1 uk2). Former Genesis frontman Peter Gabriel had a commercial breakthrough in 1986 with *So* (p2 uk1), featuring the hits "Sledgehammer" (p1 uk4) and "Big Time" (p8 uk13), both of which were the subject of innovative videos that received lots of MTV airplay. "Sledgehammer" offers an opportunity to see the roots of rock and roll in what may be considered an unlikely place. The lyrics to this track are Gabriel's tribute to the double entendre discussed in Chapter 1 with Big Joe Turner's "Shake, Rattle, and Roll," as Gabriel playfully alludes to sexuality throughout. The two-part form seems to hark back to southern soul, where the end of the song becomes a kind of loose jam of a groove, as occurs in Aretha Franklin's "Respect." Gabriel's follow-up to *So*, *Us* (p2 uk2, 1992), established him as one of the most influential songwriters of the 1990s.

Sound Check

Artist	Michael Jackson	Madonna	Prince	The Police
Title	Billie Jean	Like a Virgin	1999	Don't Stand So Close to Me
Chart peak	p1, r1, uk2 1983	p1, r9, uk3 1985	p26 1983	p10 1981
Form	Simple verse-chorus (modified)	Compound AABA	Contrasting verse-chorus	Contrasting verse-chorus
Rhythm	4/4	4/4	4/4	4/4
Instrumentation	Electric guitar Bass Drums Lead vocal Background vocal Electric piano Synthesizer	Electric guitar Bass Drums Lead vocal Synthesizer	Electric guitar Bass Drums Lead vocal Background vocal Synthesizer	Electric guitar Bass Drums Lead vocal Background vocal Synthesizer
Comments	Pre-chorus offers contrasting material Jackson performs all vocal parts Repeating bass line is central to the form	Intricate synthesizer work (bass, horns, strings, electric piano) Verse 3 is a partial repeat of verse 2 Contrast between acoustic drums and synthesized sounds	Prince performs all instruments Lead vocals alternate between several members of the Revolution The last two minutes are an extended coda	Gradual dynamic increase in introduction leading directly into verse 1 Verse two more intense because vocals are delivered in a higher octave Reggae influence in rhythm

I Will Survive: Rock Bands Continue to Thrive. If progressive rock musicians maintained a central role in rock long after their predicted demise, they were not alone. Many bands and artists from the 1960s and 1970s remained active during the 1980s without changing their stylistic approach. Foreigner, for instance, continued to dominate mainstream rock with albums such as *4* (p1 uk5, 1981) and *Agent Provocateur* (p4 uk1, 1984), the latter of which had the hit ballad "I Want to Know What Love Is" (p1 uk1). Styx continued their interest in science fiction themes with *Kilroy Was Here* (p3, 1983), including "Mr. Roboto" (p3), while Boston contributed *Third Stage* (p1, 1986), with the hit "Amanda" (p1). David Bowie's *Let's Dance* (p4 uk1, 1983) saw him returning to the rhythm and blues orientation of earlier records while enjoying a number one hit on both sides of the Atlantic. Billy Joel's *An Innocent Man* (p4 uk2, 1983) featured some of his strongest material to date, including "Tell Her About It" (p1 uk4) and "Uptown Girl" (p3 uk1).

U2	Bruce Springsteen	The Replacements	Peter Gabriel
Pride (In the Name of Love)	Born in the U.S.A.	Color Me Impressed	Sledgehammer
p33 1984	p9 1984	- 1983	p1 1986
Compound AABA	Simple verse-chorus	Contrasting verse-chorus (modified)	Contrasting verse-chorus/ Simple verse
4/4	4/4	4/4	4/4
Electric guitar Bass Drums Lead vocal Background vocal	Electric guitar Bass Drums Lead vocal Piano Synthesizer	Electric guitar Bass Drums Lead vocal	Electric guitar Bass Drums Lead vocal Background vocal Piano Synthesizer Horns
Rhythmic guitar with echo Vocal range changes intensity; verses sung lower, choruses sung higher Lyrics address social issues	Based on important two-bar melodic figure Lyrics to verses 4 and 5 are incomplete, depicting abandonment Extended coda	More intricate chord changes than stereotypical punk rock Characteristic rough vocals Only one presentation of the chorus	Two large sections (A and B), that use different formal structures Sexual innuendo in lyrics Influence of rhythm and blues in horns, rhythmic groove, and vocal improvisation

He continued his success with *Storm Front* (p1 uk5, 1989), which contained "We Didn't Start the Fire" (p1 uk7). The Rolling Stones seemed not to be slowed much by age, as *Tattoo You* (p1 uk2, 1981) produced the classic "Start Me Up" (p2 uk7), and subsequent albums like *Undercover* (p4 uk3), *Dirty Work* (p4 uk4, 1986), and *Steel Wheels* (p3 uk2, 1989) topped charts worldwide. Paul McCartney achieved notable success in the 1980s as well, hitting the number one slot in both Britain and America with 1982's *Tug of War*. In many ways, the 1980s made it clear that rock artists need no longer think of their careers as only a few years in the sun. Rock careers could in fact span decades, and acts could successfully continue even after the style with which they were originally associated had passed from popular favor.

During the 1980s, MTV and the video age challenged some of rock's deeply held values. The centrality of video images seemed to take attention away from the music itself. Viewed from a broader historical perspective, however, the ambitious scope of some music videos—and especially those of Michael Jackson, Madonna, and Eurythmics—clearly reinterpreted and redirected at least one aspect of the musical ambition that developed in the decade after *Sgt. Pepper*. Just as concept albums in the 1970s pushed at the boundaries of rock by exploring a variety of musical styles while pursuing serious-minded themes, music videos in the 1980s followed a similar path. However, the focus in the 1980s shifted to making music and image work together to create a compelling synthesis. In this case, there was certainly a strong element of artistic ambition. The music videos of the 1980s provide an important aesthetic connection to rock's past that is often missed by critics who focus more on the differences between 1970s and 1980s music than on the underlying continuities.

In addition to MTV, a generation of "new traditionalists" emerged during the early 1980s, earnestly employing the sounds and images of older forms of rock.

These groups revisited older styles at face value with a concern for returning rock to its core aesthetic values. While some aspects of the punk movement developed into commercial forms of new wave, the 1980s also saw an emerging underground hardcore movement in various locations across the United States. In the next chapter we explore how heavy metal, rap, and alternative rose from their respective underground scenes during the 1980s to emerge as important styles by the end of the decade.

FURTHER READING

Saul Austerlitz, *Money for Nothing: A History of the Music Video from the Beatles to the White Stripes* (Continuum, 2007).

Michael Azerrad, *Our Band Could Be Your Life: Scenes from the American Indie Underground, 1981–1991* (Back Bay, 2002).

Steven Blush, *American Hardcore: A Tribal History* (Feral House, 2010).

Stewart Copeland, *Strange Things Happen: A Life with the Police, Polo, and Pygmies* (It Books, 2009).

Jason Draper, *Prince: Chaos, Disorder, and Revolution* (Hal Leonard, 2011).

Bill Flanagan, *U2 at the End of the World* (Delacorte Press, 1995).

Thomas Harrison, *Music of the 1980s* (Greenwood, 2011).

Michael Jackson, *Moonwalk* (Harmony Books, 2009).

Dave Marsh, *Born to Run: The Bruce Springsteen Story, Volume 1* (Thunder's Mouth Press, 1996).

Dave Marsh, *Glory Days: Springsteen in the 1980s* (Thunder's Mouth Press, 1996).

Tom McGrath, *MTV: The Making of a Revolution* (Running Press, 1996).

June Skinner Sawyers, *Racing in the Street: The Bruce Springsteen Reader* (Penguin, 2004).

Paul Zollo, *Conversations with Tom Petty* (Omnibus, 2005).

VISIT STUDYSPACE AT WWNORTON.COM/STUDYSPACE

Access free review material such as:

- music links
- performer info
- practice quizzes
- outlines
- interactive listening guide software

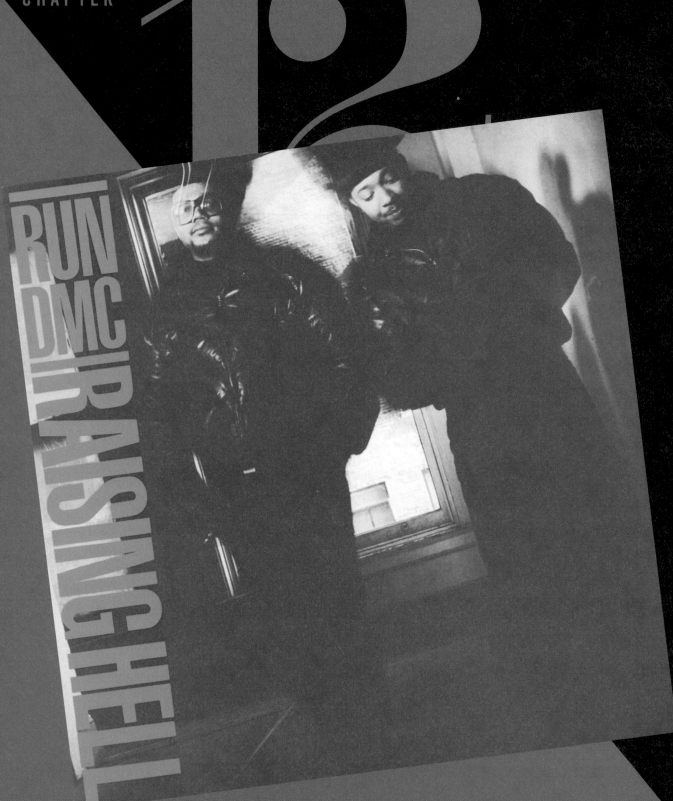

CHAPTER 12

HEAVY METAL, RAP, AND THE RISE OF ALTERNATIVE ROCK

In addition to the hardcore and indie rock movements that emerged out of punk's legacy during the early 1980s, two more underground scenes were developing that would emerge into the pop-music spotlight later in the decade: rap and heavy metal. This chapter will trace how both rap and heavy metal drew upon previous musical styles and practices throughout the 1980s. MTV played a crucial role in exposing both of these styles to a broader audience, helping them assume increasingly central positions in popular music during the second half of the decade. Moreover, as the 1980s drew to a close, the college and indie scenes also began to flirt with mainstream success under the moniker of "alternative." While rap, indie, and alternative all developed in the underground, each emerged later to enjoy tremendous commercial success. In some sense, these styles shared a common position as the voice of a disenfranchised segment of youth culture and each was able to keep that sense of identity in the midst of overwhelming popularity.

HEAVY! DUTY! HEAVY METAL IN THE 1980S

Heavy Metal Thunder. It is unclear exactly where heavy metal got its name. The phrase "heavy metal thunder" appeared in the lyrics of Steppenwolf's "Born to Be Wild," which became popular in the summer of 1968. Beat writer William Burroughs had also used the phrase in his 1962 novel *The Soft Machine*. Although the origins of the label are unclear, heavy metal's stylistic forebears are much easier to identify. Heavy metal developed out of the harder, more aggressive aspects of rock from the 1960s and 1970s. The garage band music of the Kingsmen and the early punk of the MC5 and the Stooges were early models. Progressive psychedelic songs like Iron Butterfly's "In-A-Gadda-Da-Vida" were also precursors. However, most writers cite

Run-DMC's *Raising Hell* (1986) was the first rap album to have a major impact on white audiences. This crossover appeal was driven by Run-DMC's sound, which featured strong lyrics mixed with samples from rock music. Their version of Aerosmith's "Walk This Way" exemplified this blend, and the video "duel" between Run-DMC and Aerosmith's Steven Tyler and Joe Perry brought the mix to MTV. The strong sales of *Raising Hell* to both white and black audiences and the consistent airplay of "Walk This Way" on MTV proved to industry professionals that they could make money selling rap, which in turn caused the style to explode into the mainstream.

the music of Black Sabbath as the earliest form of heavy metal. The gothic character of Sabbath's early music—driving riffs, dark themes, extended guitar solos—was an important source for later metal bands, as was the heavier side of Led Zeppelin's music. Deep Purple's blending of these same musical features with aspects of classical music also served as a model, as did the extravagant showmanship of Alice Cooper and KISS. Yet, there are aspects of the music of Led Zeppelin, Alice Cooper, and Deep Purple that heavy metal musicians did not typically adapt and, until the early 1980s, the stylistic features that would prove inspirational to metal musicians existed in music that was not set apart from other rock. Heavy metal as a separate stylistic category did not emerge in a significant way until several bands, developing as part of close-knit musical communities in England and Los Angeles, began to break out of underground venues with the help of successful albums and constant touring.

Blue-Collar Man: Image and Class. It is common to refer to heavy metal musicians and fans as "headbangers," in part owing to fans' tendency to bang their heads in the air while listening to the music. This term captures the sense, shared by many in the music world (however unfairly), that heavy metal music is primitive and its adherents are simple-minded and generally unsophisticated. This image is often compounded by a view of heavy metal as music that appealed specifically to blue-collar white audiences. Stereotypes of heavy metal listeners are prevalent throughout popular culture. More innocent characteristics, such as honesty, loyalty, and unselfish devotion to partying, are exhibited by actors Mike Myers and Dana Carvey in the *Wayne's World* movies (1992 and 1993). More negative metal stereotypes—ignorance, vulgarity, and laziness—are lampooned in the *Beavis and Butthead* cartoon series. In contrast to the general flashiness that characterized successful MTV acts during the early to mid-1980s, it is easy to see how heavy metal bands used their ragged image to oppose the status quo. Even when metal bands portrayed glamour, it was a tawdry, seedy form of glitz more closely associated with strip clubs than the various movements toward high fashion found in mainstream pop music. In any case, metal fans saw this rejection of the commercial status quo as a mark of authenticity and embraced it with enthusiasm, situating metal music as a form of cultural defiance.

The New Wave of British Heavy Metal. During the late 1970s in the UK, punk and new wave were the most visible reactions against mainstream rock released on major labels. Instead of the return-to-simplicity solution offered by punk and new wave, however, musicians that formed the nucleus of the metal scene opted for what might be termed a "return to heavy rock and roll." Many of these bands were from working-class sections of England, north of London. The various members of Black Sabbath, for example, were an important force in the growing heavy rock scene at the end of the 1970s. By 1977, Ozzy Osbourne had quit Black Sabbath to pursue a solo career. The group continued on with Ronnie James Dio taking over lead vocals (he was followed by a series of lead singers throughout the 1980s), while Osbourne recruited virtuoso guitarist Randy Rhoads and released a pair of successful solo albums, *Blizzard of Ozz* (p2 uk7, 1980) and *Diary of a Madman* (p16 uk14, 1981).

While Osbourne and Sabbath became high-profile acts, playing for stadium crowds and enjoying the benefits of past success, other English bands developed their music under the pop-industry radar. Judas Priest had formed in Birmingham in 1970, but it wasn't until 1979 that their album *Hell Bent for Leather* (uk32, 1979) earned them a broader audience in England. The group's next album, *British Steel* (p34 uk4, 1980), achieved success in the United States on the strength of tracks like "Breaking the Law" and "Living after Midnight." Iron Maiden formed outside of London in 1976, and became popular in their home country after the release of *Iron Maiden* (uk4, 1980), breaking into the American market with *The Number of the Beast* (p33 uk1, 1982). Sheffield-based Def Leppard also started from within the emerging British heavy metal scene and became internationally popular after the release of *High 'n' Dry* (p38 uk26, 1981). The group's next album, *Pyromania* (p2 uk18, 1983), showed an increasing interest in venturing into the pop field. This is apparent in the single "Photograph" (p12 uk66), which became more popular in the United States than any of the group's prior releases due, in part, to a video that became an early staple of MTV. Each of these bands, referred to collectively as the "new wave of British heavy metal," emerged into rock's mainstream in the early 1980s and continued to record and tour successfully throughout the decade. Their music was primarily guitar-driven, following the early 1970s model of Black Sabbath and Deep Purple, and often featured pyrotechnical soloing and unrelentingly heavy drumbeats.

Early Los Angeles Bands and the American Heavy Metal Underground.
While a new brand of heavy metal was developing in the north of England, American metal bands were forming their own underground networks. Although metal was not confined to a single place in America, during the 1980s the most prominent metal scene emerged in Los Angeles. In the decade before this scene emerged, Los Angeles had increasingly become the place to "make it" in the music business. As a result, musicians from all over the country migrated to Southern California seeking rock stardom and fame. The hopes and dreams of metal aspirants in Los

In addition to being talented songwriters and musicians, singer David Lee Roth (left) and guitarist Eddie Van Halen (right) were consummate showmen. Onstage, Roth projected a sense of wild, party-animal energy, while Van Halen delivered high-intensity guitar virtuosity.

Angeles were fed by the late 1970s success of Van Halen, who had worked their way up through the scene and enjoyed a series of hit albums. By 1984, however, the relationship between virtuoso guitarist Eddie Van Halen and lead singer David Lee Roth had gone sour. Roth's last album with the band was *1984* (p2 uk15, 1984). After this, Sammy Hagar joined the band as lead singer for the album *5150* (p1 uk16, 1986), and performed with the group for the remainder of the decade.

As the Van Halen personnel saga was playing out, other bands from Los Angeles began to emerge into the mainstream. Quiet Riot was among the first, as their *Metal Health* reached the top spot on the *Billboard* album charts in 1983. The album contained a version of "Cum On Feel the Noize," a hit for the British heavy rock band Slade a decade earlier. Although Quiet Riot did not like the tune and thought they turned in a poor performance, the track went to number five on the singles charts and became a staple of FM radio. Ratt was another Los Angeles metal group that entered the mainstream during the early 1980s. The group's first commercial success, *Out of the Cellar* (p7, 1984), included the hit single "Round and Round" (p12). Mötley Crüe, featuring singer Vince Neil and drummer Tommy Lee, also emerged from the Los Angeles club circuit in 1983 with *Shout at the Devil* (p17) and increased in popularity throughout the decade before releasing *Dr. Feelgood* (p1 uk4, 1989), which became their best-selling album. Mötley Crüe's "Shout at the Devil" is a good example of the kind of guitar-driven, pop-oriented metal that came out of Los Angeles in the mid-1980s. Vince Neil's singing is high, almost screaming, showing the influence of Led Zeppelin's Robert Plant, while the drumming is loud and assertive. The sing-along vocals on the chorus give the song an anthem-like quality, and the band drops out late in the track, allowing the listener to focus on the vocal hook (in live performance, the audience sings along and claps their hands).

Spectacular stage shows and outrageous costumes were a central part of 1980s heavy metal. Building on the approach of Alice Cooper, David Bowie, and Kiss from the 1970s, 1980s metal bands regularly used fiery explosions, as seen in this 1986 performance of Mötley Crüe, who often sported spandex clothes and teased hair.

Listening Guide

Get Music ⑤ wwnorton.com/studyspace

Mötley Crüe, "Shout at the Devil" Elektra 60289

Words and music by Nikki Sixx. Produced by Tom Werman. Contained on the album *Shout at the Devil*, which went to #17 on the *Billboard* "Hot LPs and Tape" chart in 1983.

FORM: Compound AABA. The A sections are made up of a verse-chorus pair, while the middle B section features a guitar solo and employs a melodic figure drawn from the introduction. The intro itself begins with 8 measures of guitar, bass, and drums, followed by a statement of the chorus, leading to 4 measures of lead guitar melody. This melody returns not only during the bridge, but also during the coda. In the last A section, the chorus occurs three times, once with only vocals and drums. This repetition places strong emphasis on the anthemic chorus, which is the song's hook. It's easy to imagine a crowd singing along to this chorus during live shows. Notice that the arrangement does not really build much, with verses and choruses throughout the song presented mostly the same way each time.

TIME SIGNATURE: 4/4.

INSTRUMENTATION: Electric guitar, bass, drums, lead and background vocals.

	0:00–0:41	**Introduction**, 16 mm.	Powerful figure played by guitar, bass, and drums in the first 8 bars, then 8 mm. that return as the song's chorus.
A	0:41–1:01	**Verse 1**, 8 mm.	Lead vocals enter. Note the high, almost screaming quality of Neil's voice, reminiscent of Led Zeppelin's Robert Plant. Note also the stops between vocal phrases. "He's a wolf screaming lonely . . ."
	1:01–1:11	**Chorus**, 4 mm.	Catchy backup vocals added. This is the material that appeared in the introduction. "Shout! Shout! . . ."
A	1:11–1:31	**Verse 2**, 8 mm.	As before. "He'll be the love in your eyes . . ."
	1:31–1:41	**Chorus**, 4 mm.	As before. "Shout!"
B	1:41–1:57	**Instrumental Bridge**, 6 mm.	Lead guitar solo over material based on the chorus.
A	1:57–2:17	**Verse 1**, 8 mm.	Repeat of first verse, done as before, "He's a wolf . . ."
	2:17–2:27	**Chorus**, 4 mm.	As before, "Shout!"
	2:27–2:37	**Chorus**, 4 mm.	Lead and backup vocals with drums only. This is where the crowd sings along in a live setting. "Shout!"
	2:37–2:47	**Chorus**, 4 mm.	Guitar and bass return. "Shout!"
	2:47–3:12	**Coda and fade**, 8 mm.+	Backup vocals continue, but music changes feel and lead guitar enters after 4 mm. with melody from introduction.

The Rise of the Metal Mega-Stars and Hair Bands. Although Def Leppard had enjoyed significant commercial success in the first half of the 1980s, no American heavy metal band had reached megastar status. The group that broke through this barrier was Bon Jovi, a group based in New Jersey and led by singer Jon Bon Jovi. The group's *Slippery When Wet* topped the U.S. album charts in 1986 (uk6), containing a handful of hit singles, including "You Give Love a Bad Name" (p1 uk14) and "Livin' on a Prayer" (p1 uk4). The band's 1988 follow-up, *New Jersey*, did even better, topping the album charts on both sides of the Atlantic and producing several hit singles, including "Bad Medicine" (p1 uk17) and "I'll Be There for You" (p1 uk18). The group's style was based on the high, soaring vocals of Jon Bon Jovi and virtuosic (but often restrained) guitar work of Ritchie Sambora. Lyrically, Bon Jovi strayed from heavy metal topics of parties and defiance, focusing instead on themes of working-class youth and Americana, revealing a close kinship with the songs of Bruce Springsteen. Despite their origins, by the late 1980s, it was clear that both Def Leppard and Bon Jovi had become too pop-oriented to be considered heavy metal. Both of these groups embraced a more mainstream style, a move that ultimately helped Bon Jovi survive the demise of metal in the 1990s.

Los Angeles–based Guns N' Roses was another American group to emerge from the metal scene as mainstream stars. Singer Axl Rose and lead guitarist Slash fronted the quintet, releasing *Appetite for Destruction* (p1 uk5) in 1987. Guns N' Roses' music often focused on the seedier side of life in Los Angeles, singing openly about drug and alcohol abuse and urban chaos. The group's music featured Rose performing in both a low baritone register and contrasting high, screaming vocals more akin to metal, along with lengthy, melodic guitar solos performed by Slash. Although *Appetite for Destruction* did not achieve success immediately, by the fall of 1988 the singles "Welcome to the Jungle" (p1 uk24) and "Sweet Child o' Mine" (p7 uk24) caught fire on the charts, making Guns N' Roses one of the most successful rock acts of the year. Relationships within the band tended to be stormy even

Guns N' Roses guitarist Slash and lead singer Axl Rose performing in concert. Guns N' Roses was one of the most popular heavy metal groups in the 1980s emerging from the Los Angeles scene to become worldwide stars. The band's sound featured Rose's multifaceted vocals and melodic guitar work from Slash.

Poison's C.C. DeVille (left), Brett Michaels (center), and Bobby Dall (right) in a 1987 concert. As representatives of what many people called "hair metal," Poison performed sexist party anthems and power ballads while wearing feminine costumes and makeup.

during the best of times, however, and while the group simultaneously released two enormously successful albums in 1991, *Use Your Illusion I* (p2 uk2) and *Use Your Illusion II* (p1 uk1), they split up just a few years later.

By the end of the 1980s, the use of costumes and stage makeup by a certain segment of metal groups prompted many listeners to designate these groups as "hair bands." Following the models of Alice Cooper, KISS, David Bowie, and many others, groups like Mötley Crüe wore makeup, outrageous clothes, and heavily teased hair, as did many other metal bands. Poison is one group that took this approach to the extreme. In an interesting contradiction to gender positioning, hair bands often attracted a disproportionate number of female fans. The Poison single "Talk Dirty to Me" (p9, 1987) represents musical and textual stereotypes of Los Angeles hair metal, with its compact form and quick, but virtuosic guitar solos and sexist lyrics. Poison's 1986 album *Look What the Cat Dragged In* hit number three in the United States, and *Open Up and Say . . . Ahh!* (p2 uk18, 1988) was even more successful. The latter album contained the hit single "Every Rose Has Its Thorn" (p1 uk13), which is a prime example of the "power ballad" genre that became popular in the context of metal during the late 1980s. Power ballads give the singer—in this case Bret Michaels—a chance to display his sensitive side, as they often begin with a quiet expressive section before the heavy guitars and drums enter, intensifying the arrangement. Other late-1980s hair bands of note are Warrant, who scored with *Dirty Rotten Filthy Stinking Rich* (p10, 1988) and *Cherry Pie* (p7, 1990); Winger, who hit with *Winger* (p21, 1988) and *In the Heart of the Young* (p15, 1990); and Skid Row, who enjoyed success on both sides of the Atlantic with *Skid Row* (p6 uk30, 1989) and *Slave to the Grind* (p1 uk5, 1991).

Metal Ambition. There was clearly a significant amount of empty showmanship in the pop-oriented sector of heavy metal toward the end of the 1980s. However, metal also had its more serious-minded, musically earnest, and ambitious practitioners during this period. Perhaps no metal band fits this description better than

Metallica in concert, 1984. Though their guitar-driven style might seem to connect them with '80s "hair bands," Metallica, led by guitarist and singer James Hetfield (right), brought a more musically complex style to heavy metal. Pictured with Hetfield is bassist Cliff Burton (left), who died tragically in a bus crash in 1986.

Listening Guide

Metallica, "One" Elektra 69329

Words and music by James Hetfield and Lars Ulrich. Produced by Metallica with Flemming Rasmussen. Single rose to #35 on the *Billboard* "Hot 100" (uk13) in 1989.

FORM: In the largest sense, this track is in two-part form, and these sections are marked "A" and "B" below. After a lengthy introduction, the A section is in contrasting verse-chorus form, with the addition of the instrumental interlude that appears three times and acts as an instrumental refrain. The fourth time this interlude occurs, it is developed and expanded musically. The second section begins as a simple verse form, but then breaks off into a through-composed instrumental composition.

TIME SIGNATURE: This track begins in 4/4, but the last 9 bars of the introduction shift to 3/4, and the A section stays in 3/4, though extra bars of 2/4 are added throughout, often at the ends of phrases. The chorus is the exception in the first section, as it mixes 4/4 and 2/4. The B section is entirely in 4/4.

INSTRUMENTATION: Two guitars, bass, drums, and lead vocal.

A	0:00–0:20	**Taped war sounds**	Machine gun fire, helicopter sounds establish the mood.
	0:20–1:31	**Introduction**, 25 mm.	Three 8-bar phrases (the last extended by a measure) then a 9-bar anticipation of the verse using quiet, clean guitar sounds.
	1:31–1:46	**Instrumental interlude**, 8 mm.	This music returns as refrain several times. Music remains quiet and this passage is sunny and might be mistaken for '70s prog-rock.
	1:46–2:13	**Verse 1**, 16 mm.	Lead vocal enters, as mood turns back to quiet and mysterious. "I can't remember anything . . ."
	2:13–2:20	**Chorus**, 4 mm.	Backup vocals enter, music contrasts strongly with verse, turning much heavier and more aggressive, using distorted guitar sounds, "Hold my breath . . ."

Metallica. The band began in Los Angeles but moved to the San Francisco area, where they felt that metal fans had a deeper appreciation of their approach. Like other metalheads, Metallica was influenced by Black Sabbath, Led Zeppelin, and Deep Purple. But the band was also influenced by some of the more serious groups associated with the new wave of British heavy metal, such as Motörhead. Formed by Lemmy Kilmister in the mid-1970s after the bassist had done a stint with Hawkwind, Motörhead brought together the guitar-dominated sound of British blues rock, the hectic tempos of punk, and a love for biker culture. Though influential, Motörhead never enjoyed marked commercial success in the United States, although albums such as *Motörhead* (uk43, 1977), *Ace of Spades* (uk4, 1980), and *Iron Fist* (uk6, 1982) were popular with audiences in England.

Get Music ⑤ wwnorton.com/studyspace

	2:20–2:34	**Instrumental interlude**, 8 mm.	Sunny, quiet music from the first interlude returns.
	2:34–3:02	**Verse 2**, 16 mm.	Mysterious, as before. "Back in the womb . . ."
	3:02–3:09	**Chorus**, 4 mm.	Heavy and aggressive, as before. "Hold my breath . . ."
	3:09–3:37	**Instrumental interlude**, 16 mm.	Twice through the returning quiet and sunny interlude music.
	3:37–3:54	**Chorus**, 10 mm.	The heavier and more aggressive 4-bar chorus is repeated once and then extended by 2 bars. "Now the world . . ."
	3:54–4:38	**Instrumental interlude (developed)**, 27 mm.	Mostly in 3/4, and in 4-bar phrases and based on the earlier interlude but now much heavier, though still melodic. Toward the end (4:20), a machine-gun rhythm begins in the drums, preparing the way for the next section, while also recalling the taped sounds that began the track.
B	4:38–4:55	**Instrumental transition**, 8 mm.	"Machine-gun" rhythm now played by entire band. This is the most aggressive and angular music so far in the track, and it sets up the mood for the second half of the song.
	4:55–5:13	**Verse 1**, 8 mm.	Lead vocal enters, as the mostly pastoral mood of the first half of the song is shattered by angry aggression. "Darkness imprisoning me . . ."
	5:13–5:22	**Verse 2**, 4 mm.	As before, "Landmine has taken my sight . . ."
	5:22–7:25	**Instrumental finale**, 57 mm.	Mostly in 4/4, this long section can be broken into sections of 12, 13, 14, and 19 measures. Note the tight playing among band members, as well as virtuosic guitar soloing.

Metallica embraced a form called speed metal, which refers to the fast tempos and blazing guitar passages featured in the music of a growing sector of metal bands. Groups such as Metallica, Megadeth, Anthrax, and Slayer explored both speed and thrash metal, the latter allowing for a broader range of musical textures and tempos. Metallica's music indeed displays a wide variety of textures, and this can be found on their early records, such as *Master of Puppets* (p29 uk41, 1986). The band's breakthrough album, . . . *And Justice for All* (p6 uk4, 1988), contains the track "One," a representative example of their music from the late 1980s. Cast in a large-scale two-part form, "One" begins quietly, but gains intensity and speed in its second section. Not to be confused with a power ballad, the complex formal design and ambitious instrumental sections in "One" are far beyond the stylistic confines of pop-oriented music made popular by hair bands, drawing more from the progressive influences on 1980s metal. The follow-up album, *Metallica* (p1 uk1, 1991), often called the "black album," marked the group's arrival as one of the most important bands in heavy metal.

Megadeth was another important thrash metal band, whose music combined metal styles and socially conscious themes. Led by former Metallica guitarist and singer Dave Mustaine, Megadeth emerged with the album *Peace Sells . . . but Who's Buying?* (1986). Later releases such as *Countdown to Extinction* (p2 uk5, 1992) and *Youthanasia* (p4 uk6, 1994) were more popular, and marked the band's move into the upper echelon of the *Billboard* charts. New York's Anthrax was another thrash metal band that developed alongside both Metallica and Megadeth. The band's 1987 album *Among the Living* (p62 uk18) also showed an interest in social themes with the song "Indians," and experimented with mixing rap and metal on "I am the Man." The Los Angeles group Slayer was also an important presence on the thrash metal scene. *Reign in Blood* (p94 uk47, 1986) was the group's first notable album, and spawned a series of moderately successful releases during the 1990s and 2000s, showing the lasting legacy of thrash metal after the 1980s.

The Role of Virtuosity and the Hippie Aesthetic.

Many metal bands embraced instrumental virtuosity, and technically demanding instrumental performance is closely associated with the genre. Virtuosic guitar was an especially important element of metal, and many metal guitarists actively cited influential players from hard rock in the 1970s. Some traced their musical pedigree back to Deep Purple's Ritchie Blackmore, for example, whose solo during "Highway Star" is a prime example of proto-metal virtuosity. Eddie Van Halen was a later influence who had developed a distinctive two-hand tapping technique, which can be heard on his solo "Eruption" from Van Halen's eponymous first album. Randy Rhoads was another important originator of guitar technique associated with the metal guitar tradition. Rhoads's style can be heard during the solo section of "Mr. Crowley," from Ozzy Osbourne's *Blizzard of Ozz*. Blackmore, Van Halen, and Rhoads became foundational figures in metal guitar during the late 1970s, inspiring a generation of performers who often took their levels of virtuosity to the extreme. Perhaps the best example of a self-consciously virtuosic metal guitarist from the generation following these leaders was Yngwie Malmsteen. Originally from Sweden, Malmsteen moved to California in 1982, where he played the Los Angeles clubs with Steeler and then Alcatrazz before forming Rising Force. The track "Dark Star," from the band's 1984 debut album, showcases Malmsteen's formidable technique, and provides an example of what many fans consider to be virtuosity gone awry.

In many ways, heavy metal—or at least the more technically oriented strain of it—offered a direct continuation of the musical ambition associated with the hippie aesthetic. In its elevation of classical-music models, extended forms, virtuosic solos, and even concept albums devoted to serious-minded issues, heavy metal can be seen as perhaps the most "traditional" style of rock music in the 1980s. Beneath the leather, chains, hairspray, and makeup, heavy metal was a physical, working-class form of rock, features that were direct extensions of 1950s rock.

THE EMERGENCE OF RAP

Rap Music and Hip-Hop Culture. The form of music that we now loosely call rap had its origins in New York's African-American and Latino communities during the late 1970s. As a musical form, rap was one element of a larger hip-hop culture, alongside graffiti art, street dance styles such as breaking and popping, and trends in fashion surrounding this movement. Graffiti artists became widespread in New York during the mid-1970s, with artists splashing their names across the city on buildings and subway cars. Subway trains were an especially effective way to broadcast graffiti, since they traveled throughout the city, reaching a wide range of residents along the way. At the same time, a style of creative movement called break dancing became extremely popular. Breaking involved performing athletic movements on a piece of cardboard or hard plastic, a style of artistic movement suited

As depicted in this image from the early 1980s in the Bronx, New York, the popularity of rap and hip-hop culture crossed racial lines. Early rap heroes like Run-DMC and LL Cool J defined the hip-hop look epitomized here: gold chains, a focus on "name brand" style, and the ubiquitous "boom box"—the portable radio/ tape deck combination that allowed people to carry their music with them, share it at a party, or even in public (whether that public wanted to hear it or not).

Rap music was part of a larger hip-hop culture that often engaged its urban surroundings in creative ways. The graffiti that sprang up on walls and subway trains often showed a high level of skill, and sometimes even a keen perception of the cultural issues at stake within the community. Many critics interpret hip-hop culture as an innovative response to urban decay and the many problems in presents.

Break dancing, which developed in the late 1970s was, along with graffiti art, a major part of hip-hop culture. As seen here, break dancers choreographed elaborate routines that showed off the acrobatic nature of the style. Like rival rap groups, break dance teams challenged each other to put on the best routine—and put down the competition at the same time.

perfectly for urban dwellers. The first break dancers were black and Hispanic teens, whose exciting displays brought the form to the attention of the general public.

The origins of rap music are best understood within this mix of urban art and dancing. The first hip-hop DJs played records at neighborhood parties, often in city parks or recreation rooms. Adapting a practice from Jamaican DJs, hip-hop DJs would often carry their own sound systems and employ an MC, or "master of ceremonies," to comment on the music and encourage the partygoers. One of the most popular early hip-hop DJs was Kool Herc, who made a practice of bringing his powerful sound system to a local park, using a city power source for electricity, and spinning records loud enough for everyone in the neighborhood to hear. Herc was perhaps the first to use an MC (Coke La Rock). These early MCs would soon develop into rappers, blending this new role with the clever patter of black radio disc jockeys.

Early hip-hop DJs such as Kool Herc and Grand-master Flash claim credit for technical innovations that would spawn important developments in modern rap. For years radio stations and dance clubs had used at least two turntables, one for the record being played and a second for the record that would follow. Using a pair of turntables, DJs were able to transition seamlessly from one record to the next, employing a mixing board or a cross-fader to decrease the volume of one record while increasing the volume of the other. Kool Herc and Grandmaster Flash employed portable turntables and mixers based on this set-up. In addition to transitioning from song to song, however, they developed techniques such as "break spinning," in which a DJ repeats a short phrase by spinning one record backward while the other is playing. "Punch phrasing" was another early technique that DJs used to feature short bursts from one record while the other was holding down the beat. The instrumental accompaniment of rap music began to feature "breaks," the catchiest instrumental breaks or passages (often drawn from disco or Latin-music recordings). This was done to incite the dancers to greater excitement, but it also began a technique of creating new music out of recorded "samples"—an idea that would form the aesthetic basis for the rap that followed. Grandmaster Flash also popularized "scratching," a technique in which the record is rotated in the reverse direction and then forward, quickly and repeatedly while manipulating the record's volume, to create a distinctive rhythm.

In addition to the technological expansions of Kool Herc and Grandmaster Flash, another early DJ, Afrika Bambaataa, expanded the range of source recordings employed within hip-hop. Bambaataa had founded Zulu Nation in the early 1970s, a gang-like organization devoted to building a sense of fraternity among

Grandmaster Flash was an important figure in the New York hip-hop scene's early years. Here, Flash performs at London's Wembley Arena in 1985.

DJ KOOL HERC: THE MAN WITH THE MASTER PLAN

by Jeff Chang

When Cindy Campbell and her brother Clive "DJ Kool Herc" Campbell threw a party in 1973, they had no idea what they were about to launch. At the end of the summer, they invited a hundred kids and kin to the modest rec room in their apartment building at 1520 Sedgwick Avenue in the Bronx.

Kool Herc started off playing some reggae dancehall tunes on his turntables, similar to the music he had heard at sound system parties in Kingston, Jamaica, where he had

lived until the age of 12. But this was the Bronx. The crowd, at first, wasn't very happy; they wanted the breaks, the kind of beats that they could move and groove to. So, like any good DJ, Herc gave the people what they wanted, and dropped some soul and funk bombs, songs like James Brown's "Give It Up or Turnit a Loose," Mandrill's "Fencewalk," and Rare Earth's "Get Ready."

Word spread quickly about the back-to-school party, and the Campbells soon found themselves throwing parties in the rec room almost every month. By the following summer, the crowds were so big they had to move outside to Cedar Park, just up the block. For electricity, they tapped lampposts and work sheds. With the loudest sound system, the hottest records, and personality for days, Herc and the Herculords, his group of rappers, DJs, and dancers, became the number one draw in the Bronx.

Herc carefully studied his audiences. The moment when the dancers went crazy was during a song's short instrumental break, when the band would drop out and the rhythm section would get elemental. Herc zeroed in on the break. He started searching for songs based on the sound of their break, songs

that he would make into his signature tunes: nonstop conga epics from the Incredible Bongo Band called "Apache" and "Bongo Rock," Johnny Pate's theme to "Shaft in Africa," Dennis Coffey's "Scorpio," black soul, Latin funk, and white rock records with an up-tempo carnival-style backbeat.

In a technique he called the "Merry-Go-Round," Herc worked two copies of the same record, back-cueing one record to the beginning of the break as the other reached the end, extending a five-second breakdown into a five-minute loop. Before

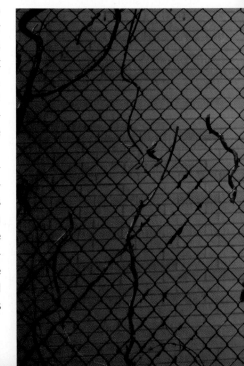

long he had tossed most of the songs, focusing on building excitement through the breaks alone. His sets drove the dancers from climax to climax on waves of churning drums. In the cyphers—the circles where they competed with each other for cheers from the crowd—the dancers became personalities in their own right. These kids had too much flavor to conform to the precision steps of group dances like the Hustle. They would simply jump in one after another to go off, take each other out, and just "break" wild on each other. Herc called them break boys—b-boys for short.

Herc's audiences were full of visionary youths. Afrika Bambaataa, a former gang leader from the Bronx River Projects, was inspired to return to his neighborhood and reach out to former enemy gangs and crews. Bambaataa's parties became common ground and from them he created the Zulu Nation, hip-hop's first official organization, and the Zulu Kings and Queens, two of hip-hop's first dance crews.

A teen from Fox Street in the South Bronx named Joseph Saddler, who would come to be known as Grandmaster Flash, went up to Cedar Park to see Herc for himself. Based on Herc's "Merry-Go-Round," he refined turntable techniques until he had helped lay the foundation for the kind of seamless beat-mixing that every DJ learns today. Along with his rap crew, the Furious 5, he perfected the art of the hip-hop musical performance.

After a period of intense gang violence, amid ongoing deindustrialization and governmental disinvestment, unrelenting white flight, and massive housing destruction, Herc's parties became a refuge for young Bronxites. He worked hard to make his audience feel welcome. He shouted out their names and kept the peace by taking a live-and-let-live policy and skillfully working the mic.

Along with his friends Coke La Rock and Dickey, he rocked entertaining rhymes like:

There's no story can't be told, there's no horse can't be rode,
and no bull can't be stopped and ain't a disco we can't rock. Herc! Herc! Who's the man with a master plan from the land of Gracie Grace? Herc Herc!

This adaptation of Jamaican sound-system toasting, jazz poetry, and soul radio host patter was called MCing, and it formed the foundation for what we now know as rap music.

Herc became a hero in the devastated Bronx, a salve to the borough's many wounds. He and his fans were kids abandoned by America, left behind in the nation's progress. But one can never underestimate the creative powers of young people. In time, hip-hop would inspire and redeem youths all around the world. And it all started with a small community party in the summer of 1973.

Jeff Chang is the author of the American Book Award–winning Can't Stop Won't Stop: A History of the Hip-Hop Generation *and editor of* Total Chaos: The Art and Aesthetics of Hip-Hop.

DJ Kool Herc (a.k.a. Clive Campbell) standing outside his former apartment at 1520 Sedgwick Avenue in the Bronx. Many say hip-hop was born at the parties held in this apartment building.

Hip-hop pioneer Afrika Bambaataa performing during the early 1980s. Note the two turntables and mixer in the photo. Bambaataa is "scratching" with his left hand and manipulating the mixer with his right.

hip-hop artists and de-emphasizing the role of fighting and crime in the urban neighborhoods of New York. Known in the community as the "master of the record," Bambaataa incorporated obscure or unlikely tracks such as the Mohawks' "Champ" and Kraftwerk's "Trans-Europe Express" into his mixes.

From the Park to the Radio: The First Rap Records. During the early years of hip-hop, there were no hip-hop records—mixing records and MCing was strictly a live affair, something you had to experience in person. In 1979, a new label called Sugar Hill Records released "Rapper's Delight," arguably the first hip-hop single. Credited to the Sugar Hill Gang, the record went to number four on the rhythm and blues charts (p36). Before this unexpected success with Sugar Hill, label owners Joe and Sylvia Robinson had run an indie label called All Platinum. Sylvia had enjoyed hit records as half of Mickey and Sylvia ("Love Is Strange," 1957) and as a solo performer ("Pillow Talk," 1973). As the story goes, Sylvia heard guests at a Harlem party chanting rhymes over the instrumental passages in disco records. Thinking this might be catchy enough to sell some records, she rounded up several young men and they "rapped" over a rhythm track drawn from Chic's "Good Times" to produce "Rapper's Delight." The success of this single demonstrated that the live hip-hop experience could indeed be transferred to vinyl. Soon after the success of "Rapper's Delight," Kurtis Blow scored with a hit for Mercury Records, "The Breaks (Part 1)," which went to number four on the rhythm and blues charts in 1980. Meanwhile, Sugar Hill developed into the most important rap label of the early 1980s, signing an impressive roster of rappers and DJs, and releasing a series of classic old-school tracks, including Grandmaster Flash and the Furious Five's "The Message" (p62 r4, 1982).

Russell Simmons and Rick Rubin: Crossing Over to White Audiences. Russell Simmons and Rick Rubin, two college students at New York University, formed another important early hip-hop label called Def Jam Records. In the mid to late 1980s, Def Jam released music by the decade's leading rappers, including LL Cool J, the Beastie Boys, and Public Enemy. Simmons's management company, Rush Entertainment, also handled some of rap's top acts including Run-DMC, Kurtis Blow, and DJ Jazzy Jeff and the Fresh Prince. Through management, label ownership, and production, Simmons and Rubin presided over the most impressive stable of talent on any indie label devoted to rap. Using a basic texture comprised of beats generated by an electronic drum machine, highlighted scratching, and the occasional sample or punch phrase, the music of Def Jam artists defined a new style of mainstream hip hop during the mid-1980s. Moreover, Simmons and Rubin were instrumental in helping popularize rap music in the mainstream.

One of the first successful artists at Def Jam was LL Cool J, whose career was jump-started in 1985 by an appearance in the movie *Krush Groove* and a hit single, "I Can't Live without My Radio" (r15). The song made reference to the growing practice of youth broadcasting music publicly using large portable "boomboxes" (also called "ghetto blasters"). The album *Radio* rose to number six on the rhythm and blues charts in 1986, hitting number forty-six on the pop charts. LL Cool J crossed over in 1987 with "I Need Love" (p14 r1), a track that is perhaps the first rap ballad, while the album *Bigger and Deffer* hit number one on the rhythm and blues album chart (p3).

Run-DMC—(from left) MC Darryl McDaniels ("DMC"), DJ Jason Mizell ("Jam Master Jay"), and MC Joseph Simmons ("Run"). Run-DMC combined traditional rap lyrics with rock breaks and samples. They were among the most important innovators in rap, influencing rap and hip-hop throughout the 1980s.

Listening Guide

Get Music Ⓢ **wwnorton.com/studyspace**

Run-DMC, "Rock Box" Profile 5045

Words and music by Larry Smith, Joseph Simmons, and Darryl McDaniels. Produced by Russell Simmons and Larry Smith. Rose to #22 on the *Billboard* "Black Singles" chart in 1984. Contained on the album *Run-DMC*, which hit #14 on the *Billboard* "Black LPs" chart.

FORM: Simple verse. This track features 2-measure vocal phrases played over a repeating 1-measure riff in the accompaniment. In the first verse sections, eight of these 2-bar vocal phrases occur, while in the second verse section twenty such phrases are heard. The last verse section is shorter than either of the previous two, containing only four 2-bar phrases. Interludes one and two create contrast by focusing the listener's attention on the background music. The coda features segments of relatively free verse, delivered over the same accompaniment found throughout the track.

TIME SIGNATURE: 4/4.

INSTRUMENTATION: Electric guitars, bass, drums, electronic percussion, vocals.

0:00–0:33	**Introduction**, 13 1/2 mm., 1 1/2 mm. pick up, then 12 mm.	Using a sampled beat and multiple distorted, hard-rock guitar melodies.
0:33–1:11	**Verse 1**, 16 mm.	Rapping begins, using eight 2-bar vocal phrases over the repeating guitar riff and beat from the introduction. "For all you sucker MCs . . ."
1:11–1:30	**Interlude 1**, 8 mm.	No vocal, focus on guitars and drums, as repeating guitar riff goes into stop time and multiple guitar melodies cascade.
1:30–3:01	**Verse 2**, 40 mm.	Twenty 2-bar phrases, the first two over only the drumbeat, then the repeated guitar riff returns. The last phrase employs scratching but no rapping. "Because the rhymes I say . . ."
3:01–3:16	**Interlude 2**, 4 mm.	No vocal, with emphasis on drumbeat as music breaks down.
3:16–3:35	**Verse 3**, 8 mm.	Four 2-bar phrases, guitar riff occurs in stop time. "We got all the lines . . ."
3:35–5:27	**Coda and fade**, 44 mm. +	Repeated guitar riff returns and is interrupted with stop time, then continues as lead guitar solos and rappers improvise, creating a long, atmospheric ending section. "Jay, Jay, Jay . . ."

About the same time, another act associated with Rubin and Simmons was crossing over in an even more direct way. Signed to Priority records but produced and managed by the Def Jam stable, Run-DMC consisted of rappers Joseph Simmons ("Run," Russell's younger brother) and Darryl McDaniels ("DMC"), and DJ Jason Mizell ("Jam Master Jay"). The group enjoyed some crossover success with the single "Rock Box" (r22, 1984), in part because the video for the song was played on MTV. Run-DMC often rapped over breaks from rock records, and this influence can be heard clearly throughout "Rock Box." The band's first album, *RUN-D.M.C.* (p53 r14, 1984), is often cited as among the most influential releases of early rap. Two years later, *Raising Hell* (p6 r1, 1986) became a mainstream hit, thrusting Run-DMC into the center of the American mainstream.

Another break Run-DMC used frequently was the opening drumbeat from Aerosmith's "Walk This Way." Rick Rubin, a big fan of hard rock and heavy metal who would later go on to produce Slayer and Danzig, invited Steven Tyler and Joe Perry to rerecord tracks for the tune rather than sampling them from the record. The resulting Run-DMC version thus featured both the rappers and the rockers. By using Aerosmith and their music, Rubin and Run-DMC brought rap to many white rockers who probably would have ignored it otherwise, and "Walk This Way" (p4 r8, 1986) became an important record for bringing rap into the pop mainstream.

Def Jam also produced a popular group comprised of white rappers. The Beastie Boys had originally been active in the New York hardcore punk scene, but transitioned into the emerging hip-hop scene in the early 1980s. After releasing a series of singles that appeared on the R&B and dance charts, the group's first mainstream single, "(You Gotta) Fight for Your Right (to Party)," hit number seven on the pop charts in 1987. Their album *Licensed to Ill* became the first rap record to hit number one on the pop album charts (r2, 1986). The Beastie Boys were also among the first bands to take advantage of the new digital sampling technology—instead of working with records and turntables, passages were recorded digitally and looped with far more precision than turntables would allow. By the end of the 1980s, digital sampling was a widespread practice among rappers, beginning a long history of lawsuits over music copyright connected to hip-hop's creative practices.

Challenging the Status Quo. Although Def Jam was a dominant force during the second half of the 1980s, other labels and artists also enjoyed success. Ice-T was born in New Jersey (as Tracy Morrow) but moved to Los Angeles as a child, where he became one of the most important representatives of West Coast rap in the late 1980s and early 1990s. "I'm Your Pusher" (r13, 1988) explores the same themes of urban life that had been addressed by black musicians decades earlier, although often in a more graphic and angry manner. The music of Ice-T and other West Coast artists that depicted these stark themes was known as "gangsta rap." Consistent with its influences from the 1970s, the track employs samples drawn from Curtis Mayfield's "Pusherman." While the 1988 album *Power* (p35 r6) did well commercially, Ice-T would enjoy much greater crossover success in the 1990s with *O.G. Original Gangster* (p15 r9, 1991) and *Home Invasion* (p14 r9, 1993).

N.W.A (Niggaz With Attitude) brought an even angrier approach to rap, creating much controversy in the process. The group's 1989 album, *Straight Outta Compton* (p37 r9), contained a track entitled "Fuck Tha Police," which earned its record company a warning letter from the FBI. In an interesting historical instance

of crossover appeal, this penchant for depicting dangerous urban life appealed strongly to white listeners, many of whom were from the American Midwest. With this support, the 1991 album *EFIL4ZAGGIN* hit number one on the pop album charts (r2), much to the consternation of many parents and community leaders. While Run-DMC used spare musical accompaniment and the Beastie Boys often incorporated samples from the rock repertoire, the music of N.W.A, created in large part by Dr. Dre, often used samples based in harder forms of funk such as Parliament and Kool and the Gang.

In addition to the stark realities explored in gangsta rap, other rap artists began to engage in social and political criticism. Boogie Down Productions (BDP), led by KRS-One (Kris Parker), is often cited as the most significant of these artists. The band's first album, *Criminal Minded* (r73, 1987), influenced many rappers who followed in its sometimes uncompromising and harsh depictions of urban life. After the death of rapper Scott La Rock in 1987, the tone of BDP's music changed drastically. In contrast to the anarchistic leanings of N.W.A, KRS-One began to portray himself as an intellectual on songs such as "My Philosophy," from the 1988 album *By All Means Necessary* (p75 r18), whose title and album cover referred directly to Malcolm X. BDP reached the peak of its crossover success with *Ghetto Music: The Blueprint of Hip-Hop* (p36 r7, 1989) and *Edutainment* (p32 r9, 1990).

Building on the rhythmic style of Run-DMC and the social and political approach of BDP, Public Enemy first stormed the rhythm and blues charts in 1988 with *It Takes a Nation of Millions to Hold Us Back* (p42 r1), containing the single "Don't Believe the Hype" (r18). "Fight the Power" (r20, 1989), which also makes direct reference to the black power movement, was featured in Spike Lee's film *Do the Right Thing*. This growing black consciousness resonated with listeners, and the group's next album, *Fear of a Black Planet* (p10 r3, 1990), sold extremely well in pop markets. Led by Chuck D and Flavor Flav, Public Enemy became one of the most influential groups in rap, enjoying their greatest crossover success with *Apocalypse 91—The Enemy Strikes Back* (p4 r1, 1991). Much like the social disarray

Listening Guide

Get Music ⑤ **wwnorton.com/studyspace**

Public Enemy, "Don't Believe the Hype" Def Jam 652833

Words and music by Carlton Ridenhour, Hank Shocklee, Eric Sadler, and Charles Drayton. Produced by Hank Shocklee and Carl Ryder. Single rose to #18 on the *Billboard* "Hot Black Singles" chart in 1988. Also contained on the album *It Takes a Nation of Millions to Hold Us Back*, which rose to #1 on the "Top Black Albums" chart (p42).

FORM: Simple verse-chorus. The verses are made up of 4-bar vocal phrases; the first verse uses four such phrases, the second uses five, and the third employs ten. The first chorus is also a 4-measure phrase, as is the third. The second and fourth choruses employ an 8-bar structure in which a 4-bar phrase is followed by a contrasting 2-bar phrase and a return to the first phrase. Note how the rhyme schemes and rhythms change often and sometimes cross over from one phrase to the next.

TIME SIGNATURE: 4/4.

INSTRUMENTATION: Vocals, guitar, bass, drums (likely sampled and looped to create a constant and repetitive backdrop). An electronic whistle sound also recurs regularly.

0:00–0:10	**Introduction**, 4 mm.	Electronically sampled and altered sounds over looped groove.
0:10–0:49	**Verse**, 16 mm.	Rapping enters in four 4-bar phrases, as looped groove continues underneath. "Bang, caught you lookin' . . ."
0:49–0:58	**Chorus**, 4 mm.	Recited two 2-bar phrases with nonverbal vocal interjections, "Don't believe the hype . . ."
0:58–1:47	**Verse**, 20 mm.	Rapping now presents five 4-bar phrases, with loop continuing with occasional stop time. "Yes was the start . . ."
1:47–2:07	**Chorus**, 8 mm.	First two 2-bar phrases as before, then one contrasting phrase, followed by a return to first 2-bar phrase.
2:07–3:44	**Verse**, 40 mm.	Rapping now presents ten 4-bar phrases, with loop continuing uninterrupted. Note the exchange of rapped phrases. "Don't believe the hype, it's a sequel . . ."
3:44–4:04	**Chorus**, 8 mm.	The first 4 mm. are without vocals, followed by two 2-bar vocal phrases.
4:04–5:00	**Verse**, 23 mm.	Rapping uses five 4-bar phrases then one 3-bar phrase, "I got flavor . . ."
5:00–5:19	**Chorus**, 8 mm.	As before, two 2-bar phrases, one contrasting phrase, then return to first 2-bar phrase.

Listening Guide

Queen Latifah, "Ladies First" Tommy Boy 1022

Words and music by Shane Faber, Mark James, Simone Johnson, Dana Owens, and Anthony Peaks. Produced by DJ Mark the 45 King. From the album *All Hail the Queen*, which rose to #6 on the *Billboard* "Soul LPs" chart in 1989 (p124).

FORM: Simple verse, divided into three sections and an ending; each section closes with the catch phrase "Ladies first," which acts like a refrain. The first section begins with the introduction and then presents verses one and two. The second section begins with a short instrumental interlude that leads into verses three and four. The interlude that leads into verses five, six, and seven is extended to 16 measures, and contains a 4/4-measure rhythm break. The ending uses the same material as the intro and interludes and fades out. Queen Latifah shares rapping duties with Monie Love and the lines are based on 4-measure units, often with a rhythm break marking the fourth bar. Note how Latifah stretches verse one by two measures and how the two rappers move between verses throughout.

TIME SIGNATURE: 4/4, with a strong funk groove.

INSTRUMENTATION: Drums, saxes, synthesizer, electric guitar, electric bass, voices. Much of the instrumental material is drawn from samples that are recombined to form the backing track. Even though the instrumental accompaniment is very repetitive, note how elements come in and out of the texture, creating constant variation behind the vocal.

0:00–0:18	**Introduction**, 8 mm.	Drums and bass establish groove, sax samples.
0:18–0:31	**Verse 1**, 6 mm.	Queen Latifah enters, the 4 mm. phrase is extended by 2 mm. "The ladies will kick it . . ."
0:31–0:49	**Verse 2**, 8 mm.	Monie Love takes over; the verse ends with the catch phrase, "Ladies first." "Excuse me but . . ."
0:49–0:54	**Interlude**, 2 mm.	Sampled "TV/radio voice" over groove. "There's gonna be some changes . . ."
0:54–1:12	**Verse 3**, 8 mm.	Monie Love continues, "Believe me . . ."
1:12–1:29	**Verse 4**, 8 mm.	Queen Latifah takes over, the verse ends with "Ladies first." "I break into . . ."
1:29–2:05	**Interlude**, 16 mm.	8 mm. of groove + 4 mm. of rhythm break + 4 mm. of groove.
2:05–2:23	**Verse 5**, 8 mm.	Queen Latifah continues, "Who said that the ladies . . ."
2:23–2:59	**Verse 6**, 16 mm.	Monie Love takes over, "Praise me not . . ."
2:59–3:17	**Verse 7**, 8 mm.	Queen Latifah takes over, the verse ends with "Ladies first." "Contact and in fact . . ."
3:17–3:52	**Ending**, 16 mm. and fade	8 mm. of groove, then 4 mm. rhythm break, then 4 mm. of groove and fade.

Public Enemy's Chuck D (left) and Flavor Flav (center) during the filming of the video for "Fight the Power," directed by Spike Lee. As seen in the bodyguards on stage, Public Enemy forwarded themes of militancy in rap during the late 1980s. Calling attention to underserved communities, Public Enemy railed against racism in the Los Angeles police department with "Burn, Hollywood, Burn" (1990) and decried attitudes toward public services in black neighborhoods in "9-1-1 is a Joke" (1990).

depicted in their lyrics, Public Enemy's music is often chaotic, featuring heavy layers of samples, drum beats, the "hype man" calls of Flavor Flav, and the deep, sanctified tone and phrasing of Chuck D's vocals.

While many popular rappers during the 1980s were male, Queen Latifah emerged as an important female voice in hip-hop with her 1989 debut, *All Hail the Queen* (r6). Born Dana Owens in Newark, New Jersey, Latifah started out in a hip-hop group called Ladies Fresh before signing as a solo artist with Tommy Boy Records. While *All Hail the Queen* was only a moderate commercial success, it made a large

Emerging from the male-dominated hip-hop industry in the late 1980s, Dana Owens (a.k.a. Queen Latifah) challenged the stereotype that women couldn't rap. She continues to enjoy a successful recording and acting career.

impact by establishing a strong female voice in hip-hop. This is exemplified on the single "Ladies First," in which Latifah shares the rapping with Monie Love. The lyrics of this track extol the pleasures of womanhood, dismiss any prejudice that women can't rap, and defiantly assert, "stereotypes, they gotta go." Latifah was nominated for a Grammy and was named Best Female Rapper by *Rolling Stone* in 1990.

Fear of a Black Planet? The Flap over Rap. Much like rock and jazz in their early years, rap faced a steady stream of controversy during the 1980s. One strain of criticism surrounded the complaint that rap was not really "music," since most rappers do not play instruments or sing. Even the lyrical content of rap music came under fire. Although it is easy to equate rap with poetry, the offensive words and images employed in some rap, which can be misogynistic, homophobic, vulgar, and violent, have sparked social and legal debate. In the context of our study of rock music, rap again trips the wires of race and class distinctions among some white listeners—a phenomenon that has emerged with many of the most important styles of popular music during the twentieth century. In the 1980s, however, this tension was often portrayed as a conflict between rock and rap, in which rock is seen as the "old guard" and rap as the newcomer.

The video for Run-DMC's "Walk This Way" displays a caricature of the racial tension between rock and rap during the mid-1980s. During the first half of the video, neither Run-DMC nor Aerosmith has much patience with the other, and it is hardly a happy moment of reconciliation when rocker Steven Tyler breaks down the wall that physically separates the two groups. While issues of race and class may have accounted for some of the tension over rap, they also accounted for some of its appeal. Many young white rap fans in the late 1980s and early 1990s were clearly fascinated by the worlds of urban violence and struggle that played a role in much of the harder-edged rap—worlds that were very different from the often affluent and mostly white suburban environment in which they lived (though perhaps not as different as is often imagined). Contrary to claims that rap is not really music, it is worth noting that rap musicians often take preexisting music and refashion it into something new, which has been an accepted aesthetic approach in the visual and musical arts at least since World War II. Many listeners might object to the music of contemporary composers such as John Cage or Karlheinz Stockhausen, but few would go so far as to say that they are not musicians. Anyone who has ever tried to compose hip-hop music can certainly attest to the artistic merits of this form, reminding us that refashioning preexisting material—even if it comes from records—can be just as "musical" as working with new material.

In many ways, rap and heavy metal might have appeared to be in opposition to one another during the second half of the 1980s, but they developed commercially along parallel paths. For example, both styles established devoted followings on MTV as the network gained a foothold as a mainstream tastemaker. *Headbangers' Ball* premiered in 1987, playing metal videos exclusively, while *Yo! MTV Raps* debuted in August 1988 and quickly became one of the most popular shows on the network. Both styles also maintained a kind of "outsider" status, depending in large part on class differences—and in the case of rap, race issues. Both styles became emblematic of the lower end of the class spectrum and used this class distinction as part of their appeal, often drawing in middle- and upper-class fans as well. While rap continued to develop throughout the 1990s, enjoying continued success (as well as inciting new criticism), heavy metal began to lose favor as a new guitar-heavy sound began to emerge, at first from Seattle, and then from around the country and from Britain.

INDIE AND ALTERNATIVE

America's Punk? In Chapters 10 and 11 we focused on the rise of punk in the late 1970s and how this scene influenced the development of a robust hardcore movement during the early 1980s. In the early 1990s, this indie-based community had its first significant move into the mainstream with a new style of mainstream rock music called "alternative." Like the punk and hardcore scenes, alternative music embraced punk's return-to-simplicity aesthetic and its directness of expression. In fact, many of the first-wave alternative artists came directly out of the hardcore scene and, for our purposes, alternative should be viewed as a marketing label rather than a distinct musical style. Like the 1970s punks who reacted against the big labels and overproduced corporate rock, alternative rockers in the 1990s appealed to listeners who began to loathe visually oriented MTV artists and flashy (often virtuosic) heavy metal bands. Alternative rock musicians dressed very casually (no spandex or teased hair), many projected themselves as amateur instrumentalists (no long guitar solos), and they often resisted the idea of recording for a major label, opting instead to work with smaller indie labels. This do-it-yourself aesthetic was one way of rejecting the crass commercialism of popular music, as well as most of the trappings of fame. Thrust much farther into the mainstream than either punk or hardcore, alternative musicians and their fans became rock's new bohemians—self-consciously scruffy and full of attitude. As we explore the transition from hardcore to alternative, through what was often called "college rock," it is important to acknowledge some of the groups that contributed to this large-scale aesthetic shift. During the 1980s, many important bands helped to ease the transition between the anarchistic attitudes and music associated punk and the more approachable views and sounds of alternative.

Massachusetts Indie: Dinosaur Jr., Sebadoah, and the Pixies.

The independent rock movement that grew out of hardcore cultivated musical scenes in many unlikely places. While we have seen the growth of regional scenes in places like Los Angeles, Minneapolis, and Washington, D.C., another regional indie center was Western Massachusetts, centered on Amherst and Northampton. These quintessential college towns became home to a thriving independent music scene in the late 1980s. Perhaps the best-known group from this area is Amherst's Dinosaur Jr. Led by guitarist J. Mascis and bassist Lou Barlow, the band released several albums on independent labels Homestead and SST in the late 1980s, including *You're Living All over Me* (1987). Soon after this album, they signed to a major label (Sire) and Barlow departed, with the group becoming a vehicle for Mascis. Although the group's tenure was relatively short, Dinosaur Jr. has held a solid place in the alternative rock pantheon, with characteristic heavy guitar, melodic vocal hooks and atmospheric guitar solos. In Boston, another independent scene was thriving, with bands such as Galaxie 500 and Morphine. The most important independent group to emerge from Boston was the Pixies, who recorded for the independent British 4AD label and then Elektra. The band was fronted by guitarist Frank Black and bassist Kim Deal, and featured catchy songs that often alternated between soft, driving verses and loud, anthemic choruses. Their albums *Surfer Rosa* (1988) and *Doolittle* (uk8, 1989) were successful in England and became landmarks of the American indie scene in the late 1980s.

College Rock Underground: R.E.M.

The return-to-simplicity credo was the working principle for a scene that would develop on U.S. college campuses in the late 1980s, known as "college rock." As an outgrowth of hardcore, this scene cel-

Listening Guide

Get Music Ⓢ **wwnorton.com/studyspace**

R.E.M., "The One I Love" I.R.S. 53171

Words and music by Bill Berry, Peter Buck, Mike Mills, and Michael Stipe. Produced by Scott Litt, Bill Berry, Peter Buck, Mike Mills, and Michael Stipe. Rose to #9 on the *Billboard* "Hot 100" in late 1987. Also contained on the album *Document*, which rose to #10 on the *Billboard* "Top Pop Albums."

FORM: Simple verse-chorus. The material for the introduction, the core of the verses, and the chorus uses the same music. The verse sections are made of a compact AABA form, with 4 measures used for each of the subsections. The single, contrasting B section within each verse acts as a mini bridge. It seems as if the verses might strictly use AABA form, while the chorus sections follow an AA pattern. Yet, an interesting derivation occurs with the instrumental solo, which uses a BA pattern, completing the AABA form started by the preceding chorus. Moreover, the final chorus is doubled in length to 16 measures. Perhaps the most fascinating aspect of the form is that there is almost no derivation in lyrics in the verse sections, creating a large-scale alternation between two sections (a verse and a chorus).

TIME SIGNATURE: 4/4.

INSTRUMENTATION: Electric guitars, bass, drums, auxiliary percussion, lead and backing vocals.

0:00–0:16	**Introduction**, 8 mm.	The track opens with a featured guitar that alternates between a low, melodic figure and a jangly rhythm guitar pattern associated closely with guitarist Peter Buck.
0:16–0:46	**Verse 1**, 16 mm.	Each verse is like a small AABA section, with each subsection lasting 4 measures. The A sections uses the music presented in the introduction, while the B begins with the lyrics "A simple prop . . ."; "This one goes out . . ."
0:46–1:01	**Chorus**, 8 mm.	A simple, one-word chorus, supported by the guitar melody presented in the introduction and a distorted rhythm guitar. "Fire . . ."
1:01–1:31	**Verse 2**, 16 mm.	The lyrics and music repeat verse 1 verbatim.
1:31–1:46	**Chorus**, 8 mm.	A backing vocal melody is added. "Fire . . ."
1:46–2:01	**Instrumental Verse**, 8 mm.	This section completes the AABA form initiated by the chorus, featuring Peter Buck's solo guitar.
2:01–2:31	**Verse 3**, 16 mm.	The lyrics and music repeat verse 1 nearly verbatim. Notice the subtle vocal effects added to Michael Stipe's voice, which create an eerie ambiance.
2:31–2:46	**Chorus**, 16 mm.	Listen closely for the multiple guitars layers in the chorus section and the added percussive shaker placed in the left speaker. "Fire . . ."
3:01–3:18	**Postlude**, 2 mm.	The song's momentum ceases, revolving around the guitar melody that plays throughout.

ebrated its lack of affiliation with major labels and corporations, with music circulating through small independent labels (or sometimes by the bands themselves), airplay on college radio stations, and live performances at clubs that formed a circuit of the country's most important college towns. In many ways, college rock got its start in Athens, Georgia, home of the University of Georgia and a local band called R.E.M. Led by guitarist Peter Buck and vocalist Michael Stipe, R.E.M. emerged from Athens to have a string of successful albums in the second half of the 1980s, marking what is perhaps the most significant instance of independent rock success in the mainstream during the decade. The band's fifth album, *Document*, rose to the number ten position on the U.S. charts in 1987 (uk28), while the single "The One I Love" hit number nine on the American charts. While many R.E.M. fans were displeased with the success of the group after "The One I Love," the driving simplicity included in this song is an example of the widespread appeal of the group. Consisting of little more than a single verse and chorus section, each repeated several times, the basic rock formula of "The One I Love" exhibited the core of R.E.M.'s aesthetic: moderately cryptic, energetic rock and roll performed by a classic rock band lineup. R.E.M. had much more chart success in the United States than in Britain, but with 1991's *Out of Time*, they finally reached the number one spot on both sides of the Atlantic, fueled in part by the success of the singles "Losing My Religion" (p4 uk19) and "Shiny Happy People" (p10 uk6).

Seattle's Grunge Scene: Nirvana. When Nirvana's second album *Nevermind* (p1 uk7) was released in late 1991, it not only rose to the top of the pop charts on both sides of the Atlantic—partly with the help of the single "Smells like Teen Spirit" (p6 uk7)—but also launched the alternative rock movement, a commercial explosion that would resonate for over a decade. Although they played their first shows in Olympia, Washington, Nirvana was perhaps the most significant of the "grunge" bands that came out of Seattle in the first half of the 1990s. Led by singer, songwriter, and guitarist Kurt Cobain, the band quickly became stars, despite Cobain's dedication to the idea that Nirvana's music rejected the rock star apparatus in show business. Accordingly, Cobain and Nirvana projected an image of amateurism, but Cobain was in fact a gifted songwriter and a tasteful guitarist. The two albums that followed *Nevermind* further solidified the band's status as one of the hottest acts in rock. *In Utero* (1993) and *Unplugged in New York* (1994) both hit the number one slot in the United States and the UK.

Nirvana's lead singer Kurt Cobain performing in England, 1992. Nirvana combined simple but intense guitar work with poetic, sometimes disturbing, longing lyrics to create a new sound: "grunge." This sound appealed especially to young, white suburbanites who felt alienated from mainstream American values. Cobain's suicide in 1994 helped turn him into an icon of "alternative" music and culture.

Listening Guide

Nirvana, "Smells like Teen Spirit" DGC 19050

Words and music by Kurt Cobain, Krist Novaselic, and Dave Grohl. Produced by Butch Vig. Single rose to #7 on the *Billboard* "Hot 100" (uk6) in early 1992. Also contained on the album *Nevermind*, which rose to #1 on the *Billboard* "200" (uk7).

FORM: Simple verse-chorus (modified). The 16-bar introduction is made up of two 2-bar phrases played solo on the guitar, then four 2-measure phrases played loudly by the entire band, followed by the same phrase played twice more but quietly and arranged differently. This last "quiet" 2-bar phrase returns again as a lead-in to the second verse and is abbreviated to 2 bars to lead into the third verse. Each verse and chorus is built on the same 2-bar phrase heard in the introduction. The 16-bar verses cycle through the phrase eight times; the first 8 bars in each case employ new lyrics while the second 8 bars repeat the "Hello/how low" lyric. The 16-bar choruses contain the 2-bar phrase six times each, with a contrasting 4 bars added to the end in each case. After the second verse-chorus pair, the verse is played instrumentally, as the guitar plays the vocal melody. The song ends with a chorus containing ten statements of the basic 2-bar phrase.

TIME SIGNATURE: 4/4.

INSTRUMENTATION: Guitars, bass, drums, vocal. Notice the contrast between the clean sounding guitar at the beginning of each sung verse and the heavily distorted guitars heard in the choruses.

0:00–0:33	**Introduction**, 16 mm.	Solo guitar plays 2-bar phrase twice through relatively quietly, then the entire band comes in playing the same music for 8 bars, followed by a return to a quiet, but differently arranged version of the same music.

"Smells like Teen Spirit" provides a representative example of Nirvana's music. The tune features a simple, catchy guitar pattern played on the low strings that repeats throughout most of the song. The lyrics are delivered with calculated care-lessness, creating a sense of tortured spontaneity in the verses while driving toward the intense and aggressive chorus. The contrast between the mellow verses and the frenetic chorus sections echoes the bipolar nature of alternative music, which evolved from often-energetic hardcore, but had gained widespread commercial appeal. Despite the rejection of commercialism that was central to alternative rock, Cobain was clearly skilled at working with the traditional elements of pop songwriting and arranging, as this and many other Nirvana tracks demonstrate. Moreover, bassist Krist Novoselic, drummer Dave Grohl, and the group's main producers, Butch Vig and Steve Albini, provided Cobain with expert support. Nirvana's career, however, was cut tragically short by Cobain's suicide in April 1994 and it would be left to others to carry the alternative torch.

Pearl Jam. In Nirvana's wake, a host of alternative rock bands began to enjoy a level of commercial success that had eluded post-punk and hardcore bands in the

0:33–1:06	**Verse 1**, 16 mm.	Lead vocal enters to the accompaniment of the "quiet" music in the first 8 bars, and to the "loud" music in the second 8 bars. "Load up on guns and bring your friends . . ."
1:06–1:47	**Chorus**, 20 mm.	Played and sung at its most aggressive, plus 4 bars of contrasting music, then a 4 mm. lead-in to the next verse using the "quiet" music, "With the lights out it's less dangerous . . ."
1:47–2:20	**Verse 2**, 16 mm.	As in verse 1, "I'm worse at what I do best . . ."
2:20–2:53	**Chorus**, 16 mm.	As before, but without the "quiet" music lead-in to the next verse. "With the lights out it's less dangerous . . ."
2:53–3:34	**Instrumental Verse**, 20 mm.	16 mm. guitar solo plays the melody almost exactly as it is sung in the verses, then the 4 mm. "quiet" music serves to lead into the verse, though this time it is a little different, allowing space for the lead guitar to die out.
3:34–4:05	**Verse 3**, 16 mm.	As in verses 1 and 2, "And I forget just why I taste . . ."
4:05–4:58	**Chorus**, 21 mm.	As before, but extended to include ten times through the 2-bar phrase, plus a last chord added to create an ending. Cobain's vocals become the most frenzied toward the end.

1980s. Also from Seattle was Pearl Jam, led by singer Eddie Vedder. The albums *Ten* (p2 uk18, 1992), *VS.* (p1 uk2, 1993), and *Vitalogy* (p1 uk6, 1994) established them as mainstream stars by mid-decade. Pearl Jam's music was in many ways closer to the heavy metal that had immediately preceded it, which made it easy to program on the mainstream rock radio stations of the mid-1990s. The group was central to the alternative rock scene, but they were also important to the anticommercial aesthetic of the alt-rock lifestyle. The band battled with Ticketmaster, a national service that handled ticket sales for many large rock concerts, because the agency was forcing individual tickets to sell for more than $20, making it difficult for some fans to attend the band's shows. (Ticketmaster merged with the concert promotion company Live Nation to become Live Nation Entertainment in 2010.) Although Pearl Jam eventually lost a long legal battle with Ticketmaster, their willingness to fight corporate interests—and lose the revenue they would have earned through concert appearances during this time—made them heroes within the alternative movement. By the end of the decade, *Yield* (1998) hit number two on the U.S. charts, and the band scored a surprise single with "Last Kiss" (p2, 1999), an unlikely cover of a 1964 splatter platter by J. Wilson and the Cavaliers.

Other Seattle Bands: Soundgarden, Alice in Chains, and Foo Fighters.
Led by the vocals of Chris Cornell and the guitar playing of Kim Thayil, Soundgarden also emerged from Seattle. Formed in the late 1980s and expected by many
in Seattle to be the band that would first break onto the national scene, Soundgarden's blend of heavy metal, 1970s blues rock, and 1960s psychedelia achieved
national commercial success in 1994 with the release of *Superunknown* (p1 uk4).
Initially signed by Columbia Records as a metal band, Alice in Chains was formed
by singer Layne Staley in the late 1980s. Staley's penchant for dark lyrics dealing
with drug addiction and death are similar to those of speed metal bands like Metallica or Megadeth, and the group's 1990 debut album, *Facelift*, was initially directed
to metal fans. In the wake of Nirvana's success, however, Alice in Chains were promoted as a "Seattle band," which helped the sales of *Facelift* and pushed the next

Sound Check

Artist	Mötley Crüe	Metallica	Run-DMC
Title	Shout at the Devil	One	Rock Box
Chart peak	1983	p35 1989	r22 1984
Form	Compound AABA	Contrasting verse-chorus (modified)/Simple verse	Simple verse
Rhythm	4/4	4/4 (3/4, 2/4)	4/4
Instrumentation	Electric guitar Bass Drums Lead vocal Background vocal	Electric guitar Bass Drums Lead vocal	Electric guitar Bass Drums Lead vocal Electronic percussion Synthesizer Turntable
Comments	High metal vocals without speed or virtuosity Audibly multitracked guitars and background vocals Anthemic chorus	Highly complex two-part form Virtuosic guitar soloing Instrumental interlude that develops each time it appears	Mainstream rock musical track with rap vocals Vocalists alternate solos and simultaneous rapping Riff-based, which becomes similar to sample-based hip hop

album, *Dirt*, to number six in the United States. In 1994, the acoustically oriented *Jar of Flies* became the first extended-play release ever to top the *Billboard* album charts, while 1995's *Alice in Chains* debuted at number one in the United States.

California Bands. Although Seattle is often thought of as the home of the alternative movement, a number of bands farther down the West Coast were developing along parallel lines. The wildly eclectic Faith No More was formed in San Francisco in 1982, and after the addition of singer Mike Patton, the band released *The Real Thing* (p11, 1990), which included the number nine single "Epic." *Angel Dust* (p10) followed in 1992 and further established the band's reputation. In many ways, Faith No More's musical approach may be more akin to the comic irreverence of Frank Zappa than to the angry rebelliousness of the Sex Pistols.

Queen Latifah	Public Enemy	R.E.M.	Nirvana
Ladies First	Don't Believe the Hype	The One I Love	Smells Like Teen Spirit
1989	r18 1988	p9 1987	p7 1992
Simple verse	Simple verse-chorus	Simple verse-chorus	Simple verse-chorus (modified)
4/4	4/4	4/4	4/4
Electric guitar Bass Drums Lead vocal Background vocal Saxophone Synthesizer	Electric guitar Bass Drums Lead vocal Background vocal Saxophone Vocal samples Turntable	Electric guitar Bass Drums Lead vocal Background vocal	Electric guitar Bass Drums Lead vocal
Much of the musical material is drawn from samples Virtuosic rapping (fast and rhythmically complex) Alternating vocals between Queen Latifah and Monie Love	Much of the musical material is drawn from samples Chuck D performs vocals for verses, while Flavor Flav performs each chorus Politically charged lyrics	Each verse is a small AABA form Listen for several different guitar parts No changing lyrics for verses	Contrast between verse and chorus (instrumentation and vocals) 2-bar phrase in the instruction is the basis for the song Short, contrasting 4-measure section added to choruses as transition

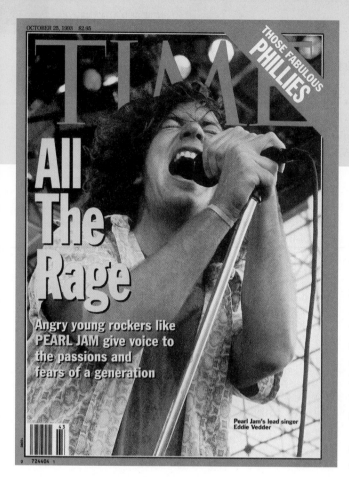

TIME

THOSE FABULOUS PHILLIES

All
The
Rage

Angry young rockers like
PEARL JAM give voice to
the passions and
fears of a generation

Pearl Jam's lead singer
Eddie Vedder

Pearl Jam's Eddie Vedder is shown here on the cover of *Time* dated October 25, 1993. Along with Nirvana, Pearl Jam represented Seattle "grunge" to the nation—a scene that had its own rebellious music and fashion sense. Pearl Jam also publicly opposed Ticketmaster over ticket prices, establishing the band's credibility within the anticommercial alternative community.

The Red Hot Chili Peppers also did not fit neatly into the alternative template. Formed in 1983 in Hollywood, the group seemed just as influenced by funk as by punk, and this is especially evident in the playing of the band's bassist, Flea. Their second album, *Freaky Styley* (1985), was produced by George Clinton, while 1989's *Mother's Milk* contained a cover version of Stevie Wonder's "Higher Ground." The band enjoyed its first commercial success with the Rick Rubin–produced *BloodSugarSexMagik*, which rose to number three in 1991. Following with hit albums such as *One Hot Minute* (p4, 1994) and *Californication* (p3, 1999), the Red Hot Chili Peppers also developed a reputation for innovative videos, many of which became staples on MTV.

Formed in 1987 even farther south in San Diego, Stone Temple Pilots drew heavily on the style of Seattle bands like Alice in Chains and Pearl Jam, while drawing in elements of 1970s guitar-oriented mainstream rock. The band was dismissed by some critics for being too derivative, but Stone Temple Pilots' first three albums—*Core* (1992), *Purple* (1994), and *Tiny Music* (1996)—all cracked the top five on the U.S. charts. After the group disbanded in 2003, singer Scott Weiland went on to form Velvet Revolver with former members of Guns N' Roses and Wasted Youth, showing the lasting connections between punk, hair metal, and alternative rock.

Some interesting questions follow the rise of alternative music in the 1990s. Why, for instance, did alternative rock have such broad appeal? Was it because it rejected the glamour of the many MTV acts that seemed to be more concerned with their looks and dance steps than with their music? Or was it because heavy metal had pushed the instrumental aspect of rock so far toward virtuosity and complexity that some kind of correction was needed to keep rock from becoming too self-involved? Could it just be that the rock public constantly requires something new? If so, why was alternative seen as new when punk and new wave acts had embraced the return-to-simplicity approach only a little more than a decade before? In the next chapter we will survey many more artists whose music became popular in the 1990s, including styles of pop and rock that embraced rock from the mainstream, the widespread popularity of jam-based music, the return of vocal-based teen groups, a resurgence in women's voices in the mainstream, extensions of the metal scene, and post-alternative indie rock. With all of this music flourishing at the end of the 1990s, it is easy to see the multiplicity of styles associated with rock at the end of the millennium, drawing on influences from the past, reacting to current trends, and pushing rock forward into unchartered territory.

FURTHER READING

Michael Azerrad, *Come As You Are: The Story of Nirvana* (Broadway Books, 1993).

Jeff Chang, *Can't Stop Won't Stop: A History of the Hip-Hop Generation* (Picador, 2005).

Ian Christie, *Sound of the Beast: The Complete Headbanging History of Heavy Metal* (Harper, 2003).

Nelson George, *Hip-Hop America* (Penguin, 1998).

Marcus Gray, *It Crawled from the South: An R.E.M. Companion* (Da Capo, 1997).

David Konow, *Bang Your Head: The Rise and Fall of Heavy Metal* (Three Rivers Press, 2002).

Pearl Jam, *Pearl Jam Twenty* (Simon and Schuster, 2011).

Glenn Pillsbury, *Damage Incorporated: Metallica and the Production of Musical Identity* (Routledge, 2006).

Tricia Rose, *Black Noise: Rap Music and Black Culture in Contemporary America* (Wesleyan University Press, 1994).

Joseph Schloss, *Foundation: B-boys, B-girls, and Hip-Hop Culture in New York* (Oxford University Press, 2009).

Russell Simmons, with Nelson George, *Life and Def: Sex, Drugs, Money, and God* (Crown, 2001).

The Vibe History of Hip-Hop, edited by Alan Light (Three Rivers Press, 1999).

Robert Walser, *Running with the Devil: Power, Gender, and Madness in Heavy Metal Music* (Wesleyan University Press, 1993).

Deena Weinstein, *Heavy Metal: The Music and its Culture* (Da Capo, 2000).

VISIT STUDYSPACE AT WWNORTON.COM/STUDYSPACE

Access free review material such as:

- music links
- performer info
- practice quizzes
- outlines
- interactive listening guide software

THE 1990s

The fall of the Berlin Wall in 1989 marked the end of the Cold War and left the United States as the world's only superpower. Clear military superiority came with responsibilities, however. In the decades that followed the Cold War, several important armed conflicts arose, and the world often looked to the United States to take the lead in both war and peacemaking efforts. In 1991 Iraq invaded oil-rich Kuwait, and American troops intervened, pushing Iraq's army back across the Kuwait border. This first Gulf War was seen as a major victory for President George Bush, but as he and his son George W. Bush would find out, this was not the last conflict the United States would have in the Middle East.

Although the Cold War was over and America was riding high after the victory in the Gulf, Bush's reelection hopes were dashed by Bill Clinton (and a recession economy) in 1992. The election of the youthful Clinton and his running mate Al Gore seemed to bring a fresh, new spirit to government. Clinton had many policy setbacks (losing a battle to reform America's health care system, most notably), but the economy boomed during his presidency and he was easily reelected in 1996. Clinton's presidency, however, was marred by one of the most public scandals since Watergate. Clinton was accused of, and finally admitted to, having a sexual affair with a White House intern and lying to Congress about it under oath. Even though Congress impeached him, Clinton (the self-proclaimed "comeback kid") stayed in office, and his approval ratings grew as the economy continued to surge.

The economy was driven by the explosion of the high-tech industry. Computer sales soared as more people used the Internet to communicate, shop, date, and do research. In the late 1990s businesses rushed to tap into the awesome power they believed the Internet held. Companies associated with the computer industry, often called dot-coms, seemed to come and go with each passing day, some making huge profits as their stock prices skyrocketed. Wall Street professionals seemed to care less about a company's ability to sell goods and services than about how well it appeared to take advantage of new technologies. High-tech innovators like Bill Gates (cofounder of Microsoft) and Steve Case (cofounder of America Online) achieved rock star status, and many investing novices became serious day traders, seeking the quick bucks the market yielded every day. Eventually, cooler heads began to outnumber irrational ones, and the market dropped nearly as quickly as it had risen.

One of the most contentious segments

of the Internet economy was in the music industry. In 1999, twenty-year-old Shawn Fanning created Napster, a file-sharing service that allowed users to exchange music, free of charge, over the Internet. Napster made music available to all, and cut record labels and artists out of the process. The Record Industry Association of America (RIAA), which represents five major record labels and a host of smaller labels, didn't like the effect of the Napster revolution on their profits, and they sued. Napster was forced to shut down (though it was eventually reborn as a legal music company). As Napster proved, many Internet users felt that anything on the Web should be free—including artistic material. The music industry continues to struggle with issues of ownership to this day.

Although the American military dominated international affairs and the economy boomed in the 1990s, all was not well at home. In 1992, four white police officers in Los Angeles stopped Rodney King for speeding and beat him senseless before arresting him. This was surely not the first instance of white police officers' brutality toward an African American but it was the first to be caught on videotape and broadcast around the country. Public outcry became public rage when the police officers in the case were acquitted on nearly all charges. To many, this confirmed the racism of white America and the Los Angeles Police Department. When the verdict was issued, riots ensued, and several neighborhoods in Los Angeles were destroyed.

Suburbia also saw its share of tragedy. In 1999 two students at Columbine High School in Colorado brought guns to school and opened fire, killing thirteen of their classmates and teachers before killing themselves. No one will ever know the true inten-

Shawn Fanning (with guitar) and Sean Parker founded Napster, the first important Internet resource to make downloading of music files possible. Napster became so popular in the late 1990s that the major record companies believed the site was hurting sales of new CDs. Lawsuits were brought against Napster, as teens and college students across the country debated the ethics of file sharing. Napster was eventually converted to a law-abiding music-downloading service, but the genie was out of the bottle, and the practice of illegal file sharing remains widespread.

After the acquittal of the four police officers who beat Rodney King, several neighborhoods in Los Angeles exploded in riots. For many, the King case confirmed the racism of white America, especially the police. This building's graffiti recalls N.W.A.'s song "Fuck tha Police." In light of the King beating and the ensuing destruction (in 1992), the song, recorded in 1988, seemed prophetic.

tions of the perpetrators, but many speculated that the boys saw themselves as social outcasts who were often harassed by the more "popular" students. Some parents blamed "grunge" and heavy metal music, gothic clothing, video games, and violent television and movies. What was clear to everyone, however, was that young people, for whatever reason, were angry at the establishment to the point of violence, and that guns in schools were a serious and widespread problem. All of this—and many of the decade's news events— was captured by twenty-four-hour cable news channels, led by CNN. The worlds of violence, entertainment, and cable news came together most noisily in the high-profile trial of football-star-turned-actor O. J. Simpson. Simpson was accused (and eventually acquitted) of the murder of his ex-wife and her friend. The country followed every moment of the proceedings on television: from the car chase, through the trial, to the verdict.

Movies in the 1990s tapped into America's high-tech and (perceived) violent culture. One of the most popular movies of the decade was Quentin Tarantino's *Pulp Fiction* (1994), which featured John Travolta and Samuel L. Jackson as thugs who would rather kill than see their boss's valuables stolen. Another innovative film was *The*

Blair Witch Project (1999), which was marketed as actual footage recovered from three student filmmakers who disappeared into the Maryland woods. The seemingly amateur camera work and true story made *Blair Witch* one of the scariest movies of the decade. To promote the myth surrounding the movie, the producers used the Internet to form an underground community, spurring the movie's popularity and making Web sites standard movie advertising tools. Mainstream films also combined fiction and reality. *Jurassic Park* (1993), *Forrest Gump* (1994), and *Titanic* (1997) topped the decade's list of box-office smashes, each exploiting quickly developing forms of digital technology to produce stunning special effects.

Television also blurred the line between fiction and reality in the 1990s. In 1992 MTV launched *The Real World*, which took young people from diverse backgrounds and made them live together, with cameras following their every move. As the network expected, the cast fought over many issues, from roommate dating to racism. CBS's hit "reality" show, *Survivor* (2000), placed strangers on a tropical island where they fought, backstabbed, and negotiated while competing for a $1 million prize. Though viewers of *The Real World*, *Survivor*, and their imitators felt like voyeurs in these strangers' lives, others felt that "reality" TV was as contrived as any soap opera.

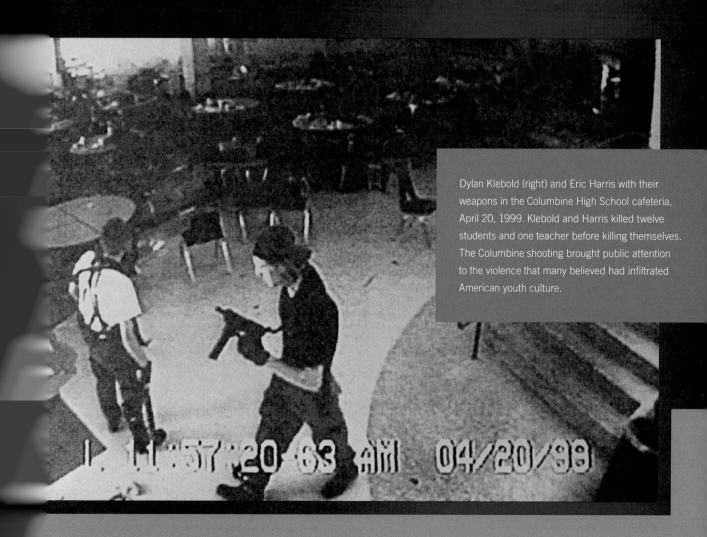

Dylan Klebold (right) and Eric Harris with their weapons in the Columbine High School cafeteria, April 20, 1999. Klebold and Harris killed twelve students and one teacher before killing themselves. The Columbine shooting brought public attention to the violence that many believed had infiltrated American youth culture.

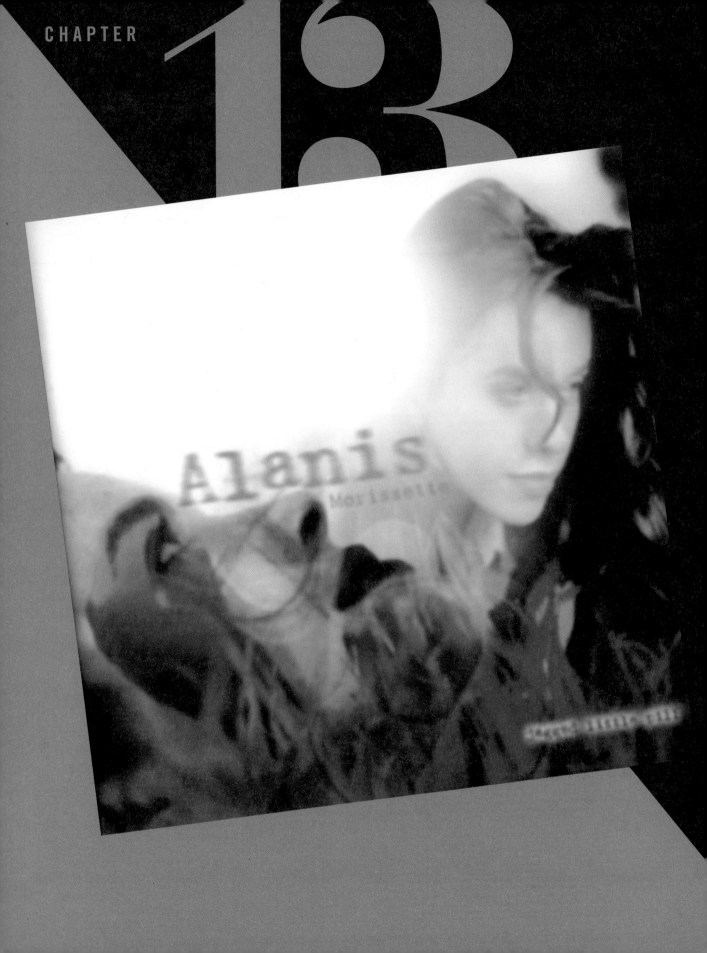

CHAPTER 13

Alanis
Morissette

WIDENING GAPS

Today, most college-age students who are fans of rock music from the 1960s and 1970s were born decades after this music was first popular. In many ways, it is the music of their parents'—or even their grandparents'—generation. Considering the role that rock music still plays in establishing a generation's sense of identity, it is fascinating that large numbers of teens still listen to decades-old rock music, in some cases even preferring it to newer and more current rock. Many of these fans of "classic rock" are first exposed to this music through their parents (or their parents' record collections), while others first encounter classic rock on the radio, on cable television, or in record stores.

This chapter will consider new industry developments in the 1990s such as the rise of the classic rock radio format and birth of the CD reissue. Musically, most of the music we will cover was indebted in some way to the rock of the past. Jam bands, the feel good rock of Hootie and the Blowfish, female singer-songwriters associated with the Lilith movement, and even a new breed of teen idol groups all had strong connections to previous movements in rock music. Other forms considered in the chapter, such as the continuation and reformation of indie rock and new styles of electronic-based music, point to newer developments that unfolded over the course of the decade, leading to important musical developments in the new millennium.

THE RISE OF CLASSIC ROCK

The Age of the CD Reissue: Selling the Same Music Again. A slow change in the standard format of the record business from records to compact discs, which began in the 1980s, was complete by the early 1990s. Compact disc technology was first introduced by Sony and Philips in 1980, and the first commercial CD was issued in late 1982. By the mid-1980s, record companies offered a small number of albums in this new format, which gradually grew over the course of the decade, as sale of cas-

It may have seemed that popular music in the 1990s was dominated by overly commercial boy bands and teen idols, but record sales indicate otherwise. Alanis Morissette's album *Jagged Little Pill* (1995) was the number three best-selling album of the 1990s (Shania Twain and Whitney Houston held the top two spots). Morissette's music is rough and in-your-face, and proved to a new generation (like Aretha Franklin, Janis Joplin, and others had in decades before) that a strong woman could be successful commercially. Artists such as Morissette, Ani DiFranco, Tori Amos, and Liz Phair drew on the personal, intimate musical legacy of female singer-songwriters like Carole King and Joni Mitchell, placing many of the impulses behind the work of these earlier artists in a 1990s context.

A CD player from 1983 made by Philips of Holland. The CD was developed by Philips in conjunction with the Japanese manufacturer Sony, and was first released in 1982. The rise of the CD reissues in the late 1980s and early 1990s was a boon to the record industry. At the time, these units were cutting-edge technology, lauded for their compact size and audio fidelity.

settes and long-play records dwindled. CDs had become the industry standard by the beginning of the 1990s, with almost one-third of all American households using them in one form or another. From a music lover's point of view, the CD constituted a major advance. Compact discs were much more portable than records, and unlike tapes, you could go directly to the song you wanted to hear without having to fuss with rewind or fast-forward buttons. And while records and tapes showed signs of wear with each use, CDs were marketed to last forever, with no appreciable degradation in audio fidelity no matter how many times you played them. (We now know that this is not true!) Add this to claims by audio experts that the digital sound of CDs was far superior to the analog sound of records or tapes—a claim that is still hotly debated—and CDs seemed to be the perfect format. Since the CD had a reputation for superior audio quality, many middle-class baby boomers—now entering middle age and with plenty of disposable income—revisited the music of their youth in a new format.

The changeover to compact discs was just the financial shot in the arm the sagging music business needed during the second half of the 1980s. Although production of CDs was limited by a small number of available pressing plants in the early 1980s, once manufacturing began to shift toward these new digital discs, companies were able to manufacture CDs in large enough volume to reduce production costs. The age of the CD reissue was in full swing in the late 1980s, often advertising features such as "digital remastering" and "bonus tracks" to tempt buyers and further sweeten the deal. Companies began to put together multi-CD boxed sets for the most serious-minded and dedicated fans, often with extensive and detailed liner notes, previously unreleased tracks or mixes, and endorsements from the original artists. The price of CDs, however, stayed higher than it had been with vinyl, and these extra profits went right into record-company coffers. Older rock albums had long ago covered their initial costs of production, so reissuing them produced easy money for the major labels.

Radio Killed the Video Star: The Classic-Rock Radio Format. About the same time record companies were beginning the compact disc switchover, radio formatting also began to reflect listener interest in a format that came to be called classic rock. Detroit radio consultant Fred Jacobs helped to create this format, which courted baby boomers to tune in to stations playing nothing but the biggest rock hits from 1966–78. Since the rapid-growth years of the mid-1970s, radio stations had relied increasingly on outside consultants like Jacobs to program their playlists. Lee Abrams, for instance, is widely credited (or blamed) for developing the stricter album-oriented-rock format that characterized rock radio in the late 1970s. Like most consultants, Abrams sold his format to stations across the country as a pre-packaged product—a tried-and-tested recipe for radio ratings success. Jacobs was trying to do the same thing when he came up with his classic-rock format. In 1985, the first classic-rock station went on the air in Lansing, Michigan, and dominated its market. As word of this early success spread, so did the format. By 1990, classic rock had become one of the most successful formats in radio and led the business of radio through the rest of the decade, sometimes with multiple stations in a single market competing against one another.

Classic-rock radio succeeded because it appealed to the same people who were buying CD reissues and, as this group aged in the 1990s, they stuck with classic rock. Programmers tweaked the format, adding songs that were less well known ("deep tracks") or recently released tracks ("fresh tracks") by the original '60s and '70s bands. The format was initially popular with record companies, since it seemed to support their rerelease of older rock. When classic rock continued to dominate in most markets and the playlists showed little change, however, the record labels began to see classic rock as squeezing out their new artists and releases. This became compounded by the fact that many younger listeners preferred classic rock to new music. Although there were many other popular radio formats, classic rock was one of the most common types of station between the mid-1980s and a large-scale radio industry transformation in 1996, when a Telecommunications Act was passed in the United States Congress that allowed station owners much more flexibility in ownership.

Behind the Music: The Rise of VH-1 and the Rockumentary. For the first few years of its existence, MTV was the only mainstream cable channel specializing in music videos. The MTV audience was young, however, and in 1985 MTV's parent company MTV Networks began broadcasting a new channel called VH-1, which targeted an older demographic—the same baby boomers who bought CD reissues and listened to classic-rock radio. Originally, the channel did not play much classic rock, preferring adult-oriented "light rock," rhythm and blues, and jazz. VH-1 did not succeed as quickly as CDs and classic-rock radio, however, and the channel struggled for over a decade until the development of several new types of shows. One of these was *Pop-Up Video*, which began in 1996. Featuring videos with onscreen facts about the music (sometimes very clever and humorous), this program drew many viewers who might not have had the patience for music videos otherwise. Many people found the factoids more fun and entertaining than the music. VH-1 then developed two quasi-historical series in 1997, *Behind the Music* and *Legends*. Both of these focused on famous rock musicians and their careers, following a predictable rags-to-riches template (with disaster sprinkled in along the way) and placing far more emphasis on the sensational aspects of their subjects' personal lives than their musical or stylistic development. Despite this, VH-1 gave viewers the sense that they were learning about rock's history, and it provided a video angle to complement CD reissues and classic-rock radio. Far from anomalous, the rise of VH-1 documentaries accompanied a large-scale international interest in rock history during the mid-1990s. In 1995 the ten-episode Time-Life series *A History of Rock and Roll* debuted, as did the ten-episode PBS series produced by Quincy Jones, *The History of Rock 'n' Roll*. By focusing on rock as a historical entity rather than a new form, VH-1 participated in a growing appreciation for rock as an important American art form. Moreover, through sales of reissued CDs, the classic-rock radio format, and new video channels focused on adult audiences, it was clear that there was big money in old music.

You're Never Too Old to Rock and Roll. While the classic-rock movement celebrated rock's past, many of the bands and artists featured in this revival enjoyed great success in the 1990s. Less than two years before VH-1 developed *Behind the Music* and *Legends*, the *Beatles Anthology* video documentary aired for the first time on ABC, featuring two unfinished John Lennon sessions completed by Paul, George, and Ringo. "Free as a Bird" hit the top ten of the "Hot 100" in late 1995, and "Real Love" reached the top five of the UK charts. The Beatles also hit the top of the album charts in 1995 and 1996 with three *Anthology* collections of rare tracks and alternate takes. Their British-invasion compatriots, the Rolling Stones, also had big albums in the 1990s with *Voodoo Lounge* (p2 uk1, 1994) and *Bridges to Babylon* (p3 uk6, 1997), and ex-Yardbird and Cream guitarist Eric Clapton released one of the

Eric Clapton proved that artists from rock's past could forge successful careers decades later. His album *Unplugged* (1992), with the somber hit "Tears in Heaven," was one of the 1990s' biggest releases. Clapton's success in the 1990s was matched by other classic rockers, including Santana and Paul McCartney.

decade's biggest-selling albums, *Unplugged* (p2 uk2, 1992), drawn from his performance on the MTV show of the same name. The album featured the tender ballad "Tears in Heaven" (p2 uk5), written for his young son, who had been killed in a tragic accident. Acts from the 1970s also stormed the charts: the reunited Eagles hit the top spot in 1994 with *Hell Freezes Over*, Peter Gabriel steamed back with *Us* (p2 uk2, 1992), and Santana hit later in the decade with *Supernatural* (p1 uk1, 1999), featuring the hit single "Smooth" (p1). Stars from the 1980s also scored big, with Sting's *Ten Summoner's Tales* (p2 uk2, 1993) and *Mercury Falling* (p5 uk4, 1996), Tom Petty's Rick Rubin–produced *Wildflowers* (p8, 1994), and Bruce Springsteen's *Greatest Hits* (p1 uk1, 1995). Perhaps most impressively, U2 hit the top spot on both sides of the Atlantic with *Zooropa* (1993) and *Pop* (1997), establishing themselves among rock's most enduring acts.

Bands without popular new material also benefitted from a resurgence of older groups. As classic-rock stations focused on hits from previous decades, many bands that had been famous in the 1960s and 1970s regrouped and toured outdoor theaters during the summer months. Bands such as Chicago, Yes, Foreigner, Styx, Kansas, and others never returned to the charts with the same force, but they were once again capable of filling large venues, especially if they shared the bill with other vintage acts. Like jazz, blues, or country, it was now possible to grow old in rock and roll—as an artist and as a fan. Moreover, the success of older groups in record stores and on concert tours reinforced the idea that rock had an important past with senior figures to act as standard-bearers.

NEW ROCK TRADITIONS

The Return of Jamming. As a younger generation of listeners embraced rock traditionalism, a new breed of younger roots rockers began to emerge. One place that traditionalism flourished during the 1990s was the "jam band scene," which had become an important underground movement across the country. The jam band phenomenon revived the idea that live performances were the central focus of the music, and that highly developed musical skill—especially in improvisation—was an important element of rock performance. While jam bands regularly released studio versions of their material, fans often considered live performances by these groups to be the most definitive. Many of these bands allowed (and even encouraged) fans to record and trade live performances. It was not uncommon for concert promoters to designate specific "taper" sections at shows, where technological savvy was apparent in a sea of tall microphone stands. Jam band performances often revealed how night after night a track could change through improvisation, heading off in any number of stylistic directions.

The heroes of the 1990s jam bands were primarily the Grateful Dead and the Allman Brothers Band, both legendary for their sprawling live shows and die-hard cultural followings. Although many new jams bands had gained regional popularity in the early 1990s, a collective summer tour in 1992 called H.O.R.D.E. (Horizons of Rock Developing Everywhere) marked the first important step toward a new generation of jam bands reaching a national audience. Among the most prominent of these was Vermont-based Phish, who arguably became the torchbearers of the jam band movement after the death of Jerry Garcia in 1995. Creating music that incorporated jazz improvisation, children's fairy tales, silly rituals (like jumping on trampolines and vacuum-cleaner solos), and high-energy rock solos, Phish garnered a huge following in the mid-1990s. Phish took control over many aspects of their

An early Dave Matthews Band lineup performing at New York's CBGB nightclub in August 1992. Featuring ethnic diversity and nonstandard instrumentation, Dave Matthews Band became popular on the jam band circuit before moving successfully into the mainstream.

John Popper (left), lead singer, guitarist, and harmonica player for Blues Traveler. Blues Traveler, like Widespread Panic and Phish, was part of the "jam band" scene. Like the Allman Brothers and Grateful Dead before them, these bands featured long, improvised solos, often making their live performances the best of these groups' productions.

concert promotion and recording efforts. Perhaps the best example of this control came in the form of the many large-scale festivals the group organized, beginning with the "Clifford Ball" in 1996. Held in remote locations such as rural Maine or the swamps of Florida, the band would create an entire town of followers for an entire weekend. Although Phish recorded many studio albums, their 1995 live album *A Live One* (p18) and the many official live concerts released through the group's Live Phish series give the best idea of how the band sounded in concert. Showing how the jam band movement and commercial radio were often disconnected, Phish consistently put together one of the highest-grossing concert tours during the late 1990s with little radio play and no hit singles. In many ways, the business practices of Phish were closely aligned with those of indie rock, as both jam bands and indie rockers worked largely outside of the mainstream music industry.

Another important group on the first H.O.R.D.E. tour was Widespread Panic, based out of Athens, Georgia. If Phish was considered an East Coast version of the Grateful Dead, Widespread Panic had a lot in common musically and culturally with the Allman Brothers. Not only was Widespread Panic from the Allmans' adopted state of Georgia, they were also the first group to sign with the newly resuscitated Capricorn Records (now based in Nashville). Featuring the swirling guitar of Michael Houser and the gritty vocals of John Bell, Widespread Panic's music embodied their southern roots, while exhibiting that the range of rock culture in the American South defied stereotypes. The group's early albums *Widespread Panic* (1991) and *Everyday* (1993) became widely known in jam band circles. Hailing from the New York metropolitan area, both Blues Traveler and the Spin Doctors also built their reputations on live performance, and anchored the H.O.R.D.E. scene in the urban mid-Atlantic region. The Spin Doctors and Blues Traveler were among the few jam-oriented groups to enjoy commercial success during the early 1990s. Featuring the offbeat vocal style of Chris Barron, the Spin Doctors' *Pocketful of Kryptonite* (1991) hit number three on the *Billboard* "Top Albums" chart in 1992 (uk2), while the single "Two Princes" rose into the Top 10 of the "Hot 100" (uk3).

Two years later, Blue Traveler's harmonica-laden "Runaround" also reached the Top 10, and has since become a staple of light rock radio and television commercials.

While Phish and Widespread Panic found success mostly in touring, and Blues Traveler and the Spin Doctors enjoyed brief stints on the pop charts, Dave Matthews Band emerged out of the jam band scene as a group that combined grass roots touring with widespread commercial success. With an unorthodox instrumental lineup consisting of drums, bass, saxophone, violin, and acoustic guitar, Dave Matthews Band combined elements of jazz, funk, bluegrass, and the singer-songwriter movement to create memorable songs to serve as the basis for large-scale improvisation. The group built a strong regional following during the early 1990s working out of Charlottesville, Virginia, and emerged on the national stage in late 1994 after the release of *Under the Table and Dreaming* (p11). The group established several connections to the jam band movement, with Blue Traveler's John Popper playing harmonica on their hit "What Would You Say" (p22, 1994). Moreover, on several occasions in 1994 they performed as an opening act for Phish, a rare occasion in itself. Unlike their jam band brethren, however, Dave Matthews Band became fixtures on the *Billboard* charts, releasing chart-topping albums such as *Crash* (p2, 1996), *Before These Crowded Streets* (p1, 1998), *Everyday* (p1, 2001), *Busted Stuff* (p1, 2002), and *Stand Up* (p1, 2005). In early 2000, Matthews and several associates formed the ATO record label, which has released recordings by groups such as David Gray, My Morning Jacket, Drive-By Truckers, and Widespread Panic.

Britpop: Oasis and Radiohead. The jam band scene was certainly not the only musical movement of the 1990s to freely reference rock music from the 1960s and 1970s. A group of bands from the UK who became popular during this time, often under the label Britpop, drew heavily upon British invasion music of the 1960s. In the United States, the most popular of these groups was Oasis, a band heavily influenced by the Beatles. Oasis reached the top of the British charts in 1994 with *Definitely Maybe*, scored a transcontinental hit the next year with *(What's the Story) Morning Glory?*, and reached the peak of their success in the United States in 1997 with the album *Be Here Now* (p2 uk1). Within the UK, the success of Oasis was more overwhelming than it was in the States, and many other groups who were virtually unknown to American audiences rose to the top of the charts in Britain, including Suede, Pulp, Supergrass, and Blur.

Perhaps the most important band to come out of England during this time was only marginally related to the Britpop movement. Drawing heavily on the atmospheric music of Pink Floyd and later British pro-

Johnny Greenwood of Radiohead performs on stage in 2003. Emerging from the Britpop movement of the early 1990s, Radiohead quickly moved away from Beatles-style pop music to focus on mixing thick rock textures with ethereal sounds created by laptops and synthesizers.

gressive rock, Radiohead first scored with *Pablo Honey* (p32 uk22, 1993), which contained the Top 40 single "Creep," and followed up with *The Bends* (p88 uk4, 1995), which sold only marginally in the United States. Their next effort, *OK Computer* (p21 uk1, 1997), made the band international critical darlings, and they won the Grammy Award for Best Alternative Album in 1998 despite not even reaching the Top 20 of the *Billboard* album charts. Often dealing with lyrical themes of isolation and alienation, Radiohead's music incorporated avant-garde noise, electronic effects, and wide dynamic shifts. Later Radiohead albums were commercially successful in the United States, including *Kid A* (p1 uk1, 2000), *Amnesiac* (p2 uk1, 2001) and *Hail to the Thief* (p3 uk1, 2003). In October 2007, the band made headlines for releasing their album *In Rainbows* to the public through their website on a pay-as-you-wish basis. Much like the jam bands, who advocated tape trading as a means of maintaining a loyal and knowledgeable fan base, Radiohead's experiment with *In Rainbows* was a legal way to expose hesitant album buyers to their newest music. And just as groups such as Phish and the Dave Matthews Band used free music to increase concert and album sales, *In Rainbows* hit the top slot on the album charts in both the United States and the UK upon its physical release in December 2007.

ROCK IS STILL POP

Feel-Good Rock: Sheryl Crow and Hootie and the Blowfish. Several groups emerged in 1994 that offered a lighter form of "feel good" rock music, seemingly as a reaction to the intensity that characterized grunge. Like the jam bands and Britpop, much of this music was clearly indebted to earlier styles. Created for the pop music market and live performances that featured literal presentations of studio recordings (and little jamming), the music of Sheryl Crow and Hootie and the Blowfish capitalized on a mainstream interest in back-to-basics rock. Based out of Los Angeles, Crow worked as a professional backing vocalist in the 1980s, appearing on a string of records and touring with Michael Jackson and Don Henley. Her 1993 album *Tuesday Night Music Club* (p3 uk8) contained the hits "All I Wanna Do" (p2 uk5, 1994) and "Strong Enough" (p5, 1995), and eventually ranked among the best-selling records of the decade. Her subsequent releases included *Sheryl Crow* (p6 uk5, 1996), *The Globe Sessions* (p5 uk2, 1998), and *C'mon C'mon* (p2 uk2, 2002). Unlike many of her roots-rock contemporaries from the mid-1990s, Crow's longevity has persisted into the 2000s as she has experimented with styles ranging from country to rhythm and blues. She has been a mainstay on the American album charts with each of her releases—including *Wildflower* (p2, 2005), *Detours* (p2, 2008), and *100 Miles from Memphis* (p3, 2010)—rising to the top of the *Billboard* album charts.

Based in the university town of Columbia, South Carolina, Hootie and the Blowfish projected a good-time, roots-rock style that featured Darius Rucker's soulful vocals (with occasional gospel influences) accompanied by happy, strummed acoustic guitar along with drums, bass, and 1970s-oriented electric guitar. Hootie and the Blowfish emerged into the mainstream in 1994, and were only in the limelight for a few years. Nevertheless, the band was among the most popular groups of

the 1990s, with album sales that reached into the stratosphere. Their breakthrough album, *Cracked Rear View* (p1 uk12, 1994), contained the hits "Hold My Hand" (p10), "Let Her Cry" (p9), and "Only Wanna Be with You" (p6) and made the band's music a staple of mainstream rock radio in the mid-1990s. To date, *Cracked Rear View* has sold more than 15 million copies, making it one of the best-selling albums of the decade. The group followed with *Fairweather Johnson* (p1 uk9, 1996) and *Musical Chairs* (p4 uk15, 1998), but did not regain the popularity of their first commercial release. Recently, lead singer Darius Rucker has remade himself as a country performer. His albums *Learn to Live* (p5 c1, 2008) and *Charleston, SC 1966* (p2 c1, 2010) have both risen to the top of the country album charts and spawned several top-selling singles.

Listening Guide

Sheryl Crow, "All I Wanna Do" A&M 0702

Words and music by Wyn Cooper, Sheryl Crow, Bill Bottrell, David Baerwald, and Kevin Gilbert. Produced by Bill Bottrell. Rose to #2 on the *Billboard* "Hot 100" chart in 1994 (uk4).

FORM: Simple verse-chorus, with pre-chorus. The verse and chorus are built on the same 3-chord, 4-bar chord progression, though the chorus diverges from that progression in the last 2 bars each time. The verses lead into a pre-chorus section, which drives the song forward to the chorus. This pre-chorus material is first heard as the introduction to the song. After the first time through the chorus, an instrumental interlude leads to the second verse; after the second chorus, that interlude—which is based on the song's 3-chord progression— is stretched to 8 bars, as a low guitar line that was first introduced during the verse sections comes to the fore. This creates a section that might be considered an instrumental verse, especially since the section leads right into the pre-chorus and forward to the final chorus. The last chorus repeats the final 4 bars—a "tag"—before heading into the ending, which is a 13-bar section that could be heard as an instrumental version of the chorus (note the ending) with an extra bar added for the last chord.

TIME SIGNATURE: 4/4. Note how the percussion and handclaps work with the drums to create a variety of rhythmic feels that help distinguish the song's sections.

INSTRUMENTATION: Electric guitar, slide guitar, acoustic guitar, electric piano, synthesizer strings, bass, drums, percussion, handclaps, lead and backing vocals.

0:00–0:14	**Introduction**, 6 mm.	This music becomes the pre-chorus later in the song, as Crow speaks over rhythmic and jazzy guitar, synthesizer strings, and handclaps. "This ain't no disco . . ."

Counting Crows and the Wallflowers. Coming out of the San Francisco area and led by songwriter and lead vocalist Adam Duritz, Counting Crows also emerged on the national stage in early 1994 during the mainstream peak of the alternative movement. The 1993 album *August & Everything After* established the band, going to number four in the United States (uk16) and containing the hit singles "Mr. Jones" (p2) and "Round Here" (p7). *Recovering the Satellites* topped the charts in 1996 (uk6), and also contained two hit singles, "Angels of the Silences" (p3) and "A Long December" (p5). The band's music-stylistic debts to earlier artists can be heard especially in Duritz's vocal style, which has often been compared to Van Morrison. At a time when electronic music was prevalent it was also notable that the band employed vintage instrumentation (clearly visible in the music video for "Mr. Jones"), including an organ, classic Gibson and Fender guitars, and an old-fashioned large diaphragm microphone. These elements contributed directly to the band's "alternative" identity in the marketplace.

0:14–0:54	**Verse 1**, 20 mm.	Full band kicks in, as slide guitar weaves in and out of the solo vocal, a low guitar melody enters toward the middle. "All I wanna do . . ."
0:54–1:06	**Pre-Chorus**, 6 mm.	Synthesizer strings return with intro music, now without jazzy guitar but with full band. "They drive their shiny . . ."
1:06–1:38	**Chorus**, 16 mm.	Harmony vocal and acoustic guitar enter, as slide guitar comes back for 12-bar chorus, which is followed by a 4-bar instrumental interlude. "All I wanna do . . ."
1:38–2:02	**Verse 2**, 12 mm.	As in verse 1, though shorter this time. Note Crow's conversational delivery of the lyrics, which don't rhyme and enhance the sense of a story told in free prose. "I like a good . . ."
2:02–2:14	**Pre-Chorus**, 6 mm.	Synthesizer strings return as before, "And a happy couple . . ."
2:14–2:54	**Chorus**, 12 + 8 mm.	Harmony vocal and acoustic guitar enter as before, but this time the instrumental interlude stretches to 8 bars, focusing on a guitar melody first introduced in the verses but now functioning almost as an instrumental verse. "All I wanna . . ."
2:54–3:10	**Pre-Chorus**, 8 mm.	As before, but a little more rhythmically active. "Otherwise the bar is ours . . ."
3:10–3:58	**Chorus**, 20 + 4 mm.	Harmony vocal and acoustic guitar return as before, but this time the chorus is stretched to 20 bars and is followed by a 4-bar tag. "All I wanna do . . ."
3:58–4:32	**Coda**, 13 mm.	This ending is a 12-bar chorus, played instrumentally, with some of the instruments dropping out in the last couple of measures.

Interestingly, both Hootie and the Blowfish ("Only Wanna Be With You") and Counting Crows ("Mr. Jones") make prominent references to Bob Dylan in their hit songs during this period. Certainly, this was a time of rekindled mainstream interest in Dylan, as he had just released his first all-acoustic album since 1964, *Good as I Been to You* (1992). Yet, both of these references seem to point to the "old" Dylan, establishing deep connections between 1990s pop and music from decades before. The connection to Bob Dylan in mainstream rock during the 1990s was even more pronounced with the success of the Los Angeles–based Wallflowers, led by singer and songwriter Jakob Dylan (son of Bob). The band splashed on the rock scene with *Bringing Down the Horse* (p4, 1996), which featured the hits "6th Avenue Heartache" (p10), "One Headlight" (p1), and "The Difference" (p3). Despite the media's desire to focus on Jakob's family ties, the younger Dylan avoided exploiting his father's fame as much as he could. However, the band's traditional rock sound would likely have led to comparisons even if there had been no blood relation.

Matchbox 20 and Third Eye Blind. By the second half of the 1990s, a wave of music became popular that merged the pop aspects of guitar-driven roots rock with the harder driving, edgier sounds of alternative rock. Florida's Matchbox 20 found a blend that combined the elemental energy of grunge with a Beatle-esque sensibility, creating a model for much of the modern guitar pop that followed in the late 1990s. The band's debut album, *You or Someone Like You* (p5), was released in 1996 and sold steadily for years after its release, making it one of the best-selling albums of the decade. Several of its tracks became staples of rock-radio playlists, including "Push" (p5), "3 A.M." (p3), and "Real World" (p9). Led by singer Rob Thomas (who sang on Santana's 1999 hit "Smooth"), the band followed up with *Mad Season* (p3, 2000).

Several other groups that created similar blends of traditional simplicity with heavier alternative sounds (and even some hip-hop influence) joined Matchbox 20 on the charts during the late 1990s. San Francisco–based Third Eye Blind enjoyed success in 1997 with "Semi-Charmed Life" (p4) and "How's It Going to Be" (p9) from the album, *Third Eye Blind* (p25). Hailing from Los Angeles, Sugar Ray softened a hard-edged approach to score hits with "Fly" (p1, 1997), "Every Morning (p3 uk10, 1999), and "Someday" (p7, 1999). Similarly, the Goo Goo Dolls morphed from a Buffalo-based post-punk band in the mid-1980s to purveyors of pop ballads such as "Name" (p5, 1995) and "Iris" (p1, 1998). Train continued the trajectory of these groups into the new millennium with the song "Drops of Jupiter" (p5 uk10, 2001), which has remained a staple of FM rock radio.

FEMALE SINGER-SONGWRITERS

Both Sides Now: Women's Perspectives in the Pop Mainstream. In the discussion of the singer-songwriters of the 1970s (Chapter 8) we traced the development of the style back to artists in the 1960s who wrote their own songs and delivered them with relatively simple accompaniment. Often featuring acoustic guitar and piano, this style focused heavily on the vocal element and the importance of the lyrics. The singer-songwriter style grew throughout the 1970s to include many artists, sometimes using simple acoustic accompaniment and at other times, as in the case of Paul Simon, Bob Seger, or Joni Mitchell, fronting bands and using more elaborate and sophisticated accompaniment. Although the initial folk revival instrumentation often merged with standard rock and jazz ensembles, the core of the singer-songwriter movement continued to thrive in mainstream pop during the 1990s. This core is based on what popular music scholars often call a perception of "authenticity." In this case, the listener has to believe the artist is singing about his or her own experiences, or reflecting his or her own thoughts and feelings. A crucial sense of authenticity is based on this projection of sincerity, and sometimes even vulnerability. Many artists from the 1970s, such as Bob Dylan and Billy Joel, thrived in the 1980s and 1990s by projecting this perception of authenticity. Perhaps the most significant development for the style in the 1990s was the emergence of a new generation of female singer-songwriters—artists whose lyrics dealt with issues that are important to women generally, and with specifically feminist issues. Influenced by well-known singer-songwriters like Carole King, Joni Mitchell, and

Carly Simon, as well as lesser-known but critically celebrated artists such as Kate Bush, Tracy Chapman, and others, the music of this new generation of younger women ranged from quiet and contemplative to angry and aggressive.

Assertive Female Voices: Tori Amos and the Indigo Girls. Among the first of this new group of singer-songwriters to emerge in the 1990s was Tori Amos. Growing up in Baltimore, Amos had been a piano prodigy who studied at the prestigious Peabody Conservatory. She eventually made her way to Los Angeles, and after a brief stint fronting a rock band, recorded her singer-songwriter debut, *Little*

Tori Amos and many female singer-songwriters of the period (Ani DiFranco and Sarah McLachlan, among others) were the antithesis of the mass-marketed pop diva. Amos, a classically trained pianist, wrote, produced, and sang songs about highly personal, intimate moments. She was also known for covering male-oriented classic rock songs in concert, injecting them with a female perspective. Although her music was originally produced on a small scale, Amos proved that such music could sell in large numbers: she had several successful albums through the 1990s and beyond.

Listening Guide

Tori Amos, "Crucify" Atlantic 82358

Words and music by Tori Amos, produced by Davit Sigerson. Contained on the album *Little Earthquakes*, which rose to number 54 on the *Billboard* "Pop Album Chart" in 1992 (uk14).

FORM: Compound AABA. The A sections are interesting in that they consist of a verse, a pre-chorus, a chorus, and an "after-chorus." (The last A section, marked A', omits the verse.) We have already seen how a pre-chorus can serve to prepare the chorus, but here we have an 8-bar passage that grows out of the chorus to become a distinctive section. If this section were shorter, we might simply think of it as an extension of the chorus, but in this case the "after-chorus" earns a label of its own. Note how the ending blends the chorus and "after-chorus" together by combining the melodies.

TIME SIGNATURE: 2/4. Most of the song can be counted in groups of 4 measures (note the 16- and 8-bar sections), except the end of the chorus, where the 4-bar pattern breaks down on the way to the "after-chorus," creating a 19-bar section.

INSTRUMENTATION: Piano, bass, drums, percussion, mandolin, ukulele, lead and background vocals.

A	0:00–0:23	**Verse 1,** 16 mm.	Lead vocals enter quietly with minimal accompaniment. "Every finger . . ."
	0:23–0:46	**Pre-Chorus,** 16 mm.	Note how the increased activity in the piano begins to open up the texture. "I've been looking . . ."
	0:46–1:13	**Chorus,** 19 mm.	The drums come to the fore here, along with a reverb-drenched percussion sound. "Why do we . . ."

Earthquakes (p54 uk14, 1991). Amos's classical training is audible in her use of harmony and melody as well as in her masterful piano playing. The first track on *Little Earthquakes*, "Crucify," provides a good example of her early style. The most striking song on the album, however, is an unaccompanied vocal track called "Me and a Gun," an intimate and gripping portrayal of a rape experience. After an extended play recording consisting of cover versions of songs by Nirvana, Led Zeppelin, and others, Amos released *Under the Pink* (p12 uk1) in 1994, and *Boys for Pele* (p2 uk2) in 1996. The success of these albums established her as one of the most talented and innovative songwriters of her generation.

The Atlanta-based Indigo Girls were a duo of female singer-songwriters from Athens, Georgia, who represented another facet of the rise of authentic female artists in the 1990s. The two women at the core of the group, Amy Ray and Emily Saliers, were openly gay from the group's inception, and supported various political movements. They broke into the mainstream in 1989 with the song "Closer to Fine" (p52), winning a Grammy Award for Best Contemporary Folk Album. Later albums enjoyed further chart success, including *Swamp Ophelia* (p6, 1994), which showcased the often-contrasting songwriting styles of Ray and

	1:13–1:25	**After-Chorus**, 8 mm.	The voice and piano join forces in a descending melody. "Chains . . ."
A	1:25–1:48	**Verse 2**, 16 mm.	The music gets quiet again, contrasting with the end of the previous section. "Got a kick . . ."
	1:48–2:11	**Pre-Chorus**, 16 mm.	The music begins to build, as it did before. "I've been looking . . ."
	2:11–2:39	**Chorus**, 19 mm.	As before, but now with background vocals added. Four-bar pattern is broken. "Why do we . . ."
	2:39–2:50	**After-Chorus**, 8 mm.	As before, but now opening into the bridge. "Chains . . ."
B	2:50–3:14	**Bridge**, 16 mm.	Note the interweaving vocal melodies that create an almost church-like atmosphere. "Please . . ."
A′	3:14–3:37	**Pre-Chorus**, 16 mm.	Music gets quiet again, though building to lead to the pre-chorus. "Looking for a . . ."
	3:37–4:04	**Chorus**, 19 mm.	As before. "Why do we . . ."
	4:04–4:16	**After-Chorus**, 8 mm.	As before, but leading to ending. "Chains . . ."
	4:16–4:57	**Ending**, 26 mm.	Combines chorus and pre-chorus, with new background vocal parts added. "Why do we . . ."

Saliers. The duo's music often features duet singing and acoustic guitar accompaniment, with Ray evincing more rock influence and Saliers projecting a gentler, folk-influenced style.

Northern Contrasts: Sarah McLachlan, Jewel, and Alanis Morissette.

Hailing from Nova Scotia, Sarah McLachlan was a female pianist who contrasted sharply with the often-harsh tone of Tori Amos. With a soft vocal delivery and lilting melodies, McLachlan's specialty became heartfelt ballads. She enjoyed moderate chart success in 1993 with *Fumbling Towards Ecstasy* (p50, 1993), but it was not until her 1997 release *Surfacing* that McLachlan broke into the pop mainstream. Popular singles like "Building a Mystery" (p13), "Adia" (p3 uk18), and "Angel" (p4) cemented McLachlan as a fixture of pop radio during the late 1990s. Her music was consistently produced by (and often written with) notable Canadian musician Pierre Marchand. As organizer of a music festival called Lilith Fair from 1997 to 1999 devoted to music by women, McLachlan became a figurehead in the female singer-songwriter movement. While initially seeming partial to white, acoustic songwriters, the festival soon included a wide range of artists and styles, including Liz Phair, the Indigo Girls, Sheryl Crow, Tracy Chapman, and Queen Latifah. Lilith Fair was relaunched in 2010, featuring a new generation of female singer-songwriters, many of whom drew inspiration from the movement in the 1990s.

Raised in Alaska, Jewel offered a pop-oriented singer-songwriter style similar to Sarah McLachlan during the last half of the 1990s. With four albums in the *Billboard* Top 10 between 1996 and 2002, Jewel was one of the best-selling artists of the period. A texture featuring acoustic guitar was used for her first two singles, "Who Will Save Your Soul" (p11, 1996) and "You Were Meant for Me" (p2, 1997). Later songs, including "Foolish Games" (p7, 1997) and "Hands" (p6, 1998) were backed by an instrumental combination that, due to a prominent piano, more closely resembled McLachlan's signature sound. This change in sonic presentation was accompanied by a move toward more adult images projected in Jewel's later music videos. Efforts to "clean up" her sound were evident in attempts to rerecord "You Were Meant for Me" after the success of her debut album *Pieces of You* (p4, 1996). As a result, the version of the song featured in the music video was much more restrained than the recording included on the album. In a fascinating reversal, Jewel abandoned her singer-songwriter roots in 2003 with the dance-oriented album *0304* (p2).

Canadian Alanis Morissette's debut album *Jagged Little Pill* (p1 uk1, 1995) was neither gentle nor delicate. Her enormously successful album contained the hits "Ironic" (p4 uk11), "You Learn" (p6) and "Head Over Feet" (p3 uk7). The album's first single, "You Oughta Know" (p13) captures the sense of anger, frustration, and outrage experienced after a romantic breakup. Although there is certainly an autobiographical element to the album's lyrics, the project was largely a collaboration with songwriter and producer Glen Ballard, an industry veteran who had written music for Michael Jackson, Paula Abdul, and Wilson Phillips. (The most famous of Ballard's songs from the earlier era is Jackson's "Man in the Mirror.") Morissette's later albums *Supposed Former Infatuation Junkie* (p1 uk3, 1998) and *Under Rug Swept* (p1 uk2, 2002) also rose to the top of the pop album charts, making her one of the most successful female singer-songwriters in the second half of the decade.

Lilith Fair, a festival devoted to women's music, was initiated in 1997. The Fair toured North America in 1997, 1998, and 1999. Sarah McLachlan was among the founders of Lilith Fair, and a long list of female artists performed during its three seasons. The poster shows the highlights of the 1998 lineup.

TEEN IDOLS

The Return of Classic Motown: Boyz II Men. While old rockers kept vintage sounds alive, a new cast of young rockers returned to these traditional approaches, and a generation of women were exploring the singer-songwriter aesthetic, a fresh sense of traditionalism was also assuming a more central place in

rhythm and blues. The most commercially successful of the many rhythm and blues artists to return to earlier styles was the Philadelphia-based vocal quartet, Boyz II Men. The band signed with Motown at the beginning of the decade, reinvigorating a label that had struggled during the 1980s. Like the Drifters or the Temptations before them, Boyz II Men's music featured highly crafted and nuanced harmony-vocal arrangements, putting the focus on the rich blending of their voices, as well as on solo passages by the band's members. They depended on others for songwriting, accompaniment, and production, returning to the Brill Building model of the early 1960s. The group's more immediate influences included New Edition and New Kids on the Block, two Boston-based vocal groups developed by songwriter-producer Maurice Starr. Both of these earlier groups enjoyed considerable chart success in the late 1980s, especially among teenage girls, and New Edition's Michael Bivens was instrumental in getting the Philadelphia band signed with Motown.

The debut Boyz II Men album, *Cooleyhighharmony* (p3 r1 uk7, 1991), contained several crossover hit singles, including "Motownphilly" (p3 r4) and "It's So Hard to Say Goodbye to Yesterday" (p2 r1). The group topped both the "Hot 100" and "Hot R&B Singles" charts for the first time with "End of the Road" (uk1, 1992), a song recorded for the movie *Boomerang* (starring Eddie Murphy) and the first to match the vocal quartet with songwriter and producer Kenneth "Babyface" Edmunds. Boyz II Men followed up in 1994 with their second album, *II*, which hit the number one spot on both the pop and R&B album charts with the help of the hit singles "I'll Make Love to You" (p1 r1 uk5) and "On Bended Knee" (p1 r2). Boyz II Men's tremendous success with a traditional vocal-harmony approach made them a model for many groups to follow in the second half of the decade, especially the Backstreet Boys and *NSYNC.

If You Build It, They Will Come: Boy Bands, Girl Groups, and Pop Divas.

From Fabian to the Monkees to David Cassidy, the history of pop music can claim a series of teen idols—performers whose images and music are carefully crafted to appeal to teenage and preteen girls. The late 1990s experienced a resurgence of

Listening Guide

Boyz II Men, "End of the Road" Motown 2178

Words and music by L.A. Reid, Babyface, and Daryl Simmons. Produced by Babyface. Rose to #1 on the *Billboard* "Hot 100" and "Hot R&B Singles" charts in 1992 (uk1).

FORM: Simple verse-chorus, with pre-chorus. The verse and chorus sections are based on the same 8-bar chord progression as the introduction. The pre-chorus section introduces contrasting material and drives toward the chorus each time. The pre-chorus acts as a bridge section that links the verse with the chorus and offers the only strong structural contrast, not only driving toward the chorus but also helping to make the return of the same material seem fresh. Each verse features a solo voice, which shifts to a different singer in the pre-chorus, while harmony vocals characterize the chorus sections. The song begins with a voice speaking over the background music, and the voice-over returns in the third verse. This last verse is the most complicated vocally, featuring 8 bars spoken, with a solo voice entering in the next 8 bars as the speaking continues and choral vocals, speaking, and solo vocals present in the pre-chorus. The song ends with four times through the chorus, the last two eventually breaking down to nothing but vocals and handclaps.

TIME SIGNATURE: 6/8. Note the strong accent on beat 4 during the chorus sections. This beat arrives just a little late and has the effect of creating a strong groove that helps distinguish the chorus from the verse sections.

INSTRUMENTATION: Electric guitar, electric piano, bass, drums, synthesizer strings, French horn, handclaps, solo and backup vocals.

0:00–0:20	**Introduction**, 8 mm.	The song's 8-bar chord progression is introduced here, with voice-over. "Girl, you know . . ."
0:20–0:59	**Verse 1**, 16 mm.	Twice through the 8-bar progression, with solo lead vocal featured

		throughout. Note the Motown-style guitar melody in the background. "We belong together . . ."
0:59–1:18	**Pre-Chorus**, 8 mm.	Contrasting material with new voice singing solo vocal, as French horn enters. "When I can't sleep . . ."
1:18–1:56	**Chorus**, 16 mm.	Twice through the 8-bar progression, with a new melody sung by harmony vocals with handclaps emphasizing beat 4 of each measure. "Although we've come . . ."
1:56–2:36	**Verse 2**, 16 mm.	As before, note the virtuosic vocal technique, with many melodic twists and turns (melismas). Horn sound enters on second 8 bars this time. "Girl, I know you really . . ."
2:36–2:55	**Pre-Chorus**, 8 mm.	New lead vocal enters, now fuller than before and supported by synth strings along with horn sound. "Will you love me . . ."
2:55–3:34	**Chorus**, 16 mm.	As before, but now with lead vocal improvising over the backup vocals, adding a sense of urgency and intensity. "Although we've come . . ."
3:34–4:12	**Verse 3**, 16 mm.	First 8 bars are spoken, as the second 8 bars add a solo vocal part behind the voice-over. "Girl, I'm there for you . . ."
4:12–4:31	**Pre-Chorus**, 8 mm.	Voice-over continues, now with new backup harmony vocals, then the urgent solo vocal reenters. "Lonely . . ."
4:31–5:48	**Chorus**, 32 mm.	Four times through the 8-bar progression, with the first two times through as before in the second chorus, but with the accompanying instruments dropping out toward the end of the third time and the fourth time performed with only vocals and handclaps. "Although we've come . . ."

Boyz II Men in concert, 1995. Like the Temptations or the Drifters before them, Boyz II Men featured highly choreographed stage shows and a polished, richly harmonized vocal style. Their album *Cooleyhighharmony* (1991) was a crossover hit and helped revitalize Motown Records, which had struggled in the 1980s.

acts designed specifically for this audience, though their musical style was more indebted to the traditionalist rhythm and blues of Boyz II Men, Babyface, and Mariah Carey than the bubbly but stiff bubblegum pop of previous decades. The two most important "boy bands" during these years were the Backstreet Boys and *NSYNC: both all-male vocal groups were modeled on Boyz II Men and managed by business mogul Lou Pearlman, who specialized in groups of this type. In 1997, Pearlman and the Backstreet Boys released *Backstreet Boys* (p4 uk12), mostly a collection of tracks that had already been successful overseas. The album was a success,

AMERICAN IDOL

by Norma Coates

Media scholar Henry Jenkins calls *American Idol* "the first killer app of media convergence." It may also be the first killer app of media globalization, as the program which originated in the UK as *Pop Idol* in 2001 now has local versions in 40 countries. Worldwide votes for *Idols* exceed 3 billion. At the same time, *American Idol* is the last killer app of old media during a time when digital technologies and the increasingly global economy rapidly undermine entrenched entertainment industry business models.

American Idol gets some of the highest ratings on current American television, consistently drawing upwards of 25 million viewers to each program. The show is propping up the major music industry during a time of inexorable change in which the traditional business model is increasingly unable to reflect and react to market reality. *American Idol* is one of the last means to produce the type of performer whose sales can keep this model going. Several *American Idol* contestants, whether they won the contest or not, have released top-selling records. First-season winner Kelly Clarkson and Season 4 winner Carrie Underwood are major stars and Grammy Award winners.

Through Season 8, the judging panel consisted of producer Randy Jackson, singer/dancer Paula Abdul, and Simon Cowell, the record industry executive whom everyone loved to hate. Abdul left after Season 8 and was replaced by songwriter Kara DioGuardi. The panel was augmented in Season 9 with the addition of American comedian and talk show host Ellen Degeneres. That season was rocked by the announcement that Cowell, the show's drawing card, would be leaving. Season 10 constituted a "reboot" of the program. Of the original judges, only Jackson remained, joined by Aerosmith lead singer Steven Tyler and pop diva Jennifer Lopez.

American Idol is, at its heart, a combination of old-style television talent contests and game shows revived as "reality programs." Reality television depicts "real people" as they participate in some sort of competition or task. Reality programs are heavily mediated and edited, yet viewers go along and identify with contestants who are "real people" like themselves. Reality television is much cheaper to produce than scripted television, given that it dispenses with writers and actors beyond hosts and occasional guest stars. Television sponsors love reality television because successful programs draw large audiences to advertisements for their products.

American Idol is "clean" family entertainment, unlike some of the competitions that revolve around romance, or that examine the bad behavior of fashion designers or chefs under stress. *American Idol* provides many different types of pleasure to viewers across age and gender. For sponsors, it provides a giant stage for product placement. In Season 6, for example, each judge drank out of a large cup that prominently featured the Coke logo. Ford commercials in each of the "final 10" episodes starred the remaining contestants, blurring the line between program and advertisement so as to render them "DVR-proof."

So why do people watch? *American Idol* is varied in format, has dramatic ups and downs, gives the at-home audience an active role in the outcome, provides different forms of entertainment, has heroes and villains and, in the immortal words of Joni Mitchell, "reveals the star-making machinery behind the popular song." In short, *American Idol* is riveting television.

Each season of *American Idol* begins with the audition process in which the judges travel to several American cities for open auditions. The first few weeks of each season then show the at-home audience the worst of the performances – and some of the best. Until he left the program after Season 9, Simon Cowell's often offensive comments in this phase sometimes attracted attention in the mainstream media. Thousands are then whittled down to a hundred, which are winnowed down to 24 in Los Angeles, where home audiences vote via phone or text message for the "final ten." Then the real drama begins, and viewers get to vicariously live out a certain type of pop star daydream by identifying with the contestants.

American Idol also has an active online culture. Fans can go to the Fox network's *American Idol* website to participate in program-related activities. Fallen idols appear on television talk shows, and draw fans to their websites. During Season 6, spoiler websites proliferated and www.votefortheworst.com, associated with radio "shock jock" Howard Stern, received national attention in its attempts to manipulate voting in favor of a contestant with a lot of charisma and penchant for interesting hairstyles, but minimal singing talent.

Records by "Idols" do sell, in part because of the exposure the buying public has to their voices over a television season, and in part because the chosen winner, and the runners up have been molded to produce "sellable" sounds. Some music fans rail against the inauthenticity of the process and the program.

Winners over the last few seasons have hewed to more conservative images and sounds than those presented by the most truly popular current pop artists, such as Lady Gaga, Katy Perry, and Beyoncé. For example, vocally and physically innocuous Kris Allen won over flamboyant Adam Lambert in Season 8. Lambert later came out as gay but to date no serious *Idol* contestant has been out during his or her time on the program. The equally milquetoast Lee DeWyse won over the Janis Joplinesque, in sound and biography, Crystal Bowersox

in Season 9. Season 10 seemed to ignore trends in pop music in 2011. Two country singers went to the finals, which crowned a 17-year-old retro-country singer, the deep-voiced Scotty McCreery, as winner. *American Idol* may be diverging from what is most popular on the internet, the radio, and iTunes, but it still taps into large market. That's enough to keep the hit-making machinery—and the entertainment industries and corporations that depend upon it—going, for now.

Norma Coates (University of Western Ontario) has written on the interaction of popular music, gender, and cultural industry. Her current book project is called Rocking the Wasteland: A Cultural History of Popular Music on American Network Television from Elvis to MTV.

Kelly Clarkson (center), winner of the first *American Idol* competition, sings "A Moment like This" to close the show's first season. Runner-up Justin Guarini is behind her, and the show's other contestants look on. Though first accepted by professional judges, Clarkson was the top choice of the millions of judges that mattered most: the viewing audience.

MUSIC VIDEO IN THE 1990S: WEEZER, "BUDDY HOLLY"

As the music video entered its second decade as the primary medium of visual promotion, many groups worked creatively within the genre. One of the most popular directors of this period was Spike Jonze. Unlike *Thriller* director John Landis, Jonze was from a generation of young filmmakers who used the music video as a means to assert their creative voice before gaining entrance into the big-budget Hollywood feature. The video for Weezer's "Buddy

of 1990s retro-hipster fashion, Jonze set *Buddy Holly* in the context of *Happy Days*, a 1970s television sitcom about the 1950s. Using the actual *Happy Days* set and actor Al Molinaro, who portrayed a character named Al on the show, Jonze alternated modern shots of Weezer with actual footage from the original show. Although the video is only four minutes long, it offers a condensed *Happy Days* episode, beginning with opening credits and ending with Al closing up the restaurant for the night (1).

TO BE CONTINUED

The band, outfitted with 1950s hairstyles and matching cardigan sweaters, performs for dancing teenagers from the diner's stage (2).

Throughout the video, Jonze uses editing to make it seem as if band members are interacting with audience members. As in many *Happy Days* episodes, the video pauses before the song's bridge as a caption informs viewers that the episode is "to be continued" (3).

In the final section of the video, Fonzie, the show's "coolest" character, enters and begins an aggressive dance that borders on absurd (4).

As a statement of Weezer's self-consciousness and Jonze's creative reading of the song, *Buddy Holly* offers a wonderful depiction of the place of the music video in early 1990s rock.

Holly," directed by Jonze, was one of the most popular videos of late 1994. Taking a cue from the song's self-aware depiction

and the singles "Quit Playing Games (with My Heart)" (p2 uk2) and "As Long As You Love Me" (p4 uk3) made the Backstreet Boys teenage heartthrobs. The band's next two albums, *Millennium* (p1 uk2, 1999) and *Black & Blue* (p1 uk13, 2000), and a string of Top 10 singles made the group mainstays of Top-40 radio, although by 1999 the group had officially split with Pearlman and his organization.

One factor that caused the split between the Backstreet Boys and Pearlman was Pearlman's attention to a new group he was developing—one that would compete directly with the Backstreet Boys as teen idols. Among the members of *NSYNC were JC Chasez and Justin Timberlake, two young men who were already familiar to the teen crowd as regular members of the Disney Channel's *The New Mickey*

Mouse Club. The new group's first album, **NSYNC* (p2, 1998), did well, producing the hit single "God Must Have Spent a Little More Time on You" (p8, 1999), but the band did not come close to challenging the Backstreet Boys with this first outing. The second album, *No Strings Attached* (p1 uk14, 2000), was **NSYNC's* blockbuster, generating the hits "Bye Bye Bye" (p4 uk3), "It's Gonna Be Me" (p1 uk9), and "This I Promise You" (p5 uk21), placing them side-by-side with the Backstreet Boys in the boy-band sweepstakes. Both bands worked from the stylistic model established earlier in the decade by Boyz II Men. As the Backstreet Boys and **NSYNC* became more popular, many other boy bands enjoyed immense success, including 98° and O-Town, while girl groups like the Spice Girls represented female versions of these industry-created vocal groups. While each of these new teen idols groups, who were comprised of mostly white singers, achieved extreme popularity in mainstream outlets, it is notable that none found success in the R&B market.

Late in 1998 female vocalist Britney Spears entered this scene, and soon became the most important artist in the burgeoning preteen movement. Like JC Chasez and Justin Timberlake, Spears had also appeared on *The New Mickey Mouse Club*, so she was an experienced performer by the time she emerged as a solo artist. In fall 1998, Britney released her debut album, *. . . Baby One More Time* (p1 uk2), produced by Swedish songwriter Max Martin. The Martin-penned single ". . . Baby One More Time" hit the number one spot on the pop charts in America and the UK, and Spears's video for the song featured her dancing suggestively in a skimpy schoolgirl outfit. A later hit, "You Drive Me Crazy" (p10 uk5), further established her as the next big thing, and her second album, *Oops . . . I Did It Again* (p1 uk2, 2000), confirmed it. Another ex-Mouseketeer, Christina Aguilera, debuted in 1999 with a more uncompromisingly sexy image, and *Christina Aguilera* topped the pop

Britney Spears performing live at the 2000 MTV Video Music Awards ceremony. In many ways a classic teen idol, Spears (and her contemporary, Christina Aguilera) also tapped into a large preteen audience. Many overlook Spears's considerable skill as a performer in light of her controversial media persona, huge global successes, and her Madonna-like style reinventions.

charts, featuring the hits "Genie in a Bottle" (p1 uk1) and "What a Girl Wants" (p1 uk3). The next year, Aguilera released *Mi Reflejo*, sung in Spanish and intended to capitalize on the boom in Latin pop, led by Ricky Martin's ubiquitous hit single "Livin' La Vida Loca" (p1 uk1, 1999) and Santana's "Smooth." The album topped the Latin charts and hit number twenty-seven on the pop charts. Aguilera was a skilled and versatile vocalist—a feature that was easy to miss in the hype over the sensual image she projected—and her approach to singing owed much to the melismatic stylings of Mariah Carey and Whitney Houston.

Critics of Britney Spears and Christina Aguilera charged them with making themselves into sexual objects, reinforcing unhealthy images of young women that are considered the source of a wide range of sociocultural problems. Proponents of this music point out that these were strong role models for women who retained significant control of their careers and provided a positive feminine image. With the simultaneous rise of female singer-songwriters and teen idols, it is certainly easy to see that there is a big difference between Tori Amos singing "Me and a Gun" and Britney Spears singing ". . . Baby One More Time." However, no matter what conclusion you draw from this disparity, by the end of the 1990s, women were playing a central role in popular music, as both the singer-songwriters and the teen idols were back.

BEAT-BASED POP

Making Beats. During the 1980s, programmable and computer-based methods of making music were widespread in a variety of popular music styles. Listening closely to the teen pop discussed above, for example, it reveals that the nonvocal elements of most of these tracks were carefully constructed using a variety of electronic instruments, including drum machines, synthesizers, and samplers. Even when traditional rock instruments were employed in these tracks, such as guitars or the electric bass, the performances were recorded to mesh with the prevailing electronic texture. This process of creating a musical track, or "making beats," was often completed independently from the vocalist or rapper before the lyrics and melodies were constructed. Beat-based production techniques were used during the 1990s to create a wide variety of popular music, including most teen pop, rap and hip-hop, and electronic dance music. While this manner of creation may at first seem to be the antithesis of the rock tradition, which valued recordings of live performance, beat-based production techniques became influential in many forms of hybrid rock in the 1990s. Moreover, by the end of the decade most rock musicians who performed live in the studio with traditional instrumentation used digital audio workstations that grew largely out of the beat-based recording movement, adding much more flexibility to the recording process.

Hip-Hop in the 1990s. In the 1990s, hip-hop culture was pervasive internationally, as rap grew into one of popular music's dominant styles both in the United States and the UK. This growth was so dramatic that hip-hop deserves to be considered as the focal point of its own history and not as one facet of the history of rock music. Yet, just as much of the popular music during the 1990s reflected heavily on earlier styles, rap music (which we will consider as part of a larger hip-hop culture that included aspects such as dancing, art, and fashion) championed eclecticism with references to older music. Early DJs like Kool Herc and Afrika Bambaataa had used a wide range of sources to create their live music in the 1970s, and the ability to combine disparate prerecorded pieces became even easier with the growth of the sampler in the late 1980s. Samplers allowed beat makers to record small sections of commercial recordings and create repetitive "loops" or present them at opportune points in a musical arrangement. Favorite early sources of music mirrored those used by live DJs in the 1980s, including artists such as James Brown and Parliament/Funkadelic. Yet, throughout the decade, sample sources were often taken from sources not usually associated with hip-hop culture, such as classical music and rock. While focused on African-American culture, most hip-hop in the 1990s was extremely popular with white suburban teenagers, a demographic group that dramatically increased record sales for rap artists and created a generation of listeners who were equally familiar with Snoop Dogg and Led Zeppelin. The use of preexisting material in hip-hop challenged notions of ownership and copyright throughout the 1990s. One of the most important cases was a ruling against rapper Biz Markie in 1991, which set a strict precedent requiring hip-hop producers to attain various levels of permission to use sampled sources. In effect, this ruling changed the way many producers approached their work, and limited access to the multitude of samples available during the 1980s.

With its growth and commercial success, rap fractured into many substyles, much as rock did during the first half of the 1970s. Within gangsta rap early in the 1990s, a rivalry developed between Southern California and New York, and this feud became the source of much controversy in the music press and eventually ended in tragedy. The West Coast faction was led by Death Row Records, owned and controlled by aspiring impresario Suge Knight. Knight signed N.W.A member Dr. Dre, whose 1993 album, *The Chronic* (p3 r1, 1993), included the rapper Snoop

One of the most successful recording teams in hip-hop history, Snoop Doggy Dogg (left) and Dr. Dre (standing). Dre was a key player in West Coast rap, where he came up with Eazy-E and Ice Cube in the group N.W.A (Niggaz with Attitude). Snoop and Dre teamed up to create *The Chronic* (1992), which became the model for West Coast gangsta rap. These two are seen here in the studio during the creation of Snoop's 1993 album *Doggy Style*.

Listening Guide

Dr. Dre, featuring Snoop Doggy Dogg, "Nuthin' but a 'G' Thang" Death Row 53816

Words and music by Cordozar Broadus, Andre Young, Leon Haywood, and Frederick Knight. Produced by Dr. Dre. Rose to #2 in the U.S. pop charts (#1 on the rhythm and blues charts) in 1993; contained on the album *The Chronic*, which rose to #3 on the U.S. pop charts (#1 on the rhythm and blues charts).

FORM: Simple verse. The verses in almost every case are built on 4-bar phrases, producing either 12- or 16-bar sections. The only exception is verse 1, which is 10 measures in length. Verses 1 and 2 are followed by a 4-bar refrain, as are verses 3, 4, and 5, and this forms a relatively regular and symmetrical formal pattern. Once the groove is set up in the accompaniment, the focus is on the rapping, which is done by both Snoop Doggy Dogg and Dr. Dre. While the rhymes are clever, the ways in which the delivery of these lines flow alternately with and against the rhythmic grouping in the accompaniment is where Snoop and Dre really display their skills. Notice how lines do not always begin or end where you might expect them to—sometimes beginning late or ending early, other times seeming to blur over the underlying 4-bar pattern. To keep the accompaniment interesting, synthesizer lines come and go throughout the track.

TIME SIGNATURE: 4/4.

INSTRUMENTATION: Electric guitars, bass, synthesizers, drums, percussion, vocals, and samples drawn from Leon Haywood's "I Wanna Do Something Freaky to You" and Kid Dynamite's "Uphill (Peace of Mind)."

0:00–0:11	**Introduction**, 4 mm.	This instrumental section establishes the laid-back groove. Note the female sighs that saturate this track and the signature synthesizer melody.

Doggy Dogg. The track "Nuthin' but a 'G' Thang" (p2 r1) provides a famous example of the album's approach. The track employs two samples: "Uphill (Peace of Mind)," a 1976 track by Kid Dynamite, and "I Wanna Do Something Freaky to You" (1979) by Leon Haywood, both drawn from late 1970s soul music. Both Snoop and Dre rap, and rather than being cast in a sing-song and predictable rhyme pattern, the lines weave in and out against the accompanying groove, often employing sophisticated rhythms and phrase groupings.

The East Coast faction of gangsta rap was led by producer, businessman, and future rap artist Sean Combs, who went by the name Puff Daddy (later changed to P. Diddy, then just Diddy). Combs had been in A&R for Uptown Records, working with artists such as Father MC and Mary J. Blige. Fired from Uptown, Combs formed his own record label, Bad Boy, and the Notorious B.I.G. was among the first to score a top crossover success for the label. B.I.G.'s *Ready to Die* reached number fifteen on the pop charts in 1995 (r3) and *Life after Death* topped the pop and rhythm and blues charts in 1997. Another group based on the East Coast (but

0:11–0:36	**Verse 1**, 10 mm.	Snoop begins the rapping, with a brief contribution from Dre. This verse consists of a 4-bar phrase, then a 2-bar phrase, followed by another 4-bar phrase. "One, two, three . . ."
0:36–1:07	**Verse 2**, 12 mm.	Snoop takes a verse solo. "Back to the lecture at hand . . ."
1:07–1:18	**Refrain**, 4 mm.	This refrain, rapped by Snoop and Dre together, signals the end of this portion of the track, setting up the next verse and introducing Dre. The synthesizer melody from the intro returns. "It's like this . . ."
1:18–1:48	**Verse 3**, 12 mm.	Dre now takes a verse solo. "Well I'm peepin' . . ."
1:48–1:58	**Refrain**, 4 mm.	The refrain again signals the end of this section. Return of synthesizer melody from intro and refrain as before. "It's like this . . ."
1:58–2:07	**Interlude**, 4 mm.	This instrumental section parallels the introduction, as synthesizer melody continues amid vocal samples and scratching.
2:07–2:38	**Verse 4**, 12 mm.	Snoop returns for another solo verse, calling on Dre at the end. "Fallin' back on that . . ."
2:38–3:19	**Verse 5**, 16 mm.	Dre again takes a solo verse. "Here's where it takes place . . ."
3:19–3:29	**Refrain**, 4 mm.	This time the refrain signals the end of the track, as the signature synthesizer melody returns as before. "Like this . . ."
3:29–3:56	**Coda**, 8 mm. and fade.	As in the introduction, this section is instrumental and fades out during the third time through the 4-bar pattern. Signature synthesizer melody continues, as vocal samples and scratching from interlude return.

not necessarily purveyors of the East Coast style) was the New York–based Wu Tang Clan, a collective of nine artists. The idea of Wu Tang Clan was to produce a smash album that would allow each of the members to spin off his own solo career. The first album, *Enter the Wu Tang (36 Chambers)*, was released in 1993 and went to number eight on the rhythm and blues charts (p41). The next release, *Wu Tang Forever* (1997), topped the pop and rhythm and blues charts in the United States and the pop album charts in the UK. Later spin-off projects produced ten top ten albums in the United States, with several more charting in the Top 40.

Emerging at the end of the decade, Eminem challenged many of the assumptions about race that the mainstream media had placed on hip-hop. Born Marshall Mathers, Eminem grew up as a poor white kid in an urban Detroit neighborhood. After establishing a reputation locally, he won a 1997 freestyle rap competition in Los Angeles and as a result, a copy of his demo tape was heard by Dr. Dre. While Dre was surprised that Eminem was white, he was soon won over by the rapper's wit and talent and produced his breakthrough album, *The Slim Shady LP* (p2 r1 uk12,

1999). While Eminem had sometimes rapped on positive themes on his first album, *Infinite* (1997), for this album he adopted the persona of Slim Shady, a character who could express his deepest emotional pain and hostility. The lead single from the album, "My Name Is" (p36 r18 uk2), provides a good example of Eminem's aggressive approach, and the rapper soon provoked widespread controversy for the violent content of his lyrics, making him rap music's preeminent bad boy. With *The Marshall Mathers LP* (p1 r1 uk1, 2000), Eminem turned his attention to the problems of his own life. The portrayal of his wife in "Kim" created a storm of public and private controversy, and his mother filed a lawsuit against him for defamation of character. The negative reaction to Eminem's music only seemed to make him more successful, partly because many fellow artists—and unlikely ones such as Elton John—strongly defended his talent and intelligence. Eminem's most recent album, *Recovery* (p1 r1 uk1, 2010), provides an about-face for the successful rapper, chronicling his years of substance abuse, which surely added to his often-erratic behavior.

In addition to "hardcore" artists like Dr. Dre and the Wu-Tang Clan, many others who participated in the hip-hop tradition were less militant and linked more closely to the rock tradition. Often employing samples from more familiar rock and soul songs, records by these artists have been consistently praised by rock critics in spite of their origins in the hip-hop community. New York's Beastie Boys are emblematic of this category of "rock approved hip-hop." Through a series of albums in the 1990s, including *Paul's Boutique* (p14 r24, 1989), *Check Your Head* (p10 r37, 1992), *Ill Communication* (p1 r2 uk10, 1994), and *Hello Nasty* (p1 uk1, 1998), the band matured from a rowdy fraternity group into socially conscious politicos who advocated Eastern religion. With samples from a wide variety of sources, including jazz and classic soul, De La Soul became critical darlings after the release of their first album *3 Feet High and Rising* (p24 r1 uk13, 1989). Through subsequent efforts, including *Stakes Is High* (p13 r4, 1996) and *Art Official Intelligence: Mosaic Thump* (p9 r3 uk22, 2000), the group focused on positive, introspective lyrics, which set them apart from the violent depictions of the ghetto used in gangsta styles. Although many hip-hop groups featured the occasional vocal melody, the Fugees were a trio that mixed two male rappers, Wyclef Jean and Pras Michel (both of Haitian origin), and female singer Lauryn Hill. Often featuring reggae-tinged accompaniments, the group's breakout single was a version of the 1971 Roberta

Dr. Dre discovered Eminem (Marshall Mathers, pictured here at a live concert) in 1997 and soon helped him produce his first album. Eminem had a distinctive vocal style and his lyrics focused not on "gangsta life" or politics, but on his personal experiences growing up as a poor white kid in Detroit. Eminem's mother and his wife Kim were only two of many targets of his aggressive and often violent rhymes.

Flack single "Killing Me Softly" (p2 rl uk1, 1996), which was also included on *The Score* (p1 rl uk2, 1996). Two years later, Hill's solo album *The Miseducation of Lauryn Hill* (p1 rl uk2, 1998) became a pop sensation on the strength of the single "Doo Wop (That Thing)" (p1 r2 uk3). The video for this song shows a particular interest in connecting with the past, as it features a split screen with Hill depicted simultaneously as a performer from 1967 (on the left side of the screen) and in modern dress (on the right side of the screen).

Electronic Dance Music. Although hip-hop was popular for dancing, an important strand of beat-based electronic dance music also entered the mainstream during the 1990s. Like other styles we have discussed so far, dance music had gone underground after its time in the pop limelight during the 1970s, and regional dance scenes developed in major cities like New York, Chicago, and Detroit. Throughout the 1980s, dance music developed away from the mainstream, as devoted dancers populated specialized clubs and DJs crafted sets designed to keep the dance floor full. By the late 1980s, America's underground dance music had made its way to England, where a dance craze began to build. The UK scene then spread back across the Atlantic to New York, San Francisco, and Los Angeles, forming the basis for the rise of electronic dance music throughout the decade. By the late 1990s, many observers of pop-music trends were predicting that electronic dance music—often referred to broadly as "techno"—would be the next big thing, replacing rock as the music of America's youth.

Much of the electronic dance movement stemmed from 1970s clubs like the Paradise Garage in New York's SoHo district, where Larry Levan established himself as one of the city's top dance DJs while disco was still popular. Employing a spectacular sound system and often controlling the lighting as well, Levan combined a wide range of music to create his sets, sometimes blending records together and at other times moving abruptly from one to another. The New York approach to dance music is often called "garage," and the New York City Peech Boys' "Don't Make Me Wait" (1982) provides a representative example of the style. However, New

All-night rave parties became extremely popular during the late 1980s. Many participants used drugs to enhance the experience of dance music, and Ecstasy was associated closely with this dance-party culture. This has led many cultural critics to label 1988 and 1989 as the "Second Summer of Love."

York was not the only city in America where dance music thrived. Frankie Knuckles, who had worked with Levan, brought the techniques and practices of the New York scene to Chicago in the late 1970s. By the early 1980s he and other Chicago DJs were developing a style that would soon be called "house," after a Chicago club. Remixes became increasingly complex, as passages from various records were spliced together and new parts were added on top, often with inexpensive synthesizers and drum machines—all in an attempt to provide a full night's worth of fresh-sounding dance music. The first recorded example of house music is probably Jesse Saunders's "On and On" (1983). In Detroit, a group of aspiring DJs, often called the Belleville Three, began blending their love for the European synthesizer music with their passion for Parliament/Funkadelic. Juan Atkins, Derrick May, and Kevin Saunderson began producing a refined, futuristic, and sonically sophisticated version of dance music that many originally called "Detroit house," though the style is more generally referred to as "techno." The Detroit approach tends not to employ traditional instruments, but rather emphasizes the drum machine, synthesizers, and sequencers. A representative example is Juan Atkins's "No UFOs" (1985), released under the name Motel 500.

One of the most important DJs in post-disco dance music was Larry Levan, pictured here in 1990 performing at Mars, an important club in the New York City house music scene. With his innovative use of multiple records, lighting, and sound effects, Levan controlled all aspects of the dance club experience. He proved that in this new genre it was not the records that were important—it was the DJ.

By the summer of 1988, all-night rave parties began to get so large they would sometimes be held outdoors, often at secret locations to avoid police intervention. The drug Ecstasy became an important part of the experience for many dancers, leading some to refer to 1988 as the "Second Summer of Love" because of the blend of trippy music, altered consciousness, and tribal sensibilities. British musicians were soon producing their own version of electronic dance music, and by the early 1990s, dance records were becoming hits on the UK pop charts. In 1990, for instance, Orbital scored with "The Chime" (uk17) and the American musician Moby hit with "Go" (uk10, 1991)—a track that samples a theme from the *Twin Peaks* television show. Other hits included the Prodigy's "Everybody in the Place" (uk2, 1992), Shut Up and Dance's "Raving I'm Raving" (uk2, 1992), and SL2's "On a Ragga Tip" (uk2, 1992). In the early 1990s, dance made its way back to the United States, as British rave culture was transplanted to New York, San Francisco, and Los Angeles. In each case, these newly founded rave scenes were driven by DJs who had experienced British rave, and each local scene had its own distinctive musical and cultural profile. In the second half of the decade, dance music became more popular as more and more local scenes sprang up and major labels began to invest in the style. The mainstream success of electronic dance music in America was driven primarily by album sales rather than singles, as had been the case in the UK earlier in the decade. MTV also played an important role, airing dance videos that were often innovative and spacey. Important hit electronic dance albums were released by the Chemical Brothers, whose *Dig Your Own Hole* (p14 uk1, 1997) made an early mark, and the Prodigy's *The Fat of the Land* (1997), which topped both the U.S. and UK charts. Moby became an important figure during these years, as every track of his 1999 album *Play* (p38 uk1, 1999) was licensed for either commercials or movie soundtracks.

METAL AND ALTERNATIVE EXTENSIONS

Rap and Rock: Rage Against the Machine. As rap was expanding into many substyles during the early 1990s, it was also gaining a firmer foothold in the world of white rock. In the years following Run-DMC's crossover cover of "Walk This Way," many rock musicians took an interest in employing aspects of rap in their music. Rap and heavy metal rose to mainstream popularity at about the same time, and cross-pollination between the two played an important role in the second half of the 1980s. Eclectic bands like Anthrax and Faith No More began to employ rapped passages in a heavy-rock context. Taking their cue from Faith No More and the Red Hot Chili Peppers, the Los Angeles–based band Rage Against the Machine blended hard-driving rock with mostly rapped vocals to establish a stylistic model many later bands would follow. Their first album, *Rage Against the Machine* (p45 uk17, 1992), evinced the group's dedication to political causes while musically drawing much from the Chili Peppers' blend of funk grooves and heavy metal riffs. Zack de la Rocha's vocals shared the spotlight with Tom Morello's innovative guitar playing, which blended metal, blues rock, and jazz, and at times imitated the sound of DJ scratching. *Evil Empire* (p1 uk4, 1996) followed and established the band as an important force in the rap-rock style, while *The Battle of Los Angeles* (p1 uk23, 1999) served to confirm this. By the end of the decade, de la Rocha had left the group and the remaining members reorganized as Audioslave, with Soundgarden's Chris Cornell performing lead vocals.

Getting Heavy: Korn, Limp Bizkit, System of a Down, and Kid Rock. Hailing from Bakersfield, California, Korn brought the sound of the seven-string guitar into rap-rock. The electric seven-string had been used by a handful of jazz guitarists over the years to make a wider range of notes available on the instrument. In most configurations, the seventh string was added below the bottom string of a conventional guitar, not only making more bass notes possible but also providing for a

Rage Against the Machine, pictured here in concert, was one of the first groups to successfully combine a rap vocal style with rock. Zack de la Rocha's (right) often political lyrics shared the spotlight with Tom Morello's innovative guitar playing, which often imitated the sound of DJ scratching. Bassist Tim Commerford is pictured left.

greater range within the grip of the guitarist's left hand. Heavy metal virtuoso Steve Vai had introduced the instrument into rock, but Korn guitarists James "Munky" Shaffer and Brian "Head" Welch practically made it into a brand name, using the low strings for heavy, angular, distortion-soaked riffs. The band's first album, *Korn* (1994), introduced the group's trademark sound, while *Life Is Peachy* (p3 uk32, 1996) and *Follow the Leader* (p1 uk5, 1998) established their reputation. As with Rage Against the Machine, Korn's lyrics are most often rapped, but also sometimes screamed, and together with the pronounced influence of heavy metal, create a more menacing stylistic blend.

Florida's Limp Bizkit picked up Korn's use of the seven-string guitar, added more screaming in the vocal dimension, and produced *Three Dollar Bill Y'all* (p22, 1997), which included a cover of George Michael's "Faith," and *Significant Other* (p1 uk26, 1999). Led by charismatic vocalist Fred Durst and guitarist Wes Borland, the band received considerable airtime on MTV. System of a Down also brought together many features of these rap-rock groups. With *System of a Down* (1998) and *Toxicity* (p1 uk13, 2001), the group continued the political and social commitment of Rage Against the Machine, while blending in the heavy, gothic tones of Korn and Limp Bizkit. Their producer was Rick Rubin, who had produced the Run-DMC records that first brought rock and rap together. Starting out as a rapper in the style of the early Beastie Boys, Detroit's Kid Rock extended the rap-rock of earlier bands by employing a wide range of styles in his music during the late 1990s. *Devil without a Cause* (p4, 1998), his major label breakthrough, uses fewer heavy metal guitar riffs and more sounds drawn from traditional blues rock. Kid Rock's vocals are both rapped and sung (at times in a very conventional manner), showing a stronger flair for pop hooks and a broad range of stylistic references, including country rock. Kid Rock's lyrics are rarely gothic or politically ambitious; instead, they are much more playful and at times ironic and comic. Unlike Korn, Limp Bizkit, and System of a Down, who were incredibly consistent in their blend of rap and metal, Kid Rock has branched out into more mainstream forms of pop.

The Menacing Sounds of Industry: Nine Inch Nails and Marilyn Manson.

While bands like Rage Against the Machine and Korn were extending 1980s heavy metal by blending in rap elements, other musicians were exploring a style often called "industrial." The roots of industrial can be traced to British bands of the mid-1970s such as Throbbing Gristle and Cabaret Voltaire, as well as to Skinny Puppy, a Canadian band from the 1980s. The genre was heavily imbued with concept art and anti-conformity, resulting in music that blended electronic sources with live performance and was decidedly avant-garde and disturbing. Mixing heavier strains of metal with industrial, Nine Inch Nails is often considered the premier 1990s group in the style, and the band's 1994 album *The Downward Spiral* (p2 uk9, 1994) brought industrial to a mainstream rock audience for the first time. In the recording studio, Nine Inch Nails is San Francisco–based composer Trent Reznor, who writes the music and performs all the parts himself, while a rotating cast of backing musicians perform with Reznor in a live setting. Nine Inch Nails' music is moody, with frequent shifts in atmosphere, and the lyrics are often concerned with the darker side of the human psyche. *The Downward Spiral*, for instance, was recorded in the house where Charles Manson and his followers committed the famous (and hideous) murders of actress Sharon Tate and her friends.

Like Alice Cooper and Ozzy Osbourne before him, Marilyn Manson used grotesque, satanic, and often vulgar lyrics and visuals in his music. Manson's outrageousness, which he flaunted at every opportunity (this picture is from a performance at the American Music Awards in 2001), appealed to a large audience of teens who longed to rebel against suburbia and the perceived commercialism of music.

A similar fascination with the grotesque can be found in the music of Marilyn Manson. Much like Alice Cooper, Marilyn Manson is the name of the band and the lead singer (who is male). Each member of the group adopted a stage name that combined the name of a glamorous female celebrity with that of a famous serial killer (the keyboardist, for instance, is Madonna Wayne Gacy). Emerging from Florida, the band made its first commercial mark with its Trent Reznor–produced third album, *Antichrist Superstar* (p3, 1996), following with the even more successful *Mechanical Animals* in 1998 (p1 uk8). Like other shock-rockers before him, Manson did all he could to outrage the more conservative segment of middle America: he dressed outrageously (as a kind of ghoulish transvestite) and included vulgar and satanic content on the albums, practically begging to be banned from the radio. And mirroring the appeal of earlier outrageous bands to previous generations of youngsters, the band's attraction was largely that it misbehaved so proudly and unabashedly, not unlike the gangsta rappers discussed above.

Alternative Impulses: Live, Lifehouse, and Creed. In the years after the grunge movement, the "alternative" style of bands such as Nirvana and R.E.M. was (ironically) fully imbedded in the mainstream. Pennsylvania-based Live is an example of a group from this period that emerged through mainstream channels, but was marketed as alternative. With records on a major label subsidiary and sales of over 8 million copies for their 1994 album *Throwing Copper* (p1), Live was a mainstay of radio and concert venues until the turn of the millennium. Similarly, the California-based trio Lifehouse created a sonic texture that drew heavily from the grunge movement. In the band's breakout single "Hanging by a Moment" (p2 uk25, 2001), there are clear allegiances to Nirvana, which are made even clearer in the music video for the song, which includes several segments that resemble the video for "Smells Like Teen Spirit." However, the transgressive nature of Nirvana and many other grunge bands was not present in the lyrics of Lifehouse songs, reflecting the band's history of playing in churches. Although not exclusively a Christian band, the lyrics for "Hanging by a Moment" can certainly be interpreted as devotional, creating a fascinating cultural combination of grunge and Christianity. With songs that alluded to Christian theology, Creed was another post-grunge band that was extremely successful in the mainstream using the heavy sound of alternative rock. Songs such as "Higher" (p7, 1999) and "My Sacrifice" (p4, 2001) clearly refer to religious themes, while the band's best-known song, "With Arms Wide Open" (p1, uk13, 2000), depicts the perspective of a new father. Although neither of these groups officially espoused the enormous side of the music industry that deals in Christian music, the conservative themes explored by both Lifehouse and Creed point to the emergence of Christian rock in the American mainstream during the 1990s.

Irony and Self-Awareness: Foo Fighters and Weezer.

Although the grunge scene influenced many bands during the mid-1990s, Foo Fighters are a band that actually grew out of the ashes of two important Seattle groups, Nirvana and Sunny Day Real Estate, after the death of Kurt Cobain in 1994. Fronted by guitarist Dave Grohl, who played drums for Nirvana, Foo Fighters has released a series of albums since the mid-1990s that placed them consistently in the upper reaches of the pop charts. Unlike Nirvana, the music of Foo Fighters is less angry and internal, perhaps owing to the personable Grohl, who served initially as the band's main songwriter and set the aesthetic tone for later releases. Also in contrast to the seriousness of Nirvana's music is the group's often-humorous tone in their music videos. "Big Me" (p13 uk19, 1996) featured the group in a pseudo-commercial for breath mints, while "Learn to Fly" (p19 uk21, 2000) showcased several band members in costume playing multiple roles. Although the band's music is rarely this slapstick, the comedic self-awareness included in these videos shows a lighter, more-accessible side of musicians who were once associated with contemplative angst. With albums such as *One by One* (p3 uk1, 2002), *In Your Honor* (p2 uk2, 2005), and *Echoes, Silence, Patience and Grace* (p3 uk1, 2007), Foo Fighters have become rock music mainstays during the past decade.

Emerging on the national scene in late 1994, the often-comedic music of Weezer embodied the self-awareness of the intelligent alternative slacker. This attitude can be found in the group's first Top-40 hit, "Buddy Holly" (p18 uk12, 1995), which depicts the song's protagonist as a geek facing threats against his girlfriend. Using slang associated with hip-hop, lead singer and songwriter Rivers Cuomo draws attention to his frailty, asking "What's with these homies dissin' my girl?" The video for the song takes the 1950s references even further, portraying the band on the set of the sitcom *Happy Days* as the entertainment at Al's Diner. Incredibly productive since their debut, the group has released a number of albums that scored very high on the *Billboard* charts, while maintaining a heavy guitar-oriented sound over a steady, danceable groove.

Pop Punk and Ska Revival.

Several bands widely influenced by punk music entered the mainstream in the early 1990s, creating a style often given the ironic label pop punk. Many of these bands were from California, showing the long lineage of heavier forms of rock in both the northern and southern parts of the state. San Francisco's Green Day, led by singer, songwriter, and guitarist Billie Joe Armstrong, enjoyed its first significant commercial success in 1994 with *Dookie* (p2 uk13) and followed in 1995 with *Insomniac* (p2 uk8). The band's music is often hard driving and aggressive, making their stylistic debt to 1970s punk, but a softer side can be heard in the ballad "Good Riddance (Time of Your Life)" (p11 uk11), which was played during the final episode of the enormously successful television show *Seinfeld*. Green Day has had the most longevity of these pop punk groups, especially after their critically acclaimed 2004 album *American Idiot* (p1 uk1), a political rock opera that has since been converted into a Broadway show. The Off- spring also emerged in 1994, releasing records on the independent Epitaph label before signing to Columbia in 1997. The group's breakthrough album was *Smash* (p4 uk21, 1994), which contained the single "Come Out and Play" (p38). This single mixes heavy riff-based punk with a simple surf guitar line during the verses, connecting to the groups' Southern California roots. San Diego's Blink-182 hit the mainstream later in the decade with the albums *Enema of the State* (p9 uk15, 1999) and *Take Off Your Pants and Jacket* (p1 uk4, 2001). A trio similar to Green Day in many ways, this group showed their comedic side in several music videos. In "What's My Age Again" (uk17, 1999) they appeared for the duration of the video running through various scenes with no clothing, while in "All the Small Things" (p6 uk2, 2000), the group parodied the video style and dress of many pop and hip- hop acts from the period.

Several years after the emergence of pop punk in the mainstream there was a similar ska revival, which produced several notable bands. Fronted by Brad Nowell,

Green Day guitarist Billie Joe Armstrong in a 1997 concert. The most popular band to emerge from the California pop punk scene, Green Day combined the speed, distortion, and style of punk with catchy pop hooks.

Sublime emerged in 1996 with an eponymous album (p13) that contained the single "What I Got" (p29). Containing elements of laid-back beach music, hip- hop, and traditional Jamaican music, Sublime's music revealed an interesting Southern California subculture of tattooed punks that were interested in West Indian roots music. Hailing from Cambridge, Massachusetts, the Mighty Mighty Bosstones also received main- stream attention during the mid-1990s. The group had been active for nearly a decade before releasing *Let's Face It* (p27 uk40, 1997), which contained the single "The Impression that I Get" (p23 uk12). Pre- senting a much more energetic mix of ska and punk (often called ska-core), the Mighty Mighty Bosstones featured a full horn section, and even employed a full- time dancer to help energize the audience. No Doubt was the mid-1990s ska revival band that made the larg- est impression on the American mainstream. On the strength of the single "Don't Speak" (p1 uk1), the group's *Tragic Kingdom* (p1 uk3, 1996) sold more than 10 million copies, making lead singer Gwen Ste- fani into a household name and a fashion icon. Later releases, such as *Return of Saturn* (p2 uk31, 2000) and *Rock Steady* (p9, 2002) explored various forms of dance music, exposing connections between American pop, Jamaican dancehall, reggae, American electronic dance styles, and even hip-hop. Stefani has also showed a wide range of musical interest, collaborating on suc- cessful singles with Moby, Eve, and Akon, in addition to releasing the multifaceted solo album *Love.Angel. Music.Baby* (p5 uk4, 2005).

INDIE ROCK

In the last several chapters we have followed the indie-rock underground, which began to develop during the early 1980s supported by a circuit of clubs and bars (often in college towns), college radio stations, and several magazines that chronicled the movement, including *College Music Journal (CMJ)*. After the rise of alternative music in the pop mainstream during the early 1990s, indie rock continued to thrive as underground music. A series of important independent record labels played an important role in the scene during this time, furthering the ideals of the punk and hardcore movements. For example, the New York–based Matador label was extremely successful during the 1990s, releasing seminal music by groups such as Yo La Tengo, Pavement, and Guided by Voices. Other important labels were Merge in Chapel Hill, North Carolina, a label run by two members of the band Superchunk, and Sub Pop in Seattle, which released early records by Nirvana, Soundgarden, and Mudhoney. In Olympia, Washington, K Records had the band Beat Happening, while Kill Rock Stars Records released material by bands such as Sleater-Kinney, Elliot Smith, and Bikini Kill. Despite the popularity of alternative music in the early 1990s, college radio stations were still the main source of radio exposure for indie rock, and *CMJ* tracked which stations were playing which records, much as *Billboard* did for mainstream pop styles. Several annual festivals that showcased live indie rock performances also emerged during the 1990s as important industry events, including the *CMJ* Music Marathon hosted in New York City and Austin's South By Southwest festival. After withstanding major label pilfering, during the 1990s indie rock was still small and off the beaten path, culturally speaking. For those who loved it, that was its charm.

Against the backdrop of a corporate machinery used to create and promote mainstream rock, perhaps the most prominent feature of indie rock in the 1990s was its do-it-yourself aesthetic: the idea that a band didn't need the machinery of a major record label to make good music. Most indie bands recorded for small labels and didn't get much mainstream attention or sell in large numbers compared to major label acts. However, with a growing infrastructure and fan base, many indie bands, even those who had the opportunity to record for major labels, found that they were happy to make a living playing music on their own terms. Even though the alternative movement grew out of the indie rock scene, with most Seattle bands moving from independent labels to major labels almost overnight, the indie scene outside of Seattle continued to thrive. In fact, many indie rock bands viewed the transformation of the Seattle scene as a negative example, and further evidence of the dangers of dealing with mainstream music conglomerates. Despite the small scale on which most of the bands enjoyed success, music critics often warmly praised indie bands and the indie scene generally. For such critics, indie music offered a purer and more direct style of rock music—a style uncorrupted by concerns about marketing and audience demographics.

Lo-Fi: Pavement, Guided by Voices and Elliot Smith. Before the digital revolution of the late 1990s made high-quality recording facilities accessible to a much wider range of musicians, one of the drawbacks to working as part of the indie scene was the lack of good recording facilities. Moreover, as aspects of musical "professionalism" were often perceived as mechanistic and inauthentic, many indie bands celebrated a recording style that revealed the impulsive nature of their music. Nowhere was this better exemplified than in the widespread "lo-fi" aesthetic that pervaded much indie rock during the early 1990s. In many ways, Pavement represented both the continuation of the indie scene during the 1990s and the celebration of the lo-fi aesthetic. Formed by childhood friends and classmates at the University of Virginia, the band eventually coalesced after moving to Hoboken, New Jersey in the early 1990s. Among the most heralded indie bands of the 1990s, Pavement's take on lo-fi can be found in their physical and lyrical embodiment of the slacker lifestyle, in addition to the loose sound on their recordings. With albums released on Matador such as *Slanted and Enchanted* (1992) and *Crooked Rain, Crooked Rain* (uk15, 1994), Pavement's style featured characteristic half-sung, half-spoken vocals from singer Stephen Malkmus, heavy distorted guitar, and a loose backing groove. Hailing from Dayton, Ohio, Guided by Voices offered another take on lo-fi, piecing together albums from amateur recordings that included audible mistakes, eclectic instrumentation, and haphazard songwriting. As older musicians from a remote location, Guided by Voices were unlikely rock musicians, which fit the indie rock profile perfectly. Led by songwriter and lead vocalist Robert Pollard, the band and its many collaborative offshoots have released hundreds of albums since emerging on the Scat and Matador labels in the early 1990s with releases such as *Bee Thousand* (1994) and *Alien Lanes* (1995), both of which have become indie classics. Portland-based Elliot Smith approached lo-fi in yet another manner, as an intimate window into the musical world of an inward-focused solo artist. Smith recorded his first solo record while part of the group Heatmiser, which was for a time signed to a major label. Far outweighing the reception of his rock-oriented work with Heatmiser, acoustic-based albums such as *Roman Candle* (1994), *Elliot Smith* (1995), and *Either/Or* (1997) featured Smith playing all the instruments by himself, often with primitive equipment, creating a homemade atmosphere that accompanied often existential lyrics. After several of his songs were featured on the soundtrack to the film *Good Will Hunting*, Smith was nominated for an Academy Award, and appeared in an incongruous setting on national television at the annual ceremony in Los Angeles backed by a full orchestra—a rare mainstream appearance for an indie rocker.

Merge: Magnetic Fields, Neutral Milk Hotel, and Superchunk. Although some indie labels cultivated a particular type of music, others highlighted a broad range of styles. In this way, it is often difficult to speak of "indie rock" as a musical style. Focusing on several of the most important bands to record for North Carolina's Merge records during the 1990s can highlight the wide range of styles proffered by a single label. Perhaps the most stereotypical group that recorded for Merge during this time was Superchunk, whose singer and guitarist Mac McCaughan and bassist Laura Balance started the label while recording several records for Matador. A high-energy group with clear roots in the punk movement, Superchunk is perhaps best known for their 1991 Matador album *No Pocky for Kitty* and the anthemic "Slack Motherfucker." Released on Merge, the single regales listeners with the story of a lowly, unmotivated employee, a typical character in the indie scene. Far from the high-energy style of Superchunk, the Louisiana-based group Neutral Milk Hotel espoused a lo-fi aesthetic to support the songwriting of group leader Jeff Mangum. Featuring cryptic instrumentation and lyrical references, and supported

Listening Guide   Get Music Ⓢ wwnorton.com/studyspace

Neutral Milk Hotel, "In the Aeroplane over the Sea" Merge 136
(also released as Blue Rose 10192 and Domino 21)

Music by Jeff Mangum. Produced by Robert Schneider. Contained on the album *In the Aeroplane Over the Sea*, which did not chart.

FORM: Simple verse, with bridge. After a short introduction, a 16-measure verse is presented. In the second verse, a series of instruments enter to enhance the musical texture. The instrumental bridge uses very similar musical material, but changed enough to offer contrast. The second bridge incorporates vocals, and repeats the musical material of the instrumental bridge, but presents the chords half as fast. This turns an 8-measure section into a 16-measure section. The interlude also presents this contrasting music at the same rate. A final 16-measure verse ends the song, with no fade out or postlude.

TIME SIGNATURE: 6/8.

INSTRUMENTATION: Acoustic guitar, drums, fuzz bass, singing saw (L and R), flugelhorn

0:00–0:07	**Introduction**, 4 mm.	Multitracked acoustic guitar.
0:07–0:40	**Verse 1**, 16 mm.	Vocals and guitar. Notice how the form of the verse is 8+8, with two distinct parts. "What a beautiful face . . ."
0:40–1:12	**Verse 2**, 16 mm.	Drums and bass enter. Notice the multitracked "singing saws," which create an ethereal sound that reflects the subject matter. "And one day . . ."
1:12–1:28	**Instrumental Bridge**, 9 mm.	Solo featuring a flugelhorn. Note how a basic 8-measure phrase adds an additional measure to prepare for the entrance of the next verse.
1:28–2:00	**Verse 3**, 16 mm.	As before with active singing saws. "What a curious life . . ."
2:00–2:32	**Bridge**, 16 mm	The flugelhorn performs multiple parts. "Now, how I remember . . ."
2:32–2:47	**Interlude**, 8 mm.	The squeaking sounds in each speaker are the saws!
2:47–3:22	**Verse 4**, 16 mm.	The flugelhorn has been added to the final verse. "What a beautiful face . . ."

by styles that range form intimate acoustic settings to avant-garde noise experiments, the 1998 album *In the Aeroplane over the Sea*, is considered one of the finest indie releases of the 1990s. A third Merge band, the Magnetic Fields, highlights the presence of perspectives from within indie rock that defy traditional male-dominated viewpoints. The group is the creative outlet for songwriter Stephin Merritt,

and the music highlights songs rather than performance, featuring inventive instrumental accompaniment provided by cellist Sam Davol and multi-instrumentalists John Woo and Claudia Gonson. Merritt's music often includes themes of gender, punctuated by his lethargic baritone voice. His crowning achievement is the three-volume collection *69 Love Songs* (1999) (23 songs per disc), which showcases his prodigious songwriting abilities.

Noise Pop: Yo La Tengo and My Bloody Valentine.
Through the lo-fi movement, we have seen that experimenting with sound was an important element of indie rock in the 1990s. While artists such as Guided by Voices and Elliot Smith often created intimate textures, other bands went to the opposite extreme, investigating the possibilities of noise, volume, repetition and droning in the recording studio and in live performance. New Jersey's Yo La Tengo offers a good example of this approach from the American indie scene. After recording a series of records for various independent labels in the late 1980s and early 1990s, the group signed to Matador and released iconic noise-rock albums such as *Painful* (1993) and *I Can Hear the Heart Beating as One* (1997). The latter contains several songs that exemplify the band's mid-1990s style. "Moby Octopad" shows the band's repetitive nature. It is built over a bass and drum groove that repeats for the length of the tune, overlaid with vocals and swaths of sound. A cover version of the Beach Boys' "Little Honda" provides an excellent example of the group's use of noise. Supported throughout by a heavy bed of distorted guitar, the formal guitar solo section consists of the band playing through the chord changes, while guitarist Ira Kaplan plays a single distorted guitar chord throughout. Although bands like Yo La Tengo often infused noise experiments into their music, other bands were known for working more thoroughly with this technique. Among these was the Irish band My Bloody Valentine, whose 1991 album *Loveless* (uk24) has become a fixture of indie rock playlists. Led by guitarist Kevin Sheilds and featuring the

vocals and guitar of Bilinda Butcher, My Bloody Valentine produced a dense sonic palette of noisy guitars supporting strong melodic material, producing what has often been called "shoegazing" music. Drawing on the 1980s legacy of groups like Sonic Youth, experiments with noise were by no means confined to Yo La Tengo and My Bloody Valentine, and were central to the work of many indie rock groups during the 1990s.

Female Perspectives: Liz Phair, Ani DiFranco, and Sleater-Kinney.

Although overwhelmingly white and upper middle class, the indie rock movement was arguably more open than the mainstream in terms of embracing varying gender perspectives. Chicago-based Liz Phair, for example, was known for her *Girly Sound* tapes, which spread as bootlegs through the indie community. She later released the Matador album *Exile in Guyville* (1993), which is a response to the Rolling Stones' *Exile on Main Street*. Containing provocative songs like "Fuck and Run," this album and the follow up *Whip-Smart* (p27, 1994) propelled Phair's lo-fi female perspective into the center of the indie community. New York–based Ani DiFranco made a mark as a female songwriter, performer, and businesswoman, resisting major label offers and releasing her music on her own indie label, Righteous Babe. Her 1995 album, *Not a Pretty Girl*, garnered critical acclaim and mainstream media attention, while *Little Plastic Castle* (1998) rose as high as number twenty-two on the pop charts. Frank and confrontational, DiFranco has been prolific as a songwriter, releasing nearly twenty studio albums since her debut in the 1990s. Portland-based Sleater-Kinney also provided a loud female voice among the indie underground.

Comprised of all female musicians, Sleater-Kinney was an integral part of the riot grrrl movement of feminist punk musicians in the Pacific Northwest, which was supported by a wide variety of self-produced zines and concert promotions. Releasing albums on seminal indie labels like Chainsaw, Kill Rock Stars, and Sub Pop, Sleater-Kinney is best known for the albums *Call the Doctor* (1996) and *Dig Me Out* (1997), which are cited consistently as important contributions to the indie scene.

Alt-Country: Uncle Tupelo and Ryan Adams.

The idea of blending country music with rock goes back at least to the second half of the 1960s with the Byrds' *Sweetheart of the Rodeo* and Dylan's *Nashville Skyline*. By the early 1970s, the Eagles and others had developed sophisticated country-rock styles, and these groups would influence not only a generation of rock musicians but also a new generation of country musicians, such as Garth Brooks. By the late 1980s, country music was undergoing a stylistic shift under the influence of rock that would lead to chart-topping albums throughout the 1990s, and a pair of friends from Belleville, Illinois, returned to the idea of blending rock and country from an indie-rock perspective, forming

Ani DiFranco performing in the Netherlands in 2001. DiFranco was staunchly independent, and acted as songwriter, performer, and producer on her numerous releases beginning in the 1990s. DiFranco also ran her own record company, Righteous Babe, which put her in control of the business aspects of her music.

the band Uncle Tupelo. Jeff Tweedy and Jay Farrar named the band's debut album *No Depression* (1990), after an old Carter Family song that they covered as the album's opening track. Released on the small label, Rockville, the album would spawn a movement within indie rock called "alt-country," as college radio stations began playing the band's music. Like many indie bands, Uncle Tupelo created the impression of musical informality and seemed to project a lack of concern for commercial appeal. But Tweedy and Farrar were highly skilled songwriters and performers, and their talent became increasingly clear as the band continued to record albums such as *Still Feel Gone* (1991), *March 16–20, 1992* (1992), and *Anodyne* (1993). The group split up in 1994, as Farrar went on to form Son Volt and Tweedy

Sound Check

Artist	Sheryl Crow	Boyz II Men	Tori Amos
Title	All I Wanna Do	End of the Road	Crucify
Chart peak	p2 1994	p1, r1 1992	1992
Form	Simple verse-chorus (modified)	Simple verse-chorus (modified)	Compound AABA
Rhythm	4/4	6/8	2/4
Instrumentation	Electric guitar Acoustic guitar Bass Drums Lead vocal Background vocal Electric piano Synthesizer strings Percussion Handclaps	Electric guitar Bass Drums Lead vocal Background vocal Electric piano Synthesizer strings French horn Handclaps	Bass Drums Lead vocal Background vocal Piano Percussion Mandolin Ukulele
Comments	The music for the introduction becomes the music for the pre-chorus Strings in introduction sound like "disco" strings Verses tell stories about Los Angeles from Crow's perspective	Verses feature solo vocals and chorus sections highlight group vocal texture Virtuosic, melismatic vocals throughout Spoken vocal section reminiscent of 1950s ballads	Piano enters in first pre-chorus and vocals add echo Odd, electronic sounds during the chorus Stark bass chords to accompany verses

formed Wilco. Both of these bands would enjoy success and critical acclaim well into the next decade. While alt-country bands like the Old-97s and the Bottle Rockets prospered in the indie scene during the 1990s, North Carolina's Ryan Adams offered a different take on the alt-country movement. With his group Whiskeytown, Adams joined fiddle player and vocalist Caitlin Cary on albums such as *Faithless Street* (1997) and *Stranger's Almanac* (1999) to replicate a pop-country sound through the palate of a former punk musician. After breaking from the group, however, Adams signed with Universal's Nashville subsidiary Lost Highway and released a string of albums including *Heartbreaker* (2000) and *Gold* (uk20, 2001) that showed his ability to perform in a wide range of styles.

Dr. Dre (featuring Snoop Doggy Dogg)	Neutral Milk Hotel
Nuthin' but a 'G' Thang	In the Aeroplane over the Sea
p2, r1 1993	1998
Simple verse	Simple verse (modified)
4/4	6/8
Electric guitar Bass Drums Lead vocal Synthesizer Percussion Turntable	Acoustic guitar Bass Drums Lead vocal Singing saw Flugelhorn
Note that the rapped vocals are sometimes double-tracked High keyboard sound characteristic of Dr. Dre "g-funk" Main sample taken from Leon Haywood's "I Wanna Do Something Freaky to You"	Interlude and bridge share a chord progression, but bridge moves half as fast Listen for musical saws Flugelhorn featured as solo instrument

Singer, songwriter, and producer Beck, in concert, 1997. For years Beck has successfully straddled the indie-major label divide. His music blends the do-it-yourself feel of indie rock with elements of hip-hop, country rock, 1970s soul, and even classical music.

Indie Music in the Mainstream: Beck. Considering the aversion to major labels within the indie world, fans were especially wary of indie bands or artists who signed with big record companies. Among the acts who successfully managed this transition was Beck Hansen, a Los Angeles–based singer-songwriter who recorded several lo-fi records on independent labels in the early 1990s. These early releases included *Golden Feelings* (1993), *Stereopathic Soulmanure* (1994), and *One Foot in the Grave* (1994), which grew out of the "anti-folk" movement in New York, a group of like-minded musicians who were shunned by the folk establishment. During the same period, Beck's single, "Loser" (1993), appeared on the indie label Bong Load to much acclaim within the Southern California indie scene. He then signed with a major label (Geffen) and the single was rereleased, going to number ten in the United States (uk15, 1994). Geffen then released *Mellow Gold* (p13, 1994) and *Odelay* (p16 uk17, 1996). Beck's music blends the lo-fi approach of bands like Guided by Voices with hip-hop, country rock, 1970s soul, and even classical music. Combined with a keen sense for pop hooks, he produced a dizzying succession of styles and stylistic references, often within the same song. Beck's music is often full of samples and rapid shifts created by editing, like much beat-based music from earlier in the decade. Beck continued to enjoy success on the charts and with critics during the second half of the decade with *Mutations* (p13 uk24, 1998) and *Midnite Vultures* (p34 uk19, 1999) and into the new century with *Sea Change* (p8 uk20, 2002) and *Guero* (p2 uk15, 2005). Much like R.E.M. in the late 1980s and Nirvana in the early 1990s, Beck maintained an indie aesthetic while transitioning into the mainstream. As we will see, many more bands began to cross this divide after the turn of the millennium, as distribution of indie records became more sophisticated and fans gained greater access to music from outside the mainstream.

Covering a wide range of music at the end of the twentieth century, this chapter has focused on several important strains. Much of the music discussed above has an outward relationship with music of the past, from the jam bands that incorporated the cultural and musical developments of the Grateful Dead and the Allman Brothers, to female singer-songwriters and teen idols, who extended the traditions of the 1970s and the Motown guy and girl groups. Not only did much of the music of the 1990s refer to older music, but classic-rock radio formatting and reissue sales also celebrated the music of the past. The vast influence of beat-based music was reflected in rock styles during the 1990s, mostly through popular rap–rock groups, which were in tune with both heavy metal and hip-hop. Moreover, the alternative movement that emerged in the early 1990s inspired a series of mainstream rock acts, which were less alternative than popular. Finally, the indie rock movement made great strides during the decade, establishing a variety of styles and aesthetic approaches to rock, such as lo-fi and experimental noise recording techniques. Although it seemed that the musical styles and approaches under the umbrella of rock were ever expanding and limitless, large-scale changes in the music business in the new millennium brought into question many of the practices used to connect popular music to its fans. This digital revolution will be the subject of the next chapter.

FURTHER READING

Bill Brewster and Frank Broughton, *Last Night a DJ Saved My Life: The History of the Disk Jockey* (Grove Press, 2000).

Mark J. Butler, *Unlocking the Groove: Rhythm, Meter, and Musical Design in Electronic Dance Music* (Indiana University Press, 2006).

Nelson George, *Hip Hop America* (Penguin, 1998).

Bruce Haring, *Off the Charts: Ruthless Days and Reckless Nights Inside the Music Industry* (Birch Lane Press, 1996).

Jeff Kitts, Brad Tolinski, and Harold Steinblatt, eds., *Alternative Rock: They Launched a Revolution—and Won!* (Hal Leonard Corporation, 1999).

Kaya Oakes, *Slanted and Enchanted: The Evolution of Indie Culture* (Holt, 2009).

Lucy O'Brien, *She Bop II: The Definitive History of Women in Rock, Pop, and Soul* (Continuum, 2002).

Dick Porter, *Rapcore: The Nu-Metal Fusion* (Plexus, 2003).

Simon Reynolds, *Generation Ecstasy: Into the World of Techno and Rave Culture* (Little, Brown, 1998).

The Vibe History of Hip Hop, edited by Alan Light (Three Rivers Press, 1999).

VISIT STUDYSPACE AT WWNORTON.COM/STUDYSPACE

Access free review material such as:

- music links
- performer info
- practice quizzes
- outlines
- interactive listening guide software

the 2000s

THE NEW MILLENNIUM

It is perhaps fitting that the new millennium began with widespread anxiety that the world's computer networks would fail at midnight on January 1, 2000. Even though this invisible threat (nicknamed Y2K) never came to fruition, the fear it prompted raised to unparalleled heights societal concerns over our reliance on technology. Ironically, less than a year after the Y2K scare, issues stemming from old-fashioned paper-based voting machines marred the United States presidential election contest between Democrat Al Gore and Republican George W. Bush. The election was one of the closest in the history of the United States, with the final tally hinging on results from the state of Florida. After a court-ordered recount, it was determined that many of the paper ballots were punched incompletely, leaving what the media called "hanging chads," which further complicated the close vote. Only after a Supreme Court decision in December, more than a month after what was arguably the most contentious general election in the history of the United States, was George W. Bush named president.

Cultural, religious, and economic differences between the United States and radical terrorist groups boiled over during the early 2000s. Tensions such as these had spawned several attacks on Americans during the 1990s, including an attempted

bombing at the World Trade Center in 1993 and an attack on the military warship USS *Cole* in October 2000. The entire world was stunned on September 11, 2001, when the terrorist network al-Qaeda completed a large-scale attack on the United States, intentionally crashing hijacked airplanes into several landmark buildings. Four airplanes were overtaken mid-flight on this Tuesday morning. One attacked the United States Pentagon building, killing nearly 200 people and severely damaging the center of United States military operations. The terrorists intended to crash a second airplane into the United States Capitol building, but several heroic passengers regained control of the craft before it crashed in rural Pennsylvania, killing all of the passengers. The two airplanes that crashed into the

World Trade Center's "twin tower" buildings, causing them to collapse from the impact and killing nearly 3,000 people, completed the most devastating portion of the attack. The events sent the entire country into a period of mourning, and incited military reactions from the United States that lasted throughout the decade. In October 2001, U.S. forces entered Afghanistan, and in May 2003 troops invaded Iraq. While this "war on terror" was a divisive issue in the United States and abroad, several important outcomes helped to mark the progress of the international effort to challenge terrorist groups, including the capture and execution of Iraqi leader Saddam Hussein.

While troops were fighting terrorism in the Middle East, a devastating natural disaster raised important issues of domestic preparedness and race relations in America. In August 2005, Hurricane Katrina ravaged the Gulf Coast of the United States, causing damage from Texas to the Florida Keys. The city of New Orleans was in the direct path of the storm, and was particularly overwhelmed. The failure of a major levee caused massive flooding in the city and destroyed thousands of homes. Public debate ensued almost immediately over local and federal preparedness for such a disaster, and how the large, mostly poor, African-American community of the Gulf Coast was treated in the aftermath of the storm. However, immediately following the storm, the American and international communities came to the aid of the Gulf Coast, seeking to help this ravaged area. The steadfastness of the region's citizens became a major rallying cry to help rebuild. Perhaps the most fitting symbol of the rejuvenation of New Orleans after Hurricane Katrina was the success of the city's professional football team. Based in the Louisiana Superdome, a structure that suffered major damage during the storm as it served as emergency shelter for thousands of local citizens, the New Orleans Saints won the Super Bowl in February 2010.

Television programming changed dramatically during the first decade of the new millennium. In the year 2000, network television experienced an explosion of "reality" programming. New series such as *Survivor* and *Big Brother* were unscripted shows starring nonactors often placed in competitive situations. Much cheaper than traditional scripted dramas and sitcoms, reality shows were favored by networks, and became extremely popular with American audiences. Throughout the decade the reality formula expanded to include entertainment competitions like *American Idol* and *Dancing with the Stars*, family based shows like *Jon & Kate Plus 8*, and travel contests such as *The Amazing Race*. The reality style even influenced traditional script-based shows, as handheld camera work became more popular, and shows like *The Office* offered reality-style

character testimonials. Amid the reality revolution, which was aimed at the masses, an important group of more ambitious television programming moved to cable networks like HBO, Showtime, and AMC. Moreover, as DVD rentals and on-demand streaming became more popular, viewers began to conceive of these programs as season-long affairs. Perhaps the most successful of these cable-based shows was *The Sopranos*, aired on HBO, which broadcast its highly anticipated final episode in June 2007.

After the dot-com boom of the 1990s, a computer-savvy society began to experiment with new avenues of communication during the 2000s. Video-based chatting over computer networks became common in the middle of the decade, aided greatly by programs like Skype, which was released to the public 2003. Perhaps more important was the concept of social media, which was strongly embraced and led to the popularity of services like Facebook, which first became popular in 2004. Originally used as a method of facilitating communication between college friends, Facebook grew to become a corporate

giant used for interaction between businesses and potential customers. More people turned to cellular phones for communication, often through the ever-growing act of text messaging. And Twitter became a popular social medium after its release in 2005, allowing users to broadcast constant updates, and follow the "tweets" of friends and celebrities alike.

The United States economy grew sharply after a technology-bust low point in early 2003. Contrary to the economic growth of the 1990s, however, this financial boom was based on speculative housing sales and "subprime" lending, or loaning large amounts of money to risky borrowers. These economic practices came to a head in late 2008 when several large financial institutions showed major signs of weakness. A global panic ensued, showing that American financial practices were heavily intertwined with the international economy. Institutions such as Bear Stearns, Lehman Brothers, Fannie Mae, and Freddy Mac, which were considered "too big to fail," were allowed to close, were acquired, or were taken over by the United States government. Two massive government stimulus packages were put into place in an effort to prevent the American economy from collapsing completely. In the process, millions of Americans lost their jobs, housing values plummeted, and many homes were foreclosed upon when borrowers could not maintain (often unfair) lending agreements.

Unlike the close election of George W. Bush at the beginning of the decade, the United States definitively elected Barack Obama as its forty-fourth president in November 2008. The first African-American president in the history of the nation, Obama's victory represented for many the culmination of the civil rights movement of the 1960s. Inheriting a financial crisis and two wars put Obama into a difficult position, and his first two years in office were marred by low approval ratings, especially after his strong endorsement of a comprehensive health care reform act in early 2010. Obama has not shied away from his love of American music, however, featuring noteworthy performances at his inauguration and later White House events by artists such as Stevie Wonder, Aretha Franklin, Paul Simon, Paul McCartney, and Beyoncé. As political and cultural developments continue into the second decade of the new millennium, there are certain constants that seem to be part of the fabric of the American experience. Issues such as technological change, race relations, class struggles, financial swings, and changing entertainment brokers have been constant since the birth of rock music. As all of these factors combined to form a rich culture during the twentieth and twenty-first centuries, rock music has lived on, reacting to change, inspiring ideas, and reflecting immense changes in American culture.

In 2008 the United States elected Barack Obama as its first African-American president. For many, Obama's success represented the culmination of the civil rights movement. Aretha Franklin is pictured here performing at Obama's inauguration in Washington, D.C., which was a fitting tribute that connected 1950s gospel and 1960s southern soul to this victory.

CHAPTER 14

A VERY DIFFERENT INDUSTRY: THE FIRST DECADE OF A NEW MILLENNIUM

We have reached a point in our survey when it becomes increasingly difficult to gain a reliable historical perspective on the development of rock music. Historians often need at least twenty years to pass before an era settles enough for them to determine what the really important elements are—or at least to begin critical and scholarly debate. In this chapter, then, we will survey a variety of styles that made their mark in the 2000s, but we will keep our eye on how these styles fit with some of the themes we have been following throughout the book. Rather than provide a comprehensive survey of the decade, this chapter will consider some important examples of recent rock music and related styles. The focus will be the ways the events and performers in the 2000s extend, repeat, or react against musical styles or other elements that are part of rock's past. While there are clear stylistic and cultural demarcations between mainstream rock, the indie community, beat-based practices, and the country industry, there have also been many important instances of crossover between these styles. More importantly, the entire music industry saw extreme changes as digital media became the preferred method of acquiring and listening to music. On par with the rock revolution of the 1950s, a global change in the way bands reach audiences and listeners enjoy music has shaken the business to its very core, causing many to question the entire infrastructure of the recording industry. It has become increasingly clear during the 2000s that rock music, once considered degenerate noise by cultural gatekeepers, has become celebrated as an integral part of American culture. Acceptance into academic fields and publications like the *New York Times* and the *New Yorker*, the creation of museums and large-scale cultural institutions, and the "canonization" of rock music in Broadway shows and other venues all show how deeply rooted this music has become in the American national identity.

The role of rock music in gaming has become highly interactive in the 2000s. The most popular video game to incorporate rock is *Guitar Hero*, an interactive game that requires players to simulate guitar performance. *Guitar Hero* and the later *Rock Band* became extremely popular methods of exposure for old and new rock. Several of the largest marketing deals of the decade have surrounded content for these interactive video games. The largest and most significant *Rock Band* release was *The Beatles: Rock Band* in 2009, which accompanied a long-awaited set of the group's remastered recordings. Here, players are pictured trying out *The Beatles: Rock Band* at a Los Angeles trade show. The popularity of interactive music games has drawn criticism from many rock purists, who see these games as an inadequate substitute for the long tradition of amateur music performance in rock. Yet, devotees maintain that interactive games have exposed millions of gamers to the joys of rock performance and distributed rock music to a wide variety of listeners.

TECHNOLOGY AND ROCK

Changing Systems of Production and Consumption. The development of digital technology has had broad and far-reaching effects on popular music. Like the wave of independent labels in the 1950s and the DIY revolution of the 1970s, during the 1990s digital recording made it possible for almost any artist or band to record an album inexpensively. Techniques associated with digital tools such as sampling and sequencing revolutionized how music was created. While the technological creation of music had become commonplace by the turn of the millennium, the next frontier became electronic distribution. One of the first important methods of Internet distribution to emerge was the traditional online sale. Rather than traveling to a physical retail space, consumers began using online retailers to purchase CDs, and have them shipped directly to a home or office. Harkening back to the days of catalog retail, which existed as far back as the late nineteenth century, this form of distribution became popular in the second half of the 1990s after the dot-com boom in the earlier part of the decade. Although this practice is widespread in today's economy, online retail took some time to gain ground, as consumers questioned the security of this form of commerce. After years of losing money, for example, the popular online shopping company Amazon turned a profit for the first time in 2001. Today, Amazon is the largest retailer in the world with sales of nearly $25 billion in 2009.

While the Internet facilitated online sales of physical CDs, an entire generation of listeners began to experiment with sharing music in the form of electronic files. Encoding music into a digital file format had been possible for some time, but several technological developments in the 1990s helped facilitate the easy transfer of music. The widespread use of the MP3, a highly compressed format that can greatly reduce the size of a music file, allowed users to send music through email or create collections of data files with hundreds of songs on a single CD. With these smaller, more manageable music files, file-sharing services emerged to facilitate trading between users. The most popular and notorious of these services was Napster, a peer-to-peer file-sharing program that allowed users to download files quickly and easily from other users. The use of Napster and other peer-to-peer file sharing services such as Limewire and Gnutella grew dramatically at the turn of the millennium, causing a massive free-for-all of music trading and changing the relationship between the music industry and its customers. There were clear advantages and disadvantages to the Napster revolution. On one hand, listeners gained access to more music than ever, sampling songs that they might not consider buying and easily suggesting music to friends. In this way, peer-to-peer networking was a democratizing force which decentralized the power of major labels, placing distribution at the fingertips of listeners. We can read evidence of this viewpoint in a widely distributed lecture-turned-article by Courtney Love called "Courtney Does the Math" from 2000, which is based on an earlier essay by indie rock producer Steve Albini called the "Problem with Music." The perspectives of both Love and Albini reflect common claims of musicians who distrust the music industry, citing specific examples of how the industry mistreats artists.

However, there were also tremendous drawbacks to these networks. For one, trading music through Napster and other peer-to-peer services was illegal, and a

decade of litigation proved that both users and those who developed these systems violated copyright laws. Several important issues arose from this widespread illegal activity. Musicians, songwriters, and record companies lost a tremendous amount of revenue. While many groups certainly received great exposure from peer-to-peer trading, they were not being paid for their services. Bands spoke out publicly against the practice and filed lawsuits to challenge Napster's activities. The most famous of these, Metallica, faced a public relations nightmare when their actions were perceived as evidence of music industry greed. When Napster was forced to shut down in July 2001, the die had already been cast. Although illegal trading continues to flourish, mostly through difficult-to-monitor decentralized networking protocols such as BitTorrent, this accounts for a much smaller share of revenue than when Napster was at its peak. In just two short years of activity, Napster challenged the very fabric of the music industry business model. The most important result of the Napster revolution was a large-scale decline in sales of physical media. Throughout the first decade of the 2000s, sales of compact discs decreased by almost two-thirds from the peak years at the end of the 1990s as listeners began to buy music in digital forms.

As digital files became an important method of consuming music, a new sector of the music industry developed to support listeners' technological needs. A variety of portable music players flooded the market in the late 1990s and early 2000s, allowing users to access an immense amount of music using an extremely small device. Users also became interested in computer software that allowed them to organize their files on a computer. In January 2001, in the midst of the controversy surrounding Napster, the computer company Apple launched a new application called iTunes. Like competitors Musicmatch and Winamp, iTunes was originally designed as Apple-only "jukebox software," which assisted users in managing their digital music files. Later that year, the company introduced the first of its revolutionary iPod music players. In 2003 Apple opened its "iTunes Store," which allowed users to purchase music files legally, downloading them directly through iTunes software, and place them on the iPod, which had become the industry-

MUSIC UNITS SHIPPED

| VINYL ALBUM | 8-TRACK ALBUM | CASSETTE ALBUM | CD ALBUM | DOWNLOAD ALBUM |

12"

| VINYL SINGLE | | | | DOWNLOAD SINGLE |

7"

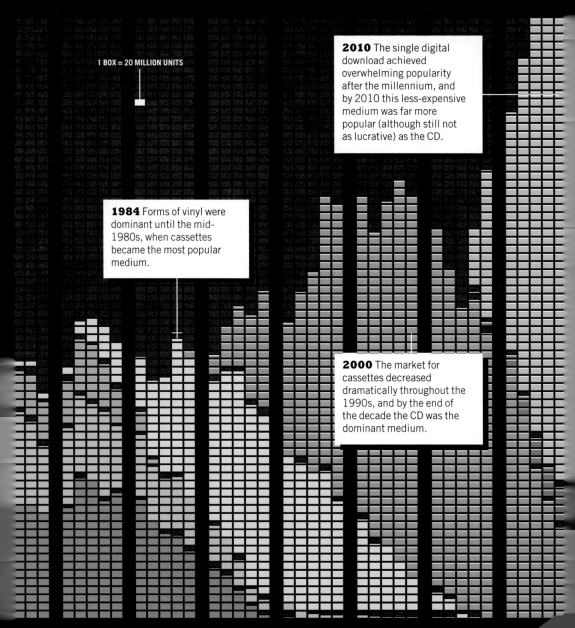

This chart uses data from the Recording Industry Association of America (RIAA) to depict large-scale trends in the number of "units" shipped to stores between 1973 and 2010. For the sake of clarity, marginal media such as CD and cassette singles have been omitted from the data. Also note that singles and albums have a much different value in the marketplace.

1 BOX = 20 MILLION UNITS

2010 The single digital download achieved overwhelming popularity after the millennium, and by 2010 this less-expensive medium was far more popular (although still not as lucrative) as the CD.

1984 Forms of vinyl were dominant until the mid-1980s, when cassettes became the most popular medium.

2000 The market for cassettes decreased dramatically throughout the 1990s, and by the end of the decade the CD was the dominant medium.

Portable music players flooded the market in the late 1990s and early 2000s, allowing users access to an immense amount of music using an extremely small device. The most popular of these was Apple's iPod. Pictured here is an early iPod from the Macworld Expo trade show in 2002. Through its "iTunes Store" Apple became the industry leader in Internet music sales. As of February 2010, the company has sold more than 10 billion music downloads through the iTunes Store.

iPod.
1,000 songs.
In your pocket.
Now with
2,000 songs.

leading portable device. Although other companies sold products to do all of these things, Apple quickly became the most popular technological music retailer, selling 25 million downloads through the iTunes Store before the end of 2003. What seemed to be a fringe industry exploded during the 2000s, as Apple quickly integrated video, gaming, and other computer applications into its iTunes Store and various handheld devices. As a result of this change in purchasing, in 2005 *Billboard* began to publish digital download charts, and incorporate these figures into its data for the "Hot 100" chart. Moreover, iTunes charts became the best place to find the pulse of the current music industry. Offering music, television and films, podcasts, audio books, educational initiatives, social networking, and a wide variety of "apps" (applications), Apple is now the largest music retailer in the United States. As of February 2010, the company has sold more that 10 billion music downloads through the iTunes Store and sales of digital singles now dwarf sales of traditional compact discs.

Changing Conceptions of Media: Rock Is Nowhere, but It's Also Everywhere. During the emergence of rock in the 1950s listeners encountered the new form in traditional places like AM radio, local dances, and record stores. Fifty years later, it is hard to find rock music in any of these places. Terrestrial radio has changed dramatically since the addition of FM, moving further into the concept of format radio that created classic-rock radio in the 1980s. Commercial stations now follow even broader formats such as "classic hits" and "hot adult contemporary," and are often nationally syndicated and out of touch with local communities. More and more listeners are turning to Internet and satellite radio as sources for rock music. The Internet allows traditional stations to stream online to anywhere in the world, and has provided a forum for thousands of new Internet-only stations. Perhaps the most interesting manifestation of the Internet radio community has been the emergence of Pandora, a service that works from data collected through a large-scale encoding initiative called the Music Genome Project. Working from a starting point entered by the user (an artist, song, or genre) and the user's taste, Pandora provides personalized radio stations and suggestions for potential new music purchases. More recent services that allow for listener-based and on-demand listening over the Internet are Spotify and last.fm. At the beginning of the 2000s, a more advanced commercial-free system of satellite radio also became available to listeners in the United States through both XM and Sirius (which have since merged into a single company). Offering more breadth than traditional commercial radio, these stations found immediate success with fans of rock music and steadily increased programming to include sports, talk, and other entertainment programming.

Rock concert promotion has also come a long way from the local sock hop or senior prom. Now a multibillion-dollar business, tickets to see a mainstream rock act are priced well beyond the budget of the average teenager, targeting instead the baby boomer generation with expendable resources. Large conglomerate corporations such as Live Nation have become the industry standard, signing artists to lucrative long-term contracts, commanding huge profits from concert tours, and purchasing (or merging with) other powerful industry players like Ticketmaster and House of Blues. Even the indie-rock circuit has become more industry savvy in the last decade, with a series of lucrative reunion tours by bands like the Pixies and Guided by Voices. We might view the October 2010 Matador Records twenty-first birthday celebration in Las Vegas as a bellwether of this change in indie values. Although marketed as an ironic venue for an independent powerhouse, a concert such as this, which featured a $400 VIP ticket option, shows the maturation and financial reach of the modern indie community. More and more, as concert promotion becomes big business, rock shows are becoming less accessible to the average fan. Rather than seeing bands live, rock listeners often make contact with their favorite groups through digital means. In the early 2000s, the advent of music-specific social networking sites such as MySpace allowed bands to communicate directly with listeners, offering up-to-the minute news, blog posts, free samples of new music, and premium tracks not offered on CDs or iTunes. The growth of You-Tube has also drastically changed how bands interact with listeners. Official music videos are now archived for instant access. Listeners participate in the creative process by creating their own videos and combinations of existing songs (often called mashups). Historic live concert footage is now widely available, new performances are often uploaded within days (or even hours) after live events, and special video broadcasts are streamed live over the Internet.

A final change has occurred in the death of the traditional record store. Once the center of rock culture, teeming with knowledgeable (and sometimes conceited) experts in the history of popular music, the independent record store has seen a slow and painful decline since the beginning of the 1990s. Mall chains, big-box stores such as Best Buy and Wal-Mart, and the rise of Internet commerce have had a crippling effect on independent record stores. The few surviving relics of this bygone age are located in college towns and large urban environments, and are mostly geared toward an indie rock audience. Even these markets have had a difficult time supporting independent music retailers, since the prices of digital downloads and CDs at large retail outlets are invariably cheaper than those offered at small record shops. Physical media itself is on the decline, as more listeners are content to purchase music in digital form. Although CD sales are still greater than digital download purchases, sales of physical units are declining while digital media are increasing year after year. Before long, the digital download will certainly become the predominant form of media in the American music industry.

All of this might lead us to believe that rock music is on the decline. Yet, while traditional rock music sales are declining, exposure to rock music is increasing. Mirroring the digital revolution at the end of the twentieth century that challenged delivery methods for most forms of entertainment media, rock music has become the center of a burgeoning industry that sells music as intellectual property. Com-

mercial advertising has come to value rock music as a means to sell products to a variety of demographics. Whether it is the Rolling Stones selling Microsoft products, Bob Dylan selling Victoria's Secret underwear, or Sting selling Jaguar automobiles, older rock musicians have grown increasingly tolerant of using their most famous songs in advertising. Modern artists like Train have even used television advertising to cross-promote their newest music: "Hey Soul Sister" was simultaneously on the record charts and featured in Samsung television commercials. This practice is by no means limited to classic rock or mainstream, as indie music has been incredibly popular with advertisers and television networks seeking a hip edge. At the beginning of the 2000s, a burgeoning cellular telephone ringtone market also exposed listeners to rock music in unconventional places, as audible ringtones pervaded public spaces and ringback tones (the sound you hear when you are waiting for someone to pick up the phone) allowed fans to share their favorite music with friends. Perhaps the most fascinating new market for rock music has been in the gaming industry, as new and old music alike have become soundtracks for the latest video games for the Xbox, PlayStation, or Wii. The role of rock music in gaming has also become highly interactive. Beginning in the early 2000s, "machine dance" games such as *Dance Dance Revolution* became important venues for new music. Perhaps the most popular video game to incorporate rock was *Guitar Hero*, which was first released in 2005. An interactive game that requires players to simulate guitar performance, *Guitar Hero* and the later *Rock Band* (which expanded instrumentation to include bass, drums, vocals, and keyboards) became extremely popular methods of exposure for old and new rock alike. Through the addition of downloadable content the library of available songs for *Rock Band* extends into the thousands, and several of the largest marketing deals of the decade have surrounded content for these interactive video games. The largest and most significant *Rock Band* release was *The Beatles: Rock Band* in 2009, which accompanied a long-awaited set of the

ROCK MUSIC AND TECHNOLOGY

by Mark Katz

In a crowded dorm room a group of students play plastic instruments while staring at a TV screen. The instruments look like toys, and for good reason: this is a video game. It could be *Guitar Hero* or *Rock Band* or any of their successors. They might be manipulating a small plastic turntable while playing *DJ Hero*; perhaps they're not using controllers at all, instead waving their limbs wildly according to onscreen instructions. How do we make sense of all this impassioned flailing? What they're doing is not exactly like playing traditional musical instruments. Their gestures are clearly connected to the music they hear, but they're activating prerecorded sounds rather than creating their own music. But if they're not true instrumentalists, they're also not mere listeners. Playing music video games might be called collaborative performance, or more simply co-performance, but whatever it's called, it's a hugely popular phenomenon that is opening up distinctive ways of engaging with music to millions of people.

In a computer lab a headphone-wearing student sits in front of a monitor, using a mouse to create and manipulate sounds. She may be using any of dozens of programs, whether free, cheap (Audacity, GarageBand), or more costly (Ableton, ProTools, Reason). She may be layering short prerecorded musical fragments, or loops, to create a new composition; she may be mixing a song recorded with her band, adjusting the balance and editing out mistakes; she may be remixing the latest dance club hit, changing the rhythm and tempo to put a new spin on it; or she may be concocting a mashup by combining the instrumental track of one song with the vocals of a different song. When she's done she's likely to share her work, whether by emailing it to friends, posting it to her blog, or uploading it to a social networking or video-sharing site. Within minutes, people she has never met are listening to and commenting on her work.

Sharing one's own music is not nearly as common as sharing other people's music, and since the late 1990s and the rise of Napster, file-sharing has been an enormously popular and hotly contested activity, especially on college campuses. At any given moment there are students sitting in front of their computers, sending and receiving MP3s and other digital music files, without payment and without permission. Some have had their campus network privileges revoked, a few have been sued, but most encounter no trouble along the way. Students are often conflicted about file-sharing—they know it can be illegal, but it doesn't feel like stealing (and technically it's unauthorized copying and distribution, not theft). Illegal file-sharing isn't the only way to experience music on the Internet without paying for it, however. More and more, students are going to video-sharing sites such as YouTube, or Internet radio and music recommendation sites like Grooveshark or Pandora, to get their fill of tunes without downloading—or paying—a thing. And of course, many are paying to download through online music stores, using Amazon, iTunes, or any of the numerous other pay sites. However the music is being acquired, this kind of activity is rapidly replacing the increasingly old-fashioned ritual of going to stores and buying physical recordings, with enormous consequences for the way we all experience and think about music.

One consequence of the move from physical recordings to sound files is that we can easily carry immense collections of music wherever we go. To walk across a typical campus is to see ear-budded students immersed in their own private soundtracks, often oblivious to their surroundings. Music was once an almost totally social activity, but now listening in solitude (even if surrounded by others) is increasingly the norm. While we may celebrate this as tremendously convenient, there are legitimate concerns about the loss of the communal aspects of music (not to mention hearing loss) arising from so much solitary listening.

A century ago, Americans debated the value of the still-young technology of sound recording. (Thomas Edison had invented the phonograph in 1877, but it hadn't come to influence musical life until the early 1900s.) Some saw great possibilities in the technology, endowing it with an almost magical ability to bring great music to the world. Others viewed it as a threat. The composer and band leader John Philip Sousa famously condemned it as a menace, declaring that no one would make music themselves when machines could do it for them. Neither side was clearly right or wrong. The type of music-making that Sousa cared about—parlor piano recitals, town band performances and the like— has clearly waned since his time. Yet he was wrong about the broad effect of technology on amateur musicians, for today millions of people are not only making music simply for the love of it, but they are using the latest technology to do so. On the other hand, it is hard to sustain the argument that technology has made America a "more musical nation"—as some contended a century ago—when the Internet music videos that enjoy the most views (often running into the tens of millions) are routinely denounced as the worst modern culture has to offer.

In the end, neither a utopian nor a dystopian view of music technology is warranted. This was true in the early twentieth century and it is true in the early twenty-first century. Technology can open up unimagined musical possibilities but can also cheapen music, rendering it an easily disposable commodity. Whatever new technologies emerge, two constants remain, one sobering, the other hopeful: the scarcity of truly great talent (and music), and the deep-seated need to seek out meaningful musical experiences. Technology will neither increase the former nor diminish the latter.

Mark Katz teaches at the University of North Carolina at Chapel Hill. He is the author of Capturing Sound: How Technology has Changed Music and Groove Music: The Art and Culture of the Hip-Hop DJ, *and is editor of the* Journal of the Society for American Music.

Performance-based video games became extremely popular during the 2000s, allowing a large community of gamers to experience amateur performance in a new way. Here, Jay-Z plays *DJ Hero* during a New York press conference in October 2009.

Viewing Rock

The music video became decentralized in the 2000s, as Internet sites such as YouTube replaced cable-based stations as the most convenient portals for video performances. Thus, documentaries, interviews, and official music videos (in addition to unofficial fan-created ones) all became available on demand in the same Internet spaces, blurring the line between historic and new performances, in addition to genres that had previously been separated on television. Yet

direct the 2006 feature film *Idlewild*, which also featured members of OutKast. "Hey Ya" depicts a live television performance by André 3000 on a 1960s-type British television show, offering a reversal of the typical British invasion appearance on television in the United States. André 3000 performed all of the instruments on "Hey Ya," and through video trickery he also performs as every member of the band in "Hey Ya." The contrast provided between a black and

white television monitor and the live band in vivid green-hued color offers a statement on the difference between classic and modern popular music (1).

Like many films that show older television shows being viewed in the home, "Hey Ya" frequently cuts to a family viewing the program in their living room and dancing along (2).

To make the British invasion connection even more clear, each member of the band is introduced through captions, drawing from the famous appearance of the Beatles on the Ed Sullivan variety show when John Lennon's photo was accompanied by the phrase "sorry girls, he's married" (3).

Eventually, the studio audience plays an important role in the video, especially during the part of the song when the lyrics encourage dancers to "shake it like a Polaroid picture" (4).

artists still made important contributions the music video genre, showing the staying power of the three-to-four minute promotional clip that had become standard in the previous twenty years. One of the most interesting examples of the early 2000s was OutKast's video for "Hey Ya," directed by Bryan Barber, who would later write and

Although the music video has become decentralized from its former MTV home, it has clearly not lost the potential to portray artists in a vivid manner, provide creative commentary on current music, and situate current music in a historical context.

group's remastered recordings. The popularity of interactive music games, especially *Guitar Hero* and *Rock Band*, has drawn criticism from many rock purists, who see these games as an inadequate substitute for the long tradition of amateur music performance in rock. However, devotees of these games maintain that the intricate musical ability required to play these games at their highest levels (especially in the area of rhythm) has exposed millions of gamers to the joys of rock performance.

Regardless of your take on the *Guitar Hero* phenomenon, it is certain that this series of games, in addition to commercial advertising and the ringtone market, have distributed rock music to a wide variety of listeners, even as rock record sales have suffered in the 2000s.

MAINSTREAM ROCK IN THE NEW MILLENNIUM

From Sk8ers to Idols: Avril Lavigne, P!nk, and Kelly Clarkson. Many popular styles of rock pervaded the American mainstream during the 2000s. Unlike rock's early years, which often featured the voices of women filtered through a male production team, the unadulterated female perspective became common after the turn of the millennium. There was a wide range of important female performers during the decade, reflecting an increasingly diverse listenership that viewed femininity from a variety of perspectives through the medium of rock music. At one end of the musical spectrum was the Canadian teenager Avril Lavigne, who emerged in the summer of 2002 with the album *Let's Go* (p2 uk1) and the single "Complicated" (p2 uk3). Lavigne wrote and performed her own music (often with the songwriting team of the Matrix), which echoed early 1990s California pop punk music. A series of number-one pop albums in the United States and United Kingdom followed, including *Under My Skin* (2004) and *The Best Damn Thing* (2007), producing hit singles like "Sk8er Boi" (p10 uk8, 2002), "I'm with You" (p4 uk7, 2002), and "Girlfriend" (p1 uk2, 2007). In light of her status as a teen sensation, Lavigne was also notable for her style of dress, often wearing dark, baggy clothing that cloaked her body. This stance served as a pillar of Lavigne's self-promotion and flew in the face of the age-old tradition of sensual female teenage artists.

While Lavigne displayed an early interest in a popular style of music indebted to the punk tradition, vocalist and songwriter P!nk became popular at the beginning of the decade with music from the beat-based community. As a protégé of R&B pioneer L.A. Reid, P!nk's debut album, *Can't Take Me Home* (p26 r23 uk13, 2000), was firmly in the tradition of pop divas and R&B girl groups like TLC and Destiny's Child. Yet, as the decade wore on, P!nk became more involved in her musical output, infusing a distinct rock element into her later albums. Singles such as "Get the Party Started" (p4 uk2, 2001) and "Don't Let Me Get Me" (p8 uk6, 2002) show a much harder vocal style, distorted guitars, and autobiographical lyrics that describe her desire to move away from cookie-cutter pop into more adventurous material. Even the title of P!nk's second album, *Missundaztood* (p6 uk2, 2002), supports this position. Later singles such as "So What" (p1 uk1, 2008), "Sober" (p15 uk9, 2008), and "Raise Your Glass" (p1 uk13, 2010) continue this powerful sense of lyrical ownership based on authenticity and stylistic diversity. Like Lavigne, P!nk's outward ownership of her music also encapsulated the treatment of her image and her stance on femininity in popular music, while still maintaining a strong connection to fashion. Perhaps the best example of her perspective can be found in the song "Stupid Girls" (p13 uk4, 2006) and its accompanying music video, which cite an "epidemic" of young women who lack individuality and ambition.

An autobiographical theme of being trapped in the music industry machine is also present in the output of Kelly Clarkson. As the winner of the first season of the television show *American Idol*, Clarkson was immediately thrust into the industry limelight, releasing her first album, *Thankful*, in the summer of 2002. Much like the diverse vocal styles required of a successful *American Idol* contestant, the music contained on *Thankful* was chock full of mainstream pop songs and covers that highlighted Clarkson's vocal acrobatics. Her next album, *Breakaway* (p3 uk3, 2004), highlighted her move away from the beat-based pop music of *American Idol* toward a more decidedly rock sound drenched with heavy drums, distorted guitars, and anthemic vocals. Singles such as "Since U Been Gone" (p2 uk5, 2004), "Behind Those Hazel Eyes" (p6 uk9, 2005), and "Because of You" (p7 uk7, 2005) highlighted Clarkson's new approach. The lead single on the album, "Breakaway" (p6 uk22, 2004), was cowritten with a group of songwriters that included Avril Lavigne, who had hoped to record the song for her own debut album. As we see in the music of Lavigne, P!nk, and Clarkson, the female voice thrived in mainstream rock music during the 2000s, as women found new avenues to assert their perspectives in a his-

Avril Lavigne performing live in 2004. Lavigne writes and performs much of her own music, which combines aspects of pop punk with mainstream rock and a unique sense of fashion.

torically chauvinistic musical style. Moreover, comparing the perspectives of these three artists with the typical female image proffered during the 1950s, we can see how dramatically different female voices have become in American society during the rock era.

Men at Work: Maroon 5, John Mayer, and Coldplay. Among the increasingly crowded field of female rockers, several middle-of-the-road male artists rose to popularity in the 2000s performing traditional brands of rock. Known as much for their good looks and personal relationships as their music, artists such as Maroon 5, John Mayer, and Coldplay found success during the decade, exhibiting clear debts to earlier styles. Maroon 5 emerged from Los Angeles in the early part of the decade after an unsuccessful stint as the band Kara's Flowers. Mixing strains of R&B and funk with heavier rock, the group featured lead singer and songwriter Adam Levine. Maroon 5's first album, *Songs about Jane* (p6 uk1), was released in the summer of 2002, along with the funk-rock single "Harder to Breathe" (p18 uk13). It took several years of incessant touring before the group achieved national popularity in early 2004 with the singles "This Love" (p5 uk3) and "She Will Be Loved" (p5 uk4). *Songs about Jane* would go on to sell more than 4 million copies in the United States and, despite the fact that the album was released two years earlier, the group won the Best New Artist Grammy Award in 2005. Debuting at the top of the *Billboard* pop album charts, the group's later albums, *It Won't Be Soon Before Long* (p1 uk1, 2007) and *Hands All Over* (p2 uk6, 2010), departed from the harder edge of *Songs about Jane*, focusing instead on dance influences. This change is apparent in the singles "Makes Me Wonder" (p1 uk2, 2007) and "Misery" (p14 uk30, 2010), which subdue heavier rock elements to focus on Levine's vocals and a more beat-based approach.

John Mayer released his first album, *Room for Squares*, through the independent Aware label in 2001 before signing to Columbia. A former student at Boston's Berklee School of Music, Mayer was no stranger to the history of rock, becoming proficient as a songwriter and guitarist in a number of styles during his studies.

With all four of his studio albums reaching the *Billboard* Top 10, and a long string of Top 20 singles, Mayer's traditional approach to pop writing and performing has made him one of the best-selling rock artists of the decade. Songs such as "No Such Thing" (p13, 2003), "Daughters" (p19, 2004), and "Waiting on the World to Change" (p14, 2006) featured some of the most intricate and audible guitar heard on mainstream radio during the 2000s, often drawing heavy influences from the blues tradition. The sonic space left on many of Mayer's recordings, which lack the layers of instruments that have become standard in twenty-first century production, makes his style seem old-fashioned.

While Mayer is clearly a student of the blues, the British group Coldplay came out of the Britpop tradition. Fronted by singer and multi-instrumentalist Chris Martin, Coldplay broke into the American market in mid-2000 with the single "Yellow" (p48 uk4). Drawing heavily on the style of Radiohead and Jeff Buckley, the group's debut album, *Parachutes* (p51 uk1, 2000), became a smash hit in the UK, and slowly sold more than two million copies in the United States. Increasing in popularity throughout the 2000s, the band released three more albums, the last of which, *Viva La Vida or Death and All His Friends* (p1 uk1, 2008) contained the hit single "Viva La Vida" (p1 uk1, 2008) and won 2009 Grammy Awards for Best Album and Best Song, respectively. The group's style changed slowly throughout the decade, morphing from a focus on Radiohead-like experimental Britpop to more mainstream concerns, all the while featuring the vocal presence of Martin, the group's leader and most visible member.

Heavy Legacies: Evanescence, Linkin Park, Hoobastank, and Nickelback.

Heavier forms of rock also thrived in the 2000s, drawing on the legacies of pop punk, rap rock, and alternative. Fronted by vocalist Amy Lee and guitarist Ben Moody (who departed the group in 2003), Arkansas-based Evanescence offered a fascinating blend of heavy music, piano-based balladry, rap, and gothic metal. The group's first album, *Fallen* (p3 uk1), sold more than 7 million copies in the United States, and contained two hit singles that differed drastically in style, showing the band's musical range. "Bring Me to Life" (p5 uk1, 2003) is based on a heavy distorted guitar riff and background rapping, and the band at times approaches the sonic quality of Korn or System of a Down. The notable difference between Evanescence and these heavier groups is the vocal style of Lee, who sings full-voiced with no characteristic Nu Metal growl. The group's next single, "My Immortal" (p7 uk7, 2003), could not have been more different. A ballad that features the piano and vocals of Lee until the full band accompaniment enters

John Mayer during a 2008 performance in England. Mayer's masterful guitar performance and simplistic production give his music an old-fashioned sense. Despite these obvious connections to the past, Mayer was one of the most popular male rock artists of the 2000s.

nearly three-quarters of the way through the track, the song resembles Sarah McLachlan more than Limp Bizkit, showing the immense diversity of the group's influences. Evanescence continued their success in 2006 with the release of *The Open Door* (p1 uk2), which included the hit single "Call Me When You're Sober" (p10 uk4).

Although Evanescence flirted with Nu Metal, Linkin Park was a group fully enmeshed in this style. Linkin Park achieved popularity alongside groups like Korn and System of a Down at the turn of the millennium, but they have persisted longer than any of these groups at the highest level of the music business, maintaining a steady career since the release of their debut album *Hybrid Theory* (p2 uk4, 2000). This might be due to their more accessible sound, which features less aggressive rapping by Mike Shinoda and more melodic vocal parts performed by Chester Bennington. This mix can be found on the group's best-known single "In the End" (p2 uk8, 2001). Later albums *Meteora* (2003), *Minutes to Midnight* (2007), and *A Thousand Suns* (2010) all rose to the top of the American album charts, producing hits such as "Numb" (p11 uk14, 2003) and "New Divide" (p6 uk19, 2009). Formed in Agoura Hills, California (the same town as Linkin Park), Hoobastank worked in a similar mainstream style of rap metal. After touring with Linkin Park in 2004, their single "The Reason" (2004) became an international hit, rising to the number two spot on the *Billboard* "Hot 100" (uk12).

The Canadian group Nickelback is another example of a popular group that focused on heavier forms of rock. Employing traditional rock instrumentation and vocal styles, Nickelback released two albums in Canada before reaching the international mainstream. The first successful Nickelback album, *Silver Side Up* (p2 uk1), appeared in stores on September 11, 2001 and included the single "How You Remind Me" (p1 uk4), which went on to become one of the most popular songs of the year. Later albums *The Long Road* (p6 uk5, 2003), *All the Right Reasons* (p1 uk2, 2005), and *Dark Horse* (p2 uk4, 2008) all rose to the upper echelons of the American charts, while consistently topping Canadian sales marks. Like many of the Nu Metal bands that mined connections between rock and hip-hop, Nickelback began to explore more of a country influence as the decade progressed. Singles such as "Rockstar" (p6 uk2, 2006) achieve this by including spoken vocal interludes by ZZ Top guitarist and vocalist Billy Gibbons. Country traditions are also apparent in the 2005 single "Photograph" (p2 uk18). Although the musical language of the

Listening Guide

Nickelback, "Photograph" Roadrunner 8300

Words by Chad Kroeger. Music by Chad Kroeger, Ryan Peake, Mike Kroeger, and Daniel Adair. Produced by Nickelback and Joey Moi. Rose to #2 on the *Billboard* "Hot 100" chart in 2006. Single available only as a digital download.

FORM: Compound AABA. Note the consistent use of four-measure phrases throughout the song, which sets the listener up for several notable exceptions to this regular pattern, most notably the shortened verse 6. After the completion of the AABA form, the last verse acts as a surprise return. Note also the use of the same instrumentation and lyrical passage "Look at this photograph" for the first and final verses, forming a cyclical structure common in country music.

TIME SIGNATURE: 4/4.

INSTRUMENTATION: Acoustic guitar, bass, electric guitar, drums, lead and background vocals. Notice in the first seconds of the song how multiple guitar and vocal performances are used simultaneously (multitracked).

A	0:00–0:27	**Verse 1**, 8 mm.	The song begins with no introduction, featuring immediately multi-tracked acoustic guitar and vocals. The lyrics draw the listener immediately to images of the past. Notice how the verses are constructed of two 4-measure groups. The full band enters at the beginning of the second group. "Look at this photograph . . ."
	0:27–0:59	**Verse 2**, 10 mm.	More specific childhood references; the same instrumentation continues. The end of the second 4-bar cycle is extended by 2 bars to create a dramatic anticipation for the chorus (0:53–0:59). "This is where I went to school . . ."

Guitarist Chad Kroeger of the group Nickelback performs with Z.Z. Top guitarist Billy Gibbons in 2008. A mainstream rock band, Nickelback explored country and southern rock influences in the mid-2000s.

Get Music ⓢ wwnorton.com/studyspace

	0:59–1:26	**Chorus**, 8 mm.	The instrumentation becomes more intense to reflect the general nature of the chorus section. It is as if in each of these sections the protagonist is stepping back from the scene to contemplate. "Every memory . . ."
	1:26–1:40	**Interlude**, 4 mm.	A simple acoustic guitar solo over a chord progression slightly different from the one used as the basis for the verse and chorus.
A	1:40–2:07	**Verse 3**, 8 mm.	Same instrumentation as verse 2. "Remember the old arcade . . ."
	2:07–2:27	**Verse 4**, 6 mm	A shorter verse with only a single cycle through the chord progression and the same extension as verse 2. "Kim's the first girl I kissed . . ."
	2:27–3:00	**Chorus**, 10 mm.	Same as first chorus with a 2-measure extension (which is similar to the end of the interlude, 1:33–1:40). "Every memory . . ."
B	3:00–3:27	**Bridge**, 8 mm.	Contrasting chord progression taken from the interlude (repeated twice). Notice the two distinct melody lines happening simultaneously singing the same lyrics. "I miss that town . . ."
A	3:27–3:35	**Verse 5**, 3 mm.	A verse segment shortened even more than verse 4. With a momentary change to the original instrumentation it seems as if this might signal the end of the song. The odd phrase length leads to a surprising return to the final chorus. Note the vocals that pan from left to right, 3:33–3:35
	3:35–4:03	**Chorus**, 8 mm.	Like the first two choruses, with an extra vocal melody over "hard to say it, time to say it . . ."
	4:03–4:18	**Verse 6**, 4 mm.	A return to the original opening line and instrumentation signals a return to the beginning, a common technique in country music that represents the "cycle of life." "Look at this photograph . . ."

song is purely mainstream rock, the subject matter draws heavily on the country tradition, reminiscing about youthful pleasures and bygone memories of high school. Filmed in Hanna, Alberta, hometown of band members Chad and Mike Kroeger, the video reinforces the sentimental quality of the song, revealing many of the actual spaces recalled in the lyrics.

In late 2004, a news story surfaced about Nickelback that is particularly revealing for our study of rock. A Canadian fan named Mikey Smith noticed similarities between the Nickelback songs "How You Remind Me" and "Someday," and after combining the two tracks into a single audio file, noticed that they shared strikingly similar musical traits. The new audio track, affectionately called "How You Remind Me of Someday," became an Internet sensation, causing many listeners to question the group's creative integrity. Reports followed accusing Nickelback of cheating fans by recycling the same song. As students of rock, we might use the tools of analyzing song form, instrumentation, and recording techniques to delve further into this controversy. What traits do these songs share, and what is original about each? Moreover, can you find other examples of music by the same artist that follows similar patterns of form and instrumentation? Members of Nickelback have attributed these likenesses to a "distinct style," similar to other classic rock bands. Given the similarities within the catalogs of artists such as Little Richard, Chuck Berry, and the Beatles, is it right to vilify a band like Nickelback for reproducing a song in their own style? If not, we may want to consider what kinds cultural forces might have inspired this attack.

COUNTRY AND BEAT-BASED STYLES

Country Rocks: Keith Urban, Taylor Swift, and Carrie Underwood. The complex relationship between rock and country continued well into the new century. Like the rockabilly of the 1950s and the 1970s music created by the avocado mafia, the last decade has offered several important examples of rock that are especially indebted to country music. Not only did many rock groups draw from the country tradition, as we have seen in the music of Nickelback, but many country artists also incorporated rock styles into their songs. In fact, as beat-based styles dominated the pop charts in the 1990s and 2000s, country music was arguably the bearer of many musical traditions that had fallen out of favor in rock. The extended guitar solo, for example, was common in country hits and rare in the pop-oriented rock of the 2000s. As much of the rock on the radio incorporated dark themes, heavy distortion, rappers and disc jockeys, the country mainstream seemed closer to classic rock than ever before. This was aided by a movement in country culture that accepted artists who did not conform to traditional western dress styles. With country artists wearing uncharacteristic clothing and performing solid pop songs supported by electric guitars and loud drum kits, the country and rock traditions melded. In the 1990s artists such as Shania Twain and Garth Brooks had made inroads into the popular mainstream while maintaining industry-leading support from country fans. But a new generation of country crossover artists in the 2000s forged even greater connections between country and rock styles.

New Zealand-born Keith Urban is one example of a crossover country artist who embodies many attributes that rock fans find attractive. In addition to his dashing good looks (and rare cowboy hat), Urban is a talented and flashy guitarist who performs in a high-energy rock style. After moving to Nashville in the early 1990s and working his way through the business, Urban became a mainstay on the country charts in the early 2000s, releasing more than twenty Top 10 singles in the last decade. His first exposure to a mainstream audience came at the end of 2004 with the song "You'll Think of Me" (p24 c1), which rose to the top of the *Billboard* "Adult Contemporary" chart. Urban continued to release songs that sold solidly in the country market and extended into the Top 40 of the "Hot 100." Moreover, each of his five studio albums released in the past decade has performed extremely well on the *Billboard* pop album charts.

In 2005, mainstream country artist Carrie Underwood emerged from one of the most unlikely places in the music business: the stage of *American Idol*. While the

Keith Urban performing in 2004. As a flashy guitarist fluent in rock styles who often demurred from stereotypical country fashion, Urban represented a new type of rock-oriented country artist that emerged during the 2000s.

producers of *Idol* had developed several notable pop stars, including Kelly Clarkson and Clay Aiken, supporting a country singer was new territory for the show. For the insular, Nashville-based country industry, it was surely a shock to see a new hit-maker come from a mainstream television show. Yet Underwood thrived in Nashville, and became one of the most successful country crossover artists of the decade. In addition to her three albums—*Some Hearts* (p2 c1, 2005), *Carnival Ride* (p1 c1, 2007), and *Play On* (p1 c1, 2009)— she has placed nine singles at the top of the country charts, and (like Urban) her music has consistently made it into the pop Top 40. Underwood's best-selling single to date, "Before He Cheats" (p8 c1, 2006), offers a great example of a crossover country song from the 2000s. The song is performed from the perspective of a woman who has caught her significant other with someone else; her reaction, naturally, is to destroy one of the cheater's most-prized possessions—his pickup truck. Taken in the context of country music, this song offers a very strong female perspective, criticizing the "other woman" for her noncountry ways, which include singing karaoke, not knowing how to play pool, and drinking a fruity cocktail instead of whiskey. Musically, the song offers heavy instrumentation featuring dark electric guitar timbres, Underwood performing in the lower part of her range, and a chord progression (in a minor key) that highlights the severity of the lyrical perspective. The music video takes the rage of the jaded lover even further. After Underwood is shown defacing the automobile and confronting the man, she stands in the streets of (what is presumably) New Orleans amidst a tempest that causes windows to shatter and sparks to fly, wreaking havoc on neighborhood buildings. The rock-tinged music and lyrics of the song combine to create a clear message: "country women" are not to be reckoned with.

Urban and Underwood saw several country compatriots make a similar mark in the pop market in the 2000s. Another prominent country crossover artist of this period was singer and guitarist Taylor Swift, who took the entire music industry

Listening Guide

Get Music Ⓢ wwnorton.com/studyspace

Carrie Underwood, "Before He Cheats" Arista Nashville 71197

Written by Chris Thompkins and Josh Kear. Produced by Mark Bright. Rose to #8 on the *Billboard* "Hot 100" chart in 2007 (c1). Single available only as a digital download.

FORM: Compound AABA. The first two A sections are comprised of a contrasting verse-chorus form, and the final A section omits the verse. The chorus differs in length due to a changing transition; when this section moves to a verse or refrain it extends to 9 measures, but the transition to the bridge happens more quickly. Notice how the bridge functions not only as contrasting material, but as a section that creates stasis in order to make the final chorus seem more powerful.

TIME SIGNATURE: 4/4.

INSTRUMENTATION: Piano, drums, electric guitars, acoustic guitar, bass, drums, fiddle, lead and background vocals.

	0:00–0:14	**Introduction**, 4 mm.	Notice how the piano and drums begin before the measure counting starts. This is called a "pickup."
A	0:14–0:39	**Verse 1**, 8 mm.	The instrumentation calms down for the verses, letting Underwood tell the story. Listen to the fiddle screeching upward at 0:20. Note how there are four phrases to each verse, the first three use the same music, while the fourth leads into the chorus. "Right now . . ."
	0:39–1:09	**Chorus**, 9 mm.	Each chorus consists of two sections, creating a structure of 4+5 (which is really 3+2). Also notice the specific references to country music culture in the lyrics, including whiskey, pool, four-wheel drive, and a Louisville Slugger. "I dug . . ."
A	1:09–1:35	**Verse 2**, 8 mm.	References to Shania Twain and Polo cologne. "Right now . . ."
	1:35–2:01	**Chorus**, 8 mm.	The transition at the end of the chorus uses only a single measure in this presentation, making the section an even 8 measures. "I dug . . ."
B	2:01–2:27	**Bridge**, 8 mm	The bridge slows the song's progress in preparation for the return to the final chorus. "I might have saved . . ."
A	2:27–3:00	**Chorus**, 9 mm.	The return to the final A section omits the verse, moving directly to the chorus. "I dug . . ."
	3:00–3:19	**Refrain**, 4 mm.	A tag (or play out) that repeats the song title allows the momentum of the song to wind down.

Carrie Underwood performing in 2007 at the Grammy Awards. Emerging from the stage of *American Idol,* Underwood released country music during the late 2000s that was popular with both the Nashville establishment and on the mainstream pop charts.

by storm in the last half of the decade. Releasing her Nashville debut in 2006 as a young teenager, Swift successfully asserted herself as a songwriter in one of the most cutthroat creative environments in the music industry. While her debut album, *Taylor Swift* (p5 cl, 2006), produced six singles that rose to the Top 10 of the country singles charts (and Top 40 pop), it was *Fearless* (p1 cl uk5, 2008) that brought her music to the masses. Singles such as "Love Story" (p4 cl uk2, 2008) and "You Belong with Me" (p2 cl uk30, 2009) became staples of pop radio, projecting a strong, young female voice and infectious melodic hooks. Swift continued her chart reign in 2010 with the release of *Speak Now* (p1 cl uk6), which rose immediately to the top of the album charts, amid a bevy of mainstream promotion. A singer who writes incisive country songs and performs in a pop style, Swift is the perfect package for country crossover, bridging the sounds of both contemporary country and mainstream rock.

Beat-Based Rockers: Kanye West, The Roots, Cee-Lo Green, and Out-Kast.
Beat-based music ranging from hip-hop to dance-oriented R&B became the most popular music in the world during the 1990s, and this popularity extended into the 2000s. Dozens of artists benefitted from this approach to creating music, reaching audiences that extended far beyond the dancers and partygoers of early New York–based hip-hop in the late 1970s. A solo artist such as Beyoncé Knowles is one example of a wildly successful beat-based performer during the 2000s. As the lead member of the girl group Destiny's Child, Knowles released a string of hit singles and albums between 1997 and 2005. After her first solo album, *Dangerously in Love* (p1 r1 uk1, 2003), Knowles has consistently placed both albums and singles at the top of the R&B and pop charts. She appears regularly in commercial advertising, is a fixture of awards shows, and starred in the 2006 motion picture *Dreamgirls.* Representing a far different area of hip-hop culture is Louisiana's Lil

Wayne, who has achieved success both as a member of the group Hot Boys and as a solo artist. As a rapper who extols his southern roots, Lil Wayne released his first solo album, *Tha Block is Hot*, in 1999 (p3 r1), and has since released seven more albums under his name (in addition to many other collaborative efforts), which have all risen to the upper reaches of the pop and R&B charts. His breakthrough album was *Tha Carter III* (p1 r1 uk23, 2008), which included the multiplatinum single "Lollipop" (p1 r1 uk26, 2008).

Yet another mainstream hip-hop artist who has achieved immense success as both a producer and performer is Kanye West. Emerging as a solo artist with the album *College Dropout* (p2 r1 uk12, 2004), West has released five albums, each of which has risen to the top of the R&B and pop album charts. West achieved notoriety for his actions at the 2009 MTV Video Music Awards, when he upstaged winner Taylor Swift in order to defend the work of Beyoncé. After a noticeable hiatus, West returned with *My Beautiful Dark Twisted Fantasy* (p1 r1 uk16, 2010), which debuted at the top spot on the *Billboard* "Top 200" album chart. In light of the styles of Knowles and Lil Wayne, West's music and persona represent a strain of hip-hop that has been especially appealing to rock listeners. Some of this may be due to West's clear projection of middle-class values, which differ sharply from the glamour of Knowles and the gritty, working-class identity created by Lil Wayne. The son of a photojournalist and a college professor, West's fashion sense favors a more clean-cut image, his vocal style lacks the growl of many southern rappers, and his lyrics often take an openly intellectual stance. Moreover, in songs such as "Gold Digger" (p1 r1 uk2, 2005, Ray Charles), "Stronger" (p1 r30 uk1, 2007, Daft Punk), and "Good Life" (p7 r3 uk23, 2007, Michael Jackson), West's music often features audible samples from sources familiar to rock listeners. West has also collaborated with rock artists such as Adam Levine, Chris Martin, and indie folk artist Bon Iver.

Within the hip-hop community, West is one of the most visible agents of a form of beat-based music that appeals to both ardent hip-hop fans and rock listeners. Yet, as we have seen in previous chapters, there has been a long tradition of rock-oriented crossover from the hip-hop community, which continued throughout the 2000s. One of the most notable groups of this type was the Roots. Formed in Philadelphia during the late 1980s, the Roots quickly became the most famous hip-hop group to perform using traditional rock instrumentation. The group released several records in the 1990s, culminating with *Things Fall Apart* (p4 r2, 1999). This album contained the most popular Roots single to date "You Got Me" (p39 r11, 1999), which was cowritten with R&B singer Jill Scott and featured neo-soul artist Erykah Badu. Similar to West, the widespread appeal of the Roots surrounded the group's thoughtful lyrics, which were concerned with middle-class themes, and the musical support of instruments that sound as if they were performed (often with a heavy jazz emphasis) rather than programmed. Five more albums by the group released in the 2000s rose to the Top 10 of both the R&B and pop album charts, cementing the Roots as one of the most consistent hip-hop crossover acts of the decade. Further exposure for the group came in 2009, when they became the house band for the NBC program *Late Night with Jimmy Fallon*, a role that allowed group members to display their range of musical ability outside of the hip-hop tradition.

As we have seen, Lil Wayne represented a growing strain of southern rap that became popular in the mainstream during the 1990s. While many of these acts

were among the most hardcore hip-hop artists, and had little interest in infusing rock styles or exploring crossover connections, this community—rappers who came from Atlanta, in particular—also produced some of the most interesting and popular hybrid forms of rock and hip-hop during the 2000s. A particularly good example of this strain is Cee-Lo Green, a rapper from Atlanta who has extensively explored strains of rock and traditional R&B that appeal to a wide listenership. As a founding member of the Goodie Mob, Cee-Lo contributed to several popular albums during the 1990s, including *Soul Food* (p64 r31, 1995). Yet, he achieved breakthrough popularity in the 2000s as a solo vocalist and member of the duo Gnarls Barkley with DJ and producer Danger Mouse. The debut Gnarls Barkley album, *St. Elsewhere* (p4 r4 uk1), was released in 2006, yielding the hit single "Crazy" (p2 r53 uk1, 2006). Although created by a DJ in a beat-based setting, the spare instrumental backing of the song featured heavy strings and lush backing vocals, and Cee-Lo's expressive vocals were more reminiscent of classic soul than modern hip-hop. Moreover, the song takes the core of its musical materials from a song called "Nel Cimitero Di Tucson," which came from an Italian spaghetti western soundtrack. Cee-Lo's later solo album, *Lady Killer* (p9 r1 uk3, 2010), was lauded for a similar infusion of classic soul sensibilities, which are at times ironic give the frank nature of the material. This conflict is most evident in the hit single "F**k You" (p2 r57 uk1, 2010), which, over a happy-go-lucky instrumental track, offers the candid perspective of a man toward his former lady friend.

As part of a collective called the Dungeon Family, Cee-Lo (through his work with the Goodie Mob) worked closely with OutKast, another Atlanta-based hip-hop group that has had a large crossover appeal with rock listeners. Comprised of Big Boi and André 3000, two multi-instrumentalists, rappers (and vocalists) and producers, OutKast similarly explored hip-hop life from a southern viewpoint, while infusing its music with a wide range of source material. Although the group released popular albums throughout the 1990s, its breakthrough came in late 2000 with the single "Ms. Jackson" (p1 r1 uk2), which chronicled André 3000's breakup with Erykah Badu. (Ms. Jackson is Badu's mother.) Revealing a quirky sense of fashion

Listening Guide

Get Music ⓢ **wwnorton.com/studyspace**

OutKast, "Hey Ya" Arista 82876-50133

Written by André Benjamin (André 3000). Produced by André 3000 and Big Boi. Rose to #1 on the *Billboard* "Hot 100" chart in 2003. Single was released as digital download, on CD, and on vinyl.

FORM: Simple verse-chorus with noncontrasting bridge. The song is constructed of seven 24-measure sections. Each 24-measure section is constructed of four 6-measure sections. The rare noncontrasting bridge, often called a "breakdown" in beat-based music, achieves contrast through a change in instrumental texture.

TIME SIGNATURE: 4/4 and 2/4. Based on a six-measure cycle that follows the following pattern: 4 4 4 2 4 4. (For the verses, you need to count: 1-2-3-4 1-2-3-4 1-2-3-4- 1-2 1-2-3-4 1-2-3-4.) Interestingly, the lyrics printed in the CD booklet provide form labels for verses, "hooks" (chorus), the "breakdown" (bridge), and "call/ response" for an improvised verse.

INSTRUMENTATION: Acoustic guitar, keyboards, programmed instruments. All performed and programmed by André 3000 and Kevin Kendricks.

0:00–0:34	**Verse 1**, 24 mm.	Four repetitions of the 6-measure verse pattern. Although André provides a "count in" at the beginning, he skips a beat. He counts "1-2-3" and you need to be ready to begin right away counting 1. "My baby . . ."
0:34–1:07	**Chorus**, 24 mm. ("Hook")	Listen for the introduction of the synth bass, a high keyboard melody, and handclaps at the end of each 6-measure section. "Hey ya . . ."
1:07–1:40	**Verse 2**, 24 mm.	Four more cycles of the same harmonic progression with a very different vocal melody. Even though the backing instrumentation stops at the end, the beat persists through the silence (keep counting!). "You think you've got it . . ."
1:40–2:14	**Chorus**, 24 mm.	The same "Hey ya" vocal chorus with an added half-sung vocal part layered over it. "Hey ya . . ."
2:14–2:47	**Verse 3**, 24 mm. ("Call/Response")	André leading a call and reposnse section between a group of "fellas" and "ladies." Notice the presence of a wah-wah keyboard sound. "Alright now fellas . . ."
2:47–3:20	**Bridge**, 24 mm. ("Breakdown")	Instrumental texture reduced to drums and bass. Although this section uses the same chord progression and structure as the verses and choruses, the reduced instrumentation functions like a bridge, leading into the next chorus section. "Shake it . . ."
3:20–3:55	**Chorus**, 24 mm.	A full instrumental texture returns, with more playful melody lines from the higher keyboard. Fade out. "Hey ya . . ."

OutKast performing at the Grammy Awards in 2002. As rappers once connected with the "dirty south," OutKast released several albums and singles that became wildly popular in mainstream pop during the 2000s.

and humor, OutKast's next album *Speakerboxxx/The Love Below* (p1 r1 uk8, 2003) contained two wildly popular singles, "Hey Ya" (p1 r9 uk3, 2003) and "The Way You Move" (p1 r3 uk7, 2003), and became one of the most popular albums of the year. While the vocal harmony and horn arrangements of "The Way You Move" sound like the 1970s group Earth, Wind, and Fire, "Hey Ya" is a deceptively simple, driving pop song. Based on a six-measure chord progression that repeats throughout, the song contains playful keyboard work, an infectious chorus, and several lines that have become standard slang in the hip-hop community (such as "shake it like a Polaroid picture"). Although the instrumental elements of the song certainly sound more like rock than hip-hop, the imagery included on the album release (picturing André 3000 as a cartoonish 1950s family man) and the later music video confirm the song's connection with music outside of the hip-hop tradition. The video features André 3000 playing each role in an eight-piece band in a setting that mirrors the Beatles' *Ed Sullivan Show* appearance. It was clear during the 2000s through the work of West, the Roots, Cee-Lo, and OutKast that a significant strain of the hip-hop community was comfortable embracing elements of rock, and that rock listeners were just as happy to support these artists with media attention and album sales.

INDIE ROCK SELLS

Indie Roots: Wilco, Vampire Weekend, and Bright Eyes. Rock music produced and released independent of large corporations has always been an important part of American popular music. This history extends from the independent rock and rhythm and blues labels that helped to establish rock in the 1950s, through garage rock in the 1960s, punk in the 1970s, hardcore in the 1980s, and the indie scene from the 1990s to the present. In each of these cases, we have seen the intermingling of independent music with the mainstream. At times, artists were thrilled to be given the opportunity to work with large companies, while in other instances

we have seen movements against this interaction. While the indie scene of the 1990s grew wary of working with major labels, during the 2000s it seemed that it was no longer necessary to worry about the risks associated with signing with a major in order to achieve mainstream success. Although the demise of traditional music distribution channels was devastating for some parts of rock culture, including the independent record store, the move toward Internet sales and digital downloading was a democratizing force in the music business. Moreover, as major label sales suffered, the indie community faithfully supported their favorite acts. All of these factors led to an interesting phenomenon during the 2000s that had not been present in the rock industry since the 1960s: independent rock was achieving record sales that regularly placed its acts at the top of the *Billboard* album charts.

A bellwether for this change came at the beginning of the decade from the band Wilco. Formed by singer, guitarist, and songwriter Jeff Tweedy after the breakup of Uncle Tupelo in the mid-1990s, Wilco maintained an affiliation with the Reprise label, which was owned by Warner Brothers. After completing the album *Yankee Hotel Foxtrot* in 2001, the group was released from its Reprise contract and negotiated to keep the rights to the recording. In September 2001, after a series of leaks, the band decided to stream the album free of charge over the Internet. Meanwhile, they had entered negotiations to sign with Nonesuch, another label owned by Warner, which eventually re-bought *Yankee Hotel Foxtrot* and released it in April 2002. Even though they were associated with Warner, the indie community had long supported Wilco, and cheered what seemed to be an example of a band's triumph over a major record company (namely that a company paid for and then repurchased the same material). Despite giving the music away to fans, *Yankee Hotel Foxtrot* sold remarkably well for a band on Nonesuch, rising to #13 on the "Billboard 200" album chart (uk40) and becoming the most successful Wilco album to date. One reason that Wilco maintained such a loyal indie following was the innovative quality of their music, which combined elements of alt-country, the singer-songwriter tradition, and experiments with sonic atmospheres and noise. A good example of this is the song "Ashes of American Flags" from *Yankee Hotel Foxtrot*. Supporting Jeff Tweedy's lonesome vocal performance are sections that vary greatly in their instrumental backing and wild atmospheric elements throughout the song.

The cover of Wilco's 2002 album *Yankee Hotel Foxtrot* depicts a stark Chicago skyline, much like the group's music explores ethereal sonic atmospheres. Paid for, then repurchased by Warner, this album helped Wilco move into the mainstream while maintaining a connection to an indie community.

Vampire Weekend and Connor Oberst have also added to the indie flood in *Billboard*. An American rock combo that emphasizes Afro-pop influences, Vampire Weekend's infectious dance rhythms and witty lyrics have made them a staple of the indie scene. After their 2008 self-titled debut slowly gained popularity, the release of *Contra* in 2010 saw a rare debut at the top slot on the *Billboard* album chart by an independent release. Nebraska-based Connor Oberst is another example of an indie musician who developed a mainstream following in the last decade. Recording mostly with the Omaha-based Saddle Creek Records, a company run by Oberst and his older brother, Oberst also worked with Merge, Rough Trade, and several other important indie labels. He released several solo albums, but was best known for his group Bright Eyes, which issued its first release (a collection of older recordings) in 1998 on Saddle Creek. Slowly gaining popularity through the 2000s, two Bright Eyes albums released on the same day in 2005, *I'm Wide Awake, It's Morning* (p10 uk23) and *Digital Ash in a Digital Urn* (p15) drew national attention. The group's later release, *Cassadaga* (uk13, 2007) rose to number four on the *Billboard* album charts. Oberst was also a member of the indie "supergroup" Monsters of Folk, along with Jim James, Mike Mogis, and M. Ward, whose eponymous debut album (2009) also charted in the Top 20.

Merge in the New Century: Arcade Fire and Spoon.
One of the most important indie labels of the 1990s, Merge Records had a stocked roster of indie artists at the end of the decade, and was poised for success during the indie explosion of the new millennium. Among the Merge bands that saw greater popularity in the 2000s was Arcade Fire. Based in Montreal and performing songs in both English and French, Arcade Fire was a newcomer to the company and an unlikely band to propel Merge into the mainstream. Nevertheless, the group's 2004 album *Funeral* slowly gained popularity, eventually selling more than a half-million copies. Later releases *Neon Bible* (p2 uk2, 2007) and *The Suburbs* (p1 uk1, 2010) were immediately successful, and the latter album shocked many in the music business by winning the Grammy Award for Album of the Year in 2011. With the success of groups like Arcade Fire, Merge had to adapt its business model to keep up with demand. This change was aided by the

Wilco front man Jeff Tweedy (right) performing in 2007 at the Montreux Jazz Festival. Combining elements of country, mainstream rock, folk, and noise, Wilco emerged during the 2000s as an important indie rock band that achieved mainstream success.

demise of independent distributor Touch and Go in 2009, which had supported indie labels for decades. Aligned since then with the Alternative Distribution Alliance (which is mostly owned by the major Warner Music Group), Merge saw a different level of distribution but lost some of its indie credibility. Merge recordings were now widely available in big-box stores like Target and Best Buy, allowing those outside of the indie community easy access to its products, and groups like Arcade Fire benefitted immensely from this larger market. Another Merge group that launched mid-decade was Spoon. Spoon released its first album on Matador in 1996 (*Telephono*) before signing to Elektra, which was part of the Warner family of labels. The 1998 Elektra album *A Series of Sneaks* was the source of a major label horror story similar to Wilco, but without the immediate happy ending. Only after signing to Merge at the beginning of the 2000s did Spoon find a happy music-industry home, releasing five albums on Merge during the decade, each of which

Listening Guide

Wilco, "Ashes of American Flags" Nonesuch 79669

Words by Jeff Tweedy. Music by Jeff Tweedy and Jay Bennett. Produced by Wilco. Not released as a single. Album *Yankee Hotel Foxtrot* rose to #13 on the *Billboard* "Top Albums" chart.

FORM: Contrasting verse-chorus, with unmeasured interlude. A four-measure vamp is used throughout the song to slow the action and introduce each verse. The complete verses (verse 1 and 2) are constructed of two four-measure sections. The third, abbreviated verse only uses the first of these sections. The second half of the verse structure is also used independently as a prechorus. The song's chorus is rather short, consisting of only two phrases and totaling four measures. An unmeasured interlude that features atmospheric noise is used a type of contrasting bridge, and returns at the end of the song to act as a segue into the next song on the album. Note how there are many familiar small segments used and recycled throughout the form, but presented rarely presented in the same order.

TIME SIGNATURE: 4/4.

INSTRUMENTATION: Various auxiliary percussion, a piano vamp, electric guitars, drums, bass, acoustic guitar, lead vocals, synthesized strings, many other electronic sounds and instruments creating a sonic wash.

0:00–0:17	**Vamp**, 4 mm.	Bell tree percussion, a piano vamp, sustained guitar and strings open the track, getting louder in anticipation of the first verse.
0:17–0:45	**Verse 1**, 8 mm.	Melodic guitar, acoustic guitar, drums and bass enter. "The cash machine . . ."
0:45–1:00	**Vamp**, 4 mm.	Notice how the melodic guitar plays a call and response in the left and right speakers. Listen also for the sonic "wind" sounds.

Tim Kingsbury (left) and Regine Chassagne (right) of Arcade Fire perform at California's Shoreline Amphitheater in 2007. A Canadian group that incorporates both English and French lyrics, Arcade Fire won a Grammy for Album of the Year in 2011 despite its indie rock origins.

Get Music ⑤ wwnorton.com/studyspace

1:00–1:14	**Pre-chorus**, 4 mm.	"I wonder why . . ."
1:14–1:28	**Chorus**, 4 mm.	Listen to the irregular snare drum pattern, which is odd for a chorus section. "All my lies . . ."
1:28–1:43	**Vamp**, 4 mm	Back to acoustic guitar, wind, and sustained electric guitar.
1:43–2:11	**Verse 2**, 8 mm.	The instrumentation of this verse is completely different. Now featuring flute sounds, before the entrance of a rhythmic acoustic guitar for the second 4 measures. "I want a good life . . ."
2:11–2:25	**Chorus**, 4 mm.	Much smaller instrumental combination for this presentation of the chorus. "All my lies . . ."
2:25–2:40	**Interlude**, unmeasured	The rhythmic element stops, leaving only special sounds.
2:40–2:54	**Pre-chorus**, 4 mm.	Now with a new piano melody in the right speaker. "I'm down on my hands and knees . . ."
2:54–3:09	**Chorus**, 4 mm.	With a new chorus of synthesizers harmonizing the vocal melody. "All my lies . . ."
3:09–3:23	**Vamp**, 4 mm.	Presented without the piano.
3:23–3:38	**Verse 3 (abbreviated)**, 4 mm.	A presentation of the first half of the verse structure. "I would like to salute . . ."
3:38–4:44	**Interlude**, unmeasured	Now the special element takes over, evolving into an experiment with avant-garde noise. (This leads seamlessly into the next track on the album.)

was more commercially successful than the one before. Released in the same year as Arcade Fire's *The Suburbs* and Vampire Weekends' *Contra*, Spoon's 2010 album *Transference* reached number four on the *Billboard* pop albums chart, helping to mark the year that indie rock stormed the mainstream. Featuring the songwriting, vocals, and guitar of Britt Daniel, Spoon's music is often stark and direct, with danceable, repetitive grooves. With an intimate and sometimes experimental production quality favored by the indie rock community, both Arcade Fire and Spoon have proven that independent bands no longer have to trade an independent aesthetic for small sales.

Michigan Calling: The White Stripes and Sufjan Stevens. One of the calling cards of the indie rock scene during the 2000s was to reveal cutting-edge local rock from unlikely places. Although Michigan was once home to internationally popular R&B and garage rock, the most notable music to emerge from Michigan in the

new millennium was hip-hop and electronic dance music. Yet the indie community also helped to popularize several important rock groups from Michigan during the 2000s, offering another example of how the grass-roots efforts of dedicated listeners could transcend the dominance of major labels. Emblematic of Detroit's new garage rock scene was the duo the White Stripes, who recorded their first three albums on the independent Sympathy for the Record Industry label around the turn of the 2000s. The White Stripes went on to sign with the less-independent V2 for the more popular releases *Elephant* (p6 uk1, 2003) and *Get Behind Me Satan* (p3 uk3, 2005), both of which rose to the upper reaches of the *Billboard* "Top 200." Although associated more closely with the major label system than many in the indie community, the White Stripes maintained a significant presence in independent music. Beginning in the early 2000s, guitarist and vocalist Jack White promoted the music of indie bands through production efforts and with his own Third Man record company. Perhaps his most famous production effort was the heavily praised 2004 Loretta Lynn album *Van Lear Rose* (p24 c2), released on the major label Universal, which won several Grammy awards in 2005. (Resurrecting the careers of forgotten roots music artists was a running theme of indie rock during the decade.) Reflecting the aesthetic interests of indie rockers, much of the music released on Third Man, including special versions of White Stripes albums, was available only in vinyl form. Also notable were Jack White's many side projects, including the Raconteurs and the Dead Weather. The music of the White Stripes was striking for several reasons. As a drums and guitar duo, with fuller instrumentation sometimes used on later releases, the group's sound included a wealth of sonic space for drummer Meg White to explore unconventional beat patterns that might otherwise be lost in a cluttered rock band sound. Moreover, Jack White used this arrangement to highlight his virtuoso blues guitar style, a throwback to 1970s arena rock.

The vast catalog of Detroit-born Sufjan Stevens shows another side of the indie community in Michigan. Originally based in the small college town of Holland, Stevens embodied aspects of the singer-songwriter movement, thematic releases akin to concept albums, and a surreal performance style that incorporated unorthodox costumes. Releasing music on Asthmatic Kitty, a label he helped to start while living in Michigan, Stevens's output often tackled large-scale projects or themes. Two of his albums, which form the basis of a rumored 50-states project, were called *Greetings from Michigan, the Great Lake State* (2003) and *Come on Feel the Illinoise* (2005), exploring various locations and aspects of these two Midwestern states. As a Brooklyn transplant, Stevens later released a multimedia project (including a CD and DVD of nonperformance footage, booklet, and View-Master reel) called *The BQE* (2009), which was a meditation on New York's Brooklyn-Queens Expressway. Although his music is often intimate, featuring a trademark banjo, Stevens also worked with nonconventional rock instrumentation ranging from simple string arrangements to large-scale orchestral textures. His 2010 release *The Age of Adz* (p7 uk30) even ventured into electronic beat-based production, while still including the lush choral and orchestral elements that became associated with his own brand of indie music. Like many of the marquee indie releases of 2010, *The Age of Adz* also reached a high position on the *Billboard* pop album charts, reflecting a growing listenership for once-obscure independent artists. Releases by the indie artists discussed above, and many others—including the National's *High Violet* (2010), Grizzly Bear's *Veckatimest* (2009), and the Black Keys' *Brothers* (2010)—show that, like many other points in the history of rock, what was once considered "alternative" had become thoroughly mainstream.

Emo Rising: Dashboard Confessional and Jimmy Eat World.
Many of the independent labels discussed above participated in the indie rock community, which was most popular with college-aged audiences and their older contemporaries. After the punk revolution of the 1980s, however, many other independent communities flourished, using similar networks of radio, clubs, and marketing. Moreover, some of these communities were targeted to, and popular with, audiences of a demographic outside of the standard indie rock market. The "emo" community is a good example of a largely independent-based network of bands that shared an audience, which was markedly younger than the average indie rock crowd. Although most bands shied away from the emo label, viewing it as a derogatory classification, the emo aesthetic that emerged in the mid-1980s grew dramatically in popularity during the 2000s, providing another example of independent music that began to make important inroads into the commercial mainstream.

Closely related to pop punk bands like Green Day and Blink-182, the emo tradition drew heavily on high-energy punk indebted to 1970s and 1980s American hardcore. However, while Blink-182 songs such as "All the Small Things" or "First Date" (and their accompanying videos) are fun and sophomoric, popular emo bands relished a more serious personal perspective and often featured heartfelt vocals. Most commentators point to the D.C. hardcore scene of the mid-1980s as the launching point for emo. Led by vocalist and guitarist Guy Picciotto, the short-lived band Rites of Spring explored the combination of hardcore and heartfelt lyrics, as did Fugazi, Picciotto's later group founded with Ian MacKaye. During the early 1990s, emo became popular with younger audiences in more regional scenes. Moving between New York, Los Angeles, and San Francisco, Jawbreaker was a local favorite that released albums and extended-play releases on several small independent labels before signing to Geffen in the mid-1990s. Sunny Day Real Estate was based in Seattle, amid the growing grunge scene, and released its most important material on Sub Pop records, the same label that held Nirvana's early releases. Milwaukee, Wisconsin, was the home of the Promise Ring, a quartet signed to the small Jade Tree label. Kansas City's the Get Up Kids, Champaign-Urbana's Braid, and Long Island's Thursday were among the many popular regional emo bands to emerge during the mid-1990s.

Independent labels such as Vagrant and Drive-Thru, in addition to a growing number of interested major companies like Interscope, drove emo into the mainstream in the late 1990s and early 2000s. Known more for marketing than music, Drive-Thru aggressively sold merchandise at mall stores such as Hot Topic and signed an agreement with MCA that helped bands such as New Found Glory reach teenage listeners nationwide. Vagrant was even more aggressive, supporting groups

Sufjan Stevens in a 2006 performance in Vancouver, Canada. Often donning odd costumes, Stevens's blend of folk guitar and banjo with album-long themes and electronic textures helped him become one of the most popular indie artists during the 2000s.

such as the Get Up Kids and Dashboard Confessional with lavish tours and Internet marketing. While the Get Up Kids became underground emo icons, Dashboard Confessional went on to release extremely successful albums such as *A Mark, A Mission, A Brand, A Scar* (p2, 2003) and *Dusk and Summer* (p2, 2005). A typical Dashboard Confessional song, "Vindicated" (2005), opens with the line "hope dangles on a string like slow spinning redemption," revealing a sensitive nature typically associated with emo. The most popular band of the emo movement was the Arizona-based quartet Jimmy Eat World. Signed to Interscope, which had also partnered with Vagrant, Jimmy Eat World released the unsuccessful *Clarity* in 1999, which has since become an emo cult classic. It was not until the album *Bleed American* (p31, 2001), later retitled *Jimmy Eat World* after September 11, 2001, that the group reached a national audience. The most successful single from the album, "The Middle" (p5 uk26, 2002), uses a typical emo formula that appealed particularly to teenagers going through life changes. Over a chunky, pop punk musical groove, singer Jim Adkins advises, "it just takes some time . . . everything will be alright." After the success of "The Middle," Jimmy Eat World continued to release popular albums throughout the decade, including *Futures* (p6 uk22, 2004), *Chase This Light* (p5 uk27, 2008), and *Invented* (p11 uk29, 2010). Although the emo movement was most popular with teenagers, issues of self-exploration commonly associated with this music reflect other movements related to the history of rock, such as the folk revival of the 1950s and 1960s, the singer-songwriter repertoire of the 1970s, and European pop of the 1980s released by bands like the Smiths. Thus, emo's blend of heavy guitars and introspective lyrics reflects the youth culture of the 1990s and 2000s while connecting with older forms of rock music and textual delivery.

ROCK AS DISCOURSE

School of Rock. As we draw to the end of this survey, it is useful to discuss some examples that illustrate the cultural impact of rock music in contemporary society. Taking as a starting point the cold reception of rock in the 1950s through the lens of racial mixing, uncouth bodily movements, and teenage rebellion, it is fascinating to watch each of these aspects turn into some of rock's most heralded qualities. After more than fifty years of slow change in societal attitudes toward civil rights, we can now view rock music as a driving force in this process. Once considered nonintellectual music of the body, rock has since seen a parallel movement as "music for listening," while still maintaining a quality that makes listeners "feel good"—a magical combination of thinking music for dancing feet. Finally, the rebellious heart of rock music has become a romanticized hallmark of nearly every teenage movement since rock's emergence in the mid-1950s. Rock continues as a soundtrack for an international tradition of each generation finding the means for its own independence.

These large-scale indications of rock's acceptance in society have been accompanied by institutional recognition. Just as jazz has become known as "America's classical music," rock is becoming institutionalized at an alarming rate. Depending on your outlook, this institutional support of rock music is either a realization of the importance of the form, or it is detrimental to the future of the art. As a college textbook used in dozens of schools internationally, this book itself is an indication of rock's acceptance into fields of higher learning. While academics have been studying the social and communicative effects of rock music since the late 1960s, there has been a slow growth in acceptance of this form of music in a wide variety of academic fields. Courses on rock music are offered as a general education option in most colleges and universities, and have increasingly grown in importance for

While actor Jack Black lampooned rock as an academic subject in the 2003 film *School of Rock*, courses and degree programs focusing on rock music have become extremely popular during the last decade.

students majoring in cultural studies, communications, gender studies, history, and music. With student interest growing in the serious study of rock music, university professors also have begun to specialize in various aspects of rock music in their research. Decades ago, courses and research on rock were limited to professors who specialized in other fields while dabbling in rock as a secondary area. Now, a growing number of doctoral programs in a wide variety of fields have accepted topics in rock (and popular music more generally) as cutting-edge research, and graduate students have become engaged in the study of rock as a primary discipline. An extreme example of the extent to which colleges and universities have fully accepted rock music is the creation of a master's program at Liverpool Hope University entitled "The Beatles, Popular Music and Society." While most colleges and universities have not risen to this level of acceptance, it is safe to say that rock music has generally become a universal addition to the many subjects available for study at institutions of higher learning.

Rock as Culture. Educational institutions are only one facet of the widespread acceptance of rock music in twenty-first-century society. Important photographers such as Alfred Wertheimer, Linda McCartney, Jim Marshall, Bob Gruen, and many others have seen their work shown at museums internationally, making the documentation of rock a noble field in itself. In addition to traveling exhibitions of photography and instruments, and growing additions to permanent collections, several museums devoted exclusively to rock music opened in the late twentieth-century. In the mid-1980s, a group of rock industry officials began a foundation called the Rock and Roll Hall of Fame, which inducted its first members in 1986. After a decade of development and fundraising, the group opened a Cleveland-based museum in 1995, which serves today as the foremost cultural institution to

The Rock and Roll Hall of Fame Museum in Cleveland, Ohio. As rock music and culture have entered into mainstream acceptance, organizations like the Rock and Roll Hall of Fame have erected museums to honor a form of music that was once considered degenerate.

promote public awareness of rock's history. With more than 600 inductees, including musicians, songwriters, and executives, the museum holds a wealth of cultural capital, confirming the importance of well-known artists, calling attention to influential figures who have been largely forgotten, and placing record company work alongside artistic endeavors. Opened in 2000 with a Frank Gehry–designed building in the shape of an electric guitar, Seattle's Experience Music Project offers a similar institutional nod to rock with an emphasis on interaction and participation. With permanent and temporary exhibitions dedicated to many aspects of rock, a variety of public programs, and an annual conference of rock critics and scholars, EMP offers another important example of the cultural institutionalization of rock.

It is understandable that baby boomers who have worked in or been influenced by rock would go on to start museums and curate exhibitions about the history of rock. Yet, there are other instances in which we can see rock music's acceptance by an even larger public, showering rock musicians with the highest levels of cultural praise in modern society. For example, each year the Kennedy Center in Washington, D.C., honors several individuals for a lifetime of achievement in the cultural arts. Attended by the President of the United States, this ceremony is televised nationally and serves as one of the greatest cultural honors offered in

As the contributions of rock musicians to modern culture are increasingly recognized through cultural awards, some of rock's seedier characters have been lionized. Here, Ozzy Osbourne speaks to the media in 2006 after his induction into the Rock and Roll Hall of Fame as a member of Black Sabbath.

the United States. In addition to famous actors, dancers, comedians, and musicians associated with the classical and jazz traditions, an increasing number of rock musicians have been among the honorees. Ray Charles (1986), Aretha Franklin (1994), Bob Dylan (1997), Elton John (2004), and many others have enjoyed this honor. In 2007, the Library of Congress created a special governmental award specifically for lifetime achievement in popular song called the Gershwin Prize. The first three honorees—Paul Simon, Stevie Wonder, and Paul McCartney—were all closely associated with rock music.

The sounds of rock have also come a long way from their humble origins, traveling hundreds of miles over AM superstations into the bedrooms of teenagers late at night under the cover of darkness and behind closed bedroom doors. Now, rock music fills some of the most hallowed halls of the world, including an increasing presence on Broadway stages. While musicals such as *Hair* and *Godspell* were unique in presenting rock styles to Broadway audiences in the late 1960s and early 1970s, musicals based on rock themes have become dominant on theatrical stages in the 2000s. Shows weaving the music of Abba, Billy Joel, and Fela Kuti into loose plots have become extremely popular, and historical shows such as *Smokey Joe's Café*, *Memphis*, *Million Dollar Quartet*, and *Jersey Boys* have romanticized the rock music of the 1950s and 1960s. Other performances, such as *Rock of Ages* and *American Idiot* have brought hair metal and pop punk to the Broadway stage.

The Canonization of Rock. Discerning readers will find that writing about rock took a very serious turn in the late 1960s. While the British press had a long tradition of covering popular music, often sensationalizing rock news for teenage fans, American magazines such as *Rolling Stone*, *Crawdaddy*, *Creem*, and a wide variety of underground publications like New York's *Village Voice*, took rock music very seriously. These publications produced fine commentary and criticism from legendary writers such as Jon Landau, Lester Bangs, Paul Williams, Richard Meltzer, and Robert Christgau. While important and insightful, this commentary was limited to a very small and focused readership, and in many ways these writers were simply writing for other devotees. In the last several decades, however, we have seen rock criticism achieve mainstream acceptance in many American publications. Prominent space is reserved for rock and other forms of popular music in the *New York Times*

Sound Check

Artist	Nickelback	Carrie Underwood
Title	Photograph	Before He Cheats
Chart peak	p2 2006	p8, c1 2007
Form	Compound AABA	Compound AABA
Rhythm	4/4	4/4
Instrumentation	Electric guitar Acoustic guitar Bass Drums Lead vocal Background vocal	Electric guitar Acoustic guitar Bass Drums Lead vocal Background vocal Piano Fiddle
Comments	Verse-chorus pairs (each A section) are in a simple verse relationship Two distinct melody lines used simultaneously in the bridge The same line is used to open and close the song	Electric guitar and fiddle announce that the song is modern country Matching the tone of the lyrics, Underwood sings in the lower, more serious register of her voice Return to A includes only a chorus and refrain (no verse)

and the *New Yorker*. Widely available anthologies of popular music criticism have become commonplace in the last decade, focusing on historical pieces, best-of-the-year collections, and conference proceedings. Moreover, with the digital revolution having similar effects on print media and the record industry, a growing number of highly skilled rock critics are maintaining blogs to document their writing.

Important themes have emerged from the explosion in rock criticism in the last decade, which are helpful to explore as currents of "rock thought" in the early twenty-first century. With the acceptance of rock music on the rise, cultural institutions and critics alike have been forced into the process of creating a "rock canon," or a loose collection of the most important works in the history of rock. We see this most literally in "best of" lists like the *Rolling Stone* "500 Greatest Albums of All Time" and the myriad countdowns aired on VH-1. The list of Rock and Roll Hall

OutKast	Wilco
Hey Ya	Ashes of American Flags
p1, r9 2003	2002
Simple verse-chorus (modified)	Contrasting verse-chorus (modified)
4/4 (2/4)	4/4
Acoustic guitar Keyboards Programmed instruments	Electric guitar Acoustic guitar Bass Drums Lead vocal Piano Auxiliary percussion Synthesized strings Electronic noise
The same 6-measure cycle repeats for the entire song (28 times) Instruments build throughout the arrangement (synth bass, wah wah keyboard) Call and response between men and women in verse 3	Highly modified form that includes a pre-chorus, a floating vamp, and an interlude Verses often feature different arrangements Electronic noise is present throughout the track, and is featured in the final interlude

of Fame inductees offers another concrete example of individuals who have been accepted into a canon of rock history. While we treasure the albums, artists, and songs that most often appear on these lists, the process of creating such a body is necessarily exclusionary. Far more than a simple popularity contest, not including certain music in this constructed history can have detrimental effects on the availability of music for purchase, dramatically changing the lives of forgotten musicians and arguably altering history. A growing number of music critics have been instrumental in fighting the canonization of rock. One of the most powerful tools that has emerged to combat this trend is the concept of "rockism," or understanding how the history of popular music has often been viewed as if rock has been the central form of pop music since 1954. Although many readers may question whether this book falls into the trap of "rockism," it is helpful to understand that the preceding survey has clearly named rock as the center of our study (not the entire field of popular music), and that we have been careful to consider the music in these pages as mere representations of various forms of rock. Nevertheless, as rock moves into the twenty-first century and rock writing moves from a means of entertainment to a form of organizing history, it will become essential to continually revisit and reevaluate the music of the past, forcing ourselves to stay as objective as possible about how our place in history effects our perception in the present.

In looking at these issues, this study ends much like it began, with the struggle to define rock. If we have learned anything from studying this form of music and its various manifestations over the last six decades, we should understand that rock music is in a constant state of change, and to define it—to place borders around what is, and what is not, rock—requires us to account for ourselves as much as the music. Rock is intertwined with social, political, and cultural issues. Defining rock depends on who we are, where and when we live, and what we know. Rock has been presented to listeners very specifically by a complex and multifaceted music industry, which has drastically shaped the creation of music and how fans understand it. As a movement dependent upon mass media, rock has been formed and reformed again and again through changing technologies. These new developments have altered the ways in which we make music, enjoy it through listening and viewing, document musicians, and facilitate interaction between musicians and fans. No matter how we define this music and its many styles and sounds, it is safe to say that rock has been the dominant cultural force of the last half-century. Through close study, intent listening, and broad cultural understanding, readers of this text are now poised to better understand rock as a historical subject, a developing field, and a lifelong pursuit.

FURTHER READING

Dean Budnick and Josh Baron, *Ticket Masters: The Rise of the Concert Industry and How the Public Got Scalped* (ECW, 2001).

John Cook, Mac McCaughan, and Laura Ballance, *Our Noise: The Story of Merge Records, the Indie Label That Got Big and Stayed Small* (Algonquin, 2009).

Matthew David, *Peer to Peer and the Music Industry: The Criminalization of Sharing* (Sage, 2009).

Andy Greenwald, *Nothing Feels Good: Punk Rock, Teenagers, and EMO* (St. Martin's Griffin, 2003).

Barry Kernfeld, *Pop Song Piracy: Disobedient Music Distribution since 1929* (University of Chicago Press, 2011).

Greg Kot, *Wilco: Learning How to Die* (Broadway, 2004).

Katherine L. Meizel, *Idolized: Music, Media, and Identity in American Idol* (Indiana University Press, 2011).

Kiri Miller, *Playing Along: Digital Games, YouTube, and Virtual Performance* (Oxford University Press, 2012).

Roni Sariq, *Third Coast: OutKast, Timbaland, and How Hip-Hop Became a Southern Thing* (Da Capo, 2007).

Ⓢ VISIT STUDYSPACE AT WWNORTON.COM/STUDYSPACE

Access free review material such as:

- music links
- performer info
- practice quizzes
- outlines
- interactive listening guide software

GLOSSARY

AABA form. A song form that uses two verses (A A), a bridge (B), and a return to the verse (A) as its basic organizational pattern. Once the complete AABA pattern is presented, a song may repeat all of the pattern (full reprise) or only part of it (partial reprise). AABA form is strongly associated with the Tin Pan Alley popular song style, though it also occurs frequently in rock music.

Arpeggio. When the individual notes of a chord are played separately, an arpeggio results. While any instrument can play an arpeggio, they are frequently found in guitar and piano parts as a way of providing variety in the accompaniment.

Bar. Musicians often count out a song, saying "1, 2, 3, 4." This is a bar of music, and the numbers represent beats. These bars usually have the same number of beats in them throughout a song (though not always). The term "bar" is synonymous with "measure." See also, "meter."

Beat. A regular rhythmic pulse in music is called a "beat." Beats are organized into "measures" or "bars" to create "meter."

Blues (as in "blues-based"). The blues is an important style in popular music that displays a series of musical features. When such features occur in rock, we use the term "blues-based" to highlight the influence of this style. Blues-based features might include the use of the "12-bar blues" pattern, string bends on the guitar, or bluesy inflections of pitch in any lead instrument or voice.

Bridge. The bridge is a section in a song that provides contrast to other, more salient sections of the same song, such as the verse or the chorus. While bridge sections can be quite interesting musically, they are almost never the focal section of a song.

Call and response. When an instrumental or vocal line is immediately answered or repeated by other instruments or vocals, we refer to this as "call and response."

Chords. A chord is a combination of three or more notes played simultaneously. A limited number of such combinations make up the majority of chords heard in rock music. Musicians classify these combinations, using such terms as "major," "minor," "dominant seventh," "minor seventh," among others.

Chorus. The chorus is usually the most important or easily remembered section of a song, containing the title and the catchiest musical material. Not all songs have a chorus, but when one is present, it is usually the focus of the song.

Coda. Some songs contain an ending section called the "coda." The coda often uses musical material from earlier in the song to provide an ending, which is sometimes a fade-out. Some musicians refer to the coda as an "outro," paralleling the beginning section in a song, which is often called the "intro."

Compound (meter). When we subdivide the basic beat into three equal parts, this creates a compound feel, which is notated using compound meters such as 6/8, 9/8, or most commonly, 12/8. See the Introduction for an explanation of simple and compound meters.

Compound AABA form. In a compound AABA form, each A section contains at least one verse and a chorus section (these can be contrasting or not). After two presentations of this verse-chorus unit (A A), a contrasting bridge section occurs (B), followed by a return to some version of the verse-chorus pair (A). Sometimes this return can consist only of the chorus and repetitions of it.

Contrasting verse-chorus form. In contrasting verse-chorus form, the verse and chorus sections employ contrasting musical material. The form consists of these contrasting verses and choruses presented in alternation, though more than one verse may occur before the chorus.

Duple (meter). When there are two beats in a bar (or measure) of music, the meter is classified as duple. Duple meter is commonly notated as 2/4 if it is a simple feel, or 6/8 if it is a compound feel. See the Introduction for an explanation of meter classifications.

Falsetto. When a male singer uses his highest vocal register, this is referred to as the falsetto. The highest vocal parts on Beach Boys records, for example, are often sung in falsetto. A good example is the line "everybody's gone surfing" in the song "Surfin' U.S.A." Frankie Valli has a more aggressive sounding falsetto, as can be heard in "Big Girls Don't Cry."

Formal diagram. A formal diagram, such as the ones used in the Listening Guides throughout this book, provides an overview of the formal design of a song, or how the different parts of the song fit together to create what is often a familiar pattern. These familiar patterns are organized into the five song forms described in the Introduction.

Full reprise. In an AABA form, playing once through the AABA structure often does not create a song that is long enough. When the entire AABA structure is repeated, this is called a "full reprise." Some songs may use more than one repeat of the entire AABA structure.

Instrumental verse. A verse section that repeats the music of the verse, without the singing and with an instrument soloing, is an instrumental verse. Guitar, saxophone, and keyboard solos are common, though any instrument can solo in an instrumental verse.

Interlude. An interlude is a brief instrumental passage in a song that separates the other sections (verse, bridge, or chorus) from one another. Frequently the musical material of such interludes is drawn from the Introduction.

Introduction. An introduction is a section of a song that precedes the start of the first verse or chorus (when the chorus appears before the verse). Introductions are frequently instrumental, but may also contain singing. Some musicians refer to this section as the "intro."

Key. Most rock songs are in a specific key. This refers to the fact that all of the notes in the song bear a subordinate relationship to some central note. The actual note that is central is identified using a note name (A, B♭, F#) and the way in which the other notes relate to that central note is identified using terms such as "major" or "minor." When musicians refer to the key of D major, for instance, they mean that the note D is the central note and that the other notes relate to it in a specific way that we hear as major.

Lick. A lick is a short and distinctive melodic figure. A lick is not a complete melody, but it may be employed as part of a melody, either vocally or instrumentally. A lick may also be used anywhere in the accompaniment, often as part of a repeated pattern, but not necessarily. The guitar lick from the beginning of the Rolling Stones' "(I Can't Get No) Satisfaction" is a famous example. For the purposes of this book, "lick" and "riff" are synonymous.

Measure. Musicians often count out a song, saying "1, 2, 3, 4." This is a measure of music, and the numbers represent beats. These measures usually have the same number of beats in them throughout a song (though not always). The term "measure" is synonymous with "bar." See also, "meter."

Meter. A meter establishes how we will notate music within a certain meter classification. Each of the meter classifications discussed in the Introduction can be represented with several meters, but some meters are far more common than others, especially in rock music. Of the simple meters, 2/4, 3/4, and 4/4 are most common, and among the compound meters, 6/8, 9/8, and 12/8 are most common. See "meter classification" and the Introduction.

Meter classification. A meter classification classifies how we feel the organization of the rhythm for a particular song or passage. In this book, meters are classified as either simple or compound, and then as either duple, triple, or quadruple. A meter classification can be notated using a

specific meter, and though there are several meters than can be used with each classification, there are six meters that are most common. See "meter," and the Introduction.

Overdubbing. Overdubbing is a recording process in which new recorded parts are added to previously recorded ones. One benefit to overdubbing is that it allows parts of a song to be recorded at different times, and even makes it possible for the same person to perform multiple parts in a way that would be impossible in real time.

Partial reprise. In an AABA form, playing once through the AABA structure often does not create a song that is long enough. When only a portion of AABA structure is repeated, this is called a "partial reprise." Most partial reprises repeat the BA or the ABA sections of the AABA structure.

Phrase. A phrase is a short passage of music; often in rock music, phrases are four measures in length (sometimes eight measures). A phrase is akin to a sentence in spoken language and divides the music into units that make it easier to comprehend. Vocal phrases often correspond to obvious points of division and articulation in the lyrics being sung.

Pre-chorus. Some songs employ a pre-chorus, which is a section that connects the verse to the chorus. The purpose of a pre-chorus is to build up the musical movement toward the chorus, and in that way it is a special kind of bridge. Many times, the lyrics on each occurrence of the pre-chorus are the same or only slightly varied.

Quadruple (meter). When there are four beats in a bar (or measure) of music, the meter is classified as quadruple. Quadruple meter is commonly notated as 4/4 if it is a simple feel, or 12/8 if it is a compound feel. See the Introduction for a fuller explanation of meter classifications.

Refrain. A refrain is a subsection that often occurs in a verse. It functions much as a chorus does except that it is too brief to be considered a separate section and is otherwise clearly part of a larger section. The refrain will often occur as the last phrases or phases of a verse, but may also constitute the opening phrase or phases of a verse. A song that employs a refrain will most often not also employ a chorus. Refrains are thus most commonly found in the verses of AABA forms, since an AABA form does not employ a chorus.

Reprise. Generally speaking, a reprise is simply a repeat of music that has already been heard; the reprise of "Breathe" on Pink Floyd's *Dark Side of the Moon* or of the title track on *Sgt. Pepper's Lonely Hearts Club Band* are famous examples. In this book, "reprise" is routinely used to describe an aspect of return that occurs within an AABA form. See "full reprise" and "partial reprise."

Rhythm. In the broadest sense, the word "rhythm" refers to the organized patterning of the temporal dimension in music. More specifically, we can refer to a rhythmic figure in the music, which is usually a short segment with a clearly defined profile of some kind. Meter and meter classification are aspects of the broader aspect of rhythmic organization and are discussed at greater length in the Introduction.

Riff. A riff is a short and distinctive melodic figure. A riff is not a complete melody, but it may be employed as part of a melody, either vocally or instrumentally. A riff may also be used anywhere in the accompaniment, often as part of a repeated pattern, but not necessarily. The guitar riff from the beginning of the Rolling Stone's "(I Can't Get No) Satisfaction" is a famous example. For the purposes of this book, "riff" and "lick" are synonymous.

Roman numerals. Roman numerals are used by music theorists to identify chords within a key. The chord based on the first note of the scale in a major key is labeled "I," while the chord built on the fifth note of the same scale is labeled "V." Some theorists use upper-case Roman numerals for major chords and lower-case numerals for minor chords. Thus, the chord built on the first note of a minor key is "i." Once one learns the way chords are formed in major and minor keys, the Roman numerals help to generalize how the chords work in any major key or in any minor key. See Interlude One for further discussion.

Sampling. Sampling is a practice, perhaps most prominent in hip-hop, in which a segment of some existing recording is excerpted and mixed into a new recording. Such samples can be quite long, or they can be much shorter segments. Sometimes shorter segments are made to immediately repeat numerous times, creating a loop. The advent of digital recording made sampling very easy, though the growth and development of this practice gave rise to a series of lawsuits over claims of copyright infringement.

Scale. In the simplest sense, a scale merely takes the notes that are available for use in any given key and puts them in order, starting and ending on the most important note. In the key of C major, for instance, the notes available are A, B, C, D, E, F, and G (these are the white keys on the piano). A C-major scales arranges these notes in relation to C, so that the scale is C D E F G A B C.

Shuffle. A shuffle rhythm is often a way of playing 4/4 that transforms it into something closer to 12/8. The four beats in a measure of 4/4 are each divided into two equal parts, making for a scheme that goes 1 & 2 & 3 & 4 &. In 12/8, the same measure would divide the beats into three equal parts, resulting in 1 & ah 2 & ah 3 & ah 4 & ah. A shuffle uses the second of these schemes, but the & is often silent, so we get 1 (&) ah 2 (&) ah 3 (&) ah 4 (&) ah. This sounds somewhat like the first scheme (4/4), since it has two elements per beat, but unlike the first scheme, the elements do not evenly divide the beat.

Sectional chorus and sectional verse. In the decades before rock music, popular songs often featured two large sections. The first of these was a kind of lengthy introduction to the song proper, employing lyrics that set the scene for the song itself. The second large section was the song itself. Through the years, many of these introductions have been all but forgotten, while the songs themselves have remained familiar. Writers who work in Tin Pan Alley-style pop often call the first section of such songs the "verse," and the second section the "chorus." This usage conflicts with the established use of these terms in rock music, however, and can lead to great confusion. To address this, we will call these introductory sections "sectional verses" and the song proper "sectional chorus," reserving the use of "verse" and "chorus" for use as they are defined in this Glossary and in the text.

Simple (meter). When we subdivide the basic beat into two equal parts, we create a simple feel, which is notated using simple meters such as 2/4, 3/4, or most commonly, 4/4. See the Introduction for a fuller explanation of simple and compound meters.

Simple verse-chorus form. In simple verse-chorus form, the verse and chorus sections employ the same underlying musical material, though the lyrics and sung melodies of each section are different. The form consists of these verses and choruses presented in alternation, though more than one verse may occur before the chorus.

Simple verse form. A simple verse form consists of a series of verses, all of which use the same underlying music. A simple verse form contains no chorus or bridge sections, though the verses may contain a refrain.

Tag. A tag usually occurs at the end of a song or large section and consists of repeating the last few measures of the concluding section up to two times.

Triple (meter). When there are three beats in a bar (or measure) of music, the meter is classified as triple. Triple meter is commonly notated as 3/4 if it is a simple feel, or 9/8 if it is a compound feel. See the Introduction for a fuller explanation of meter classifications.

Twelve-bar blues. The twelve-bar blues is a structure that forms the musical basis for many verses, choruses, and even bridges in rock music. It can be divided into three 4-bar phrases. The lyrics to the first phrase are frequently repeated in the second phrase, with new lyrics appearing in the third phrase, creating a kind of question/question repeated/answer model as the words unfold. The twelve-bar blues also employs a specific arrangement of chords, and this is explained in greater detail in Interlude One. In the history of rock, the twelve-bar blues is strongly associated with 1950s rock and rhythm & blues. Even when this structure arises in later rock, the reference to the 1950s is often clear.

Verse. A verse is a section that most often features new lyrics with each repetition within a song, unlike a chorus, which tends to repeat the same lyrics with each recurrence. The verse is often used to tell a story or describe a situation. In an AABA form, the verse is the focal point of the song, and may also include a refrain. In a verse-chorus type form, the verse sets up the chorus, which is the focus of the song.

CREDITS

Every effort has been made to contact the copyright holders of the material used in **What's That Sound: An Introduction to Rock and Its History**. Please contact us with any updated information.

PHOTOS

Introduction

p. 2: From the collection of John Tefteller www.tefteller .com; **p. 5 top:** Douglas Kent Hall/Zuma/Corbis; **p. 5 bottom left:** Mark Metcalfe/Getty Images; **p. 5 bottom right:** Bettmann/Corbis; **p. 8:** Michael Ochs Archives/ Getty Images; **p. 20:** Henry Diltz/Corbis; **p. 21:** Fin Costello/Redferns/Getty Images; **p. 22:** Kevin Cummins/ Getty Images; **p. 27 top left:** Ray Avery/Redferns/Getty Images; **p. 27 top right:** Richard E. Aaron/Redferns/ GettyImages; **p. 27 bottom:** Courtesy AVID; **p. 32 all:** Motown: The DVD © 2009 Historic Music, Inc. under exclusive license to Universal Music Enterprises.

Chapter 1

p. 35: Library of Congress; **p. 36:** Bettmann/Corbis; **p. 38 both:** © Copyright 1940, 1942 by Irving Berlin; **p. 41:** *The Wizard of Oz* 1939 Victor Fleming Metro-Goldwyn-Mayer (MGM); **pp. 43–44:** Bettmann/Corbis; **p. 45:** Pictorial Press Ltd/Alamy; **p. 47:** Michael Ochs Archives/Getty Images; **p. 48 top:** Pictorial Press Ltd/ Alamy; **p. 48 bottom:** Robert Johnson Estate/Hulton Archive/Getty Images; **p. 51:** GAB Archives/Redferns/ Getty Images; **p. 53:** Bernard Hoffman/Time Life Pictures/ Getty Images; **p. 54:** John Springer Collection/Corbis; **p. 55:** Michael Ochs Archives/Getty Images; **p. 58 left:** Benoit Tessier/Reuters/Corbis; **p. 58 right:** Justin Lane/ epa/Corbis; **p. 59:** Yale Joel/Time Life Pictures/Getty Images; **p. 61:** Michael Ochs Archives/Getty Images; **p. 64:** GAB Archive/Redferns/Getty Images; **p. 65:** Michael Ochs Archives/Getty Images; **p. 68:** Bettmann/ Corbis.

Chapter 2

p. 75: J. R. Eyerman/Life Magazine/Time & Life Pictures/ Getty Images; **p. 76:** Bettmann/Corbis; **p. 78:** From the collection of John Tefteller www.tefteller.com; **p. 81 from top down:** *The Wild One* 1953 László Benedek Stanley Kramer Productions Distributor: Columbia Pictures; *Rebel Without a Cause* 1955 Nicholas Ray Warner Brothers; *Blackboard Jungle* 1955 Richard Brooks Metro-Goldwyn-Mayer (MGM), **p. 83:** GAB Archive/Redferns/Getty Images; **p. 88:** ABC Photo Archives/Getty Images; **p. 89:** Michael Ochs Archives/Getty Images; **p. 91:** GAB Archive/ Redferns/Getty Images; **p. 93:** Bettmann/Corbis; **p. 94:** Michael Ochs Archives/Getty Images; **p. 99 all:** from DVD: *Elvis: The Ed Sullivan Show, the Classic Performances* © Sofa Entertainment, Inc. All Rights Reserved. © 2009 Image Entertainment; **p. 101:** AP Photo; **p. 102:** Time Life Pictures/Getty Images; **p. 103:** Michael Ochs Archive/ Getty Images; **p. 106:** CBS Photo Archive/Getty Images; **p. 110:** Bettmann/Corbis.

Chapter 3

p. 112: From the collection of John Tefteller www.tefteller .com; **p. 117:** Bettmann/Corbis; **p. 118:** GAB Archive/ Redferns/Getty Images; **p. 119:** Hulton Archive/Getty Images; **p. 121:** Michael Ochs Archives/Getty Images; **p. 122:** Michael Ochs Archives/Getty Images; **p. 125:** PhotoQuest/Getty Images; **p. 127:** Michael Ochs Archives/ Getty Images; **p. 128:** Michael Ochs Archives/Getty Images; **p. 131:** Michael Ochs Archives/Getty Images; **p. 133:** Ray Avery/Getty Images; **p. 135:** Michael Ochs Archives/Getty Images; **p. 140:** Michael Levin/Corbis; **p. 143:** David Redfern/Getty Images; **p. 146:** Michael Ochs Archives/Getty Images; **p. 152:** Capitol/EMI.

Chapter 4

p. 155: Bettmann/Corbis; **p. 156:** Bob Adelman/Corbis; **p. 158:** Capitol; **p. 162:** CA/Redferns/Getty Images; **p. 164 both:** Michael Ochs Archives/Getty Images; **p. 169:** Bettmann/Corbis; **p. 170 all:** From DVD: Miramax Films Collector Series: *A Hard Day's Night*. Distributed by Buena Vista Home Entertainment; **p. 175:** GAB Archive/ Redferns/Getty Images; **p. 180:** David Redfern/Getty Images; **p. 181:** Bettmann/Corbis; **p. 183:** Pace/Getty Images; **p. 184:** BG070-PO © Bill Graham Archives, LLC and available at www.wolfgangsvault.com; **p. 185:** David Redfern/Getty Images; **p. 187:** Michael Ochs Archives/Corbis.

Chapter 5

p. 192: Columbia Records; **p. 195:** RB/Redferns/Getty Images; **p. 197:** Alice Ochs/Michael Ochs Archives/Getty Images; **p. 199:** Michael Ochs Archives/Getty Images; **p. 200:** David Redfern/Getty Images; **p. 201:** Michael Ochs Archives/Getty Images; **p. 203:** Capitol/EMI; **p. 205:** Jan Olofsson/Redferns/Getty Images; **p. 206:** Michael Ochs Archives/Getty Images; **p. 207:** Henry Diltz/Corbis; **p. 208:** Michael Ochs Archives/Getty Images; **p. 211:** GAB Archive/Redferns/Getty Images; **p. 212:** Michael Ochs

Archives/Getty Images; **p. 214:** Elektra Records; **p. 215:** Everett Collection Inc/Alamy; **p. 217:** Moviestore collection Ltd/Alamy.

Chapter 6

p. 222: From the collection of John Tefteller www.tefteller .com; **p. 226:** Michael Ochs Archives/Getty Images; **p. 227:** Michael Ochs Archives/Stringer/Getty Images; **p. 228:** Michael Ochs Archives/Getty Images; **p. 231:** Michael Ochs Archives/Getty Images; **p. 234:** David Redfern/Getty Images; **p. 237:** GAB Archives/Redferns/Getty Images; **p. 239:** Michael Ochs Archives/Getty Images; **p. 240:** Michael Ochs Archives/Getty Images; **p. 242:** Universal Music; **p. 243:** Michael Ochs Archives/Getty Images; **p. 247:** James Brown live in Boston (from TV) 1968 www.thevideobeat.com; **p. 248 all:** From DVD: *The Temptations: Get Ready. Definitive Performances 1965–1972.* (2006) Universal Music Group International; **p. 252:** Chuck Stewart.

Chapter 7

p. 254: Courtesy Capitol/EMI; **p. 258:** Hulton Archive/Getty Images; **p. 260:** Michael Ochs Archives/Getty Images; **p. 265:** Avico Ltd/Alamy; **p. 266:** George Hunter (707) 388-3983 GHD@vom.com; **p. 267:** www .wolfgangsvault.com; **p. 269:** www.wolfgangsvault.com; **p. 272 top:** Courtesy of Sony BMG Music Entertainment; **p. 272 bottom:** Ted Streshinsky/Corbis; **p. 274:** Reprinted through the courtesy of the Editors of Time Magazine © 2011; **p. 276:** Nigel Weymouth & Michael English; **p. 279:** Pictorial Press Ltd/Alamy; **p. 280:** David Redfern/Getty Images; **p. 282:** Ed J. Caraeff; **p. 283:** Courtesy Warner Brothers; **p. 285:** Jan Persson/Redferns/Getty Images; **p. 287:** AP Photo; **p. 288:** Ralph Ackerman/Getty Images; **p. 289:** Time Life Pictures/Getty Images; **p. 290 all:** From DVD: *Woodstock: 3 Days of Peace and Music. The Director's Cut.* © 2009 Warner Bros. Entertainment Inc; **p. 291:** Bettmann/Corbis.

Chapter 8

pp. 297–298: Bettmann/Corbis; **p. 300:** Courtesy Atlantic/Warner Brothers; **p. 303:** Robert Knight Archive/Redferns/Getty Images; **p. 307:** Pictorial Press LTD/Alamy; **p. 308:** Peter Tarnoff/Retna Ltd./Corbis; **p. 311:** Richard Upper; **p. 315:** Henry Diltz/Corbis; **p. 317:** Tom Hill/WireImage/Getty Images; **p. 319 top:** David Redfern/Getty Images; **p. 319 bottom:** Rhino/Elektra; **p. 321:** Pictorial Press Ltd/Alamy; **p. 323:** Courtesy Capitol/EMI; **p. 324:** Michael Ochs Archives/Getty Images; **p. 325:** Jan Persson/Redferns/Getty Images; **p. 326:** Michael Ochs Archives/Getty Images; **p. 328:** Michael Ochs Archives/Getty Images; **p. 329:** Pictorial Press Ltd/Alamy; **p. 330:** Michael Ochs Archives/Getty Images; **p. 332:** David J. & Janice L.Frent Collection/Corbis; **p. 334:** Anwar Hussein/Getty Images; **p. 335:** Henry Diltz/Corbis; **p. 339:** Henry Diltz/Corbis.

Chapter 9

p. 342: Motown/Universal; **p. 345:** Pictorial Press Ltd/Alamy; **p. 346:** Pictorial Press Ltd/Alamy; **p. 347:** Charlyn Zlotnick/Redferns/Getty Images; **p. 350:** Michael Ochs Archives/Getty Images; **p. 351:** RB/Redferns/Getty Images; **p. 354:** Michael Ochs Archives/Getty Images; **p. 357 both:** Archives du 7eme Art/Photos 12/Alamy; **p. 358:** Pictorial Press Ltd/Alamy; **p. 360:** Richard E. Aaron/Redferns/Getty Images; **p. 364:** Andrew Putler/Redferns/Getty Images; **p. 367:** *Saturday Night Fever* 1977 John Badham, Paramount Pictures Robert Stigwood Organization (RSO); **p. 370:** Richard E Aaron/Redferns/Getty Images; **p. 372:** AP Photo.

Chapter 10

p. 374: Pennie Smith/Sony; **p. 378:** Richard E. Aaron/Redferns/Getty Images; **p. 379:** Richard E. Aaron/Redferns/Getty Images; **p. 381:** Rogers Ressmeyer/Corbis; **p. 383 top:** Ebet Roberts/Redferns/Getty Images; **p. 383 bottom:** Richard E. Aaron/Redferns/Getty Images; **p. 386:** Pictorial Press Ltd/Alamy; **p. 387:** Denis O'Regan/Corbis; **p. 388:** Richard E. Aaron/Redferns/Getty Images; **p. 391:** Mick Gold/Redferns/Getty Images; **p. 392 top:** Denis O'Regan/Corbis; **p. 392 bottom:** Lynn Goldsmith/Corbis; **p. 394:** Lynn Goldsmith/Corbis; **p. 396:** Michael Ochs Archives/Getty Images; **p. 399:** Roberta Bayley/Redferns/Getty Images; **p. 401:** Elvis Costello, "Less Than Zero/Radio Radio" (screen grab from *Saturday Night Live* performance) 1977 NBC Studio; **p. 403:** Lynn Goldsmith/Corbis; **p. 408 left:** Michael Ochs Archives/Getty Images; **p. 408 right:** Pictorial Press Ltd/Alamy.

Chapter 11

p. 411: Bettmann/Corbis; **p. 412:** Jacques M. Chenet/Corbis; **p. 414:** MJJ Productions, LLC; **p. 416:** The Buggles, "Video Killed the Radio Star" (music video) 1980 From a DVD titled, *"The Best of Alternative 80s—The DVD Collection"* distributed by Universal Music Group; **p. 418:** Roger Ressmeyer/Corbis; **p. 419:** Rob Verhorst/Redferns/Getty Images; **p. 423:** Everett Collection; **p. 424 all:** From DVD: *Thriller 25: The World's Biggest Selling Album of All Time, Michael Jackson.* © 1982, 2008 MJJ Productions, Inc; **p. 426:** Richard E. Aaron/Redferns/Getty Images; **p. 428:** Ian Dickson/Redferns/Getty Images; **p. 429:** Peter Still/Redferns/Getty Images; **p. 430:** Henry Diltz/Corbis; **p. 431:** Ebet Roberts/Redferns/Getty Images; **p. 432:** Bettmann/Corbis; **p. 435:** Lynn Goldsmith/Corbis; **p. 437:** Richard E. Aaron/Redferns/Getty Images; **p. 439:** Lynn Goldsmith/Corbis; **p. 440:** Ian Dickson/Redferns/Getty Images; **p. 450:** Peter Gabriel, *Sledgehammer* (music video) 1986 dir. Stephen R. Johnson Production Company: Aardman Animation.

Chapter 12

p. 452: Courtesy of Sony BMG Music Entertainment; **p. 455:** Michael Ochs Archives/Getty Images; **p. 456:** Corbis; **p. 458:** Joe Giron/Corbis; **p. 459:** Ebet Roberts/Redferns/Getty Images; **p. 460:** Pete Cronin/Redferns/Getty Images; **p. 463:** Jamel Shabazz; **p. 464 top:** Jamel Shabazz; **p. 464 bottom:** Michael Ochs Archives/Corbis; **p. 465:** David Corio/Michael Ochs Archives/Getty Images; **p. 467:** Tyler Hicks/The New York Times/Redux; **p. 468:** David Corio/Michael Ochs Archives/Getty Images; **p. 469:** Ebet Roberts/Redferns/Getty Images; **p. 472:** Al Pereira/Michael Ochs Archives/Getty Images; **p. 474:** Michael Ochs

INDEX